CW00820383

ADVANCED MATHEMATICS

BOOK 2

THE SCHOOL MATHEMATICS PROJECT

ADVANCED MATHEMATICS

BOOK 2

CAMBRIDGE UNIVERSITY PRESS
CAMBRIDGE
LONDON · NEW YORK · MELBOURNE

Published by the Syndics of the Cambridge University Press
The Pitt Building, Trumpington Street, Cambridge CB2 1RP
Bentley House, 200 Euston Road, London NW1 2DB
32 East 57th Street, New York, NY 10022, USA
296 Beaconsfield Parade, Middle Park, Melbourne 3206, Australia

Library of Congress catalogue card number: 67-28685

ISBN 0 521 07677 3

First published 1968
Metricated 1970
Reprinted 1973, 1974, 1976

Printed in Great Britain
at the
University Printing House, Cambridge
(Euan Phillips, University Printer)

THE SCHOOL MATHEMATICS PROJECT

When the SMP was founded in 1961, its main objective was to devise radically new secondary-school mathematics courses (and corresponding GCE and CSE syllabuses) to reflect, more adequately than did the traditional syllabuses, the up-to-date nature and usages of mathematics.

This objective has now been realized. SMP *Books 1–5* form a five-year course to the O-level examination 'SMP Mathematics'. *Books 3T, 4* and *5* give a three-year course to the same O-level examination (the earlier *Books T* and *T4* being now regarded as obsolete). *Advanced Mathematics Books 1–4* cover the syllabus for the A-level examination 'SMP Mathematics' and five shorter texts cover the material of the various sections of the A-level examination 'SMP Further Mathematics'. Revisions of the first two books of *Advanced Mathematics* are available as *Revised Advanced Mathematics Books 1* and *2*. There are two books for 'SMP Additional Mathematics' at O-level. All the SMP GCE examinations are available to schools through any of the Examining Boards.

Books A–H, originally designed for non-GCE streams, cover broadly the same development of mathematics as do the first few books of the O-level series. Most CSE Boards offer appropriate examinations. In practice, this series is being used very widely across all streams of comprehensive schools, and its first seven books, followed by *Books X, Y* and *Z*, provide a course leading to the SMP -O-level examination. An alternative treatment of the material in *SMP Books A, B, C* and *D* is available as *SMP Cards I* and *II*.

Teachers' Guides accompany all series of books.

The SMP has produced many other texts, and teachers are encouraged to obtain each year from the Cambridge University Press, Bentley House, 200 Euston Road, London, NW1 2DB, the full list of SMP books currently available. In the same way, help and advice may always be sought by teachers from the Director at the SMP Office, Westfield College, Hampstead, London NW3 7ST, from which may also be obtained the annual Reports, details of forthcoming in-service training courses and so on.

The completion of this first ten years of work forms a firm base on which the SMP will continue to develop its research into the mathematical curriculum, and is described in detail in Bryan Thwaites's *SMP: The First Ten Years*. The team of SMP writers, numbering some forty school and university mathematicians, is continually evaluating old work and preparing for new. But at the same time, the effectiveness of the SMP's future work will depend, as it always has done, on obtaining reactions from a wide variety of teachers – and also from pupils – actively concerned in the class-room. Readers of the texts can therefore send their comments to the SMP, in the knowledge that they will be warmly welcomed.

January 1974

The S.M.P. texts are based on the original contributions of

A. B. Bolt
*P. G. Bowie
*H. M. Cundy
*J. H. Durran
*L. E. Ellis
A. G. Gallant
*C. C. Goldsmith
B. J. W. Heath

D. A. Hobbs
S. W. Hockey
D. J. Holding
G. S. Howlett
A. Hurrell
*T. A. Jones
*M. J. Leach

P. G. T. Lewis
T. D. Morris
*D. A. Quadling
G. D. Stagg
A. R. Tammadge
*B. Thwaites
J. V. Tyson
J. S. T. Woolmer

and are edited by Dr H. Martyn Cundy assisted by Mr P. G. Bowie.

* Those primarily concerned with this book are indicated by the asterisk.

Many other schoolteachers have been directly involved in the further development and revision of the material and the Project gratefully acknowledges the contributions which they and their schools have made.

CONTENTS

Preface *page* ix

Glossary of symbols xii

11 Σ-Notation and Finite Series 305

12 Position and Spread 316

13 Further Vectors 347

14 Further Trigonometry 386

15 The Quadratic Function 417

Revision Exercises 441

16 Local Approximation 445

17 The Technique of Differentiation 471

18 Units and Dimensions 492

19 Kinematics 504

Revision Exercises 541

20 Probability 546

21 Linear Equations 582

22 Area 603

23 Techniques of Integration 640

24 Introduction to Mechanics 672

Revision Exercises 719

Index 731

PREFACE

This is the second of a series of four books which together will cover the single-subject course in S.M.P. A-level mathematics. A fifth book is planned to cover the additional material for the double-subject Further Mathematics.

This Book 2 is in many ways the 'core' book of the Advanced course. Its most obvious feature is its physical size: it is a very much larger book than its predecessor in the series, or than either of its planned successors. The reason for this is twofold; partly it arises by chance because certain chapters which might conceivably have been included in Book 1 were not in their final form by the time that book had to go to press; but also it is to some extent deliberate, because this is the stage at which foundations are being laid down in all the departments of the course; hard, deep, and thorough work is thus called for on the part of the student. One cannot embark on Applied Mathematics until there is a substantial body of mathematics to apply; hence the deferment of any consideration of statistics and mechanics to this book, and the consequent need for space to treat them as fully as they deserve.

There are those who would wish to interpret the statement that 'no candidate need cover more than roughly three-quarters of the published A-level syllabus' as a permission to exclude entirely any consideration of one of the applications of mathematics in the syllabus, for example, statistics or mechanics. The authors would repudiate such an interpretation as implying a misunderstanding of the nature of the course and the purpose of the examination, nor would they consider it to be in the best interests of the candidate, likely as it is to enhance neither his interest, his mathematical education, nor his examination prospects. They would consider that all students should make themselves familiar, at least in broad outline, with the contents of the whole of this present book.

The algebra in the book is designed with two main ends—to introduce some basic techniques, and to adumbrate developments to come. Thus Chapter 11 introduces a convenient shorthand notation and uses it to state and prove some familiar results about series; but these are set in a context where their statistical applications are immediately of value. We learn to solve a quadratic equation in Chapter 15, but again in a setting of transformation of functions and graphs which is of fundamental mathematical importance. In Chapter 21 we discuss linear equations in a way which leads us up to the threshold of the ideas of linear dependence and vector space, which will be taken up more fully in Book 4. Vectors here find geometrical applications; the scalar product appears in Chapter 13 and is shown to characterize Euclidean space; many interesting classic geometrical theorems are now seen as obvious consequences of simple algebraic results. Chapter 14, on Trigonometry, looks at first very traditional, and necessarily so, but here again new ideas are bringing fresh light; the emphasis is throughout on the circular functions as the mathematical model of periodic phenomena.

In the analysis chapters we develop the main techniques of the calculus in Chapters 17 and 23, but introducing these are two chapters which help to show the point of these techniques. The first, Chapter 16, shows that differentiation really provides us with a local linear approximation to a function which may be much more tractable than the function itself. This is a fruitful idea, leading to such useful results as the finding of small changes, and the Newton–Raphson method of solving equations of all kinds. The second introductory chapter, Chapter 22 on area, gives an unusually full discussion of the problem of defining an area function for a region, and of evaluating such a function for general regions with curved boundaries. The definite integral is carefully defined, and its properties established. The area under a parabola and a few other simple curves is treated exactly, and the approximate rules are discovered. Only then are we introduced to the fundamental theorem, which is therefore seen in its true importance, and the enormous simplification it brings can be better appreciated.

There remain the two main fields of application in this book: statistics, and mechanics. The former has two chapters, 12 and 20, which not only introduce simple rules and techniques, but, what is of much greater significance, strive throughout to inculcate a critical attitude to the whole idea of constructing mathematical models of chance events. The relation of the mathematical model to the physical world is taken up in Chapter 18, which brings in the idea of dimension. Two extensive chapters, 19 and 24, begin the mechanics part of the course. With the development of the vector behind us, we can be as much interested in the world of two and three dimensions from the outset as in the rather arid field of the straight line, and the treatment gains in power and interest accordingly. Newton's laws are seen to be fundamental, in their vector form, and the problems of mass and weight, of frames of reference, units and dimensionality, are thoroughly discussed.

A word should be said about the matter of units and notation. The British universities have agreed that all students entering from 1972 onwards will take examinations in which none but S.I. units will be used; the various schools examination boards are accordingly phasing in the use of S.I. units so that in 1972 the A-levels will be wholly in S.I. This metricated version therefore uses S.I. units and notation throughout. It recognizes, however, that the centimetre, while not strictly belonging to

S.I., remains a useful practical measure of length; it appears in a number of examples. A short starred section has been included in Chapter 24 which gives details of the obsolescent imperial units and others, together with a set of exercises. It is hoped that these will not long be needed. Incidentally, S.I. practice confirms our long-held belief that Newton's law should be used in the form $\boldsymbol{F} = m\boldsymbol{a}$, and that absolute units alone should be used in mechanics. This is true even in the starred section; the old gravitational unit lbf should now die a natural death.

Much important material appears in this book in the form of exercises. These have, wherever possible, been indicated by bold type. Harder sections and exercises have, as usual, been distinguished by the asterisk. Miscellaneous exercises are usually more difficult than those in the body of the chapters. Perhaps we should say that we do not expect all students to work all the exercises. Many are suitable for allocation to different members of the class, the results being pooled for discussion.

Answers to exercises will be given in the first of the Teachers' Guides which accompanies this book. A further Guide giving the mathematical background to the Advanced Course is in process of preparation.

ACKNOWLEDGEMENTS

We acknowledge with gratitude permission received from the Oxford and Cambridge Schools Examination Board to reproduce examination questions. Our sincere thanks go to Mrs Catherine Young and Mrs Elizabeth Muir for their painstaking typing of the MSS. Finally, we again express our debt of gratitude to the staff of the Cambridge University Press for their care, helpfulness and co-operation in this whole enterprise.

GLOSSARY OF SYMBOLS

Additional to those in Book 1

ALGEBRA

$u_1, u_2, \ldots u_n$	Successive terms of a sequence
$u_1+u_2+\ldots+u_n$	Series derived from this sequence
$S_1, S_2, \ldots$	Partial sums of this series: $S_1 = u_1$, $S_2 = u_1+u_2$, etc.
$\sum_{i=1}^{i=n} u_i\ \sum_{i=1}^{n} u_i,\ \sum_{1}^{n} u_i$	Alternative notations for $S_n = u_1+u_2+u_3+\ldots+u_n$
j	Root of $j^2+1 = 0$; new element adjoined to real field R which generates the complex number field C
$\sqrt{}$	The positive square root of
$0!$	1

VECTORS AND MATRICES

$\mathbf{i}, \mathbf{j}, \mathbf{k}$	The unit vectors $\begin{pmatrix}1\\0\\0\end{pmatrix}, \begin{pmatrix}0\\1\\0\end{pmatrix}, \begin{pmatrix}0\\0\\1\end{pmatrix}$
$\hat{\mathbf{u}}$	Arbitrary unit vector
p	Magnitude of $\mathbf{p}$
$\mathbf{p}.\mathbf{q}$	Scalar product of $\mathbf{p}$ and $\mathbf{q}$
$\mathbf{a}.\hat{\mathbf{u}}$	Resolved part of $\mathbf{a}$ in direction of $\hat{\mathbf{u}}$
$\mathbf{n}$	Normal vector to the plane $\mathbf{p}.\mathbf{n} = d$
$\mathbf{I}$	The unit matrix $\begin{pmatrix}1&0&0\\0&1&0\\0&0&1\end{pmatrix}$
$\mathbf{E}$	Elementary matrix, obtained from I by an elementary row-operation
$\mathbf{L}$	Lower triangular matrix, of form $\begin{pmatrix}a&0&0\\b&c&0\\d&e&f\end{pmatrix}$
$\mathbf{U}$	Upper triangular matrix, of form $\begin{pmatrix}a&b&c\\0&d&e\\0&0&f\end{pmatrix}$
$\mathbf{A}^{-1}$	Inverse of the matrix $\mathbf{A}$, such that $\mathbf{AA}^{-1} = \mathbf{A}^{-1}\mathbf{A} = \mathbf{I}$
$\perp$	Is perpendicular to
$\parallel$	Is parallel to

CALCULUS

δx	Small increment in x
δy	Consequent increment in y
f''	Derived function of f'; second derived function of f
f'''	Derived function of f''; third derived function of f
$f^{(r)}$	rth derived function of f
$\int_a^b f(x)\,dx$, $\int_a^b f$	Area under the graph of f over the interval $[a, b]$
$\int f$	Primitive or indefinite integral of f; any function F such that $F' = f$
$\Big[F(x)\Big]_a^b$, $\Big[F\Big]_a^b$	$F(b) - F(a)$
$\sin^{-1}$ etc.	Inverse function to sin, etc., with restricted range

PROBABILITY AND STATISTICS

m, $\bar{x}$	Mean value of x
$f(x_i)$	Frequency of x_i; number of occurrences in population of $x = x_i$
s	Standard deviation
s^2, v_x	Variance (of x); mean square deviation from m
v_{xy}	Covariance of x and y
$m_2, m_3, m_4, \ldots$	Second, third, fourth, ... moments about the mean; mean square, cube, fourth-power deviations from m
$\mathscr{E}$	Possibility space
A	Subset of $\mathscr{E}$ associated with event **A**
$p(\mathbf{A})$	Probability of event **A** $(= n(A)/n(\mathscr{E}))$
E	Certain event
O	Impossible event
$p(\sim \mathbf{A})$	Probability of (not-**A**)
$p(\mathbf{A} \wedge \mathbf{B})$	Probability of both **A** and **B**
$p(\mathbf{A} \vee \mathbf{B})$	Probability of at least one of **A** and **B**
$p(\mathbf{A} \mid \mathbf{B})$	Probability of **A** given **B**

MECHANICS

$\mathbf{r}$	Position vector of a particle
$\dot{\mathbf{r}}$, $\mathbf{v}$	$d\mathbf{r}/dt$, velocity of particle
$\ddot{\mathbf{r}}$, $\mathbf{a}$	$d\mathbf{v}/dt$, acceleration of particle
m	mass of particle
F, **N**, **T**	Forces acting on a body
ω, $\dot{\theta}$	Angular velocity, $d\theta/dt$
$\dot{\omega}$, $\ddot{\theta}$	Angular acceleration, $d\theta^2/dt^2$
$\mathbf{g}$	Acceleration of local gravity
$\mathbf{g}_0$	Acceleration of standard gravity
μ	Coefficient of friction
λ	Angle of friction, $\tan^{-1}\mu$
M, **L**, **T**	Dimensions of mass, length, and time

UNITS

Metric prefixes:	mega	kilo	milli	micro	nano	pico
Multiplier:	10^{6}	10^{3}	10^{-3}	10^{-6}	10^{-9}	10^{-12}

Mechanical units in consistent sets:

	Mass	Length	Time	Force	Acceleration
m.k.s.	kg	m	s	N	m/s²
c.g.s.	g	cm	s	dyne	cm/s²
British	lb	ft	s	pdl	ft/s²
British	ton	ft	s	tonnal	ft/s²
Technical	kg	m	s	kgf	$g_0 = 9{\cdot}80665$ m/s²
Technical	lb	ft	s	lbf	$g_0 = 32{\cdot}174$ ft/s²

The first of these has been adopted as standard by the Système Internationale d'Unités (S.I.), and may be expected to supersede all the others.

11

Σ-NOTATION AND FINITE SERIES

In statistics we shall often be considering the sums of many terms, the essential feature of such sums being that they are of 'families' of terms. Either all the terms are particular cases of a certain general form for which a formula can be given, or all are particular values of a certain variable such as height, age, number of goals, output of a machine and so on, for which a table of values can be given. The power of the notation we now develop will be demonstrated immediately in the chapter on statistics, but extends to many other branches of mathematics.

1. THE Σ-NOTATION

1.1 $1^2+2^2+3^2+4^2+5^2+6^2+7^2+8^2$ might well be written as

$$1^2+2^2+3^2+\ldots+8^2$$

without much danger. A perverse reader, however, might think that the latter form indicated $1^2+2^2+3^2+5^2+8^2$, using the pattern $1+2 = 3$, $2+3 = 5$, $3+5 = 8$. To avoid this danger the sum is often written $1^2+2^2+\ldots+i^2+\ldots+8^2$, but this still assumes the convention that i takes *consecutive* integral values.

The standard way of writing this particular sum is $\sum\limits_{i=1}^{i=8} i^2$. Σ is said 'Sigma'. It is the Greek capital letter corresponding to 'S' which begins the English word 'Sum'. We read the whole symbol as 'Sigma, i equals 1 to 8, of i-squared'—or words to that effect; sometimes we say 'the sum, ...' instead of 'Sigma, ...'.

The symbol Σ indicates that a summation is to be carried out. The general type of term is to be i^2. The first value of i is to be $i = 1$. *Consecutive integral* values of i are to be taken. The last value of i is to be $i = 8$. The summation is said to be taken between the *limits* 1 and 8. The *lower* limit of i is written *below* the Σ.

We usually abbreviate the symbol to $\sum\limits_{1}^{8} i^2$ if there is no ambiguity as to which letter is doing the counting.

Note that $\sum\limits_{i=1}^{i=8} i^2 = \sum\limits_{j=1}^{j=8} j^2$, since the counting letter or counter does not appear in the final evaluation, which in this case is 204. (For this reason the counter is known as a *dummy variable*.)

Note also that the notation is no help in actually carrying out the summation; indeed it can be used to indicate a sum for which there is no short method of summation available, such as $\sum_{1}^{100} 1/i$.

There is no formula which gives $\sum_{1}^{n} 1/i$ in terms of n. In the example given, when $n = 100$, the sum exceeds 5. In a general numerical case, unless some particular formula for the answer is known or some short method devised, the evaluation is done by writing out the sum in full.

Example 1. Evaluate $\sum_{0}^{3} (2i+1)$.

$$\begin{aligned}\sum_{0}^{3} (2i+1) &= (2.0+1)+(2.1+1)+(2.2+1)+(2.3+1)\\ &= 1+3+5+7\\ &= 16.\end{aligned}$$

Example 2. Given that $\sum_{1}^{n} 2^i = 2^{n+1}-2$, find the sum of the first ten integral powers of 2.

The required sum is

$$\begin{aligned}\sum_{1}^{10} 2^i &= 2^{11}-2\\ &= 2048-2\\ &= 2046.\end{aligned}$$

A sum can, in fact, be expressed in Σ-notation in many ways. For example, it is easily verified that $2^2+4^2+6^2+8^2+10^2$ can be written as

$$\sum_{1}^{5} (2i)^2, \quad \text{or} \quad \sum_{0}^{5} (2i)^2, \quad \text{or} \quad \sum_{0}^{4} (2i+2)^2.$$

1.2 Suffixes. Suppose we wish to find the average age of the people at a dance. We would require the sum of their ages. To express this symbolically, we take the people in some order and let the age of the jth person be y_j years. Then the age total in years can be written $\sum_{j=1}^{j=N} y_j$, where N is the number of people.

If there are 20 people aged 16, 40 aged 17, 25 aged 18 and 5 aged 20, the age total is, of course, more easily worked out from

$$16\times 20+17\times 40+18\times 25+20\times 5.$$

If we call the different ages involved x_1, x_2, x_3, x_4 and the number of times these occur (that is, their *frequencies*) q_1, q_2, q_3, q_4, the age total can be written

$$x_1 q_1+x_2 q_2+x_3 q_3+x_4 q_4, \quad \text{i.e.} \sum_{i=1}^{i=4} x_i q_i.$$

We see that the notation helps us to write succinctly expressions involving terms of a sequence. The dummy variable then occurs as a suffix.

In our example, there is a one-one correspondence between the ages and the frequencies, and we can define a function f—the frequency function—under which $f(x_i) = q_i$ for all i. The number of people present is then $\sum_1^n f(x_i)$, the age total is $\sum_1^n x_i f(x_i)$, and the average age is

$$\sum_1^n x_i f(x_i) \Big/ \sum_1^n f(x_i),$$

where n is the number of different ages.

It is important to realize that with the Σ-notation and suffixes we have not introduced any new mathematical concepts—they are simply aids in a mathematical shorthand.

Exercise A

1. Write out the sums involved and when they are numerical evaluate them.

(*a*) $\sum_2^4 i$; (*b*) $\sum_1^3 i^3$; (*c*) $\sum_1^4 2^i$; (*d*) $\sum_{-2}^1 2^{i+3}$;

(*e*) $\sum_1^4 (-1)^i i^3$; (*f*) $\sum_0^3 i(i+1)$; (*g*) $\sum_1^5 (-1)^i i x^{i+1}$.

2. Express the following in Σ-notation. Do each part twice, once beginning the summation at $i = 0$ and once at $i = 1$. In part (*a*), express the sum also in such a way that a term of zero value begins the expanded form.

(*a*) $1.3+2.4+3.5+\ldots+10.12$;
(*b*) $\frac{1}{4}+\frac{1}{5}+\frac{1}{6}+\ldots+(1/n)$;
(*c*) $64+64\times(\frac{3}{4})+64\times(\frac{3}{4})^2+\ldots+\frac{243}{16}$;
(*d*) $x-2x^2+3x^3-4x^4+5x^5$;
(*e*) $1-x+x^2-x^3+\ldots+(-1)^n x^n$;
(*f*) $ar^p+ar^{p+1}+\ldots+ar^{p+q}$;
(*g*) $ar^{p-1}+ar^p+\ldots+ar^n$.

3. Investigate whether the following are true or false:

(*a*) $\sum_1^3 i^3 = \sum_0^5 (2i+1)$;

(*b*) $\sum_1^8 (3i+4) = \sum_0^7 (28-3i)$;

(*c*) $\sum_1^5 i^2 = \left(\sum_1^5 i\right)^2$;

(*d*) $\sum_1^6 (2i+8) = \left(\sum_1^6 2i\right)+8$;

(*e*) $\sum_1^n (2i+8) = 2\sum_1^n (i+4)$;

(*f*) $\sum_1^n (i^2+3i) = \sum_1^n i^2+\sum_1^n 3i$;

(*g*) $\sum_1^n (3i+4) = 3\sum_1^n i+4n$;

(*h*) $\sum_1^n i.\sum_1^n i^2 = \sum_1^n i^3$;

(*j*) $\sum_{-3}^4 (x^i-x^{i-1}) = x^4-x^{-4}$;

(*k*) $\sum_0^6 (i+4)(i-2) = \sum_{-3}^3 (i+1)(i+7)$.

4. Assuming $x_1 = 12$, $x_2 = 7$, $x_3 = 9$, $x_4 = 15$, $x_5 = 12$, $x_6 = 10$, $x_7 = 12$, $x_8 = 9$, evaluate:

(*a*) $\sum_1^8 x_i$; (*b*) $\sum_1^4 x_{2i}$; (*c*) $\sum_1^4 2x_i$; (*d*) $\sum_1^4 x_{2i-1}$;

(*e*) $\sum_1^4 (x_{2i}-1)$.

5. Let f be the function $f: x \to 3x+1$ and u_1, u_2, u_3, u_4 be 4, 1, 3, 5. Find:

(*a*) $f(u_2)$; (*b*) $u_4 f(u_4)$; (*c*) $\sum_1^4 f(u_i)$; (*d*) $\sum_1^4 u_i f(u_i)$;

(*e*) $\sum_1^4 (u_i - 3) f(u_i)$.

What is the connection between your last three answers?

6. If $f(x) = 2x+3$, find $\sum_1^4 f(i^2)$, $\sum_1^4 (f(i))^2$, $\left(\sum_1^4 f(i)\right)^2$.

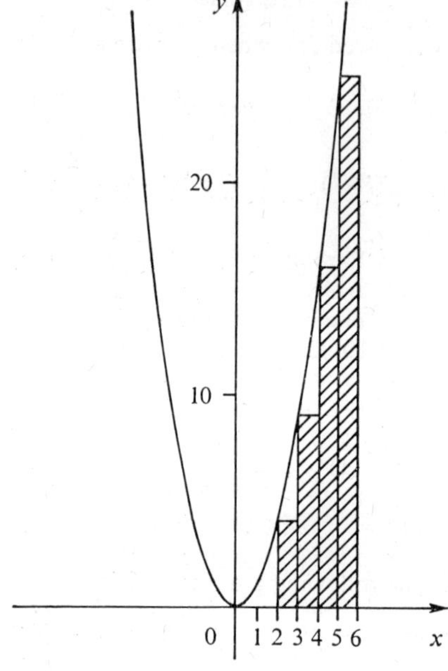

Fig. 1

7. In this question $x_i = x_0 + ih$, $g(x) = x^2$. Evaluate the sums concerned in each part. Show that the sum in (*a*) represents the shaded area in Figure 1, and illustrate the other sums similarly.

(*a*) $x_0 = 2$, $h = 1$; $\sum_0^3 g(x_i)$. (*b*) $x_0 = 2$, $h = \frac{1}{2}$; $\sum_0^7 (\frac{1}{2}g(x_i))$.

(*c*) $x_0 = 3$, $h = 0{\cdot}1$; $\sum_0^9 (0{\cdot}1 g(x_i))$.

8. Let a_{ij} denote the element in the ith row and the jth column of the matrix

$$\begin{pmatrix} 1 & 4 & 6 & 3 \\ 2 & 0 & 7 & 1 \\ 8 & 3 & 2 & 0 \end{pmatrix}.$$

Write down the values of

$$\sum_{i=1}^{i=3} a_{ij} \quad \text{when} \quad j = 3, \quad \text{and} \quad \sum_{j=1}^{j=3} \left(\sum_{i=1}^{i=2} a_{ij} \right).$$

9. If a_{ij}, b_{ij} are the elements in the ith row and jth column of two 3×3 matrices **A** and **B**, show that the element in the second row and third column of the product **AB** is $(a_{21} b_{13} + a_{22} b_{23} + a_{23} b_{33})$. Express this in sigma notation, and write down an expression for the element in the ith row and jth column of the product.

10. Generalize Question 9, taking **A** as an $l \times m$ matrix and **B** as an $m \times n$ matrix.

1.3 Some useful results. It is worth generalizing some of the results suggested in Question 3 of the last exercise.

(i) $\sum_1^n af(i) \equiv a \sum_1^n f(i)$;

(ii) $\sum_1^n (f(i)+b) \equiv \left(\sum_1^n f(i)\right) + nb$;

(iii) $\sum_1^n (f(i)+g(i)) \equiv \sum_1^n f(i) + \sum_1^n g(i)$.

Each identity is proved by writing out in full the expressions implied by the sigma notation. The only one which looks surprising is (ii), and the proof of this is as follows.

$$\begin{aligned} \sum_1^n (f(i)+b) &= (f(1)+b)+(f(2)+b)+(f(3)+b)+\ldots+(f(n)+b) \\ &= (f(1)+f(2)+f(3)+\ldots+f(n))+(b+b+\ldots+b) \\ &= \left(\sum_1^n f(i)\right) + nb. \end{aligned}$$

2. SOME FINITE SERIES

2.1 $\sum_1^n i$. With any clearly defined sequence $u_1, u_2, u_3, u_4, \ldots$ we can associate an infinite series $u_1+u_2+u_3+\ldots$. We shall meet many examples of such infinite series. We shall find that certain series have a 'sum', for example, $1+\frac{1}{2}+\frac{1}{4}+\frac{1}{8}+\ldots = 2$, and that for other series, for example, $1+\frac{1}{2}+\frac{1}{3}+\frac{1}{4}+\ldots$ there is no such sum.

Determining whether or not an infinite series has a sum is a difficult problem which we cannot fully consider now. However, the way in which one approaches the matter is to consider the *partial sums*:

$$S_1 = u_1,$$
$$S_2 = u_1+u_2,$$
$$S_3 = u_1+u_2+u_3,$$
$$\dots\dots\dots\dots\dots\dots$$
$$S_n = u_1+u_2+u_3+\dots+u_n.$$

If these partial sums S_1, S_2, ... tend to a limit S, then S is said to be the sum of the infinite series $u_1+u_2+u_3+\dots+u_n+\dots$. If the partial sums do not tend to a limit, then we say that the infinite series cannot be summed.

It is important then to be able to evaluate the partial sums, that is, to sum finite series, and we shall now look at one method of doing this which also establishes a result important in its own right.

Consider the series $1+2+3+\dots$ and let S_n, as usual, denote the nth partial sum. Then we can draw up the following table of values.

n:	1	2	3	4	5	6	7	8	9	10	11
S_n:	1	3	6	10	15	21	28	36	45	55	66

All the later values of S_n are composite, i.e. are not prime numbers. This suggests investigating the factors of S_n. When n is prime, S_n contains n as a factor: 5 is a factor of 15, 7 is a factor of 28, 11 is a factor of 66. This may or may not be a coincidence, but in any case it seems a good idea to investigate the other factors, so we add an S_n/n line to our table.

n:	1	2	3	4	5	6	7	8	9	10	11
S_n/n:	1	$1\frac{1}{2}$	2	$2\frac{1}{2}$	3	$3\frac{1}{2}$	4	$4\frac{1}{2}$	5	$5\frac{1}{2}$	6

It is now clear that $S_n/n = \frac{1}{2}(n+1)$, that is $S_n = \frac{1}{2}n(n+1)$.

For this statement we have shown that 1, 2, 3, ..., 11 are elements of its truth set, but the result is not yet proved generally. We use the method of induction to do this.

Suppose k belongs to the truth set T. This means $\sum_1^k i = \frac{1}{2}k(k+1)$. Then

$$\sum_1^{k+1} i = \left(\sum_1^k i\right)+(k+1)$$
$$= \tfrac{1}{2}k(k+1)+(k+1)$$
$$= \tfrac{1}{2}(k+1)(k+2).$$

This expression is of the right form with $(k+1)$ in place of n.

So $$k \in T \Rightarrow k+1 \in T.$$

But $$1, 2, 3, \dots, 11 \in T, \quad \text{so} \quad 12, 13, \dots \in T.$$

Hence $\sum_1^n i = \frac{1}{2}n(n+1)$ for all natural numbers n.

This is taking a sledgehammer to crack a nut, and the result could be proved with less fuss. However, it provides a simple example of an experimental method yielding a result which is then proved by induction. It is possible, of course, that one will hit upon an incorrect formula. In which case an attempted inductive proof breaks down.

2.2 Arithmetic progressions. Finite series in which the difference between successive terms is constant are called *arithmetic progressions.* They are easily summed using the results of Sections 1.2 and 2.1.

Example 3. Sum the first 20 terms of the series $8+14+20+26+\ldots$.

$$\begin{aligned} S_{20} &= 8+14+20+26+\ldots+122 \\ &= \sum_0^{19}(8+6i) \qquad \text{(notice that the upper limit is 19, not 20)} \\ &= 20\times 8+6\sum_0^{19} i \\ &= 160+6(\tfrac{1}{2}.19.20) \\ &= 160+1140 \\ &= 1300. \end{aligned}$$

Notice that the twentieth term of the sequence is $8+6\times 19 = 122$, and that S_n is $n.$(average of the first and last terms), i.e. $20.\frac{1}{2}(8+122)$.

If the first term is called a and the common difference d, then

$$\begin{aligned} S_n = \sum_0^{n-1}(a+id) &= na+d.\tfrac{1}{2}(n-1)n \\ &= \tfrac{1}{2}n(2a+(n-1)d). \end{aligned}$$

The last term is $a+(n-1)d$, so we see again that $S_n = n(\frac{1}{2}(u_1+u_n))$.

Exercise B

1. In each of the following cases investigate whether k being a member of the truth set implies $(k+1)$ being also a member.

(*a*) $\sum_1^n (2i+1) = n^2+2n$;　　(*b*) $\sum_1^n 3.4^i = (4^{n+1}+2)$;

(*c*) $\sum_1^n (3i^2-3i) = n^3-n$;　　(*d*) $\sum_1^n \dfrac{2}{i(i+1)} = 3-\dfrac{4}{n+1}$;

(*e*) $\sum_1^n 3i(i-1) = (n-1)(n)(n+1)$.

2. In each part of Question 1, find whether or not 1 is a member of the truth set, and hence state whether the statements are true for all natural numbers.

3. Let $S_n = \sum_1^n i^3$. Construct a table of values showing n and S_n for values of n from 1 to 6. Guess a formula for S_n, and check that it is correct using induction.

4. Obtain values of $S_n = \sum_1^n i^2$ for $n = 1, 2, 3, \ldots, 11$. Guess a formula for S_n in terms of n, and check that it is correct using induction.

5. Explain each step of the following proof.

$$\sum_1^n i = \sum_1^n (n+1-i) = \tfrac{1}{2}\left[\sum_1^n i + \sum_1^n (n+1-i)\right] = \tfrac{1}{2}\sum_1^n (i+n+1-i) = \tfrac{1}{2}n(n+1).$$

To what simple process is this method of proof equivalent?

6. Evaluate:

(*a*) $\sum_1^{15} (i+5)$; (*b*) $\sum_{10}^{20} (2i+1)$; (*c*) $\sum_{i=1}^{i=n} (r+3i)$;

(*d*) $\sum_{i=1}^{i=n} (n-i)$.

7. Find:

(*a*) $\sum_{n+1}^{2n} i$; (*b*) $\sum_0^{n-1} i$; (*c*) $\sum_{n-k}^{n+k} i$.

8. Express the following in sigma notation, and find their sums.

(*a*) $1+4+7+\ldots+94$; (*b*) $22+17+12+\ldots+(-28)$;
(*c*) $12+14+16+\ldots$, 39 terms; (*d*) $80+71+62+\ldots$, 14 terms.

9. (*a*) If $S_n = \sum_1^n u_i$, show that $S_n - S_{n-1} = u_n$.

(*b*) If $S_n = n^3$, what is u_n? What is u_i? Deduce the formula for $\sum_1^n i^2$.

10. Use the method of Question 9 to find $\sum_1^n i^3$.

11. Prove that $\sum_1^n i(i+1) = \frac{1}{3}n(n+1)(n+2)$ by induction or otherwise.

Find formulae for

$$\sum_1^n i(i+1)(i+2) \quad \text{and} \quad \sum_1^n i(i+1)(i+2)\ldots(i+r).$$

12. Find a, b, c such that

$$i^3+12i^2+17i = ai(i+1)(i+2)+bi(i+1)+ci.$$

Hence find $\sum_1^n (i^3+12i^2+7i)$, using the results of Question 11.

13. Find:

(*a*) $\sum_1^{19} (i^2+7i)$; (*b*) $\sum_1^{9} (i^3+2i+1)$; (*c*) $\sum_1^n (4i^3-12i^2)$;

(*d*) $\sum_1^n (i+2)^3$; (*e*) $\sum_1^n (n-i)^2$.

Check your answers to (*c*) and (*d*) by putting $n = 2$.

(The formulae found in earlier questions of this exercise should be used for this question. These are not discussed in the text, but are set out in the summary at the end of the chapter.)

14. Show that $n(n+1)(2n+1)$ is divisible by 6 for all natural numbers n.

15. If $x_i = x_0 + ih$, $x_0 = 2$, $h = 4/n$, $g(x) = x^2$, display $\sum_{i=0}^{n-1} h.g(x_i)$ as in Question 7 of Exercise A, and carry out the summation.

What is the limit of this sum as $n \to \infty$? What does this represent?

16. Repeat Question 15 if $x_0 = a$, $h = (b-a)/n$.

***17.** Repeat Question 16 for different functions $g(x)$.

***18.** Three non-concurrent lines divide a plane into 7 regions (see Figure 2). Prove, by induction or otherwise, that n lines (no two parallel and no three concurrent) divide the plane into $\frac{1}{2}(n^2+n+2)$ regions.

(*Hint.* Consider how many extra regions result from adding one more line.)

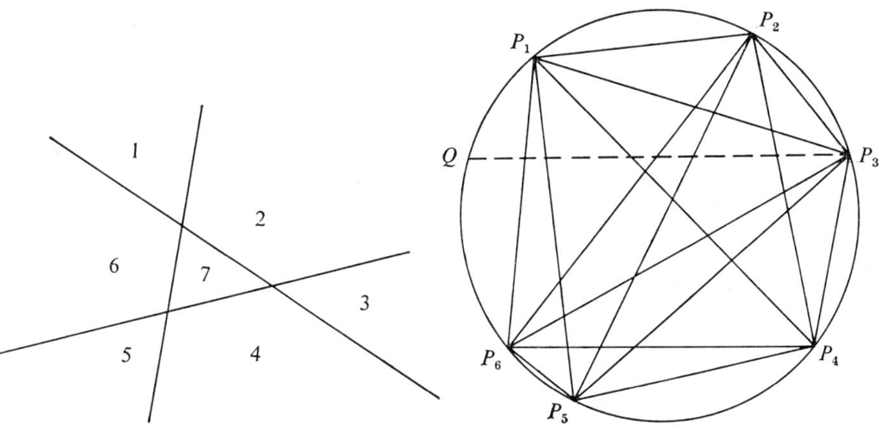

Fig. 2

Fig. 3

***19.** We are now in a position to find a formula for the number of regions a circle is divided into by the sides and diagonals of an n-sided polygon inscribed in it (see Figure 3). It is assumed that no three line segments are concurrent. (See Chapter 2, p. 45.) Denote the number of regions by S_n, and let u_k be the *extra* number of regions created by increasing the number of points on the circle from k to $k+1$.

In the diagram the number of regions is increased by 7 when Q is joined to P_3. This is one more than the number of existing lines crossed.

If Q is joined to P_i explain why the number of regions is increased by $(i-1)(k-i)+1$.

Show that
$$u_k = \sum_{i=1}^{i=k} ((i-1)(k-i)+1),$$
and sum the series.

Show that
$$S_n = 1 + \sum_{k=1}^{n-1} u_k,$$
and hence prove that
$$S_n = \tfrac{1}{24}n(n-1)(n-2)(n-3) + \tfrac{1}{2}n(n-1) + 1.$$

2.3 Geometric progressions. A series like $2+6+18+54+\dots$ in which the ratio between consecutive terms is always the same (in this case 3) is called a *geometric progression* (GP). Such series occur frequently in connection with mortgages, life insurance, annuities, hire purchase and in other contexts.

The nth partial sum of a GP can be written

$$S_n = a+ar+ar^2+\dots+ar^{n-1} = \sum_0^{n-1} ar^i$$

and can be summed by various methods.

(i) $$\begin{aligned} S_{n+1} &= a+ar+ar^2+\dots+ar^n \\ &= (a+ar+\dots+ar^{n-1})+ar^n \quad \text{or} \quad a+(ar+ar^2+\dots+ar^n) \\ &= S_n+ar^n \quad \text{or} \quad a+r(a+ar+\dots+ar^{n-1}). \end{aligned}$$

We see that $$S_n+ar^n = a+rS_n;$$

hence $$S_n = a\left(\frac{1-r^n}{1-r}\right).$$

(ii) In Chapter 7 we required the identity

$$\frac{b^n-a^n}{b-a} = b^{n-1}+b^{n-2}a+b^{n-3}a^2+\dots+a^{n-1}.$$

If $b = 1$ and $a = r$, this reduces to

$$\frac{1-r^n}{1-r} = 1+r+r^2+\dots+r^{n-1}.$$

If this result is quoted, the formula for S_n is arrived at immediately.

Example 4. Find the sum of the first ten terms of the series

$$2+6+18+54+\dots.$$

Putting $a = 2$, $r = 3$, $n = 10$ in the formula, we obtain

$$S_n = a\left(\frac{1-r^n}{1-r}\right) = 2\left(\frac{1-3^{10}}{1-3}\right) = 3^{10}-1 \simeq 59000.$$

Exercise C

1. Write down the sums of the following GP's. Simplify but do not evaluate your answers.

(*a*) $7+14+28+56+\dots$, 10 terms; (*b*) $2+\frac{1}{2}+\frac{1}{8}+\dots$, 12 terms;
(*c*) $3-6+12-24+\dots$, 19 terms; (*d*) $-3+1-\frac{1}{3}+\frac{1}{9}-\dots$, 16 terms.

2. Show that £A, invested at r % per annum compound interest, is worth £Ax^n after n years, where $x = 1+r/100$.

If I invest £40 each year on 1 January for ten years, and my money earns a steady 5 % compound interest, what is my total investment worth exactly ten years after the first instalment?

3. (*a*) A mortgage of £4000 on a house is paid off in 20 equal annual instalments of £y. Interest of 6% is charged each year on the remaining part of the debt. Show that after two years the amount owed is £$(4000x-y)x-y$ where $x = 1{\cdot}06$. Find an expression for the amount owed after 20 years, and by equating this with zero evaluate y.

(*b*) Using your answer to (*a*), find how much was still owing after ten years. How would you check whether or not your answer is reasonable?

4. Let $S_n = 1+\frac{1}{2}+\frac{1}{4}+\frac{1}{8}+\ldots$. Draw the graph of S_n against n for $n = 1, 2, 3, 4, 5$. (The graph will be a set of isolated points, of course.) Write down the formula for S_n and consider what happens as $n \to \infty$. Does your graph confirm this?

5. Repeat Question 4 for the series

$$(a)\ 1-\tfrac{1}{2}+\tfrac{1}{4}-\tfrac{1}{8}+\ldots,$$

and

$$(b)\ \tfrac{1}{2}+\tfrac{1}{3}+\tfrac{2}{9}+\tfrac{4}{27}+\ldots.$$

6. A certain ball is dropped from a height of 3 m. The first bounce takes 1 second (this is the interval between the instants when the ball hits the ground for the first and second times), and each subsequent bounce takes two-thirds of the time of the previous bounce. Find the total times taken (*a*) by the first 3 bounces, (*b*) by the first 10 bounces (use logarithms), and (*c*) until bouncing stops.

Is there anything paradoxical in an infinite number of bounces taking place in a finite time?

Summary. If g is a function,

$$\sum_1^n g(x_i) \quad \text{is a shorthand for} \quad \sum_{i=1}^{i=n} g(x_i), \quad \text{or} \quad \sum_{i=1}^{n} g(x_i),$$

which is itself a shorthand for

$$g(x_1)+g(x_2)+g(x_3)+\ldots+g(x_n),$$

where the suffix of x takes all integral values from 1 to n.

$$\sum_1^n (af(i)+bg(i)+c) = a\sum_1^n f(i)+b\sum_1^n g(i)+cn.$$

Some finite series

$$\sum_1^n i = \tfrac{1}{2}n(n+1),$$

$$\sum_1^n i^2 = \tfrac{1}{6}n(n+1)(2n+1),$$

$$\sum_1^n i^3 = \tfrac{1}{4}n^2(n+1)^2,$$

$$\sum_1^n i(i+1)(i+2)\ldots(i+r) = \frac{1}{r+2}n(n+1)(n+2)\ldots(n+r+1).$$

Arithmetic progressions:

$$a+(a+d)+\ldots+\{a+(n-1)d\} = \tfrac{1}{2}n(\text{first term}+\text{last term}).$$

Geometric progressions:

$$a+ar+ar^2+\ldots+ar^{n-1} = a\left(\frac{1-r^n}{1-r}\right).$$

12

POSITION AND SPREAD

1. POPULATIONS

1.1 In the elementary course, we met various statistics—mean, median, mode, quartiles, interquartile range—and discussed how to calculate them in simple cases. In the first three sections of this chapter, these elementary ideas are revised; a new and more useful measure of spread is then introduced.

First, consider a situation in which a sum of money is shared among ten people as follows: Alice £4, Brian £3½, Cynthia £4, David £0, Elizabeth £4, Frank £3½, Kate £2, Victor £3, Jean £1, Geoffrey £3.

This information is about a set and a function. The set consists of the ten people concerned; the function has this set for its domain. The image of a person of the domain consists of a number, namely the number of pounds received by that person.

From a mathematical standpoint, the names of the people (and the order in which they are listed) are irrelevant; so we discard this information and concentrate on their images under the function. Since there are repetitions amongst these (because two or three people receive the same sum of money), the ten images (4, 3½, 4, 0, 4, 3½, 2, 3, 1, 3) do not constitute a set. Such a collection of numbers with possible repetitions and no notion of order we shall call a *population*. This is one of the basic notions of the branch of mathematics called 'Statistics'. Just as 'Calculus' deals with functions, and 'Geometry' deals with points, lines and planes, so 'Statistics' deals with populations.

1.2 If we have data of any sort—cricket scores, census returns, car production figures, numbers of spots on butterfly wings—we can calculate various quantities from them—greatest scores, number of children per family, average number of spots. Any such number is called a *statistic*.

A statistic may be devised for one of three main purposes:

(i) *Comparison of two or more populations*

If we have two populations of similar measurements, we may wish to be able to assess how they differ from one another. Of two football clubs, which tends to score more goals? Of two countries, which has the larger industrial capacity? Of two experimenters working at the same task, whose readings are more consistent? Do the heights or masses of 16-year-old girls vary more?

This chapter is largely concerned with *Descriptive Statistics*, the branch of study which devises and calculates measures of comparison. The aim is well summed up in the words of R. A. Fisher:

'A quantity of data which by its mere bulk may be incapable of entering the mind is to be replaced by relatively few quantities which shall adequately represent the whole, or which, in other words, shall contain as much as possible, ideally the whole, of the relevant information contained in the original data.'

(ii) *Forecasting*

How much electricity will the country need in five years time? How many temporary extra postmen will be needed in Bristol next Christmas? Statistics play an important part in answering such questions; but many other considerations enter into the calculation, of course.

(iii) *Deriving information from samples*

If we took a set of households in a city, say Nottingham, and counted the number of rooms in each household (with suitable definitions of rooms and households), we would again get a population—of numbers of rooms. This population might be thought of as only a part of the larger population which would be obtained by listing the number of rooms to a household throughout the U.K. When we particularly want to concentrate on a population as part of a larger one, we call it a *sample* from the larger population, and the larger population we call the *parent population.*

Now in our example the population of rooms-to-a-household in the U.K. is itself merely a sample of the population obtained from households in Western Europe, and so on. The terms 'sample' and 'parent population' are not absolute.

We shall discuss sampling in a later chapter. The aim of this is to estimate properties of a parent population from the statistics of samples.

1.3 How reliable a sample is, or how *significant* a statistic, requires careful consideration. Answers to such questions will depend, among other things, upon the size of a population. In this chapter, populations are mostly kept small, but it must be understood that this is in order to keep the calculations within reasonable bounds in the hope that the meanings of the terms and statistics will not be obscured by heavy arithmetic.

2. FREQUENCY FUNCTIONS

2.1 We are familiar with the process of drawing up a *frequency* table. For the population of the money-sharing situation of Section 1.1, this is:

Number of pounds	Frequency
0	1
1	1
2	1
3	2
$3\frac{1}{2}$	2
4	3

We have here a function defined as follows. If x is a number, then $f(x)$ is defined to be the number of times x occurs in the population. If x does not occur in the population, then $f(x) = 0$. The value of $f(x)$ is, of course, the *frequency* of x, and f is called the *frequency function*. Its range is obviously a set of non-negative integers. In this case we can write, for example, $f(3\frac{1}{2}) = 2$.

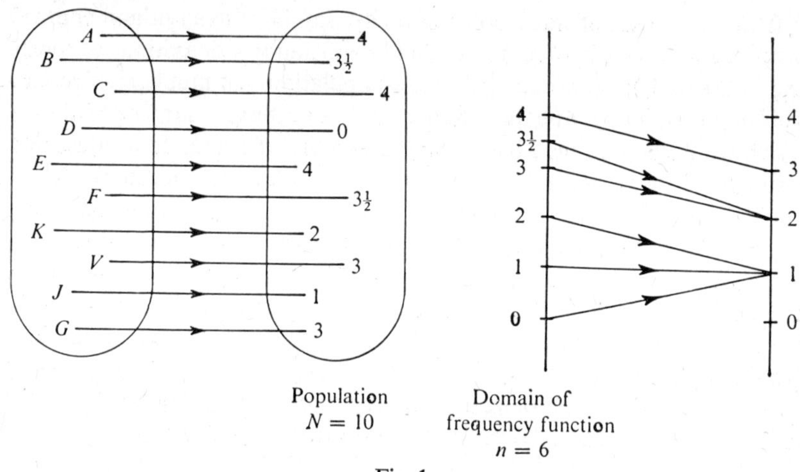

Fig. 1

We see that two mappings are involved. One measures a property of the original set of individuals or events, and so produces a population of numbers; the other is the frequency function defined by the population. These mappings are illustrated in Figure 1.

The following notation will be used:

N denotes the size of the population,

n is the number of different values of x that occur in the population,

$x_1, x_2, x_3, \ldots, x_n$ are elements of the domain of the frequency function that occur in the population.

Then, $$N = \sum_{i=1}^{i=n} f(x_i).$$

In our example, $n = 6$ and $N = 10$. It is usually convenient to arrange the values of x in ascending order. Check that here this would mean that $x_5 = 3\frac{1}{2}$ and $f(x_6) = 3$.

2.2 Frequency diagrams. The graph of the frequency function would be a set of isolated points. A more useful display is a frequency diagram, such as we have used in the elementary course. In our example it appears

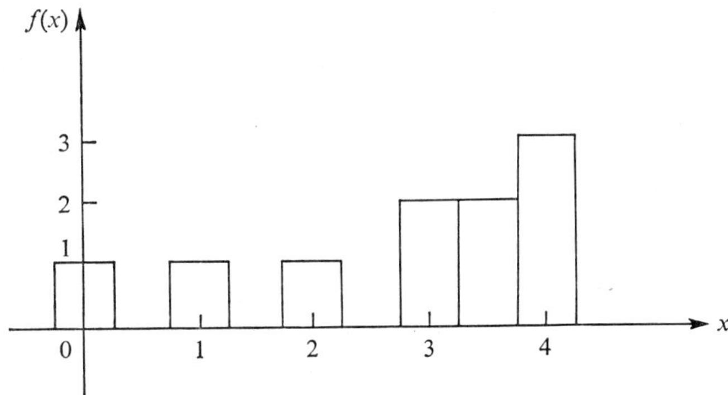

Fig. 2

that we should think of the unit of issue as £$\frac{1}{2}$, and extend the frequency table to display that $f(x) = 0$ for $x = \frac{1}{2}, 1\frac{1}{2}, 2\frac{1}{2}$. The diagram is then as shown in Figure 2.

Exercise A

(Keep the results of this exercise for use in later exercises.)

1. Draw frequency diagrams for each of the frequency functions, f, g and h.

x_i	$f(x_i)$	$g(x_i)$	$h(x_i)$
3	1	1	1
4	2	1	1
5	3	2	2
6	2	4	3
7	1	5	3
8	0	2	6

2. The following data were obtained from a class.

	A	B	C	D	E	F	G	H	I	J	K	L	M
Age	16	16	16	15	16	16	15	16	14	15	16	16	15
Number of brothers/sisters	3	4	0	0	2	1	6	1	0	2	3	2	1
Number of letters in Christian name	4	5	11	5	4	5	6	7	4	4	5	8	4
Height (in cm)	165	163	167	167	155	175	165	172	158	165	175	163	165

For each population, draw up a frequency table, draw a frequency diagram, and state the values of N and n (as defined above).

3. POSITION AND AVERAGE

3.1 In this section and in Section 4 we shall consider two simple comparisons of measurements—to speak loosely: 'Which are the bigger?', 'Which are the more varied?' For instance, 'Are Frenchmen taller than Spaniards?', 'Are incomes more varied in Italy than in Britain?'.

In this section we discuss *position* and *average*, summarizing ideas already dealt with in earlier books. To fix our attention we shall consider data derived from the following two sets of objects:

the first 27 sentences of *The History of Mr Polly*;
the first 27 sentences of *The Way of All Flesh.*

We take x to be the length in words of a sentence and so we have two populations of values of x. We call these populations THOMP and TWOAF. They give rise to two frequency functions which we denote by h and w respectively. We obtain the tables:

x	3	4	5	6	7	10	11	12	14	15	16	17	18	19	20	21	22
$h(x)$	2	2	2	1	1	1	1	1	2	2	1	2	0	0	1	3	1
$w(x)$	0	1	0	0	0	1	0	0	1	1	0	0	2	1	0	0	0

x	23	24	25	26	27	28	29	31	32	35	37	39	40	41	46	73	122
$h(x)$	0	2	0	0	1	0	0	0	0	0	1	0	0	0	0	0	0
$w(x)$	1	2	2	1	0	1	2	1	1	1	0	1	2	1	2	1	1

3.2 Comparison of positions. Our question is 'Which set contains the longer sentences?' A glance shows that the sentences of TWOAF are longer than those of THOMP. If the frequency diagrams were plotted on the same scale, the main bulk of the ordinates for TWOAF would be to the right of that of THOMP. The position of the bulk of the ordinates is an indication of the average sentence-length. We can describe this more precisely in many ways. For instance, by comparing one of the four following statistics:

(i) *Mean of the extreme values of x*

In THOMP, the extreme values are 3 and 37 with mean 20.
In TWOAF, the extreme values are 4 and 122 with mean 63.

(ii) *The Mode*

The modes of x in a population are those values of x that occur most frequently.

Here they are the commonest sentence lengths.

In THOMP the mode is unique. It is 21 and $h(21) = 3$.

In TWOAF the modes are 18, 24, 25, 29, 40, 46, each with frequency 2. THOMP is *unimodal*, TWOAF is *multimodal*. Clearly, in an example like this the mode is a worthless statistic.

(iii) *The Median*

To find the median of x in a population, arrange the population in ascending order of x. Then if N—the population size—is odd, the median is unique and is the value of x of the $\frac{1}{2}(N+1)$th member of the population. If N is even, the median may be indeterminate, being any value between the values of x of the $(\frac{1}{2}N)$th and $(\frac{1}{2}N+1)$th members of the population. Roughly speaking, the median is the value of x for the 'middle' member of the population.

In THOMP and TWOAF the medians are 15 and 28.

(iv) *The Mean*

The mean is the average (in the usual sense) of all the numbers in the population. Since x_i occurs $f(x_i)$ times in the population, it contributes $x_i f(x_i)$ to the total of the numbers in the population.

The total is then

$$x_1 f(x_1) + x_2 f(x_2) + \ldots + x_n f(x_n) = \sum_1^n x_i f(x_i).$$

So the mean

$$m = \frac{1}{N}\sum_1^n x_i f(x_i) = \sum_1^n x_i f(x_i) \Big/ \sum_1^n f(x_i).$$

It is uniquely defined for any population.

In THOMP and TWOAF the means are 14·6 and 32·3. The calculations are tedious and some short cuts will be shown later.

3.3 The merits of each statistic. Almost all our later work in this course will use the mean as the measure of position. It is easily handled algebraically and has important properties which will emerge when we discuss sampling. However, the other statistics are all easier to find, and have certain other advantages. For purely descriptive work, the following points should be noted:

(i) *Mean of extremes.* Easy to calculate, even without sorting the data, but not often a useful statistic.

(ii) *Modes.* If a frequency table has been drawn up, no calculation is required to find the modes.

(iii) *Median.* Not much affected by abnormal members of a population, i.e. by values of x exceptionally large or small. Used commonly, for instance, in describing 'average' salaries, when the mean would be considerably affected by a few tycoons.

(iv) *Mean.* (*a*) Takes into account every member of the population. This is usually an advantage, but not always (see (iii) above).

(*b*) Can be calculated without ordering or sorting out the data. This is useful when working with a desk calculator or computer.

In advanced work, the mean is used most, but the median comes into its own when samples are taken from a population for which the frequency function is completely unknown—such methods are called 'distribution-free'.

3.4 Discrete and continuous.

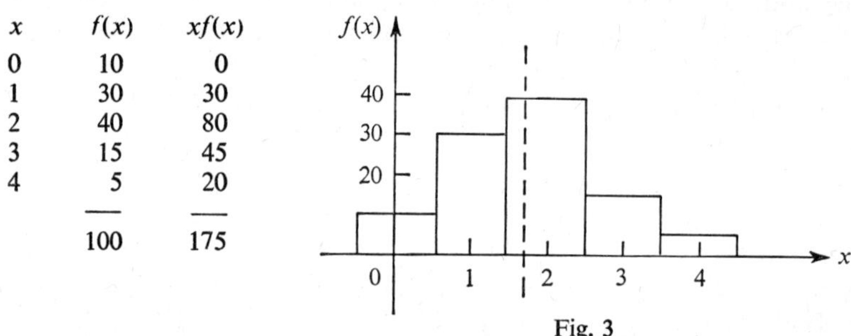

x	$f(x)$	$xf(x)$
0	10	0
1	30	30
2	40	80
3	15	45
4	5	20
	100	175

Fig. 3

The frequency function given in the table above and shown in the frequency diagram, might arise from many different situations; for instance, x might be the number of goals scored by 100 football clubs on a particular Saturday, or perhaps the height (in cm, to the nearest cm) of a collection of seedlings. There is an important difference between these cases from a statistical standpoint, the populations being drawn respectively from a *discrete* domain, and an interval of the real number-line. (This latter case is usually loosely described by the word 'continuous'.) Discrete domains contain only isolated numbers, usually (but not necessarily) integers. In measuring heights, lengths, masses, temperatures and other quantities, however, we are dealing with domains in which possible values could be any real numbers within reasonable limits, and need not be isolated from one another, at any rate in principle. We can, however, only measure these quantities to within a certain degree of accuracy, and so inevitably our data are grouped between upper and lower bounds imposed by the lack of precision in measurement. If the table above refers to heights of seedlings, it is assumed that measurements have only been made to the nearest cm, and $f(1) = 30$ implies that 30 seedlings had heights between 0·5 cm and 1·5 cm. With a discrete domain grouping is not inevitable but it is often desirable nonetheless.

The table above gives exact information in the discrete case, and the working gives a mean of exactly 1·75. Also we can say without hesitation that the median number of goals is 2. In the 'continuous' case the table gives us approximate information, and the same working gives us an approximate mean height of 1·75 cm. In this calculation we are assuming that the heights are fairly evenly spaced within each class, and that any errors will tend to cancel each other out.

To find a value for the median in the 'continuous' case, we require the ordinate which will divide the area of the frequency diagram into equal halves, i.e. the middle block must be divided in the ratio 10:30. This is shown by the dotted line above; the median is approximately 1·75. The fact that this coincides with the mean is an accident of the data, and has no special significance.

3.5 Grouped data—smoothing irregularities. In the tables of Section 3.1, the populations of sentence-length were seen to be very irregular in detail. We can smooth these irregularities by grouping the sentence-lengths. Such a group we call a class, and the mid-point of its interval on the x-axis is called the *class-mark*. Shown below are the grouped frequencies for THOMP, taking equal *class-lengths* of 5, with the subsequent calculation of the mean. Because of the grouping, the value found will be only an approximation, but the result is in fact within 0·1 of the correct value.

Class-interval	Class-mark (x_i)	$f(x_i)$	$x_i f(x_i)$
$\frac{1}{2}$–$5\frac{1}{2}$	3	6	18
$5\frac{1}{2}$–$10\frac{1}{2}$	8	3	24
$10\frac{1}{2}$–$15\frac{1}{2}$	13	6	78
$15\frac{1}{2}$–$20\frac{1}{2}$	18	4	72
$20\frac{1}{2}$–$25\frac{1}{2}$	23	6	138
$25\frac{1}{2}$–$30\frac{1}{2}$	28	1	28
$30\frac{1}{2}$–$35\frac{1}{2}$	33	0	0
$35\frac{1}{2}$–$40\frac{1}{2}$	38	1	38
		27	396

$$m \simeq \tfrac{396}{27} = 14{\cdot}7.$$

The choice of class length is a matter for judgement, and no hard and fast rules can be laid down, but taking between 7 and 10 classes nearly always proves satisfactory. Note that if the class-length is an odd number, the class-marks are integral.

Just where we impose the regular class-marks is another matter at our disposal. Obviously a class-interval from $-1\frac{1}{2}$ to $8\frac{1}{2}$ is rather bizarre, but then a genuine sentence of length 1 word is impossible, so a class-interval of $\frac{1}{2}$–$5\frac{1}{2}$ is not much better. Perhaps an interval $1\frac{1}{2}$–$6\frac{1}{2}$ would be best for the first class in our example.

3.6 Histograms. Suppose two girls, Ann and Zena, were asked independently to record the lengths of the first 100 calls after 6 p.m. to pass through their telephone exchange. They might produce the following frequency tables, which are consistent with each other; the only difference is that Ann has produced more detailed information than Zena.

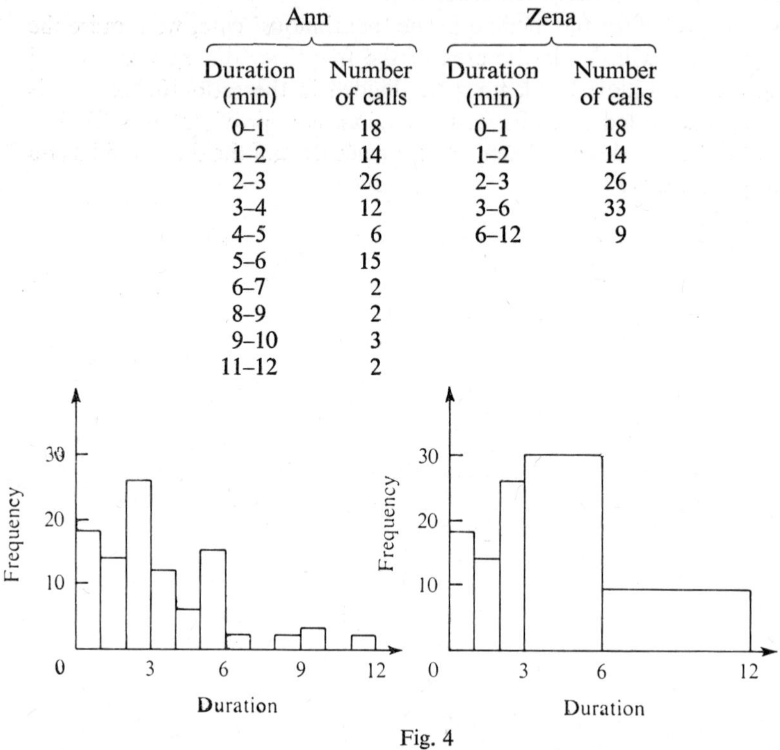

Ann		Zena	
Duration (min)	Number of calls	Duration (min)	Number of calls
0–1	18	0–1	18
1–2	14	1–2	14
2–3	26	2–3	26
3–4	12	3–6	33
4–5	6	6–12	9
5–6	15		
6–7	2		
8–9	2		
9–10	3		
11–12	2		

Fig. 4

Figure 4 shows the frequency diagrams corresponding to the two frequency tables. The second is clearly misleading; it gives the impression that a large proportion of the calls were between 3 and 6 minutes in length.

We can remedy this by representing the frequency corresponding to each class by the *area* of the rectangle with the class-interval as base, and *not* by the height of the rectangle. The axis up the page in our example will then represent the number of calls per minute. The new diagrams are then as in Figure 5.

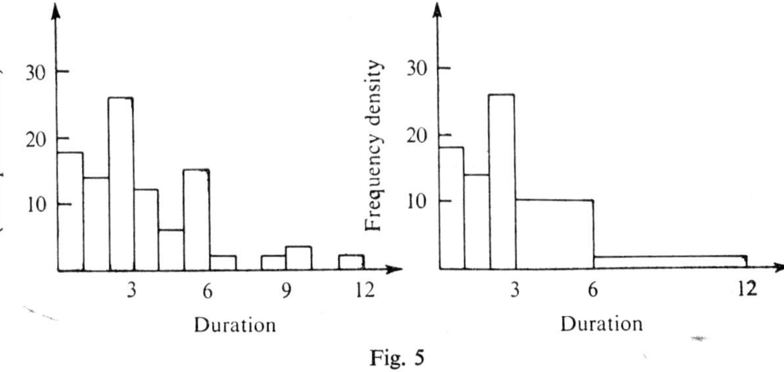

Fig. 5

Such diagrams are called *histograms*. These two convey broadly the same impression as, of course, they should.

Up the page we measure *frequency density*, and the function which relates the value of x to the frequency density is the *frequency density function*. So for each class,

$$\text{frequency density} = \frac{\text{frequency in the class}}{\text{length of class interval}}.$$

Note that if all the class lengths are equal, then the frequency diagram and histogram differ only in scale. If the class lengths vary, the histogram gives the more accurate impression of the data.

Exercise B

1. For which populations of Exercise A, Question 2, are the domains discrete? Find the means and medians. Where the domain is continuous, calculate the approximate means and medians, and mark them on the frequency diagrams. What is the greatest possible error in these values? Explain.

2. Find the means, medians and modal classes for each population of Exercise A, Question 1, assuming the domain to be continuous. Mark these on your frequency diagrams, and note their relative positions. f, g and h are, respectively, typical frequency functions of (i) a *symmetrical* population, (ii) a *negatively-skewed* population (so called because the long tail of the frequency diagram is to the left-hand or negative side), and (iii) a *negatively-J-shaped* population. Explain why you would expect the mean of a negatively-J-shaped population to be less than the median. Is the mean of the negatively-skewed population greater or less than the median? Would your answer be altered if the domain were discrete?

3. Construct simple frequency functions to fit each of the following sets of statistics, and draw the frequency diagrams. (The populations need, in fact, have no more than 7 members each.)

(*a*) mode = -1, median = 1, mean = 0;
(*b*) mode = -2, median = 0, mean = -1;
(*c*) mode = 1, median = 0, mean = 2;
(*d*) mode = 1, median = 2, mean = 1.

4. Calculate the mean length of a telephone call from the data supplied by Zena (see Section 3.6). How inaccurate would you expect this to be? Calculate the mean from Ann's data, and compare your two answers.

5. Two chains were examined and their links individually broken in succession to determine their breaking strains. The measurements (N) were as follows:

First chain	70000	72000	68000	74000	71000	69000
Second chain	71000	74000	69000	75000	73000	67000

Find the mean breaking strain of the links of each chain. Which chain was the stronger?

6. The following average monthly rainfalls (in cm) occur in the seaside resorts of Puddling Regis and Llandrwnch:

	Jan.	Feb.	Mar.	Apr.	May	June	July	Aug.	Sept.	Oct.	Nov.	Dec.
P.R.	9	7	5	5	5	5	5	5	5	5	5	7
Ll.	10	9	9	4	4	3	3	3	4	6	9	11

Draw up the frequency tables. Which town has the higher average monthly rainfall? Which gives the better holiday prospects?

7. Group the data of THOMP (Section 3.1) into classes of length 5 beginning with the class interval $2\frac{1}{2}$–$7\frac{1}{2}$, and hence calculate the mean sentence length. Repeat with class length 7, beginning with the class interval $\frac{1}{2}$–$7\frac{1}{2}$; and yet again, beginning with the interval $2\frac{1}{2}$–$9\frac{1}{2}$.

8. A batsman's scores during a season when grouped were as follows:

No. of runs	0	1–9	10–29	30–49	50–59	60–99
Frequency	6	9	15	10	8	4

Draw a histogram to show these figures. How will you label the vertical axis?

9. The annual wages and salaries of a small firm are shown grouped in the following table.

Wages or salary £	Frequency
600–800	50
800–1000	35
1200–2000	10
2000–3000	4
8000	1

Find an estimate of the mean. Draw a histogram, and mark on it the mean. Roughly how many men earn more than the mean?

10. The ages of people on a holiday tour are given by the following table.

Ages in years	Under 13	13	14	15	Over 16
Frequency	6	8	7	6	8

It is known that some of the people (included in the table) were adult guides. Select two statistics to describe the 'average' age, and invent a measure of the spread of ages.

11. Two judges mark 11 candidates for a competition, each judge using his own marking methods, and the raw marks are:

Candidate	A	B	C	D	E	F	G	H	I	J	K
Judge 1	15	11	6	4	3	3	3	2	1	1	0
Judge 2	12	15	10	6	5	7	5	8	6	8	6

(*a*) Transform the populations of marks to 2 populations with the same range.

(*b*) Transform the populations of marks to 2 populations with the same interquartile range.

(*c*) Convert the populations of marks to two orders of merit.

Assume that the orders of merit from each judge are similar enough to justify combining their marks in some way and use the three transformed populations above to produce three possible final orders of merit of the candidates.

4. SPREAD AND VARIABILITY

4.1 Comparison of spreads. In Section 3 we looked at the data for THOMP and TWOAF and considered how we might answer the question 'Which author wrote the longer sentences?'. We now consider ways of answering the question 'Which author varied his sentence-length more in the passages under consideration?'. It is virtually useless to know merely the mean value for a population without knowing how clustered round that mean are the numbers in the population. A good example of this is provided by the following pair of experiments:

(1) A single die is thrown 72 times and the scores recorded. These form a population with mean about 3·5 and the extremes are probably 1 and 6.

(2) Two dice are thrown 72 times as a pair and half-the-score recorded. These also form a population with mean about 3·5, and the extremes are again probably 1 and 6.

The reader should perform these experiments and keep the results for later reference and use.

A glance at the table of Section 3.1 shows that the sentence-length in TWOAF is more varied than the sentence-length in THOMP. If histograms were drawn for each, the rectangles for TWOAF would be more spread out along the x-axis than those for THOMP. The spread of the rectangles along the x-axis gives an indication of the variability of the sentence length. We can describe this more precisely in many ways. We list two in this section and consider other ways later.

(1) *The range.* This is the difference of the extremes of x. In THOMP it is $37-3$, that is 34; in TWOAF it is 118. It is dependent only on two of the values of x, and this makes it almost useless unless the histogram is very compact. It is no help in distinguishing between the populations produced by the two experiments above.

(2) *The semi-interquartile range.* The quartiles are those three values of x which (roughly speaking) quarter the population. Details are unnecessary here, but the same trivial difficulties arise as when finding the median. The quartiles in THOMP are the $\frac{1}{4}(27+1)$th, $\frac{1}{2}(27+1)$th, and $\frac{3}{4}(27+1)$th values of x; they are 6, 15, 21. Roughly half the population will lie between the first and third quartiles; here the semi-interquartile range is $\frac{1}{2}(21-6)$, that is 7·5. In TWOAF the semi-interquartile range is $\frac{1}{2}(40-19)$, that is 10·5.

These two measures of spread correspond to the mean of extremes and median as 'averages', and have the same advantages and disadvantages. They are quick and easy to calculate, but are often misleading. What we need to develop is a measure of spread which, like the mean as an 'average', takes into account every member of the population.

4.2 Deviations from an average value. An altogether more fruitful approach is to consider deviations from the mean, and to devise a statistic representing in some way the average deviation. We could equally well choose to consider deviations from some other central measure of x (the median perhaps), and the choice of the mean in this context will be considered later.

Consider the population of the nine numbers (2, 2, 2, 3, 5, 6, 7, 9, 9). We shall discuss ways of indicating the spread of this population. Calculations are shown in the following table:

x_i	x_i-m	$\|x_i-m\|$	$(x_i-m)^2$
2	−3	3	9
2	−3	3	9
2	−3	3	9
3	−2	2	4
5	0	0	0
6	1	1	1
7	2	2	4
9	4	4	16
9	4	4	16
9)45	0	9)22	9)68
5		2·44	7·56

(Notice that on this occasion repeated numbers of the population have been listed separately; this can, of course, always be done, though it often shortens the work to use a frequency function. This point is discussed in detail in the following section.)

The first column lists the population and shows that the mean is 5. (In general, the mean is called m.) The second column can then be filled in, showing deviations from this mean; these are defined as $(x_i - m)$. We might then define the average deviation as $(1/N)\Sigma(x_i - m)$; but adding up the second column gives zero, and a moment's reflection shows that this will always be so. So a sensible suggestion is to ignore the minus signs before averaging, as in the third column. This gives us the *mean absolute deviation from the mean*, i.e. $\frac{1}{N}\sum_{1}^{N}|x_i - m|$.

Compare the population with another population of nine numbers y_i: (1, 2, 4, 5, 5, 5, 7, 7, 9). The population mean is again 5, but it is clear by inspection that the numbers are less spread out than the previous ones; and indeed the mean absolute deviation from the mean is 1·78, compared with 2·44 for the x_i. This is an adequate statistic for comparing the spreads of two populations; however, it is tiresome to calculate unless the populations are small or have integral means, and it has other more serious disadvantages.

There is another way of coping with the minus signs in the column of deviations. This is to square each deviation before taking the average. The fourth column shows the calculation of the mean square deviation, which comes to 7·56. In order to obtain a statistic in the same units as those of the original population values we must take the square root of this. This gives us the *standard deviation* (or S.D.). This function of the deviations is the 'root mean square' function familiar to electrical engineers. In our example, the standard deviation is $\sqrt{7{\cdot}56} = 2{\cdot}75$. This is an 'average' deviation worked out in a different way from before, and we should expect a different answer.

It is only possible to interpret a statistic when one has seen the values it can take in particular cases; Exercises C and D are designed with this in mind.

Exercise C

1. Verify that the mean absolute deviation from the mean of the population y_i in Section 4.2 is 1·78 and calculate the standard deviation.

2. 15 sacks of coal were taken from a merchant's lorry and their mass checked. These were 51, 52, 49, 53, 51, 51, 49, 50, 55, 48, 54, 53, 49, 47, 53 kg. Show that the mean mass was 51 kg, and calculate the mean absolute deviation from the mean, and the standard deviation.

3. The ages of the children at a Christmas party were 2, 3, 3, 4, 6, 6, 6, 7, 8, 8, 9, 9, 9, 10 years. Find the standard deviation of this population.

4.3 Calculation of standard deviation. The last section gives us the definition of the standard deviation, and this is expressed algebraically as

$$s = \sqrt{\left[\frac{1}{N}\sum_{1}^{N}(x_i - m)^2\right]}.$$

Observe that the notation is a somewhat simplified version of that introduced in Section 2, in that here we consider the population $(x_1, x_2, ..., x_N)$, and do not introduce a frequency function (in fact, we could interpret this as $f(x_i) = 1$ for all $i = 1, ..., n$ and $n = N$). Repetitions may occur, as in the example of the last section.

You will have found that the arithmetic needed to answer the last question of Exercise C was tiresome. This working can be simplified as we shall now show. This is done by obtaining an alternative formula for the standard deviation.

$$\begin{aligned} s = \sqrt{\left[\frac{1}{N}\Sigma(x_i-m)^2\right]} \Leftrightarrow Ns^2 &= \Sigma(x_i-m)^2 \\ &= \Sigma(x_i^2-2mx_i+m^2) \\ &= \Sigma x_i^2 - \Sigma 2mx_i + m^2N \\ &= \Sigma x_i^2 - 2m\Sigma x_i + m^2N \\ &= \Sigma x_i^2 - 2m.mN + m^2N \text{ (since } m = \Sigma x_i/N) \\ &= \Sigma x_i^2 - m^2N. \end{aligned}$$

So

$$s = \sqrt{\left(\frac{1}{N}\Sigma x_i^2 - m^2\right)}.$$

If you find this working fearsome, try writing it out in full for the population of Section 4.2 starting with

$$s^2 = \tfrac{1}{9}\{(2-m)^2+(2-m)^2+(2-m)^2+(3-m)^2+(5-m)^2+(6-m)^2 \\ +(7-m)^2+(9-m)^2+(9-m)^2\}.$$

Expand each term and then add, without yet replacing m by 5. This should make the vital steps of the algebra clearer.

In the more general notation, using a frequency function, the appropriate version of the standard deviation definition is

$$s = \sqrt{\left[\frac{1}{N}\sum_1^n (x_i-m)^2 f(x_i)\right]}.$$

All that is involved here is, for example, replacing

$$(2-m)^2+(2-m)^2+(2-m)^2$$

in the expression above by $(2-m)^2 \times 3$.

The corresponding alternative version of this is

$$\sqrt{\left[\frac{1}{N}\sum_1^n x_i^2 f(x_i) - m^2\right]}.$$

The following example demonstrates the calculation of the standard deviation from this formula.

Example 1.

x_i	$f(x_i)$	$x_i f(x_i)$	$x_i^2 f(x_i)$
1	10	10	10
2	10	20	40
3	20	60	180
4	40	160	640
5	50	250	1250
6	20	120	720
	150	620	2840

$$m = \frac{620}{150} = 4{\cdot}133, \quad s = \sqrt{\left(\frac{2840}{150} - 4{\cdot}133^2\right)} = 1{\cdot}36.$$

Note that the fourth column in the table is most easily found by multiplying each number in the third column by the corresponding number in the first column.

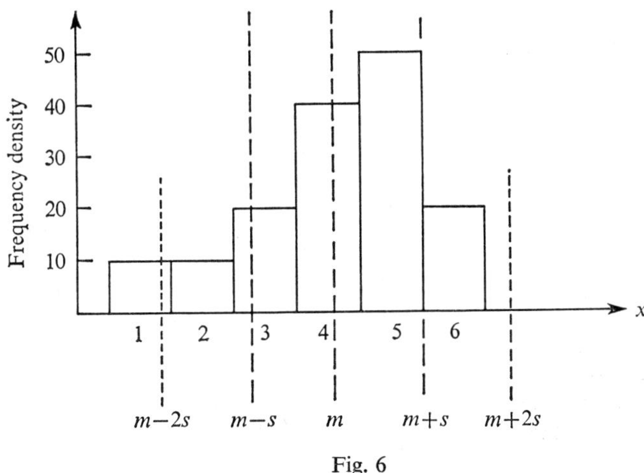

Fig. 6

4.4 Figure 6 shows the histogram for the population in the last example. Some idea of the meaning of standard deviation is given by the lines superimposed on the diagram at $x = m, m-s, m+s, m-2s$ and $m+2s$. Thus the area of the histogram between the lines $x = m-s$ and $x = m+s$ gives an estimate of the number in the population between these values (assuming the population to be drawn from a continuous domain). In this example it is about

$$\tfrac{7}{10} \times 20 + 40 + 50 = 104,$$

or 69 % of the population size. Between $m-2s$ and $m+2s$ the corresponding figure is 141, representing 94 % of the population. These are typical results for fairly symmetrical well-humped histograms.

4.5 Collected formulae.

	Population fully listed as $(x_1, x_2, \ldots, x_N)$	Population in which $x_1, x_2, \ldots, x_n$ occur with frequency $f(x_1), f(x_2), \ldots, f(x_n)$
Population size	N	$N = \sum_1^n f(x_i)$
Mean	$m = \frac{1}{N}\sum_1^N x_i$	$m = \frac{1}{N}\sum_1^n x_i f(x_i)$
Standard deviation	$s = \sqrt{\left[\frac{1}{N}\sum_1^N (x_i - m)^2\right]}$ (1)	$s = \sqrt{\left[\frac{1}{N}\sum_1^n (x_i - m)^2 f(x_i)\right]}$ (3)
	$= \sqrt{\left[\frac{1}{N}\sum_1^N x_i^2 - m^2\right]}$ (2)	$= \sqrt{\left[\frac{1}{N}\sum_1^n x_i^2 f(x_i) - m^2\right]}$ (4)

4.6 Calculation of standard deviation with the aid of a computer.

The mean and standard deviation both have the property that they can be calculated without first sorting out the numerical data. The flow diagram shows how this can be done. V, W, X, Y and Z are working stores, A and B accumulate Σx and Σx^2, and C counts how many numbers have been taken from the data. Once each member of the population has contributed to A, B, C it is forgotten. (It is assumed here that the size N of the population is known beforehand.) The five instructions after the loop work out the mean and standard deviation from the appropriate formulae, using form (2) of Section 4.5.

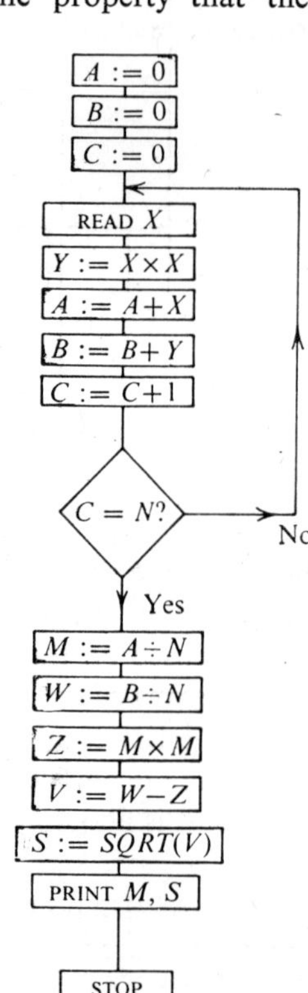

The flow diagram is also relevant if desk calculators are being used. In the first instance, it is probably best for one machine to be used to find Σx; its accumulator then acts as store A, while its counter acts as store C. A second machine simultaneously finds Σx^2.

Notice that the mean absolute deviation could not be found in this way; the numbers must be read and then stored while the mean is calculated, then brought out again in order to calculate the deviations. The formula (1) expressing the *definition* of standard deviation is equally awkward for computer purposes.

4.7 Variance. Standard deviation has been defined as the 'root mean square deviation from the mean'; but the mean square deviation itself, $(1/N)\,\Sigma(x_i-m)^2$, is also of course a measure of the spread of a population. This quantity, known as the *variance*, is just the square of the standard deviation, and is denoted by s^2; no new symbol is introduced. It is an advantage that no square roots are required in its calculation; notice, for example, that in Section 4.3 the working was carried out in terms of the variance to avoid writing square roots in each line.

On the other hand, variance requires unfamiliar units for its measurement: thus if the population is of masses measured in kilograms, the variance is in square kilograms! This means that variance cannot be added to the mean, as was done with standard deviation in expressions such as $m+s$ in Section 4.4. It should also be noticed that if the spread of one population is twice that of a similar population, its variance will be four times as great (for example, consider the populations 2, 3, 4 and 1, 3, 5).

One advantage of using the variance is indicated in Exercise D, Question 10. Certain general results are expressed more easily in terms of the variance than the standard deviation.

Exercise D

1.

x_i	$f(x_i)$	$g(x_i)$	$h(x_i)$	$p(x_i)$	$q(x_i)$	$r(x_i)$
1	1	20	10	50	10	10
2	6	50	20	40	50	10
3	15	40	30	30	20	10
4	20	20	30	10	60	10
5	15	10	40	30	30	10
6	6	10	70	40	20	10
7	1	0	0	50	10	0

Find the mean and standard deviation for each of the populations whose frequency functions are given above. Draw the histograms, mark in the lines $x = m-2s$, $m-s$, m, $m+s$, $m+2s$. Find in each case what percentage of the population lies (*a*) within one standard deviation of the mean, (*b*) within two standard deviations of the mean.

2. For the population in the worked example of Section 4.3, calculate the mean absolute deviation from the mean, $\Sigma|x-m|\,f(x_i)/N$. Also check the standard deviation by using formula 3 of Section 4.5; slide rule accuracy is sufficient.

3. Consider the following data representing the same information grouped in two different ways (the x_i are class-marks):

x_i	1	2	3	4	5	6	7	8	9	10	11	12	13	14	15
$f(x_i)$	12	12	12	30	30	30	30	30	30	20	20	20	8	8	8

x_i	2	5	8	11	14
$g(x_i)$	36	90	90	60	24

Draw histograms for each of the frequency functions, using the same scales for both x-axes, and also for both frequency density axes. Calculate the mean and standard deviation of each population. Comment on the effect that grouping data has on the calculated value of the standard deviation.

4. Construct a frequency function for another population having the same size, mean, and standard deviation as the first one in Question 1.

5. Construct an unsymmetrical frequency diagram for a population with mean 0 and standard deviation 4.

6. The following table shows (fictional, but typical) counts of the number of spots on the hind wing of the butterfly *Maniola jurtina*:

No. of spots	0	1	2	3	4
No. of butterflies (male)	4	15	61	17	3
No. of butterflies (female)	18	15	38	7	2

Find the mean and standard deviation of each population of number of spots.
Split the females into 2 groups, one of which has spot-counts as follows:

No. of spots	0	1	2
No. of butterflies	16	8	6

Find the mean and standard deviation of the number of spots in each group of females and compare them with the group of males.

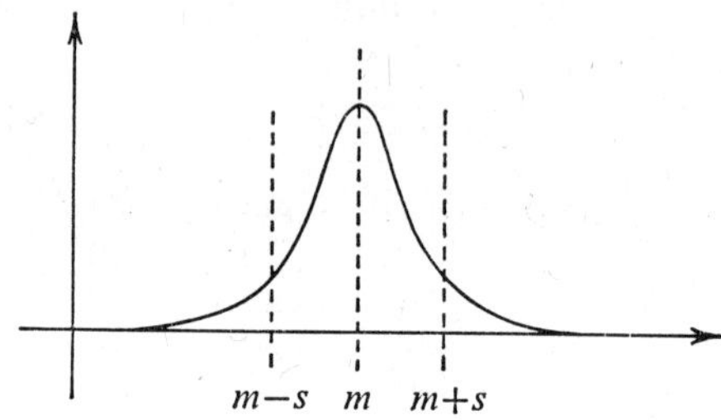

Fig. 7

7. In Figure 7, a continuous curve has been drawn to suggest the general shape of a histogram. The population has size N, mean m, and standard deviation s. Draw four freehand diagrams to show frequency density functions for populations with the statistics listed in the table below. Each diagram must contain a copy of Figure 7 for comparison. Only the continuous general outlines need be drawn.

	Size	Mean	Standard deviation
(*a*)	$\frac{1}{2}N$	m	s
(*b*)	N	$\frac{1}{2}m$	s
(*c*)	N	m	$\frac{1}{2}s$
(*d*)	N	m	$2s$

8. A greengrocer mixes a batch of 100 apples of mean mass 150 g and standard deviation 30 g with another batch of 400 apples of mean mass 150 g and standard deviation 20 g. What is the standard deviation for the combined batch of 500 apples?

9. Two populations are to be combined to give a single larger population. If the sizes, means and standard deviations of the two separate populations are as given below, find in each case the mean and standard deviation of the combined populations.

	First population			Second population		
	N	m	s	N	m	s
(*a*)	10	15	4	10	15	6
(*b*)	10	12	4	10	16	4
(*c*)	10	12	4	30	16	6

10. The following figures show moisture-content, in arbitrary units, of samples from various positions in 4 coke wagons at a steel works.

Wagon \ Position	1	2	3	4	5
1	5	7	4	6	3
2	8	12	7	7	1
3	5	9	19	4	3
4	0	2	0	7	1

Find the mean and variance of the moisture-content for each wagon separately. Find the mean of these variances and the variance of these means. (These are called the average variance *within* classes and the variance *between* classes; they become of value in the branch of statistics called 'Analysis of Variance' and in the design of experiments.)

Verify that the sum of the last two statistics calculated is the variance of the whole population of 20 measurements. (No such simple relation connects the standard deviations, of course.)

11. If $N = \Sigma f(x_i)$ and $m = \frac{1}{N}\Sigma x_i f(x_i)$, show (as in Section 4.3) that:

(*a*) $\frac{1}{N}\Sigma(x_i - m)^2 f(x_i) = \frac{1}{N}\Sigma x_i^2 f(x_i) - m^2$;

(*b*) $\frac{1}{N}\Sigma(x_i - m) f(x_i) = 0$;

(*c*) $\frac{1}{N}\Sigma(x_i - k) f(x_i) + k = m$, where k is any constant;

(*d*) $\frac{1}{N}\Sigma(x_i - k)^2 f(x_i) - (m-k)^2 = \frac{1}{N}\Sigma x_i^2 f(x_i) - m^2$.

Interpret these results in terms of a population and a frequency function.

12. In a mixed school there are 200 boys of mean height 175 cm with standard deviation 10 cm, and 100 girls of mean height 166 cm with standard deviation 7 cm. Find the mean height and standard deviation for all the pupils in the school.

(*Hint.* It simplifies the calculation to use the results of Question 11 (*c*) and (*d*) with a suitably chosen value of k.)

13. Given that $x_i = k+ct_i$, $\bar{x} = \frac{1}{N}\Sigma x_i f(x_i)$ and $\bar{t} = \frac{1}{N}\Sigma t_i f(x_i)$, show that

(*a*) $\bar{x} = k+c\bar{t}$, (*b*) $\sqrt{\left[\frac{1}{N}\Sigma(x_i-\bar{x})^2\right]} = c\sqrt{\left[\frac{1}{N}\Sigma(t_i-\bar{t})^2\right]}$.

Interpret these results in terms of a change of origin and unit of measurement for a population.

14. Calculate the mean and standard deviation from each of the following tables:

x_i	$f(x_i)$	$g(x_i)$	$h(x_i)$
−3	0	1	1
−2	3	1	2
−1	6	5	5
0	7	11	6
1	6	5	10
2	3	1	1
3	0	1	0

(This question shows that even the mean and standard deviation may not give enough information. Other statistics are discussed in Exercise G, Questions 1–3.)

15. Write a flow diagram to calculate the mean and standard deviation of a population from formula (4), where the elements of the population and their frequencies are specified.

5. AIDS TO CALCULATION

5.1 'Two-standard-deviation' check. It is clear that if we take intervals

$$m-s < x < m+s,$$
$$m-2s < x < m+2s,$$
$$m-3s < x < m+3s, \quad \text{and so on,}$$

then an increasing fraction of the total population will be included. Tchebychev (1821–94) showed, in a famous inequality that bears his name, that if we take an interval $m-\lambda s < x < m+\lambda s$, then less than $1/\lambda^2$ of the population can lie outside this interval, however 'eccentric' the frequency function may be.

Very often, however, we shall be dealing with populations whose histograms are humped. If they are not too unsymmetrical, the figures will approximate to those of Normal populations†, which we shall discuss in later chapters. For these it is possible to be more precise about the proportion of the population lying within various intervals. The relevant figures are:

	Normal populations	Tchebychev
Within 1 standard deviation either side	68% of the population	*Not* none of the population
Within 2 standard deviations from the mean	95%	At least $\frac{3}{4}$
Within 3 standard deviations from the mean	Effectively all	At least $\frac{8}{9}$

† 'Normal' is a technical term here and not a descriptive adjective.

The population of Section 4.4 gave figures very similar to those for Normal populations, even though its histogram was by no means symmetrical, and most of the examples of Exercise D should have done so too, with the notable exceptions of the fourth and last populations of Question 1.

The 'two-standard-deviation' check is a quick way of ensuring that our answers for standard deviations are reasonable. This involves that about 5% of the population lies outside the interval $m-2s < x < m+2s$.

5.2 Working zero. Figure 8 shows a histogram for the sentence-lengths of THOMP, suitably grouped as in Section 3.5. By any of the methods discussed so far, calculating the standard deviation would involve tiresome arithmetic. This is much reduced if a *working zero* is used. The idea is to select a class-mark that is roughly central in the population, and to give all population values relative to this class-mark. Thus in our example we might select 18 as a working zero; the transformation $X = x-18$ is then applied to all the x_i, and the calculations carried out with the population of X_i rather than x_i.

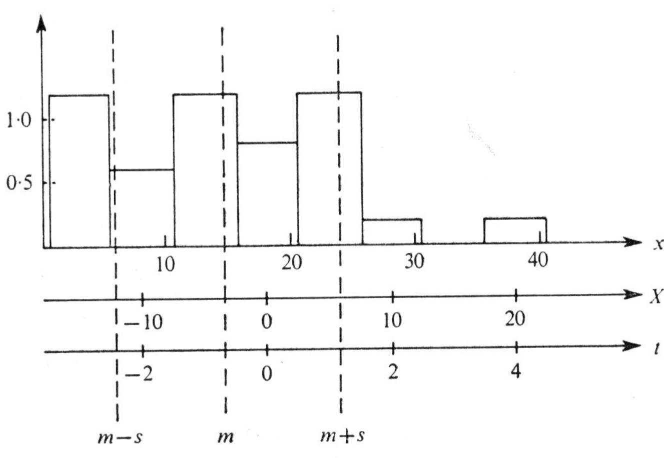

Fig. 8

To avoid ambiguity we shall now use the symbol $\bar{x}$ rather than m for the mean of the population of x_i; the mean of the population of X_i will then be denoted by $\bar{X}$. We shall write for each population value, $f(x_i) = F(X_i)$, the frequency of X_i. Thus the histogram in Figure 8 can be regarded as applying to the X-population by replacing the x-axis by an X-axis. It is clear at once from the diagram that, for this example, $\bar{x} = \bar{X}+18$, and if s_x, s_X denote the standard deviations, that $s_x = s_X$.

The results of Exercise D, Question 10(*c*) and (*d*), form the basis of an algebraic proof that, for an arbitrary working zero k,

$$\bar{x} = \bar{X}+k \quad \text{and} \quad s_x = s_X.$$

The working for THOMP is now given

Class-interval	x_i	$X_i = x_i - 18$	$f(x_i) = F(X_i)$	$X_i F(X_i)$	$X_i^2 F(X_i)$
$\frac{1}{2}$– $5\frac{1}{2}$	3	−15	6	−90	1350
$5\frac{1}{2}$–$10\frac{1}{2}$	8	−10	3	−30	300
$10\frac{1}{2}$–$15\frac{1}{2}$	13	− 5	6	−30	150
$15\frac{1}{2}$–$20\frac{1}{2}$	18	0	4	0	0
$20\frac{1}{2}$–$25\frac{1}{2}$	23	5	6	30	150
$25\frac{1}{2}$–$30\frac{1}{2}$	28	10	1	10	100
$30\frac{1}{2}$–$35\frac{1}{2}$	33	15	0	0	0
$35\frac{1}{2}$–$40\frac{1}{2}$	38	20	1	20	400
			27	−90	2450

$\bar{X} = -\frac{90}{27} = -3{\cdot}3,\quad \bar{x} = -3{\cdot}3+18 = 14{\cdot}7$ (as in Section 3.5).

$$s_X = \sqrt{[\tfrac{2450}{27} - (-3{\cdot}3)^2]} = 8{\cdot}9, \quad s_x = s_X = 8{\cdot}9.$$

The area of the histogram outside the lines $x = m-2s$ and $x = m+2s$ is 1, representing $\frac{1}{27}$, or 4% of the population. So the 'two standard deviation' check is satisfied.

A warning is in order here about finding the standard deviation from grouped data. If two or more contiguous classes with equal frequencies are amalgamated, the value found for the mean is not affected. Exercise D, Question 3 shows that this is not true of the standard deviation. Sheppard's correction, which we only mention here, is designed to reduce the errors likely to result from grouping. It is frequently employed as a matter of routine by persons who do not know when it is likely to help or even that it may not. This sort of attitude to statistics is comparable to preparing the Sunday joint by finding in a dictionary that 'to roast' is 'to cook or heat by exposure to open fire or sun'.

We shall resign ourselves to accepting some uncertainty in a value for the standard deviation found from a grouped table, and answers will be given to 2 significant figures.

5.3 Change of scale. A further reduction in the magnitude of the numbers handled can be effected by a change of scale. This means using the transformation $X = 5t$ in the example of the last section, and so bringing into play the t-axis of Figure 8. Such a step is of value only where the differences between successive x_i are all multiples of some number c. The working of Exercise D, Question 13, establishes the results we should expect:

$$\bar{x} = k+c\bar{t}; \quad s_x = cs_t.$$

x_i	$t_i = (x_i - 18)/5$	$f(x_i) = g(t_i)$	$t_i g(t_i)$	$t_i^2 g(t_i)$
3	−3	6	−18	54
8	−2	3	−6	12
13	−1	6	−6	6
18	0	4	0	0
23	1	6	6	6
28	2	1	2	4
33	3	0	0	0
38	4	1	4	16
		27	−18	98

$$\bar{t} = -\tfrac{18}{27} = -0{\cdot}67, \quad \bar{x} = 18 - 5 \times 0{\cdot}67 = 14{\cdot}7;$$

$$s_t = \sqrt{[\tfrac{98}{27} - (-0{\cdot}67)^2]} = 1{\cdot}78, \quad s_x = 5 \times 1{\cdot}78 = 8{\cdot}9.$$

5.4 Charlier's checks. The reader will have discovered in the previous exercises how easy it is to make an arithmetical slip in these long calculations. Good checks are provided by using:

$$\Sigma(x_i + 1) f(x_i) = \Sigma x_i f(x_i) + \Sigma f(x_i)$$

and
$$\Sigma x_i(x_i + 1) f(x_i) = \Sigma x_i^2 f(x_i) + \Sigma x_i f(x_i).$$

Since the right-hand sides of these identities are quantities which occur elsewhere in the table, we can check our results by appending columns for $(x_i + 1) f(x_i)$ and $x_i(x_i + 1) f(x_i)$. The population in the example of Section 4.3 is used to show the operation of these checks.

x_i	$f(x_i)$	$x_i f(x_i)$	$x_i + 1$	$(x_i + 1) f(x_i)$	$x_i^2 f(x_i)$	$x_i(x_i + 1) f(x_i)$
1	10	10	2	20	10	20
2	10	20	3	30	40	60
3	20	60	4	80	180	240
4	40	160	5	200	640	800
5	50	250	6	300	1250	1500
6	20	120	7	140	720	840
	150	620		770	2840	3460

$$\Sigma x_i f(x_i) + \Sigma f(x_i) = 620 + 150 = 770 = \Sigma(x_i + 1) f(x_i),$$

$$\Sigma x_i^2 f(x_i) + \Sigma x_i f(x_i) = 2840 + 620 = 3460 = \Sigma x_i(x_i + 1) f(x_i).$$

The third and fifth columns should be summed and the first check verified before the sixth and seventh columns are worked out.

These checks should be used also when a working zero and change of scale are employed. The next example illustrates this. Note carefully the way the working is laid out.

Exercise C contained artificially simple questions, but we are now ready to find the mean and standard deviation for any population likely to be encountered. If you can obtain some local data—populations of ages, heights, weights, I.Q.'s, examination marks, etc.—it will be more interesting to use these in preference to the questions of Exercise E.

Example 2. In a certain year percentages obtained in O-level mathematics at one school were distributed as follows. Find the mean and standard deviation, employing Charlier's checks and the two standard deviation check.

Class interval	x_i	$t_i = \dfrac{x_i - 54{\cdot}5}{10}$	$f(x_i) = g(t_i)$	$t_i g(t_i)$	$(t_i+1)\,g(t_i)$	$t_i^2 g(t_i)$	$t_i(t_i+1)\,g(t_i)$
10–19	14·5	−4	1	−4	−3	16	12
20–29	24·5	−3	4	−12	−8	36	24
30–39	34·5	−2	11	−22	−11	44	22
40–49	44·5	−1	25	−25	−22	25	0
50–59	54·5	0	41	−63	41	0	0
60–69	64·5	1	29	29	58	29	58
70–79	74·5	2	37	74	111	148	222
80–89	84·5	3	14	42	56	126	168
90–99	94·5	4	3	12	15	48	60
				+157	+281		
				−63	−22		
			165	94	259	472	566

$$\Sigma t_i\, g(t_i) + \Sigma g(t_i) = 94+165 = 259 = \Sigma(t_i+1)\, g(t_i),$$

$$\Sigma t_i^2\, g(t_i) + \Sigma t_i\, g(t_i) = 472+94 = 566 = \Sigma t_i(t_i+1)\, g(t_i).$$

$$\bar{t} = \tfrac{94}{165} = 0{\cdot}57, \quad \bar{x} = 54{\cdot}5 + 10\bar{t} = 60 \text{ (to 2 s.f.)};$$

$$s_t = \sqrt{[\tfrac{472}{165} - (0{\cdot}57)^2]} = 1{\cdot}59, \quad s_x = 10 \times 1{\cdot}59 = 16 \text{ (to 2 s.f.)};$$

$$\bar{x} - 2s_x = 28, \quad \bar{x} + 2s_x = 92.$$

About 7 out of 165, i.e. 4 % of the candidates, scored less than 28 or more than 92. The 'two standard deviation' check is therefore satisfied.

Notes:

(i) The class intervals should strictly be labelled $9\frac{1}{2}$–$19\frac{1}{2}$, $19\frac{1}{2}$–$29\frac{1}{2}$, etc.

(ii) The $(t_i+1)\,g(t_i)$ column is obtained by multiplying each $g(t_i)$ by the number in the *next* row of the t_i column.

(iii) The seventh column is obtained by multiplying together corresponding numbers in the third and fifth columns.

(iv) The eighth column is obtained by multiplying together corresponding numbers in the third and sixth columns.

(v) The zero line in columns 5 and 6 is a convenient place to enter the negative totals.

Exercise E

1. Seven girls' schools *A*, *B*, ..., *G* were asked to supply statistics of performance in the same O-level examination. The passmark was 40 out of 100.

	A	B	C	D	E	F	G
No. of candidates	50	100	150	90	60	160	100
Mean mark	50	55	60	50	60	55	60
Median mark	55	45	—	—	—	50	50
Standard deviation	—	—	15	10	20	15	10

Compare the results of schools *A* and *B*, and of schools *C*, *D* and *E*. Which school probably had most girls getting over 80 %? Which had the largest proportions getting over 80 %? Estimate, where possible, the approximate number who failed in each school. Do you think an error has been made in the calculation of the statistics for school *G*?

2. In 1881, statues of Gudea, who in about 2170 B.C. ruled the Sumerian city Lagash, were excavated. One of them now in the Louvre shows him holding a scale graduated with the following intervals, measured in mm:

17·5, 17·7, 16·5, 16·8, 16·0, 17·7, 16·6, 17·2, 16·5, 16·5, 16·5,
17·3, 16·7, 17·0, 16·5, 16·5.

(These figures and those in Question 3 are given in A. E. Berriman's *Historical Metrology*, Dent, 1953.)

Find the mean and standard deviation of these lengths. Assuming that the mean length is a Sumerian Shustri, find the length of 10 Sumerian cubits in English inches. (25·4 mm = 1 inch, 30 Shustri = 1 cubit.) Identify this length in the old-fashioned English system of measures.

Now taking the limits of error of the true values of the Shustri to be two standard deviations on either side of the mean, find the limits of the length of 10 cubits in inches.

3. 276 small cuboids of chert found in archaeological diggings in the Indus Valley had the following masses *x* g with frequencies *f*(*x*).

x	*f*(*x*)	*x*	*f*(*x*)	*x*	*f*(*x*)	*x*	*f*(*x*)
1·7	6	3·2	2	6·6	1	13·4	6
1·8	4	3·3	4	6·7	3	13·5	9
1·9	2	3·4	17	6·8	22	13·6	23
2·1	1	3·5	6	6·9	10	13.7	17
2.3	1	3·6	3	7·0	2	13·8	7
		3·8	1	7·3	3	13·9	7
26·6	1	3·9	1			14·0	5
26·8	5	4·0	2			14·1	1
27·0	11					14·2	1
27·2	31	53·6	1				
27·4	17	53·8	1				
27·6	5	54·0	6	134	1		
27·8	4	54·4	8	135	3		
28·0	2	54·6	4	136	6		
28·2	1	55·0	1	138	1		

Find the mean mass in each group and comment on the significance of the results.

4. Group the data of THOMP (Section 3.1) into classes of length 7 beginning with the interval $1\frac{1}{2}$–$8\frac{1}{2}$. Repeat beginning with the interval $2\frac{1}{2}$–$9\frac{1}{2}$. In each case estimate the mean and variance of sentence lengths in THOMP. Use a working zero, change of scale, and Charlier's checks. Repeat (as a class project) with intervals of length 3, 4, 6.

5. Measurements of height (in cm) in a certain species of thistle are as follows:

Height	116–124	124–132	132–140	140–148	148–156	156–164
Frequency	4	18	26	31	15	6

Estimate the standard deviation in cm. Use Charlier's checks.

6. The maximum heights (in cm) cleared by a group of high jumpers are as follows:

x	160·0	162·5	165·0	167·5	170·0	172·5	175·0	177·5
$f(x)$	1	5	13	20	22	17	9	3

Find the mean and standard deviation. Use Charlier's checks.

7. Find the mean and variance from the frequency tables produced by each of the experiments of Section 4.1.

Construct the theoretically ideal frequency tables for these experiments, and calculate the mean and variance from these tables. What would have been the likely effects on your four answers if instead of using 72 throws you had used (*a*) 36 throws, (*b*) 7200 throws?

(This question shows the usefulness of the variance in distinguishing between two significantly related populations.)

8. Examine the first 200 words of The Acts of the Apostles in the Authorized Version and in the New English Bible. (Exclude all words beginning with a capital letter even when the first word of a sentence. This is to exclude any words used as proper names.) Find the means and standard deviations of the lengths of the words measured by number of letters.

9. Examine the first 200 words of books in Latin, French and German, and compare the means and standard deviations of the word lengths.

6. MEAN VALUE

In this chapter, we have already considered several different averages defined for a population:

1. The mean
$$=\frac{1}{N}\sum_{1}^{n} x_i f(x_i).$$

2. The mean absolute deviation from the mean
$$=\frac{1}{N}\sum_{1}^{n} |x_i-m|\, f(x_i).$$

3. The mean square deviation from the mean
$$=\frac{1}{N}\sum_{1}^{n} (x_i-m)^2 f(x_i).$$

All these are special cases of the general expression

$$\frac{1}{N}\sum_{1}^{n} g(x_i)\, f(x_i);$$

this is called the *mean value of* $g(x)$ in the population, and is often written $\overline{g(x)}$.

Taking $g(x) = x$, we get

$$\frac{1}{N}\sum_{1}^{n} x_i f(x_i) = \text{the mean value of } x = \bar{x},$$

so the notation just introduced is consistent with our previous use of the symbol $\bar{x}$.

A further example is provided by

$$\frac{1}{N}\sum_{1}^{n} x_i^2 f(x_i),$$

which has featured in calculations of standard deviation. This is the mean value of x^2, written $\overline{x^2}$. Notice that $\overline{x^2} \neq \bar{x}^2$; indeed the variance can be written as $\overline{x^2} - \bar{x}^2$.

In general, $\overline{g(x)} \neq g(\bar{x})$.

6.1 Regression lines.

Figure 9 illustrates a situation that often arises in experimental science. An experiment that was expected to lead to a straight-line graph has been carried out. However, because of experimental errors, the observed values

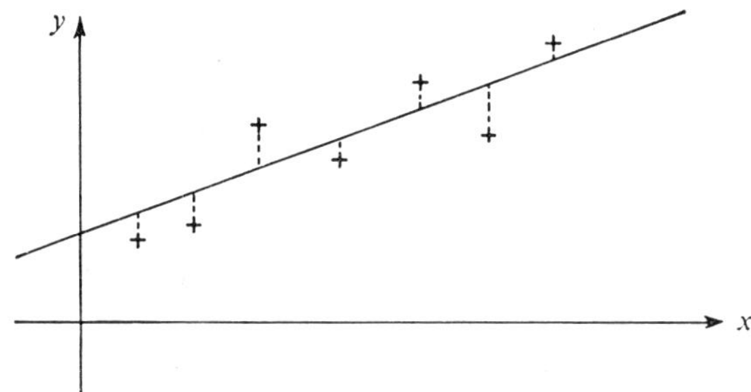

Fig. 9

the of variables give non-collinear points. In practice the next step is generally to draw the 'best straight line through the points'. It is instructive to discuss how to define the 'best' line, and to devise a statistic representing the 'average error'.

Let us tackle the second problem first. Given a straight line, and a set of points near the line, we wish to define the average error. This is almost exactly the situation of Section 4.2, and, as in the definitions of a measure of spread of a single variable, there are many different sensible suggestions. The one normally chosen is the *root mean square* of the displacements parallel to the y-axis of the points from the line; that is, of the differences between the observed values of y_i and the values of y given by the linear equation $y = kx+l$ for the corresponding x_i. We therefore define

$$z = \sqrt{\left[\frac{1}{N}\Sigma(kx_i+l-y_i)^2\right]}$$

as the measure of divergence of the set of points from the line.

This is a function of k and l, and provides us with a measure of the average error for straight lines corresponding to all values of k and l. It is reasonable now to define the 'best' line as that which minimizes z. This is called a *regression line*, and can be found algebraically without even plotting the points on a graph (see Exercise F, Question 5).

The mean values of various other functions of the coordinates might have been chosen as the 'average error'. One's first instinct might have been to consider the perpendicular distances of the points from the line rather than vertical displacements. A sufficient reason why this is not done is that the resulting algebra is excessively complicated; and on closer examination other drawbacks will also be found.

6.2 Alternative definitions of measures of position and spread.

With a single variable, a similar approach could be adopted. An average distance along the number line of $x_1, x_2, x_3, \ldots, x_N$ from an arbitrary number k could be defined as

$$z = \sqrt{\left[\frac{1}{N}\Sigma(x_i-k)^2\right]}.$$

Measures of position and spread could then be defined simultaneously—as the value of k making this a minimum, and the corresponding value of z.

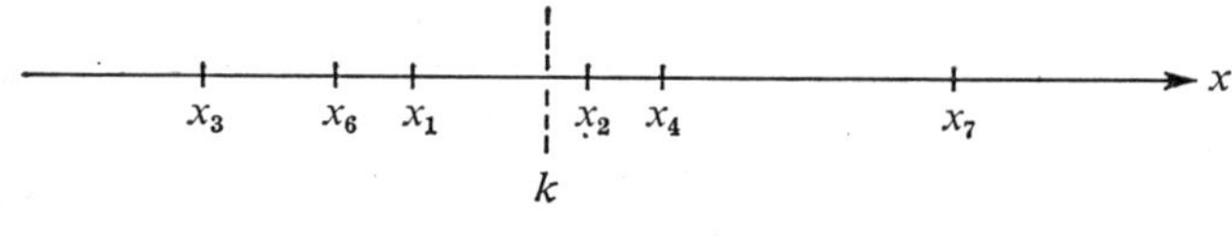

Fig. 10

An alternative pair of statistics could be defined in a similar way, taking $(1/N)\,\Sigma|x_i-k|$ as the average deviation from k. These possibilities are explored in Exercise F.

Exercise F

1. (The calculations of this question may suitably be split among the class.) With $x_1 = 3$, $x_2 = 4$, $x_3 = 7$, $x_4 = 8$, $x_5 = 8$, we define:

$p(k)$ = the mean deviation from k $(= \frac{1}{5}\Sigma(x_i - k))$,
$q(k)$ = the mean absolute deviation from k $(= \frac{1}{5}\Sigma|x_i - k|)$,
$r(k)$ = the mean square deviation from k $(= \frac{1}{5}\Sigma(x_i - k)^2)$.

(*a*) Calculate $p(k)$, $q(k)$ and $r(k)$ for $k = 2, 3, 4, 5, 6, 7, 8, 9$, and draw the graph of each function.

(*b*) What values of k minimize (i) the mean absolute deviation, (ii) the mean square deviation? Are these the mean, mode or median of the population?

(*c*) What value of k makes the mean deviation zero? Comment.

2. Using the notation of the last question, show that the result of Exercise D, Question 11(*d*) could be written $r(k) = s^2 + (m-k)^2$. Hence prove the result suggested in Question 1(*b*), (ii).

3. Given that $x_1, \ldots, x_5$ have the same values as in Question 1, $x_6 = 6$, and $q(k) = \frac{1}{6}\Sigma|x_i - k|$, find $q(5)$, $q(6)$, $q(6\frac{1}{2})$, $q(7)$. How should the median be defined for a population of even size?

4. (*a*) On a graph, plot the nine points whose coordinates are given in the following table.

x	-4	-3	-2	-1	0	1	2	3	4
y	$-6{\cdot}1$	-6	$-3{\cdot}3$	-2	$0{\cdot}4$	$1{\cdot}7$	$3{\cdot}9$	$4{\cdot}4$	$7{\cdot}0$

(*b*) Work out Σx_i, Σy_i, Σx_i^2, Σy_i^2, $\Sigma x_i y_i$, and so write $\Sigma(kx_i + l - y_i)^2$ in as simple a form as possible.

(*c*) Find the values of k and l which minimize this expression. With these values, draw the graph of $y = kx + l$. Would you agree that this is the 'best straight line' through the nine points?

***5.** The regression line of Section 6.1 is found most easily by changing the origin to the point $(\bar{x}, \bar{y})$, i.e. using the transformation $x = X + \bar{x}$, $y = Y + \bar{y}$. The coefficients of the regression line $Y = aX + b$ result then from minimizing $(1/N)\Sigma(aX_i + b - Y_i)^2$, where $\Sigma X_i = 0$, $\Sigma Y_i = 0$. Find these values of a and b, and hence show that the equation of the line is

$$(y - \bar{y}) = \frac{v_{xy}}{v_x}(x - \bar{x}),$$

where v_x is the variance of the x_i's, and v_{xy} (the covariance of x and y) is defined as $(1/N)\Sigma(x_i - \bar{x})(y_i - \bar{y})$.

6.3 Minimum property of variance

The results of Exercise F, Questions 1, 2 and 3 can be summed up as follows:

(*a*) The mean square deviation is least if the deviations are taken from the mean.

(*b*) The excess when any other point is used is the square of the difference between that point and the mean.

(*c*) The mean absolute deviation is least when the deviations are taken from the median.

*Exercise G

1. The rth moment of a population about the mean is defined as

$$m_r = (1/N)\,\Sigma(x_i - \bar{x})^r f(x_i).$$

Thus $m_1 = 0$, $m_2 = s^2$. The *skewness* is defined as m_3/s^3, and the *kurtosis* is defined as $m_4/s^4 - 3$. The latter indicates the length and heights of the tails of the histogram, and is zero for the Normal curve.

Calculate the skewness and kurtosis for each of the frequency functions of Exercise D, Question 14.

2. If $m'_r = (1/N)\,\Sigma x_i^r f(x_i)$, show that

$$m_3 = m'_3 - 3s^2\bar{x} - \bar{x}^3 \quad \text{and} \quad m_4 = m'_4 - 4m_3\bar{x} - 6s^2\bar{x}^2 - \bar{x}^4.$$

Use these forms to calculate the skewness and kurtosis for some of the populations of Exercise D, Question 1.

3. Describe a Charlier-type check for the columns involved in calculating the skewness as in Question 2.

4. The following classic data refer to deaths by horse-kick of Prussian cavalry in 10 corps during 1875–1894.

Number of deaths per corps per year	Frequency with which a corps had this death-rate
0	109
1	65
2	22
3	3
4	1

Calculate the mean, variance and skewness.

(This is the frequency function of a population which is nearly a so-called *Poisson* population. Such populations arise in cases like this, where it is possible to count how many times during the year a death from horse-kick occurs but *not* how many times such a death does not occur.)

5. In a population, the values 0, 1, 2, ..., n occur with frequencies $f(0)$, $f(1)$, $f(2)$, ..., $f(n)$. We define a function $G: t \to \Sigma f(i) t^i$, where t is a variable introduced arbitrarily.

Show that

$$G(1) = N,$$
$$G'(1) = mN,$$

and

$$G''(1) = s^2N + m^2N - mN.$$

6. Show that for the first population of Exercise D, Question 1, $G(t) = (1+t)^6$. Use the results of Question 5 to find the variance of this population.

7. Find an expression for the skewness in terms of the values of $G(t)$ and its derived functions.

(G is called a *generator*, or *generating function*.)

13

FURTHER VECTORS

The main purpose of this chapter is to express the geometrical results of Chapter 9 in algebraic terms. We shall cover much of the same ground in a rapid survey, and then add the new idea of scalar product which will enable us to handle the properties of Euclidean space associated with perpendicularity.

1. BASE-VECTORS AND COORDINATES

Exercise A

1. Figure 1 shows a 'grid' of equal parallelograms. Selecting a vertex, O, we name the vectors $\mathbf{OA} = \mathbf{a}$ and $\mathbf{OB} = \mathbf{b}$. Express in terms of $\mathbf{a}$ and $\mathbf{b}$

(*a*) **OP**; (*b*) **OQ**; (*c*) **OR**; (*d*) **OS**; (*e*) **OT**;
(*f*) **PS**; (*g*) **TR**; (*h*) **QA**; (*i*) **UR**; (*j*) **AU**.

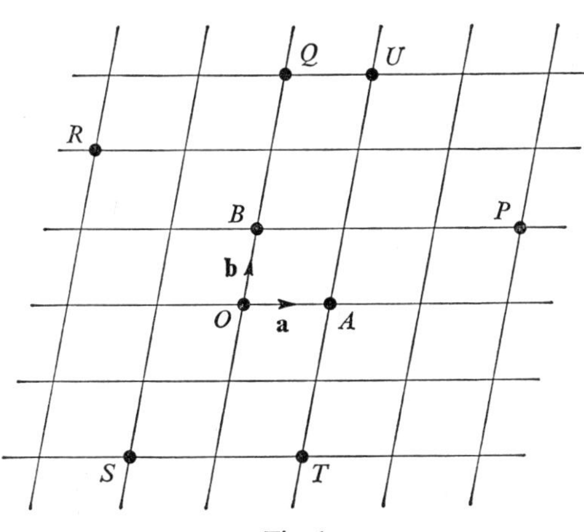

Fig. 1

2. $\mathbf{i}$ and $\mathbf{j}$ are unit vectors along the axes of an ordinary system of rectangular Cartesian coordinates.

(*a*) Let P be the point $(5, -3)$, and express **OP** in terms of $\mathbf{i}$ and $\mathbf{j}$.
(*b*) If $\mathbf{OQ} = -7\mathbf{i}+4\mathbf{j}$, what are the coordinates of Q?
(*c*) Express **PQ** in terms of $\mathbf{i}$ and $\mathbf{j}$.

3. In Figure 1, what is $\mathbf{OP}+\mathbf{OR}$? Express the sum in terms of $\mathbf{a}$ and $\mathbf{b}$.

4. With the notation of Question 2, if $\mathbf{OL} = x_1\mathbf{i}+y_1\mathbf{j}$ and $\mathbf{OM} = x_2\mathbf{i}+y_2\mathbf{j}$, and $\mathbf{ON} = \mathbf{OL}+\mathbf{OM}$, what are the coordinates of N?

1.1 Base vectors and coordinates. From this exercise it should be clear that we can express any vector in a plane in terms of two *base vectors* **a** and **b**, or **i** and **j**. As a matter of convenience we can take **i** and **j** to be of unit length and in perpendicular directions; conventionally we take **i** pointing to the right and **j** upwards (see Figure 2).

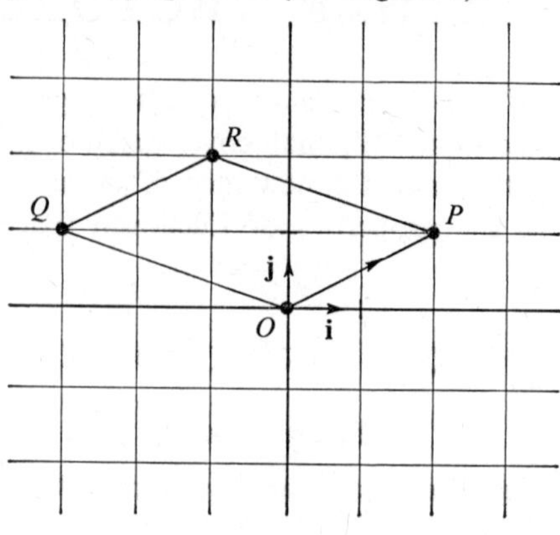

Fig. 2

For a point such as P, $\mathbf{OP} = 2\mathbf{i}+\mathbf{j}$. We say that P has *coordinates* (2, 1). We can specify the vector **OP** in several different ways. We may write

$$\begin{aligned}\mathbf{OP} &= \mathbf{p}, \text{ using a single letter;}\\ &= 2\mathbf{i}+\mathbf{j}, \text{ in terms of the base vectors;}\\ &= \begin{pmatrix}2\\1\end{pmatrix}, \text{ as an algebraic column vector.}\end{aligned}$$

This last notation is really a 2×1 matrix; it is particularly useful when we are dealing with transformations and with linear equations. In this notation

$$\mathbf{i} = \begin{pmatrix}1\\0\end{pmatrix} \quad\text{and}\quad \mathbf{j} = \begin{pmatrix}0\\1\end{pmatrix}.$$

Since the notation $\mathbf{OP} = 2\mathbf{i}+\mathbf{j}$ conveys the same information as

$$\mathbf{OP} = \begin{pmatrix}2\\1\end{pmatrix}$$

and is easier to print, we shall normally use it in preference to the second notation, except when dealing with matrices.

In Figure 2, corresponding to $\mathbf{OP}+\mathbf{OQ} = \mathbf{OR}$, we have

$$\begin{pmatrix}2\\1\end{pmatrix}+\begin{pmatrix}-3\\1\end{pmatrix} = \begin{pmatrix}-1\\2\end{pmatrix}; \quad\text{and, in general,}\quad \begin{pmatrix}a\\b\end{pmatrix}+\begin{pmatrix}c\\d\end{pmatrix} = \begin{pmatrix}a+c\\b+d\end{pmatrix}.$$

1.2 Three-dimensional coordinates. Any point in three-dimensional space requires three coordinates to specify its position in relation to three non-coplanar lines or *axes* drawn from an *origin* O. It is convenient for these axes to be mutually perpendicular. For example, we may think of the first two as perpendicular axes lying in a horizontal plane, and the third as drawn vertically.

Mathematically there is no distinction between our real world and the 'looking-glass' world that would result from reflecting it in a plane mirror. But physically and biologically there is a distinction—we should be quite unable to assimilate food grown in a looking-glass world, and of course right-handed people would find difficulty in driving looking-glass screws.

If we wish to make this distinction—and in constructing models or diagrams we must do—it is convenient to establish the convention that our axes form what is called a RIGHT-HANDED set. The easiest way to explain this is to say that a right-handed screw, turned through a quarter-turn from Ox to Oy, would be advanced in the direction of Oz (see Figure 3).

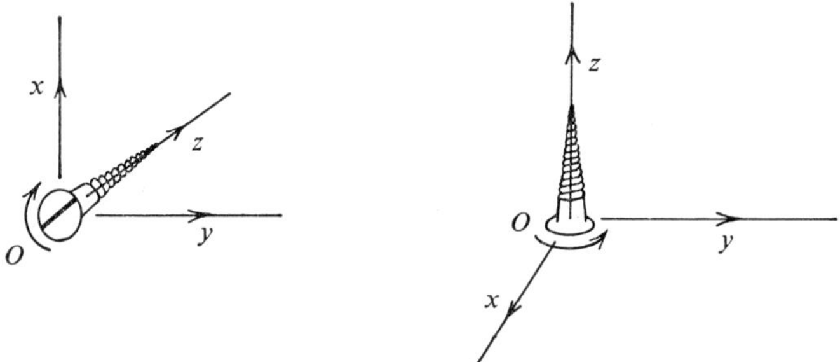

Fig. 3. Right-hand axes.

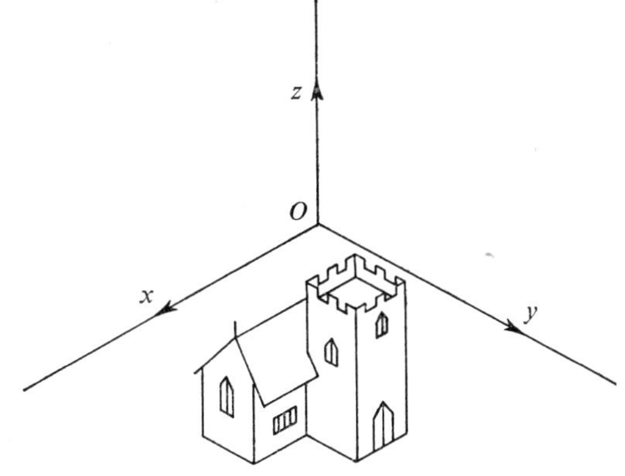

Fig. 4. Isometric axes.

A little experiment will soon show that in this case a quarter-turn from Oy to Oz will drive the screw in the direction Ox, and a quarter-turn from Oz to Ox will drive it in the direction Oy.

The usual diagram has the axes of y and z in the plane of the paper—to the right and upwards respectively—when the axes of x will be found to be directed out towards the reader. Or the axes may be drawn *isometrically* (see Figure 4), it being understood that the inclined axes point forwards. In the drawing, the axes meet at angles of 120°, and the scales along all three axes are the same.

We may now specify any vector **p** in three dimensions by taking the segment representing it starting out from the origin O; if the terminus of this segment is P, we write $\mathbf{p} = \mathbf{OP}$, and **p** is the position vector of P.

If P has coordinates (x, y, z) referred to the coordinate axes, and **i, j, k** are unit vectors along these axes, then

$$\mathbf{p} = \mathbf{OP} = x\mathbf{i}+y\mathbf{j}+z\mathbf{k}$$

$$= \begin{pmatrix} x \\ y \\ z \end{pmatrix} \quad \text{in } 3\times 1 \text{ matrix notation.}$$

Exercise B

1. Let P be $(5, -1, 3)$ and Q $(-2, 4, -1)$. Write down **OP** and **OQ** in terms of **i, j, k**. If $\mathbf{OP}+\mathbf{OQ} = \mathbf{OR}$, what are the coordinates of R?

2. In Question 1, write down **PQ** in terms of **i, j, k**.

3. $ABCD$ is a parallelogram. Write down the coordinates of D if:
(*a*) B is $(0, 0, 0)$, A is $(3, 1, 0)$, C is $(2, 5, 0)$.
(*b*) B is $(0, 0, 0)$, A is $(3, 1, -2)$, C is $(2, 5, 4)$;
(*c*) B is $(0, 0, 0)$, A is $(-1, 2, 4)$, C is $(2, -3, -4)$;
(*d*) B is $(1, 2, 3)$, A is $(2, 3, 4)$, C is $(-1, 5, -3)$.

4. Write each of **i, j, k** in column matrix form.

5. Figure 5 shows a cube of side 2 units. Take an origin at its centre, the axis of x in the direction of AB, and the axis of y in the direction of BC.

Choose the axis of z to make a right-handed set, and write down the coordinates of the eight vertices.

Which is the plane $\{(x, y, z): x = 1\}$? The equation $x = 1$ is called the equation of the plane. Which is the plane with equation $z = -1$?

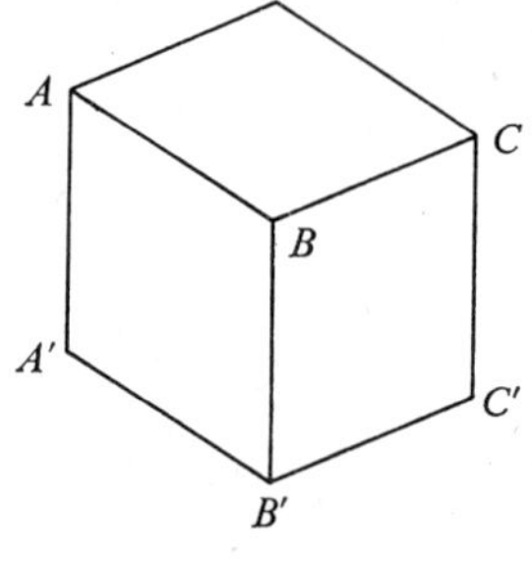

Fig. 5

6. What is the figure formed by the points whose position vectors are **0, i, j, k, i+j, j+k, i+k, i+j+k**?

Where is the point whose position vector is $\frac{1}{3}\mathbf{i}+\frac{1}{3}\mathbf{j}+\frac{1}{3}\mathbf{k}$ in relation to the points whose position vectors are **i, j,** and **k**?

The identity $\frac{1}{3}(\mathbf{i}+\mathbf{j}+\mathbf{k}) = \frac{1}{3}\mathbf{i}+\frac{1}{3}\mathbf{j}+\frac{1}{3}\mathbf{k}$ tells us a fact about a cube. What is it? Would this fact also be true for any parallelepiped (that is, a 'squashed cube', all of whose six faces are parallelograms)?

7. Identify the figure whose four points have position vectors

$$\mathbf{p} = \mathbf{i}+\mathbf{j}+\mathbf{k}, \quad \mathbf{q} = \mathbf{i}-\mathbf{j}-\mathbf{k}, \quad \mathbf{r} = -\mathbf{i}+\mathbf{j}-\mathbf{k}, \quad \mathbf{s} = -\mathbf{i}-\mathbf{j}+\mathbf{k}.$$

Deduce a geometrical fact about the figure from the identity $\frac{1}{2}(\mathbf{p}+\mathbf{q}) = -\frac{1}{2}(\mathbf{r}+\mathbf{s})$.

8. Let

$$\mathbf{p} = \begin{pmatrix} 5 \\ -1 \\ 2 \end{pmatrix}, \quad \mathbf{q} = \begin{pmatrix} -10 \\ 9 \\ 7 \end{pmatrix} \quad \text{and} \quad \mathbf{r} = \begin{pmatrix} 2 \\ 1 \\ 3 \end{pmatrix}.$$

Write down the vectors $4\mathbf{p}+\mathbf{q}$ and $5\mathbf{r}$.

If **p**, **q** and **r** are the position vectors of points P, Q and R, what conclusion do you draw?

9. The six points $A(1, 0, 0)$, $B(0, 1, 0)$, $C(0, 0, 1)$, $D(-1, 0, 0)$, $E(0, -1, 0)$ and $F(0, 0, -1)$ are joined by twelve lines other than the axes. Describe the figure so formed.

***10.** What is the shape of the quadrilateral whose vertices have position vectors $2\mathbf{i}$, $\mathbf{i}+\mathbf{j}+\mathbf{k}$, $2\mathbf{j}$ and $\mathbf{i}+\mathbf{j}-\mathbf{k}$? How many faces of this shape are on the surface of the polyhedron whose vertices have position vectors

$$\pm 2\mathbf{i}, \quad \pm 2\mathbf{j}, \quad \pm 2\mathbf{k}, \quad \pm\mathbf{i}\pm\mathbf{j}\pm\mathbf{k},$$

taking all permutations of the signs (that is, 14 points in all)? Do you know a name for this polyhedron? What is its volume?

2. VECTOR ALGEBRA IN TERMS OF COMPONENTS

Definition. If a vector **p** is expressed in terms of base vectors **i**, **j**, **k** in the form $\mathbf{p} = x\mathbf{i}+y\mathbf{j}+z\mathbf{k}$, then the numbers x, y, z are called the *components* of **p** with respect to this base.

In column vector form we write $\mathbf{p} = \begin{pmatrix} x \\ y \\ z \end{pmatrix}$.

In the previous exercise we have employed two rules:

If $\mathbf{p}_1 = x_1\mathbf{i}+y_1\mathbf{j}+z_1\mathbf{k}$ and $\mathbf{p}_2 = x_2\mathbf{i}+y_2\mathbf{j}+z_2\mathbf{k}$, then:

Vector-sum $\quad \mathbf{p}_1+\mathbf{p}_2 = (x_1+x_2)\mathbf{i}+(y_1+y_2)\mathbf{j}+(z_1+z_2)\mathbf{k}$;

Scalar-multiple $\quad \lambda\mathbf{p}_1 = (\lambda x_1)\mathbf{i}+(\lambda y_1)\mathbf{j}+(\lambda z_1)\mathbf{k}$;

which are easily established using the associative, commutative and distributive laws.

The results of Chapter 9 can now be expressed in terms of components. For example, in Section 4.3 we showed that the point R with position vector $\mathbf{r} = (\lambda\mathbf{p}+\mu\mathbf{q})/(\lambda+\mu)$ lies on $\overleftrightarrow{PQ}$ and divides $\overline{PQ}$ in the ratio $\mu:\lambda$. If P is (x_1, y_1, z_1) and Q is (x_2, y_2, z_2), then

$$\begin{aligned} \lambda\mathbf{p}+\mu\mathbf{q} &= \lambda x_1\mathbf{i}+\lambda y_1\mathbf{j}+\lambda z_1\mathbf{k}+\mu x_2\mathbf{i}+\mu y_2\mathbf{j}+\mu z_2\mathbf{k} \\ &= (\lambda x_1+\mu x_2)\mathbf{i}+(\lambda y_1+\mu y_2)\mathbf{j}+(\lambda z_1+\mu z_2)\mathbf{k}. \end{aligned}$$

We conclude that the point R, which divides the join of $P(x_1, y_1, z_1)$ to $Q(x_2, y_2, z_2)$ in the ratio $\mu:\lambda$, is

$$\left(\frac{\lambda x_1+\mu x_2}{\lambda+\mu}, \quad \frac{\lambda y_1+\mu y_2}{\lambda+\mu}, \quad \frac{\lambda z_1+\mu z_2}{\lambda+\mu}\right).$$

The general principle is now obvious: vector-algebra operations on the vectors correspond to ordinary algebraic operations on the components. Details are worked out in the following exercise.

Exercise C

1. What is $x\begin{pmatrix}1\\0\\0\end{pmatrix}+y\begin{pmatrix}0\\1\\0\end{pmatrix}+z\begin{pmatrix}0\\0\\1\end{pmatrix}$?

2. What is $3\begin{pmatrix}5\\-4\\2\end{pmatrix}+4\begin{pmatrix}-4\\3\\-1\end{pmatrix}$?

3. Show that $\frac{3}{5}\begin{pmatrix}4\\-1\\3\end{pmatrix}+\frac{2}{5}\begin{pmatrix}-1\\9\\8\end{pmatrix}=\begin{pmatrix}2\\3\\5\end{pmatrix}$.

What do you conclude about the points

$$(4, -1, 3), \quad (2, 3, 5) \quad \text{and} \quad (-1, 9, 8)?$$

4. What is the mid-point of $\overline{AB}$ where $A = (3, -5)$ and $B = (-2, 7)$?

5. What is the mid-point of $\overline{PQ}$ where $P = (3, -5, 4)$ and $Q = (-2, 7, 7)$?

6. What are the coordinates of the centroid of the triangle ABC, where

$$A = (x_1, y_1), \quad B = (x_2, y_2) \quad \text{and} \quad C = (x_3, y_3)?$$

(see Chapter 9, Section 5.1).

7. Let $P = (1, 3, -2)$, $Q = (3, 4, 6)$; $R = (-2, 5, 1)$ and $S = (1, -1, 0)$. Write down the coordinates of

(*a*) U, the mid-point of $\overline{PQ}$; (*b*) V, the mid-point of $\overline{RS}$;

(*c*) G, the mid-point of $\overline{UV}$; (*d*) X, the centroid of triangle QRS.

Verify that G divides $\overline{PX}$ in the ratio 3:1.

8. $OABC$ is a square plate of mass $4m$, with small masses $4m$, $3m$, $2m$, m attached to it at O, A, B, C respectively. Take O as origin, A as $(2a, 0)$, C as $(0, 2a)$, and find the coordinates of the centre of mass of the system.

9. A tetrahedron of six equal light rods links rigidly together four small heavy spheres of masses 5, 6, 7, and 8 units. If the mass 5 is at $(1, 1, 1)$, 6 at $(-1, -1, 1)$, 7 at $(1, -1, -1)$, and 8 at $(-1, 1, -1)$, locate the centre of mass of the framework.

3. PARAMETERS IN ONE DIMENSION

3.1 Lines through the origin. Let A be any point on the straight line which passes through the origin O and a fixed point B. If $\mathbf{OA} = 7\mathbf{OB}$, then $\mathbf{a} = 7\mathbf{b}$; if $\mathbf{OA} = \frac{1}{2}\mathbf{OB}$, then $\mathbf{a} = \frac{1}{2}\mathbf{b}$; if $\mathbf{OA} = -3\mathbf{OB}$, then $\mathbf{a} = -3\mathbf{b}$; and so on. In general the vector $\mathbf{r}$ occurring in the relation

$$\mathbf{r} = t\mathbf{b}$$

can be made to represent any point R of the line by choosing t such that $\mathbf{OR} = t\mathbf{OB}$. There is, in fact, a one-one correspondence between the points of the line and the real numbers: to any point of the line there corresponds a unique value of t, and to any value of t there corresponds a unique point of the line. The scalar t, with this property, is called a *parameter* of the point R, and the equation $\mathbf{r} = t\mathbf{b}$ is called a parametric equation of the line.

Although the line is one-dimensional, it can be 'embedded' in two or three dimensions. For example, it may be that $\mathbf{b} = 2\mathbf{i}+5\mathbf{j}$, in which case the line becomes $\mathbf{r} = t(2\mathbf{i}+5\mathbf{j})$. If $\mathbf{b} = 2\mathbf{i}+5\mathbf{j}+3\mathbf{k}$, then the line becomes $\mathbf{r} = t(2\mathbf{i}+5\mathbf{j}+3\mathbf{k})$. So we see that a line can be defined by expressing the position vector of a point on it in terms of a single vector, and that it can also be defined in terms of two or three vectors. However, we shall find later that, when a position vector is related in a less restricted way to two or three vectors, figures other than straight lines can be obtained.

3.2 Components in two dimensions in terms of parameters. The line $\mathbf{r} = t(\mathbf{i}+\mathbf{j})$ can be written $\mathbf{r} = t\mathbf{i}+t\mathbf{j}$, and if, for example, $t = 8$, the position vector of the corresponding point is $8\mathbf{i}+8\mathbf{j}$; if therefore we denote the components of a vector with respect to the base vectors $\mathbf{i}, \mathbf{j}$ by x, y, we have $x = 8$, $y = 8$. In general, the components of the position vector of any point of the line are $x = t$, $y = t$, so that $x = y$.

Take as a second example the equation $\mathbf{r} = t(2\mathbf{i}+5\mathbf{j}) = 2t\mathbf{i}+5t\mathbf{j}$; here we have $x = 2t$, $y = 5t$, so that $y = 5x/2$. This gives us a link with the more familiar Cartesian equation of the line, from which we might notice that its gradient is 5/2.

3.3 Lines not through the origin. If A is a point and $\mathbf{b}$ is a vector, then the position vector of a point $2\mathbf{b}$ from A is $\mathbf{r}_2 = \mathbf{a}+2\mathbf{b}$, and this can be drawn using the triangle rule. So can the points $\mathbf{r}_7 = \mathbf{a}+7\mathbf{b}$, $\mathbf{r}_{\frac{1}{2}} = \mathbf{a}+\frac{1}{2}\mathbf{b}$, $\mathbf{r}_{-3} = \mathbf{a}-3\mathbf{b}$, and so on.

Using the idea of the parameter t, the equation of the line through A parallel to $\mathbf{b}$ is $\mathbf{r} = \mathbf{a}+t\mathbf{b}$.

In two dimensions, using the base vectors $\mathbf{i}, \mathbf{j}$ we might be given that $\mathbf{a} = 3\mathbf{i}+\mathbf{j}$ and $\mathbf{b} = 2\mathbf{i}+5\mathbf{j}$, in which case the line is

$$\mathbf{r} = 3\mathbf{i}+\mathbf{j}+t(2\mathbf{i}+5\mathbf{j}).$$

If we wish to express the equation of the line in terms of ordinary Cartesian coordinates, we see that it is a line of gradient 5/2 (as before), that passes through the point (3, 1). Hence the equation is $y = 5x/2-13/2$.

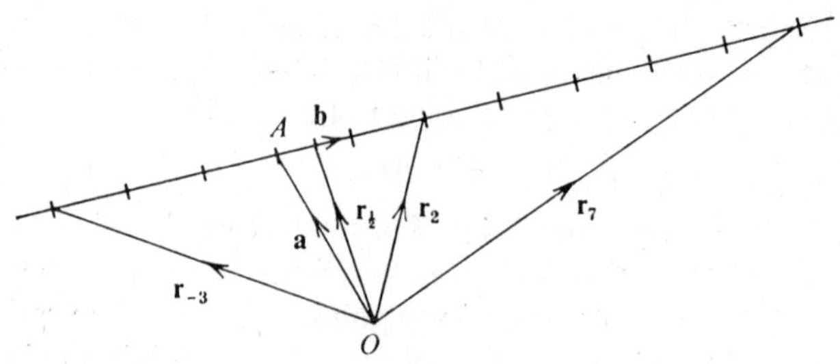

Fig. 6

Alternatively, using the same method as in Section 3.2, we write

$$x = 3+2t, \quad y = 1+5t,$$

and eliminating t from these equations we obtain

$$y = \frac{5x}{2}-\frac{13}{2}.$$

3.4 Intersection. If R is the point of intersection of the lines

$$\begin{cases} \mathbf{r} = t\mathbf{b}, \\ \mathbf{r} = \mathbf{a}+s\mathbf{c}, \end{cases}$$

then the value of the scalars is fixed by the equations

$$\mathbf{r}_i = t_i\mathbf{b},$$
$$\mathbf{r}_i = \mathbf{a}+s_i\mathbf{c}.$$

(Note that different parameters must be used here, for each will have its own different value at the point of intersection.)

Nothing more can be found unless the vectors are expressed in terms of the base vectors of the system. Suppose, for example, that

$$\mathbf{b} = \mathbf{i}+\mathbf{j}, \quad \mathbf{a} = 3\mathbf{i}+\mathbf{j} \quad \text{and} \quad \mathbf{c} = 2\mathbf{i}+5\mathbf{j}.$$

Then
$$\mathbf{r}_i = t_i(\mathbf{i}+\mathbf{j}),$$
$$\mathbf{r}_i = 3\mathbf{i}+\mathbf{j}+s_i(2\mathbf{i}+5\mathbf{j}).$$

These are expressions for the same vector and so the components must be the same in each expression. If we equate the components, that is, the coefficients of **i** and **j**, we can find the particular values of the parameters giving the point of intersection:

$$\text{coefficients of } \mathbf{i}\text{: } t_i = 3+2s_i,$$
$$\text{coefficients of } \mathbf{j}\text{: } t_i = 1+5s_i,$$

from which $s_i = \frac{2}{3}$, $t_i = \frac{13}{3}$. With these values, either equation will give $\mathbf{r}_i = \frac{13}{3}\mathbf{i}+\frac{13}{3}\mathbf{j}$.

In a similar way in three dimensions we can try to find where the lines

$$\mathbf{r} = t\mathbf{i} \quad \text{and} \quad \mathbf{r} = \mathbf{k}+s(\mathbf{j}+\mathbf{k})$$

intersect. Equating coefficients:

$$\text{coefficients of } \mathbf{i}\text{:} \quad t = 0,$$

$$\text{coefficients of } \mathbf{j}\text{:} \quad 0 = s,$$

$$\text{coefficients of } \mathbf{k}\text{:} \quad 0 = 1+s.$$

The solution set of these equations is empty, so the lines do not intersect.

3.5 In the following sections and exercises we shall often wish to specify lines and planes associated with the unit tetrahedron and the unit cube positioned in the join of the positive axes (see Figures 7 and 8). The convention that we shall adopt for lettering their vertices is shown in the figures.

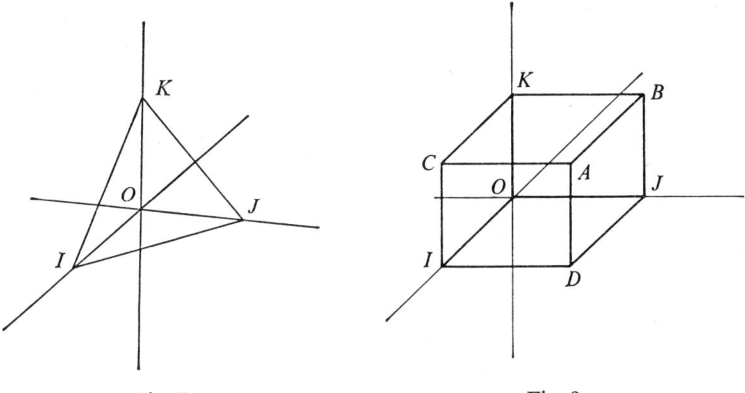

Fig. 7 Fig. 8

Exercise D

1. Express in terms of **i** and **j** the equations of the lines:

(*a*) through the origin and the point $\mathbf{r} = 3\mathbf{i}+\mathbf{j}$;

(*b*) through the origin and the point (2, 3);

(*c*) through the origin and the point with position vector $\mathbf{b}+2\mathbf{c}$, where

$$\mathbf{b} = \begin{pmatrix} 1 \\ 1 \end{pmatrix}, \quad \mathbf{c} = \begin{pmatrix} -1 \\ 0 \end{pmatrix};$$

(*d*) through the point (2, 1) parallel to **j**;

(*e*) through the points $D(1, 1)$ and $E(4, 2)$ (that is, through D in the direction of DE).

2. Express in terms of **i**, **j** and **k** the equations of the lines:

(*a*) the *x*-axis;

(*b*) through the origin and the point with position vector $\mathbf{b}+\mathbf{c}$, where

$$\mathbf{b} = \begin{pmatrix}0\\1\\1\end{pmatrix}, \quad \mathbf{c} = \begin{pmatrix}1\\0\\1\end{pmatrix};$$

(*c*) through the point $F(2, 0, 1)$, parallel to **k**;

(*d*) through the points $D(1, 1, 0)$ and $C(1, 0, 1)$;

(*e*) through the points $A(1, 1, 1)$ and $I(1, 0, 0)$;

(*f*) through the point $B(0, 1, 1)$, parallel to the line joining $I(1, 0, 0)$ and $E(0, 2, 0)$.

3. (*a*) Rewrite the following using Cartesian coordinates:

(i) $\mathbf{p} = \mathbf{i}+3\mathbf{j}$; (ii) $\mathbf{q} = 3\mathbf{i}+7\mathbf{j}$; (iii) $\mathbf{r} = t(\mathbf{i}+3\mathbf{j})$;
(iv) $\mathbf{r} = t(4\mathbf{i}+3\mathbf{j})$; (v) $\mathbf{r} = 2\mathbf{i}+t(\mathbf{i}+\mathbf{j})$; (vi) $\mathbf{r} = \mathbf{i}+3\mathbf{j}+t(\mathbf{i}+3\mathbf{j})$.

(*b*) Give vector equations of the following:

(i) $y = 2x$; (ii) $y = -x$; (iii) $y = 4x/5$; (iv) $y = 3x+1$.

4. Find the magnitude of **b** and then the distance between the points represented by $\mathbf{p} = 3\mathbf{b}$ and $\mathbf{q} = 5\mathbf{b}$, where:

(i) $\mathbf{b} = \mathbf{i}+\mathbf{j}$; (ii) $\mathbf{b} = 2\mathbf{i}+5\mathbf{j}$; (iii) $\mathbf{b} = 2\mathbf{i}+5\mathbf{j}+3\mathbf{k}$.

(Do not evaluate the square roots occurring in your answers.)

5. Find where the lines $\mathbf{r} = t(2\mathbf{i}+\mathbf{j})$ and $\mathbf{r} = 3\mathbf{i}+s(\mathbf{i}+\mathbf{j})$ intersect.

6. Does the line joining the point I to the mid-point of JK intersect the line $\mathbf{r} = t(\mathbf{i}+\mathbf{j}+\mathbf{k})$? If so, where?

7. Prove that the medians of the triangle IJK intersect at a point. (Use the idea of intersection just developed. Confirm your answer using the idea of centroid from Chapter 9.)

8. Use the technique of Section 3.4 to show whether or not the following lines intersect (drawing the unit cube will give the answers immediately):

(*a*) KC and OJ; (*b*) CB and KD;

(*c*) IB and the line joining the mid-point of the face $OKCI$ to the mid-point of the face $BADJ$.

4. PARAMETERS IN TWO DIMENSIONS

4.1 Planes through the origin. Consider a plane through the origin O and the points B and C. Then if $\mathbf{a} = 2\mathbf{b}+3\mathbf{c}$, $\mathbf{p} = \mathbf{b}-\mathbf{c}$ and $\mathbf{q} = 7\mathbf{b}+\mathbf{c}$, it is easy to see that A, P and Q will be points which lie in the plane. In general, any point in the plane OBC has a position vector **r** satisfying the relation $\mathbf{r} = t\mathbf{b}+s\mathbf{c}$, where t and s are any pair of real numbers. The relation is said to be the equation of the plane.

As before, although the plane is two-dimensional, it can be embedded in three dimensions. For example, if $\mathbf{b} = 2\mathbf{i}+5\mathbf{j}+3\mathbf{k}$ and $\mathbf{c} = \mathbf{i}+\mathbf{j}+\mathbf{k}$, then the plane through these points and the origin is

$$\mathbf{r} = t(2\mathbf{i}+5\mathbf{j}+3\mathbf{k})+s(\mathbf{i}+\mathbf{j}+\mathbf{k}).$$

4.2 Planes not through the origin. Consider a plane through a point D parallel to the plane OBC (see Figure 9). If $\mathbf{p}$ is the position vector *relative to D* of any point in the plane, then $\mathbf{p} = t\mathbf{b}+s\mathbf{c}$. Hence, the equation of the plane *relative to O* is $\mathbf{r} = \mathbf{d}+\mathbf{p}$, that is $\mathbf{r} = \mathbf{d}+t\mathbf{b}+s\mathbf{c}$.

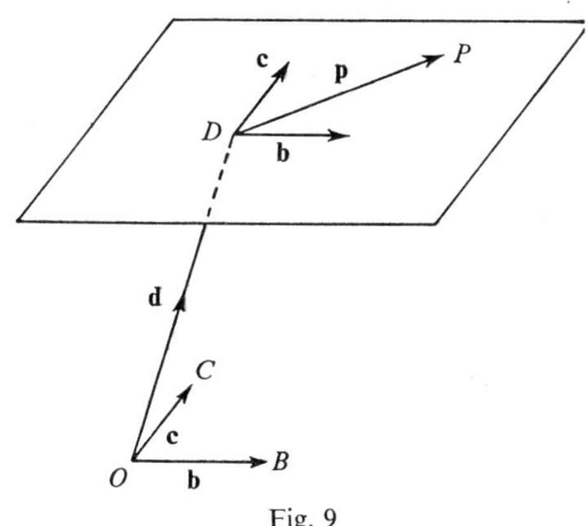

Fig. 9

For example, the plane through the points I, J, K can be found in this way. Two vectors through I in this plane are $\mathbf{IJ} = \mathbf{j}-\mathbf{i}$ and $\mathbf{IK} = \mathbf{k}-\mathbf{i}$; hence the plane IJK has the equation $\mathbf{r} = \mathbf{i}+t(\mathbf{j}-\mathbf{i})+s(\mathbf{k}-\mathbf{i})$, that is, $\mathbf{r} = (1-t-s)\mathbf{i}+t\mathbf{j}+s\mathbf{k}$.

Next, let us find the equation of the plane $ABJD$. Here $\mathbf{JD} = \mathbf{i}$ and $\mathbf{JB} = \mathbf{k}$, so that the equation is $\mathbf{r} = \mathbf{j}+t\mathbf{i}+s\mathbf{k}$.

The technique for discovering points or lines of intersection is the same as that for lines discussed in Section 3.4. For instance, the intersection of the line $\mathbf{r} = u(\mathbf{i}+\mathbf{j}+\mathbf{k})$ with the plane IJK given by

$$\mathbf{r} = (1-t-s)\mathbf{i}+t\mathbf{j}+s\mathbf{k}$$

is found by equating coefficients:

$$\left.\begin{array}{ll}\text{coefficients of } \mathbf{i}\text{:} & u = 1-t-s \\ \text{coefficients of } \mathbf{j}\text{:} & u = t \\ \text{coefficients of } \mathbf{k}\text{:} & u = s,\end{array}\right\} \quad \text{from which } u = t = s = \tfrac{1}{3},$$

so that the point is
$$\mathbf{r} = \tfrac{1}{3}(\mathbf{i}+\mathbf{j}+\mathbf{k}).$$

In a similar way we can deal with the intersection of two planes. We will show that the plane IJK meets the x, y plane in the line IJ. Now the plane IJK is

$$\mathbf{r} = (1-t-s)\mathbf{i}+t\mathbf{j}+s\mathbf{k},$$

and the plane $OIDJ$ is $\mathbf{r} = u\mathbf{i}+v\mathbf{j}$.

Equating coefficients:

$$\left.\begin{aligned} u &= 1-t-s, \\ v &= t, \\ s &= 0, \end{aligned}\right\} \text{ from which } u = 1-t,\ v = t.$$

Hence the line of intersection is

$$\begin{aligned} \mathbf{r} &= (1-t)\mathbf{i}+t\mathbf{j}, \\ &= \mathbf{i}+t(-\mathbf{i}+\mathbf{j}). \end{aligned}$$

and this is the line through the point I parallel to IJ, that is the line IJ.

Exercise E

1. Write down the equations of the planes through the origin and the following points:

(*a*) $I(1, 0, 0)$, $K(0, 0, 1)$;
(*b*) $I(1, 0, 0)$, $A(1, 1, 1)$;
(*c*) $C(1, 0, 1)$, $D(1, 1, 0)$.

2. Write down the equations of the planes:
(*a*) through K parallel to the x, y plane;
(*b*) through the point with position vector $\frac{1}{2}(\mathbf{i}+\mathbf{j})$ parallel to $OJBK$;
(*c*) through the points C, B, D;
(*d*) through the points C, K, J, D.

3. What is the point of intersection of the line OA with the plane IJK?

4. Write down the coordinates of the centroid, G, of the tetrahedron $OIJK$. Show that the line OG intersects the plane IJK at the centroid of the face IJK.

5. In what ratio does the plane joining the mid-points of KB, AB and AD divide the line segment CI?

6. What is the equation of the line of intersection of the planes BCD and $OKAD$?

7. Does the point $(\frac{1}{6}, \frac{1}{3}, \frac{1}{2})$ lie in the plane IJK? (That is, can the values of the parameters be chosen to give a point in the plane with position vectors $\frac{1}{6}\mathbf{i}+\frac{1}{3}\mathbf{j}+\frac{1}{2}\mathbf{k}$?)

8. What relation connects x, y and z if the point (x, y, z) lies in:
(*a*) the plane IJK; (*b*) the plane BCD; (*c*) the plane $OIAB$?
(Compare Question 7.)

5. SCALAR PRODUCT

We now introduce a most important idea which provides us with a very powerful tool. The basic idea is to define a function of two vectors that is proportional to their lengths and will be zero when the vectors are perpendicular. We shall come to it as an extension of the idea of the projection of a segment onto a line.

5.1 Projection

In two dimensions, we call $\overline{P'Q'}$ (see Figure 10) the *projection* of the segment $\overline{PQ}$ onto the line $\overleftrightarrow{HK}$, if $\overleftrightarrow{PP'}$, $\overleftrightarrow{QQ'}$, are perpendicular to $\overleftrightarrow{HK}$. The projection is said to be positive if $\overrightarrow{P'Q'}$ has the same direction as $\overrightarrow{HK}$, and negative otherwise.

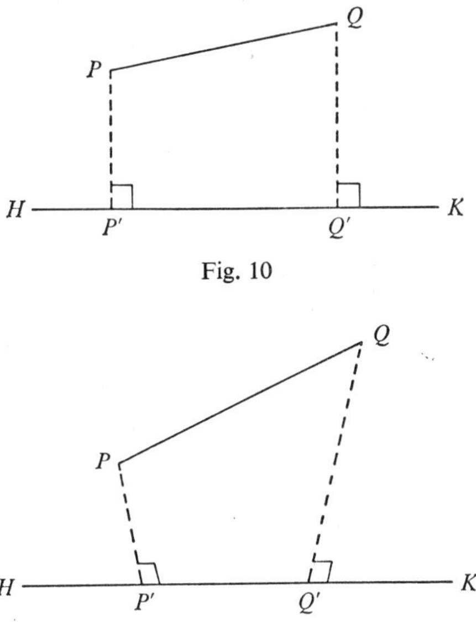

Fig. 10

Fig. 11

In three dimensions, the same definition holds, but the figure is harder to visualize (see Figure 11), since PQ and $P'Q'$ are not necessarily coplanar. In both cases, the length of the projection depends only on the directions of $\overleftrightarrow{PQ}$ and $\overleftrightarrow{HK}$, and the length (but not the location) of $\overline{PQ}$. For example, if the coordinates of P and Q in a rectangular Cartesian system are (x_1, y_1, z_1) and (x_2, y_2, z_2), and $\overleftrightarrow{HK}$ is the x-axis, then the projection of $\overline{PQ}$ is of magnitude $x_2 - x_1$, and this is unaltered under any translation of $\overline{PQ}$, since the result of such a translation would be to change x_1 and x_2 by the same amount. As the length of the projection depends only on the direction of HK and the magnitude and direction of $\overline{PQ}$, we must be able to express it in terms of $\mathbf{u}$ (the unit vector in the direction of $\overrightarrow{HK}$) and the vector $\mathbf{PQ}$. We shall denote the magnitude of the projection by the symbol $\mathbf{PQ}.\mathbf{u}$.

If $\overline{PQ}$ is of length l and $\overline{OL}$ is a parallel segment through the origin, then, denoting a unit vector in the x-direction by $\mathbf{i}$ and the angle between $\overline{OL}$ and the x-axis by θ, we have $\mathbf{PQ}.\mathbf{i} = \mathbf{OL}.\mathbf{i} = l \cos \theta$. (See Figure 12.)

We see that the idea of projection involves two vectors (one of which is a unit vector) and the cosine of the angle between them. Now there are other physical quantities which involve a pair of vectors and the cosine of the angle between them. For example, in mechanics the 'work' done by a force **P** which moves its point of application through a displacement **d** is

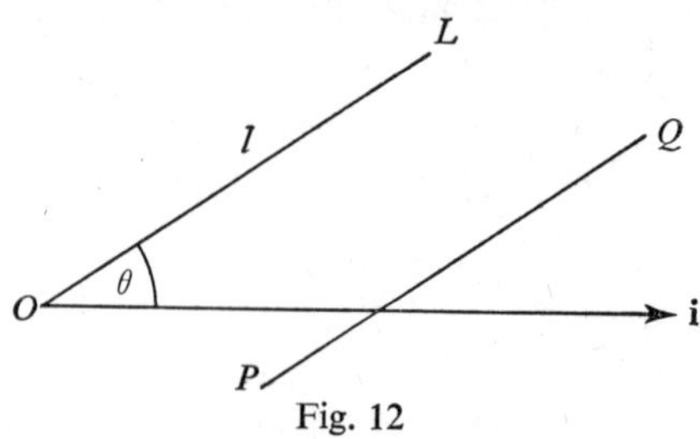

Fig. 12

given by $Pd \cos\theta$ where P and d are the magnitudes of the force and the displacement, and θ is the angle between their directions. Here it will be seen that neither vector is necessarily a unit vector. We are therefore led to the following definition.

5.2 The scalar product of two vectors.

The *scalar* or *dot product* of two vectors is defined to be the product of their lengths and the cosine of the angle between their directions. If the vectors are **p** and **q**, of lengths p and q, and θ is the angle from **p** to **q**, we write

$$\mathbf{p}.\mathbf{q} = pq\cos\theta.$$

We observe that $\cos\theta = \cos(-\theta) = \cos(360°-\theta)$, so that it is irrelevant which way we rotate from **p** to **q**, the short way or the long way; and it is also irrelevant whether we rotate from **p** to **q** or from **q** to **p**, that is, $\mathbf{p}.\mathbf{q} = \mathbf{q}.\mathbf{p}$. Also when one of the vectors is a unit vector, we can interpret the scalar product in terms of a projection.

We have called $\mathbf{p}.\mathbf{q}$ a 'product' because it has some of the usual properties of a product.

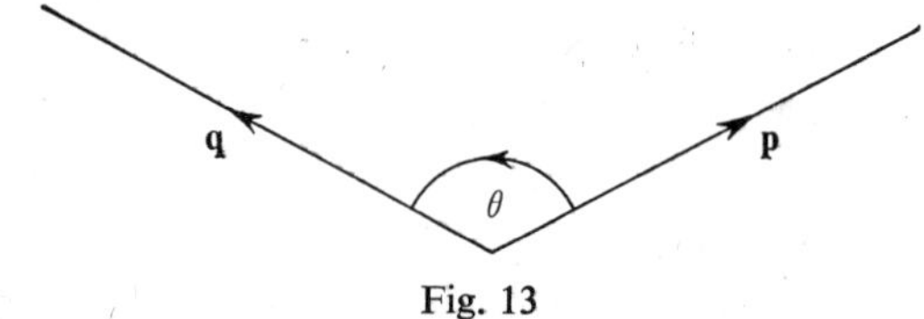

Fig. 13

(i) We have proved it is commutative: $\mathbf{p}.\mathbf{q} = \mathbf{q}.\mathbf{p}$.

(ii) The associative law does not apply, since $\mathbf{p}.\mathbf{q}$ is a number (or scalar—hence the name scalar product) and we cannot form its dot product with a third vector.

(iii) $(k\mathbf{p}).(l\mathbf{q}) = (kl)\mathbf{p}.\mathbf{q}$. It is easy to see that this is true if k and l are positive, since the length of $k\mathbf{p}$ is k times the length of $\mathbf{p}$, and so on. A proof in the cases when k or l is negative can be obtained by using the fact that $(-\mathbf{p}).\mathbf{q} = -(\mathbf{p}.\mathbf{q})$, since $\cos(180°-\theta) = -\cos\theta$.

(iv) The distributive law holds: $\mathbf{p}.(\mathbf{q}+\mathbf{r}) = \mathbf{p}.\mathbf{q}+\mathbf{p}.\mathbf{r}$. To demonstrate this, let us take **OP** to represent $\mathbf{p}$, **OQ** to represent $\mathbf{q}$, and **QS** to represent $\mathbf{r}$; and $\mathbf{u}$ a unit vector along $\mathbf{p}$ (see Figure 14).

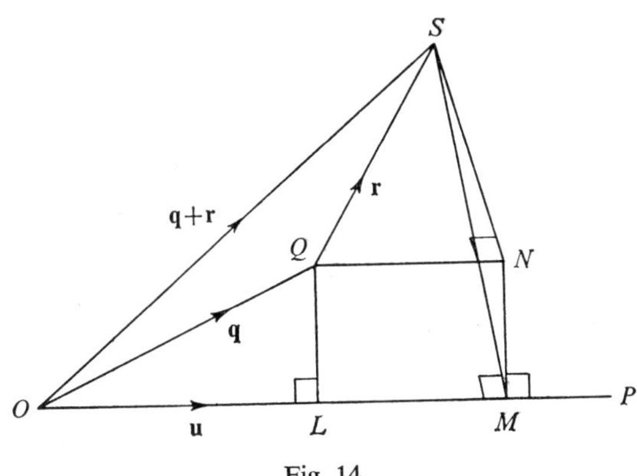

Fig. 14

The projections of **OQ**, **QS** and **OS** onto OP are $\overline{OL}$, $\overline{LM}$, $\overline{OM}$ respectively, and, as $\overline{OL}+\overline{LM} = \overline{OM}$,

$$\mathbf{q}.\mathbf{u}+\mathbf{r}.\mathbf{u} = (\mathbf{q}+\mathbf{r}).\mathbf{u};$$

and if $\mathbf{p}$ is of length p,

$$\begin{aligned} \mathbf{q}.\mathbf{p}+\mathbf{r}.\mathbf{p} &= \mathbf{q}.p\mathbf{u}+\mathbf{r}.p\mathbf{u} \\ &= p\mathbf{q}.\mathbf{u}+p\mathbf{r}.\mathbf{u} \\ &= p(\mathbf{q}.\mathbf{u}+\mathbf{r}.\mathbf{u}) \quad \text{(this is the distributive law for } \textit{numbers}\text{)} \\ &= p(\mathbf{q}+\mathbf{r}).\mathbf{u} = (\mathbf{q}+\mathbf{r}).\mathbf{p}. \end{aligned}$$

Since the dot product is commutative, we also have

$$\mathbf{p}.\mathbf{q}+\mathbf{p}.\mathbf{r} = \mathbf{p}.(\mathbf{q}+\mathbf{r}).\dagger$$

Some important uses of the dot product are as follows:

(i) $\mathbf{p}.\mathbf{p} = p^2$, the square of the length of $\mathbf{p}$;

(ii) if $\mathbf{p}$ is perpendicular to $\mathbf{q}$, then $\mathbf{p}.\mathbf{q} = 0$;

(iii) if $\mathbf{p}.\mathbf{q} = 0$ and $\mathbf{p}$ and $\mathbf{q}$ are neither of them zero, then $\mathbf{p}$ is perpendicular to $\mathbf{q}$. (We shall write '$\mathbf{p} \perp \mathbf{q}$'.)

† Since we are assuming as intuitive the 'theorem'

$$(OM \perp NM \quad \text{and} \quad QN \perp SN) \Rightarrow OM \perp SM$$

(Figure 14) in order to achieve this demonstration, we cannot call it a proof. Indeed it is more in accord with modern practice to take the distributive law as an axiom and to derive the geometrical properties of Euclidean space from it.

These last two results are immediately obvious from the definitions, since

$$\cos\theta = 0 \Leftrightarrow \theta = 90^\circ \text{ or } 270^\circ \quad (0^\circ \leqslant \theta \leqslant 360^\circ).$$

5.3 Scalar product in terms of components; Pythagoras's Theorem. In two dimensions, if $\mathbf{i}, \mathbf{j}$ are unit vectors along perpendicular axes, then $\mathbf{i}.\mathbf{i} = \mathbf{j}.\mathbf{j} = 1$, and $\mathbf{i}.\mathbf{j} = 0$.

Any vector **OP** in their plane can be written as $\mathbf{p} = x\mathbf{i}+y\mathbf{j}$, where x and y are the components of $\mathbf{p}$ (see Figure 15).

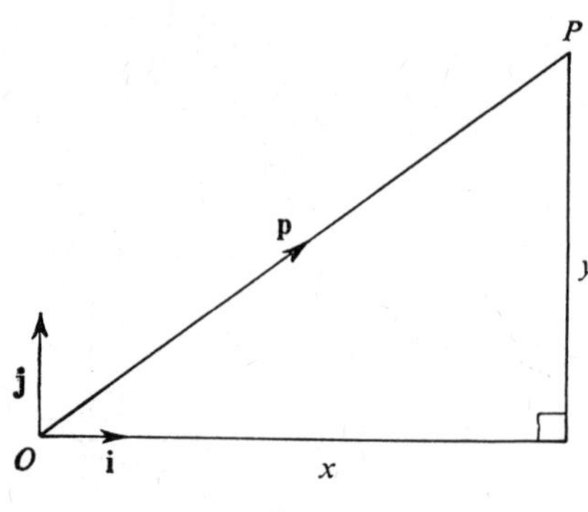

Fig. 15

Then
$$\begin{aligned} p^2 = \mathbf{p}.\mathbf{p} &= (x\mathbf{i}+y\mathbf{j}).(x\mathbf{i}+y\mathbf{j}) \\ &= x^2\mathbf{i}.\mathbf{i}+y^2\mathbf{j}.\mathbf{j}+xy\mathbf{i}.\mathbf{j}+xy\mathbf{j}.\mathbf{i} \\ &= x^2+y^2, \end{aligned}$$

which is Pythagoras's Theorem.

Also if
$$\mathbf{p}_1 = \begin{pmatrix} x_1 \\ y_1 \end{pmatrix} \text{ and } \mathbf{p}_2 = \begin{pmatrix} x_2 \\ y_2 \end{pmatrix},$$

then
$$\begin{aligned} \mathbf{p}_1 \cdot \mathbf{p}_2 &= (x_1\mathbf{i}+y_1\mathbf{j}).(x_2\mathbf{i}+y_2\mathbf{j}) \\ &= x_1x_2+y_1y_2. \end{aligned}$$

In three dimensions we have exactly similar results.

If $\mathbf{i}, \mathbf{j}, \mathbf{k}$ are unit vectors along mutually perpendicular axes, then

$$\mathbf{i}.\mathbf{i} = \mathbf{j}.\mathbf{j} = \mathbf{k}.\mathbf{k} = 1$$

and
$$\mathbf{i}.\mathbf{j} = \mathbf{j}.\mathbf{k} = \mathbf{k}.\mathbf{i} = 0.$$

The equivalent of Pythagoras's Theorem is $p^2 = x^2+y^2+z^2$ (see Figure 16), and the proof follows the same pattern as in two dimensions.

Also if
$$\mathbf{p}_1 = \begin{pmatrix} x_1 \\ y_1 \\ z_1 \end{pmatrix} \text{ and } \mathbf{p}_2 = \begin{pmatrix} x_2 \\ y_2 \\ z_2 \end{pmatrix},$$

then

$$\mathbf{p}_1 . \mathbf{p}_2 = (x_1\mathbf{i}+y_1\mathbf{j}+z_1\mathbf{k}).(x_2\mathbf{i}+y_2\mathbf{j}+z_2\mathbf{k})$$
$$= x_1x_2+y_1y_2+z_1z_2 \quad \text{(all other products being zero).}$$

Further, $\mathbf{p}_1 . \mathbf{i} = x_1, \quad \mathbf{p}_1 . \mathbf{j} = y_1, \quad \mathbf{p}_1 . \mathbf{k} = z_1,$

so that the components themselves are expressible in terms of scalar products. Similar equations, of course, hold in two dimensions.

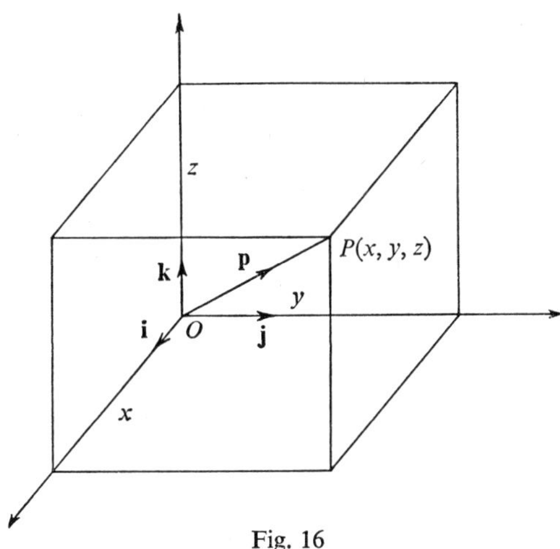

Fig. 16

5.4 Angle between two vectors.

Example 1. Find the angle between the vectors

$$\begin{pmatrix} 2 \\ 1 \\ -2 \end{pmatrix} \text{ and } \begin{pmatrix} 6 \\ -2 \\ 3 \end{pmatrix}.$$

Call the vectors **p** and **q**, and write their scalar product in two different ways.

(1) $\mathbf{p}.\mathbf{q} = pq\cos\theta$, where θ is the angle between the vectors. Now

$$p^2 = 2^2+1^2+2^2 = 9 \quad \text{and} \quad q^2 = 6^2+(-2)^2+3^2 = 49,$$

so that $p = 3$ and $q = 7$. Hence $\mathbf{p}.\mathbf{q} = 21\cos\theta$.

(2) By components

$$\mathbf{p}.\mathbf{q} = 2\times6+1\times(-2)+(-2)\times3 = 4.$$

Hence $21\cos\theta = 4 \quad \text{and} \quad \cos\theta = \frac{4}{21}.$

Hence $\theta = 79^\circ\ 1'.$

The method is quite general.

If
$$\mathbf{p}_1 = \begin{pmatrix} x_1 \\ y_1 \\ z_1 \end{pmatrix} \quad \text{and} \quad \mathbf{p}_2 = \begin{pmatrix} x_2 \\ y_2 \\ z_2 \end{pmatrix},$$
then
$$p_1 = \sqrt{(x_1^2+y_1^2+z_1^2)}, \quad p_2 = \sqrt{(x_2^2+y_2^2+z_2^2)},$$
$$p_1 p_2 \cos\theta = \mathbf{p}_1 . \mathbf{p}_2 = x_1x_2+y_1y_2+z_1z_2,$$
from which $\cos\theta$ can be found.

Example 2. Express $\begin{pmatrix} 2 \\ 3 \end{pmatrix}$ in the form $a\begin{pmatrix} 1 \\ 2 \end{pmatrix}+b\begin{pmatrix} 2 \\ -1 \end{pmatrix}$.

First method. Since $a\begin{pmatrix} 1 \\ 2 \end{pmatrix}+b\begin{pmatrix} 2 \\ -1 \end{pmatrix} = \begin{pmatrix} a+2b \\ 2a-b \end{pmatrix}$,

we must have $a+2b = 2$, $2a-b = 3$; which on solution give
$$a = \tfrac{8}{5}, \quad b = \tfrac{1}{5}.$$

Second method. If
$$a\begin{pmatrix} 1 \\ 2 \end{pmatrix}+b\begin{pmatrix} 2 \\ -1 \end{pmatrix} = \begin{pmatrix} 2 \\ 3 \end{pmatrix},$$
then
$$a\begin{pmatrix} 1 \\ 2 \end{pmatrix}.\begin{pmatrix} 1 \\ 2 \end{pmatrix}+b\begin{pmatrix} 2 \\ -1 \end{pmatrix}.\begin{pmatrix} 1 \\ 2 \end{pmatrix} = \begin{pmatrix} 2 \\ 3 \end{pmatrix}.\begin{pmatrix} 1 \\ 2 \end{pmatrix};$$
that is $5a = 8$ or $a = \frac{8}{5}$. Similarly, $b = \frac{1}{5}$. This makes use of the fact that
$$\begin{pmatrix} 1 \\ 2 \end{pmatrix} \quad \text{and} \quad \begin{pmatrix} 2 \\ -1 \end{pmatrix}$$
are perpendicular vectors.

Exercise F

1. Figure 17 shows a number of vectors in a plane. What are the values of the scalar products:

(*a*) **p**.**q**; (*b*) **p**.**r**; (*c*) **p**.**s**;
(*d*) **q**.**r**; (*e*) **q**.**s**; (*f*) **q**.(**r**+**s**)?

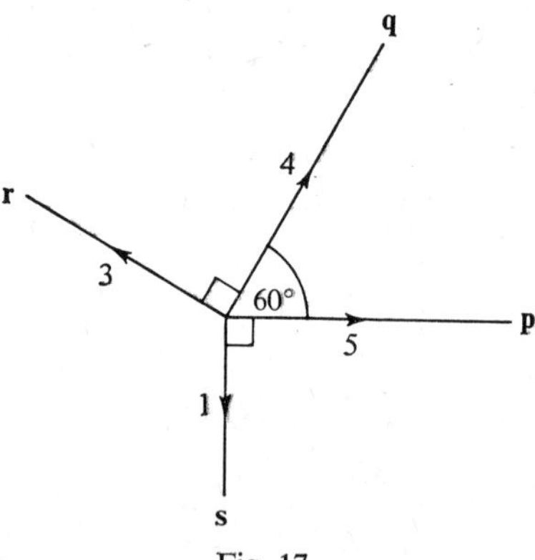

Fig. 17

2. If $\mathbf{u}.\mathbf{v}$ is negative, what can you say about the vectors $\mathbf{u}$ and $\mathbf{v}$?

3. If $\mathbf{a}$, $\mathbf{b}$ are of equal length, show that $(\mathbf{a}+\mathbf{b}).(\mathbf{a}-\mathbf{b}) = 0$. Deduce from this a fact about the diagonals of a rhombus.

4. Explain why $(-\mathbf{p}).(-\mathbf{q}) = \mathbf{p}.\mathbf{q}$. (Remember that $-\mathbf{p}$ is equal and opposite to $\mathbf{p}$.)

5. Work done by a force

If $\mathbf{F}$ is a force acting in a fixed direction, applied to a body at A (see Figure 18), and the body moves to B, then the work done by the force $\mathbf{F}$ is defined as the product of the force and the distance moved by the body in its direction. Prove that if $\mathbf{AB} = \mathbf{x}$, the work done is $\mathbf{F}.\mathbf{x}$.

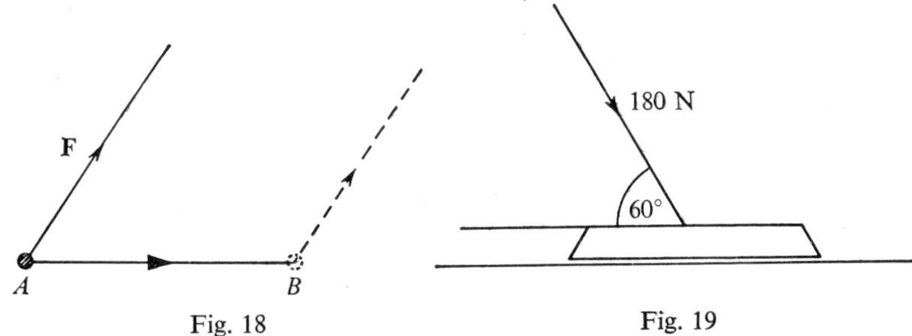

Fig. 18

Fig. 19

If I push down on the handle of a floor polisher, inclined at 60° to the horizontal, with a force of 180 N (see Figure 19), how much work do I do in moving the polisher 4 m? (1 N does 1 J of work when it moves its point of application 1 m in the direction of the force.)

6. A block of mass 20 kg is pulled 8 m up a slope of 1 in 5 by a rope parallel to the slope, the tension in which is 60 N. How much work is lost in overcoming friction? ($g \approx 10\ \text{m/s}^2$.)

7. Does the work done in raising a truck of mass 10 tonnes through a vertical distance of 100 m up a sloping track depend on the slope of the track? Explain your answer.

8. Find the magnitudes of $\mathbf{OP}$ and $\mathbf{OQ}$ and the angle POQ when:

(*a*) P is $(12, 1, -12)$, and $Q(8, 4, 1)$;
(*b*) P is $(4, -1, -8)$ and $Q(7, 4, -4)$;
(*c*) P is $(-9, 2, 6)$ and $Q(3, 6, -2)$;
(*d*) P is $(3, 4, -5)$ and $Q(12, -13, 5)$;
(*e*) P is $(-6, 2, 7)$ and $Q(3, -5, 4)$.

9. Write down the coordinates of the vertices of a cube, whose centre is at the origin and whose sides, of length 2 units, are parallel to the coordinate axes. Hence find the angle between two cube diagonals.

10. In Question 9, find the angles of the triangle formed by the mid-points of the three edges that pass through (1, 1, 1).

11. Find the values of the following products:

(*a*) $(2\mathbf{i}+\mathbf{j}).(3\mathbf{i}-4\mathbf{j})$;
(*b*) $(\mathbf{i}+2\mathbf{j}).(\mathbf{i}-2\mathbf{j})$;
(*c*) $\mathbf{i}.(9\mathbf{i}-11\mathbf{j})$;
(*d*) $(2\mathbf{i}-\mathbf{j})^2$, or $(2\mathbf{i}-\mathbf{j}).(2\mathbf{i}-\mathbf{j})$;
(*e*) $(2\mathbf{i}+\mathbf{j}-3\mathbf{k}).(4\mathbf{i}+3\mathbf{j}-5\mathbf{k})$;
(*f*) $(\mathbf{i}+\mathbf{j}-\mathbf{k})^2$.

12. If $\mathbf{a}.\mathbf{b} = 0$, what can you say about a and b? (There are three possibilities.)

13. If the components of a vector $\mathbf{p}$ with respect to three mutually perpendicular unit vectors $\mathbf{i}$, $\mathbf{j}$ and $\mathbf{k}$ are x, y and z, prove, by squaring $\mathbf{p} = x\mathbf{i}+y\mathbf{j}+z\mathbf{k}$, that $p^2 = x^2+y^2+z^2$.

14. Show that

$$\begin{pmatrix} 3 \\ -4 \end{pmatrix} \text{ and } \begin{pmatrix} 4 \\ 3 \end{pmatrix}$$

are perpendicular vectors, and then express $\mathbf{i}$ and $\mathbf{j}$ each in the form

$$a\begin{pmatrix} 3 \\ -4 \end{pmatrix}+b\begin{pmatrix} 4 \\ 3 \end{pmatrix}.$$

15. If

$$x\mathbf{i}+y\mathbf{j} = p\begin{pmatrix} 3 \\ -4 \end{pmatrix}+q\begin{pmatrix} 4 \\ 3 \end{pmatrix},$$

find p and q in terms of x and y, and verify that $x^2+y^2 = 25(p^2+q^2)$.

16. Show that the vectors

$$\mathbf{u} = \begin{pmatrix} 1 \\ 2 \\ 2 \end{pmatrix}, \quad \mathbf{v} = \begin{pmatrix} 2 \\ -2 \\ 1 \end{pmatrix}, \quad \mathbf{w} = \begin{pmatrix} 2 \\ 1 \\ -2 \end{pmatrix}$$

are mutually perpendicular and are each of length 3 units.

17. With $\mathbf{u}$, $\mathbf{v}$, $\mathbf{w}$ defined as in Question 16, let $\mathbf{i} = a\mathbf{u}+b\mathbf{v}+c\mathbf{w}$, and hence write down a set of three equations involving a, b and c. Solve them, and so express $\mathbf{i}$ in terms of $\mathbf{u}$, $\mathbf{v}$ and $\mathbf{w}$.

18. If $\mathbf{i} = a\mathbf{u}+b\mathbf{v}+c\mathbf{w}$, with $\mathbf{u}$, $\mathbf{v}$, $\mathbf{w}$ defined as in Question 16, form the scalar products $\mathbf{i}.\mathbf{u}$, $\mathbf{i}.\mathbf{v}$, $\mathbf{i}.\mathbf{w}$, and hence find a, b and c.

Do likewise for $\mathbf{j}$ and $\mathbf{k}$, and then express each of $\mathbf{i}$, $\mathbf{j}$ and $\mathbf{k}$, in terms of $\mathbf{u}$, $\mathbf{v}$, $\mathbf{w}$. What is $3\mathbf{i}+4\mathbf{j}-\mathbf{k}$ in terms of $\mathbf{u}$, $\mathbf{v}$ and $\mathbf{w}$?

19. Write down in column matrix form the *unit* vectors $\hat{\mathbf{u}}$, $\hat{\mathbf{v}}$, $\hat{\mathbf{w}}$, in the directions of the vectors $\mathbf{u}$, $\mathbf{v}$, $\mathbf{w}$, defined in Question 16. Write down, in the form of scalar products, the components of $\mathbf{i}$, $\mathbf{j}$, $\mathbf{k}$ with respect to the mutually perpendicular base vectors $\hat{\mathbf{u}}$, $\hat{\mathbf{v}}$, $\hat{\mathbf{w}}$, and then evaluate these components.

20. For the triangle PQR, where P is $(5, -3, 1)$, Q is $(-2, 1, 5)$ and R is $(9, 5, 0)$, write down $\mathbf{QR}$, $\mathbf{RP}$ and $\mathbf{PQ}$, and hence calculate the angles of the triangle.

21. Repeat Question 20, where P is $(6, -7, -3)$, Q is $(3, -3, 2)$ and R is $(2, 4, 2)$

22. ABC is a triangle. Denote $\mathbf{CB}$, $\mathbf{CA}$, $\mathbf{AB}$ by $\mathbf{a}$, $\mathbf{b}$, $\mathbf{c}$ and use the relation $\mathbf{a} = \mathbf{b}+\mathbf{c}$ to find a formula for a^2 in terms of b, c and angle A. By means of this formula calculate the largest angle in the triangle whose sides are 3 cm, 5 cm and 7 cm.

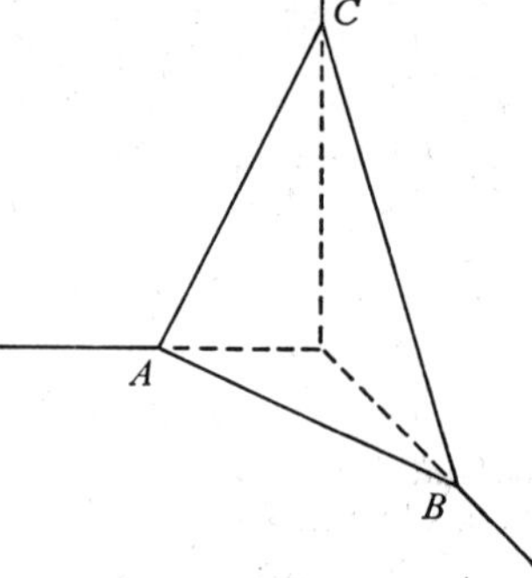

Fig. 20

23. A triangular flap is to fit into a corner of a rectangular room as shown in Figure 20; A is 9 cm from the corner, B is 12 cm from the corner, and C is 16 cm above the floor. Find the sides and angles of the triangle ABC.

24. **OP** is the position vector of the point (x, y, z) and makes angles α, β and γ with the x-, y- and z-axes. Prove that $\cos^2\alpha+\cos^2\beta+\cos^2\gamma = 1$. (Use $x = \mathbf{p}.\mathbf{i}$, $y = \mathbf{p}.\mathbf{j}$, $z = \mathbf{p}.\mathbf{k}$.)

25. P_1 and P_2 have coordinates (x_1, y_1, z_1) and (x_2, y_2, z_2). If OP_1 makes angles α_1, β_1 and γ_1 with the coordinate axes and OP_2 makes angles α_2, β_2 and γ_2 with them, prove, by considering $\mathbf{p}_1.\mathbf{p}_2$, that if θ is the angle between OP_1 and OP_2, then

$$\cos\theta = \cos\alpha_1\cos\alpha_2+\cos\beta_1\cos\beta_2+\cos\gamma_1\cos\gamma_2.$$

6. PERPENDICULARITY

6.1 Perpendicular vectors in a plane. We have seen that two vectors in a plane are perpendicular if their scalar product is zero; that is,

$$\mathbf{p}_1 = \begin{pmatrix} x_1 \\ y_1 \end{pmatrix} \quad \text{and} \quad \mathbf{p}_2 = \begin{pmatrix} x_2 \\ y_2 \end{pmatrix}$$

are perpendicular if

$$\mathbf{p}_1.\mathbf{p}_2 = x_1x_2+y_1y_2 = 0.$$

For example $\begin{pmatrix} 5 \\ -2 \end{pmatrix}$ is perpendicular to $\begin{pmatrix} 2 \\ 5 \end{pmatrix}$ and so is $\begin{pmatrix} 5k \\ -2k \end{pmatrix}$ for any k. This in fact is often the easiest way of handling perpendicular vectors in a plane:

Any vector perpendicular to $\begin{pmatrix} a \\ b \end{pmatrix}$ can be written in the form $\begin{pmatrix} kb \\ -ka \end{pmatrix}$.

The gradients of these vectors are

$$\frac{b}{a} \quad \text{and} \quad \frac{-ka}{kb}, \quad \text{that is} \quad \frac{b}{a} \quad \text{and} \quad \frac{-a}{b},$$

whose product is -1.

Hence if two vectors in a plane are perpendicular, the product of their gradients is -1.

There is an exceptional case, namely the base vectors themselves. $\begin{pmatrix} 1 \\ 0 \end{pmatrix}$ and $\begin{pmatrix} 0 \\ 1 \end{pmatrix}$ are perpendicular by definition, but the second does not have a gradient.

The converse is, however, true without exception; if two vectors have gradients whose product is -1, they are perpendicular. The proof is immediate.

6.2 Vectors and lines (two dimensions). We begin with the familiar fact that the equation

$$3x+2y = 6$$

represents a line passing through (2, 0) and (0, 3). We have hitherto assumed without much justification that the set

$$\{(x, y): 3x+2y = 6\}$$

is a straight line. We can now prove this and also re-interpret the equation.

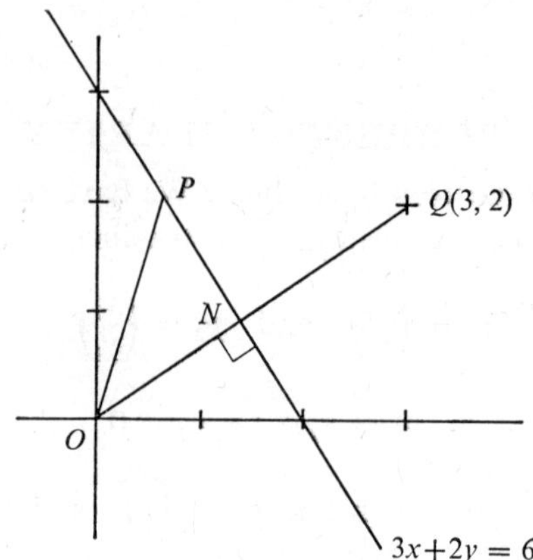

Fig. 21

Let Q be the point (3, 2). Then if P is (x, y), the equation $3x+2y = 6$ states that $\mathbf{OP}.\mathbf{OQ} = 6$.

But if PN is drawn perpendicular to OQ,

$$\mathbf{OP}.\mathbf{OQ} = OP.OQ \cos \angle POQ = \mathbf{OQ}.\mathbf{ON},$$

the product being positive when OQ and ON are in the same direction and negative when they are in opposite directions.

Now OQ is a fixed length ($\sqrt{(3^2+2^2)}$) and if $\mathbf{OQ}.\mathbf{ON} = 6$, then ON is the fixed distance $6/\sqrt{13}$. This means that N is a fixed point and the locus of P, $\{P: \mathbf{OP}.\mathbf{OQ} = 6\}$, is the line through N perpendicular to OQ. We have incidentally proved that the perpendicular distance from O to the line is $6/\sqrt{13}$.

Generally, the line $ax+by = c$ can be interpreted in the same way. If Q is (a, b), then

$$\{(x, y): ax+by = c\} \text{ is } \{P: \mathbf{OP}.\mathbf{OQ} = c\},$$

which is a line perpendicular to OQ whose distance from the origin is

$$\frac{|c|}{OQ} = \frac{|c|}{\sqrt{(a^2+b^2)}}.$$

It follows at once that for different values of c the lines $ax+by = c$ are all parallel.

6.3 Perpendicular distance (two dimensions). Suppose we require the perpendicular distance from the point $P_1(x_1, y_1)$ to the line $ax+by = c$. Let $\mathbf{q}$ be the vector $\begin{pmatrix} a \\ b \end{pmatrix}$ normal to the line, whose equation can be written as $\mathbf{p}.\mathbf{q} = c$. Let N be the foot of the perpendicular from P_1; let $\mathbf{ON} = \mathbf{n}$, $\mathbf{NP_1} = \mathbf{h}$.

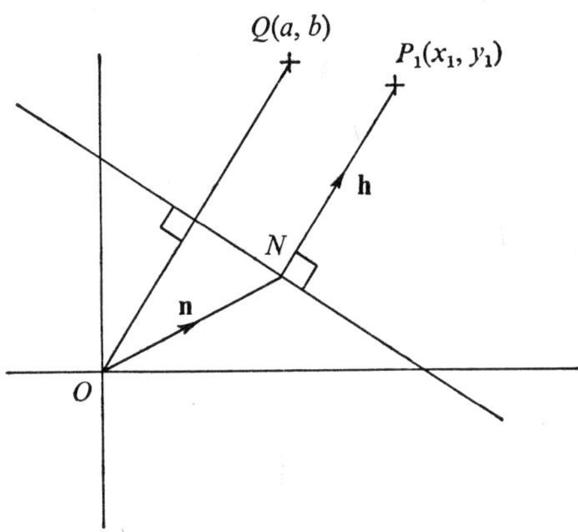

Fig. 22

Then $\mathbf{h} = \mathbf{p}_1 - \mathbf{n}$, so that

$$\mathbf{h}.\mathbf{q} = (\mathbf{p}_1 - \mathbf{n}).\mathbf{q} = \mathbf{p}_1.\mathbf{q} - \mathbf{n}.\mathbf{q}$$
$$= ax_1 + by_1 - c,$$

since $\mathbf{n}.\mathbf{q} = c$ as N is on the line.

But $$|\mathbf{h}.\mathbf{q}| = hq, \quad \text{since } \mathbf{h} \text{ and } \mathbf{q} \text{ are parallel,}$$
$$= h\surd(a^2+b^2).$$

Hence:

The perpendicular distance from (x_1, y_1) onto $ax+by = c$ is

$$h = \frac{|ax_1+by_1-c|}{\surd(a^2+b^2)}.$$

It is sometimes necessary to determine the sign of ax_1+by_1-c when it is known on which side of the line $ax+by-c = 0$ the point (x_1, y_1) lies, although x_1, y_1 are not specified numerically. Now $\mathbf{h}.\mathbf{q} = hq$ if $\mathbf{h}$ and $\mathbf{q}$ have the same direction and $\mathbf{h}.\mathbf{q} = -hq$ if the directions are opposite. It follows that $\mathbf{h}.\mathbf{q}$, and therefore ax_1+by_1-c, is positive for all points (x_1, y_1) on one side of the line and negative for all points (x_1, y_1) on the other side. In particular we notice that, for lines not through the origin, the sign of ax_1+by_1-c is the same as the sign of $-c$ for all points (x_1, y_1) on the 'origin side' of the line, since ax_1+by_1-c reduces to $-c$ when $x_1 = y_1 = 0$.

Example 3. How far is the point (100, −134) from the line $4x+3y-3 = 0$, and on which side of the line does it lie?

When $x = 100$ and $y = -134$, the value of $4x+3y-3$ is -5; and at the origin its value is -3. The perpendicular distance is

$$\frac{5}{\sqrt{(4^2+3^2)}} = 1.$$

Hence, the point lies on the *origin* side of the line, at unit distance from it.

6.4 Parallel lines (two dimensions). In Section 6.2 it was shown that the line $ax+by = c$ is perpendicular to the vector $\begin{pmatrix} a \\ b \end{pmatrix}$. We call this vector a *normal vector* to the line. It will also be a normal vector to any parallel line. Hence:

The equation of a line parallel to $ax+by = c$ is of the form

$$ax+by = k, \text{ for some value of } k.$$

Example 4. Find the equation of the line through (2, −3) parallel to $4x-y = 1$.

The equation is of the form $4x-y = k$. It goes through (2, −3), and therefore $4\times 2-(-3) = k$, which gives $k = 11$.

This working can be abbreviated to the following: the parallel line is

$$4x-y = 4\times 2-(-3) = 11.$$

The equation can be found in another way. If A is the point (2, −3) and $P(x, y)$ a point on the line through A parallel to $4x-y = 1$, then **AP** is perpendicular to $\begin{pmatrix} 4 \\ -1 \end{pmatrix}$. Hence $\begin{pmatrix} x-2 \\ y+3 \end{pmatrix}\cdot\begin{pmatrix} 4 \\ -1 \end{pmatrix} = 0$, which reduces to $4x-y = 11$.

6.5 Perpendicular lines (two dimensions).

Since a vector perpendicular to $\begin{pmatrix} a \\ b \end{pmatrix}$ is $\begin{pmatrix} b \\ -a \end{pmatrix}$, a line perpendicular to $ax+by = c$ has $\begin{pmatrix} b \\ -a \end{pmatrix}$ as a normal vector.

The equation of the line will therefore be of the form

$$bx-ay = k, \text{ for some } k.$$

Example 5. Find the equation of the line through (2, −3) perpendicular to $4x-y = 1$.

The equation is of the form $-x-4y = k$. It goes through (2, −3), and therefore $-2-4\times(-3) = k$, which gives $k = 10$. Hence the equation required is $-x-4y = 10$ or $x+4y+10 = 0$.

In abbreviated style: the perpendicular line is

$$-x-4y = -2-4\times(-3) = 10.$$

Alternatively, with the same notation as in the previous example, **AP** is perpendicular to $\begin{pmatrix} b \\ -a \end{pmatrix}$, and the equation of the line is obtained by reducing

$$\begin{pmatrix} x-2 \\ y+3 \end{pmatrix} \cdot \begin{pmatrix} -1 \\ -4 \end{pmatrix} = 0.$$

6.6 Angle between two lines (two dimensions). The angle between two lines in two dimensions can be found as shown in the following example.

Example 6. What is the angle between the lines

$$3x+4y = 5 \quad \text{and} \quad 8x+15y = 22?$$

These lines have normal vectors

$$\begin{pmatrix} 3 \\ 4 \end{pmatrix} \quad \text{and} \quad \begin{pmatrix} 8 \\ 15 \end{pmatrix},$$

and the angle between the lines is equal to the angle between these vectors.

If

$$\mathbf{p} = \begin{pmatrix} 3 \\ 4 \end{pmatrix} \quad \text{and} \quad \mathbf{q} = \begin{pmatrix} 8 \\ 15 \end{pmatrix},$$

$$p^2 = 3^2+4^2 = 25, \quad \text{and} \quad q^2 = 8^2+15^2 = 289,$$

so that $p = 5$ and $q = 17$. The formula $\mathbf{p}.\mathbf{q} = pq \cos \theta$ now gives

$$3.8+4.15 = 5.17 \cos \theta \quad \text{or} \quad 84 = 85 \cos \theta,$$

from which $\theta = 9°$ (to the nearest degree).

Exercise G

1. Write down the equations of the lines through the given points parallel and perpendicular to the given lines:

(*a*) $(2, 3)$, $3x-y = 5$; (*b*) $(-3, -1)$, $x+y = 2$;
(*c*) $(4, -5)$, $2x+y = 3$; (*d*) $(-3, 4)$, $x = 2$;
(*e*) $(1, -1)$, $7x+5y+6 = 0$; (*f*) $(0, -4)$, $13x-8y = 17$.

2. Interpret the statement

$$\begin{pmatrix} x-x_1 \\ y-y_1 \end{pmatrix} \cdot \begin{pmatrix} x-x_2 \\ y-y_2 \end{pmatrix} = 0,$$

in terms of the points $P(x, y)$, $P_1(x_1, y_1)$ and $P_2(x_2, y_2)$. Describe the set of points P defined by this equation, where P_1 and P_2 are fixed points.

3. Find the equation of the circles with the given points at ends of a diameter:

(*a*) $(1, -2)$, $(-3, 5)$; (*b*) (p, q), $(-q, p)$.

4. Find the angle between the lines:

(*a*) $3x+y = 2$ and $4x-3y = 1$;
(*b*) $2x-y = 5$ and $x+2y+3 = 0$;
(*c*) $5x+12y+3 = 0$ and $12x+5y = 11$;
(*d*) $7x-4y+1 = 0$ and $y+8x = 0$;
(*e*) $x-3y-7 = 0$ and $x+2y+6 = 0$.

5. Find the perpendicular distance of the point from the line:

(*a*) (0, 0), $3x+4y = 5$; (*b*) (0, 0), $5x+12y+3 = 0$;
(*c*) (2, −3), $15x-8y-3 = 0$; (*d*) (−5, 1), $y = x-7$.

6. Find the point of intersection of the altitudes of the triangle with vertices (3, 2), $(-2, 2\frac{1}{2})$ and (−7, −3).

6.7 Perpendicular vectors (three dimensions). We can test if a straight line is perpendicular to a plane by placing a set-square along the line and seeing if the perpendicular edge rests on the plane. A verdict can be given by testing twice in this way, provided the set-square is not held in the same plane both times, but the planes of the set-square need not be perpendicular to one another. What we are saying is that if a line is perpendicular to each of two intersecting lines, then it is perpendicular to every line in the plane which contains the two lines. The proof is straightforward, assuming the distributive law (see p. 361, footnote):

Let **p**, **q**, **r** be the position vectors of P, Q, R relative to an origin O. If **OP** is perpendicular to **OQ** and to **OR**, then $\mathbf{p}.\mathbf{q} = 0$ and $\mathbf{p}.\mathbf{r} = 0$. Now if $\overline{XY}$ is any line segment in the plane of OQR, **XY** is of the form $\lambda\mathbf{q}+\mu\mathbf{r}$, for some λ and μ. But $\mathbf{p}.(\lambda\mathbf{q}+\mu\mathbf{r}) = \lambda\mathbf{p}.\mathbf{q}+\mu\mathbf{p}.\mathbf{r} = 0$, and therefore **OP** is perpendicular to **XY**.

A line which is perpendicular to two intersecting lines in a plane, and therefore to every line in the plane, is said to be *normal* to the plane.

A plane is uniquely determined if we know a normal vector to it and a point through which it passes. The equation of the plane through the origin for which

$$\mathbf{OQ} = \begin{pmatrix} a \\ b \\ c \end{pmatrix}$$

is a normal vector (that is, **OQ** is normal to the plane) can be found by expressing the fact that if (x, y, z) are the coordinates of any point P of the plane then **OQ** is perpendicular to **OP** (see Figure 23). That is

$$\begin{pmatrix} a \\ b \\ c \end{pmatrix} . \begin{pmatrix} x \\ y \\ z \end{pmatrix} = 0, \quad \text{or} \quad ax+by+cz = 0.$$

As a second example we shall find the equation of the plane through the point A (2, -1, 3) with a normal vector

$$\mathbf{n} = \begin{pmatrix} 1 \\ 1 \\ 4 \end{pmatrix}.$$

If $P(x, y, z)$ is any point in the plane, then

$$\mathbf{AP} = \begin{pmatrix} x-2 \\ y+1 \\ z-3 \end{pmatrix}.$$

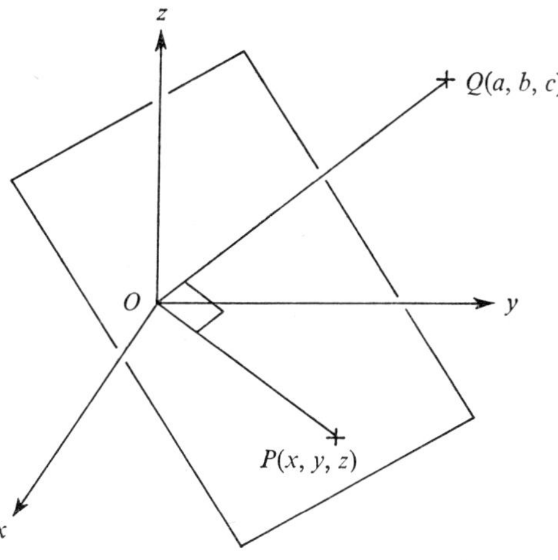

Fig. 23

But $\mathbf{AP}.\mathbf{n} = 0$, that is,

$$\begin{pmatrix} x-2 \\ y+1 \\ z-3 \end{pmatrix} . \begin{pmatrix} 1 \\ 1 \\ 4 \end{pmatrix} = 0,$$

which reduces to $x+y+4z-13 = 0$.

In general, the equation of the plane through (x_1, y_1, z_1) for which a normal vector is $\begin{pmatrix} a \\ b \\ c \end{pmatrix}$ is

$$\begin{pmatrix} x-x_1 \\ y-y_1 \\ z-z_1 \end{pmatrix} . \begin{pmatrix} a \\ b \\ c \end{pmatrix} = 0,$$

which can be written $ax+by+cz-(ax_1+by_1+cz_1) = 0$ and is of the form $ax+by+cz = d$. This shows that the equation of a plane is of the first degree in x, y, z; we shall return to this in Section 7.

6.8 Orthocentres.

Example 7. *The orthocentre of a triangle. ABC* is any triangle and D is a point such that $\overline{DB}$ is perpendicular to $\overline{CA}$ and $\overline{DC}$ is perpendicular to $\overline{AB}$. Prove that $\overline{DA}$ and $\overline{BC}$ are also perpendicular (Figure 24).

With D as origin, let the position vectors of A, B, C be **a**, **b**, **c**. Then

$$\mathbf{DB} \perp \mathbf{CA} \Rightarrow \mathbf{b}.(\mathbf{a}-\mathbf{c}) = 0 \quad \text{or} \quad \mathbf{b}.\mathbf{a} = \mathbf{b}.\mathbf{c};$$

and

$$\mathbf{DC} \perp \mathbf{AB} \Rightarrow \mathbf{c}.(\mathbf{b}-\mathbf{a}) = 0 \quad \text{or} \quad \mathbf{c}.\mathbf{b} = \mathbf{c}.\mathbf{a}.$$

But $\mathbf{b}.\mathbf{c} = \mathbf{c}.\mathbf{b}$, so $\mathbf{b}.\mathbf{a} = \mathbf{c}.\mathbf{a}$, and this is equivalent to $(\mathbf{c}-\mathbf{b}).\mathbf{a} = 0$, which implies $\mathbf{DA} \perp \mathbf{BC}$.

Hence the altitudes of a triangle meet in a point, called its *orthocentre*.

Nowhere in this example have we assumed that A, B, C and D must lie in a plane. If they do not, the figure represents a tetrahedron. If the vectors represented by $\overline{AD}$ and $\overline{BC}$ are perpendicular, we still say that $\overline{AD}$ and $\overline{BC}$ are perpendicular, even though they are skew (not coplanar).

We thus have the theorem:

> If two pairs of opposite edges of a tetrahedron are perpendicular, so is the third pair.

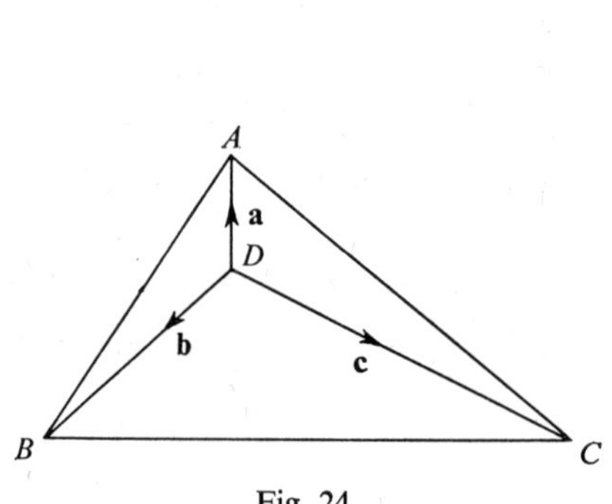

Fig. 24

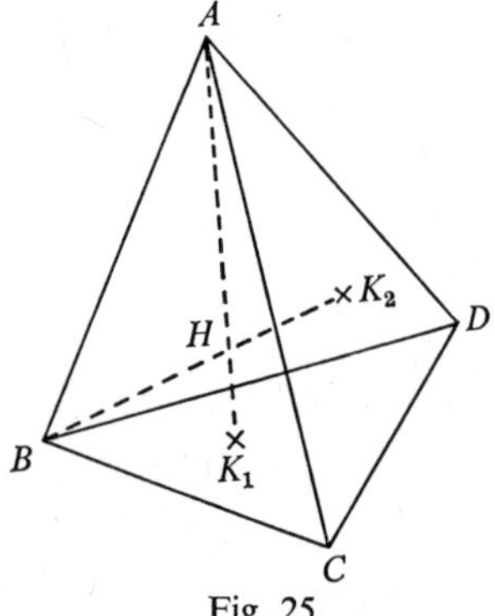

Fig. 25

We can also show that if the opposite edges of $ABCD$ are perpendicular, then the normals to the faces through the opposite vertices meet at a point. We select a new origin at the centre O of the circumsphere of $ABCD$, and denote position vectors of points by the corresponding small letters.

Now **a**, **b**, **c**, **d** are of equal length and, for example, $\mathbf{b}+\mathbf{c}$ is perpendicular to $\mathbf{b}-\mathbf{c}$, since $(\mathbf{b}+\mathbf{c}).(\mathbf{b}-\mathbf{c}) = b^2-c^2 = 0$.

Let H be the point with position vector $\frac{1}{2}(\mathbf{a}+\mathbf{b}+\mathbf{c}+\mathbf{d})$. Then

$$\begin{aligned}(\mathbf{h}-\mathbf{a}).(\mathbf{b}-\mathbf{c}) &= \tfrac{1}{2}(\mathbf{b}+\mathbf{c}+\mathbf{d}-\mathbf{a}).(\mathbf{b}-\mathbf{c}) \\ &= \tfrac{1}{2}(\mathbf{b}+\mathbf{c}).(\mathbf{b}-\mathbf{c})+\tfrac{1}{2}(\mathbf{d}-\mathbf{a}).(\mathbf{b}-\mathbf{c}) = 0,\end{aligned}$$

since $\overline{AD} \perp \overline{BC}$. Hence $\overline{AH} \perp \overline{BC}$, and by the symmetry between B, C and D, $\overline{AH} \perp \overline{CD}$ and so on, so that $\overline{AH}$ is normal to the plane BCD. In the same way it can be shown that $\overline{BH}$, $\overline{CH}$ and $\overline{DH}$ are normal to the other faces, so that H is the orthocentre of the tetrahedron.

In general, however, a tetrahedron does not have an orthocentre, as the following argument shows. Suppose the normals AK_1, BK_2 to the faces BCD, CDA do meet at H (see Figure 25). Then if B, C and D are fixed and A moves parallel to CD, BK_2 is fixed but AK_1 no longer meets it.

Exercise H

1. Show that if P is $(2, 5, -3)$, Q is $(4, -1, 1)$ and R is $(-2, 5, 7)$, then OP is normal to the plane QOR. Verify that if S is $(2, 4, 8)$, then OS lies in this plane, and express $\mathbf{s}$ in terms of $\mathbf{q}$ and $\mathbf{r}$.

2. Show that if A is $(1, 3, -5)$, B is $(3, 8, -2)$, C is $(-1, 0, -3)$ and D is $(-11, 10, -13)$, then $ABCD$ is a tetrahedron in which each edge is perpendicular to the opposite edge.

3. Show that if P, Q, R and S are the points whose coordinates are $(\pm 1, \pm 1, \pm 1)$ with an *even* number of $-$ signs, then $PQRS$ is a regular tetrahedron with its opposite edges perpendicular. What can you say about the four points with an *odd* number of $-$ signs?

4. What is the equation of the plane through the origin normal to the vector $\begin{pmatrix} 2 \\ 3 \\ -4 \end{pmatrix}$? What is the equation of the plane parallel to this plane through the point $(-3, 4, 1)$?

5. Find a vector which is perpendicular to both the vectors

$$\begin{pmatrix} 5 \\ 2 \\ 3 \end{pmatrix} \text{ and } \begin{pmatrix} 3 \\ 4 \\ 1 \end{pmatrix}.$$

6. Show that

$$\begin{pmatrix} b_1c_2-b_2c_1 \\ c_1a_2-c_2a_1 \\ a_1b_2-a_2b_1 \end{pmatrix}$$

is always perpendicular to both

$$\begin{pmatrix} a_1 \\ b_1 \\ c_1 \end{pmatrix} \text{ and } \begin{pmatrix} a_2 \\ b_2 \\ c_2 \end{pmatrix}.$$

Solve Question 5 again, using this result.

(This result will be found useful in some of the following exercises.)

7. If G is the centroid of the tetrahedron $ABCD$, express its position vector $\mathbf{g}$ in terms of $\mathbf{a}$, $\mathbf{b}$, $\mathbf{c}$ and $\mathbf{d}$ (see Chapter 9, Section 5). Compare with Section 6.8 above, and state what this tells you about O, G and H.

7. LINES AND PLANES

7.1 A plane defined by a linear equation. In Section 6.7 we showed that a plane, conceived as a set of lines through a point at right-angles to a normal vector, has an equation of the form $ax+by+cz = d$; and that this argument can be reversed (see Exercise I, Question 8). For what follows it will be more natural to start from the linear equation, and indeed define a plane to be the set of points $\{(x, y, z): ax+by+cz = d\}$ where a, b, c, d are any four real numbers, and to develop its properties from this.

We take $\mathbf{OQ}$ to be the vector $\begin{pmatrix} a \\ b \\ c \end{pmatrix}$ (see Figure 26). If P is (x, y, z) and $\overline{PN}$ is perpendicular to $\overline{OQ}$, then $ax+by+cz = d \Rightarrow \mathbf{OP}.\mathbf{OQ} = d$, and therefore $ON.OQ = d$, so that $ON = d/OQ$, which is constant.

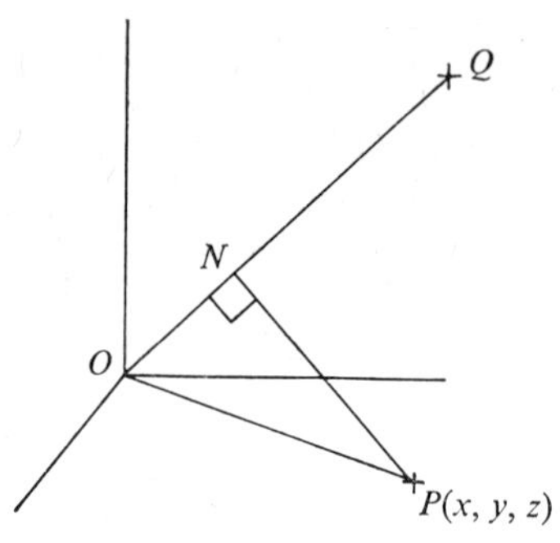

Fig. 26

The plane is therefore the set of points P for which $\mathbf{PN}$ is perpendicular to $\mathbf{OQ}$, where $\mathbf{OQ}$ is a fixed vector and N a fixed point of $\overleftrightarrow{OQ}$.

We have shown that the perpendicular distance, ON, of the origin from $ax+by+cz = d$ is

$$\frac{|d|}{\sqrt{(a^2+b^2+c^2)}}.$$

The perpendicular distance of any point P from the plane can be found in a similar manner.

Example 8. What is the equation of the plane through (1, 2, 3) normal to the vector

$$\mathbf{q} = \begin{pmatrix} 3 \\ -1 \\ 4 \end{pmatrix}?$$

The plane has an equation of the form $\mathbf{p}.\mathbf{q} = k$, that is, $3x-y+4z = k$. Since (1, 2, 3) lies in it, $k = 3\times 1-2+4\times 3 = 13$. Hence the equation is $3x-y+4z = 13$.

Alternatively the equation can be found from

$$\begin{pmatrix} x-1 \\ y-2 \\ z-3 \end{pmatrix} . \begin{pmatrix} 3 \\ -1 \\ 4 \end{pmatrix} = 0.$$

7.2 Perpendicular distance from a plane. Let N be the foot of the perpendicular from $P_1(x_1, y_1, z_1)$ to the plane $ax+by+cz = d$ (see Figure 27) and let $\mathbf{ON} = \mathbf{n}$, $\mathbf{NP}_1 = \mathbf{h}$. Then if

$$\mathbf{q} = \begin{pmatrix} a \\ b \\ c \end{pmatrix},$$

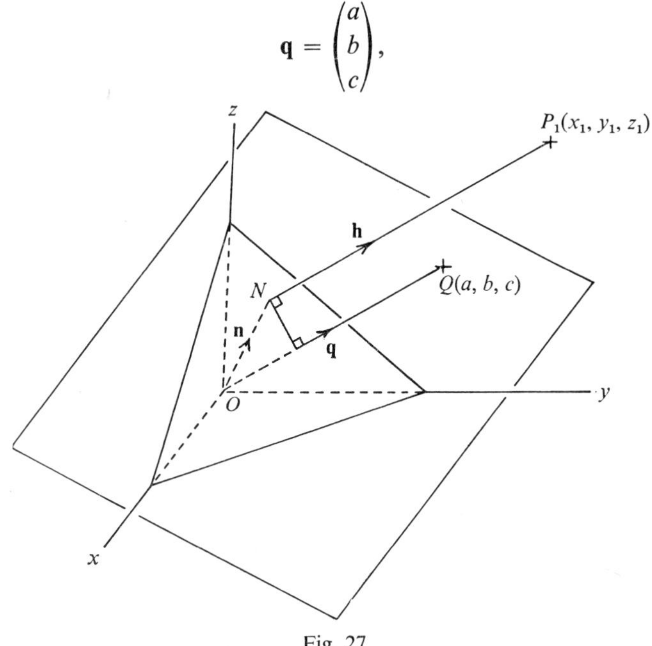

Fig. 27

we have $\mathbf{h} = \mathbf{p}_1 - \mathbf{n}$, so that

$$\begin{aligned} \mathbf{h}.\mathbf{q} &= \mathbf{p}_1.\mathbf{q} - \mathbf{n}.\mathbf{q} \\ &= \mathbf{p}_1.\mathbf{q} - d, \quad \text{since } N \text{ is in the plane,} \\ &= ax_1+by_1+cz_1-d. \end{aligned}$$

But $\mathbf{h}.\mathbf{q} = hq = h\sqrt{(a^2+b^2+c^2)}$, since h and q are parallel. Hence the perpendicular distance of the point (x_1, y_1, z_1) from the plane

$$ax+by+cz = d$$

is

$$h = \frac{|ax_1+by_1+cz_1-d|}{\sqrt{(a^2+b^2+c^2)}}.$$

It can be shown, by an argument similar to that of Section 6.3, that the expression $ax+by+cz-d$ is positive for all points (x, y, z) on one side of the plane and negative on the other side. For planes that do not pass through the origin the sign for all points on the origin side of the plane is that of $-d$.

7.3 The axial planes. The equation $x = 0$, of the first degree, represents a plane. Its normal vector is

$$\begin{pmatrix} 1 \\ 0 \\ 0 \end{pmatrix},$$

which is $\mathbf{i}$, and it contains the axes Oy and Oz: it is the plane yOz. Similarly, $y = 0$ and $z = 0$ are planes perpendicular to the y- and z-axes, the planes zOx and xOy.

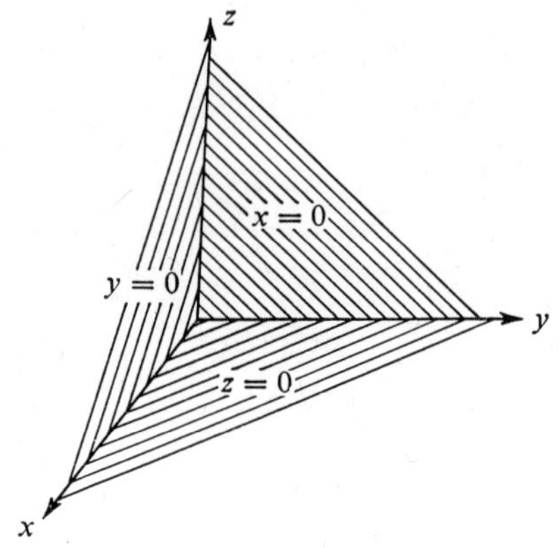

Fig. 28

7.4 Intercepts on the axes and the axial planes. The plane

$$ax+by+cz = d$$

evidently meets the plane $x = 0$ in the line whose equation in the plane $x = 0$ is $by+cz = d$. In space the two equations are needed to specify the line

$$\begin{cases} by+cz = d, \\ \quad\;\; x = 0. \end{cases}$$

The intercepts of the plane on the y-axis and z-axis are therefore d/b and d/c respectively, and similarly the intercept on the x-axis is d/a.

Example 9. Find the equation of the plane through the points (1, 0, 0), (0, 2, 0) and (0, 0, −3).

If the equation is $ax+by+cz = d$, we have at once that $a = d$, $2b = d$,

$-3c = d$, and hence setting $d = 6$ (to avoid fractions) we have for the equation

$$6x+3y-2z = 6.$$

(*Note* that the equation of the plane is not determined uniquely: for example, the equations $6x+3y-2z = 6$ and $12x+6y-4z = 12$ both represent the same plane. This accounts for the freedom we had in selecting a suitable value for d.)

Example 10. A plane meets the plane $x = 0$ in the line $x = 0$, $4y-3z = 10$; and the plane $z = 0$ in the line $z = 0$, $7x+2y = 5$. What is its equation?

This is simply a matter of constructing an equation which will reduce to $4y-3z = 10$ when $x = 0$, and to $7x+2y = 5$ when $z = 0$. It is obviously

$$14x+4y-3z = 10.$$

Exercise I

1. A plane is normal to the vector $\begin{pmatrix} 4 \\ -1 \\ -3 \end{pmatrix}$ and contains the point (1, 1, 1). What is its equation?

2. A regular tetrahedron has vertices at (1, 1, 1), (1, −1, −1), (−1, −1, 1) and (−1, 1, −1). Find the equations of the planes of its faces, and the lengths of the perpendiculars from the origin to the faces.

3. Find the lengths of the perpendiculars from the following points to the given planes:

(*a*) from (1, 0, 0) to $x+y+z = 4$;
(*b*) from (4, 2, −3) to $2x-y+z = 3$;
(*c*) from (−2, −3, 7) to $4x-3y = 2$;
(*d*) from (6, 5, 4) to $7x-4y-4z+3 = 0$;
(*e*) from (4, 0, −1) to $3x+6y-2z+7 = 0$;
(*f*) from (−11, 17, −10) to $5x-y-8z-26 = 0$.

4. The plane $ax+by+cz+d = 0$ divides space into two regions, in one of which $ax+by+cz+d > 0$ and in the other $ax+by+cz+d < 0$. Is (3, −8, −9) on the same side of $7x-10y+13z+15 = 0$ as the origin, or not? Are the points (−5, 3, 4) and (4, 1, −2) on the same or opposite sides of this plane?

5. Find the plane which bisects that angle between the planes $2x+8y-4z = 11$ and $4x-y+2z+7 = 0$ in which the origin lies. (This is the locus of points from which the perpendiculars onto the two planes, with the appropriate signs, are equal.)

6. Write down the equation of the plane through (3, 1, −2) parallel to $5x-2y+7z = 0$.

7. Find the equation of the plane through $P(1, -1, 0)$ and $Q(2, 0, -3)$ perpendicular to the plane $x-y+z = 0$. (Its normal vector must be perpendicular both to **PQ** and to the normal vector of the given plane.)

8. Show that if $P_1(x_1, y_1, z_1)$ is a point of the locus $ax+by+cz = d$, then the locus is the set of points P such that PP_1 is perpendicular to a fixed line.

9. For what value of λ can

$$\begin{pmatrix} -1 \\ 3 \\ \lambda \end{pmatrix}$$

be a normal vector to a plane through the line $x = 0$, $6y-5z = 30$? Find the equation of this plane for this value of λ, and the line in which it meets the plane $y = 0$.

7.5 Lines (three dimensions). If P_1 is a point on a line, and P is any other point on it, then $\mathbf{P_1P}$ is in a fixed direction. If $\mathbf{u}$ is a unit vector in this direction and the segment P_1P is of length t, then $\mathbf{p} = \mathbf{p}_1 + t\mathbf{u}$, and this is a parametric equation for the line. If

$$\mathbf{u} = \begin{pmatrix} l \\ m \\ n \end{pmatrix},$$

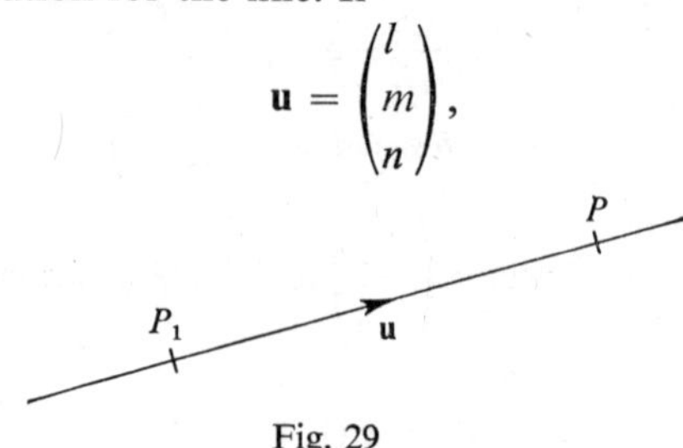

Fig. 29

then the equation $\mathbf{p} = \mathbf{p}_1 + t\mathbf{u}$ can be written in component form as:

$$\left.\begin{aligned} x &= x_1 + tl, \\ y &= y_1 + tm, \\ z &= z_1 + tn. \end{aligned}\right\}$$

The same equations hold if $\mathbf{u}$ is not a unit vector, but then t is not the length of P_1P.

In a plane, where there are only two component equations, we can eliminate t between them and obtain the single equation

$$\frac{x-x_1}{l} = \frac{y-y_1}{m},$$

which represents the line. In space this cannot be done—or rather it does not give complete information. In space such an equation represents a plane, a plane through the line. The line itself is defined by two such planes, and these can be found by equating any pair of the three equal quantities,

$$\frac{x-x_1}{l} = \frac{y-y_1}{m} = \frac{z-z_1}{n} (= t),$$

which are the three different expressions for t.

Example 11. Do the pairs of equations

$$\frac{x-1}{3} = \frac{y+2}{4} = \frac{z-4}{5}$$

and
$$\frac{x+2}{6} = \frac{y+6}{8} = \frac{z+1}{10}$$
represent the same line?

To begin with, their direction vectors
$$\begin{pmatrix}3\\4\\5\end{pmatrix} \quad \text{and} \quad \begin{pmatrix}6\\8\\10\end{pmatrix}$$
are parallel, which is a necessary condition.

It only remains now to check whether or not the lines are coincident. We do this by seeing if there is a common point. If we put
$$\frac{x-1}{3} = \frac{y+2}{4} = \frac{z-4}{5} = 0,$$
we see that $(1, -2, 4)$ lies on the first line (which is also obvious from the definition of the standard equations). We now determine whether $(1, -2, 4)$ satisfies the second pair of equations. If $x = 1$, $\frac{1}{6}(x+2) = \frac{1}{2}$; if $y = -2$, $\frac{1}{8}(y+6) = \frac{1}{2}$; and if $z = 4$, $\frac{1}{10}(z+1) = \frac{1}{2}$, so that the same point lies on the second line. The lines are therefore identical.

Example 12. Where does the line
$$\frac{x+1}{2} = \frac{y-3}{5} = \frac{z+2}{-1}$$
meet the plane $x+y+z = 12$?

We first express the equation of the line in parametric form
$$\left.\begin{aligned} x &= -1+2t, \\ y &= 3+5t, \\ z &= -2-t. \end{aligned}\right\}$$
The point with parameter t will lie on the plane if
$$(-1+2t)+(3+5t)+(-2-t) = 12.$$
This equation is satisfied when
$$6t = 12, \quad \text{that is} \quad t = 2.$$
The point of intersection is therefore $(3, 13, -4)$.

Example 13. Find parametric equations for the line joining $A(2, 1, 4)$ to $B(5, -1, -2)$.

We have only to find the vector **AB**. This is
$$\begin{pmatrix}3\\-2\\-6\end{pmatrix}.$$

Suitable parametric equations are therefore

$$x = 2+3t, \quad y = 1-2t, \quad z = 4-6t.$$

If we wish the parameter to represent length, we must choose a *unit* vector along the line. Since $3^2+2^2+6^2 = 7^2$, such a vector could have components

$$\frac{3}{7}, \frac{-2}{7}, \frac{-6}{7}$$

and any point P of the line is given by

$$x = 2+\tfrac{3}{7}r, \ y = 1-\tfrac{2}{7}r, \ z = 4-\tfrac{6}{7}r,$$

where r is the length of the segment AP.

Exercise J

1. Find parametric equations for the edges of the tetrahedron with vertices (1, 1, 1), (1, −1, −1), (−1, 1, −1) and (−1, −1, 1).

2. Find parametric equations for the line joining $(u, 0, 0)$ to $(0, 1, u)$. Show that every point of this line lies on the surface $z = y(x+z)$, whatever u may be. Show also that every point on the line joining $(0, v, 0)$ to $(1-v, v, v)$ lies on the same surface for all values of v.

3. Find where the line joining the given points meets the given plane.

(*a*) (0, 1, 0), (1, 0, 1), $x+y+z = 1$;
(*b*) (3, −1, 2), (5, −4, 1), $4x-y+3z = 5$;
(*c*) (2, 1, 4), (−1, 0, 5), $3x-2y+z = 4$;
(*d*) (4, 3, 5), (7, −4, 6), $5x+2y-z = 10$;
(*e*) (4, 3, 5), (7, −4, 6), $5x+2y-z = 21$.

4. Find a vector perpendicular to each of the vectors

$$\begin{pmatrix} 3 \\ 4 \\ 5 \end{pmatrix} \text{ and } \begin{pmatrix} +2 \\ -1 \\ +1 \end{pmatrix}.$$

Hence find the equation of the plane through the origin parallel to each of the lines

$$\frac{x-1}{3} = \frac{y+2}{4} = \frac{z-2}{5} \quad \text{and} \quad \frac{x+4}{2} = \frac{2-y}{1} = \frac{z-2}{1}.$$

Does the plane contain either of the lines?

5. Show that the line $\mathbf{p} = \mathbf{p}_1 + t\mathbf{u}$ meets the plane $\mathbf{p}.\mathbf{n} = d$ in the point whose position vector is

$$(\mathbf{p}_1(\mathbf{u}.\mathbf{n}) - \mathbf{u}(\mathbf{p}_1.\mathbf{n}) + d\mathbf{u})/(\mathbf{u}.\mathbf{n}).$$

7.6 Lines parallel to a plane. We shall now consider some more important special relationships between lines and planes. We have seen how to find the point of intersection, if any, of a line and a plane. However, the line may be parallel to the plane. If it is, its vector must be perpendicular to the plane's normal vector. This can be tested in the usual way by examining the scalar product.

For instance,

$$\frac{x-1}{3} = \frac{y-2}{4} = \frac{z-3}{5}$$

is parallel to $2x+y-2z = 0$, since the vectors

$$\begin{pmatrix}3\\4\\5\end{pmatrix} \quad \text{and} \quad \begin{pmatrix}2\\1\\-2\end{pmatrix}$$

are perpendicular (their scalar product is zero). The line

$$\frac{x-1}{4} = \frac{y-2}{-2} = \frac{z-3}{3}$$

is also perpendicular to the normal vector and, hence, parallel to the plane. Both these lines contain the point (1, 2, 3). They therefore determine a plane parallel to the given one. Its equation is obviously

$$2x+y-2z = 2\times 1+2-2\times 3 = -2.$$

If we write the lines parametrically, we have $x = 1+3t$, $y = 2+4t$, $z = 3+5t$ for the first, and $x = 1+4s$, $y = 2-2s$, $z = 3+3s$ for the second. Substitution in $2x+y-2z = -2$ reveals that in each case the equation is satisfied for all values of t and s. The lines lie completely in the plane. So, in fact, will any line through (1, 2, 3) whose vector is a linear combination of the vectors

$$\begin{pmatrix}3\\4\\5\end{pmatrix} \quad \text{and} \quad \begin{pmatrix}4\\-2\\3\end{pmatrix}.$$

In general, the line $\mathbf{p} = \mathbf{p}_1 + t\mathbf{u}$ will be parallel to the plane $\mathbf{p}.\mathbf{q} = d$ if $\mathbf{u}.\mathbf{q} = 0$, and will lie *in* the plane if, in addition, $\mathbf{p}_1.\mathbf{q} = d$. In that case, $(\mathbf{p}_1 + t\mathbf{u}).\mathbf{q} = d$ for all values of t.

***7.7 A sheaf and a prism of planes.** As an example, consider the equation $2x+y-2z-1+k(x+3y-3z-1) = 0$, where k belongs to the set of real numbers. For any particular value of k it is a linear equation which therefore represents a plane π (say). If $p_1(x_1, y_1, z_1)$ is any point on l, the line of intersection of the planes α and β, whose equations are

$$2x+y-2z-1 = 0 \quad \text{and} \quad x+3y-3z-1 = 0,$$

then $$2x_1+y_1-2z_1-1 = 0 \quad \text{and} \quad x_1+3y_1-3z_1-1 = 0.$$

Hence also $$2x_1+y_1-2z_1-1+k(x_1+3y_1-3z_1-1) = 0;$$

so that P_1 lies in π. For example, the point (1, 1, 1) lies in both α and β, and clearly satisfies the equation we are considering, whatever the value of k. It follows therefore that π is a plane through the line l where α and β intersect. By varying k we get different planes through the line l, and we can describe any set of these planes as a 'sheaf' of planes through l.

If we take the case where $k = 1$ we have the sheaf of planes

$$\begin{cases} 2x+y-2z-1 = 0, \\ x+3y-3z-1 = 0, \\ 3x+4y-5z-2 = 0, \end{cases}$$

and we may notice that their normal vectors

$$\mathbf{u} = \begin{pmatrix} 2 \\ 1 \\ -2 \end{pmatrix}, \quad \mathbf{v} = \begin{pmatrix} 1 \\ 3 \\ -3 \end{pmatrix} \quad \text{and} \quad \mathbf{w} = \begin{pmatrix} 3 \\ 4 \\ -5 \end{pmatrix}$$

are linearly dependent; that is, we can find real numbers a, b and c (not all zero) such that $a\mathbf{u}+b\mathbf{v}+c\mathbf{w} = 0$. (In this case we could take $a = b = 1$, $c = -1$.)

In general, for any value of k, the normal vectors α, β and π are linearly dependent because

$$\begin{pmatrix} 2 \\ 1 \\ -2 \end{pmatrix} + k\begin{pmatrix} 1 \\ 3 \\ -3 \end{pmatrix} - \begin{pmatrix} 2+k \\ 1+3k \\ -2-3k \end{pmatrix} = 0.$$

This is also clear because their normal vectors are each perpendicular to l, and therefore, as position vectors, are coplanar.

The converse is not true, because although

$$\begin{pmatrix} 2 \\ 1 \\ -2 \end{pmatrix}, \quad \begin{pmatrix} 1 \\ 3 \\ -3 \end{pmatrix}, \quad \begin{pmatrix} 3 \\ 4 \\ -5 \end{pmatrix}$$

are linearly dependent, the three planes

$$2x+y-2z+4 = 0,$$

$$x+3y-3z-1 = 0,$$

$$3x+4y-5z-2 = 0,$$

for which these are normal vectors, do not meet in a line. This is easily seen by observing that the first equation is that of a plane parallel to the plane $2x+y-2z-1 = 0$, which we know to pass through l. These three planes form a triangular tunnel, which we shall call a *prism*.

When three planes form a prism they are all parallel to some common line. (In our example, it is easy to verify that the planes are parallel to the line $x = 3t$, $y = 4t$, $z = 5t$, for instance.) Their normal vectors are therefore linearly dependent. By considering the following questions we can establish the converse result:

> If for three planes the normal vectors are linearly dependent, then the planes form a prism or a sheaf.

(1) Is there always a line parallel to two given planes?

(2) Given $\mathbf{q}$ and $\mathbf{r}$, can you always find a vector $\mathbf{u}$ to make $\mathbf{u}.\mathbf{q} = 0 = \mathbf{u}.\mathbf{r}$?

(3) Given three linearly dependent vectors, $\mathbf{q}$, $\mathbf{r}$ and $\mathbf{s}$, can you always express $\mathbf{s}$ in the form $\lambda\mathbf{q}+\mu\mathbf{r}$?

(4) Is it true that $\mathbf{u}.\mathbf{q} = 0$ and $\mathbf{u}.\mathbf{r} = 0 \Rightarrow \mathbf{u}.\mathbf{s} = 0$, if $\mathbf{q}$, $\mathbf{r}$ and $\mathbf{s}$ are linearly dependent?

(5) If $\mathbf{u}.\mathbf{q} = 0 = \mathbf{u}.\mathbf{r} = \mathbf{u}.\mathbf{s}$, what can you say about the planes $\mathbf{p}.\mathbf{q} = d$, $\mathbf{p}.\mathbf{r} = e$ and $\mathbf{p}.\mathbf{s} = f$?

Exercise K

1. Verify that the line

$$\frac{x-1}{3\lambda+4\mu} = \frac{y-2}{4\lambda-2\mu} = \frac{z-3}{5\lambda+3\mu}$$

lies in the plane $2x+y-2z = -2$ for all values of λ and μ.

(Put each ratio equal to t and substitute in the equation of the plane for x, y, z.)

2. Find equations of the form

$$x = at,\ y = bt,\ z = ct,$$

for the lines through the origin, one in each of the coordinate planes, which are parallel to $x+y+z = 1$. What is the equation of the plane in which they all lie?

3. Verify that $x = 3t$, $y = 4t$, $z = 5t$ lies in the plane

$$2x+y-2z+k(3x+4y-5z) = 0$$

for all values of t and k. What does this imply?

4. Do the planes $2x+y-2z = 3$, $3x+4y-5z = 1$ and $12x+11y-16z = 7$ form a sheaf or a prism?

5. Show that the planes $2x-y+5z = 7$, $5x+3y-z = 4$ and $3x+4y-6z = k$ have a line in common for some value of k, and find this value.

6. Find a vector parallel to the planes $x+y = 0$ and $y+z = 0$.

***7.** Show that the planes $x+y = 0$, $y+z = 0$ and $x = z+1$, form a prism, and find the direction of its 'axis'.

***8.** What is the condition for the planes $x+y = a$, $y+z = b$ and $z-x = c$, to form a sheaf?

14

FURTHER TRIGONOMETRY

In this chapter we extend the work of Chapter 8, and especially examine the consequences of the addition formulae and the periodic property of the circular functions.

1. THE ADDITION FORMULA FOR TANGENTS

From the formulae of Chapter 8 for $\sin(\theta+\phi)$ and $\cos(\theta+\phi)$ we can derive a formula for $\tan(\theta+\phi)$ which is expressed in terms of tangents alone. This is of some advantage in computing the function $\tan x$. We have

$$\tan(\theta+\phi) = \frac{\sin(\theta+\phi)}{\cos(\theta+\phi)}$$

$$= \frac{\sin\theta\cos\phi+\cos\theta\sin\phi}{\cos\theta\cos\phi-\sin\theta\sin\phi}.$$

Dividing the numerator and denominator of this fraction by $\cos\theta\cos\phi$, we obtain

$$\tan(\theta+\phi) = \frac{\dfrac{\sin\theta\cos\phi}{\cos\theta\cos\phi}+\dfrac{\cos\theta\sin\phi}{\cos\theta\cos\phi}}{\dfrac{\cos\theta\cos\phi}{\cos\theta\cos\phi}-\dfrac{\sin\theta\sin\phi}{\cos\theta\cos\phi}}$$

$$= \frac{\tan\theta+\tan\phi}{1-\tan\theta\tan\phi},$$

which is entirely expressed in terms of tangents. For completeness we add the formula for $\tan(\theta-\phi)$. Remembering that 'tan' is an 'odd' function, i.e. $\tan(-\phi) = -\tan\phi$, we obtain

$$\tan(\theta-\phi) = \frac{\tan\theta-\tan\phi}{1+\tan\theta\tan\phi}.$$

This last formula can be used to find the angle between two vectors, or between two lines in a plane whose gradients are known (cf. p. 371).

Example 1. What is the angle between the lines $y = 3x$ and $2y+5x = 0$? The gradient of the first is 3, and if we write the second as $y = -\frac{5}{2}x$, we see that its gradient is $-\frac{5}{2}$ (see Figure 1). We require $\alpha-\beta$, where

$$\tan\alpha = -\tfrac{5}{2}, \quad \tan\beta = 3.$$

The formula gives

$$\tan(\alpha-\beta) = \frac{-\frac{5}{2}-3}{1+(-\frac{5}{2})(3)} = \frac{-\frac{11}{2}}{1-\frac{15}{2}} = \frac{11}{13}.$$

Hence $\alpha-\beta = 40^\circ\,15'$ approximately.

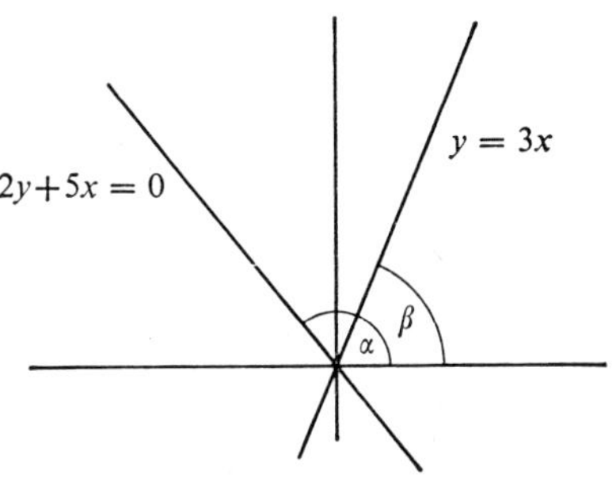

Fig. 1

Example 2. Find the angle between the vectors

$$\begin{pmatrix}1\\3\end{pmatrix} \text{ and } \begin{pmatrix}3\\-4\end{pmatrix}.$$

The tangents of the angles which these vectors make with the x-axis are 3 and $-\frac{4}{3}$ respectively. Hence if θ is the angle required

$$\tan\theta = \frac{3+\frac{4}{3}}{1-3\times\frac{4}{3}} = -\frac{13}{9},$$

so that $\theta = 180^\circ - 55{\cdot}3^\circ = 124{\cdot}7^\circ$. We cannot tell without a figure whether this obtuse angle, or the acute angle $55{\cdot}3^\circ$, is the true angle between the vectors.

This method avoids finding the length of the vectors, which is necessary if the scalar product method is used. On the other hand its use is restricted —it could not be used to find the angle between the vectors

$$\begin{pmatrix}1\\1\\3\end{pmatrix} \text{ and } \begin{pmatrix}2\\3\\1\end{pmatrix}.$$

Exercise A

1. Find $\tan 2A$ ($= \tan(A+A)$) in terms of $\tan A$. (Compare the method used for finding $\sin 2A$ and $\cos 2A$ in earlier work.)

2. Prove that

$$\tan\left(\frac{\pi}{4}+\theta\right) = \frac{1+\tan\theta}{1-\tan\theta}.$$

3. Find the acute angle between:

(*a*) $y = x$ and $y = 2x$; (*b*) $y = 3x$ and $y = -2x$;
(*c*) $2y = 7x$ and $y+x = 0$; (*d*) $3y = 4x$ and $5y+6x = 0$;
(*e*) $3y = 4x+5$ and $5y+6x = 11$.

4. Find the angle between the vectors:

$$(a)\ \begin{pmatrix}2\\5\end{pmatrix} \text{ and } \begin{pmatrix}3\\7\end{pmatrix}; \qquad (b)\ \begin{pmatrix}4\\-3\end{pmatrix} \text{ and } \begin{pmatrix}3\\4\end{pmatrix}.$$

5. Find the acute angle between the lines joining the points (2, 5, 3) and (3, 7, 3), and (6, 3, 3) and (4, 2, 3).

2. MULTIPLE ANGLES

2.1 If in the formula for $\sin(\theta+\phi)$ we put $\theta = \phi = x$, we obtain

$$\sin 2x = 2 \sin x \cos x.$$

In the same way, from the formula for $\cos(\theta+\phi)$ we get

$$\cos 2x = \cos^2 x - \sin^2 x.$$

There are two other forms for this last result which are much more useful, since they do not involve both sines and cosines. Using

$$\left.\begin{aligned} 1 &= \cos^2 x + \sin^2 x, \\ \cos 2x &= \cos^2 x - \sin^2 x, \end{aligned}\right\}$$

and adding and subtracting, we find

$$1+\cos 2x = 2\cos^2 x,$$

$$1-\cos 2x = 2\sin^2 x.$$

These formulae are very interesting. They tell us that $\sin^2$ and $\cos^2$ are not different kinds of function from sin and cos themselves—different, that is, in the same way as $x \to x^2$ (which, for example, has a curved graph and not a linear one) is a different kind of function from $x \to x$.

The functions $x \to \sin x$ and $x \to \cos x$ are periodic functions: if x is increased by 2π, or any multiple of 2π, the images under the mapping $x \to \sin x$ are repeated. That is, $\sin(x+2n\pi) = \sin x$ for all $n \in Z$. Now $\sin^2 x$ behaves in a similar way, except that in this case the values repeat after an interval of only π in x. $\sin^2$ is the composite mapping

$$x \to 2x \to \cos 2x \to \tfrac{1}{2}\cos 2x \to \tfrac{1}{2}-\tfrac{1}{2}\cos 2x \ (= \sin^2 x),$$

and the graphs show this relationship clearly (see Figure 2).

2.2 For $\tan 2x$ we have

$$\tan 2x = \tan(x+x)$$
$$= \frac{\tan x + \tan x}{1 - \tan x . \tan x}$$
$$= \frac{2\tan x}{1-\tan^2 x}.$$

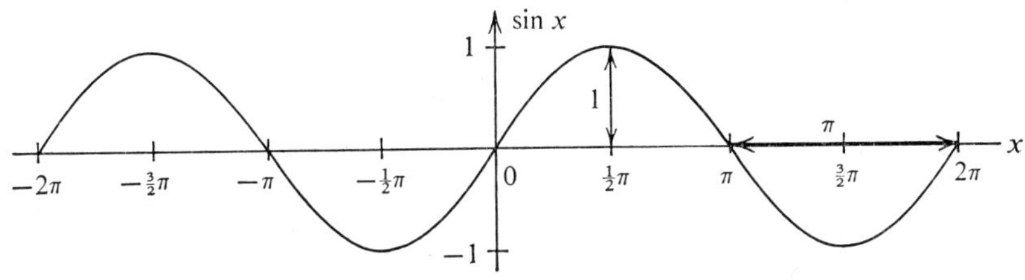

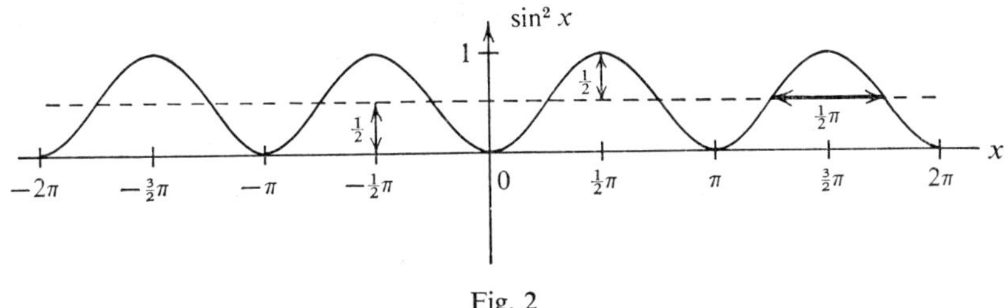

Fig. 2

Remarkably enough, $\sin 2x$ and $\cos 2x$ can also be expressed entirely in terms of $\tan x$. For

$$\sin 2x = 2\sin x . \cos x = \frac{2\sin x\cos x}{\sin^2 x + \cos^2 x} \quad (\text{since } \sin^2 x + \cos^2 x = 1)$$
$$= \frac{\dfrac{2\sin x}{\cos x}}{\dfrac{\sin^2 x}{\cos^2 x}+1} = \frac{2\tan x}{1+\tan^2 x};$$

and

$$\cos 2x = \frac{\cos^2 x - \sin^2 x}{\cos^2 x + \sin^2 x}$$
$$= \frac{1-\dfrac{\sin^2 x}{\cos^2 x}}{1+\dfrac{\sin^2 x}{\cos^2 x}}$$
$$= \frac{1-\tan^2 x}{1+\tan^2 x}.$$

These formulae are very useful, because they give an *algebraic* mapping from the set of values of t ($= \tan \frac{1}{2}\theta$) onto the set of values of $\sin \theta$ and $\cos \theta$.

In fact, if we put $2x = \theta$, we have

$$\sin \theta = \frac{2t}{1+t^2},$$

$$\cos \theta = \frac{1-t^2}{1+t^2},$$

$$\tan \theta = \frac{2t}{1-t^2}.$$

Thus $\sin \theta$, $\cos \theta$, $\tan \theta$ are three rational algebraic functions of t. Further, as θ takes values in the domain $0 \leqslant \theta \leqslant \frac{1}{2}\pi$, t takes values in the range $0 \leqslant t \leqslant 1$, and t increases monotonically, though not of course uniformly, with θ.

Algebraic equations involving $\sin \theta$ and $\cos \theta$, can often be solved easily in terms of t, and θ may then be found from the equation $t = \tan \frac{1}{2}\theta$.

The graphs of the functions $t \to \sin \theta$, $t \to \cos \theta$ are shown in Figure 3, and it is instructive to investigate their behaviour as t increases beyond 1.

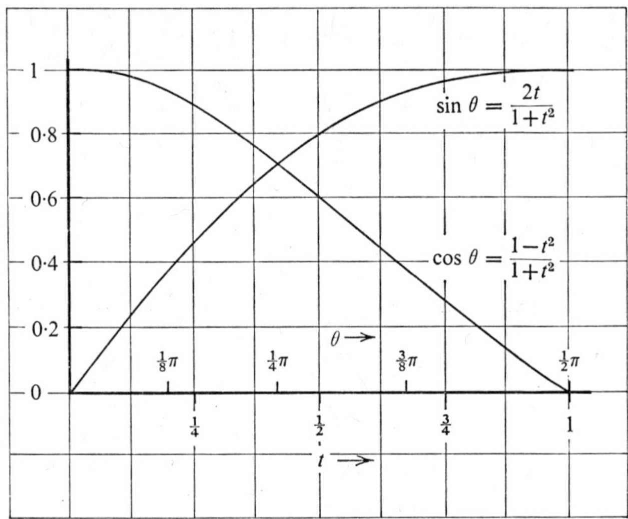

Fig. 3

Exercise B

1. Writing $\sin 3A = \sin(2A+A)$, find a formula for $\sin 3A$ in terms of $\sin A$ only. (Use $\cos^2 A + \sin^2 A = 1$.)

Do the same for $\cos 3A$, in terms of $\cos A$.

2. Find simpler forms for:

(*a*) $\cos^4 x - \sin^4 x$; (*b*) $\dfrac{1-\cos 2x}{1+\cos 2x}$;

(*c*) $(\cos x + \sin x)^2$; (*d*) $\sin^2 x \cos^2 x$ (in terms of $\cos 4x$).

3. Check the formulae for $\sin 2\theta$ and $\cos 2\theta$ when $\theta = 60°$.

4. What happens to the formula for $\tan 2\theta$ when $\tan\theta = 1$? Why? Explain the result when $\tan\theta = \sqrt{3}$.

5. If $A + B = \frac{1}{2}\pi$, show that $\tan A \tan B = +1$.
(*Hint.* Draw a right-angled triangle containing the angles A and B.)

6. Given that θ is acute and $\tan\theta = \frac{1}{5}$, work out $\tan 4\theta$ by two applications of the formula for $\tan 2\theta$. Is 4θ greater or less than 45°?

7. If $0° < \theta < 90°$, $90° < \phi < 180°$, and $\cos\theta = \frac{3}{5}$, $\sin\phi = \frac{5}{13}$, calculate (as fractions) the values of:

(*a*) $\sin(\theta+\phi)$; (*b*) $\cos 2\theta$; (*c*) $\cos(2\theta+\phi)$;
(*d*) $\tan 2\phi$; (*e*) $\tan(2\phi+\theta)$.

In what quadrants are the angles $(2\theta+\phi)$ and $(2\phi+\theta)$?

8. If $\cos\theta = \frac{12}{17}$ and θ is acute, evaluate $\cos 2\theta$. Without using tables, show that θ is very nearly 45°. Is it greater or less?

9. By a method similar to Question 8, show that if $\cos\theta = \frac{13}{15}$, and θ is acute, then θ is very nearly 30°, and decide without tables whether it is greater or less.

10. Express $3\sin\theta + 4\cos\theta$ in terms of $t = \tan\frac{1}{2}\theta$, and hence find the solution set of angles θ for which

$$0° < \theta < 360° \quad \text{and} \quad 3\sin\theta + 4\cos\theta = 2.$$

11. By putting $x = \cos\theta$, and using the result of Question 1, find the three solutions of $12x^3 - 9x = 1$. Discuss the possibility of using this substitution generally, to solve cubic equations.

3. COMBINED FUNCTIONS

3.1 Periodic oscillations. In Chapter 8 (Book, 1, p. 235 ff.) we looked at the periodic property of the simple sin and cos functions, and showed how they could be used to describe oscillations such as those of a loaded

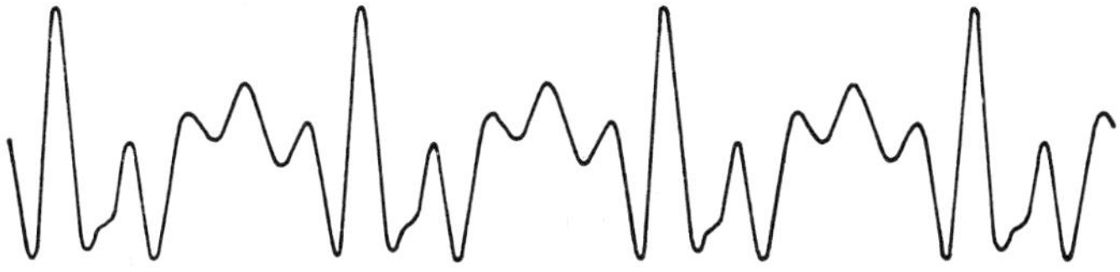

Fig. 4. From Sir James Jeans, *Science and Music*, C.U.P.

helical spring or the variation in alternating current. Most oscillations, however, which occur in practice are not of this simple type; such a pattern, for example, as is shown in Figure 4, which represents the sound wave produced by a single note on the oboe, is clearly quite unlike a simple sine curve. Yet it is a remarkable fact that even so complicated a pattern as this, provided it is truly periodic, can be represented by a suitable combination of simple sine waves. To analyse such a pattern is the difficult task of a branch of mathematics called *harmonic analysis*; here we shall merely build up by trial one or two simple patterns.

3.2 Superposition of waves of the same period. Consider two simple sine graphs with the same period, which are not just carbon copies of one another (Figure 5). They will differ in two ways: their maxima—the 'peaks' of the waves—may be of different heights, and may occur in different places. The height of the peak (and the depth of a trough) measured from the x-axis is called the *amplitude* of the wave, and the difference in the values of x at two successive maxima is called the *phase-difference* between the waves. The earlier questions in the following exercise are designed to help you discover what happens when two such waves are combined together by adding the ordinates of the two graphs. When you have worked through them, it will be obvious that patterns like that in Figure 4 can never be obtained in this way.

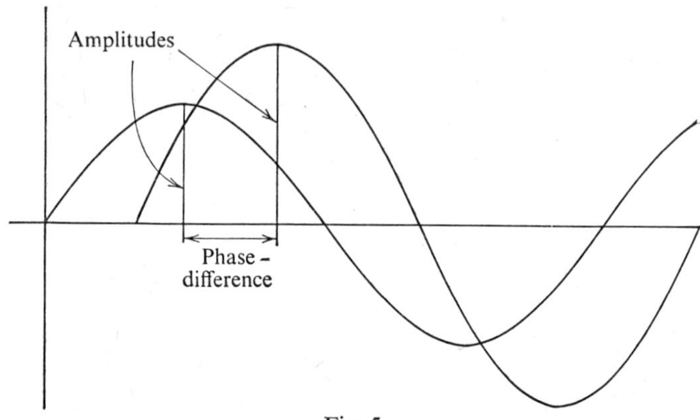

Fig. 5

3.3 Superposition of waves with different periods. The most interesting, and indeed the most important, case is when one period is an exact multiple of the other, or when the ratio of the two periods is that of two small natural numbers. When this happens, the period of the combined wave is easily found. For example, $\sin x$ has period 2π; $\sin 5x$ has period $\frac{2}{5}\pi$, since if x is increased by this amount, $5x$ is increased by 2π and $\sin 5x$ returns to its former value. What then will be the period of $\sin x + \sin 5x$? Evidently, since one period divides exactly into the other, it will simply be the longer of the two periods, namely 2π. What happens in the case of sin $3x+\sin 5x$? The periods of the separate wave-functions are $\frac{2}{3}\pi$ and $\frac{2}{5}\pi$. Can you tell what the period of the combined wave will be?

The effect of combining such wave-functions by adding together their ordinates is most easily shown graphically. Figure 6 shows the graphs of $\sin x$ and $\sin 2x$, and the graph of $\sin x+\sin 2x$, obtained by adding the

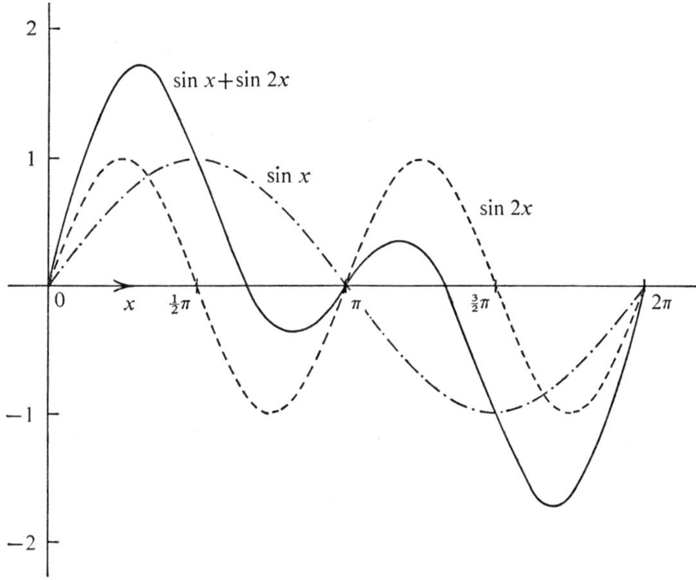

Fig. 6

ordinates of the first two graphs. Unlike the situation in the previous section, a new pattern has now appeared. You can obtain more interesting patterns of this kind by working through the later questions of the following exercise.

Exercise C

To draw the graphs in this exercise it may help to prepare pieces of card with their edges cut in the forms of the graphs of sin *x*, sin 2*x*, *and* sin 3*x*.

1. Draw the graphs of $\sin x$ and $\cos x$. What is their phase-difference? Add the ordinates to obtain the graph of the function $x \to \sin x+\cos x$. From your graph find:

(*a*) the amplitude of this function;
(*b*) its period;
(*c*) the phase-difference between it and $\sin x$.

2. Repeat Question 1 for the graphs of $\sin x$ and $\sin(x+\frac{1}{3}\pi)$. Is the combined graph still a sine-curve?

3. Draw on the same axes the graphs of $3\sin x$ and $5\sin(x-\frac{1}{3}\pi)$. From them obtain the graph of $3\sin x+5\sin(x-\frac{1}{3}\pi)$. Is it a sine-curve?

What is its amplitude and period?

4. Use the addition formulae to express $3\sin x+5\sin(x-\frac{1}{3}\pi)$ in the form $a\sin x+b\cos x$ and show that $a^2+b^2 = 49$.

(Remember that $\sin\frac{1}{3}\pi = \frac{1}{2}\sqrt{3}$ and $\cos\frac{1}{3}\pi = \frac{1}{2}$.)

5. Draw the graph of the function $\theta \to 4\sin\theta+7\cos\theta$. Read off from your graph the maximum and minimum values of $4\sin\theta+7\cos\theta$ and the values of θ at which these occur.

6. Cut out of thin card a triangle ABC, where $AB = 4$ cm, $BC = 7$ cm, and the angle ABC is a right-angle.

(*a*) Calculate for this triangle the length of AC and the angle CAB.

(*b*) Place the triangle on centimetre graph paper with A at a convenient origin, AB along the x-axis and BC in the direction of the positive y-axis. Rotate the triangle through a positive angle; call this angle θ. What is the height of C above the x-axis in this position?

Answer this in two ways: without using your answer to (*a*), and then more shortly, using this result.

(*c*) Turn the triangle so that C has its maximum height above the x-axis, still keeping A at the origin. What is this maximum height and what is now the value of the angle θ? Compare with your answers to Question 5.

(*d*) Use the result you found in part (*b*) to write $4\sin\theta+7\cos\theta$ in the form $k.\sin(\theta+\alpha)$, giving the values of k and α.

It is suggested that the following questions are allocated to different members of the class, and the results displayed for general discussion.

7. Draw on one diagram the graphs of:

(*a*) $\cos x$; (*b*) $\cos x+\cos 2x$; (*c*) $\cos x+\cos 2x+\cos 3x$.

8. Draw on one diagram the graphs of:

(*a*) $\sin 4x$; (*b*) $\sin 4x+\sin(2x+\frac{1}{4}\pi)$;

(*c*) $\sin 4x+\sin(2x+\frac{1}{4}\pi)+\sin(x+\frac{1}{4}\pi)$.

9. Draw on one diagram the graphs of:

(*a*) $\sin x$; (*b*) $\sin x+\sin 3x$; (*c*) $\sin x+\sin 3x+\sin 5x$.

10. Draw on one diagram the graphs of:

(*a*) $(4/\pi)\sin x$; (*b*) $(4/\pi)(\sin x+\frac{1}{3}\sin 3x)$;

(*c*) $(4/\pi)(\sin x+\frac{1}{3}\sin 3x+\frac{1}{5}\sin 5x)$.

What do you think the graph of

$$(4/\pi)(\sin x+\tfrac{1}{3}\sin 3x+\tfrac{1}{5}\sin 5x+\ldots)$$

would look like?

4. THE FUNCTION $a\sin x+b\cos x$

The functions of the type $a\sin x+b\cos x$ which arose in Exercise C will now be investigated by means of a few examples.

Example 3. Express $5 \cos x - 12 \sin x$ as a cosine function.

Draw a right-angled triangle with sides 5 and 12. By Pythagoras's Theorem, the hypotenuse will be 13 (see Figure 7). Let the angle marked be α. Then $5 = 13 \cos \alpha$ and $12 = 13 \sin \alpha$.

We have

$$5 \cos x - 12 \sin x = 13 \cos \alpha \cos x - 13 \sin \alpha \sin x$$

$$= 13 \cos (x + \alpha).$$

From the triangle, $\tan \alpha = 2{\cdot}4$ which implies $\alpha = 67{\cdot}4^\circ$. Hence,

$$5 \cos x - 12 \sin x = 13 \cos (x + 67{\cdot}4^\circ).$$

Example 4. Express $4 \sin x + 7 \cos x$ as a sine function.

Since we want a sine function, we need $4 = h \cos \beta$ and $7 = h \sin \beta$; we therefore draw the triangle as in Figure 8. Clearly $h = \sqrt{65}$ by Pythagoras's Theorem. Also $\tan \beta = 1{\cdot}75$ and $\beta = 60^\circ\ 15'$. Accordingly

$$4 \sin x + 7 \cos x = h \cos \beta \sin x + h \sin \beta \cos x$$

$$= \sqrt{65} \sin (x + 60^\circ\ 15').$$

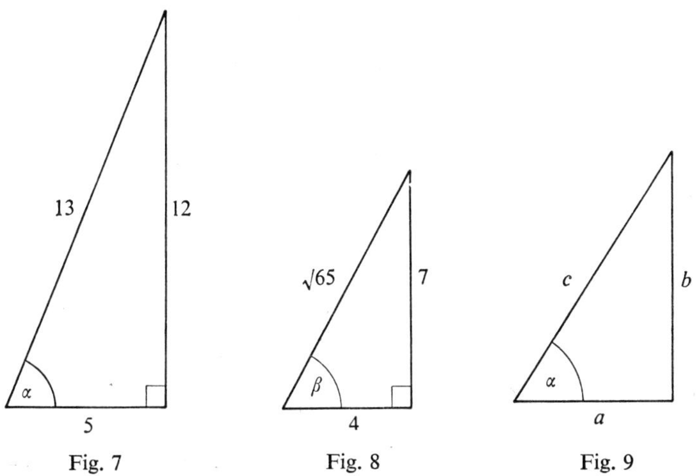

Fig. 7 Fig. 8 Fig. 9

Example 5. Express $a \cos x + b \sin x$ in the form $c \cos (x - \alpha)$.

We must have $c \cos \alpha = a$, $c \sin \alpha = b$, so the figure is Figure 9. From this,

$$c = \sqrt{(a^2 + b^2)}$$

and

$$\cos \alpha = \frac{a}{c}, \quad \sin \alpha = \frac{b}{c}.$$

This will still be true if a and b are not positive, although α is then not an acute angle.

Exercise D

1. Express $3\cos x+4\sin x$ in the form $a\sin(x+\alpha)$, and hence sketch its graph.

2. What is the greatest value of $8\sin x-15\cos x$?

3. Prove that $\sin x+\cos x = \sqrt{2}\cos(x-\frac{1}{4}\pi)$ and hence sketch the graph of the function $x\to\sin x+\cos x$. For what values of x $(0\leqslant x\leqslant 2\pi)$ is

$$\sin x+\cos x = 1?$$

4. If $24\cos x-7\sin x = 8$, find values of x which lie between 0 and 2π and satisfy this equation by expressing $24\cos x-7\sin x$ in the form $a\cos(x+\alpha)$ and

(i) drawing its graph,
(ii) using tables.

5. A rectangular chest measuring $1{\cdot}5\text{ m}\times 0{\cdot}9\text{ m}$ is turned until it just wedges in a passage w m wide (see Figure 10).
(*a*) If $\alpha = 12°$, what is the width of the passage?
(*b*) If $w = 1{\cdot}35$, through what angle is it turned?

6. Find x if $20\cos x+21\sin x = 29$. Is there more than one answer in the interval $(0, 2\pi)$?

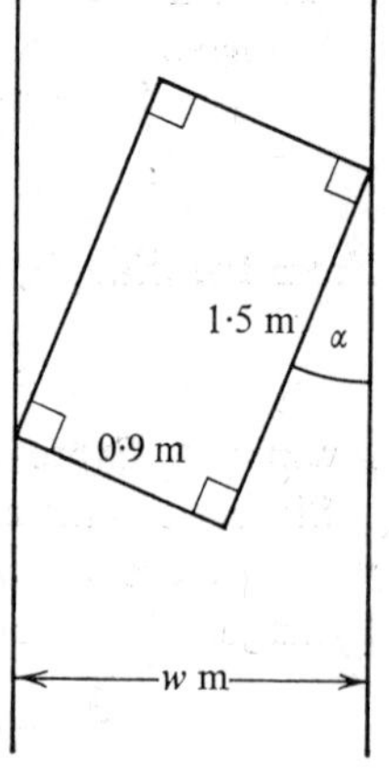

Fig. 10

5. SIMPLE TRIGONOMETRICAL EQUATIONS

5.1 The basic equations. Since the functions $x\to\sin x$, $x\to\cos x$, $x\to\tan x$ are *periodic*, with values recurring at regular intervals, the *inverse image* of an element of the range of one of these functions will usually be an *infinite set* of values of x. In practical problems, where x is a rotation, we may only be interested in values in the interval $0\leqslant x\leqslant 2\pi$, but not all problems are of this kind. In any case it is best to consider first the infinite set before choosing the finite subset which is relevant to the problem on hand.

(*a*) What is the solution set of $\cos x = \cos\alpha$? Consider the graph of $\cos x$ (see Figure 11).

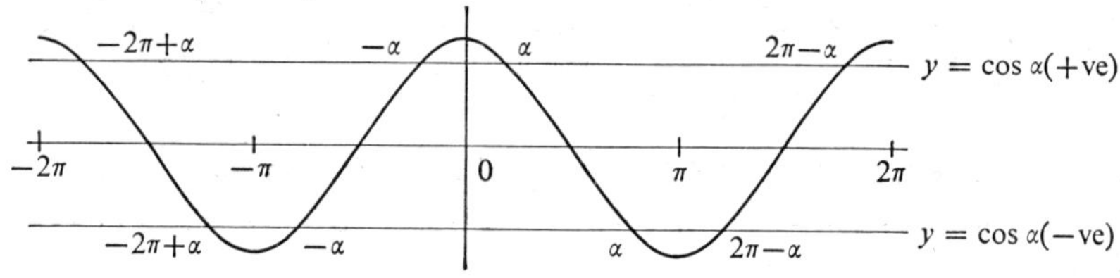

Fig. 11

It is clear that whether $\cos\alpha$ is positive or negative, the line $y = \cos\alpha$ will meet the graph twice in every period of 2π, and that the solution set is

$$\{\ldots, -2\pi+\alpha, -\alpha, \alpha, 2\pi-\alpha, 2\pi+\alpha, \ldots\};$$

in other words $\{x\colon x = 2n\pi\pm\alpha, \quad \text{where} \quad n\in Z\}$.

(*b*) What is the solution set of $\sin x = \sin\alpha$? The graph of $\sin x$ is shown in Figure 12 and again the line $y = \sin\alpha$ is drawn, for $\sin\alpha$ positive

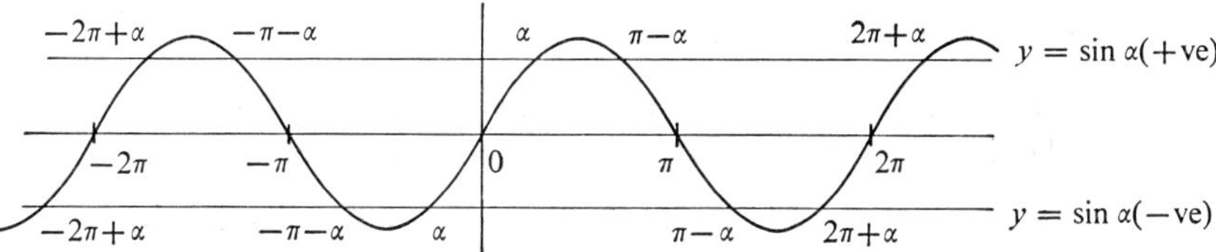

Fig. 12

and negative. In the second case α itself is negative. Again there are two solutions in every period of 2π, and the solution set is

$$\{\ldots, -\pi-\alpha, \alpha, \pi-\alpha, 2\pi+\alpha, \ldots\};$$

in other words

$$\{x\colon x = 2n\pi+\alpha, n\in Z\} \cup \{x\colon x = (2n+1)\pi-\alpha, n\in Z\}.$$

(*c*) Finally, if $\tan x = \tan\alpha$, we draw the graph of $\tan x$ as shown in Figure 13, remembering that tan has period π. Here the solution set is obviously

$$\{\ldots, -2\pi+\alpha, -\pi+\alpha, \alpha, \pi+\alpha, 2\pi+\alpha, \ldots\};$$

in other words

$$\{x\colon x = n\pi+\alpha, \quad n\in Z\}.$$

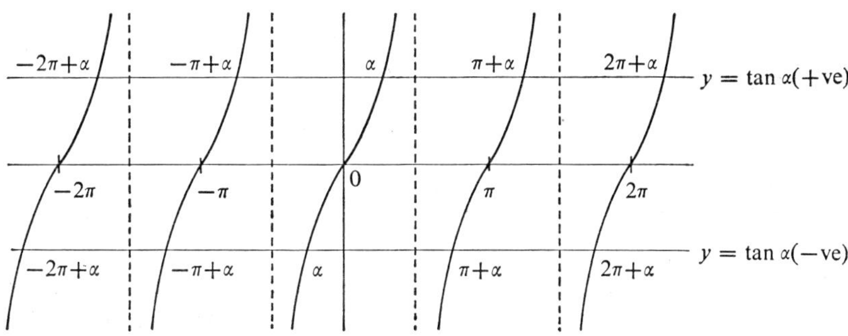

Fig. 13

Summarizing:

Equation	Solution set: Degree measure	Solution set: Radian measure	
$\cos x = \cos\alpha$	$\{360n^\circ \pm \alpha\}$	$\{2n\pi \pm \alpha\}$	$(n \in Z)$
$\sin x = \sin\alpha$	$\{360n^\circ + \alpha\} \cup$ $\{360n^\circ + 180^\circ - \alpha\}$	$\{2n\pi + \alpha\} \cup$ $\{(2n+1)\pi - \alpha\}$	
$\tan x = \tan\alpha$	$\{180n^\circ + \alpha\}$	$\{n\pi + \alpha\}$	

In these equations $\cos\alpha$, $\sin\alpha$, $\tan\alpha$ will usually be known numbers, and α can be found from tables. If $\cos\alpha$, $\sin\alpha$, or $\tan\alpha$ is positive, we may take $0° \leqslant \alpha \leqslant 90°$; if $\cos\alpha$ is negative, we take $90° < \alpha \leqslant 180°$; if $\sin\alpha$ or $\tan\alpha$ is negative, then $-90° \leqslant \alpha < 0°$.

Example 6. Find the solution set of x given that $\cos x = -\frac{1}{2}$.

Here $-\frac{1}{2}$ is the cosine of 120°, so that the solution set is

$$\{x: x = 360n° \pm 120°\}, \quad \text{or in radians} \quad \{x: x = 2n\pi \pm \tfrac{2}{3}\pi\}.$$

Example 7. Solve $\sin x = -0{\cdot}45$.

From tables, $\sin 26{\cdot}8° = +0{\cdot}45$ and hence $\sin(-26{\cdot}8°) = -0{\cdot}45$. The solution set is accordingly

$$\{360n° - 26{\cdot}8°, n \in Z\} \cup \{360n° + 206{\cdot}8°, n \in Z\}.$$

If we want only the solutions between 0 and 360° they are 206·8° (the element of the second set corresponding to $n = 0$) and 333·2° (the element of the first set corresponding to $n = 1$).

Example 8. Find the solutions of $\tan 4x = 1$ in the interval $0° \leqslant x \leqslant 360°$.

Here care is needed, for even though x lies in the interval [0°, 360°] it does not follow that $4x$ does; in fact, all we know about $4x$ is that $0° \leqslant 4x \leqslant 1440°$.

In cases such as this it is safer to write down first the infinite solution set. Since $1 = \tan 45°$, it follows that $4x = 180n° + 45°$, and hence

$$x = 45n° + 11\tfrac{1}{4}°.$$

The intersection of this solution set with

$$\{x: 0° \leqslant x \leqslant 360°\}$$

is now seen to be

$$x = \{11\tfrac{1}{4}°, 56\tfrac{1}{4}°, 101\tfrac{1}{4}°, 146\tfrac{1}{4}°, 191\tfrac{1}{4}°, 236\tfrac{1}{4}°, 281\tfrac{1}{4}°, 326\tfrac{1}{4}°\}.$$

5.2 An extension. In the above examples we solved equations such as $\cos x = \cos\alpha$ where $\cos\alpha$ was a given number. However, we shall often want to solve more complicated equations where $\cos\alpha$, etc., are no longer known numbers but are functions of x.

Example 9. Solve $\cos 3x = \cos 2x$.

Here we may write at once

$$3x = 2\pi n \pm 2x \quad \text{where} \quad n \in Z.$$

Taking the plus sign, $x = 2\pi n \quad (n \in Z)$.

Taking the minus sign, $5x = 2\pi n \quad (n \in Z)$

$$\Leftrightarrow x = 2\pi n/5 \quad (n \in Z).$$

But $\{2\pi n: n \in Z\} \subset \{2\pi n/5: n \in Z\}$ and so the full solution set is

$$\{2n\pi/5: n \in Z\}.$$

Example 10. Find angles x between 0 and 2π for which $\cos 2x = \sin x$.

Since the solution set for $\cos x = \cos \alpha$ can be expressed more simply than that for $\sin x = \sin \alpha$, we begin by putting $\sin x = \cos(\frac{1}{2}\pi - x)$. Then

$$\begin{aligned} \cos 2x &= \cos(\tfrac{1}{2}\pi - x) \\ \Leftrightarrow 2x &= 2n\pi \pm (\tfrac{1}{2}\pi - x) \\ \Leftrightarrow 3x &= 2n\pi + \tfrac{1}{2}\pi \quad \text{or} \quad x = 2n\pi - \tfrac{1}{2}\pi \\ \Leftrightarrow \quad x &= \frac{2n\pi}{3} + \frac{\pi}{6} \quad \text{or} \quad x = 2n\pi - \frac{\pi}{2}. \end{aligned}$$

If $0 < x < 2\pi$, we have therefore

$$x \in \left\{\frac{\pi}{6}, \frac{5\pi}{6}, \frac{3\pi}{2}\right\}.$$

Note in fact that

$$\left\{x: x = 2n\pi - \frac{\pi}{2}, n \in Z\right\} \subset \left\{x: x = \frac{2n\pi}{3} + \frac{\pi}{6}, n \in Z\right\}.$$

5.3 The linear equation. This is the name given to the equation of the form

$$a \cos x + b \sin x = c.$$

We can solve this equation by the use of an *auxiliary angle*, as we shall now show (compare Question 4 in Exercise D, p. 396 and Examples 3–5, page 395).

Example 11. Solve the equation

$$5 \sin x - 3 \cos x = 4.$$

There is an angle α whose tangent is $\frac{3}{5}$; from Figure 14 we see at once that $\sin \alpha = 3/\sqrt{34}$ and $\cos \alpha = 5/\sqrt{34}$. Dividing the given equation through by $\sqrt{34}$, we obtain

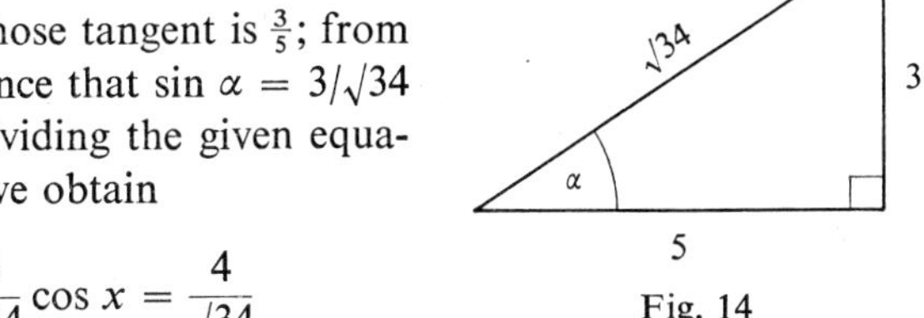

Fig. 14

$$\begin{aligned} \frac{5}{\sqrt{34}} \sin x - \frac{3}{\sqrt{34}} \cos x &= \frac{4}{\sqrt{34}} \\ \Leftrightarrow \cos \alpha \sin x - \sin \alpha \cos x &= \frac{4}{\sqrt{34}} \\ \Leftrightarrow \sin(x - \alpha) &= \frac{4}{\sqrt{34}} = 0{\cdot}686 \\ \Leftrightarrow \sin(x - \alpha) &= \sin 43{\cdot}3^\circ. \end{aligned}$$

Now $\tan\alpha = \frac{3}{5}$ and $\alpha = 31{\cdot}0°$. (We need not write down the most *general* value of α; that will be taken care of by the final general solution.)

Hence
$$x = 31{\cdot}0°+43{\cdot}3°+360n°,$$
$$\text{or}\quad 31{\cdot}0°+180°-43{\cdot}3°+360n°$$
$$= 360n°+74{\cdot}3° \quad\text{or}\quad 360n°+167{\cdot}7°.$$

In the general case, since the general solution of $\cos x = \cos\beta$ is simpler than that of $\sin x = \sin\beta$, it is usually better to use an auxiliary angle to throw the left-hand side into the form $\cos(x-\alpha)$ rather than $\sin(x+\alpha)$.

If $a\cos x+b\sin x = c$, let d be the *positive* square root of a^2+b^2. Then, whatever the signs of a and b, there is always an angle α ($0 \leqslant \alpha < 360°$) such that
$$\cos\alpha = a/d, \quad \sin\alpha = b/d,$$

Hence
$$a\cos x+b\sin x = c$$
$$\Leftrightarrow \frac{a}{d}\cos x+\frac{b}{d}\sin x = \frac{c}{d}$$
$$\Leftrightarrow \cos x\cos\alpha+\sin x\sin\alpha = c/d$$
$$\Leftrightarrow \cos(x-\alpha) = c/d.$$

Provided $c \leqslant d = \sqrt{(a^2+b^2)}$, c/d is the cosine of some angle β in the interval $0° \leqslant \beta \leqslant 180°$, and, finally, $x = \alpha+360n° \pm \beta$.

Exercise E

Write down the general solution of the equations in Questions 1–8.

1. $\cos x = 0{\cdot}891$.

2. $\sin x = -0{\cdot}891$.

3. $\tan x = 1{\cdot}54$.

4. $3\sin x = 4\cos x$.

5. $\cos x = -0{\cdot}075$.

6. $\cos x+\sin x = 0$.

7. $2\sin x+1 = 0$.

8. $5\cos x+1 = 0$.

Find all the solutions in the interval $0 \leqslant x < 360°$ of the equations in Questions 9–14.

9. $\sin 2x = \sin 44°$.

10. $\cos 3x = -0{\cdot}809$.

11. $\tan 5x = 1$.

12. $\sin 3x = \sin 2x$.

13. $\sin 4x = \cos x$.

14. $\sin x+\cos x = 1$.

Write down (*a*) the general solution, (*b*) the set of solutions in $\{x: 0° \leqslant x < 360°\}$ for the equations in Questions 15–18.

15. $3\cos x-4\sin x = 2$.

16. $\cos x+2\sin x = 1$.

17. $7\sin x-5\cos x = 4$.

18. $\cos 2x = 2\sin 2x+2$.

6. FURTHER DEVELOPMENTS

There are a large number of relations between the circular functions of the same or different angles which come in useful at some time or other. Exploration of these relations and the establishing of 'identities', or the writing of the same expressions in different ways, has been a rich source of students' exercises in the past. While this can easily be overdone, some facility with the commoner of such relations is useful, and we shall here give the various formulae and a few illustrative examples.

6.1 The factor formulae. These express the sums and differences of sines and cosines in factors, unlike the addition formulae of Section 2 of Chapter 8 (from which they are derived), which express the sines and cosines of sums and differences as sums. For convenience, all the formulae are set out below:

(i) $\sin(x+y) = \sin x \cos y + \cos x \sin y$,

(ii) $\sin(x-y) = \sin x \cos y - \cos x \sin y$,

(iii) $\cos(x+y) = \cos x \cos y - \sin x \sin y$,

(iv) $\cos(x-y) = \cos x \cos y + \sin x \sin y$,

(v) $2\sin x \cos y = \sin(x+y) + \sin(x-y)$ by adding (i) and (ii),

(vi) $2\cos x \sin y = \sin(x+y) - \sin(x-y)$ by subtracting (ii) from (i),

(vii) $2\cos x \cos y = \cos(x+y) + \cos(x-y)$,

(viii) $2\sin x \sin y = \cos(x-y) - \cos(x+y)$.

Putting

$$x = \frac{u+v}{2} \quad \text{and} \quad y = \frac{u-v}{2},$$

which are equivalent to $x+y = u$ and $x-y = v$, in equations (v) to (viii) we get

$$\text{(ix)} \quad \sin u + \sin v = 2\sin\frac{u+v}{2}\cos\frac{u-v}{2},$$

$$\text{(x)} \quad \sin u - \sin v = 2\cos\frac{u+v}{2}\sin\frac{u-v}{2},$$

$$\text{(xi)} \quad \cos u + \cos v = 2\cos\frac{u+v}{2}\cos\frac{u-v}{2},$$

$$\text{(xii)} \quad \underline{\cos v - \cos u} = 2\sin\frac{u+v}{2}\sin\frac{u-v}{2}.$$

Note carefully the sign of the left-hand side of equation (xii). It is reasonable because, as x increases, $\cos x$ decreases $(0 \leqslant x \leqslant \pi)$; hence $0 \leqslant v < u \leqslant \pi \Rightarrow \cos u < \cos v \Rightarrow \cos v - \cos u > 0 \Rightarrow \sin \frac{1}{2}(u-v) > 0$.

These last formulae are easily proved directly by vector methods. In Figure 15 let **OP** and **OQ** be unit vectors. Then

$$\mathbf{OP} = \begin{pmatrix}\cos x\\ \sin x\end{pmatrix} \quad \text{and} \quad \mathbf{OQ} = \begin{pmatrix}\cos y\\ \sin y\end{pmatrix}.$$

Also $\mathbf{OP}+\mathbf{OQ} = 2\mathbf{OR}$ (R is the mid-point of $\overline{PQ}$). We shall express **OR** in terms of x and y. Since $P\widehat{O}Q = x-y$, it follows that

$$Q\widehat{O}R = \frac{x-y}{2} \quad \text{and} \quad U\widehat{O}R = \frac{x+y}{2}$$

(the mean of x and y).

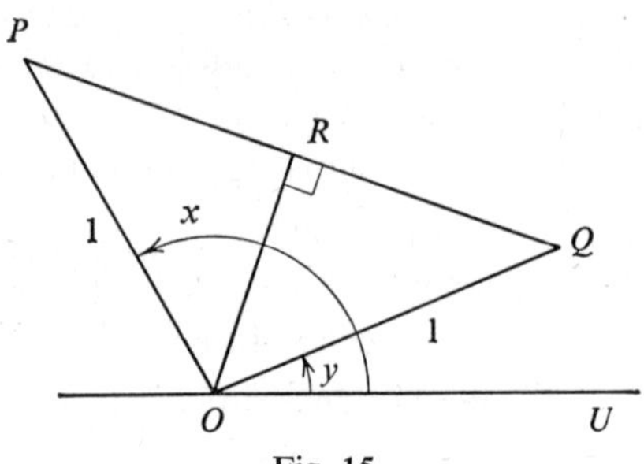

Fig. 15

But $$OR = OQ\cos\frac{x-y}{2} = \cos\frac{x-y}{2},$$

and so $$\mathbf{OR} = \cos\frac{x-y}{2}\begin{pmatrix}\cos\dfrac{x+y}{2}\\ \sin\dfrac{x+y}{2}\end{pmatrix}.$$

However, $$\mathbf{OP}+\mathbf{OQ} = 2.\mathbf{OR},$$

hence $$\begin{pmatrix}\cos x\\ \sin x\end{pmatrix}+\begin{pmatrix}\cos y\\ \sin y\end{pmatrix} = 2\cos\frac{x-y}{2}\begin{pmatrix}\cos\dfrac{x+y}{2}\\ \sin\dfrac{x+y}{2}\end{pmatrix}.$$

Formulae (ix) and (xi) follow by simply equating components of these vectors. Formula (x) follows by reversing the sign of y in (ix), remembering that 'sin' is an odd function. Formula (xii) is rather more difficult to derive but substitution of $y+\pi$ for y will give the required form. This is left as an exercise.

6.2 Alternative demonstration of the derivative of sin *x*. We can now give the second proof of $\sin' = \cos$ in an alternative form (compare Section 3 of Chapter 8).

By definition, if $f(x) = \sin x$, then

$$f'(a) = \lim_{b\to a} \frac{f(b)-f(a)}{b-a}$$

$$= \lim_{b\to a} \frac{\sin b - \sin a}{b-a}$$

$$= \lim_{b\to a} \frac{2\cos\frac{1}{2}(b+a)\sin\frac{1}{2}(b-a)}{b-a}, \quad \text{by formula (x)}$$

$$= \lim_{b\to a} \cos\tfrac{1}{2}(b+a) \times \lim_{b\to a} \frac{\sin\frac{1}{2}(b-a)}{\frac{1}{2}(b-a)} \quad \text{(assuming that this is legitimate)}$$

$$= \cos a \times 1.$$

Hence $f'(x) = \cos x$.

6.3 Use of tan $\frac{1}{2}x$ formulae in equations. If, in the equation

$$a\cos x + b\sin x = c,$$

we make the substitutions (see Section 2)

$$\cos x = \frac{1-t^2}{1+t^2}, \quad \sin x = \frac{2t}{1+t^2}, \quad \text{where} \quad t = \tan\tfrac{1}{2}x,$$

we obtain

$$\frac{a(1-t^2)}{1+t^2} + \frac{2bt}{1+t^2} = c,$$

$$\Leftrightarrow a(1-t^2) + 2bt = c(1+t^2)$$

$$\Leftrightarrow (c+a)t^2 - 2bt + (c-a) = 0.$$

This quadratic equation can be solved by the usual methods, and from this t and x can be found.

There is, however, one difficulty about this method of solution; the mapping $x \to t$ is not defined for all x in $0 \leqslant x < 2\pi$, there being *no image* of $x = \pi$. If $x = \pi$ is a solution of the original equation, it will therefore be lost in the process.

For example, $x = \pi$ is clearly a solution of the equation

$$3\cos x - 4\sin x + 3 = 0.$$

The auxiliary angle method gives

$$\cos\alpha\cos x - \sin\alpha\sin x = -\tfrac{3}{5},$$

where $\cos\alpha = \frac{3}{5}$ and $\sin\alpha = \frac{4}{5}$, so that $\alpha = 53{\cdot}1° = 0{\cdot}927$ radians.

Hence $\quad \cos(x+\alpha) = -\cos\alpha$

and $\quad x+\alpha = 2n\pi \pm (\pi-\alpha)$

giving $\quad x = (2n+1)\pi \quad \text{or} \quad 2n\pi+\pi-2\alpha$

or, in degrees, $\quad x = 360n° + 180° \quad \text{or} \quad 360n° + 73{\cdot}8°.$

If, however, we use the method of this section we get

$$3(1-t^2)-8t+3(1+t^2) = 0$$
$$\Leftrightarrow 6-8t = 0$$
$$\Leftrightarrow t = \tfrac{3}{4},$$

giving only $\frac{1}{2}x = 180n^\circ + 36{\cdot}9^\circ$, or $x = 360n^\circ + 73{\cdot}8^\circ$.

The other set of solutions has dropped out. For this reason, and also because it usually involves less work, the auxiliary angle method is to be preferred. In theoretical discussion of the linear equation, however, the method of this section is often useful.

[Another 'method', sometimes used by beginners, is to write the equation as $a\cos x - c = -b\sin x$ and square, using $\sin^2 x = 1-\cos^2 x$. The trouble is that in the mapping $x \to \pm\sqrt{(1-\cos^2 x)}$, every x has *two* images which have the same square; a number of 'solutions' will therefore appear which are in fact the solutions of $a\cos x - c = +b\sin x$. This procedure is therefore a very troublesome one, since all solutions need to be checked and sorted.]

6.4 The reciprocal functions, sec *x*, csc *x*, cot *x*. On many occasions it is useful to have abbreviations for the reciprocals of $\sin x$, $\cos x$ and $\tan x$, and the notation $\sin^{-1} x$ is reserved for another purpose. We write

$$\frac{1}{\cos x} = \sec x \quad \text{(the \textit{secant} of } x\text{)},$$

$$\frac{1}{\sin x} = \csc x \quad \text{(or cosec } x\text{, the \textit{cosecant} of } x\text{)},$$

$$\frac{1}{\tan x} = \cot x \quad \text{(the \textit{cotangent} of } x\text{)}.$$

$\sec x$, of course, will not be defined when $\cos x = 0$, that is, when $x = (2n+1)\pi/2$, $n \in Z$.

$\cot x$ and $\csc x$, in the same way, are not defined when $\sin x = 0$, that is when $x = n\pi$, $n \in Z$.

All six functions can be expressed in terms of $\sin x$ and $\cos x$ alone, as follows:

$$\tan x = \frac{\sin x}{\cos x}, \quad x \neq (2n+1)\pi/2 \quad (n \in Z);$$

$$\sec x = \frac{1}{\cos x}, \quad x \neq (2n+1)\pi/2 \quad (n \in Z);$$

$$\csc x = \frac{1}{\sin x}, \quad x \neq n\pi \quad (n \in Z);$$

$$\cot x = \frac{\cos x}{\sin x}, \quad x \neq n\pi \quad (n \in Z).$$

The names of these functions arose as follows:

(*a*) *Sine* comes from the Latin *sinus*, a fold, which is in turn a translation from the Arabic name.

(*b*) *Secant* and *Tangent* derive from the diagram shown in Figure 16; if the radius $\overline{OU}$ has unit length, and angle $UOP = x$, then $\overline{UT}$, cut off on the *tangent*, has length $\tan x$, and $\overline{OT}$, cut off on the *secant* has length $\sec x$.

(*c*) The functions whose names are prefixed with *co* are the corresponding functions of the complementary angles; thus

$$\cos x = \sin(\tfrac{1}{2}\pi - x),$$
$$\csc x = \sec(\tfrac{1}{2}\pi - x),$$
$$\cot x = \tan(\tfrac{1}{2}\pi - x).$$

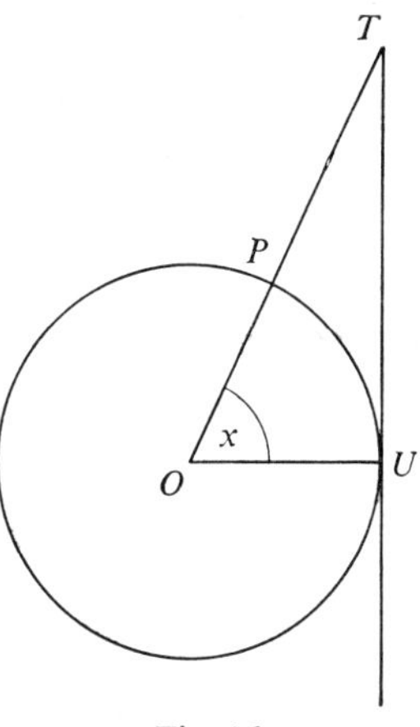

Fig. 16

Exercise F

1. Use the relation $\sin^2 x + \cos^2 x = 1$ to obtain the identities

$$\mathbf{1 + \tan^2 x = \sec^2 x \text{ and } 1 + \cot^2 x = \csc^2 x.}$$

2. Sketch the graphs of $\sec x$, $\csc x$ and $\cot x$.

3. Express in factors:

(*a*) $\sin 3x - \sin x$; (*b*) $\cos 5x + \cos 3x$;

(*c*) $\sin 54° + \sin 36°$; (*d*) $\cos 75° - \cos 15°$.

4. For Figure 17, write expressions for x and y in terms of a and θ without trigonometrical functions in the denominator.

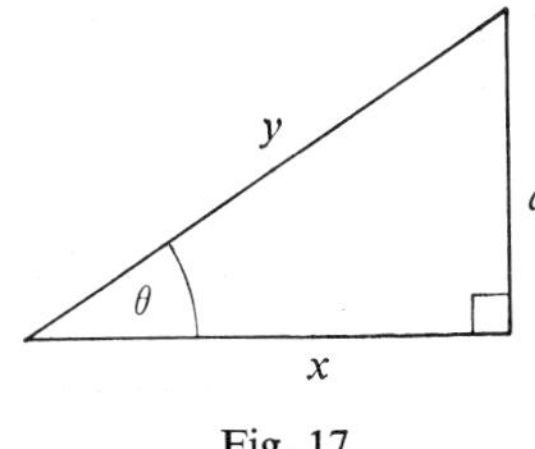

Fig. 17

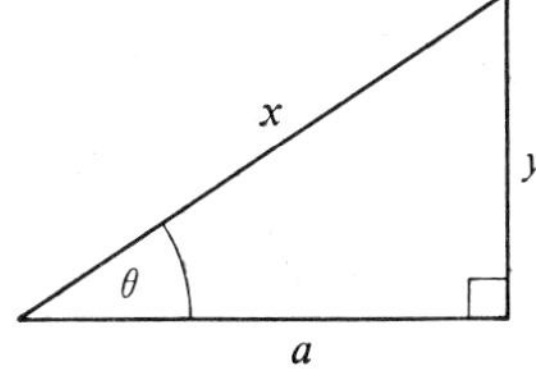

Fig. 18

5. Answer Question 4 for Figure 18, giving x, y in terms of a and θ.

6. Simplify

$$\frac{1+\cos 2x}{\sin 2x} \text{ and } \frac{\sin 2x}{1-\cos 2x}.$$

7. Find all the values of x in the interval $0° \leqslant x < 360°$ for which

$$\cos x + \cos 3x = \cos 2x.$$

(Use factor formula (xi) on the left-hand side.)

8. Prove that

$$4 \sin x . \sin\left(\frac{\pi}{3}+x\right) . \sin\left(\frac{2\pi}{3}+x\right) = \sin 3x,$$

by first using formula (viii) on

$$2 \sin\left(\frac{\pi}{3}+x\right) . \sin\left(\frac{2\pi}{3}+x\right).$$

9. Simplify

$$\sin x + \sin\left(\frac{2\pi}{3}+x\right) + \sin\left(\frac{4\pi}{3}+x\right)$$

by first using formula (ix) on the outer pair.

10. Solve, using the substitution $t = \tan \frac{1}{2}\theta$, the equation

$$4 \cos \theta - 7 \sin \theta = 8.$$

11. ADB is a semicircle with centre C, and DO is perpendicular to AB. The angle $BAD = x$ (see Figure 19).

Use the vector equation $\mathbf{OA}+\mathbf{OB} = 2\mathbf{OC}$ to show that

$$\cot x - \tan x = 2 \cot 2x$$

and verify this result by the formulae of this chapter.
[Take $OD = h$, and express everything in terms of h.]

Find a simpler form for $\cot x + \tan x$.

12. ABC is an equilateral triangle and AB is inclined at an angle x to OU (see Figure 20). Use $\mathbf{AB}+\mathbf{BC}+\mathbf{CA} = \mathbf{0}$ to deduce the result of Question 9. What is the similar result for cosines?

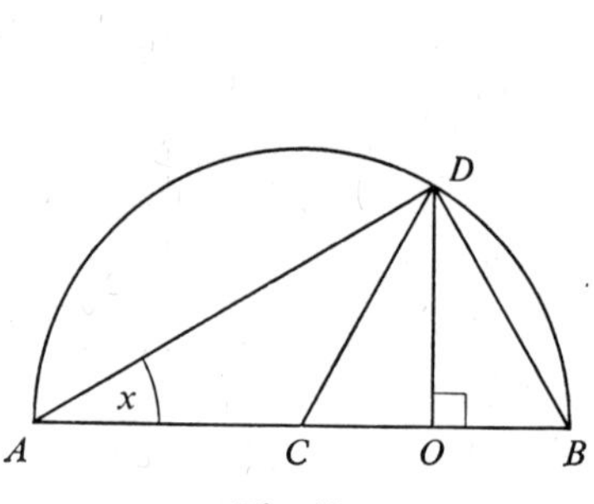

Fig. 19

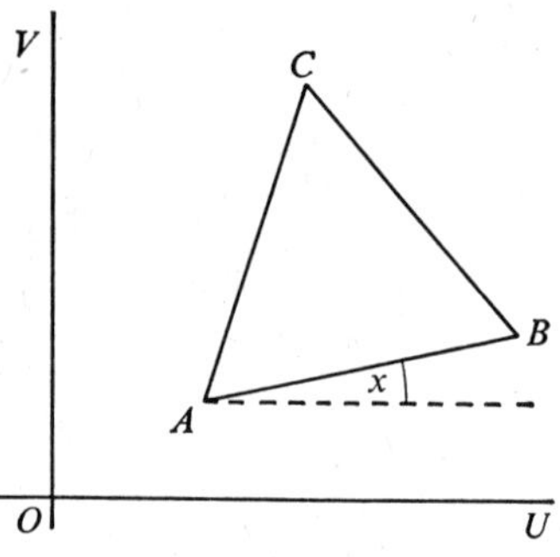

Fig. 20

***13.** By the method of Question 12 prove that

$$\sum_{k=0}^{n-1} \cos\left\{x + \frac{2k\pi}{n}\right\} = 0.$$

***14.** Establish the result of Question 13 as follows:

(*a*) Multiply

$$\cos\left\{x+\frac{2k\pi}{n}\right\} \text{ by } 2\sin\frac{\pi}{n}$$

and use formula (vi).

(*b*) Prove that

$$\begin{aligned} 2\sin\frac{\pi}{n}\sum_{k=0}^{n-1}\cos\left\{x+\frac{2k\pi}{n}\right\} &= \sum_{k=0}^{n-1}\left[\sin\left\{x+\frac{2k+1}{n}\pi\right\}-\sin\left\{x+\frac{2k-1}{n}\pi\right\}\right] \\ &= \sin\left\{x+\frac{2n-1}{n}\pi\right\}-\sin\left\{x-\frac{\pi}{n}\right\} = 0. \end{aligned}$$

Prove a similar result for

$$\sum_{k=0}^{n-1}\sin\left\{x+\frac{2k\pi}{n}\right\}.$$

7. POLAR COORDINATES

To specify the position of a point P in a plane relative to an origin O we must know the position vector **OP**. There are two simple ways of doing this: we must know the *components* of this vector relative to two fixed axes—say $\mathbf{OP} = \begin{pmatrix} x \\ y \end{pmatrix}$, which gives the *Cartesian coordinates* of P, (x, y); or else we must know the magnitude of OP and its direction relative to some fixed direction, $\overrightarrow{OU}$. If OP has length r, and angle $UOP = \theta$, then (r, θ) are called the *polar coordinates* of P (Figure 21).

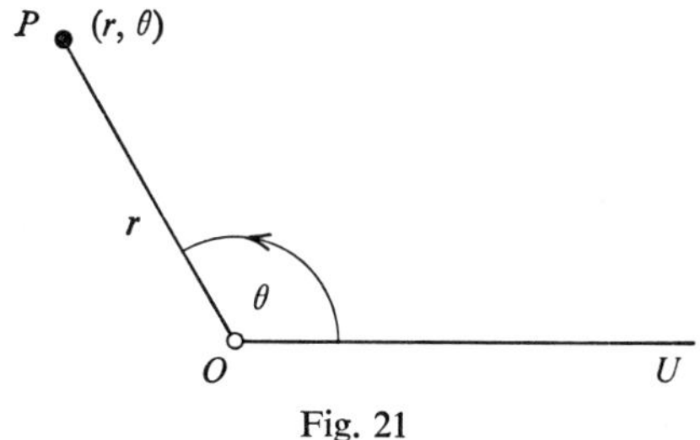

Fig. 21

The polar coordinates of a point are not unique. Not only will the same point P be given by the pair $(r, \theta+2\pi)$, and therefore by $(r, \theta+2n\pi)$ for every integer n; but also if we allow r to be negative then $(-r, \theta+\pi)$ also gives rise to P, since a displacement $-OP$ in the direction opposite to **OP** is clearly **OP** itself.

We could of course make the coordinates unique by restricting r to be positive and θ to lie in the range $0 \leqslant \theta < 2\pi$. But many loci can be more simply expressed if we do not do this, but allow r and θ to continue unrestricted until the locus begins to be traced again. A simple example will make the matter clear.

Example 12. Sketch the locus

$$C = \{(r, \theta): r \geqslant 0,\ 0 \leqslant \theta < 2\pi,\ r = a \cos \tfrac{1}{2}\theta\}.$$

As θ increases from 0 to π, r decreases from a to 0.

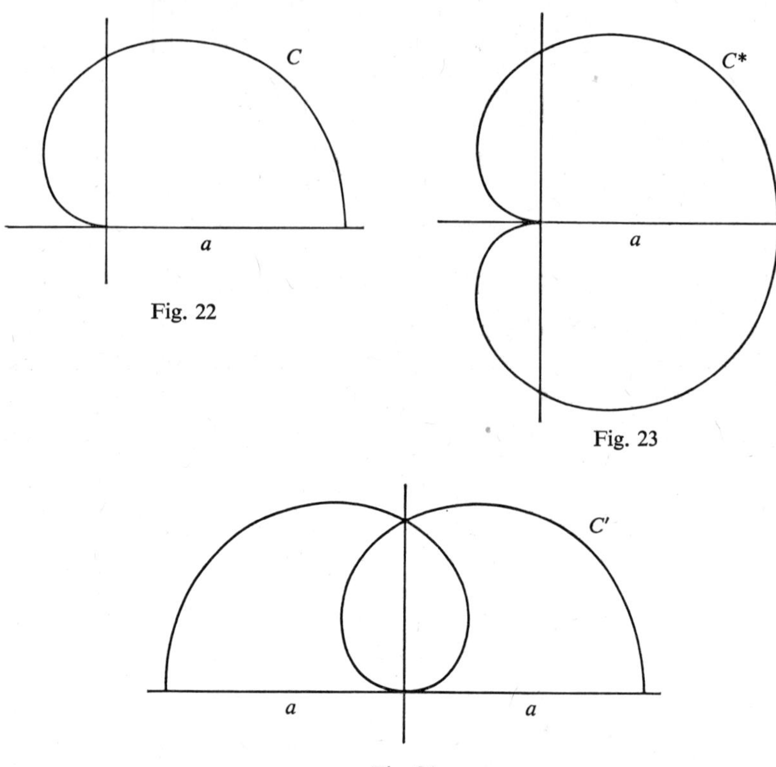

Fig. 22

Fig. 23

Fig. 24

For $\pi < \theta < 2\pi$, $\cos \frac{1}{2}\theta < 0$ and there are no points of C defined as we have defined it. C is sketched in Figure 22. But if we consider the locus

$$C^* = \{(r, \theta): r \geqslant 0, \quad r = a \cos \tfrac{1}{2}\theta\}$$

we find that for $3\pi \leqslant \theta \leqslant 4\pi$, r increases again from zero to a, and the sketch of C^* is the symmetrical curve shown in Figure 23. If we consider

$$C' = \{(r, \theta): 0 \leqslant \theta \leqslant 2\pi, \quad r = a \cos \tfrac{1}{2}\theta\},$$

where r may be negative, we obtain the locus shown in Figure 24. Finally, if we allow r and θ to be quite unrestricted, we obtain the 'complete' locus C^{**} with symmetry about both axes (see Figure 25).

$$C^{**} = \{(r, \theta): r = a \cos \tfrac{1}{2}\theta\}.$$

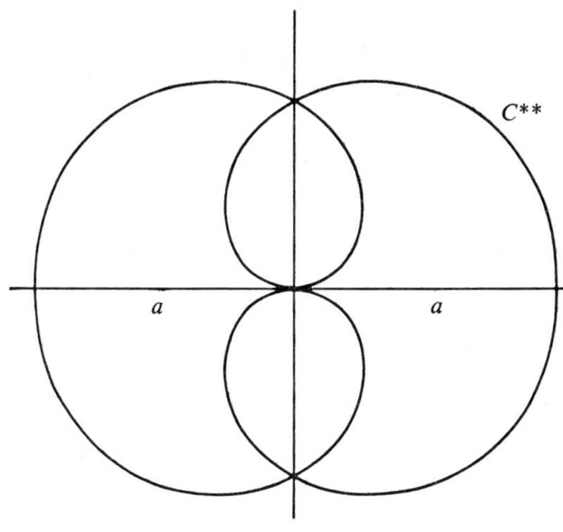

Fig. 25

7.1 Connection between Cartesian and polar coordinates. This is merely the definition of sine and cosine; from Figure 26 we have at once

$$\left.\begin{aligned} x &= r\cos\theta \\ y &= r\sin\theta \end{aligned}\right\}, \quad \left.\begin{aligned} x^2+y^2 &= r^2 \\ \tan\theta &= y/x \end{aligned}\right\}.$$

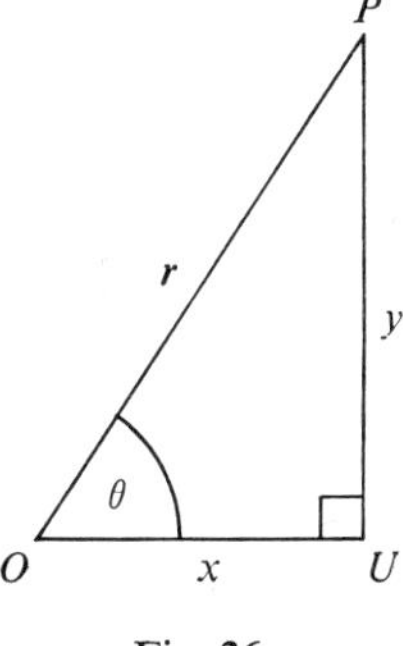

Fig. 26

It will be noted that while the first pair of equations define x and y unambiguously in terms of r and θ, the second pair do not define r and θ unambiguously in terms of x and y. To do this we must introduce the restrictions $r \geqslant 0$, $0 \leqslant \theta < 2\pi$, and then we have

$$r = +\sqrt{(x^2+y^2)},$$

$$\cos\theta : \sin\theta : 1 = x : y : r.$$

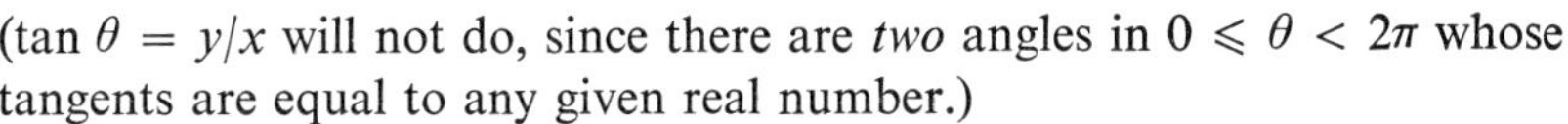

($\tan\theta = y/x$ will not do, since there are *two* angles in $0 \leqslant \theta < 2\pi$ whose tangents are equal to any given real number.)

It is of interest to note that the ordered pair (r, θ) is not a vector in the same way as the ordered pair (x, y) can be so regarded. The rules for combination of vectors do not apply, e.g.

$$\begin{pmatrix} a \\ \theta \end{pmatrix} + \begin{pmatrix} b \\ \phi \end{pmatrix} \neq \begin{pmatrix} a+b \\ \theta+\phi \end{pmatrix}.$$

7.2 Polar loci. We conclude this section with a few curves of special interest given by polar equations. The sketching of most of them is left as an exercise. For further information about them and other curves, see Lockwood, *A Book of Curves* (C.U.P.).

Example 13. Sketch the locus $r \cos \theta = a$.

This is merely the straight line, $x = a$ (see Figure 27).

Example 14. Sketch the locus $r = a \cos \theta$.

If $OA = a$, $OP = r$, angle $AOP = \theta$, $-\frac{1}{2}\pi \leqslant \theta \leqslant \frac{1}{2}\pi$, then

$$\text{angle } APO = \text{a right-angle} \Leftrightarrow r = a \cos \theta.$$

By considering values of θ outside the range $-\frac{1}{2}\pi \leqslant \theta \leqslant \frac{1}{2}\pi$ one can readily check that the double implication is still true. The locus is the circle on OA as diameter (see Figure 28).

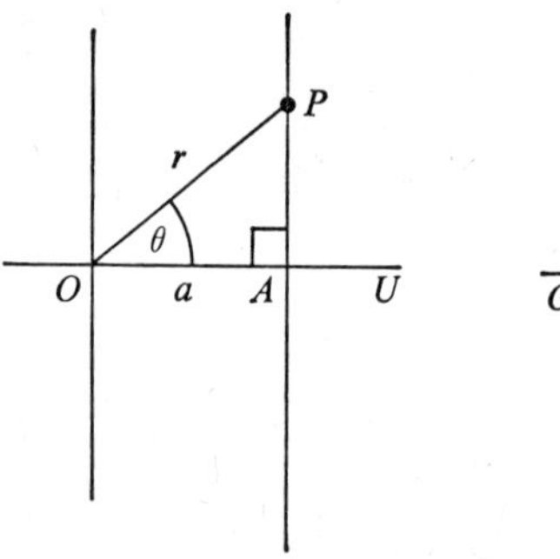

Fig. 27

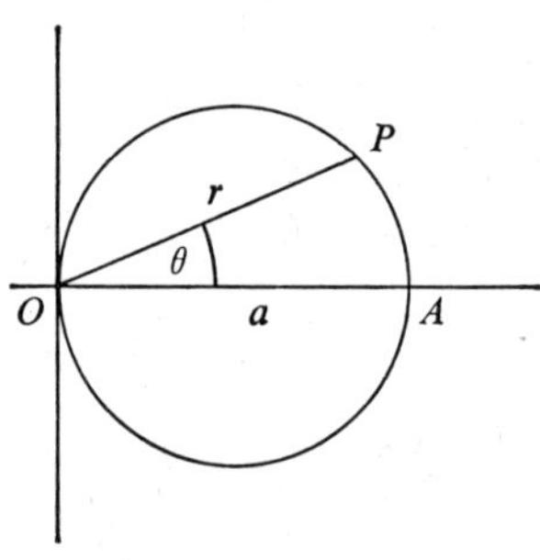

Fig. 28

Example 15. Sketch the locus $r = a \cos^2 (\frac{1}{2}\theta)$.

If $a > 0$, then $r \geqslant 0$ always. As θ increases from 0 to π, r decreases from a to 0, and increases again to a as θ increases from π to 2π. For further increase in θ the locus will be retraced.

When

$$\theta = \frac{\pi}{2} \quad \text{or} \quad \frac{3\pi}{2}, \quad r = \tfrac{1}{2}a;$$

when

$$\theta = \frac{\pi}{3} \quad \text{or} \quad \frac{5\pi}{3}, \quad r = \tfrac{3}{4}a;$$

when $$\theta = \frac{2\pi}{3} \text{ or } \frac{4\pi}{3}, \quad r = \tfrac{1}{4}a.$$

The locus is symmetrical about OA. It is called the *cardioid* (heart-shaped) (see Figure 29).

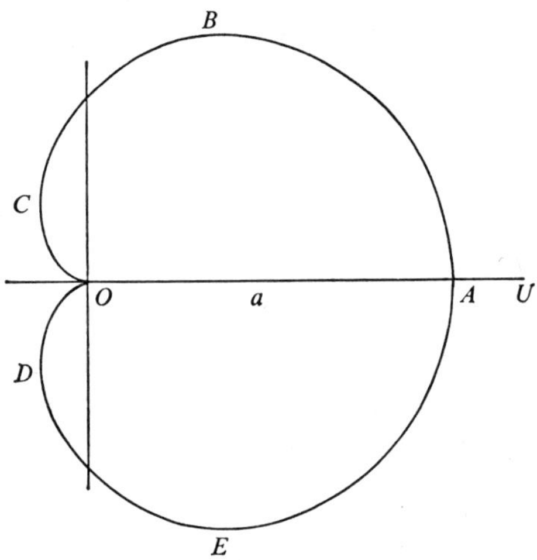

Fig. 29

Exercise G

1. Prove that the locus $r = f(\cos\theta)$ is always symmetrical about OU ($\theta = 0$). (Use $\cos(-\theta) = \cos\theta$.)

What can be said about $r = f(\sin\theta)$?

Sketch the following curves (polar graph paper is useful, but not essential):

2. The *lemniscate* $r^2 = a^2\cos 2\theta$.

3. The *limaçon with a loop* $r = 2+3\cos\theta$.

4. The *limaçon with a dimple* $r = 3+2\cos\theta$.

5. The *Archimedean spiral* $r = a\theta$ ($\theta \geqslant 0$).

6. The *trifolium* $r = a\cos 3\theta$.

7. The *rose-curve* $r = a\cos 4\theta$.

8. The *hyperbola* $r = \dfrac{3}{1+2\cos\theta}$.

9. The *cissoid* $r = a\sin\theta\tan\theta$. (What is the limit of $x = r\cos\theta$ as $\theta \to \frac{1}{2}\pi$?)

10. The *reciprocal spiral* $r\theta = a$. (What is the limit of $y = r\sin\theta$ as $\theta \to 0$?)

8. THE SOLUTION OF TRIANGLES

The classical problem of trigonometry, from which the subject takes its name, is that of calculating the remaining sides and angles of a triangle when a suitable set of these quantities is given. Many formulae have been devised to handle the various cases that can arise, and to render them amenable to different methods of computation. We shall content ourselves with proving the two most useful and important results, leaving one or two others as exercises.

8.1 The cosine rule. Basically, this is a rule to find the magnitude of the difference (or the sum) of two vectors whose magnitudes and directions are known. If the vectors **b**, **c** are represented by the line-segments $\overline{AC}$, $\overline{AB}$ (Figure 30), then $\overline{BC}$ will represent the vector $\mathbf{b}-\mathbf{c}$. Hence, if a is the length of BC, b the length of AC, and c the length of AB, we have

$$\begin{aligned} a^2 &= (\mathbf{b}-\mathbf{c}).(\mathbf{b}-\mathbf{c}) \\ &= \mathbf{b}.\mathbf{b}-2\mathbf{b}.\mathbf{c}+\mathbf{c}.\mathbf{c} \\ &= b^2-2bc\cos A+c^2. \end{aligned}$$

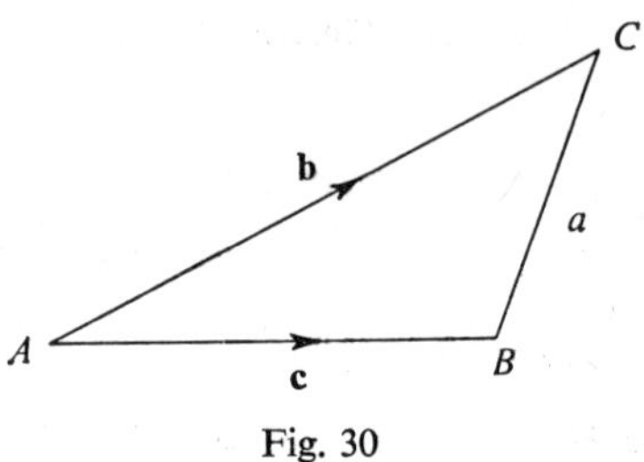

Fig. 30

Note that, if A is obtuse, $\cos A$ will be negative; if A is a right-angle, $\cos A = 0$, and then $a^2 = b^2+c^2$, the familiar conclusion of Pythagoras's Theorem.

Any formula such as this one, connecting the sides, a, b, and c, and the angles A, B, and C of a triangle, cannot be essentially affected by the particular choice of sides and angles made. If we apply to it any permutation of the letters a, b, and c, and the same permutation of the letters A, B, and C, it must remain true. We therefore can write down at once two further formulae, giving the trio

$$\begin{aligned} a^2 &= b^2+c^2-2bc\cos A; \\ b^2 &= c^2+a^2-2ca\cos B; \\ c^2 &= a^2+b^2-2ab\cos C. \end{aligned}$$

We can also rearrange these formulae to give us the cosines of the three angles in terms of the sides, thus:

$$\cos A = \frac{b^2+c^2-a^2}{2bc};$$

$$\cos B = \frac{c^2+a^2-b^2}{2ca};$$

$$\cos C = \frac{a^2+b^2-c^2}{2ab}.$$

8.2 The sine rule. This is a formula connecting the lengths of the sides with the opposite angles. We might at first have conjectured that the sides would be proportional to the opposite angles; if two angles are very small, so that the third is nearly a straight angle, this is true approximately for the two shorter sides, but obviously false for the longest side. A triangle with angles of 1°, 2°, and 177° plainly cannot have its longest side 177 times as long as its shortest. The truth is more subtle, but none the less remarkable: the sides are proportional to the sines of the opposite angles. This we shall now show.

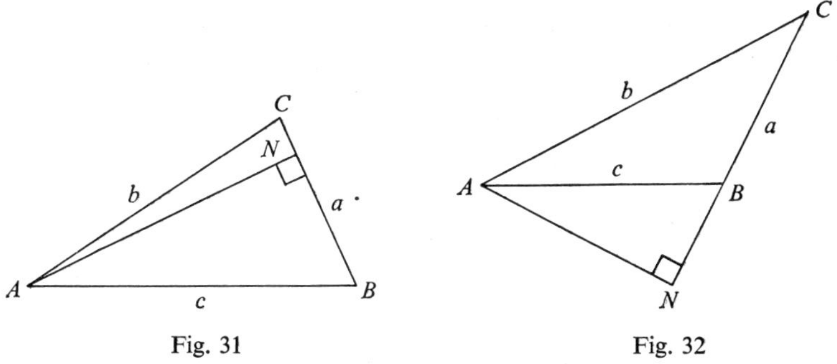

Fig. 31 Fig. 32

We revert to Figure 30, but now consider the components of **b** and **c** perpendicular to **BC**. These components are equal, being (in both Figure 31 and Figure 32) each equal to AN, the length of the perpendicular from A to $\overleftrightarrow{BC}$. In each figure the component of **b** is $b \sin C$; in Figure 31 the component of c is $c \sin B$, whereas in Figure 32 it is $c \sin (180° - B)$; but, since $\sin (180° - B) = \sin B$, we have in both cases

$$b \sin C = c \sin B.$$

This can be written in the symmetrical form

$$\frac{b}{\sin B} = \frac{c}{\sin C},$$

and, by permuting the letters in this result, we find that each of these ratios is equal to $a/\sin A$. The full sine rule is therefore

$$\frac{a}{\sin A} = \frac{b}{\sin B} = \frac{c}{\sin C}.$$

8.3 The choice of rule. To fix a triangle, we must know the length of one side, and two more of the five remaining quantities: the lengths of the other two sides and the magnitudes of the three angles. Further, if we know two of the angles we can calculate the third at once from the fact that the sum of the angles is 180°. There are therefore four cases to consider:

(*a*) given two sides and the angle between them;
(*b*) given three sides;
(*c*) given one side and two angles (hence all the angles);
(*d*) given two sides and an angle not between them.

In case (*a*) the cosine rule in its first form can be used to find the third side, and reduces the situation to case (*b*). In case (*b*) the cosine rule in its second form will find all the angles.

In case (*c*) the sine rule will find the remaining sides. In case (*d*) the sine rule will find the sine of one of the remaining angles. But the angle of a triangle is not completely determined if its sine is known (why not?). Careful examination of a figure is necessary in this case; there may be two possible triangles, or one, or none. This case is considered in Exercise H, Question 7. These two rules will therefore suffice to find the sides and angles of a triangle in all cases.

Practically, however, the cosine rule is awkward for computation because of the many different operations it involves—squaring, addition and subtraction, multiplication and extraction of square root. This means that unless the lengths of the sides are small integers, it is best to use the sine rule whenever possible. In cases (*a*) and (*b*) the cosine rule must be used once, but after that we can continue with the sine rule, taking care to use it only to find the sines of angles known to be acute.

If you have a Rietz pattern (or similar) slide-rule, in which the trigonometrical scales are marked, the sine rule can be used with great ease. The procedure differs slightly according to whether the sine scale is on the slide or on the stock, but the basic idea is the same. To calculate b, for example, where

$$\frac{3{\cdot}57}{\sin 36{\cdot}9^\circ} = \frac{b}{\sin 55{\cdot}4^\circ},$$

we use the cursor to align 36·9° on the sine scale with 3·57 on the C (or D) scale, and then opposite 55·4° on the sine scale we read b on the C (or D) scale. To find B from

$$\frac{3{\cdot}57}{\sin 36{\cdot}9^\circ} = \frac{5{\cdot}28}{\sin B},$$

the setting of the slide is the same as before, and B is read direct from the sine scale opposite 5·28 on scale C or D (Figure 33). $180° - B$ may of course also be an appropriate solution. There are other formulae that have been devised for use in cases (*a*) and (*b*) where logarithms or a slide-rule are used as aids to calculation: see, for example, Exercise H, Questions 12–16.

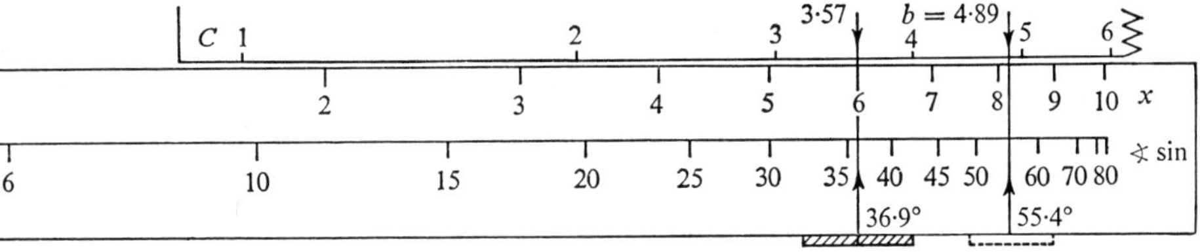

Fig. 33

Exercise H

1. Use the cosine rule to find the largest angle of the triangle, given the sides as follows:

(*a*) 6 cm, 7 cm, 8 cm; (*b*) 3 mm, 5 mm, 7 mm;
(*c*) 4·5 km, 20 km, 20·5 km; (*d*) 10 m, 17 m, 16 m.

2. What is the condition for a triangle to be obtuse-angled?

3. Find the remaining sides of a triangle by means of the sine rule, given:
(*a*) $a = 10$ cm, $B = 50°$, $C = 70°$;
(*b*) $b = 6$ cm, $A = 105°$, $B = 28°$;
(*c*) $a = 6$ cm, $A = 105°$, $B = 28°$;
(*d*) $c = 10$ km, $B = 27°$, $C = 131°$.

4. ABC is a triangle in which $BC = 8$ cm, $CA = 6$ cm, $AB = 7$ cm, and M is the mid-point of BC. Suppose the angle $AMC = \theta$; write down by the cosine rule formulae for AB^2 and AC^2 in terms of $\cos\theta$ and add the results. Hence calculate the length of AM.

5. Find the length of the side BC of a triangle if $AB = 7$ cm, $AC = 11$ cm, and the angle A is

(*a*) 37°; (*b*) 83°; (*c*) 143°.

6. Find the angle B of a triangle in which the angle A is 57°, the length of AC is 10 cm, and the length of BC is

(*a*) 9 cm; (*b*) 8 cm; (*c*) 11 cm.

Draw sketches to help you discover when there is more than one answer.

***7.** If the sides a, b and the *acute* angle A of a triangle are given, how many possible triangles can be drawn in the cases

(*a*) $a < b \sin A$; (*b*) $b \sin A < a < b$; (*c*) $b < a$?

Can there ever be two possible triangles if A is obtuse?

8. If **a** and **b** are vectors of lengths 5·1 and 7·2 units, calculate the angle between them if **a**+**b** has length 8·8 units, and find the length of **a**−**b**.

9. A plane flies north-east with an air speed of 640 km/h. If the wind is blowing at a steady speed of 80 km/h from the west, calculate the ground speed and the course made good.

10. The wind force on a racing dinghy beating to windward is equivalent to a force of 350 N from 21° abaft the beam; the water resistance is equivalent to 323 N from 8° ahead of the beam; what is the accelerating force on the dinghy, and in what direction is it acting?

11. A pilot in a plane capable of 480 km/h is instructed to fly from Gloucester to Rugby on a ground bearing of 049°. The wind is blowing at 80 km/h from 260°. What course should he set?

***12.** Prove, by using the factor formulae, that

$$\frac{b-c}{b+c} = \frac{\sin B - \sin C}{\sin B + \sin C} = \frac{\tan \frac{1}{2}(B-C)}{\tan \frac{1}{2}(B+C)}.$$

Given $b = 13{\cdot}6$ cm, $c = 6{\cdot}4$ cm, and the angle A is 53·4°, find in turn,

(*a*) $\dfrac{B+C}{2}$; (*b*) $\dfrac{B-C}{2}$; (*c*) B and C.

***13.** In Figure 34, the circle touches the sides of the triangle ABC. Prove that

$$v+w = a,$$

$$w+u = b,$$

$$u+v = c,$$

and solve these equations for u, v and w in terms of a, b and c.

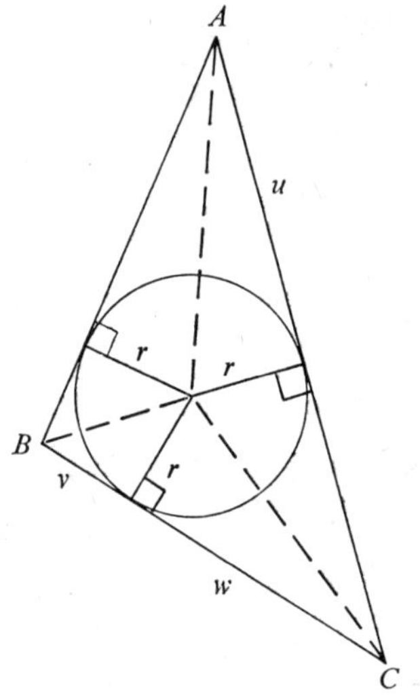

Fig. 34

***14.** In Figure 34, prove that if r is the radius of the circle, then

$$r = u \tan \tfrac{1}{2}A = v \tan \tfrac{1}{2}B = w \tan \tfrac{1}{2}C.$$

***15.** Use the fact that $\frac{1}{2}C = 90° - \frac{1}{2}A - \frac{1}{2}B$ to prove that

$$\tan \tfrac{1}{2}B \tan \tfrac{1}{2}C + \tan \tfrac{1}{2}C \tan \tfrac{1}{2}A + \tan \tfrac{1}{2}A \tan \tfrac{1}{2}B = 1,$$

and hence, from the result of the preceding question, that

$$r^2 = uvw/(u+v+w).$$

***16.** Use the results of the previous exercises to prove that

$$\tan^2 \frac{A}{2} = \frac{vw}{su}, \quad \text{where} \quad s = \tfrac{1}{2}(a+b+c).$$

Find in turn the values of u, v, w, s and A, given $a = 5{\cdot}73$, $b = 2{\cdot}85$, $c = 6{\cdot}08$.

15

THE QUADRATIC FUNCTION

In Chapters 3 and 4 we saw that a polynomial may be used to define a function. A polynomial of the second degree such as

$$3x^2+x-4$$

is called a *quadratic* polynomial or a *quadratic form*; and the function

$$f: x \to 3x^2+x-4$$

defined by it is called a *quadratic function.*

The general quadratic function is, therefore,

$$f: x \to ax^2+bx+c,$$

where a, b, c are numbers.

1. GRAPHS OF QUADRATIC FUNCTIONS

1.1 The graphs of a quadratic function were plotted in Chapter 5. In particular you will recognize the graph of $y = x^2$ or the square function $f: x \to x^2$.

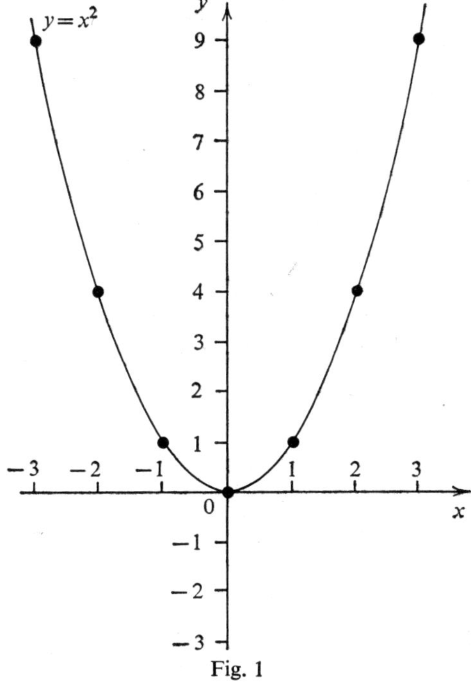

Fig. 1

From the way in which the function is defined, we can see two things immediately:

(i) *Symmetry*. We can pair off points thus: (2, 4) with (−2, 4), (3, 9) with (−3, 9), and so on.

In other symbols, if T is the set of ordered pairs satisfying the relation $y = x^2$, then
$$(p, q) \in T \Rightarrow (-p, q) \in T$$
because
$$q = p^2 \Rightarrow q = (-p)^2.$$
Now, $(-p, q)$ is the image of (p, q) on reflection in the y-axis. So the image in the y-axis of every point on the graph is also on the graph, and the graph is symmetrical about the y-axis.

(ii) *Range*. Whereas x can take any value, x^2 is never negative; and as x increases from zero x^2 passes through all positive values.

So if we let the domain of the function be the set of all real numbers, then the range of the function is the set of non-negative numbers.

The function is continuous, and derivable everywhere; also its derived function is continuous.

This means that the points of the graph will lie on a smooth curve. This curve is called a parabola. The point of the graph which is on the axis of symmetry (at the origin in this case) is called the vertex of the parabola.

1.2 It is possible to obtain the graph of *any* quadratic function by applying, to the graph of $y = x^2$, the transformations which are discussed in Chapter 5. The following examples will demonstrate this.

Example 1. What is the image of $y = x^2$ under a translation $\begin{pmatrix} 0 \\ -2 \end{pmatrix}$, that is a shift of 2 units downwards? Adding the relevant column vectors we obtain
$$\begin{pmatrix} x' \\ y' \end{pmatrix} = \begin{pmatrix} x \\ y \end{pmatrix} + \begin{pmatrix} 0 \\ -2 \end{pmatrix} = \begin{pmatrix} x \\ y-2 \end{pmatrix};$$
hence
$$x' = x \quad \text{and} \quad y' = y-2.$$
Accordingly
$$y = x^2 \Leftrightarrow y'+2 = x'^2 \quad \text{or} \quad y' = x'^2-2.$$

This set of points $\{(x', y'): y' = x'^2-2\}$ is, of course, the same set as $\{(x, y): y = x^2-2\}$ and this is the simpler, and more usual form.†

The equation of the new curve is thus $y = x^2-2$ and its graph is as shown in Figure 2.

Example 2. What is the image of $y = x^2$ under a one-way stretch of 3 parallel to Oy? This time the origin is invariant and hence the 2×2 matrix which effects this operation is
$$\begin{pmatrix} 1 & 0 \\ 0 & 3 \end{pmatrix}.$$

† This process is usually called 'dropping the dashes' and will be referred to as such in subsequent cases.

Hence,
$$\begin{pmatrix} x' \\ y' \end{pmatrix} = \begin{pmatrix} 1 & 0 \\ 0 & 3 \end{pmatrix} \begin{pmatrix} x \\ y \end{pmatrix} = \begin{pmatrix} x \\ 3y \end{pmatrix}.$$

Thus
$$x' = x \quad \text{and} \quad y' = 3y$$
$$\Leftrightarrow y = \tfrac{1}{3}y' \quad \text{and} \quad x = x'.$$

Hence,
$$y = x^2 \Leftrightarrow \tfrac{1}{3}y' = x'^2$$
$$\Leftrightarrow y' = 3x'^2.$$

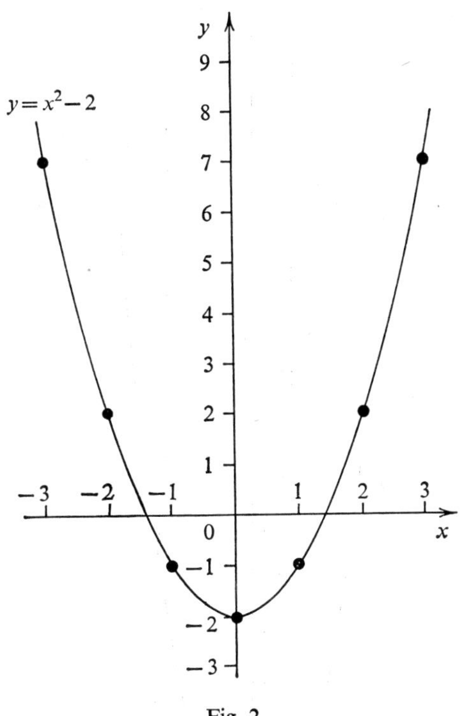

Fig. 2

'Dropping the dashes' gives $y = 3x^2$ for the equation of the graph shown in Figure 3.

Example 3. What is the image of $y = x^2$ under the translation $\begin{pmatrix} 2 \\ 1 \end{pmatrix}$? As in Example 1
$$\begin{pmatrix} x' \\ y' \end{pmatrix} = \begin{pmatrix} x \\ y \end{pmatrix} + \begin{pmatrix} 2 \\ 1 \end{pmatrix} = \begin{pmatrix} x+2 \\ y+1 \end{pmatrix}$$
$$\Leftrightarrow x' = x+2 \quad \text{and} \quad y' = y+1.$$

Hence,
$$y = x^2 \Leftrightarrow y'-1 = (x'-2)^2$$
$$= x'^2 - 4x' + 4.$$

Dropping the dashes, we obtain

$$y = x^2 - 4x + 5$$

as the equation of the graph in Figure 4.

There is now symmetry about the line $x = 2$.

Example 4. If we now reflect the graph of the last example in the x-axis, then $x' = x$ and $y' = -y$.

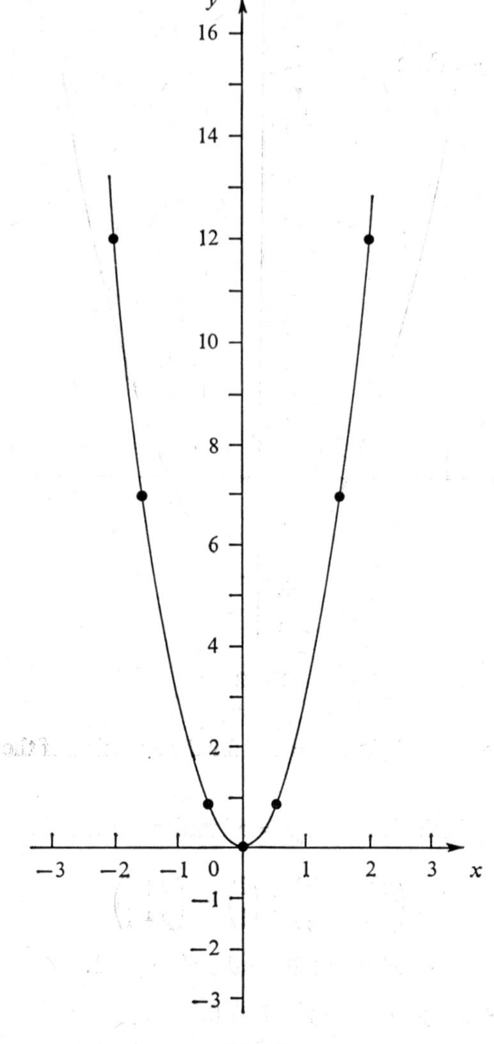

Fig. 3

So $y = x^2-4x+5 \Leftrightarrow -y' = x'^2-4x'+5$.

Dropping the dashes, $\qquad y = -x^2+4x-5$

is the equation of the graph shown in Figure 5.

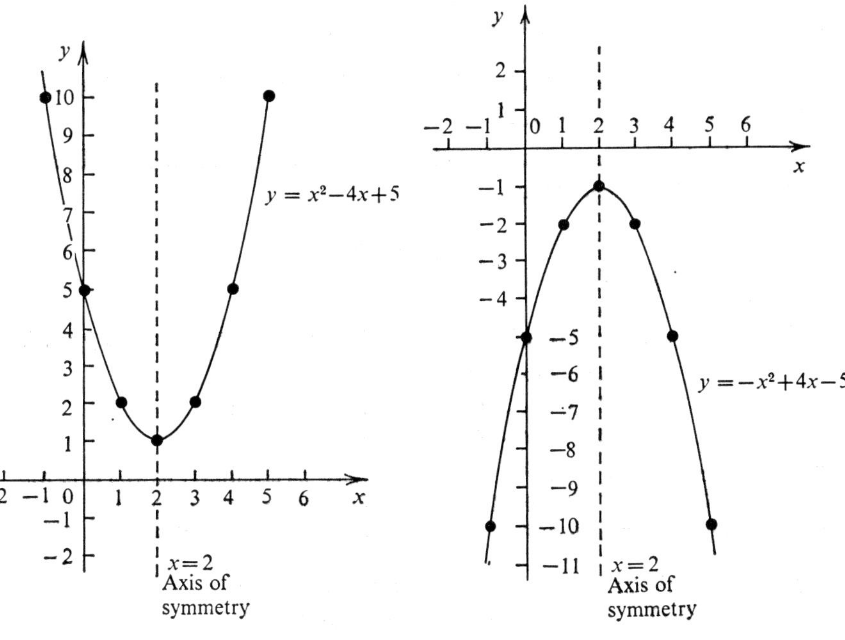

Fig. 4 Fig. 5

1.3 Locating the graph. The problem we are faced with is more often the opposite to that considered in the previous examples. In the course of some investigation a quadratic function arises, and we wish to sketch its graph. We shall discuss this problem more generally in the next section, but here we revise briefly what was said in Book 1, Chapter 5.

Let G be the graph of $y = x^2$, and, for example, let G' be the graph of $y = (x+3)^2+2$. How are G and G' related? Precisely, what transformation must be applied to G to give G'? We proceed as follows (cf. Book 1, p. 136 and following pages):

$$(p, q) \in G \Leftrightarrow q = p^2;$$

$$(p', q') \in G' \Leftrightarrow q'-2 = (p'+3)^2;$$

these relations become identical if we put

$$\begin{cases} p = p'+3, \\ q = q'-2. \end{cases}$$

The transformation

$$\begin{pmatrix} p' \\ q' \end{pmatrix} \to \begin{pmatrix} p \\ q \end{pmatrix}$$

is therefore the translation $\begin{pmatrix} 3 \\ -2 \end{pmatrix}$, and the transformation $G \to G'$ is the *inverse* of this, namely the translation $\begin{pmatrix} -3 \\ 2 \end{pmatrix}$.

The graph of $y = (x+3)^2+2$ is the graph of $y = x^2$ translated so that its vertex is moved to $(-3, 2)$.

As a check, we see at once that there is symmetry about $x+3 = 0$, and that y has 2 as its least value.

Exercise A

1. For each function:
(*a*) sketch its graph;
(*b*) describe the transformation under which it would be the image of $y = x^2$.

(1) $x \to x^2-3$; (2) $x \to 2x^2$;
(3) $x \to -x^2$; (4) $x \to 2x^2-3$;
(5) $x \to 4-x^2$; (6) $x \to (x-3)^2$.

2. Draw the graph of $y = 3x^2-2$ on graph paper, as accurately as you can, for values of x between -2 and $+2$ $(-2 \leqslant x \leqslant 2)$. Find points on the graph whose y-coordinates are -1, 0, and 5, and hence solve as accurately as your graph allows:

(*a*) $-1 = 3x^2-2$; (*b*) $0 = 3x^2-2$;
(*c*) $5 = 3x^2-2$; (*d*) $1 > 3x^2-2$.

3. The equation of the graph drawn in Question 2 was $y = 3x^2-2$.

$$y = 3x^2-2 \Leftrightarrow y+2 = 3x^2$$
$$\Leftrightarrow x^2 = \frac{y+2}{3}$$
$$\Leftrightarrow x = \pm\sqrt{\left(\frac{y+2}{3}\right)}.$$

Draw a flow diagram, and use this formula to *calculate* the answers to Question 2 as a check on the accuracy of your graph. (Use a slide rule or desk calculator.)

4. If $y = 5-2x^2$, express x in terms of y and calculate the value of x when $y = 2{\cdot}76$.

5. If $x^2+6x-5 = (x+3)^2+k$, find the value of k.

6. Put each of the following quadratic polynomials into the form $(x+p)^2+q$ (find the numbers p and q):

(*a*) x^2-2x+3; (*b*) x^2+4x-3; (*c*) x^2-3x-2.

7. If $3x^2-9x+2 = 3(x-1\tfrac{1}{2})^2+k$, find the value of k.

8. Put each of the following into the form $p(x+q)^2+r$:

(*a*) $5x^2+10x-2$; (*b*) $3x^2+2x+1$; (*c*) $-2x^2+6x-7$.

2. COMPLETING THE SQUARE

2.1 If we apply the translation $\begin{pmatrix}\alpha\\ \beta\end{pmatrix}$ to the graph of $y = x^2$, then the point (x, y) is moved to (x', y'), where

$$x' = x+\alpha, \quad \text{that is} \quad x = x'-\alpha,$$

and

$$y' = y+\beta, \quad \text{that is} \quad y = y'-\beta.$$

So $y = x^2$ is mapped onto $y'-\beta = (x'-\alpha)^2$ or

$$y = x^2-2\alpha x+\alpha^2+\beta \quad \text{(dropping the dashes).}$$

This is now the equation of the graph shown in Figure 6. The curve has symmetry about the line $x = \alpha$ and has (α, β) as its vertex.

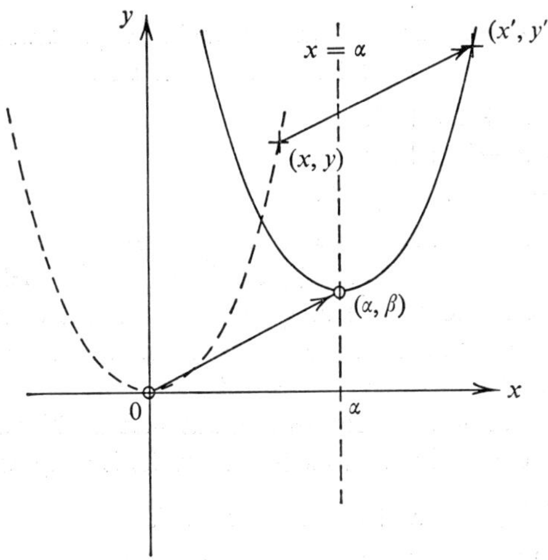

Fig. 6

2.2 It is often more useful to perform the above process in reverse; that is, given an equation such as

$$y = x^2-4x+5,$$

to find under which transformation it is the image of $y = x^2$, as we did in Question 1 of Exercise A.

We use the method of Questions 5 and 6 of Exercise A to isolate the terms in x and x^2 in a squared linear factor. This process is called *completing the square.*

Since $$x^2-4x+4 = (x-2)^2,$$

we have $$x^2-4x+5 = (x-2)^2+1,$$

so that the equation may be written in the form

$$y = (x-2)^2+1 \quad \text{or} \quad y-1 = (x-2)^2.$$

This shows that its graph is the image of $y = x^2$ under the translation $\begin{pmatrix}2\\1\end{pmatrix}$ (compare Figure 4).

Looking at the equation in the form

$$y = (x-2)^2+1.$$

we can see two things:

(i) There is symmetry about the line $x = 2$, since reflection in this line maps the point $(2-a, b)$ onto $(2+a, b)$ and if one of these points lies on the graph so does the other.

(ii) The *least* value of y is 1, occurring when $x = 2$, since

$$(x-2)^2 \geqslant 0 \Rightarrow (x-2)^2+1 \geqslant 1.$$

2.3 When we wish to 'complete the square' in a quadratic polynomial it helps to bear the following results in mind: for all x

(i) $(x+a)^2 = x^2+2ax+a^2$;
(ii) $(x-a)^2 = x^2-2ax+a^2$;
(iii) $(px+q)^2 = p^2x^2+2pqx+q^2$.

Expressions of this type are called *perfect squares.*

Notice that in the perfect squares (i) and (ii) where the coefficient of x is 1, the constant term is the square of half the coefficient of x. In the more general type (iii), the product of the constant term and the coefficient of x^2 equals the square of half the coefficient of x.

x^2+6x+5 is thus not a perfect square, but with a different constant we can complete the expression $x^2+6x+\ldots$ to make it a square.

In fact, for all x

$$x^2+6x+9 = (x+3)^2.$$

The 9 is formed by squaring half of 6. If the coefficient of x^2 is not 1 then we may take this out as a factor first of all. For example,

$$\begin{aligned}3x^2+2x+4 &= 3(x^2+\tfrac{2}{3}x+\tfrac{4}{3})\\ &= 3(x^2+\tfrac{2}{3}x+\tfrac{1}{9}+\tfrac{4}{3}-\tfrac{1}{9})\\ &= 3(x+\tfrac{1}{3})^2+4-\tfrac{1}{3}\\ &= 3(x+\tfrac{1}{3})^2+3\tfrac{2}{3}.\end{aligned}$$

Example 5. Find the maximum (or minimum) value of

$$4-3x-2x^2,\quad x \in R.$$

Write y for the value of $4-3x-2x^2$ and complete the square:

$$\begin{aligned}y &= 4-2(x^2+\tfrac{3}{2}x)\\ &= 4-2(x^2+\tfrac{3}{2}x+\tfrac{9}{16})+\tfrac{9}{8}\\ &= 5\tfrac{1}{8}-2(x+\tfrac{3}{4})^2.\end{aligned}$$

This tells us that y has a *greatest value*, $5\frac{1}{8}$, at $x = -\frac{3}{4}$, and that the graph is symmetrical about the line $x = -\frac{3}{4}$. (It is perhaps worth noting here that the greatest or least values could have been obtained by finding the derived function, although by that method the rest of the information obtained here would not have come to light.)

Exercise B

1. Rewrite the following by completing the square:

(*a*) x^2-8x+5; (*b*) $3x^2+8x-1$;

(*c*) $5x^4+4x^2-2$; (*d*) $5-6x-9x^2$.

2. In the section above we found that

$$x^2+6x+5 = (x+3)^2-4.$$

Now use the difference of two squares to factorize this quadratic form.

3. Use the method of Question 2 to factorize:

(*a*) x^2-x-6; (*b*) $6x^2-x-2$.

4. For each of the following quadratic functions,

(i) find the greatest or least value of y by any method;
(ii) find the axis of symmetry of the graph;
(iii) sketch the graph.

(*a*) $y = x^2-8x+18$; (*b*) $y = 1+6x-3x^2$;

(*c*) $y = 2x^2+3x+1$; (*d*) $y = 2-x-x^2$;

(*e*) $y = 2x-x^2$.

Produce the successive transformations which will map $y = x^2$ onto (*a*), and express them by means of algebraic equations as in Examples 1–4, pp. 418 f. Repeat (i), (ii) and (iii) by this means.

5. Factorize:

(*a*) x^2+5x+6; (*b*) x^2-x-6; (*c*) $3x^2+x-10$.

6. (*a*) Factorize the polynomial $x^2-7x+12$ and *then* evaluate it at $x = 0, 1, 2, 3, 4, 5, 6$, and 7.

(If a quadratic polynomial factorizes, it is usually easier to evaluate in the factorized form.)

(*b*) Repeat (*a*) for the polynomial x^2-4x-5.

7. Factorize the polynomials in parts (*c*), (*d*) and (*e*) of Question 4. Use your results to find where the graphs cut the x-axis.

8. Express $x^2+y^2-4x+2y-20 = 0$, in the form $(x-\alpha)^2+(y-\beta)^2 = r^2$.
What transformation will map the circle $\{(x, y): x^2+y^2 = 25\}$ onto

$$\{(x, y): x^2+y^2-4x+2y-20 = 0\}?$$

9. Draw the ellipse

$$\frac{x^2}{4}+\frac{y^2}{9} = 1.$$

Prove that the equation of its image under a translation $\begin{pmatrix} 2 \\ -1 \end{pmatrix}$ is

$$9x^2+4y^2-36x+8y+4 = 0.$$

10. Find the coordinates of the centre of the ellipse

$$16x^2+36y^2+80x-36y-35 = 0.$$

3. QUADRATIC EQUATIONS

An equation such as $3x^2+2x-4 = 0$ is called a *quadratic equation*. Such equations occur in many branches of mathematics. For example, calculating the frequency of oscillations in an electrical circuit requires the solution of a quadratic equation.

We now look at some ways of solving these equations. When doing this we shall naturally think of $x \in R$, although from time to time it may be that $x \in Q$ or N. Again, x might be the cosine or the sine of an angle, in which case we must have $-1 \leqslant x \leqslant 1$. However, in the work which follows, unless stated otherwise, we shall assume $x \in R$.

3.1 Solution by factors.

Example 6. Consider the equation

$$2x^2+3x-5 = 0.$$

This may be written $$(2x+5)(x-1) = 0.$$

Now $$ab = 0 \Leftrightarrow \text{either } a = 0 \quad \text{or} \quad b = 0.$$

So either $2x+5 = 0$ or $x-1 = 0$; that is, either $x = -2\frac{1}{2}$ or $x = 1$.

Thus $-2\frac{1}{2}$ and 1 are the roots of the equation $2x^2+3x-5 = 0$, and

$$\{x\colon 2x^2+3x-5 = 0\} = \{-2\tfrac{1}{2}, 1\}.$$

This can be seen from the graph of $y = 2x^2+3x-5$ in Figure 7 which cuts the x-axis at the points $(-2\frac{1}{2}, 0)$ and $(1, 0)$.

When this method of factorization *can* be used, this is the best way to solve a quadratic equation.

Can you say for what values of x

$$2x^2+3x-5 < 0?$$

3.2 Solution by graph. Figure 7 shows part of the graph of the equation

$$y = 2x^2+3x-5.$$

It is a simple matter to calculate y when the value of x is given. The reverse process, of finding x when y is known, is more difficult.

(*a*) If $y = -3$, for example, then x must satisfy

$$-3 = 2x^2+3x-5$$

or, more simply, $2x^2+3x-2 = 0.$

We can solve this quadratic equation by finding the points on the graph where

$$y = -3.$$

There are two such points, with x-coordinates -2 and $\frac{1}{2}$.

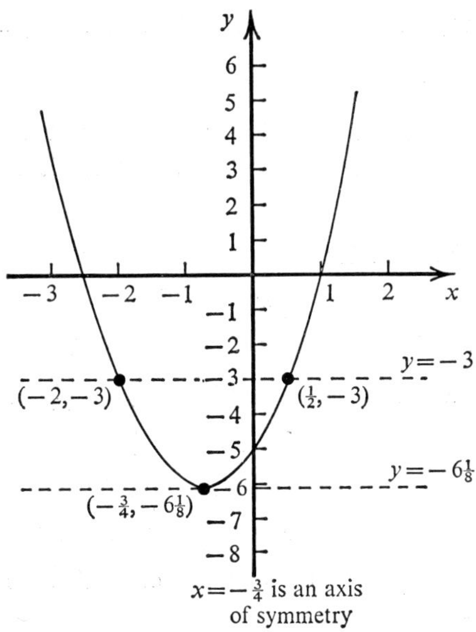

Fig. 7

So the solution to the equation

$$2x^2+3x-2 = 0$$

is $$x = -2 \quad or \quad x = \tfrac{1}{2}.$$

Thus the equation has the two roots, -2 and $\frac{1}{2}$. That is,

$$\{x: 2x^2+3x-2 = 0\} = \{-2, \tfrac{1}{2}\}.$$

(*b*) The line with equation $y = -6\frac{1}{8}$

meets the graph in only *one* point (where $x = -\frac{3}{4}$).

So the equation $$2x^2+3x-5 = -6\tfrac{1}{8}$$

has only *one* root, $-\frac{3}{4}$. That is,

$$\{x: 2x^2+3x+1\tfrac{1}{8} = 0\} = \{-\tfrac{3}{4}\}.$$

(*c*) To solve the equation

$$2x^2+3x+3 = 0,$$

that is

$$2x^2+3x-5 = -8,$$

we must see where the graph cuts the line with equation

$$y = -8.$$

The intersection of these two sets of points is empty, so this quadratic equation has no real roots. That is,

$$\{x: 2x^2+3x+3 = 0\} = \varnothing.$$

What can you say about the number of roots of a quadratic equation where $x \in R$?

3.3 Solution by completing the square. If the quadratic form cannot easily be factorized, then we first transform it by completing the square (see Example 5).

Example 7. Solve the equation

$$2x^2+3x-6 = 0.$$

This equation may be rewritten $2(x^2+\frac{3}{2}x)-6 = 0.$

$$\begin{aligned} 2(x^2+\tfrac{3}{2}x)-6 = 0 &\Leftrightarrow 2(x^2+\tfrac{3}{2}x+\tfrac{9}{16})-2.\tfrac{9}{16}-6 = 0 \\ &\Leftrightarrow 2(x+\tfrac{3}{4})^2 = 7\tfrac{1}{8} \\ &\Leftrightarrow (x+0{\cdot}75)^2 = 3{\cdot}5625 \\ &\Leftrightarrow x+0{\cdot}75 = \pm 1{\cdot}89 \text{ (3 s.f.)} \\ &\Leftrightarrow x = 1{\cdot}14 \quad \text{or} \quad -2{\cdot}64 \text{ (3 s.f.)}. \end{aligned}$$

On the graph of

$$y = 2x^2+3x-5$$

these roots are found on the line $y = 1$, since $2x^2+3x-6 = 0$ is the same equation as

$$2x^2+3x-5 = 1.$$

Example 8. Solve the equation

$$2x^2+3x+3 = 0.$$

(This is equation (*c*) in Section 3.2, which was found to have no real roots.) We now have

$$2(x+\tfrac{3}{4})^2 = -3+\tfrac{9}{8},$$

$$(x+\tfrac{3}{4})^2 = -\tfrac{15}{16}.$$

No value of x satisfies this equation, since

$$(x+\tfrac{3}{4})^2 \geqslant 0$$

for all values of x. This equation, therefore, has no roots with $x \in R$.

Exercise C

Solve the equations in Questions 1–10.

1. $2x^2-5x-12 = 0.$

2. $x^2+4x-7 = 0.$

3. $x^2-4x+4 = 0.$

4. $x^2+3x+2 = 0.$

5. $x^2+2x+3 = 0.$

6. $3x^2-2x+1 = 0.$

7. $5x^2+6x+4 = 0.$

8. $5x^2-3x = 0.$

9. $5x^2+3x = 0.$

10. $5x^2-3 = 0.$

11. The number of metres, s, between a railway engine and a bridge, and the time in seconds after the start, t, are related by the equation

$$3s = 400+20t+t^2.$$

How far is the engine from the bridge after 5 s? When is there 200 m between them?

12. What can you say about numbers p and q if pq is: (*a*) positive; (*b*) zero; (*c*) negative?

13. What can you say about x if $(x+1).(x-2)$ is: (*a*) positive; (*b*) zero; (*c*) negative?

14. Can you solve Questions 3 and 4 if '$= 0$' is replaced by '< 0'?

15. Solve the simultaneous equations

$$s+t = 3,$$
$$st = 2.$$

16. Solve the simultaneous equations

$$p+q = 2,$$
$$pq = -3.$$

4. QUADRATIC INEQUALITIES

4.1 Graphical solutions. We can use Figure 7, the graph of

$$y = 2x^2+3x-5,$$

to solve inequalities in much the same way as for equations.

For example, we have already seen that the least value of y is $-6\frac{1}{8}$. So

$$\{x: 2x^2+3x-5 < -6\tfrac{1}{8}\} = \emptyset$$

or, more simply, $$\{x: 2x^2+3x+1\tfrac{1}{8} < 0\} = \emptyset.$$

Example 9. Use the graph to solve

$$2x^2+3x-2 < 0.$$

This inequality can be written $2x^2+3x-5 < -3$.

We therefore want the values of x for which $y < -3$. These are clearly the values between -2 and $\frac{1}{2}$.

Thus
$$\{x: 2x^2+3x-2 < 0\} = \{x: -2 < x < \tfrac{1}{2}\}.$$

What are $\{x: 2x^2+3x-2 \leqslant 0\}$ and $\{x: 2x^2+3x-2 > 0\}$?

4.2 Algebraic solution. To illustrate this important method we shall consider the sign of
$$2x^2+3x-5.$$

Factorizing, this polynomial gives $(2x+5)(x-1)$. Now this is *positive* if $(2x+5)$ and $(x-1)$ are *both* positive or *both* negative. It is *zero* if either $(2x+5)$ or $(x-1)$ is zero.

By solving simple inequalities, we can find for what values of x the factors $(2x+5)$ and $(x-1)$ are positive, zero and negative. The results are shown in Figure 8.

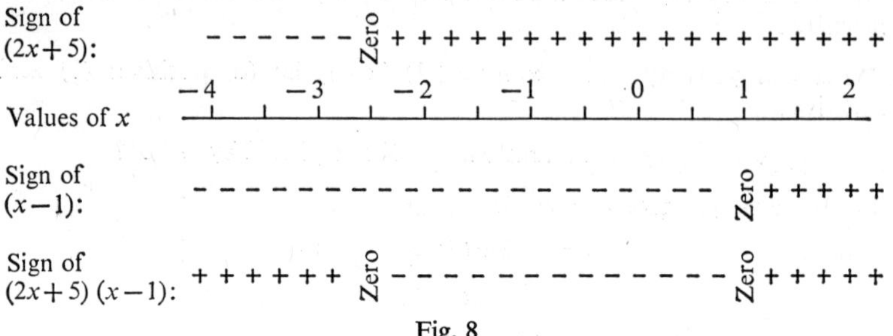

Fig. 8

It is clear from the figure that the two factors are of *different* sign only when x lies between $-2\frac{1}{2}$ and 1, and we obtain the following results:

(*a*) $\{x: 2x^2+3x-5 < 0\} = \{x: -2\frac{1}{2} < x < 1\}$;

(*b*) $\{x: 2x^2+3x-5 = 0\} = \{-2\frac{1}{2}, 1\}$;

(*c*) $\{x: 2x^2+3x-5 > 0\} = \{x: x < -2\frac{1}{2}\} \cup \{x: x > 1\}$.

What is $\{x: 2x^2+3x-5 \leqslant 0\}$?

The information in Figure 8 could be conveyed by shading the parts of the number line (values of x) for which each expression is *positive*. For $(2x+5)$ this would give the diagram in Figure 9.

Fig. 9

The open circle indicates that $-2\frac{1}{2}$ is not a member of the set under consideration.

Complete Figure 8 in the form of Figure 9.

Exercise D

1. Express the two statements at the beginning of Section 4.2 in set notation.

2. Solve $(x+3)(3x-1) < 0$.

3. Solve: (*a*) $(2-x)(x+1) > 0$; (*b*) $(2-x)(x+1) \geqslant 0$.

4. Solve $4x^2-4x-3 > 0$.

5. Solve $4(x^2-x) < 3$.

6. Solve $5+5x-2x^2 > 0$.

7. Solve $x^2-2x+1 > 0$.

8. Solve $(x-1)(x+2) < 4$.

9. Solve $x^2-5x+5 \geqslant 0$.

10. Solve $x^2+3x+7 < 0$.

5. DOMAIN AND RANGE OF A QUADRATIC FUNCTION

5.1 In the last sections we have kept to $x \in R$ when dealing with the domain of the quadratic function. However, it was mentioned at the outset that there were other possibilities for the domain and range, and this is a very important question, especially when we are discussing quadratic equations.

For the function in Example 3,

$$f: x \to x^2-4x+5$$

we could take the domain to be the set of all *rational* numbers. Then the range is a set of rational numbers, all greater than or equal to 1. But the range is not the set of *all* rational numbers greater than or equal to 1.

That is to say, equations of the form

$$x^2-4x+5 = c,$$

where c is a rational number, do not always have a root in the system of rational numbers, even when c is greater than 1.

5.2 At each stage in extending the number system from the natural numbers to the rational numbers we have found that more equations are soluble in the extended system.

Equations of the form $q+x = p$ do not always have a solution in the natural numbers N.

For example, $3+x = 2$ has no solution in N, but all equations of this type have a solution in the integers Z.

In Z, equations of the form $ax+b = 0$ where $a, b \in Z$ are not always soluble. For example, there is no integer satisfying

$$2x-3 = 0.$$

But all such equations having rational coefficients are soluble in the rational numbers, Q. We say that all *linear* equations are soluble in Q. But quadratic equations are not always soluble in Q.

5.3 Irrational numbers. First we will show that the equation

$$x^2 - 2 = 0$$

does not have a rational root.

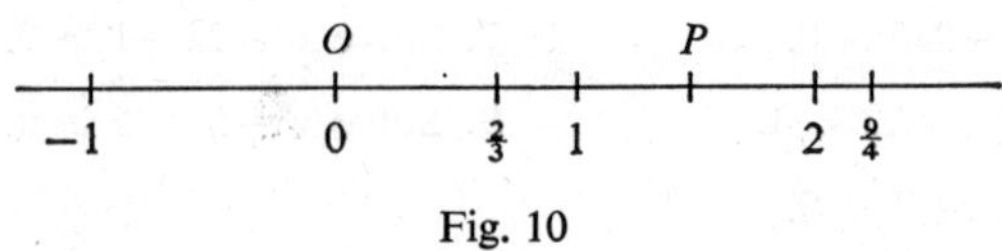

Fig. 10

You have been used to writing the solution $x = \pm\sqrt{2}$. So we have to show that $\sqrt{2}$ is not a rational number.

Suppose $\sqrt{2}$ were rational. Then we could put $\sqrt{2} = m/n$ where m and n are *integers* and with no common factor (that is, the number has been 'cancelled down' and m/n is the simplest fraction).

Then, squaring the equation we get

$$2 = m^2/n^2$$

$$\Rightarrow 2n^2 = m^2 \qquad \text{(i)}$$

$$\Rightarrow m^2 \text{ is even}$$

$$\Rightarrow m \text{ is even (since } m \text{ odd} \Rightarrow m^2 \text{ odd)}$$

$$\Rightarrow m = 2p \text{ where } p \text{ is an integer.}$$

Equation (i) becomes $$2n^2 = 4p^2,$$

or $$n^2 = 2p^2$$

$$\Rightarrow n^2 \text{ is even}$$

$$\Rightarrow n \text{ is even.}$$

Thus, *both* m and n are even. But this is impossible since we assumed that m and n had no common factor. We must conclude that the original supposition was false and that $\sqrt{2}$ cannot be expressed as a rational number.

Secondly, we can construct the point P on the number line (Figure 10) which corresponds to $\sqrt{2}$. For if we draw a triangle ABC in which $\angle C = 90°$ and $AC = CB = 1$ unit (Figure 11), then $AB = \sqrt{2}$ units by Pythagoras's Theorem. So if we mark off $AB = OP$ on the number line then P is at the point corresponding to the number $\sqrt{2}$. And so P is a point which does not correspond to a rational number.

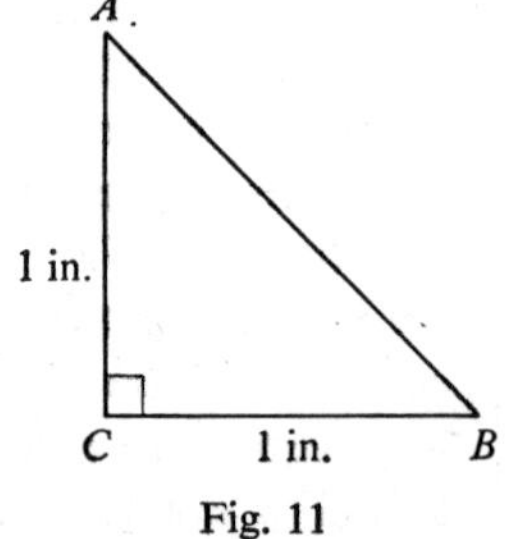

Fig. 11

A number which is not rational, but which corresponds to a point on the number line in this way, is called *irrational.*

There is, however, a close connection between rational and irrational numbers. In the case of $\sqrt{2}$ for example, the rational numbers can be divided into two sets—those less than $\sqrt{2}$ and those greater than $\sqrt{2}$ (that is, according to whether their corresponding point is to the left or right of P). And we can find a rational number as close as we please to $\sqrt{2}$, either above or below.

On a slide rule you might read $\sqrt{2}$ as 1·41. But 1·41 is a *rational* number (why?), so it can only be an approximation of $\sqrt{2}$. In fact it is the closest approximation possible using a number with 3 significant figures, and we should of course write

$$\sqrt{2} \approx 1{\cdot}41 \text{ (3 S.F.)}.$$

With more significant figures it is always possible to get closer.

5.4 The real numbers. So far we have talked about the real numbers without ever really defining them, and we have used an intuitive picture of them arranged like the points on a line—the real number line. We have just proved in the last paragraph that there is at least one number, $\sqrt{2}$, whose position on the number line we can construct geometrically (ideally, of course), which is not a rational number. Its position would never coincide exactly with any division of a measuring rule marking the integers 0, 1, 2, ..., however finely the rule were divided. A moment's thought should convince us (and we shall prove it in Question 4 of the next Exercise) that there are infinitely many numbers like this; for example, $2+\sqrt{3}$, $\frac{7}{3}-\sqrt{29}$, and so on, are all irrational numbers. Numbers like this involving square roots are called *quadratic surds.*

We might imagine that when we had included all the conceivable quadratic surds with the rational numbers we would have covered the number-line completely, but in fact this is not the case. To give only one example, a number like π does not appear in either category, for it is neither rational nor a quadratic surd; indeed more than this was proved at the end of the last century: it is not the root of any polynomial equation with rational coefficients. Intuition here is a most unsafe guide. A full treatment of the real numbers is a difficult undertaking which is beyond our scope here. All we can say is that when we have included with the rational numbers the quadratic surds, and even the zeros of all rational polynomial equations (the *algebraic irrationals*), we still have not begun to exhaust the real numbers. We fall back again, for the time being, on our earlier intuitive idea of the densely-packed, ordered set of points on a line; this will be sufficient so long as we realize how hopelessly inadequate it really is.

Real numbers form a *field* (see Book 1, p. 27). That is to say, the sum, product, difference and quotient of any two real numbers (excluding zero as the denominator of a quotient) is always a real number. All real numbers have positive squares; therefore there are real numbers—all the negative real numbers—that have no square roots. In the real-number system R we may solve all linear equations $ax+b = 0$, $a, b \in R$; also all equations $x^2 = a$, where $a \in \{R^+, 0\}$, the set of non-negative reals; but we cannot solve $x^2+1 = 0$, or $x^2 = a$, when $a \in R^-$. The next step will be to invent a number system in which such equations have a solution.

Exercise E

1. Write out a proof that $\sqrt{5}$ is irrational (similar to the proof given above for $\sqrt{2}$).

2. (*a*) Is $(R, +)$ a group? (*b*) Is $(R, \times)$ a group?

3. Consider the set of numbers derived by combining $\sqrt{2}$ with all the rational numbers, that is

$$\{a+b\sqrt{2}: a, b \in Q\}.$$

Show that this is closed under addition and multiplication. Find the negative and reciprocal of $2+3\sqrt{2}$, each in the form $a+b\sqrt{2}$.

4. Let k be a prime number. Show that if $kp^2 = q^2$ for integers p and q, then this would contradict the Fundamental Theorem of Arithmetic (which says that every integer n, greater than 1, can be factorized into a product of primes in only one way).

Explain how this proves that the square root of a prime number is always irrational.

6. THE GENERAL QUADRATIC FUNCTION

All that we have done in the previous sections can be done in general terms. We shall now revise the various methods by applying them to the general quadratic polynomial

$$ax^2+bx+c,$$

where a, b and c can be replaced by any numbers. The resulting formulae are often useful.

6.1 Roots of $ax^2+bx+c = 0$.

$$x^2+\frac{b}{a}x+\frac{c}{a} = 0 \quad \text{(dividing by } a\text{, assumed} \neq 0)$$

$$\Leftrightarrow x^2+\frac{b}{a}x+\left(\frac{b}{2a}\right)^2+\frac{c}{a} = \frac{b^2}{4a^2} \quad \text{(completing the square)}$$

$$\Leftrightarrow \left(x+\frac{b}{2a}\right)^2 = \frac{b^2-4ac}{4a^2}$$

$$\Leftrightarrow x+\frac{b}{2a} = \pm\frac{\sqrt{(b^2-4ac)}}{2a}$$

$$\Leftrightarrow x = \frac{-b\pm\sqrt{(b^2-4ac)}}{2a}.$$

There are three cases to consider:

(i) If $b^2-4ac > 0$, then $\sqrt{(b^2-4ac)}$ exists and is not zero, and the equation has *two* roots.

(ii) If $b^2-4ac = 0$, there is *one* root, $-b/2a$. In this case, the quadratic form factorizes as a squared linear polynomial and the equation becomes

$$a\left(x+\frac{b}{2a}\right)^2 = 0.$$

We sometimes say that this equation has *two coincident roots.*

(iii) If $b^2-4ac < 0$, then $\sqrt{(b^2-4ac)}$ does not exist, and the equation has *no* real roots.

The expression b^2-4ac is called the *discriminant* of the quadratic form ax^2+bx+c.

6.2 Graph of $y = ax^2+bx+c$. By completing the square, we get

$$y = a\left(x+\frac{b}{2a}\right)^2-\frac{(b^2-4ac)}{4a}.$$

Symmetry. The axis of symmetry is the line with equation

$$x = \frac{-b}{2a}.$$

Range. $\left(x+\frac{b}{2a}\right)^2 \geqslant 0$ for all values of x, so if $a > 0$, then

$$a\left(x+\frac{b}{2a}\right)^2 \geqslant 0$$

for all values of x, so that y has a *least* value

$$\frac{-(b^2-4ac)}{4a}$$

when

$$x = \frac{-b}{2a}.$$

Figure 12 shows the six possible types of graph, according to the values of a, b and c. (Only the x-axis is indicated.)

In each case the greatest or least value of y is

$$\frac{-(b^2-4ac)}{4a}$$

(which is zero when $b^2-4ac = 0$).

6.3 Sign of y (or ax^2+bx+c). Let α and β be the roots of

$$ax^2+bx+c = 0 \quad \text{when} \quad b^2-4ac \geqslant 0.$$

Then from the graphs in Figure 12 we can see that:
(i) if $a > 0$, then $y < 0$ only when $\alpha < x < \beta$;
(ii) if $a < 0$, then $y > 0$ only when $\alpha < x < \beta$, and so on.

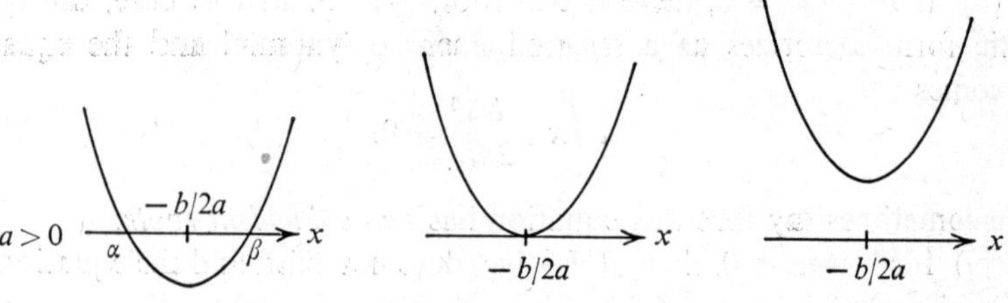

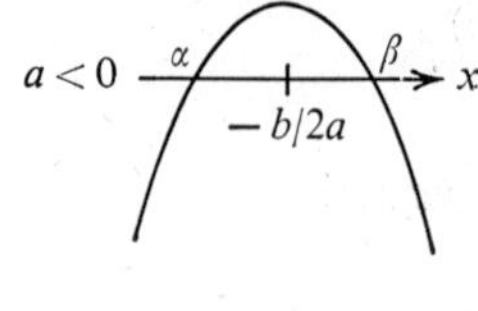

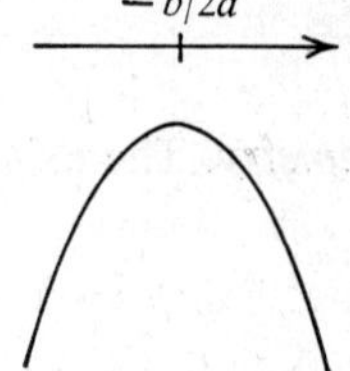

Fig. 12

Exercise F

1. Use the formula of Section 6.1 to solve the following equations (unless you can use the factor method—always try this first):

(*a*) $3x^2-x-1 = 0$; (*b*) $3x^2+2x-1 = 0$; (*c*) $3x^2+2x+1 = 0$.

2. When will the equation

$$ax^2-2x+3 = 0$$

have

(*a*) *two* distinct roots;
(*b*) only *one* root (or two coincident roots);
(*c*) no roots?

3. Use the formula of Section 6.1 to solve the equations in Questions 1–10 of Exercise C.

4. *Sum and product of roots.*

(*a*) Let s and t be the roots of

$$ax^2+bx+c = 0. \tag{i}$$

Then the equation can be written

$$a(x-s)(x-t) = 0.$$

But this is $$ax^2 - a(s+t)x + ast = 0 \qquad \text{(ii)}$$

By comparing the coefficients of (i) and (ii) show that:

the sum of the roots, $s+t$, equals $-b/a$

and **the product of the roots, st, equals c/a.**

(*b*) Show that these results can also be obtained by adding and multiplying the roots found by the formula of Section 6.1.

(*c*) Use the sum and product formulae to check the roots of some of the quadratic equations which you have solved in this chapter.

(*d*) If you solve a quadratic equation and the roots you find satisfy *both* the sum and the product formulae, then you can be sure that the solution is correct. Can you construct an example to show that checking one formula alone is *not* sufficient?

5. Write down the quadratic equation which has roots whose sum is 7 and product is 3. A second equation is such that its roots are twice the roots of the first one. What are the sum and product of these new roots? Hence write down the second equation.

6. Let the roots of $$2x^2 - 5x + 1 = 0$$

be s and t. Find the quadratic equation with roots $s+1$ and $t+1$.

(*Hint*. Find the sum and product of the old and of the new roots.)

7. Let the roots of the equation
$$3x^2 - x - 1 = 0$$

be t and s. Then $t+s = \frac{1}{3}$ and $ts = -\frac{1}{3}$. We can find sequences of numbers

$$t_1, t_2, t_3, \ldots \quad \text{and} \quad s_1, s_2, s_3, \ldots$$

which converge to t and s by using the relations

$$t_n + s_n = \tfrac{1}{3} \quad \text{and} \quad t_{n+1}s_n = -\tfrac{1}{3}.$$

If we start with $t_1 = 0$,

$$t_1 + s_1 = \tfrac{1}{3}$$
$$\Rightarrow 0 + s_1 = \tfrac{1}{3},$$
$$\Rightarrow s_1 = 0{\cdot}33 \quad \text{(2 decimal places).}$$

Then $$s_1 t_2 = -\tfrac{1}{3} \Rightarrow t_2 = -1,$$

and so on. The beginning of this sequence is given below. Continue the table until you consider that you have found t and s to 2 decimal places.

n	t_n	s_n
1	0	0·33
2	−1	1·33
3	−0·25	0·58

This is an example of an *iterative* method. Draw a computer flow diagram for this process.

8. Use the iterative method of Question 7 with a different choice of t_1 at the beginning.

9. Solve $2x^2 + x - 6 = 0$ by an iterative process.

7. COMPLEX NUMBERS

7.1 In the real number system, R, it was always possible to solve a quadratic equation of the form
$$x^2 - a = 0$$
so long as $a > 0$ (i.e. the square root of a positive number always exists in R).

7.2 We will now assume

(1) that we can extend R to a system in which the equation
$$x^2 + 1 = 0$$
has a solution;

(2) that the extended system contains the real numbers as before; and

(3) that the same rules for addition and multiplication apply for all elements in the extended system, i.e. that the extended system forms a *field* (see Chapter 1, Book 1, p. 27).

Now this system must contain a root of
$$x^2 + 1 = 0.$$
Denote this by the letter j, so that
$$j^2 + 1 = 0.$$

If we combine j with the real numbers we shall find that under the operations of addition, subtraction, multiplication, and division (excluding 0 as divisor) we always obtain numbers of the form $a + bj$, a and $b \in R$.

Two examples are given here:

Example 10. $(3 - j) + (5 + 4j)$
$$= 3 + 5 - j + 4j$$
$$= 8 + 3j.$$

Example 11. $(2 + 3j)(1 - 5j)$
$$= 2 - 7j - 15j^2$$
$$= 2 - 7j + 15, \quad \text{since } j^2 = -1$$
$$= 17 - 7j.$$

Numbers of this form are called *complex numbers*, and the extended system is called the *complex number field C*. That is,
$$C = \{a + bj\colon \quad a, b \in R\}.$$

7.3 Argand diagram. Because each number has two parts, we cannot now represent them on a single line (which has only *one* dimension); we need two dimensions. For this we use a plane (Figure 13) with the usual axes of Cartesian coordinates, and make the point (a, b) correspond to the complex number $a+jb$. This is sometimes called the *Argand diagram*, or, better, the *complex number plane*.

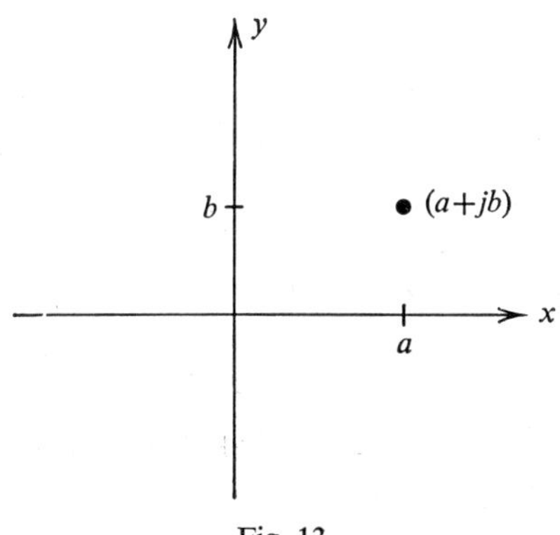

Fig. 13

7.4 In the complex number field C we can now solve all equations of the form

$$x^2 = a.$$

For example,

$$x^2 = -4$$

$$\Rightarrow \quad \text{either} \quad x = 2j \quad \text{or} \quad x = -2j.$$

In fact it can be shown that any polynomial equation of the form:

$$a_0x^n + a_1x^{n-1} + \ldots + a_{n-1}x + a_n = 0$$

has a root in C.

Exercise G

1. $\{a+0.j : a \in R\}$ is a subset of C. Is this isomorphic to R under $+$ and $\times$?

2. In an Argand diagram, plot the points corresponding to the two numbers $(2+3j)$ and $(1+2j)$. Now mark a third point, corresponding to the sum of these two numbers. What sort of figure do these three points make with the origin?

3. Mark the points $(3+2j)$ and $(3+2j).j$ in a diagram. What is the effect in the diagram corresponding to multiplying by j?

4. Mark the points corresponding to the two complex numbers

$$Z_1 = 2-3j \quad \text{and} \quad Z_2 = 2+j$$

in an Argand diagram.

Show the points corresponding to

$$-Z_1, \quad -Z_2, \quad Z_1+Z_2, \quad Z_1Z_2, \quad Z_1-Z_2.$$

5. If $a+jb = c+jd$, where a and b are *real* numbers, then

$$(a-c) = j(d-b) \Rightarrow (a-c)^2 = -(d-b)^2.$$

What can you deduce from this?

6. Verify that the numbers $1+j$ and $1-j$ are each a root of the equation

$$x^2-2x+2 = 0.$$

Does this equation have a root in the field of real numbers?

7. For each of the following equations, say whether it has a root, or roots, in each of N, Z, Q, R and C, and find the roots if they exist:

(*a*) $x+3 = 5$; (*b*) $x+7 = 2$; (*c*) $2(x+2) = 3x-5$;
(*d*) $4x+1 = 3-2x$; (*e*) $x^2-17 = 0$; (*f*) $x^2-9 = 0$;
(*g*) $x^2-18 = 0$; (*h*) $x^2+25 = 0$; (*i*) $x^2+2 = 0$;
(*j*) $x^3-1 = 0$; (*k*) $x^4-1 = 0$.

The subject of complex numbers is dealt with more fully in a later chapter.

Miscellaneous Exercise

1. Factorize $2x^3-x^2-2x+1$ given that $(x+1)$ is a factor. For what values of x will this polynomial be zero?

2. Draw a graph of $y = 4-3x-2x^2$ (see Example 5 above) for values of x between $-2\frac{1}{2}$ and 1 $(-2\frac{1}{2} \leqslant x \leqslant 1)$. Use the graph to solve the equations:

(*a*) $2-3x-2x^2 = 0$; (*b*) $3x+2x^2 = 0$; (*c*) $4-3x-2x^2 = 0$;
(*d*) $5-3x-2x^2 = 0$; (*e*) $-1\frac{1}{8}-3x-2x^2 = 0$.

3. In sketch graphs, show points whose coordinates (x, y) satisfy the following relations $(x, y \in R)$:

(*a*) $y > x^2$; (*b*) $y > x^2$ *and* $y = x$;
(*c*) $y = x^2$ *and* $y = x$; (*d*) $y < x^2$ *and* $y = x$;
(*e*) $y > x^2$ *and* $y < x$ (that is, $x > y > x^2$);
(*f*) $0 < y < x(2-x)$; (*g*) $2 < y < x(2-x)$;
(*h*) $x < y < x(2-x)$; (*i*) $x < y$ *or* $y < x(2-x)$;
(*j*) $(x+1)(x-2) < y < x(3-x)$.

4. Solve the following inequalities $(x \in R)$:

(*a*) $3x^2-x-1 < 0$; (*b*) $3x^2+2x+1 < 0$;
(*c*) $3x^2+2x-1 < 0$; (*d*) $3x^2+2x+1 \geqslant 0$;
(*e*) $3+2x-x^2 > 0$; (*f*) $3+2x-x^2 < 0$;
(*g*) $2+x-3x^2 > 2-2x-2x^2$; (*h*) $3x^2+x-1 \leqslant 2x^2+3x-2$.

5. Solve the following equations $(x \in R)$:

(*a*) $x^2-4x+3 = 0$; (*b*) $x^2-4x+1 = 0$; (*c*) $x^2-4x+5 = 0$.

6. Express the following complex numbers in the form $a+bj$ where a, b are both real:

(i) $(2-j)^2-(3+2j)^2$; (ii) $(2+j)^3$.

7. Prove that

(*a*) $\dfrac{1}{1+j} = \frac{1}{2}(1-j)$; (*b*) $\dfrac{1}{3-4j} = \frac{1}{25}(3+4j)$.

REVISION EXERCISES

11. Σ-NOTATION AND FINITE SERIES

1. (*a*) Express in sigma notation and find the sum of $52+45+38+31+\ldots$ to 10 terms.

(*b*) Find $\sum_{i=1}^{i=n}(2^i-3i)$.

2. Show by considering the terms that

$$\sum_{i=0}^{i=n} i = \sum_{i=0}^{i=n}(n-i).$$

What is $\sum_{i=0}^{i=n} n$?

(*a*) Hence show that

$$2\sum_{0}^{n} i = n(n+1).$$

(*b*) If $g(i) = i(i+1)$, show by induction that

$$3\sum_{1}^{n} g(i) = n(n+1)(n+2).$$

3. (*a*) Establish a similar result to that in Question 2(*b*) for

$$4\sum_{1}^{n} i(i+1)(i+2).$$

(*b*) Use the results of 2(*a*), (*b*) and 3(*a*) to find $\sum_{1}^{n} i^3$.

4. (*a*) Prove that
$$\sum_{0}^{n-1} i^2(i+1)^2 = \sum_{1}^{n} i^2(i-1)^2.$$

(*b*) Prove that
$$\sum_{1}^{n} i^2(i+1)^2 - \sum_{1}^{n} i^2(i-1)^2 = 4\sum_{1}^{n} i^3.$$

(*c*) Use the results of (*a*) and (*b*) to find $\sum_{1}^{n} i^3$.

5. Which of the following statements are true, and which are false? Give brief reasons.

(*a*) $\sum_{1}^{n}(3i^2+1) = 3\sum_{1}^{n} i^2+1$;

(*b*) $\sum_{1}^{9} i^3 = \sum_{1}^{9}(10-i)^3$;

(*c*) $\sum_{i=1}^{100}(x^i-x^{i-1}) = x^{100}-1$;

(*d*) $\sum_{1}^{n} 1/i = \dfrac{2}{n+1}$;

(*e*) $\sum_{1}^{n} i^2 . \sum_{1}^{n} i^3 = \sum_{1}^{n} i^5$.

6. Given that

$$\sum_1^n f_i = 1, \quad \sum_1^n (x_i-\alpha) f_i = 0 \quad \text{and} \quad \sum_1^n (x_i-\alpha)^2 f_i = \beta^2,$$

show that

(*a*) $\sum_1^n x_i f_i = \alpha$; (*b*) $\sum_1^n x_i^2 f_i = \alpha^2+\beta^2$.

12. POSITION AND SPREAD

1. Calculate the standard deviation of the numbers 3, 6, 9, 12, 15. What will be the standard deviation of the numbers 130, 160, 190, 220, 250?

2. In a class of 10 children the marks in an examination are 14, 18, 21, 25, 29, 29, 30, 31, 35, 38. Find the mean and the standard deviation, giving your answers to the nearest integer. (OC)

3. The boys in a certain school in 1967 were counted according to their year of birth, with the following results:

Year of birth	Number of boys
1948	15
1949	115
1950	175
1951	180
1952	165
1953	140
1954	10
	800

Calculate the average age of these boys on 1 July 1967 and the standard deviation.

4. A random sample of 100 skirts was measured at Ascot. Their lengths (to the nearest 5 cm) were as follows:

Length in cm:	35	40	45	50	55	60	65
Number of skirts:	3	15	9	17	30	20	6

(*a*) Work out the mean length (m) and standard deviation (s).

(*b*) Any skirt longer than $m+s$ is regarded as 'square'. Approximately how many 'square' skirts were there in the sample?

(*c*) Any skirt shorter than $m-1\frac{1}{2}s$ is considered indecent. How many of these were there?

(*d*) Draw a histogram and show on it your answers to (*b*) and (*c*).

5. Marks out of 100 for a test taken by 100 boys were:

Range:	0–9	10–19	20–29	30–39	40–49
Frequency:	2	4	6	18	24
Range:	50–59	60–69	70–79	80–89	90–100
Frequency:	19	8	10	7	2

(*a*) Calculate the mean, median and sextiles.

(*b*) Calculate the standard deviation.

Check that roughly $\frac{2}{3}$ of the candidates are within one standard deviation of the mean.

6. The distances from Polebourne of the homes of the 70 boys in Friar House are indicated by the following frequency table:

Distance in km:	0–20	20–40	40–60	60–80	80–100
Number of boys:	7	13	17	12	6

Distance in km:	100–150	150–200	200–500	Over 500
Number of boys:	8	2	2	3

Display this information in a histogram.

The median distance is 58 km. Indicate this on your diagram, and state what geometrical property the median has in relation to the histogram.

Without doing any calculation, but giving a brief reason, say whether you would expect the mean to be greater or less than 58 km.

13. FURTHER VECTORS

1. (*a*) Write down a parametric vector equation for the line l through the point $(-1, 1, -2)$ parallel to the vector $3\mathbf{i}-4\mathbf{j}$.

(*b*) Write down the equation of the plane π through the point $(1, -1, 2)$ perpendicular to the vector $2\mathbf{i}-\mathbf{j}+\mathbf{k}$.

(*c*) Find the coordinates of the point of intersection of l and π.

2. Find the angle between the lines

$$\frac{x-10}{4} = \frac{y-3}{1} = \frac{z+3}{-3} \quad \text{and} \quad \frac{x-3}{1} = \frac{y-6}{5} = \frac{z-6}{3}.$$

Do these lines intersect?

3. Find a vector which makes the same angle with each of the vectors

$$\begin{pmatrix}4\\3\\0\end{pmatrix}, \quad \begin{pmatrix}3\\0\\4\end{pmatrix} \quad \text{and} \quad \begin{pmatrix}0\\0\\5\end{pmatrix}.$$

Is there more than one answer?

4. Find the equation of the plane through (1, 2, 3), (0, 0, 1), and (0, 1, 0). Find also the equation of the parallel plane through $(-1, 2, 0)$.

What is the volume enclosed between these planes and the planes $x = 0$, $y = 0$, $z = 0$?

5. Give a geometrical interpretation of the following matrices in terms of transformations of three-dimensional space:

$$(a)\ \begin{pmatrix}1 & 0 & 0\\0 & 0 & -1\\0 & 1 & 0\end{pmatrix}; \qquad (b)\ \begin{pmatrix}1 & 0 & 0\\0 & 0 & 1\\0 & -1 & 0\end{pmatrix}; \qquad (c)\ \begin{pmatrix}0 & 0 & -2\\0 & -2 & 0\\-2 & 0 & 0\end{pmatrix}.$$

6. Explain how to use the scalar product to calculate the angle between two vectors.

Greenwich (G) is 51·5° N, 0° E; Karachi (K) is 25° N, 67° E. Taking axes OX, OY, OZ where X is 0° N, 0° E, Y is 0° N, 90° E and Z is the North Pole, express the vectors $\mathbf{OG}$ and $\mathbf{OK}$ in terms of R, the earth's radius, and calculate the great-circle distance GK in nautical miles.

14. FURTHER TRIGONOMETRY

1. Find the general solution of $\cos 2x = \frac{1}{2}$, giving your answer in radians.

2. (*a*) Express $\dfrac{\sin 2A}{1+\cos 2A}$ in terms of $\tan A$.

(*b*) Factorize $\cos 5A+\cos 3A$. For what values of A is it zero?

(*c*) Illustrate your answer to (*b*) by sketching the graphs of $\cos 5x$ and $-\cos 3x$ for $0 \leqslant x \leqslant 2\pi$.

3. Find the set of values of x for which $2 \sin x+\sin 2x > 0$. What is the greatest value of $2 \sin x+\sin 2x$?

4. Sketch the graphs of the following, on the same axes:

(*a*) $r = 2$; (*b*) $r = 3 \cos \theta$; (*c*) $r = 2+3 \cos \theta$.

Explain in geometrical terms the connection between the three loci.

5. By multiplying the series $\left[\frac{1}{2}+\sum_{n=1}^{N} \cos nx\right]$ by $\sin \frac{1}{2}x$, find a formula for its sum. Discuss the formula when $x = 0$. (OC)

6. Three needles of lengths 6 cm, 7 cm, and 8 cm are soldered together at their ends to form a triangle, which is then fixed in a horizontal plane. A ball of radius 4 cm rests on them. Find the height of its centre above their plane.

15. THE QUADRATIC FUNCTION

1. Find all values of x (which may be complex) satisfying the equations:

(*a*) $x^2-4x+3 = 0$; (*b*) $x^2+x+1 = 0$;

(*c*) $x^2+5x+1 = 0$; (*d*) $x^3+6x^2+5x = 0$.

2. Express $x^2+4x+13$ in the form $(x+a)^2+b$ and hence discover whether $x^2+4x+13$ has a maximum or a minimum value, its actual value, and the value of x for which it occurs. Sketch the graph of $f: x \to x^2+4x+13$.

3. (*a*) Find $S = \{x: x^2-13x-7{\cdot}2 < 0\}$ and illustrate your answer by a sketch.

(*b*) Express in set notation the set of values of x for which $(4-3x)(5x+2)$ is negative.

4. If the roots of $4x^2-6x+1 = 0$ are α and β, find the values of

(*a*) $(\alpha-\beta)^2$; (*b*) $\alpha^2+\beta^2$; (*c*) $\left(\alpha^2+\dfrac{1}{\beta^2}\right)\left(\beta^2+\dfrac{1}{\alpha^2}\right)$.

5. Factorize x^2+2x+2 when the coefficients are in arithmetic modulo 5. Deduce from your answer the factors of $4x^2+3x+3$.

6. Write the quartic function $x^4+2x^3+2x^2-4x-8$ in the form

$$(x^2+x+\alpha)^2-ax^2-bx-c,$$

choosing α so that ax^2+bx+c is a perfect square. Hence find the solution set of the equation $x^4+2x^3+2x^2-4x-8 = 0$.

16

LOCAL APPROXIMATION

1. APPROXIMATION BY MAPS

When a map is made of a portion of the earth's surface (which we shall assume for simplicity to be near enough a perfect sphere) there is inevitably distortion, since the surface of a sphere cannot be flattened out on a plane.

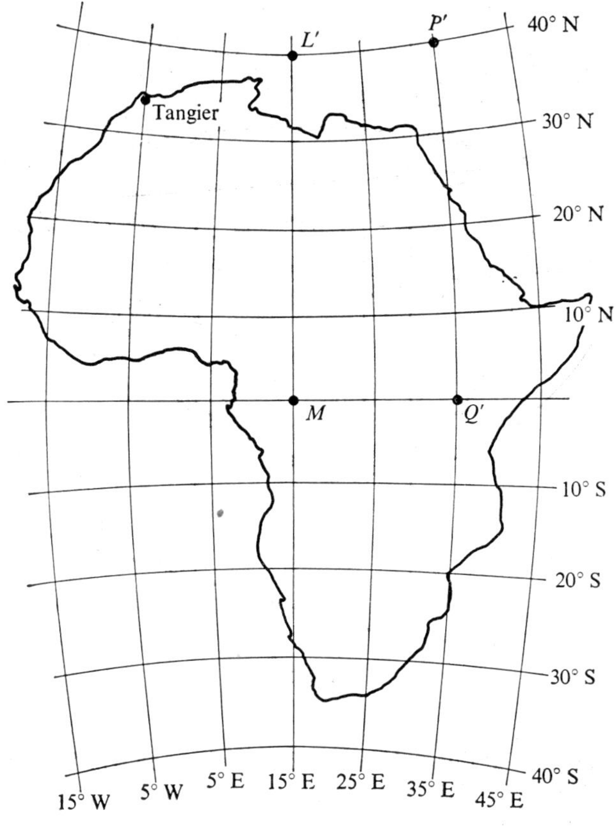

Fig. 1

One of the features that is distorted is the distance between points; so that, although it is common for maps to carry a 'scale', this scale can give only an approximate indication of distances.

Figure 1 shows a map of Africa made by stereographic projection. The method of construction is as follows. First, an exact map is supposed made on a globe of convenient radius, which we have taken to be $1/10^8$ of the radius of the earth. A point M on the globe near the centre of the region to be mapped is then selected, and we imagine a plane to be drawn

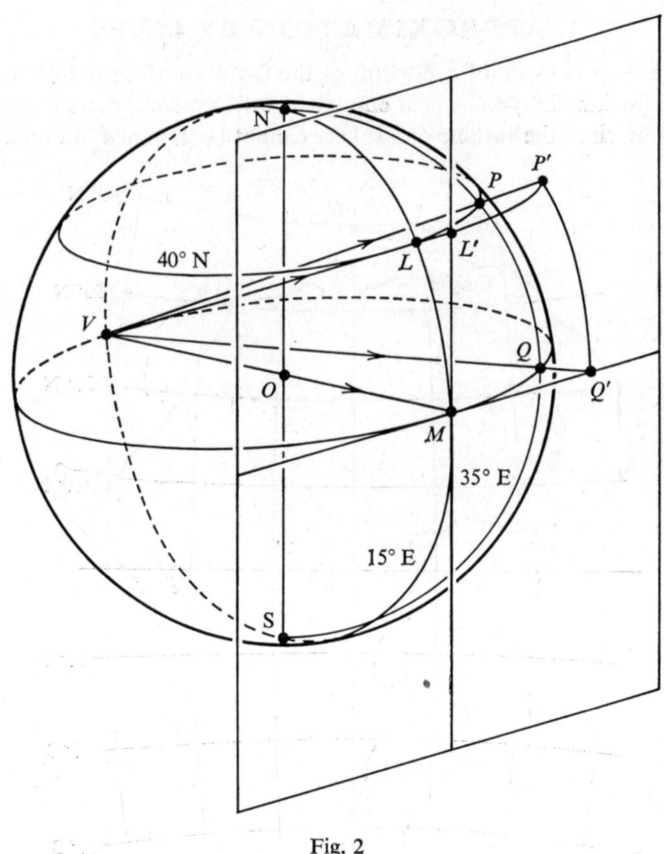

Fig. 2

to touch the globe at this point. This is the plane on which the map is to be made. The point V on the globe is now defined to be the point antipodal to M; in the given example M is a point in the north-eastern Congo, on the equator and with longitude 15° E, so that V is on the equator and 165° W. V is now used as the vertex of a geometrical projection; that is, if P is any point of the globe, its image P' on the map is found as the point of intersection of the ray VP produced and the plane of the map.

This kind of map projection has some important properties. For example, it preserves the *local* mapping accurately; that is, small regions appear accurately to scale. Thus if two rivers meet at an angle of 30°, this will be shown correctly on the map. But the actual 'local scale factor' varies considerably at different places on the map. At M it is the same as that of the globe, that is 1:100000000. But around Tangier, for example, it is 1:88000000, a difference of 14 %. If the map is used to compare areas, the situation is even less satisfactory; for if the linear scales are in the ratio 1·14, the surface scales are in the ratio $(1{\cdot}14)^2$, or 1·30, so that there is a percentage difference of 30 % in area representation, enough to give a very misleading impression of the relative sizes of two countries. Such a map therefore gives a good approximation in a restricted region, but is less satisfactory if used to show a large area.

We may say that the plane map is a *local approximation* to the map on the globe in a neighbourhood of a particular point, the quality of that approximation improving as the size of the neighbourhood is reduced.

2. LINEAR APPROXIMATION TO A FUNCTION

2.1 In this chapter we shall apply the process of local approximation to functions whose domain and range are subsets of the real numbers. It is useful to begin by recalling two results from previous chapters:

(i) The local scale factor for a function f at a value $x = p$ of the domain is measured by the derivative $f'(p)$.

(ii) Any linear function

$$x \to ax+b$$

has a constant scale factor a.

We shall first investigate the possibility of finding a local approximation to a given function by means of a linear function. Our method is to find the value of the derivative at the point in question, and then to find the linear function which has this derivative for its scale factor, and which also has the same value as the given function at the point round which the local approximation is required.

Example 1. Use a linear function to serve as a local approximation to the square root function

$$f\colon x \to \sqrt{x}$$

in a neighbourhood of $x = 9$.

The image of 9 under the square root function is 3. A number near to 9 is conveniently denoted by $9+\alpha$, where α is small, and its image is $\sqrt{(9+\alpha)}$. This mapping is illustrated in Figure 3(a); the interval of the domain of length α, from 9 to $9+\alpha$, is mapped onto an interval of the codomain of length $\sqrt{(9+\alpha)}-3$.

In the linear approximation the same interval of the domain of length α is mapped onto an interval whose length is proportional to α. The constant of proportion is chosen to be the local scale factor for the given function at the point $x = 9$; that is, the derivative $f'(9)$.

Now it was pointed out in Chapter 7 (Section 3.1) that the derived function of the square root function is

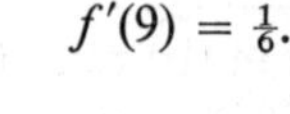

$$f': x \to \frac{1}{2\sqrt{x}}.$$

It follows that
$$f'(9) = \tfrac{1}{6}.$$

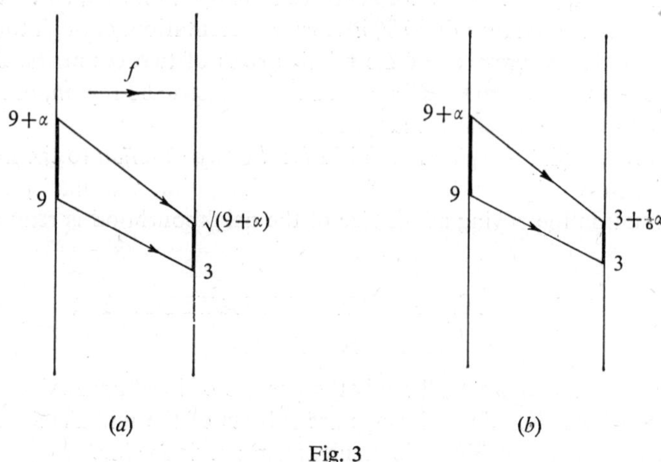

Fig. 3

For the linear approximation, therefore, the interval of length α is mapped onto an interval of length $\frac{1}{6}\alpha$; that is, the image of $9+\alpha$ is $3+\frac{1}{6}\alpha$. This is illustrated in Figure 3(*b*).

It is important to remember that this is merely a *local* approximation, which is useful only for numbers close to 9; that is, when α is small. We say that, for small α,
$$\sqrt{(9+\alpha)} \approx 3+\tfrac{1}{6}\alpha.$$

The closeness of the approximation can be shown by means of a table of values:

α	$\sqrt{(9+\alpha)}$	$3+\frac{1}{6}\alpha$	Difference
−1·0	2·8284	2·8333	0·0049
−0·8	2·8636	2·8667	0·0031
−0·6	2·8983	2·9000	0·0017
−0·4	2·9326	2·9333	0·0007
−0·2	2·9665	2·9667	0·0002
+0·2	3·0332	3·0333	0·0001
+0·4	3·0659	3·0667	0·0008
+0·6	3·0984	3·1000	0·0016
+0·8	3·1305	3·1333	0·0028
+1·0	3·1623	3·1667	0·0044

(The final figures are, of course, subject to rounding errors.) It is apparent that in a small region surrounding the value $x = 9$ the correspondence between the true value and the approximation is very close indeed, but that as the distance from $x = 9$ increases the distortion becomes more significant.

2.2 The method of Example 1 can be applied to any function for which a derivative can be found. Let such a function be denoted by f, and suppose that a linear approximation to the function is required in the region around a value p in the domain. For this function the image of the number p is $f(p)$, and the derivative $f'(p)$.

We choose, therefore, for the approximating linear function that one for which the number p maps onto $f(p)$ and for which the (constant) scale factor is $f'(p)$. For this function the interval of length α, from p to $p+\alpha$, maps onto an interval of length $f'(p).\alpha$ (see Figure 4). The image of the number $p+\alpha$ under this linear function is therefore

$$f(p)+f'(p).\alpha.$$

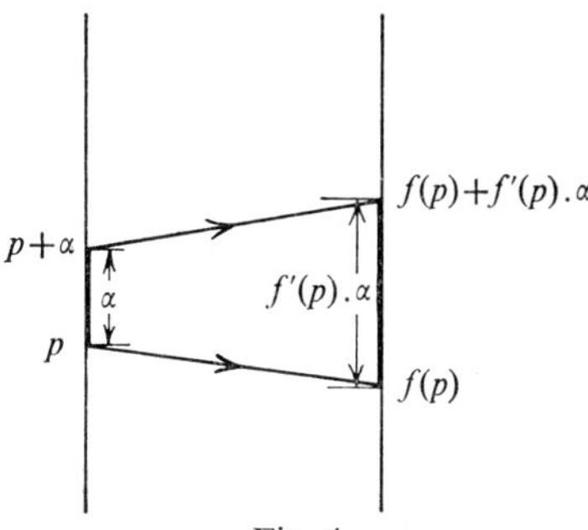

Fig. 4

The image of $p+\alpha$ under the given function f is, of course, $f(p+\alpha)$. We therefore say that, for small α,

$$f(p+\alpha) \approx f(p)+f'(p).\alpha.$$

Example 2. Find a local approximation to the sine function in the neighbourhood of $\frac{1}{3}\pi$, and hence estimate the value of sin 61°.

The derived function is cos, so that substitution in the formula established above gives

$$\begin{aligned}\sin(\tfrac{1}{3}\pi+\alpha) &\approx \sin(\tfrac{1}{3}\pi)+\cos(\tfrac{1}{3}\pi).\alpha\\ &= \tfrac{1}{2}\sqrt{3}+\tfrac{1}{2}\alpha\\ &= 0{\cdot}866+\tfrac{1}{2}\alpha.\end{aligned}$$

This is the equation giving the approximation required.

We now apply this for a particular value of α. In circular measure 60° corresponds to $\frac{1}{3}\pi$ radians and 1° to $\frac{1}{180}\pi$, or 0·017 radians. Therefore

$$\begin{aligned}\sin(61°) &= \sin(\tfrac{1}{3}\pi+0{\cdot}017)\\ &\approx 0{\cdot}866+\tfrac{1}{2}\times 0{\cdot}017\\ &= 0{\cdot}874.\end{aligned}$$

2.3 It was shown in Section 2.1 that, for small α,

$$\sqrt{(9+\alpha)} \approx 3+\tfrac{1}{6}\alpha.$$

This result can be re-cast into another form, so as to give a function of x, which approximates to the function $\sqrt{x}$ in the neighbourhood of $x = 9$.

If we write $9+\alpha$ as x, then α is $x-9$, and the approximation can be written as

$$\sqrt{x} \approx 3+\tfrac{1}{6}(x-9)$$
$$= \tfrac{1}{6}x+\tfrac{3}{2}$$

when $x-9$ is small. We therefore have two functions: the given function

$$f\colon x \to \sqrt{x},$$

and the linear function $$x \to \tfrac{1}{6}x+\tfrac{3}{2}$$

and we say that the second is a local linear approximation to the first in the neighbourhood of $x = 9$.

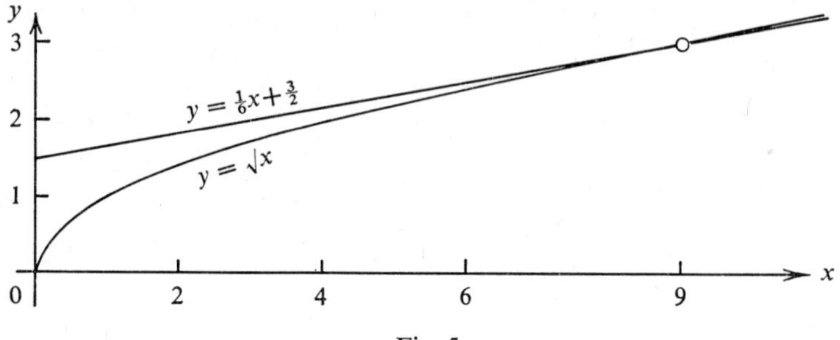

Fig. 5

It is interesting to illustrate this by drawing the graphs of the equations $y = \sqrt{x}$ and $y = \frac{1}{6}x+\frac{3}{2}$ (Figure 5). At $x = 9$ the values of the two functions are exactly equal to each other; and the graphs show that for numbers x close to 9 the images of x under the two functions are very nearly equal. In fact, since the scale factor (or gradient) of the linear function was chosen to be equal to the derivative of the function $\sqrt{x}$ at $x = 9$, the linear graph is the tangent at the point (9, 3) to the graph $y = \sqrt{x}$.

We can easily demonstrate that the same is true of the linear approximation to a general function f in the neighbourhood of a value p in the domain. Figure 6 shows the graph of the equation $y = f(x)$. P is the point with coordinates $(p, f(p))$, and PT is the tangent to the graph at P. Q is a point of the graph corresponding to some other number x in the domain, whose coordinates are $(x, f(x))$; and T is the point of the tangent corresponding to the same number x. To find the equation of the tangent we need to find an expression for the length NT.

Now the gradient of the tangent is $f'(p)$, so that

$$RT = f'(p).PR = f'(p).(x-p).$$

Hence $$NT = MP+RT = f(p)+f'(p).(x-p).$$

The equation of the tangent is therefore

$$y = f(p)+f'(p).(x-p);$$

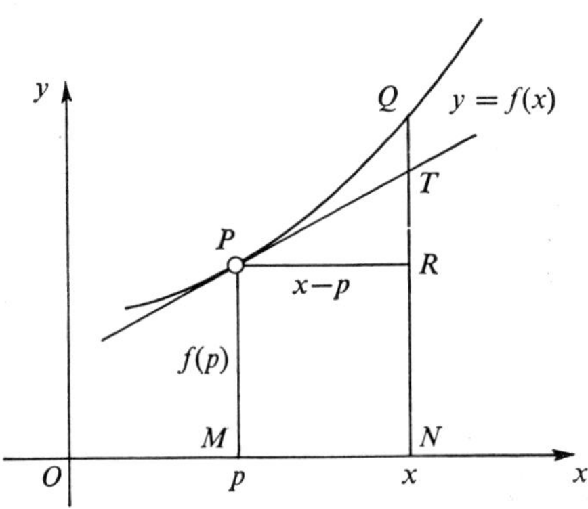

Fig. 6

and we are asserting that, in the neighbourhood of $x = p$, the linear function

$$x \to f(p)+f'(p).(x-p)$$

is a local approximation to the given function

$$x \to f(x).$$

To derive this from the approximation

$$f(p+\alpha) \approx f(p)+f'(p).\alpha$$

obtained in Section 2.2, we have merely to write $p+\alpha$ as x, so that $\alpha = x-p$. We deduce that, for numbers x close to p,

$$f(x) \approx f(p)+f'(p).(x-p).$$

2.4 The increment notation δy, δx described in Chapter 7, Section 7, suggests yet another way of writing the local linear approximation to values of a function. If we write

$$y = f(x),$$

and consider the mapping of the interval of the domain from p to $p+\alpha$, then we commonly write δx in place of α, and the corresponding increase in y as

$$\delta y = f(p+\alpha)-f(p).$$

If we also write the scale factor $f'(p)$ as dy/dx, the approximation

$$f(p+\alpha)-f(p) \simeq f'(p).\alpha$$

takes the form $$\delta y \approx \frac{dy}{dx}\delta x,$$

where dy/dx is evaluated at the point from which the increments are taken. This form is frequently used in physical applications.

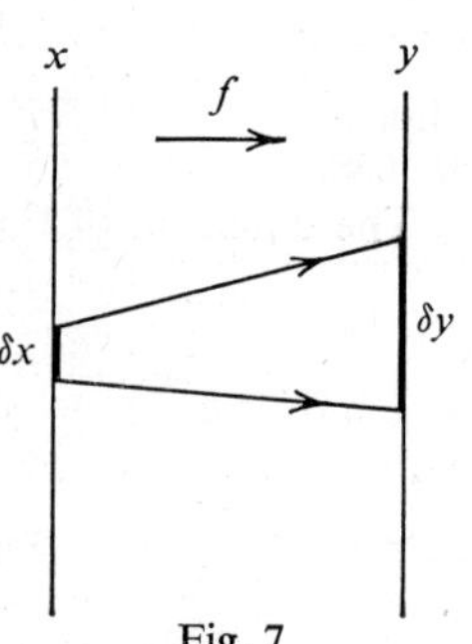

Fig. 7

Example 3. Estimate the decrease in the gravitational pull of the earth between sea level and the top of Mount Everest.

The pull of the earth is described by the 'inverse square law'

$$P \propto \frac{1}{x^2},$$

where x is the distance from the centre of the earth (in km, say). For a given body we may therefore write

$$P = \frac{k}{x^2}.$$

Taking the radius of the earth as about 6380 km, the weight of the body is given by this formula as $k/6380^2$.

Our problem is to find how much this force changes when x increases by 8·9 km, the height of the summit of Everest. That is, we wish to calculate δP for a value $\delta x = 8{\cdot}9$.

Now

$$\frac{dP}{dx} = -\frac{2k}{x^3},$$

so that at sea level the rate of change of weight with height is

$$-\frac{2k}{6380^3}.$$

The formula of linear approximation therefore gives

$$\begin{aligned}\delta P &\approx \frac{dP}{dx}.\delta x \\ &= -\frac{2k}{6380^3}.8{\cdot}9 \\ &= -\frac{17{\cdot}8k}{6380^3}.\end{aligned}$$

This result is most easily understood in terms of proportional increase. A pull of $k/6380^2$ is diminished by $17{\cdot}8k/6380^3$; that is, by a fraction

$$\frac{17{\cdot}8}{6380}$$

of itself, about 0·28%.

Exercise A

1. Find a linear approximation to $\sqrt{(49+\alpha)}$ when α is small, and hence find approximate values for $\sqrt{50}$ and $\sqrt{48}$. Deduce approximations for $\sqrt{2}$ and $\sqrt{3}$.

2. Apply the method of Example 1 to the reciprocal function

$$r: x \to \frac{1}{x},$$

and hence find approximations, for small α, for (i) $1/(10+\alpha)$, (ii) $1/(a+\alpha)$, where $a \neq 0$. Use the first answer to give an approximate value for $1/9{\cdot}9$.

Prove that the difference between the approximate and the exact value in (i) is

$$\frac{\alpha^2}{100(10+\alpha)}.$$

Hence show that the error in the estimated value of $1/9{\cdot}9$ is about 10^{-5}.

3. Find a linear function $x \to L(x)$ which approximates to the function $x \to \sqrt{x}$ for values of x near to 1. Draw a large-scale diagram to illustrate the mapping $x \to \sqrt{x}$ over the interval $0{\cdot}6 < x < 1{\cdot}4$, drawing arrows at points of the domain distant 0·1 apart. Then draw on tracing paper to the same scale a diagram of the mapping $x \to L(x)$. Illustrate the approximation by placing the tracing paper diagram on top of the first diagram.

4. Find a linear approximation for $\cos(p+\alpha)$ when α is small. Hence estimate cos 1. State whether this estimate is too high or too low, giving a reason.

5. Use the linear approximation to $\sin(\frac{1}{3}\pi+\alpha)$ to estimate (in radian measure) the acute angle whose sine is 0·9.

6. For the function

$$f: x \to 1/x^2,$$

show (either from first principles or by using the general rule for differentiating x^n) that the derived function is

$$f': x \to -2/x^3.$$

Find a linear function which approximates to f in a neighbourhood of $x = 2$. Use this to estimate the difference between $1/2^2$ and $1/2{\cdot}05^2$. If a measurement x is given correctly as 2·0 centimetres, within what percentage accuracy can the value of $1/x^2$ be relied on?

7. Find the equation of the tangent to the graph of $y = x^3$ at the point (2, 8). Plot accurately the graph of $y = x^3$ and this tangent over the interval

$$1{\cdot}5 < x < 2{\cdot}5,$$

and from the graphs estimate the interval over which the linear approximation is accurate to within 0·1.

8. Find a linear approximation to the function

$$s: x \to x^2$$

in a neighbourhood of $x = 5$. Use this to estimate the square root of 27. Then, by finding a linear approximation in some other neighbourhood suggested by your first answer, improve on the first estimate.

9. By applying the result in Section 2.2 to the function

$$x \to x^n,$$

where n is a positive integer, find an approximation for $(p+\alpha)^n$ for small α. Verify that the same result would be obtained by multiplying out the expression $(p+\alpha)(p+\alpha)\ldots(p+\alpha)$ with n brackets and discarding all terms involving powers of α higher than the first. What is the point of the restriction that n should be a positive integer? Can the result be generalized?

10. Re-draw Figure 6, labelling it according to the δy, δx notation.

11. A car is timed over a measured kilometre. Write a formula for calculating the speed in m/s from the time in seconds. If the time is 6·250 seconds, measured with an instrument accurate to the nearest thousandth of a second, use a linear approximation to find with what accuracy the speed (160 m/s) can be given.

12. The time T for the swing of a clock pendulum is proportional to the square root of its length l. Express this algebraically, and find an approximate equation connecting δT and δl. Deduce that

$$\frac{\delta T}{T} \approx \frac{1}{2}\frac{\delta l}{l}.$$

If the length of the pendulum goes up by 0·1% on a hot day, what effect will this have on the timekeeping?

13. When a substance is heated, all its linear dimensions are increased by α% and its mass remains unchanged. Use linear approximations to estimate the percentage changes in the volume, the surface area and the density.

14. An aircraft crosses the Atlantic (4800 km) at a speed of 800 km/h. Use a linear approximation to estimate how much time would be saved by travelling 30 km/h faster. If the cost of the journey per passenger is given by the formula

$$£\left(50+\frac{v}{40}+\frac{8000}{v}\right),$$

find how much difference the extra 30 km/h would make to the cost.

3. SOLUTION OF EQUATIONS

3.1 An important application of the method of local approximation is to the solution of equations. Some equations, such as quadratic equations and certain equations which arise in trigonometry, can be solved by exact methods (although some approximation will usually be necessary in the final computation); but many of the equations which occur in practice are not of these special kinds, and these must be solved by a method of successive approximation. The labour of computation is often reduced by using a computer. Indeed, even when an equation can be solved by an exact method, it may well be more efficient to obtain the answer to a desired degree of accuracy by a method of approximation.

Any equation involving just one unknown can be written in the form

$$f(x) = 0,$$

where f is some function. For example, an equation such as

$$x = \cos x$$

can be re-cast as

$$x - \cos x = 0,$$

which is of the given form with the function f defined by the mapping

$$x \to x - \cos x.$$

The values of x which make the equation true are called the *roots* of the equation, or the *zeros* of the function. The problem of solution is to identify these roots with some specified degree of accuracy.

The location of the real number roots is clearly illustrated by the graph of the relation

$$y = f(x).$$

We are looking for the numbers whose image under the given function is zero, and these are represented by the points where the graph meets the x-axis. When solving an equation the first step is usually to make a sketch of this graph, and hence to find 'first approximations' to the roots. Figure 8 shows the graph of the relation

$$y = x - \cos x,$$

from which we see that there is only one root of the equation

$$x - \cos x = 0$$

in real numbers, and that its value is between 0 and 1, probably fairly near to 0·7. In fact,

$$\begin{aligned} f(0{\cdot}7) &= 0{\cdot}7 - \cos(0{\cdot}7) \\ &= 0{\cdot}7 - 0{\cdot}7648 \\ &= -0{\cdot}0648. \end{aligned}$$

A glance at the graph shows that, in this case, the fact that $f(0{\cdot}7)$ is a small negative number indicates that the root is near to, but rather larger than, 0·7.

Our problem now is to improve the accuracy with which this root can be estimated, and this is where the concept of linear approximation is useful. For although the root is not exactly 0·7, it could be written as $0{\cdot}7+\alpha$, where α is a small number. We are aiming to find the value of α for which

$$f(0{\cdot}7+\alpha) = 0.$$

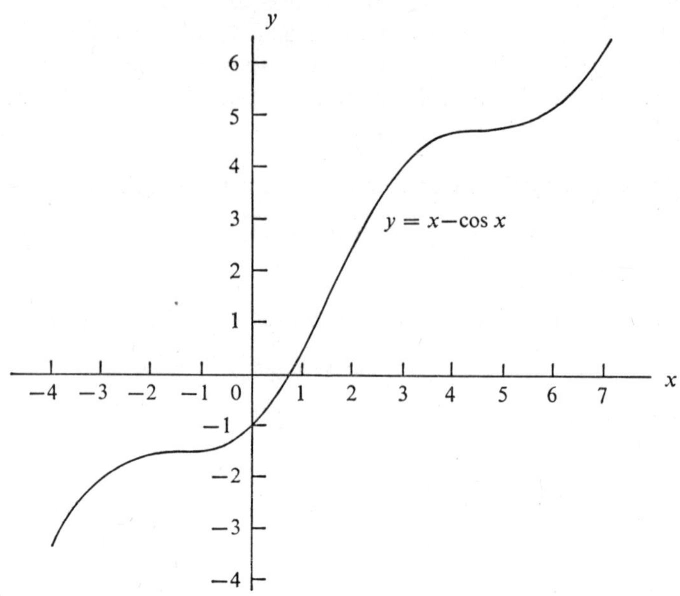

Fig. 8

This equation for α is in itself no easier to solve than the original equation for x. Since α is small, however, we know that

$$f(0{\cdot}7+\alpha) \approx f(0{\cdot}7)+f'(0{\cdot}7).\alpha,$$

so that

$$f(0{\cdot}7)+f'(0{\cdot}7).\alpha \approx 0.$$

If therefore we solve for α the *exact* linear equation

$$f(0{\cdot}7)+f'(0{\cdot}7).\alpha = 0,$$

it is likely that the number $0{\cdot}7+\alpha$ will be close to the root of the original equation $f(x) = 0$.

We therefore continue the computation as follows. For the function

$$f: x \to x - \cos x$$

the derived function is $\quad f': x \to 1 + \sin x,$

so that $\quad f'(0{\cdot}7) = 1 + \sin(0{\cdot}7) = 1{\cdot}6442.$

We deduce that the linear approximation, for small α, to $f(0{\cdot}7+\alpha)$ is

$$-0{\cdot}0648 + 1{\cdot}6442\alpha.$$

We therefore solve for α the equation

$$-0{\cdot}0648 + 1{\cdot}6442\alpha = 0,$$

obtaining $\quad \alpha = \dfrac{0{\cdot}0648}{1{\cdot}6442} = +0{\cdot}0394.$

Then it is expected that $0{\cdot}7+0{\cdot}0394$, or $0{\cdot}7394$, will be close to the root required.

3.2 It is instructive to follow through the work of the preceding section graphically. Figure 9 shows a magnification of the relevant part of the graph of $y = x - \cos x$, with the tangent to the curve at $(0{\cdot}7, -0{\cdot}0648)$.

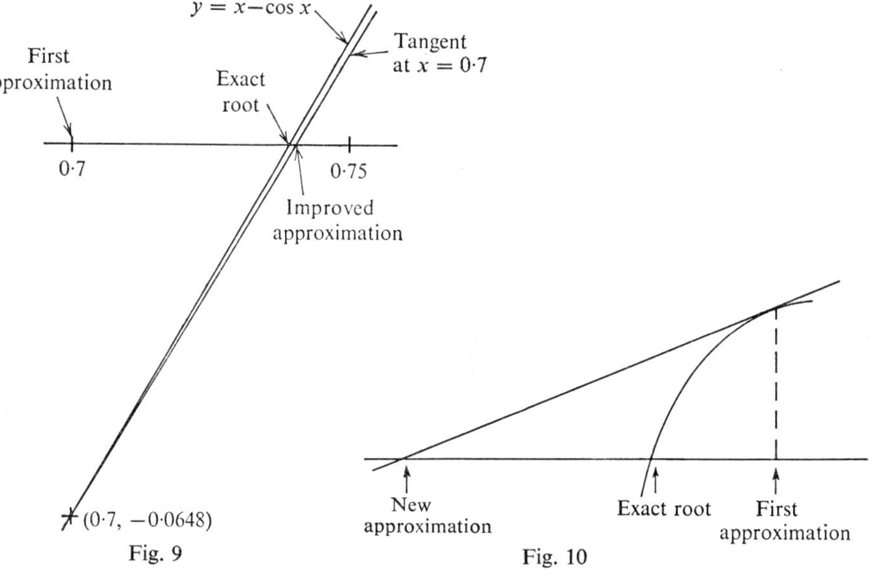

Fig. 9

Fig. 10

We saw in Section 2.3 that the local linear approximation is equivalent to replacing the curve by the tangent, so that the calculation performed above locates the point where this tangent cuts the x-axis. Now the exact root of the equation is represented by the point where the curve itself cuts the axis, and it is intuitively clear that, in general, we have by this method come closer to the root than our original first approximation.

A warning should, however, be given that there are equations for which the method may break down. Figure 10 shows a graph for which the derivative at the point considered is small and the curve is changing direction rapidly. It will be seen that in this example the interval over which the local linear approximation is adequate is too small to include the root we are seeking, and that the point where the tangent cuts the axis is still a long way from the root. In this case, however, the difficulty could have been overcome by choosing a better first approximation, and for most functions the method can be expected to furnish an efficient means of approximating to the root.

3.3 The method of Section 3.1 can be expressed in general terms in the following way. For an equation

$$f(x) = 0,$$

a first approximation to a root is taken, which we shall denote by p_1. The exact root can then be expressed in the form $p_1+\alpha$, where α may be expected to be small. We are seeking the value of α for which

$$f(p_1+\alpha) = 0.$$

Now, for small α,

$$f(p_1+\alpha) \approx f(p_1)+f'(p_1).\alpha$$

so that we may expect to find a closer approximation to the root by finding the value of α for which

$$f(p_1)+f'(p_1).\alpha = 0;$$

that is,

$$\alpha = -\frac{f(p_1)}{f'(p_1)}.$$

This is not the *exact* value of α, since we have replaced $f(p_1+\alpha)$ by its local linear approximation for small α. But in this way we arrive at a new value of x,

$$p_2 = p_1-\frac{f(p_1)}{f'(p_1)},$$

which we may reasonably expect to be very close to the desired root.

3.4 Although we have developed a method of obtaining a close approximation to a root, we have yet to meet the requirement of evaluating the root *to any desired degree of accuracy*. However, the result established in Section 3.3 leads at once to a simple iterative process by which this can be achieved. It is merely necessary to repeat the calculation, replacing the first approximation p_1 by the newly calculated closer approximation p_2, and to find a third number p_3, defined by

$$p_3 = p_2-\frac{f(p_2)}{f'(p_2)},$$

which will normally be closer to the root than p_2. This in turn can be used to calculate p_4, given by

$$p_4 = p_3 - \frac{f(p_3)}{f'(p_3)},$$

and so on. It can be shown that the limit of the sequence, $p_1, p_2, p_3, \ldots$—if such a limit exists—is a root of the equation $f(x) = 0$, so that this root can be found as closely as we please (with the appropriate computational aids) by carrying the calculation sufficiently far.

This procedure is known as the *Newton–Raphson* method (or sometimes merely as *Newton's method*). A process equivalent to this, developed in geometrical terms, was used by Newton to solve the problem of time in a planetary orbit, which leads to equations which cannot be solved by exact methods.

As an example, we may proceed further with the solution of the equation

$$x - \cos x = 0,$$

which was discussed in Section 3.1. Taking p_1 to be 0·7, we found that $p_2 = 0{\cdot}7394$. The calculation now continues as follows. Since

$$f(0{\cdot}7394) = 0{\cdot}7394 - 0{\cdot}7389 = 0{\cdot}0005$$

and
$$f'(0{\cdot}7394) = 1 + 0{\cdot}6738 = 1{\cdot}6738,$$

we calculate
$$p_3 = 0{\cdot}7394 - \frac{0{\cdot}0005}{1{\cdot}6738} = 0{\cdot}7391.$$

Repeating the calculation yet again, we find that

$$p_4 = 0{\cdot}7391.$$

We have now found two consecutive numbers of the sequence

$$p_1, p_2, p_3, \ldots$$

which are the same, and it follows that, unless we change our tables, all succeeding numbers will also have the value 0·7391. This does not imply that the root of the equation $x - \cos x = 0$ is exactly 0·7391, but that this is the closest approximation to the root which can be obtained within the limitations imposed by the tables available. If a more accurate value is required, we must use tables giving the values of the trigonometric functions to more figures.

Example 4. Find an approximate value for the cube root of 10 with a maximum error of 0·001.

The cube root of 10 is the solution of the equation

$$x^3 - 10 = 0.$$

We shall use the Newton–Raphson method, taking for f the function

$$x \to x^3 - 10.$$

The derived function is $f': x \to 3x^2.$

Therefore, if the letter p is used to denote any member of the sequence $p_1, p_2, p_3, \ldots,$ the next member will be

$$p - \frac{p^3 - 10}{3p^2}$$
$$= p - \tfrac{1}{3}p + \frac{10}{3p^2}$$
$$= \frac{1}{3}\left\{2p + \frac{10}{p^2}\right\}.$$

For a first approximation we may take $p_1 = 2$, which is clearly the nearest integer to the root. The calculation then proceeds as follows:

$$p_2 = \frac{1}{3}\left\{2 \times 2 + \frac{10}{2^2}\right\} = 2{\cdot}167,$$
$$p_3 = \frac{1}{3}\left\{2 \times 2{\cdot}167 + \frac{10}{2{\cdot}167^2}\right\} = 2{\cdot}154,$$
$$p_4 = \frac{1}{3}\left\{2 \times 2{\cdot}154 + \frac{10}{2{\cdot}154^2}\right\} = 2{\cdot}154.$$

Since p_3 and p_4 are indistinguishable within the specified degree of accuracy, we need not carry the computation further. We deduce that the cube root of 10 is approximately equal to 2·154.

As a check on this calculation, we observe that

$$2{\cdot}154^3 \approx 9{\cdot}994,$$

and
$$2{\cdot}155^3 \approx 10{\cdot}008$$

so that the cube root lies in fact between 2·154 and 2·155.

Exercise B

1. Estimate graphically the positive root of the equation

$$x = 2 \sin x,$$

and then use the method of Section 3.1 to improve on your estimate.

2. Use the method of Section 3.1 to find approximately the roots of the quadratic equation

$$x^2 - 4{\cdot}1x + 2{\cdot}9 = 0.$$

3. Draw a diagram similar to that of Figure 4 (p. 449) to illustrate Newton's approximation to a root of $f(x) = 0$.

4. Explain how you know that the equation

$$x^3 + x = 1$$

has only one root. Use a graph and a linear approximation to estimate its value. Write a flow diagram for your computation.

5. Find the square root of 5 with a maximum error of 0·001.

6. Find the roots of the equation

$$\cos x = x^2$$

as accurately as your tables permit.

7. Find the roots of

$$1{\cdot}29x^2 + 8{\cdot}36x - 5{\cdot}41 = 0$$

to within 0·05 of the exact values.

8. Draw a diagram to show the generation of the sequence $p_1, p_2, p_3, \ldots$ of Section 3.4 in relation to the graph of $y = f(x)$.

9. The Newton–Raphson method is sometimes modified by using the sequence $p_1, p_2, q_3, q_4, \ldots$ given by

$$p_2 = p_1 - \frac{f(p_1)}{f'(p_1)},$$

$$q_3 = p_2 - \frac{f(p_2)}{f'(p_1)},$$

$$q_4 = q_3 - \frac{f(q_3)}{f'(p_1)}, \quad \text{etc.}$$

Show with the help of a diagram similar to that of Question 8 how this differs from the method described in Section 3.4. What is the advantage and the disadvantage of this modified method? Use it to solve the equation $x = \cos x$, discussed in Section 3.4.

10. Figure 10 (Section 3.2) shows the graph of a function for which the first application of Newton's method does not give an appreciably better approximation to the root of $f(x) = 0$ than the original guess (and might even give a worse one). Describe the circumstances, in terms of the sizes and signs of $f(p)$, $f'(p)$ and $f''(p)$, in which you would expect this situation to arise. In what circumstances is the method certain to give a better approximation to the root than the original guess?

11. Explain with the help of graphs why the sequence $p_2, p_3, p_4, \ldots$ of successive approximations after the first (with the notation of Section 3.4) will in almost all circumstances get steadily closer to the root. Can you suggest any exceptions to this general rule?

12. Show by the method of Section 3.4 that the square root of any positive number k can be found to any desired degree of accuracy from the sequence $p_1, p_2, p_3, \ldots$ where p_{n+1} is the average of p_n and k/p_n.

Write a flow diagram for computing the square root of a positive number k.

13. A semicircular window of radius 1 m is covered with small insects spread uniformly over the surface. Find the median distance of an insect from the diameter of the window, within an accuracy of 1 mm.

(*Hint.* It is easier to use the method to find an angle than a distance in this question.)

4. OTHER LINEAR APPROXIMATIONS

4.1 The method of linear approximation developed in Section 2 is useful when we are concerned with the nature of the function in a small neighbourhood; but, as Example 1 of Section 2.1 shows, it may give a distorted picture outside such a neighbourhood. It is important to realize that this kind of approximation is not always the best for a particular situation; indeed, when we are interested in the behaviour of a function *over a specific interval,* it is almost always true that a more suitable approximation can be obtained by other means.

We shall illustrate this by comparing two different linear approximations over the interval $4 < x < 6$ to the reciprocal function r, defined by the formula

$$r(x) = \frac{1}{x}.$$

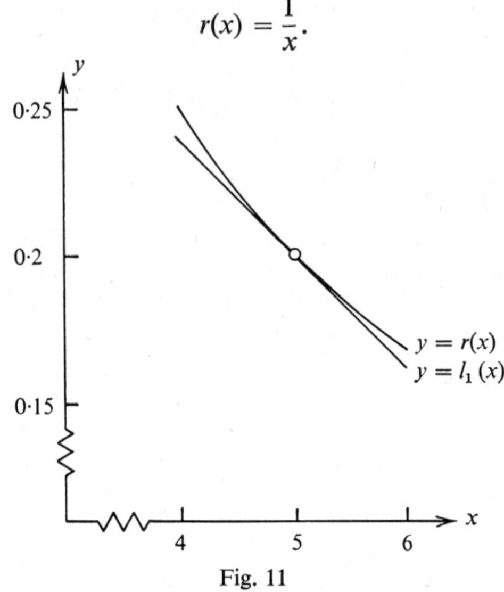

Fig. 11

One possibility would be to use the local linear approximation at $x = 5$, the mid-point of the interval. It was shown in Section 2.3 that this is the function

$$x \to r(5) + r'(5).(x-5).$$

Since

$$r'(x) = -\frac{1}{x^2},$$

this is

$$x \to \tfrac{1}{5} + (-\tfrac{1}{25}).(x-5),$$

or

$$x \to 0{\cdot}4 - 0{\cdot}04x.$$

We denote this function by l_1.

Figure 11 shows the graphs of $y = r(x)$ and $y = l_1(x)$ in the interval $4 < x < 6$. (The y-scale has been much exaggerated in order to show the difference more clearly.) It will be noticed that although the approximation is very close near to $x = 5$, there would be a substantial error involved in using the approximation near the ends of the interval.

It can be shown, however, that an approximation which would be far more suitable for application over the whole interval is afforded by the linear function

$$l_2: x \to 0{\cdot}4079 - 0{\cdot}0410x.$$

(An explanation of the derivation of this function is given in a later chapter of this course.) The value of this function does not coincide with

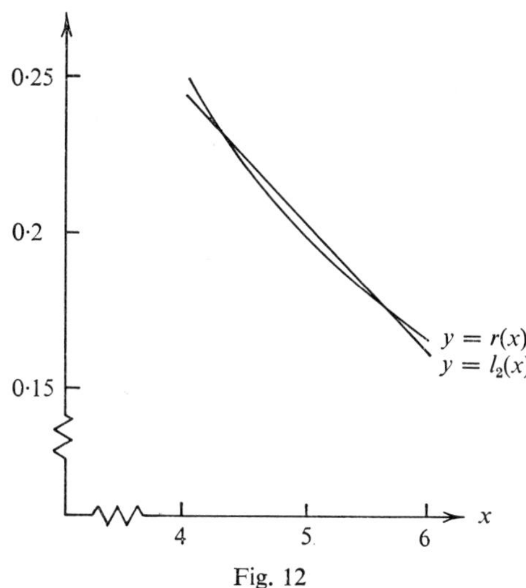

Fig. 12

that of the reciprocal function when $x = 5$; and the errors are sometimes positive and sometimes negative. Over the complete interval from $x = 4$ to $x = 6$ the maximum deviation from the value of r is 0·0061, compared with 0·01 for the function l_1. This linear approximation is illustrated in Figure 12.

A comparison between the two approximations is afforded by the following table:

Value of x	$r(x)$	$l_1(x)$	Difference $r(x)-l_1(x)$	$l_2(x)$	Difference $r(x)-l_2(x)$
4·1	0·2439	0·2360	+0·0079	0·2398	+0·0041
4·3	0·2326	0·2280	+0·0046	0·2316	+0·0010
4·5	0·2222	0·2200	+0·0022	0·2234	−0·0012
4·7	0·2128	0·2120	+0·0008	0·2152	−0·0024
4·9	0·2041	0·2040	+0·0001	0·2070	−0·0029
5·1	0·1961	0·1960	+0·0001	0·1988	−0·0027
5·3	0·1887	0·1880	+0·0007	0·1906	−0·0019
5·5	0·1818	1·1800	+0·0018	0·1824	−0·0006
5·7	0·1754	0·1720	+0·0034	0·1742	+0·0012
5·9	0·1695	0·1640	+0·0055	0·1660	+0·0035

4.2 It is convenient to devise a measure for the closeness of an approximation over an interval, a kind of 'average error over the interval'. An error must, of course, make a similar contribution to this measure whether it is positive or negative; and a simple way of ensuring this is to take the average of the *squares* of the errors, which are always positive. Finally, in order to preserve the correct dimension, we take the square root of this average. This gives the 'root mean square difference': thus to estimate the closeness of the approximation of $l(x)$ to $r(x)$ over an interval, we take the differences between the values of the functions at points $x_1, x_2, \ldots, x_n$ evenly spread over the interval, and calculate

$$\sqrt{\left(\frac{\sum_{i=1}^{i=n}\{r(x_i)-l(x_i)\}^2}{n}\right)}.$$

This measure was introduced in Chapter 12, p. 344, in connection with regression lines. A regression line is in fact the 'best' linear approximation to a set of observations over an interval.

For the approximations l_1, l_2 to the function r over the interval

$$4 < x < 6,$$

the calculation of the root mean square differences is carried out as follows:

Value of x	Squared difference ($\times 10^8$) $\{r(x)-l_1(x)\}^2$	$\{r(x)-l_2(x)\}^2$
4·1	6241	1681
4·3	2116	100
4·5	484	144
4·7	64	576
4·9	1	841
5·1	1	729
5·3	49	361
5·5	324	36
5·7	1156	144
5·9	3025	1225
	10)13461	10)5837
	1346	584

Thus using l_1 and l_2 as approximations for r over the interval

$$\{x: 4 < x < 6\},$$

the root mean square differences are respectively $\sqrt{(1346\times 10^{-8})} = 0{\cdot}0037$ and $\sqrt{(584\times 10^{-8})} = 0{\cdot}0024$. This demonstrates clearly the superiority of l_2 to the local approximation for use over this interval.

Exercise C

1. Draw the graph of the equation $y = \sin x$ over the interval $0 < x < 2$. Find the equation of the tangent at the point (1, 0·84), and draw this tangent on your diagram. Draw also the line which you estimate to be the 'best' linear approximation to the function over the interval $0 < x < 2$. Use the 'root mean square' criterion to compare this approximation with the local linear approximation represented by the tangent.

2. Could you suggest any other criteria than the 'root mean square difference' and the 'maximum deviation over the interval' for comparing the two linear approximations in Section 4? Obtain some numerical assessment of the comparison according to your new criterion.

3. Explain with the help of the graph of $y = r(x)$ how you could get another linear approximation over the interval $4 < x < 6$ by making the maximum deviation of the linear function from the reciprocal function in the interval as small as possible. Prove that this function would be given by the formula

$$l_3(x) = 0{\cdot}4125 - 0{\cdot}0417x,$$

and calculate the root mean square difference for this approximation.

4. The following readings were observed as the result of an experiment:

x	1	3	4	7	9
y	2·3	3·4	4·0	6·0	8·1

There is reason to expect the variables x and y to be associated by a law of the form

$$y = ax + b,$$

and it is decided to find values of a and b which make the sum of the squared differences between the observed and the 'theoretical' values of y as small as possible. Write down the expression which it is desired to minimize, and then use calculus to find the most appropriate values of a and b.

*5. HIGHER DEGREE APPROXIMATIONS

5.1 If the general formula for local linear approximation derived in Section 2.2 is applied to the functions x^2, x^3, x^4, etc., we obtain the following series of results:

$$\text{For small } \alpha \begin{cases} (p+\alpha)^2 \approx p^2 + 2p\alpha, \\ (p+\alpha)^3 \approx p^3 + 3p^2\alpha, \\ (p+\alpha)^4 \approx p^4 + 4p^3\alpha, \end{cases}$$

and so on. Comparing these with the exact forms

$$\begin{cases} (p+\alpha)^2 = p^2 + 2p\alpha + \alpha^2, \\ (p+\alpha)^3 = p^3 + 3p^2\alpha + 3p\alpha^2 + \alpha^3, \\ (p+\alpha)^4 = p^4 + 4p^3\alpha + 6p^2\alpha^2 + 4p\alpha^3 + \alpha^4, \end{cases}$$

and so on, we notice that the linear approximation is derived from the exact expansion by omitting all those terms in which α appears to a power higher than the first. That this is reasonable may be seen from the fact that, if α is a small number, then α^2, α^3, etc., are by comparison smaller still, so that a fair measure of accuracy can be retained by dropping the terms which involve these factors.

If a closer local approximation is required for small α, this could be obtained by retaining from the exact expansions not merely the terms involving the factor α but also those involving α^2. For the function x^2 the local approximation is now the same as the exact expansion; but for the functions x^3 and x^4 we obtain:

$$\text{For small } \alpha, \quad \begin{cases} (p+\alpha)^3 \approx p^3+3p^2\alpha+3p\alpha^2, \\ (p+\alpha)^4 \approx p^4+4p^3\alpha+6p^2\alpha^2. \end{cases}$$

We call these 'local quadratic approximations' for the functions in a neighbourhood of $x = p$.

The form of these approximations is made clearer by displaying the coefficients of 1, α and α^2 in a table:

	Coefficients of:		
Function	1	α	α^2
x^2	p^2	$2p$	1
x^3	p^3	$3p^2$	$3p$
x^4	p^4	$4p^3$	$6p^2$

We have already seen that, for any function f, the coefficients in the first two columns are $f(p)$ and $f'(p)$ respectively. It appears from the table that the coefficients of α^2 are the respective values of $\frac{1}{2}f''(p)$.

Thus for these special functions we have the result:

$$\text{For small } \alpha, \quad f(p+\alpha) \approx f(p)+f'(p).\alpha+\tfrac{1}{2}f''(p).\alpha^2.$$

Verify in the same way that this approximation holds good for the functions x^5, x^6.

5.2 Suppose now that f is any function. We have seen already that the local linear approximation for this function in the neighbourhood of p is

$$x \to f(p)+f'(p).(x-p);$$

and that at $x = p$ this function has value $f(p)$ and derivative $f'(p)$.

The process of generalizing this result should now be plain. For a local quadratic approximation we shall seek a function q defined by a mapping of the form

$$x \to A+B(x-p)+C(x-p)^2$$

and satisfying the conditions that at p this function and the function f should have the same value, first derivative and second derivative; that is,

$$q(p) = f(p), \quad q'(p) = f'(p) \quad \text{and} \quad q''(p) = f''(p).$$

The first and second derived functions of q are

$$q': x \to B + C.2(x-p)$$

and

$$q'': x \to 2C.$$

[Note that the derivative of $(x-p)^2$, or $x^2-2px+p^2$, is $2x-2p$, or $2(x-p)$. This result will appear more elegantly and in more general form in the next chapter.]

It follows that

$$q(p) = A, \quad q'(p) = B \quad \text{and} \quad q''(p) = 2C;$$

but we have specified that, for the local quadratic approximation, we should have

$$q(p) = f(p), \quad q'(p) = f'(p) \quad \text{and} \quad q''(p) = f''(p).$$

Therefore the coefficients A, B, C must be given by

$$A = f(p), \quad B = f'(p) \quad \text{and} \quad C = \tfrac{1}{2}f''(p).$$

That is, the local quadratic approximation to the function f at p is

$$q: x \to f(p) + f'(p).(x-p) + \tfrac{1}{2}f''(p).(x-p)^2.$$

Since the image of $p+\alpha$ under this function is

$$q(p+\alpha) = f(p) + f'(p).\alpha + \tfrac{1}{2}f''(p).\alpha^2,$$

this result leads at once to the approximation given at the end of Section 5.1.

Example 5. Obtain a quadratic approximation for $\cos\alpha$ when α is small.

If f is cos, the first and second derived functions are $-\sin$ and $-\cos$ respectively. Therefore

$$f(0) = \cos 0 = 1, \quad f'(0) = -\sin 0 = 0, \quad f''(0) = -\cos 0 = -1,$$

so that, for small α,

$$\cos\alpha \approx 1 + 0.\alpha + \tfrac{1}{2}.(-1).\alpha^2$$
$$= 1 - \tfrac{1}{2}\alpha^2.$$

5.3 The extension to still more refined approximations can now be made. For example, the cubic approximation to f at p is that, for small α,

$$f(p+\alpha) \approx f(p) + f'(p).\alpha + \frac{f''(p)}{2!}.\alpha^2 + \frac{f'''(p)}{3!}.\alpha^3.$$

The general form for these approximations is

$$f(p+\alpha) \approx f(p) + f'(p).\alpha + \frac{f''(p)}{2!}\alpha^2 + \dots + \frac{f^{(n)}(p)}{n!}.\alpha^n;$$

or, more concisely,

$$f(p+\alpha) \approx \sum_{r=0}^{n} \frac{f^{(r)}(p)}{r!}\alpha^r.$$

[We define $f^{(0)}(p)$ as $f(p)$, and $0!$ as 1.]

This is known as *Taylor's approximation.* It is easily derived by a generalization of the argument given for the quadratic approximation in Section 5.2.

5.4 Because these higher degree approximations take account not merely of the local scale factor, but also of the rate at which this scale factor varies, the quadratic, cubic, etc. approximations are useful over a wider range of values than the linear approximation.

We shall illustrate this by means of the reciprocal function r, for which the derived functions are

$$r': x \to -1/x^2,$$

$$r'': x \to +2/x^3,$$

$$r''': x \to -6/x^4, \text{ etc.}$$

Taking approximations in neighbourhoods of 5, and observing that $r(5) = 0{\cdot}2$, $r'(5) = -0{\cdot}04$, $r''(5) = 0{\cdot}016$, $r'''(5) = -0{\cdot}0096$, we obtain the following series of approximations for $1/(5+\alpha)$:

Linear $0{\cdot}2-0{\cdot}04\alpha.$

Quadratic $0{\cdot}2-0{\cdot}04\alpha+0{\cdot}008\alpha^2.$

Cubic $0{\cdot}2-0{\cdot}04\alpha+0{\cdot}008\alpha^2-0{\cdot}0016\alpha^3.$

The quality of the various approximations is demonstrated by the following table of values:

Value of α	$r(\alpha)$	Linear approx.	Diff.	Quadratic approx.	Diff.	Cubic approx.	Diff.
$-1{\cdot}0$	0·2500	0·2400	+0·0100	0·2480	+0·0020	0·2496	+0·0004
$-0{\cdot}5$	0·2222	0·2200	+0·0022	0·2220	+0·0002	0·2222	+0·0000
0	0·2000	0·2000	0	0·2000	0	0·2000	0
$+0{\cdot}5$	0·1818	0·1800	+0·0018	0·1820	−0·0002	0·1818	+0·0000
$+1{\cdot}0$	0·1667	0·1600	+0·0067	0·1680	−0·0013	0·1664	+0·0003

It is, however, necessary to repeat the warning given in Section 3. The quadratic and cubic approximations obtained are still *local* approximations, appropriate for use in neighbourhoods of $x = 5$. If the 'best' approximation of the second or third degree is required for use over the interval $\{x: 4 < x < 6\}$, the quadratic and cubic approximations given above will not serve this purpose.

Exercise D

1. Find a quadratic function which approximates to the function $x \to x^3$ around $x = 1$.

Illustrate your answer with a graph.

2. Find a cubic approximation for $\sqrt{(1+\alpha)}$, where α is small. Find a similar approximation for $\sqrt{(4+\beta)}$, where β is small; and then show how this answer could in fact have been derived from the first one.

3. Find a quadratic approximation for $\cos(\frac{1}{3}\pi+\alpha)$ for small α, and use it to estimate the value of $\cos 61{\cdot}4^\circ$ to five places of decimals.

4. Find a quadratic approximation for $1/(10+\alpha)^2$, where α is small. Find in as simple a form as you can an exact expression for the error involved in the approximation.

5. Obtain a cubic approximation for $\sin\alpha$ when α is small. Show on a graph the comparison between the exact values and those given by the approximation, and estimate over what range of values of α the approximation is within 5% of the exact value.

6. Using the quadratic approximation for $f(p_1+\alpha)$, show that, when the method of Section 3.3 is applied to improve on an estimate, p_1, for the root of $f(x) = 0$, the order of magnitude of the residual error in the value of α is likely to be about

$$\frac{f''(p_1).\{f(p_1)\}^2}{2\{f'(p_1)\}^3}.$$

Does this fit in with your conclusions of Question 10 of Exercise B, and if so how?

Apply the method to the solution of the equation

$$x^3+4x = 40,$$

using 3 as a first estimate and giving your answer to as many figures as you consider warranted by the method.

7. Write out in detail the argument leading to the cubic approximation

$$f(p+\alpha) \approx f(p)+f'(p).\alpha+\frac{f''(p)}{2!}\alpha^2+\frac{f'''(p)}{3!}\alpha^3$$

given in Section 5.3.

Summary.

Local linear approximation

$$f(p+\alpha) \approx f(p)+f'(p).\alpha \quad \text{for small } \alpha;$$

or $$f(x) \approx f(p)+f'(p).(x-p) \quad \text{for values of } x \text{ near to } p;$$

or $$\delta y \approx \frac{dy}{dx}\delta x \quad \text{for small } \delta x.$$

Newton–Raphson method

If p is an approximation to a root of $f(x) = 0$, then normally $p-\dfrac{f(p)}{f'(p)}$ is a better approximation.

The limit of a sequence defined by

$$p_{n+1} = p_n - \frac{f(p_n)}{f'(p_n)}$$

(when this limit exists) is a root of $f(x) = 0$.

Higher degree approximations (*Taylor approximations*)

Quadratic: $f(p+\alpha) \approx f(p)+f'(p).\alpha+\frac{1}{2}f''(p).\alpha^2.$

Cubic: $f(p+\alpha) \approx f(p)+f'(p).\alpha+\frac{1}{2}f''(p).\alpha^2+\frac{1}{6}f'''(p).\alpha^3.$

In general $f(p+\alpha) \approx \sum_{r=0}^{n} \frac{f^{(r)}(p)}{r!}\alpha^r$ for small α.

17

THE TECHNIQUE OF DIFFERENTIATION

1. COMPOSITE FUNCTIONS

In this chapter, we consider methods of dealing with more complicated functions than we have met hitherto, and in particular *composite functions* and *products of functions.* These methods will in fact enable us to differentiate almost any function which we can break down into simpler parts, and Exercise A suggests how we should proceed.

Exercise A

1. Differentiate the functions named, and express the derived functions in a natural form. For example,

$$x \to (x+2)^3$$

$$f(x) = x^3+6x^2+12x+8 \Rightarrow f'(x) = 3x^2+12x+12 = 3(x+2)^2;$$

this is the natural form of the answer, because of its close relationship to the form in which f is given.

(*a*) $x \to (x-1)^2$; (*b*) $x \to (3x+2)^2$; (*c*) $x \to (x-3)^3$;

(*d*) $x \to (2x+5)^3$; (*e*) $x \to (x^2+3)^2$; (*f*) $x \to (2x^2-1)^3$.

2. Differentiate from first principles—that is, find

$$\lim_{b\to a} \frac{f(b)-f(a)}{b-a}:$$

(*a*) $x \to \dfrac{1}{x+3}$; (*b*) $x \to \dfrac{1}{2x-1}$; (*c*) $x \to \dfrac{1}{x^2+1}$;

(*d*) $x \to \sin 2x$; (*e*) $x \to \sqrt{(3x+1)}$; (*f*) $x \to \sqrt{(1-x^2)}$.

3. From your experience of Questions 1 and 2, *write down* what you think will be the derived function of:

(*a*) $x \to (2x-1)^3$; (*b*) $x \to (4x+1)^4$; (*c*) $x \to \dfrac{1}{(x+3)^2}$;

(*d*) $x \to \dfrac{1}{(x^2+1)^2}$; (*e*) $x \to \sin 4x$; (*f*) $x \to \sin x^2$;

(*g*) $x \to \cos(3x+\pi)$; (*h*) $x \to (\sin x)^2$; (*i*) $x \to (\cos 3x)^2$.

4. Write down flow diagrams which show how the functions of Questions 1–3 are built up from simpler functions. For example, $x \to \sin(x^2-1)$ may be expressed by the flow diagram:

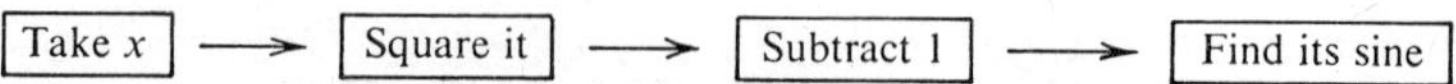

5. If $h(x) = ax+b$, and $k(x) = px+q$, what is the scale factor of the function kh?

It was shown in the previous chapter that near $x = a$, $f(x)$ is approximately equal to $f_1(x)$, where f_1 is a linear function. What is the scale factor of f_1?

Deduce the approximate scale factor of gf, if $f(a) = b$ and $g(b) = c$.

6. By considering the graphs of $y = x^2$, $y = x^3$, $y = 1/x$, $y = \sin x$, and transforming them by translations and stretches where necessary, confirm the answers to Question 1 (*a*)–(*d*), and Question 2 (*a*), (*b*), (*d*).

(*Hint.* If the graph G is transformed into G_1 by a stretch of factor $\frac{1}{2}$ parallel to Ox, so that $y = f(x)$ is transformed into $y = f(2x)$, how is the gradient of G_1 at $\frac{1}{2}a$ related to the gradient of G at a?)

2. COMPOSITE FUNCTIONS—THE CHAIN RULE

Example 1. Differentiate the function $p: x \to (2x+5)^3$.

This is a composite function, described by the flow diagram

Take x → Double it → Add 5 → Cube it

and therefore by the mapping diagram of Figure 1, drawn to illustrate the

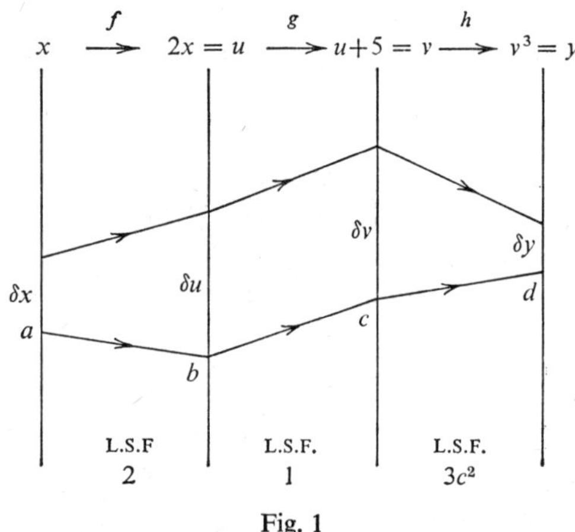

Fig. 1

behaviour of the function near $x = a$. Notice that an (x, y) diagram is bound to obscure the composition of the function, though in this case the method of Exercise A, Question 6 could be applied.

The average scale factor of $p = hgf$ is $\delta y/\delta x$. This is equal to

$$\frac{\delta y}{\delta v}\times\frac{\delta v}{\delta u}\times\frac{\delta u}{\delta x},$$

that is to the *product* of the average scale factors of h, g, f respectively.

This suggests, correctly, that the local scale factor dy/dx of p will be equal to

$$\frac{dy}{dv}\times\frac{dv}{du}\times\frac{du}{dx},$$

that is to the *product* of the local scale factors of h, g, and f. We cannot prove this by 'cancelling' du and dv, as we could cancel δu and δv to find the average scale factor, because du and dv have been given no meaning except in expressions like dy/dv and du/dx. The proof is too difficult for this course, but it follows from the theorem that the limit of a product is equal to the product of the limits; the principal difficulty is to ensure that δu, δv do not vanish during the limiting process.

The derivative may therefore be read off as

$$\frac{dy}{dv}\times\frac{dv}{du}\times\frac{du}{dx},$$

or as $h'(c).g'(b).f'(a)$. In this case (see Figure 1) it is $3c^2.1.2 = 6c^2$; since $c = b+5 = 2a+5$, it follows that the derivative $p'(a)$ is $6(2a+5)^2$, and that the derived function is $p'\colon x \rightarrow 6(2x+5)^2$.

For linear functions $f_1\colon x \rightarrow a_1x+b_1$ and $f_2\colon x \rightarrow a_2x+b_2$, the scale factor of f_2f_1 is a_2a_1. Since Taylor's approximation gives

$$f(x+h) \approx f'(h).x+f(h),$$

for small x, we can also explain the Chain Rule in the way suggested by Exercise A, Question 5.

2.1 The Chain Rule. The Chain Rule, for differentiating composite functions, can now be stated as follows:

> The local scale factor of a composite mapping is equal to the product of the local scale factors of the component mappings.

This rule applies to any number of component mappings, but for two mappings it can be expressed in either of the two equivalent forms (provided that suitable derivatives exist):

(i) If $h = gf$ and $f(a) = b$, then $h'(a) = g'(b).f'(a)$.

(ii) If $x \xrightarrow{f} u \xrightarrow{g} y$, then

$$\frac{dy}{dx} = \frac{dy}{du}\times\frac{du}{dx}.$$

Example 2 shows a convenient way of presenting these equivalent techniques.

Example 2. Differentiate (*a*) $x \to \sin(x^2)$; (*b*) $x \to (\sin x)^2$.†

A flow diagram shows that (*a*) applies the square function and the sine function in that order, and (*b*) in the opposite order. We use (*a*) to illustrate form (i), and (*b*) to illustrate form (ii).

(*a*) The scale factor of the composite mapping, by the Chain Rule, is $g'(b).f'(a) = \cos b.2a = 2a\cos(a^2)$ (see Figure 2), so that the derived function h' is $x \to 2x\cos(x^2)$.

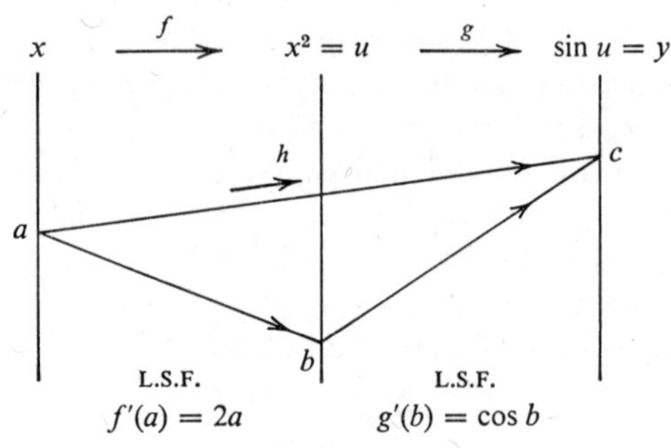

Fig. 2

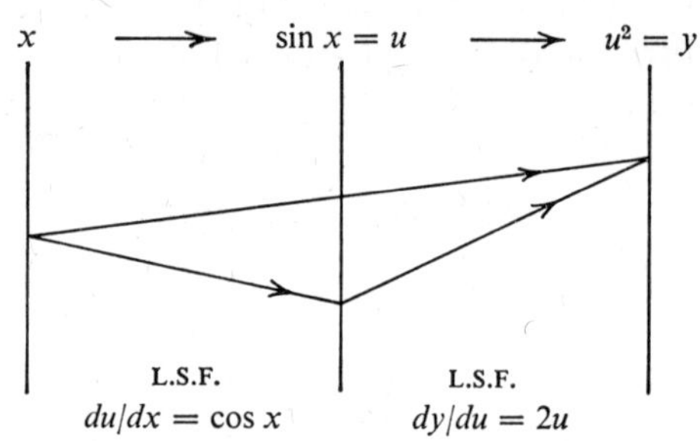

Fig. 3

(*b*) The scale factor of the composite mapping, by the Chain Rule, is

$$\frac{dy}{du}\times\frac{du}{dx} = 2u.\cos x = 2\sin x.\cos x$$

(see Figure 3) and this is the form required for the derived function.

It is possible to do much of this mentally, if we begin with the *last* function to be applied. For (*a*), think: 'Differentiate *sin* to get *cos* (x^2); now differentiate the *square* to get *twice* x; answer, *cos* $(x^2).2x$.'

† Ambiguity and the use of brackets are avoided if we follow the convention of writing $\sin(x^2)$ as $\sin x^2$ and $(\sin x)^2$ as $\sin^2 x$.

Exercise B

1. Find the derivative at a for each of the following functions, using the notation of Example 2(a).

(a) $x \to (2x+3)^4$; (b) $x \to (x^2-1)^5$;

(c) $x \to \dfrac{1}{2x+1}$; (d) $x \to \dfrac{1}{2x^2+5x+1}$;

(e) $x \to \sqrt{(3-2x)}$; (f) $x \to (2x^2+3)^{-\frac{1}{2}}$;

(g) $x \to \sin 4x$; (h) $x \to \sin^3 \frac{1}{2}x$ (that is, $(\sin \frac{1}{2}x)^3$).

2. Find the derived function of each of the following functions, using the notation of Example 2(b):

(a) $x \to (x^2-2x+4)^3$; (b) $x \to (1-2x^3)^4$;

(c) $x \to (1+x^2)^{-1}$; (d) $x \to (1-x^2)^{\frac{1}{2}}$;

(e) $x \to \sqrt{\left(\dfrac{1}{1-x^2}\right)}$; ($f$) $x \to \sin^4 x$;

(g) $x \to \cos^2 3x$; (h) $x \to \sin^2 x + \cos^2 x$;

(i) $x \to (\cos x + \sin x)^3$.

3. Differentiate:

(a) $x \to \left(x-\dfrac{1}{x}\right)^4$; ($b$) $x \to \dfrac{1}{x(x+1)}$;

(c) $x \to (x^3-1)^{\frac{1}{3}}$; ($d$) $x \to \sec x$;

(e) $x \to \sec^2 x$; (f) $x \to \sqrt{(\sec^2 x - 1)}$.

Note: $\sec x$ is defined as $1/(\cos x)$; $\sec^2 x - \tan^2 x = 1$. What light does this relation shed on part (f)?

4. Use the Newton–Raphson method to find a root of $\sin 3x - 2x = 0$ (where x is in radian measure).

(*Hint.* Take 0·5 as your first approximation and make one correction.)

5. Find the x-coordinates of the points of $y = \sin^2 x$ for which $dy/dx = 0$, and find the corresponding values of y. Hence sketch the curve.

6. Find the point of

$$y = \frac{1}{(x-1)(x-2)}$$

for which the gradient is zero. Can it be more easily found by another method? Sketch the curve.

3. PRODUCTS OF FUNCTIONS— THE PRODUCT RULE

The reader will probably remember the rule for the error in a product caused by small errors in the factors. (See Book T, p. 102.) It was convenient to use the idea of a *fractional change* or *fractional error* $\delta a/a$ for the purpose.

It is natural to try to build up from this some sort of rule for differentiating a product, and Exercise C suggests a possible line of development.

We shall use the notation $f.g: x \to f(x).g(x)$; $f.g$ must be clearly distinguished from $fg: x \to f(g(x))$.

Exercise C

1. A car was said to travel at 14 m/s for 15 s, and these figures were subject to errors of $\pm 1\%$, $\pm 3\%$ respectively. Show that an estimate of the distance gone is subject to an error of approximately $\pm 4\%$.

2. If in Question 1 both measurements were given correct to two significant figures, what would be the greatest and least distances the car could actually have covered?

3. If the speed of the car in Question 1 was u m/s and the time t s, and these were subject to fractional errors up to $\delta u/u$ and $\delta t/t$, what would be the greatest possible fractional error in ut? (You may assume that δu and δt are positive.)

Draw a diagram to illustrate your result, in which u, t are the sides of a rectangle.

4. Deduce from Question 3 the change in the product $y.z$ if y and z are increased by δy, δz respectively. If y, z are functions of x, can you suggest a formula for $\dfrac{d}{dx}(y.z)$?

5. Write down flow diagrams for the functions given below. For example, $x \to x^2 \cos x$ may be expressed by

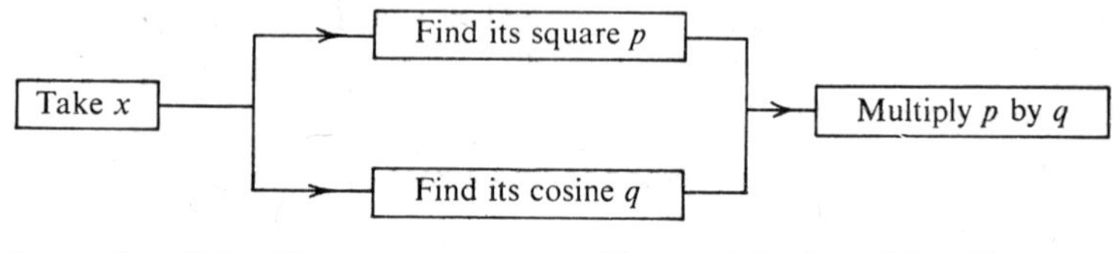

(*a*) $x \to (x+1)(x+2)$;

(*b*) $x \to (x^2-2x+4)(x+2)$;

(*c*) $x \to x \sin x$;

(*d*) $x \to \dfrac{x}{x+1}$;

(*e*) $x \to \dfrac{x}{(x+1)(x+2)}$;

(*f*) $x \to \dfrac{\sin x}{\cos x}$.

What differences are there between the flow diagrams of this question and those of Question 4 of Exercise A?

6. Use your suggested rule from Question 4 to differentiate the functions of Question 5, and check the answers to parts (*a*), (*b*) and (*d*) by other means.

7. Can you produce a function which you cannot differentiate, by using the operations of composition, addition and multiplication, on simpler functions which you can differentiate?

3.1 The product rule.

Example 3. Differentiate $x^2 \sin x$.

(*a*) Let $u = x^2$ and $v = \sin x$. We draw two perpendicular lines Ou and Ov, and use them, as in Figure 4, to represent the mappings $f\colon x \to u$ and $g\colon x \to v$. Then the product $f.g$ is represented by mapping x to the area of the rectangle $OPQR$.

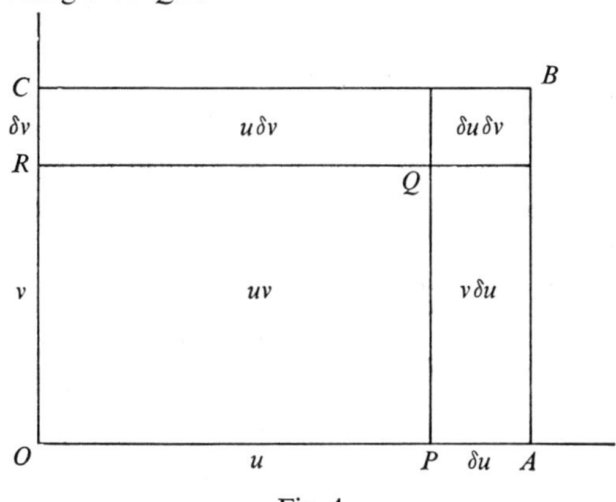

Fig. 4

When x is increased by δx, and hence u is increased by δu and v by δv, the area $OPQR$ is increased by $PABCRQ$, that is, by

$$u\,\delta v + v\,\delta u + \delta u\,\delta v;$$

so that the average scale factor of the mapping of x to the area is

$$u.\frac{\delta v}{\delta x} + v.\frac{\delta u}{\delta x} + \frac{\delta u}{\delta x}.\frac{\delta v}{\delta x}.\delta x.$$

When δx tends to O, the local scale factor is then

$$u.\frac{dv}{dx} + v.\frac{du}{dx}.$$

In this example, since

$$\frac{du}{dx} = 2x \quad \text{and} \quad \frac{dv}{dx} = \cos x,$$

the derived function is $x^2 \cos x + 2x \sin x$.

(*b*) It is interesting to approach this 'from first principles', finding directly the limit

$$\lim_{b\to a}\left(\frac{b^2 \sin b - a^2 \sin a}{b-a}\right).$$

There is no immediately obvious line of attack but since the fraction

$$\frac{\sin b - \sin a}{b-a},$$

whose limit is cos a, is familiar, we introduce two terms whose sum is zero, to make the limit

$$\lim_{b\to a}\left(\frac{b^2\sin b-b^2\sin a}{b-a}+\frac{b^2\sin a-a^2\sin a}{b-a}\right)$$

$$=\lim_{b\to a}\left(b^2.\frac{\sin b-\sin a}{b-a}+\frac{b^2-a^2}{b-a}.\sin a\right)$$

$$=a^2.\cos a+2a.\sin a.$$

3.2 Statement of the rule. The working in Example 3 above is perfectly general, and can immediately be applied to the product of any differentiable functions u, v. The result is then as follows:

If $y = u.v$, then

$$\mathbf{\frac{dy}{dx}=\frac{d}{dx}(u.v)=u\frac{dv}{dx}+v\frac{du}{dx}.}$$

Alternatively, if $h=f.g$, $h'(a)=f(a).g'(a)+f'(a).g(a)$, or abbreviating,

$$\mathbf{h'=f.g'+f'.g.}$$

We may express the result in words as follows:

> To differentiate a product, take the sum of all the terms obtained by differentiating one factor only, leaving the other factors unchanged.

3.3 Extension of the Product Rule. The Product Rule extends readily to functions with three (or more) factors to give:

If $y = u.v.w$, then

$$\frac{dy}{dx}=vw\frac{du}{dx}+uw\frac{dv}{dx}+uv\frac{dw}{dx}.$$

Alternatively, this result can be written

$$\frac{1}{y}\frac{dy}{dx}=\frac{1}{u}\frac{du}{dx}+\frac{1}{v}\frac{dv}{dx}+\frac{1}{w}\frac{dw}{dx}.$$

Example 4. Differentiate $x.\cos 2x$.

If $u=x$, and $v=\cos 2x$, $du/dx=1$ and $dv/dx=-2\sin 2x$ (by the Chain Rule). So

$$\frac{dy}{dx}=u.\frac{dv}{dx}+v.\frac{du}{dx}=x.(-2\sin 2x)+\cos 2x.(1)$$

$$=\cos 2x-2x.\sin 2x.$$

Example 5. Differentiate $\dfrac{\sin x}{2x+3}$.

Let $u=\sin x$ and $v=\dfrac{1}{2x+3}$.

Then $\dfrac{du}{dx} = \cos x$ and $\dfrac{dv}{dx} = \dfrac{-2}{(2x+3)^2}$ (Chain Rule),

So $$\frac{dy}{dx} = u.\frac{dv}{dx}+v.\frac{du}{dx} = \sin x.\frac{-2}{(2x+3)^2}+\frac{1}{2x+3}.\cos x$$

$$= \frac{(2x+3)\cos x-2\sin x}{(2x+3)^2}.$$

3.4 The Quotient Rule. Example 5 shows that a quotient may always be treated as a product, and that a separate 'Quotient Rule' is unnecessary.

It is, however, often more convenient to use the result

$$\mathbf{\frac{d}{dx}\left(\frac{u}{v}\right) = \frac{v.\frac{du}{dx}-u.\frac{dv}{dx}}{v^2}}.$$

Notice how, in Example 5, we used the Chain Rule to differentiate $1/(2x+3)$. Similarly, when we differentiate $1/v$, the result will be

$$-(1/v^2).(dv/dx).$$

This helps us to remember the order of the terms in the expression above; for differentiating u gives the positive term $v.(du/dx)$, and differentiating $1/v$ gives the negative term.

Thus, by the Product Rule, we may say

$$\frac{d}{dx}\left(u.\frac{1}{v}\right) = u\left(-\frac{1}{v^2}\right)\frac{dv}{dx}+\frac{1}{v}.\frac{du}{dx},$$

which can immediately be written in the form above.

Example 5 (*continued*). It is now more convenient to write $u = \sin x$, $v = 2x+3$, and to quote

$$\frac{d}{dx}\left(\frac{u}{v}\right) = \frac{v.\frac{du}{dx}-u.\frac{dv}{dx}}{v^2} = \frac{(2x+3)\cos x-2\sin x}{(2x+3)^2}.$$

Example 6. Differentiate

$$\tan x = \frac{\sin x}{\cos x}.$$

If we write $u = \sin x$, $v = \cos x$,

$$\frac{d}{dx}(\tan x) = \frac{\cos x.\cos x-\sin x.(-\sin x)}{\cos^2 x} = \frac{1}{\cos^2 x}$$

$$= \sec^2 x.$$

This is an important result.

Exercise D

1. Find the derivatives of the following functions:

(*a*) $x \to x(x^2+1)$; (*b*) $x \to (2x-1)^2(3x+2)$;
(*c*) $x \to (x-2)^3(x+2)^4$; (*d*) $x \to x^2 \cos x$;
(*e*) $x \to x.\sin^2 x$; (*f*) $x \to x\sqrt{(a^2-x^2)}$;
(*g*) $x \to \dfrac{\sin x}{x}$; (*h*) $x \to \dfrac{x}{1+x}$;
(*i*) $x \to \dfrac{x}{x^2+c^2}$.

2. Find the derivatives of the following functions:

(*a*) $x \to (x^3-a^3)(x^3+a^3)$; (*b*) $x \to x^5(a-x)^7$;
(*c*) $x \to \sin^5 x.\cos^7 x$; (*d*) $x \to x \sin 3x$;
(*e*) $x \to (x^2-2)\sin x + 2x \cos x$; (*f*) $x \to x^2\sqrt{(2x+3)}$;
(*g*) $x \to \dfrac{x}{\sin x}$; (*h*) $x \to \dfrac{x}{\sqrt{(b^2+x^2)}}$;
(*i*) $x \to x(x-1)(x-2)(x-3)$.

3. Find the derivatives of the following functions:

(*a*) $x \to \sin x.\sec x$; (*b*) $x \to \dfrac{1-\sin^2 x}{1-x^2}$;
(*c*) $x \to \dfrac{x}{(1+x^2)^3}$; (*d*) $x \to \dfrac{x}{(1-x^2)^{\frac{3}{2}}}$;
(*e*) $x \to \dfrac{\sqrt{(b-x)}}{\sqrt{(b+x)}}$; (*f*) $x \to \cos 3x.\cos x + \sin 3x.\sin x$;
(*g*) $x \to x^p(a-x)^q$; (*h*) $x \to \sin^p x.\cos^q x$.

4. Find the maxima and minima (if any) of the following functions, and sketch their graphs:

(*a*) $x \to \dfrac{x}{1+x^2}$; (*b*) $x \to \dfrac{x}{x^2-1}$; (*c*) $x \to \dfrac{x-1}{x^2(x-2)}$.

5. Find the smallest positive number x for which $x.\cos 2x$ is a maximum (use the Newton–Raphson method, taking two corrections to the first approximation, 0·5).

6. By using the product rule for $\mathbf{u}.\mathbf{v}^{-n}$, prove the more general form of the quotient rule:

$$\frac{d}{dx}\left(\frac{u}{v^n}\right) = \frac{v.\dfrac{du}{dx} - nu.\dfrac{dv}{dx}}{v^{n+1}}.$$

(*Hint.* First differentiate, say, $\dfrac{3x+2}{(2x+1)^4}$ by this method, and then think how it will work in the general case.)

Confirm your answers to Question 2(*h*), and Question 3(*c*), (*d*), (*e*) by using suitable values of n.

***7.** Use the method of Example 3(*b*) to find the derived function of $f.g$ and of f/g.

4. FUNCTIONS DEFINED INDIRECTLY

4.1 Inverse functions.

Example 7. Use the scale factor of the square function to differentiate the square root function.

We restrict the domain of the square function to non-negative numbers. Since the scale factor for the mapping f at a is $2a$, the scale factor for f^{-1} is, as suggested by Figure 5, $1/2a$. Now, since $a = \sqrt{p}$, the derivative of f^{-1} at p is $1/(2\sqrt{p})$.

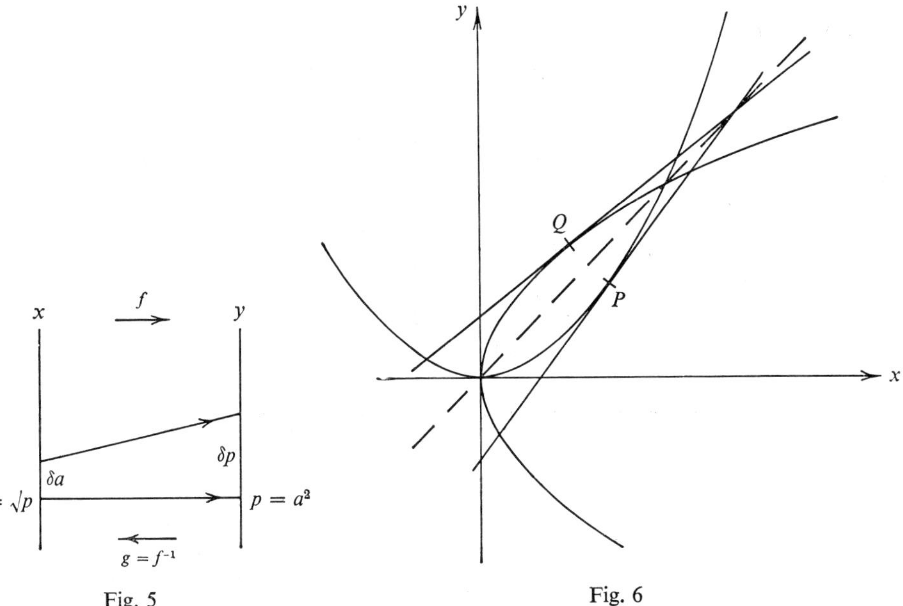

Fig. 5

Fig. 6

Notice that if g is f^{-1}, the square root function, gf must be the identity function, whose derivative is everywhere 1. By the chain rule, then, $g'(p).f'(a) = 1$, which justifies the intuitive suggestion that

$$g'(p) = \frac{1}{f'(a)}$$

suggested by the figure. Notice also (see Figure 6) that since the tangent at Q on the (x, y) graph is the image under reflection in $x = y$ of the tangent at P, the product of their gradients must be 1. This time, the Chain Rule gives

$$\frac{dx}{dy}\cdot\frac{dy}{dx} = \frac{dx}{dx} = 1,$$

not, of course, by cancelling.

Example 8. Differentiate $\tan^{-1} x$, where the domain of tan is restricted to $\{x: -\frac{1}{2}\pi < x < +\frac{1}{2}\pi\}$.

We first sketch Figure 7. Now, since the scale factor of tan at a is $\sec^2 a$ (see Example 6), the scale factor of $\tan^{-1}$ as above must be

$$\frac{1}{\sec^2 a} = \frac{1}{1+\tan^2 a} = \frac{1}{1+b^2}.$$

The derived function is therefore

$$x \to \frac{1}{1+x^2}.$$

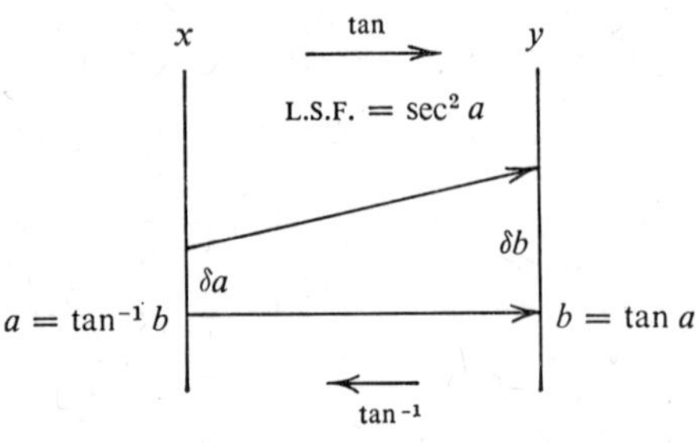

Fig. 7

As an example of this, notice that when $a = \frac{1}{4}\pi$, $b = 1$; the scale factors are

$$\sec^2 \frac{\pi}{4} = 2 \quad \text{and} \quad \frac{1}{1+1^2} = \frac{1}{2}$$

respectively. Similarly, when $a = b = 0$, the scale factors are both 1. What approximations, to $\tan x$ and $\tan^{-1} x$ for small x, do we obtain from these results?

This technique can be applied to any inverse functions, such as $\sin^{-1}$ and $\sqrt[3]{\ }$; the inverse trigonometrical functions will come into their own when we need to reverse the process of differentiation later in the book, though the need to differentiate them is not at present at all obvious.

4.2 Functions defined by a parameter. Some useful functions are easier to handle parametrically—that is, with x and y expressed in terms of a *parameter*, t, say.

Example 9. The *cycloid* illustrated in Figure 8 may be defined as the locus of a point on the rim of a wheel of radius a rolling along the line Ox, though it has a number of other applications. Its equation cannot be expressed conveniently in terms of x and y, but it can be written down usefully in the form $x = a(t - \sin t)$, $y = a(1 - \cos t)$.

Figure 9 suggests, correctly, that

$$\frac{dy}{dx} = \frac{dy}{dt} \div \frac{dx}{dt}.$$

Since $$\frac{dx}{dt} = a(1-\cos t) \quad \text{and} \quad \frac{dy}{dt} = a \sin t,$$

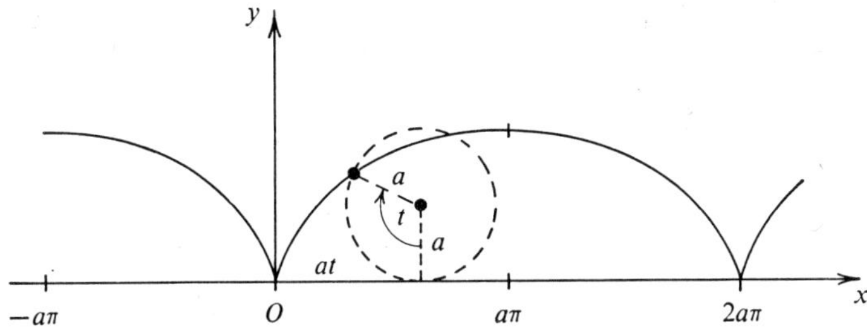

Fig. 8

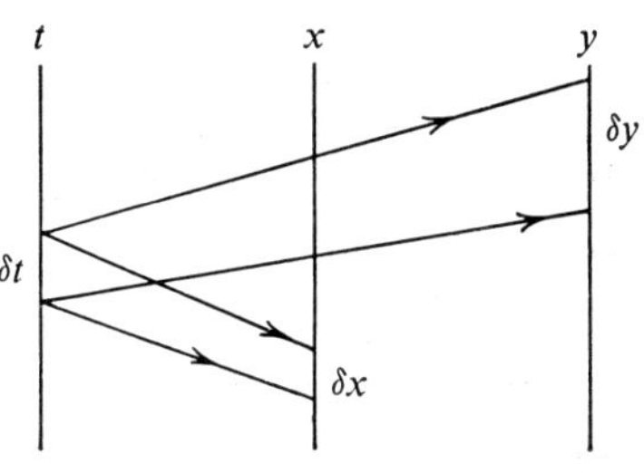

Fig. 9

it follows that $$\frac{dy}{dx} = \frac{\sin t}{1-\cos t} = \frac{2 \sin \frac{1}{2}t \cos \frac{1}{2}t}{2 \sin^2 \frac{1}{2}t} = \cot \tfrac{1}{2}t,$$

the gradient at the point t.

4.3 Other types of indirectly defined functions. There are a number of occasions when it is interesting and useful to differentiate such expressions as xy, or even $x^2(dy/dx)$. As an illustration, we re-consider Example 5, and also prove the Quotient Rule by another method.

Example 5 (*concluded*). Differentiate

$$\frac{\sin x}{2x+3}.$$

If we put $y = \sin x/(2x+3)$, then this relation can be rewritten in the form $(2x+3)y = \sin x$. That is to say, if y is the image of x under the function $x \rightarrow \sin x/(2x+3)$ at every point where it is defined, the two sides of this equation are identical functions of x. Their derivatives must therefore have the same value.

By the Product Rule

$$\frac{d}{dx}(u.y) = u.\frac{dy}{dx}+y.\frac{du}{dx}.$$

Here, setting $u = 2x+3$, it follows that

$$(2x+3)\frac{dy}{dx}+2y = \cos x, \quad \text{whence} \quad \frac{dy}{dx} = \frac{(2x+3)\cos x-2\sin x}{(2x+3)^2}.$$

Example 10. Differentiate u/v.

If $y.v = u$, as above,

$$y.\frac{dv}{dx}+v.\frac{dy}{dx} = \frac{du}{dx};$$

so, since $y = u/v$, it follows that

$$\frac{dy}{dx} = \frac{v.\frac{du}{dx}-u.\frac{dv}{dx}}{v^2}.$$

Exercise E

1. Use the method of Example 7 to differentiate $x^{\frac{1}{3}}$.

2. Use the method of Example 8 to show that

$$\frac{d}{dx}(\sin^{-1} x) = \frac{1}{\sqrt{(1-x^2)}}.$$

3. Find the inverse function g of

$$f: x \to \frac{x^3+5}{2},$$

and the derived functions f' and g'. If $f(a) = b$, check that $f'(a).g'(b) = 1$.

4. Repeat Question 3 for the function

$$\frac{p}{q-2x}.$$

5. Deduce from the results of Example 8 and Question 2 the derivatives of the following functions:

(*a*) $x \to \cos^{-1} x$; (*b*) $x \to \tan^{-1}(1/x)$;
(*c*) $x \to \cot^{-1} x$; (*d*) $x \to \sec^{-1} x$.

6. Find the gradients of these curves at the points named.

(*a*) $y^2 = 4ax$; $(at^2, 2at)$, $(4a, 4a)$.
(*b*) $4x^2+9y^2 = 36$; $(3\cos t, 2\sin t)$, $(1{\cdot}8, 1{\cdot}6)$.
(*c*) $xy = c^2$; $(ct, c/t)$, (c, c).
(*d*) $x^2-4y^2 = 4$; $(2\sec t, \tan t)$, $(5{\cdot}2, 2{\cdot}4)$.
(*e*) $x^3 = y^2$; (t^2, t^3), $(4, 8)$.
(*f*) $y = x^{1/q}$; (t^q, t), $(1, 1)$.

7. Consider what information you can deduce from Question 6 about the shape of the curves when t has 'large' and 'small' values, and how far you can use the parametric form to sketch their general shape.

8. There is a function $\mathscr{E}$ for which, for all real a, $\mathscr{E}'(a) = \mathscr{E}(a)$ and $\mathscr{E}(0) = 1$. If $\mathscr{L}$ denotes its inverse function, prove that $\mathscr{L}'(a) = 1/a$.

5. POWERS OF x

This section extends the rule for differentiating x^m, where m has any *rational* value. The extension to all *real* values is also possible, but is beyond the scope of this chapter.

In each part, we establish the general result $(d/dx)(x^m) = mx^{m-1}$ for a wider class of numbers; finally, we are able to differentiate *any* function built up from rational powers of x and from trigonometrical functions.

5.1 Positive integral index—direct method. The derivative of x^m at a is, by definition,

$$\lim_{b\to a}\frac{(b^m-a^m)}{b-a}.$$

When m is a positive integer, by division, the fraction reduces to

$$(b^{m-1}+ab^{m-2}+a^2b^{m-3}+\ldots+a^{m-1}),$$

provided $b \neq a$.

There are m terms in this expression, each of which tends to a^{m-1} as b tends to a in the limit, so that the derivative is ma^{m-1}, and the derived function is $x \to mx^{m-1}$.

5.2 Method of induction. Alternatively, we may use the method of induction explicitly; it was, of course, used implicitly above in the reduction of the fraction 'by division'.

(*a*) The result is true when $m = 1$, since $\dfrac{d}{dx}(x^1) = 1.x^0$.

(*b*) If the result is true for an integer $k \in N$, then

$$\frac{d}{dx}(x^{k+1}) = \frac{d}{dx}(x^k.x) = x^k.1+kx^{k-1}.x \quad \text{(by the Product Rule)},$$

$$= (k+1)x^k,$$

so that the result is also true for the integer $(k+1) \in N$.

It follows, by the principle of induction, that

$$\frac{d}{dx}(x^m) = mx^{m-1},$$

for all positive integral m.

5.3 Negative integral index. If $m = -n$, where n is a positive integer, $x^m = (1/x)^n$. So

$$\frac{d}{dx}(x^m) = \frac{d}{dx}\left(\frac{1}{x}\right)^n = n.\left(\frac{1}{x}\right)^{n-1}.\frac{-1}{x^2} \quad \text{(by the Chain Rule),}$$

$$= \frac{-n}{x^{n+1}} = mx^{m-1}, \quad \text{as before.}$$

5.4 Rational index. If $m = p/q$, where p, q are integers with no common factor,

$$y = x^m \Leftrightarrow y^q = x^p$$

(with x and y restricted to positive values if q is even). Differentiating, by the Chain Rule,

$$qy^{q-1}\frac{dy}{dx} = px^{p-1} = p.\frac{y^q}{x}.$$

So $$\frac{dy}{dx} = \frac{p}{q}.\frac{y}{x} = mx^{m-1}, \quad \text{once more.}$$

6. SUMMARY OF RESULTS

(*a*) *Powers of x*

$$f(x) = x^m \Rightarrow f'(x) = mx^{m-1}, \quad \text{for all rational } m.$$

(*b*) *Composite functions*

(i) If $h = gf$ and $b = f(a)$, then

$$h'(a) = g'(b).f'(a).$$

(ii) If $x \xrightarrow{f} u \xrightarrow{g} y$, then

$$\frac{dy}{dx} = \frac{dy}{du}.\frac{du}{dx}.$$

(*c*) *Product Rule*

(i) If $h = f.g$, then

$$h'(a) = f(a).g'(a)+g(a).f'(a).$$

(ii) If $y = u.v$, then

$$\frac{dy}{dx} = u.\frac{dv}{dx}+v.\frac{du}{dx}.$$

(*d*) *Parameters*

If $y = f(t)$, and $x = g(t)$, then

$$\frac{dy}{dx} = \frac{f'(t)}{g'(t)} = \frac{dy}{dt} \div \frac{dx}{dt}.$$

(*e*) *Inverses*

If $f(a) = b$, and g is an inverse function of f, then

$$g'(b) = \frac{1}{f'(a)}.$$

(f) Trigonometrical functions and their inverses

$f(x)$	$f'(x)$	$f(x)$	$f'(x)$
$\sin x$	$\cos x$	$\cos x$	$-\sin x$
$\tan x$	$\sec^2 x$	$\cot x$	$-\csc^2 x$
$\sec x$	$\sec x \tan x$	$\csc x$	$-\csc x \cot x$
$\sin^{-1} x$	$\dfrac{1}{\sqrt{(1-x^2)}}$	$\cos^{-1} x$	$\dfrac{-1}{\sqrt{(1-x^2)}}$
$\tan^{-1} x$	$\dfrac{1}{1+x^2}$	$\cot^{-1} x$	$\dfrac{-1}{1+x^2}$
$\sec^{-1} x$	$\dfrac{1}{x\sqrt{(x^2-1)}}$	$\csc^{-1} x$	$\dfrac{-1}{x\sqrt{(x^2-1)}}$

Note the strong family resemblance between the results in the two columns. Notice that (when x lies between 0 and $\frac{1}{2}\pi$) sin, tan and sec have positive derivatives because they are increasing functions; the co-functions (sin, tan and sec of the complement) are obtained by a reflection in $x = \frac{1}{4}\pi$, and are therefore decreasing. Can you find a simpler form for $(\frac{1}{2}\pi - \cot^{-1} x)$?

Miscellaneous Exercise

Questions on the whole of the calculus so far

1. A lidless wooden box is to be made with the sides of the base in the ratio 3:5, and its capacity is to be 450 cm³. Find the dimensions which will minimize the area of wood used, stating clearly what assumptions you make.

2. A cylindrical mast is to be cut from a tree 8 m high which tapers uniformly so that its diameter decreases from 30 cm to 20 cm. What is the greatest volume possible?

3. The mast in Question 2 is itself to be tapered, so that the diameter at the top is four-fifths of the diameter at the bottom. What is the greatest volume now possible?

4. A conical cap of the least possible curved surface area is to rest on the ground and cover a hemisphere of radius 1 cm, with its plane face in contact with the ground. What is its vertical angle?

5. The stiffness of a beam h cm deep and k cm wide is given by Akh^3, where A is a constant. What are the dimensions of the stiffest beam that can be cut out of a cylindrical log 30 cm in diameter?

6. The cost of fuel for a reasonably calm Atlantic crossing at V km/h in the Veronica is £$A(V+\frac{1}{100}V^2)$, and the food and staff costs are £$1250A/V$. What is the most economic speed overall? Draw up an account for speeds of 50 km/h and 55 km/h, and find an approximation for the rate at which the cost changes with the speed, when the speed is 50 km/h.

7. The distance between vehicles passing along a busy road at an average speed of v m/s is about $(8+v+v^2/18)$ m. How many vehicles pass a given point in an hour? What speed makes this number a maximum?

8. Two large square plates lie on top of each other and can turn about a pivot 2·5 cm from each side, so that they remain parallel and partly in contact. Prove that when the plates have the minimum area in contact they are symmetrically placed.

9. A circular safety zone of radius 10 m is to be denied to the public by four fences surrounding it in the shape of a rhombus. Find the minimum length of fencing needed, and show that this length also encloses the minimum possible area.

10. If C is the cost of producing Q units of a commodity, the marginal cost is defined to be dC/dQ. Explain the idea of marginal cost to someone who knows no calculus.

Prove that the average cost is a minimum when it is equal to the marginal cost, provided that d^2C/dQ^2 is positive, and explain this to the non-mathematician.

11. If $f(x) = a \cos nx + b \sin nx$, find $f'(x)$ and $f''(x)$. Explain the result by expressing $f(x)$ in the form $R \sin(nx+\theta)$, where R, θ are constant.

12. Two corridors, of widths 1·5 m and 2 m, meet at right-angles. What is the longest pole that can be carried round horizontally?

(*Hint.* Use an angle as variable.)

If the corridors are 2·5 m high, what is the longest pole that can go round in any position?

13. Differentiate $2 \sin x \cos x$, first as it stands, and then in another form (using the double angle formulae). Compare your two answers.

14. If $f(x) = \cos^2 x - \sin^2 x$ and $g(x) = \cos^2 x + \sin^2 x$, find $f'(x)$ and $g'(x)$ without simplification, and explain your answers in terms of the double angle formulae.

15. (*a*) If $y = \sin x \cos\theta + \cos x \sin\theta$ (where θ is constant), find dy/dx *without* simplifying y first, and explain why your answer is as expected.

(*b*) Find d^2y/dx^2 as before, and comment on your answer.

16. Differentiate (*a*) $\tan^2 x$, (*b*) $\sec^2 x$, and explain your answers.

17. Differentiate $\tan x + \cot x$, express your answer in terms of the double angle $2x$, and explain your result.

18. Find the second derivatives of

(*a*) $\sin ax \cos bx - \cos ax \sin bx$,

(*b*) $\cos 2(\pi - x)$, and

(*c*) $\cos x + \cos(x+2\pi/3) + \cos(x+4\pi/3)$

without simplifying, and explain your results in terms of simpler functions.

19. Draw an equilateral triangle which will explain the result of Question 18(*c*).

20. Deduce the form of $d(\tan^{-1} x)/dx$ by using the Chain Rule to differentiate $\tan(\tan^{-1} x)$.

21. Find the maximum and minimum points of the graph of $y = 2t/(1+t^2)$, and sketch the graph. Sketch also the graph of $y = \sin x$ for $-\pi \leqslant x \leqslant \pi$ and compare your two graphs. Then solve the equations $\sin x = -0{\cdot}3$ and

$$2t/(1+t^2) = -0{\cdot}3,$$

and show the connection between your two sets of answers.

$$\left(\text{Remember that } \sin x = \frac{2\tan\frac{1}{2}x}{1+\tan^2\frac{1}{2}x}\right).$$

22. Show that the fact that, for $0 < x < \frac{1}{2}\pi$, $\sec x > x/(\sin x) > 1$ determines the shape of all six trigonometrical curves near $x = \frac{1}{2}n\pi$, and sketch their graphs, with due attention to all their symmetries.

23. Use the results of Question 21 to sketch the graphs of the six ratios between $2t$, $1+t^2$, and $1-t^2$, and explain how a 'variable stretch' parallel to Ox can transform them into the graphs of Question 22 over the interval $-\pi < x < \pi$.

24. Let

$$f(x) = \frac{1}{2}\left(\frac{1}{x}+x\right), \quad \text{and} \quad g(x) = \frac{1}{2}\left(\frac{1}{x}-x\right).$$

Sketch the graphs of

$$f,\ g,\ \frac{1}{f},\ \frac{1}{g},\ \frac{f}{g},\ \frac{g}{f},$$

and comment on the results. What is the difference of the squares of $f(a)$ and $g(a)$?

25. Given that

$$y = \frac{5+6t+5t^2}{1-t^2},$$

sketch the graph of y against t, considering first:

(*a*) the values of t for which y is undefined, and the size of y when t is just greater or just less than these values;

(*b*) what happens when t is very large (positive or negative);

(*c*) the value of y at the maximum and minimum points.

26. Find the minimum value of $y = 3\tan x + 5\sec x$ in the interval $(-\frac{1}{2}\pi, +\frac{1}{2}\pi)$, and comment on the connection with Question 25.

27. Given that $f(x) = \cos x - 1 + \frac{1}{2}x^2$, find

$$f(0),\quad f(\tfrac{1}{4}\pi),\quad f(\tfrac{1}{2}\pi),\quad f'(0),\quad f''(0),\quad f'''(0),$$

sketch the graph of $y = f(x)$ in the interval $(-\frac{1}{2}\pi, +\frac{1}{2}\pi)$, and comment.

28. By using the derivatives as an approximation to the average scale factor, find

(*a*) $\tan 46°$; (*b*) $\sin 29°$; (*c*) $\tan^{-1}(1{\cdot}75)$.

Explain the connection of this method with the Taylor approximation, and estimate how accurate your results are.

29. If $A: r \to \pi r^2$ is the area function of a circle, explain why A' is the circumference function, and state under what conditions a similar result will be true for:

(*a*) a sphere; (*b*) a cylinder; (*c*) a right circular cone.

30. $\sqrt{120}$ is near 11. Use a linear approximation to find $\sqrt{30}$, and a quadratic approximation to say roughly how large your error is.

Devise similar methods for finding $\sqrt{11}$, $\sqrt[3]{37}$, $\sqrt{7}$, $\sqrt{10}$, $\sqrt[3]{2}$, $\sqrt{5}$ and $\sqrt{6}$. (24, 63, 80, 99, 128, 999 and 1024 are interesting numbers.)

31. *Write down* the fourth degree Taylor approximation to $1/(1+x)$ when x is small, and use this result to *write down* successively approximations for $1/(1+x^2)$ and $\tan^{-1}x$.

32. Find approximations of the form $a_0+a_1x+a_2x^2+a_3x^3+a_4x^4$, when x is small, for

(*a*) $\sec x$;   (*b*) $\sin^{-1}x$;   (*c*) $\sqrt{(1-x)}$;   (*d*) $\dfrac{x^2}{\sqrt{(1-x^2)}}$.

33. Find fourth degree Taylor approximations for: (*a*) $\sin x$, (*b*) $\cos x$, (*c*) $\cos 2x$. Deduce from (*c*) a fourth degree approximation for $\sin^2 x$. Check this result by squaring the result of (*a*) and neglecting all terms of degree greater than 4.

34. Find the third derivative of: (*a*) $x\cos x$; (*b*) $x^2\sin x$, and (*c*) $x^3\sin 2x$, and write down what you think will be the fourth and fifth derived functions. Check your results by comparing with the Taylor approximations for $\cos x$, $\sin x$ and $\sin 2x$.

35. Show that $1/\sqrt{(1-x^2)}$ is a solution of the differential equation

$$(1-x^2)\frac{d^2y}{dx^2}-3x\frac{dy}{dx}-y = 0.$$

36. Show that for *Legendre's Equation*

$$(1-x^2)\frac{d^2y}{dx^2}-2x\frac{dy}{dx}+n(n+1)\,y = 0,$$

(*a*) when $n = 1$, $y = x$ is a solution;
(*b*) when $n = 2$, $y = \frac{1}{2}(3x^2-1)$ is a solution;
(*c*) when $n = 3$, $y = \frac{1}{2}(5x^3-3x)$ is a solution.
Confirm that

$$\frac{1}{2^n.n!}\cdot\left(\frac{d}{dx}\right)^n(x^2-1)^n$$

gives the same solutions, and see whether it still gives a solution when $n = 4$.

37. Use the Newton–Raphson method to solve, correct to three significant figures:
(*a*) $x^2-2 = 0$;
(*b*) $x^4-10x^2+1 = 0$ (take ± 3 and $\pm 0{\cdot}3$ as first approximations);
(*c*) $x = 4\sin x$.

38. Solve to the nearest degree the equations (which occur in certain statical problems):
(*a*) $\tan\theta+\sin\theta = \frac{1}{2}$;   (*b*) $\tan\theta = \cos^2\theta$;
(*c*) $4\cos^3\theta-14\cos^2\theta+9 = 0$.
(In (*c*), solve for $\cos\theta$, taking $+1$ and $-0{\cdot}7$ as first approximations.)

39. Draw graphs of the functions $x\to\sin x$ and $x\to x-\frac{1}{6}x^3$, and use four-figure tables to find out roughly when their values first differ by as much as $0{\cdot}001$, and to compare their maximum and minimum values and intercepts with Ox.

40. Prove that the graph of $y = ax^3 - 3bx^2 + 3cx - d$ is symmetrical about its point of inflexion.

41. Sketch the graphs of the following functions, taking care about the form near O, the form at infinity, and all maxima, minima, and points of inflexion:

(a) $x \to \dfrac{x}{x^2+4}$; (b) $x \to \dfrac{x}{x^2-9}$;

(c) $x \to x - \dfrac{1}{x}$; (d) $x \to x^2 + \dfrac{2a^3}{x}$;

(e) $x \to \dfrac{1}{(x-1)(x+4)}$; (f) $x \to \dfrac{x(x-1)}{(x-2)(x-3)}$.

42. Can you define an inverse function, together with its domain, for

$$f: x \to 2x^3 - 9x^2 + 12x - 3,$$

when the range of f is restricted to the interval:

(a) (1, 2), (b) $(\frac{1}{2}, 1\frac{1}{2})$, (c) (0, 2), (d) (0, 3)?

Is the inverse function in each case (i) unique, (ii) continuous?

43. Prove the quotient rule for differentiating $k = f/g$:

(a) from first principles (using an average scale factor);
(b) using δx, δu and δv;
(c) by differentiating $f.h$, where h is the function $1/g$;
(d) by differentiating $k.g$.

Extend each of these methods to differentiate f/g^n.

44. Prove the product rule for three functions by using the product rule for two functions twice. Extend this by the method of induction to prove the product rule for $f_1.f_2.f_3.\ldots.f_n$.

45. Let $x = t^2+1$ and $y = t^3+3t$. Find dy/dx and hence d^2y/dx^2 in terms of t.

46. Differentiate $x \to (x+2)\sqrt{(x-1)}$ directly and explain the connection between this answer and the answer to Question 45.

47. Find d^2y/dx^2 for the parabola whose typical point is $(at^2, 2at)$ at the point whose parameter is t, and compare with the result obtained from the Cartesian equation.

48. If $x = f(t)$ and $y = g(t)$, find d^2y/dx^2 in terms of f', g', f'' and g''.

49. Assuming only that the derived function of $f: x \to x^m$ is $f': x \to mx^{m-1}$ when x is a positive integer, prove that the same formula holds when m is a positive rational number p/q, by considering the point (t^q, t^p). Why must the domain be restricted if q is even? Must p/q be in its lowest terms for this formula to work?

50. Use a method similar to Question 49 to extend the rule:

(a) to negative integers; (b) to fractions $1/q$;
(c) to all rational numbers.

What is the difficulty about the extension to all real numbers? Can you attach any significance to the number 2^π, or to the statement that, if

$$y = x^\pi, \quad \text{then} \quad \frac{dy}{dx} = \pi.\frac{y}{x}?$$

18

UNITS AND DIMENSIONS

1. PHYSICAL MEASUREMENTS

Much of the mathematics we have been studying so far has been concerned with the set of real numbers and with the properties of the common operations defined on this set. One particular structure, namely the group, has been singled out for special treatment, and we have seen examples of this structure being applied to sets other than those of the real numbers. Other structured sets, too, are familiar to you and the common feature of them all is that the logic of the operations is well defined.

In contrast to this, quantities arising from measurements of physical phenomena have not been treated to quite the same degree of rigour. For example, we have been happy to assert that 'two metres plus one metre makes three metres' without examining too closely what is meant by 'one metre', 'two metres', or 'three metres'. These quantities are certainly not numbers, or vectors, or matrices, or geometrical transformations, and the definition of the operation of addition on them has not yet been made, even though it may be intuitively obvious. Moreover, combinations of, or operations on, physical quantities are constantly used even when the quantities are manifestly of different kinds: thus one often interprets 'twelve metres divided by three seconds' as 'four metres per second'. It seems desirable therefore to put operations such as these two examples on a rather less intuitive basis, and this is the main aim of this short chapter.

The quantities with which we shall deal here will all be abstract or idealized in the sense that no observation can be said to yield an *exact* measurement such as '40 cm'. All physical measurements *necessarily* involve, if only implicitly, inequalities. Thus

$$228 \text{ millimetres} < \text{the height of this page} < 229 \text{ millimetres},$$

and no refinement of apparatus can ever reduce this statement to an equality, partly because all measurement is essentially digital and partly because the height of the paper is not, in any case, a determinate quantity if molecular distances are to be contemplated. Such problems, of measurement and of the errors involved, are not, however, dealt with here.

Exercise A

1. Discuss what meaning can be attached to the statement that the Sun is 150000000 kilometres from the Earth.

2. Suggest various uses of a spherical ball of diameter of about 3 cm which necessitate the diameter being given to 0·1 cm, 0·01 cm, 0·001 cm and 0·0001 cm.

3. How many physical quantities can you construct from various combinations of two seconds, five metres, ten kilograms?

4. A road engineer is wondering whether to make the surface of a new road plane to an accuracy of a centimetre, a millimetre, or a tenth of a millimetre. Discuss the relative merits and demerits of these three possibilities.

5. With what degree of accuracy do you think you could measure, with the apparatus available in your school, the following:

(*a*) the length of a day;
(*b*) your own mass;
(*c*) the roughness on your blackboard;
(*d*) the height of the roof ridge of your classroom block;
(*e*) the height of a gas-jet flame;
(*f*) the pitch of middle C on your piano;
(*g*) the length of cotton on a new reel?

2. PHYSICAL UNITS

We all think we know what 'one metre' is. Until recently, it was the distance between two marks on a platinum bar preserved in Paris. It is now defined as 1650763·73 vacuum wavelengths of orange light (of wavelength 6058 Ångstrom units) from a krypton-86 discharge lamp! But such definitions suffer from the difficulties mentioned in Section 1, and from others, too. Nevertheless, we shall proceed by regarding 'one cm' (being one-hundredth' of 'one metre') as a perfectly definite quantity of length: we feel that we have a very good notion of what length is, what kind of physical character it has; and we also accept the notion of a *unit* of length, in terms of which other lengths may be measured.

In the same way, we feel certain about what is meant by 'one second' as a unit of time. (It is, in fact, recognized internationally, as

$$\frac{1}{31\,556\,925{\cdot}9747}$$

of the tropical year starting at noon on 31 December 1899!)

It is not immediately obvious that other physical units, if any, are as basic as the two units of length and time. You might say the speed of 'one metre per second' is a natural unit; but it is presumably derivable from 'one metre' and 'one second', and so is not a new, independent unit. Are there, therefore, any other units which are independent of those of time and length?

A unit of weight seems a possible candidate for a third unit, say a 'one kilogram weight' as measured on a spring balance. But a disadvantage of that unit is its variability: if the kilogram bag of sugar is taken, together with its spring balance, to the moon, it will record only about 150 g there; while in a satellite orbiting the earth, it would weigh nothing. This disadvantage could be overcome by defining the 'one kilogram weight' as the gravitational force on a given body at a given place at a given time, but this is hardly convenient. After all, the units of time and length are not restricted in any way to position on earth or in the heavens.

A better method of defining a unit of force would be to construct a standard spring on which the required unit of force would produce a certain extension (or compression); presuming that the compressibility-characteristics of a spring will not vary from one place to another. And in fact the standard unit of force—'one kilogram force' (or '1 kgf')—*could* be defined in this manner, but it would be extremely difficult to achieve in this way a degree of accuracy of the order of one part in 10^{12} parts which characterizes the definition of, say, the second of time. A different definition is, however, usually used, as is described in a later chapter.

There are many other units of physical measurement: just to give a few—1 hectare, 1 cubic metre, 1 joule, 1 newton, 1 metre per second per second, and so on. All these are regarded as units which are derived, through defining equations, from a small set of basic units; and it is one of the most important functions of the equations of physics that they define a wide variety of physical quantities.

Exercise B

1. Write down a list of all the units of length you can think of, and in each case give an example in which that particular unit might be used in preference to others. (Do you know what units are used in astronomy?)

2. Repeat Question 1 (*a*) for time, (*b*) for angle.

3. The chances are that the ratio of any two of the units you have mentioned in Questions 1 and 2 is a rational number. Can you think of some good reasons for this? In cases where this is not so, explain why such different units are used side by side.

4. Under what circumstances might the following be useful units?

(i) 1 centimetre per year;
(ii) 1 cubic kilometre;
(iii) 1 square millimetre;
(iv) 1 kilometre per second;
(v) 1 second per kilometre;
(vi) 1 second per day;
(vii) 1 square kilometre per month;
(viii) 1 month per square kilometre.

3. SCALARS AND OTHER QUANTITIES

If we seek to structure physical quantities in a mathematical fashion, a start can be made by listing various typical operations involving a single unit such as 'one metre'. In everyday language we might write, for example,

$$2 \text{ metres} = 2\times(1 \text{ metre}),$$
$$3 \text{ metres} = 1 \text{ metre}+2 \text{ metres},$$

or

$$8 \text{ metres} \div 4 = 2 \text{ metres};$$

and there is an obvious likeness between these equations and the following:

$$(2x) = 2\times(x),$$
$$3x = x+2x,$$

or

$$(8x) \div 4 = 2x.$$

Thus we are considering the (infinite) set of quantities

$$\{(1 \text{ metre}), (2 \text{ metres}), (3 \text{ metres}), ...\}$$

whose general member is (n metres) where n is real. On this set are imposed laws of:

(*a*) addition and subtraction;

(*b*) multiplication and division by real numbers, the set being closed under all four operations (with the exception of division by zero).

It is useful to refer to the real numbers as scalars and tempting to refer to the length-quantities as vectors. It is, however, best perhaps to avoid 'vector' in this context, since in a different context it is not nonsense to write

$$1 \text{ metre}+2 \text{ metres} = 2 \text{ metres};$$

this could make sense if each of the three quantities has an appropriate direction attached to it, the addition being defined as in Chapter 9 (Book 1) and the two sides of the equation being interpreted as magnitudes. More accurately, in this case, one might write $|1 \text{ metre}+2 \text{ metres}| = |2 \text{ metres}|$. 'Sum by accumulation' is a preferable term to describe the operation in our second equation, a term which carries with it the implicit property of commutativity.

Exercise C

1. A typical member of the set of all lengths is (n metres) where $n \in R$. Consider the four subsets defined by

(i) $n \in N$;
(ii) $n \in Q^+$;
(iii) $n \in R^+$;
(iv) $n \in R^-$.

Is each closed under the operation of 'sum by accumulation'? What stages of civilization correspond to these sets?

2. What meaning, if any, would you attach to the quantity (-3 metres)? Is such a quantity useful, from either a practical point of view or from a mathematical?

3. Make, where possible, as many interpretations as you can of:

(i) 1 metre per second + 2 metres per second = 3 metres per second;
(ii) 2 metres per second + 1 metre per second = $2\frac{1}{2}$ metres per second;
(iii) 2 kg + 4 kg = 6 kg;
(iv) 2 kg + 5 kg = 6 kg;
(v) 2 kgf + 5 kgf = 6 kgf;
(vi) 1 cubic metre + 1 cubic metre = 2 cubic metres;
(vii) 1 cubic metre + 2 cubic metres = 2 cubic metres.

4. UNITS AND CHANGE OF UNITS

The word *unit* most naturally refers to a quantity such as (1 metre) or (1 cubic metre) or (1 kilogram), the numeral being unity in each case. The meaning can, however, be generalized without any confusion to denote any quantity in terms of which others are measured as scalar multiples. Thus, in this sense, (20 metres) or (10 cubic metres) or (70 kilograms) could be used as units in situations in which they would be convenient. In such situations, convenience is best served if the numeral unity is once again restored; thus one might invent new units of (20 metres) as 1 pitch, the unit of (10 cubic metres) as 1 lorry load, or the unit of (70 kilograms) as 1 man mass.

Such new units may satisfy the self-importance of their creators but, despite what has been said already, they cannot be recommended. To have to describe 3 metres as 0·15 pitch is not helpful and for similar reasons one can only be thankful that the British coinage is now based on a decimal system, and that the familiar system of British units—masses and measures—which was hallowed by history is now being superseded by the metric system. In fact, since the numbers we normally use are expressed in decimal form, the most sensible system of units is the metric system in which successive units of, say, length are connected by factors which are multiples of ten; thus 10 millimetres = 1 centimetre, 10 centimetres = 1 decimetre, 10 decimetres = 1 metre, 10 metres = 1 dekametre, 10 dekametres = 1 hectametre, 10 hectametres = 1 kilometre.

In many scientific applications, the most common factors are 10^6, 10^3, 10^{-3}, 10^{-6}, 10^{-9}, 10^{-12}, and these are represented by the prefixes mega-, kilo-, milli-, micro-, nano- and pico-. Thus 1 microsecond = 10^{-6} seconds, a unit of time which is useful in connection with the operation of electronic computers; again, 1 megatonne = 10^6 tonnes, a term commonly used in connection with atomic weapons.

To express a quantity in terms of a certain unit when it is given already in terms of another unit, one has to follow the rules suggested in Section 3. Thus, for example, to express 80 minutes of arc in degrees, one might write

$$80 \text{ minutes} = \tfrac{4}{3}\times(60 \text{ minutes}) = \tfrac{4}{3}\times(1 \text{ degree}) = \tfrac{4}{3} \text{ degree},$$

or

$$80 \text{ minutes} = 80\times(1 \text{ minute}) = 80\times(\tfrac{1}{60} \text{ degree}) = \tfrac{4}{3} \text{ degree},$$

in which the role of the scalars is clarified. In practice, no-one would write a 'conversion of units' at such length and the mental process would probably follow the second equation abbreviated as

$$80 \text{ minutes} = 80.\tfrac{1}{60} \text{ degree} = \tfrac{4}{3} \text{ degree.}$$

Exercise D

1. Give as many examples as you can think of in ten minutes, of sensible uses of the various metric prefixes, describing briefly the physical circumstances of each.

2. If 02143 is a symbol for the angle 21° 43′, draw up a flow diagram for the addition of the two general angles *abcde* and *vwxyz*, and give the answer.

3. Invent a series of magnitudes appropriate to a system of measurement using the binary scale. How many units would be required to measure distances between 1 cm and 1 km? What are the advantages and disadvantages of such a system?

5. DIMENSIONS: SUMS

In Section 3, we thought of scalars as multipliers, and we considered addition of two quantities expressed in the same units. We need to examine other possible binary operations which could be defined on various sets of scalars and physical quantities. In this section, let us consider the operation of summation (and, by implication, the inverse operation of subtraction).

First, consider a summation involving different units such as

$$3 \text{ metres} + 140 \text{ centimetres.}$$

This will cause you no difficulty. For example

$$3 \text{ m} + 140 \text{ cm} = 3 \times (100 \text{ cm}) + 140 \text{ cm} = 300 \text{ cm} + 140 \text{ cm} = 440 \text{ cm.}$$

This has been written out at undue length and you would probably obtain the final result very quickly in your head.

Another way of writing 3 m + 140 cm would simply be 3 m 140 cm, by analogy with the 21 degrees 43 minutes of Exercise D. The convention used in a compound quantity such as 21 degrees 43 minutes implies, however, rather more than just the addition: 21 degrees + 43 minutes. First, it implies that the two units named degree and minute are of the same physical character; indeed that the whole quantity is a single physical quantity obtained as a sum by accumulation. Secondly, it is normally written in such a way that none of the component quantities exceeds one unit of the next greater quantity used; thus 43 minutes does not exceed 1 degree. You should consider for yourself why this is the convention and, in doing so, consider the analogous situation in systems of counting wherein numbers expressed in base N use digits chosen only from $1, 2, 3, \ldots, N-1$. According to these conventions, therefore, 3 metres + 140 centimetres would not normally be written as 3 m 140 cm, as was suggested a little earlier, but as 4 m 40 cm (or preferably as 4·40 m).

Now in considering the equation 3 metres + 140 cm = 440 cm, we note that the three quantities are all of the same physical character and it is often thought that such an equation can only make sense if this condition of homogeneity is satisfied. Thus (it is suggested) homogeneous quantities—that is, those of the same character—can be summed but non-homogeneous quantities cannot be.

In fact, it is doubtful whether this can be laid down as a metaphysical principle. Consider, for example,

$$4 \text{ girls} + 3 \text{ boys} = 7 \text{ pupils}.$$

Does this make sense in view of the fact that the girls and boys do not have 'the same physical character' in all respects? It could be argued that the 'girls', the 'boys' and the 'pupils' all do have some characteristic in common—for example, they are all in the same class—and so it is reasonable to sum them. But even if we are satisfied with the concept of a sum in such a case, the meaning and properties of the quality sign as it is used here are not wholly conventional. For consider the following argument

$$\begin{aligned} & 4 \text{ girls} + 3 \text{ boys} = 7 \text{ human beings}, \\ & 4 \text{ girls} + 3 \text{ boys} = 7 \text{ pupils}, \\ \Rightarrow\ & 7 \text{ human beings} = 7 \text{ pupils}, \\ \Rightarrow\ & 1 \text{ human being} = 1 \text{ pupil}. \end{aligned}$$

Every human being is certainly not a pupil and so these manipulations are clearly not valid. You should examine, as an exercise, which of the symmetric, reflexive and transitive properties of the conventional '=' relation hold for the equality as it is used in the above argument.

Nevertheless, some such principle as the 'consistency of physical character' *is* usually adopted in the mathematical models which we construct to represent physical phenomena and it is best to regard it as an integral part of the model. The technical term for 'physical character' is *dimension*: a centimetre has the same dimension as a metre, or 5 metres per second has the same dimension as 2000 kilometres per hour. An equation such as 3 m + 140 cm = 440 cm is said to be *dimensionally consistent* whereas 4 metres − 1 second = 3 metres per second is dimensionally inconsistent and is therefore usually regarded as nonsense.

Exercise E

1. Make up your own examples of inequations or equations such as:

2 men $\times$ 3 hours $=$ 6 man-hours,
2 turtles $\times$ 3 doves $\neq$ 6 turtle-doves,
2 turtles $+$ 3 doves $=$ 5 animals,
5 turtle-doves $=$ 5 animals,

which indicate that the principle of dimensional consistency is itself a matter of interpretation.

2. An equation such as
2 kilocycles per second $+$ 3 kilocycles per second $=$ 5 kilocycles per second is dimensionally consistent; it is not easy, however, to envisage a physical system in which there are two observable frequencies, 2 and 3 kilocycles per second, which are summable by some means to give 5 kilocycles per second. Describe such a system.

3. Invent other examples similar to Question 2.

6. DIMENSIONS: PRODUCTS

The formalism introduced so far into operations has been almost instinctive. Operations involving *products* of physical quantities, however, require not only additional mathematical structure but also a deeper understanding of 'physical character' or of dimensions.

Suppose we write 2 metres $\times$ 3 metres $=$ 6 square metres. There are two aspects to this. We note, first, that the scalars 2, 3 and 6 satisfy the multiplication $2 \times 3 = 6$; secondly, that the product of two similar dimensions results in a quantity of different dimensions. The principle of dimensional consistency, if it is still to hold, therefore, must be extended to deal with such products. Now the idea of a length multiplied by a length giving an area could be formalized as $\mathbf{L} \times \mathbf{L} = \mathbf{L}^2$ where the symbol $\mathbf{L}$ denotes the dimension of length and the notation follows convention. Extensions are immediately suggested. For example, $\mathbf{L} \times \mathbf{L}^2 = \mathbf{L}^3$ can be interpreted as length $\times$ area $=$ volume, the dimension of volume being $\mathbf{L}^3$.

The process of division follows naturally. $\mathbf{L} = \mathbf{L}^3 \div \mathbf{L}^2$, for volume divided by area equals length. Thus in the three equations involving the dimension $\mathbf{L}$ we see examples of the idea of dimensional consistency being extended to products.

It is important to realize that the statement 3 cubic metres $\div$ 0·6 metres $=$ 5 square metres does not necessarily make sense, just because the scalar calculation is correct—$3 \div 0{\cdot}6 = 5$—and the equation is dimensionally consistent. Whether it makes sense or not depends also on whether it is a model of a sensible physical situation. Thus if a rectangular water tank of volume 3 cubic metres had one side of 0·6 metres, then we would certainly know that one of the faces was 5 square metres in area. However, a 3 cubic metres load of topsoil divided by the 60-cm waist of my elder sister does not result in any identifiable area of 5 square metres.

But the dimensional equation $\mathbf{L}^3 \div \mathbf{L} = \mathbf{L}^2$ can be said always to make sense: if a volume is divided by a *relevant* length, the result is bound to be a *relevant* area.

We are thus led to the tentative conclusion that, provided the quantities in an equation are all strictly relevant to some identifiable physical situation, the principle of dimensional consistency is a valuable, even an indispensable, guide to the result and to the meaning of a product (or of a quotient).

Further combinations of dimensions can be derived by the introduction of **T**, the dimension of time. Thus $\mathbf{L} \div \mathbf{T} = \mathbf{LT}^{-1}$ may be said to be the dimension of speed and $\mathbf{LT}^{-1} \div \mathbf{T} = \mathbf{LT}^{-2}$ that of acceleration.

$$\mathbf{L}^3 \div \mathbf{T} = \mathbf{L}^3\mathbf{T}^{-1}$$

is a less obvious dimension but is the dimension of the time-rate-of-change of volume: for example, the flow of water pouring at 4 litres per second has dimension $\mathbf{L}^3\mathbf{T}^{-1}$.

What physical quantity has dimension $\mathbf{T}^2$? The answer is 'none'; at least there is no recognized name for a unit of physical quantity whose dimension is $\mathbf{T}^2$. But from a mathematical viewpoint, there is no objection to the concept of a quantity of dimension $\mathbf{T}^2$, and we could establish a unit of 2 squarsecs if the fit so took us.

Then 6 metres ÷ 2 squarsecs = 3 metres per second per second makes at least some sense. On the whole, however, the fewer the total number of different types of unit the better and squarseconds will not be found in other books.

The structure of the dimensions formed by the two fundamental dimensions **L** and **T** is that of a multiplicative group. The members of the group are $\mathbf{L}^a\mathbf{T}^b$ where a, b are integers (positive, negative or zero); $\mathbf{L}^0\mathbf{T}^0 = \mathbf{1}$ is the identity element.

Exercise F

Write down as complete a list as you can of recognized units whose dimensions are members of the group generated by **L** and **T**.

7. QUOTIENTS: DERIVATIVES

Already in this chapter, for example, in Exercise B, Question 4 and in Section 6, we have met quotients of physical quantities in which either a single dimension is involved (as in 3 cubic metres ÷ 0·6 metres = 5 square metres), or in which the numerator and denominator have different dimensions (as in 3 metres ÷ 0·6 seconds = 5 metres per second).

More complicated examples of this are the following:

8 litres ÷ 4 litres per second = 2 seconds;
6 metres per second ÷ 3 metres per second per second = 2 seconds;
60 kilometres ÷ 15 kilometres per hour = 4 hours;
4 square metres per second ÷ 2 metres per second = 2 metres.

The dimensional forms of these four examples are, respectively,

$$\mathbf{L}^3 \div (\mathbf{L}^3\mathbf{T}^{-1}) = \mathbf{T};$$
$$(\mathbf{L}\mathbf{T}^{-1}) \div (\mathbf{L}\mathbf{T}^{-2}) = \mathbf{T};$$
$$\mathbf{L} \div (\mathbf{L}\mathbf{T}^{-1}) = \mathbf{T};$$
$$(\mathbf{L}^2\mathbf{T}^{-1}) \div (\mathbf{L}\mathbf{T}^{-1}) = \mathbf{L}.$$

A particularly important application of dimensions to quotients occurs when the derivative of some variable physical quantity is taken with respect to another, different, physical quantity. Now the concept of a derivative has been developed in Chapters 7 and 17 primarily in terms of real numbers—that is, the derivative dy/dx has been defined with some rigour when y is a numerical (and differentiable) function of the numerical variable x.

But cases have also been given in earlier chapters in which, for example, a distance has been differentiated with respect to time to obtain a speed. Thus you are familiar with the idea that if a car is moving in a straight line so that its distance, s, measured in metres from a fixed point is given by the formula $s = 3t^2-2t+1$ where t is time measured in seconds, then its speed at any time is given by $ds/dt = (6t-2)$ metres per second. The process used here needs a formalized description.

Before we try to describe the process of differentiation, however, we need to comment on the unsatisfactory nature (at least in the context of dimensional considerations) of a formula such as $s = 3t^2-2t+1$. If s and t are *numerical* measures, then there are no difficulties. But when one talks of s as distance measured in metres, it customarily means that s has the dimension of length. Thus (in our example) $3t^2-2t+1$ also has the dimension of length. Therefore the symbols 3, 2, 1 are *not* numbers, but have dimensions $\mathbf{LT}^{-2}$, $\mathbf{LT}^{-1}$, $\mathbf{L}$ respectively. This then represents a thoroughly undesirable system of notation and a much better form for the formula $s = 3t^2-2t+1$ is

$$\frac{s}{s_0} = 3\left(\frac{t}{t_0}\right)^2 - 2\left(\frac{t}{t_0}\right) + 1,$$

where s_0, t_0 are *constant* quantities, characteristic of the system under consideration, of dimensions **L** and **T** respectively. The formula now is dimensionally consistent. If we take s_0 to be 1 m and t_0 to be 1 s, we could then write

$$\frac{s}{\mathrm{m}} = 3\left(\frac{t}{\mathrm{s}}\right)^2 - 2\left(\frac{t}{\mathrm{s}}\right) + 1,$$

as is sometimes done.

As to the dimension of a derivative, it is clear from the definition of a derivative as a limit that the dimension of dy/dx is the same as that of $y \div x$.

Thus, in our example,

$$v = \frac{ds}{dt} = \frac{s_0}{t_0}\left(6\frac{t}{t_0} - 2\right),$$

and every term of this equation has, as it should, the dimension $\mathbf{LT}^{-1}$. What is more, the *units* of the derivative dy/dx are the same as those of $y \div x$. Thus in our example, if s, s_0 are measured in metres, and t, t_0 in seconds, then the speed v given by

$$\frac{s_0}{t_0}\left(\frac{6t}{t_0} - 2\right)$$

is measured in metres per second. If $s_0 = 1$ m, $t_0 = 1$ s, we can write

$$v = \frac{\text{m}}{\text{s}}\left(6\frac{t}{\text{s}} - 2\right).$$

If, for example, $t = 4$ s, then this gives

$$v = \frac{\text{m}}{\text{s}}(6 \times 4 - 2) = 22 \text{ m/s}.$$

Exercise G

1. In the example discussed in the text suggest other suitable values for the constants s_0 and t_0.

2. A formula for the volume of water remaining in a bath at time t after the plug has been pulled out has been given by

$$V = 6000 - 40t - t^2.$$

(*a*) Suggest units for V and t;
(*b*) At what time is the bath empty?;
(*c*) How much water was originally in the bath?;
(*d*) Suggest appropriate constants V_0 and t_0 of dimensions $\mathbf{L}^3$ and $\mathbf{T}$ respectively;
(*e*) Rewrite the formula by introducing V_0 and t_0, so that it is dimensionally consistent;
(*f*) What is the initial rate of flow down the waste pipe: (i) in terms of V_0 and t_0, (ii) as a definite number of units of flow?
(*g*) Repeat (*f*) but for the final rate of flow.

3. A spherical balloon is expanding. Prove that the rate of change of volume V with respect to surface area A is $\frac{1}{4}\sqrt{(A/\pi)}$. Verify the dimensional consistency of the equations you have written down. What is the value of this rate-of-change when $V = 36\pi$ cubic centimetres?

8. DERIVATIVES OF POLYNOMIALS

It is worth remarking that the ideas of the previous section may be applied to the derivatives of polynomials. Consider $(d/dx)(x^n) = f(x)$ and let us regard x as a length, that is with dimension $\mathbf{L}$. Then $f(x)$ is of dimension $\mathbf{L}^n \div \mathbf{L} = \mathbf{L}^{n-1}$ and since x is the only dimensional quantity (n being a number), $f(x)$ is of the form $k(n)x^{n-1}$ where $k(n)$ is a numerical function of n. In fact, as you know, $k(n) = n$, but this result can only be obtained by a full calculation of the derivative.

It should be mentioned that all results derived from dimensional arguments depend upon the group property of the dimensions of various physical quantities. In the case of $(d/dx)(x^n)$, you may argue that to have regarded x as a length was an artificial device and that the whole argument of the last paragraph would collapse if x were regarded as a number—as would be entirely legitimate. To meet this criticism one can fall back on rather more abstruse group-theoretic ideas or alternatively proceed as follows:

If
$$\frac{d}{dx}(x^n) = f(x),$$

then
$$f(cx) = \frac{d}{d(cx)}(cx)^n = \frac{1}{c}\frac{d}{dx}(c^n x^n)$$
$$= \frac{c^n}{c}\frac{d}{dx}(x^n)$$
$$= c^{n-1} f(x).$$

Thus
$$\frac{f(x)}{(cx)^{n-1}} = \frac{f(x)}{x^{n-1}},$$

whatever the value of c.

Hence $\{f(x)\}/x^{n-1}$ takes the same value for all values of x, and so is a constant.

It is not possible to apply a dimensional analysis with any rigour to the derivatives of other functions. The elementary functions such as $\sin x$, e^x or $\log x$ are not amenable to such treatment since they are functions which map the reals into the reals, that is, they refer to quantities which are essentially dimensionless.

19

KINEMATICS

Kinematics is the analysis of motion. It is not concerned with the causes or effects of motion. The chapter deals with velocity and acceleration and their expression in mathematical terms. Most of the work will be in two dimensions though the ideas and definitions apply equally well in three.

From earlier chapters, we already know that speed and size of acceleration can be obtained by differentiating expressions for distance: also that position, velocity and acceleration can be expressed by means of vectors. Now consider the following situation:

A circuit for go-kart racing is semicircular with the start at the mid-point of the diameter. Suppose that a kart travels so that its distance from the start is given by $s = 2t+t^2$ (metre-second units), the size of its velocity (speed) by $v = 2+2t$ (differentiating), and the size of its acceleration by $a = 2$ (differentiating).

It reaches the end of the straight when $t = 12$. The distance travelled is then 168 m; its speed is 26 metres per second; its acceleration is 2 metres per second per second.

Suppose now that the kart travels with a constant speed of 26 metres per second along the curved part of the track. Its distance from the starting point no longer varies—it is now constant at 168 m. The distance from the start is given by $s = 168$. Differentiating to obtain the size of the velocity, we find $v = 0$ (and not 26).

It seems that v, the derivative of s, is not necessarily the actual speed of the object. (What is it, in this case?) Our method breaks down once the direction of motion starts to change and this tells us that we need to consider both magnitude and the direction of the kart's displacement, that is, we must consider vector quantities.

It would be useful if we could find some vector expression for the position of a moving body and an associated expression that would give its velocity. Can we learn to differentiate vectors so as to find the rate of change both of magnitude and direction and thus obtain the actual velocity of a body?

Throughout the chapter, the mathematical expressions will refer to the position, velocity, etc., of points. In the examples, we shall take points as models of particles, electrons, bodies, stones, people, vehicles of all kinds and even planets. It is worth questioning, in the context of each example, whether this simplification is really justified.

1. AVERAGE VELOCITY

Consider the line given by $\mathbf{r} = t(\mathbf{i}+3\mathbf{j})$. In Chapter 13, the parameter t was stated to be a scalar which could take any real value and which, as it varied, determined the position of the point.

This parameter can be given physical significance—t can represent time. So, above, when the time is 1, the point is at P where $\mathbf{p} = (\mathbf{i}+3\mathbf{j})$; when the time is 3, the point is at Q where $\mathbf{q} = 3(\mathbf{i}+3\mathbf{j})$.

> If a point moves from position P at time t_1, to position Q at time t_2 (see Figure 1), then the *average velocity* will be given by the displacement $\mathbf{PQ}$ divided by the time interval (t_2-t_1).

On the above line the average velocity is given by

$$\frac{\mathbf{PQ}}{t_2-t_1} = \frac{\mathbf{q}-\mathbf{p}}{t_2-t_1} = \frac{3(\mathbf{i}+3\mathbf{j})-(\mathbf{i}+3\mathbf{j})}{3-1} = \mathbf{i}+3\mathbf{j}.$$

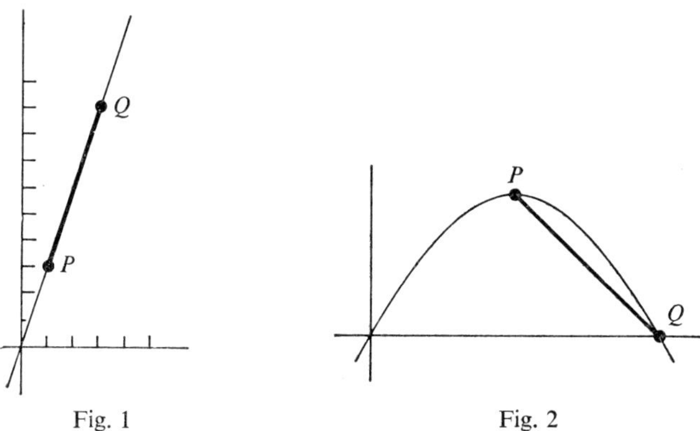

Fig. 1

Fig. 2

On the curve $\mathbf{r} = t\mathbf{i}+(2t-t^2)\mathbf{j}$ (see Figure 2), where P is the position when the time is 1 and Q that when the time is 2, the average velocity is

$$\frac{\mathbf{q}-\mathbf{p}}{t_2-t_1} = \frac{[2\mathbf{i}+0\mathbf{j}]-[\mathbf{i}+1\mathbf{j}]}{2-1} = \mathbf{i}-\mathbf{j}.$$

Average velocities are vector quantities and can be expressed in terms of their magnitude and their inclination to the x-axis. In these cases, the magnitudes are $\sqrt{(1^2+3^2)} = \sqrt{10}$ and $\sqrt{(1^2+1^2)} = \sqrt{2}$, and the inclinations are $\tan^{-1}(3/1) = 71{\cdot}5°$ and $\tan^{-1}(-1/1) = -45°$.

Although the parameter t has been given physical meaning, the above examples have been about graphs. In this case, no units need be stated. But whenever the context is a physical situation, all units must be stated. We shall usually use kilometres per hour or metres per second. In accordance with the recommendations of the British Standards Institution, we shall denote these by km/h and m/s.

Exercise A

In each of Questions 1–6 prepare axes for a sketch graph and:

(*a*) mark the positions P and Q of the point at the given times;
(*b*) sketch the curve near P and Q;
(*c*) show the displacement **PQ** with a heavy line;
(*d*) state the average velocity:
 (i) in vector form,
 (ii) by giving its magnitude and direction relative to the x-axis.

1. $\mathbf{r} = t\mathbf{i}$ between $t = 1$ and $t = 7$.

2. $\mathbf{r} = t^3(\mathbf{i}+\mathbf{j})$ between $t = 1$ and $t = 2$.

3. $\mathbf{r} = \mathbf{i}+t\mathbf{j}$ between $t = 0$ and $t = 3$.

4. $\mathbf{r} = (2+t)\mathbf{i}+(1-t)\mathbf{j}$ between $t = 0$ and $t = 3$.

5. $\mathbf{r} = t\mathbf{i}+t^2\mathbf{j}$ between $t = 1$ and $t = 4$.

6. $\mathbf{r} = t\mathbf{i}+\cos t\mathbf{j}$ between $t = 0$ and $t = \frac{1}{2}\pi$.

7. The useful, everyday idea of average speed can be defined as the total distance travelled divided by the time taken.

(*a*) If A and B are 15 km apart in a straight line, and 20 km apart by road and if the journey by road takes 20 minutes, calculate the average speed and the magnitude of the average velocity.

(*b*) A man ran one complete circuit of a 400 m track in 50 seconds. Calculate his average speed in m/s and his average velocity.

(*c*) Describe circumstances under which the average speed and the magnitude of the average velocity are equal.

8. Suppose that a particle moves along a straight line so that its distance, d cm, from a point O after t seconds is given by

$$d = 2^t.$$

Calculate the magnitude of the average velocity over the following time intervals and so estimate this magnitude as t approaches 0.

(*a*) $t = 0$ to 4; (*b*) $t = 0$ to 3; (*c*) $t = 0$ to 2;
(*d*) $t = 0$ to 1; (*e*) $t = 0$ to $\frac{1}{2}$; (*f*) $t = 0$ to $\frac{1}{4}$.

9. A particle describes a circle of radius 3 cm at a steady speed. If at zero time it is in position A and moves through a quadrant in one second, find by drawing and measurement the average velocity in the first: (*a*) second, (*b*) $\frac{1}{2}$ second, (*c*) $\frac{1}{4}$ second, (*d*) $\frac{1}{8}$ second. Estimate the velocity at A.

2. VELOCITY: $v = dr/dt$

From the diagrams of Exercise A, it is obvious that the average velocity is not necessarily along either the radius vector or the curve. What happens to the average velocity as one takes shorter and shorter time intervals?

Consider a particle moving along the curve shown in Figure 3 so that it passes position A at zero time, and positions B, C and D at successive second intervals when AB, AC, AD are of lengths 0·5 m, 1·1 m, 1·7 m, in the directions shown. The average velocities over the 3, 2 and 1 s intervals from A to D, C and B are 0·57 (1·7/3), 0·55 (1·1/2) and 0·5 m/s in the directions shown.

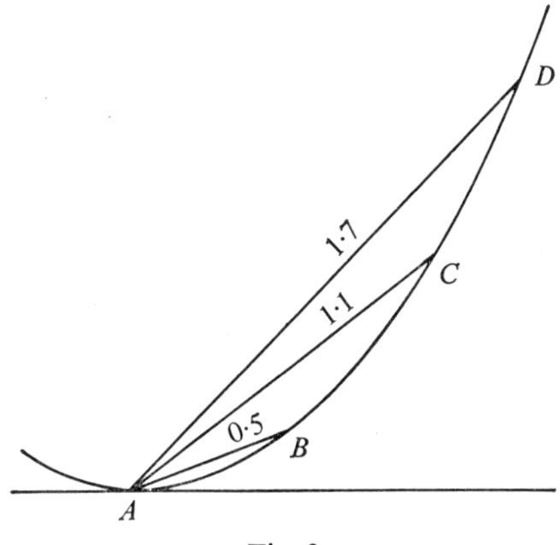

Fig. 3

If, by taking shorter and shorter intervals we can make the average velocity as close to 0·49 m/s as we please, then we should say that the velocity *at A* was 0·49 m/s in the direction of the tangent at A, since this is the direction towards which the direction of the average velocity tends.

In general, we can denote the displacement or change in position $\mathbf{r}_{\frac{1}{2}} - \mathbf{r}_1$ by $\delta\mathbf{r}$. If the corresponding time interval is denoted by δt, then the average velocity will be $\delta\mathbf{r}/\delta t$.

If as $\delta t \to 0$, $\delta\mathbf{r}/\delta t$ tends to a limit both in magnitude and direction, then we denote this limit by $d\mathbf{r}/dt$ and this, by definition, is the velocity of the point at the time t and position $\mathbf{r}$. Denoting this velocity by $\mathbf{v}$, we have $\mathbf{v} = d\mathbf{r}/dt$.

Now the limiting direction of the chord $\overline{PP'}$ of Figure 4 is of course the direction of the tangent at P, so the direction of $\mathbf{v}$ will be tangential to the path. Moreover, it is reasonable to suppose that the ratio of the arc length to the chord length PP' tends to unity as P' approaches P, so the magnitude of the velocity at P is the rate of change of distance with time along the path, or what we would understand by the speed of P along its path.

This result cannot be used in a calculation unless **r** can be expressed as a function that can be differentiated with regard to t. The vector equations of curves are just such functions. For example

$$\mathbf{r} = t\mathbf{i}+t^2\mathbf{j}$$

$$\Rightarrow \mathbf{v} = \frac{d\mathbf{r}}{dt} = \mathbf{i}+2t\mathbf{j}.$$

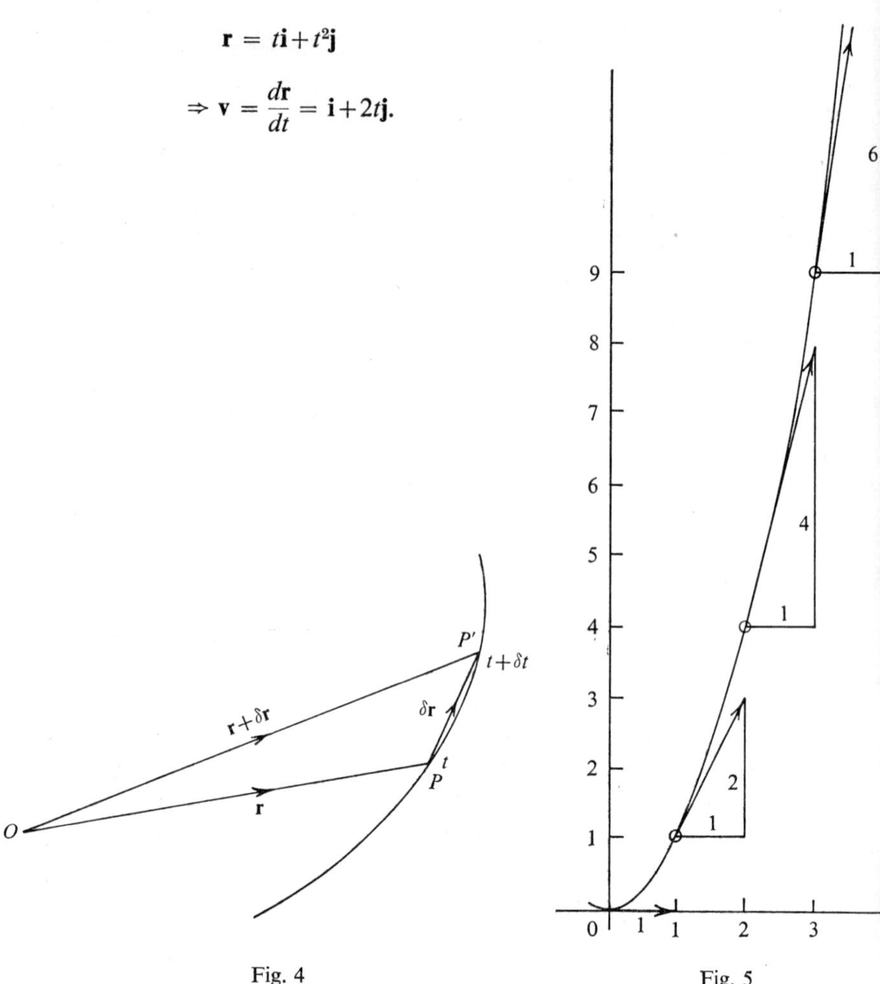

Fig. 4

Fig. 5

Perhaps it is easier to think of this as a velocity with magnitude

$$\sqrt{\{1^2+(2t)^2\}}$$

and making an angle of $\tan^{-1}(2t/1)$ with the x-axis.

Figure 5 is a sketch of the curve. The points and velocities marked are for $t = 0, 1, 2$, and 3. Writing the vectors in column form, check that the entries in the following table are correct.

Time	Position	Velocity
$t = 0$	$\begin{pmatrix} t \\ t^2 \end{pmatrix} = \begin{pmatrix} 0 \\ 0 \end{pmatrix}$	$\begin{pmatrix} 1 \\ 2t \end{pmatrix} = \begin{pmatrix} 1 \\ 0 \end{pmatrix}$
1	$\begin{pmatrix} 1 \\ 1 \end{pmatrix}$	$\begin{pmatrix} 1 \\ 2 \end{pmatrix}$
2	$\begin{pmatrix} 2 \\ 4 \end{pmatrix}$	$\begin{pmatrix} 1 \\ 4 \end{pmatrix}$
3	$\begin{pmatrix} 3 \\ 9 \end{pmatrix}$	$\begin{pmatrix} 1 \\ 6 \end{pmatrix}$

The following miscellaneous points should be noticed:

(i) The velocity vectors, though they may be associated with or derived from position vectors, are themselves free vectors and do not refer to an origin.

(ii) If we write the general expression for a position vector in two dimensions as

$$\mathbf{r} = x\mathbf{i}+y\mathbf{j}, \quad \text{then} \quad \mathbf{v} = \frac{d\mathbf{r}}{dt} = \frac{dx}{dt}\mathbf{i}+\frac{dy}{dt}\mathbf{j}.$$

The direction of the velocity will be given by

$$\tan^{-1}\left(\frac{dy}{dt}\bigg/\frac{dx}{dt}\right)$$

and this is the same as $\tan^{-1}(dy/dx)$, which is the inclination of the curve for the same values of t. This result has been more generally stated at the foot of p. 507.

(iii) The relation between the vector and the magnitude and direction form (for positions, or velocities, or accelerations) can easily be illustrated.

Suppose $\mathbf{b} = \begin{pmatrix} p \\ q \end{pmatrix}$. Then $b = \sqrt{(p^2+q^2)}$ and, setting $\tan\theta = q/p$, the triangle shown in Figure 6 can be drawn either from (p and q) or from (b and θ).

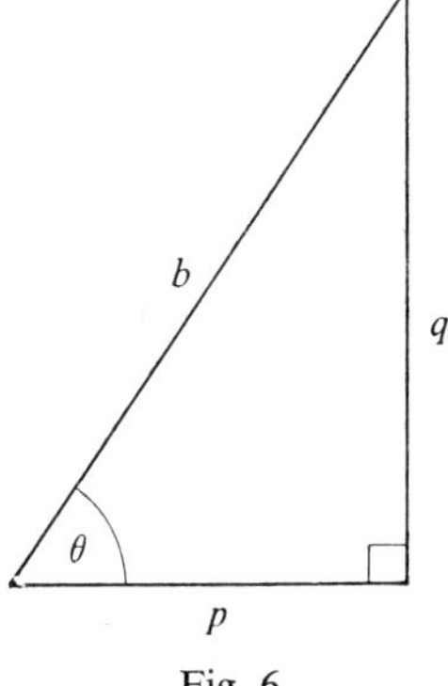

Fig. 6

(iv) In most applications, the scalar involved in the derivative of a vector is 'time', and, for these, a particularly simple notation is reserved whereby the derivative is denoted by placing a dot above the variable. For example

$\frac{d\mathbf{r}}{dt}$ may be written $\dot{\mathbf{r}}$, so $\mathbf{v} = \dot{\mathbf{r}}$ (read as 'r dot').

The second derivative of $\mathbf{r}$ with respect to t is shown as $\ddot{\mathbf{r}}$ (read as 'r double dot') and this, as we shall see, gives the acceleration:

$$\mathbf{a} = \dot{\mathbf{v}} = \ddot{\mathbf{r}}.$$

Also if $\mathbf{r} = x\mathbf{i}+y\mathbf{j}$, then

$$\dot{\mathbf{r}} = \dot{x}\mathbf{i}+\dot{y}\mathbf{j} \quad \text{and} \quad \ddot{\mathbf{r}} = \ddot{x}\mathbf{i}+\ddot{y}\mathbf{j}.$$

For example, if

$$\mathbf{r} = t^3\mathbf{i}+\sin \tfrac{1}{2}\pi t\mathbf{j},$$

$$\dot{\mathbf{r}} = 3t^2\mathbf{i}+\tfrac{1}{2}\pi \cos \tfrac{1}{2}\pi t\mathbf{j},$$

$$\ddot{\mathbf{r}} = 6t\mathbf{i}+(\tfrac{1}{2}\pi)^2 (-\sin \tfrac{1}{2}\pi t)\mathbf{j}.$$

In this section we have been making assumptions about vector differentiation which have yet to be proved. For example, in differentiating the term $t^3\mathbf{i}$, can we assume that we get $3t^2\mathbf{i}$ just as if we were differentiating $7t^3$ to get $7.3t^2 = 21t^2$? And what would happen if the expressions contained variable vectors unlike $\mathbf{i}$ and $\mathbf{j}$? The next Sections 2.1 and 2.2 contain the necessary proofs.

***2.1 The derivative.** Before we come to prove theorems on vector differentiation, a formal definition of the derivative of a vector with respect to a scalar is given for the sake of completeness. It can, however, be omitted at this stage.

Let S be a set of scalars $\{s\}$ and $\mathbf{V}$ a set of vectors $\{\mathbf{v}\}$ and suppose there is a function $F\colon S \to \mathbf{V}$, then we can write $\mathbf{v} = F(s)$. If for a particular s there exists a fixed vector $\mathbf{L}$ such that

$$\left|\frac{\delta\mathbf{v}}{\delta s}-\mathbf{L}\right| \to 0 \quad \text{as} \quad \delta s \to 0,$$

then we say

$$\lim_{\delta s\to 0} \frac{\delta \mathbf{v}}{\delta s} = \mathbf{L},$$

and denote this limit by

$$F'(s) \quad \text{or} \quad \frac{d\mathbf{v}}{ds}.$$

Thus we have

$$\frac{d\mathbf{v}}{ds} = \mathbf{L} \quad \text{or} \quad F'(s) = \mathbf{L}.$$

In particular when defining the velocity $\mathbf{v}$ as the limit of $\delta\mathbf{r}/\delta t$ it is implied that the modulus of the vector difference between the average velocity $\delta\mathbf{r}/\delta t$ and $\mathbf{v}$ tends to zero as δt tends to zero.

Although we can define a function from set A to set B, where the elements $\mathbf{a}$ and $\mathbf{b}$ of A and B are both vectors, it is not possible, in general, to define its derivative since this would involve $\delta\mathbf{b}/\delta\mathbf{a}$, and this is something to which we cannot attach a meaning.

2.2 Theorems on vector differentiation. For convenience of writing, the differentiation in the following theorems is with respect to t, but the theorems apply to any scalars for which the derivatives exist.

(i) $d\mathbf{b}/dt = \mathbf{0}$ where $\mathbf{b}$ is a constant vector and $\mathbf{0}$ the zero vector. The proof is left as an exercise.

(ii) If $\mathbf{b}$ and $\mathbf{c}$ are functions of t then $(d/dt)(\mathbf{b}+\mathbf{c}) = \dot{\mathbf{b}}+\dot{\mathbf{c}}$.

Suppose that as t changes from t to $t+\delta t$, $\mathbf{b}$ and $\mathbf{c}$ change from $\mathbf{b}$ to $\mathbf{b}+\delta\mathbf{b}$ and from $\mathbf{c}$ to $\mathbf{c}+\delta\mathbf{c}$; then

$$\delta(\mathbf{b}+\mathbf{c}) = (\mathbf{b}+\delta\mathbf{b}+\mathbf{c}+\delta\mathbf{c})-(\mathbf{b}+\mathbf{c}) = \delta\mathbf{b}+\delta\mathbf{c}.$$

The result follows by considering the limits after dividing through by δt.

(iii) If p and $\mathbf{b}$ are functions of t, then $(d/dt)(p\mathbf{b}) = \dot{p}\mathbf{b}+p\dot{\mathbf{b}}$.

$$\delta(p\mathbf{b}) = (p+\delta p)(\mathbf{b}+\delta\mathbf{b})-p\mathbf{b} = p\,\delta\mathbf{b}+\delta p\,\mathbf{b}+\delta p\,\delta\mathbf{b}.$$

Hence
$$\frac{\delta(p\mathbf{b})}{\delta t} = p\frac{\delta\mathbf{b}}{\delta t}+\frac{\delta p}{\delta t}\mathbf{b}+\delta p\frac{\delta\mathbf{b}}{\delta t}.$$

As $\delta t \to 0$, $\dfrac{\delta\mathbf{b}}{\delta t}\to\dfrac{d\mathbf{b}}{dt}$, $\dfrac{\delta p}{\delta t}\to\dfrac{dp}{dt}$ and $\delta p\dfrac{\delta\mathbf{b}}{\delta t}\to 0\dfrac{d\mathbf{b}}{dt} = \mathbf{0}$,

from which the result follows. In particular, if p is constant

$$\frac{d}{dt}(p\mathbf{b}) = p\dot{\mathbf{b}}$$

and if $\mathbf{b}$ is constant
$$\frac{d}{dt}(p\mathbf{b}) = \dot{p}\mathbf{b}.$$

(iv) If $\mathbf{b}$ and $\mathbf{c}$ are functions of t, then

$$\frac{d}{dt}(\mathbf{b}.\mathbf{c}) = \dot{\mathbf{b}}.\mathbf{c}+\mathbf{b}.\dot{\mathbf{c}}.$$

Here $\mathbf{b}.\mathbf{c}$ represents the scalar product of the vectors $\mathbf{b}$ and $\mathbf{c}$.

Now
$$\delta(\mathbf{b}.\mathbf{c}) = (\mathbf{b}+\delta\mathbf{b}).(\mathbf{c}+\delta\mathbf{c})-\mathbf{b}.\mathbf{c}$$
$$= \mathbf{b}.\delta\mathbf{c}+\delta\mathbf{b}.\mathbf{c}+\delta\mathbf{b}.\delta\mathbf{c}.$$

Hence,
$$\frac{\delta(\mathbf{b}.\mathbf{c})}{\delta t} = \mathbf{b}.\frac{\delta\mathbf{c}}{\delta t}+\frac{\delta\mathbf{b}}{\delta t}.\mathbf{c}+\frac{\delta\mathbf{b}}{\delta t}.\delta\mathbf{c}.$$

In the limit as $\delta t \to 0$,

$$\frac{\delta\mathbf{c}}{\delta t}\to\frac{d\mathbf{c}}{dt},\quad \frac{\delta\mathbf{b}}{\delta t}\to\frac{d\mathbf{b}}{dt}\quad\text{and}\quad \frac{\delta\mathbf{b}}{\delta t}.\delta\mathbf{c}\to\frac{d\mathbf{b}}{dt}.\mathbf{0} = 0,$$

from which the result follows.

It should be noted that in the first stage of this proof use has been made of the distributive and commutative laws for scalar products of vectors and in the final stage, as well as in the proof of (iii), we have assumed that $\lim(\mathbf{l}.\mathbf{m}) = \lim\mathbf{l}.\lim\mathbf{m}$; including the special cases of this where either $\mathbf{l}$ or $\mathbf{m}$ is constant. The truth of this theorem can be deduced from the corresponding theorem for scalars.

Exercise B

(Some questions may be solved by drawing)

In each of Questions 1–5:

(*a*) Sketch the curve from $t = 0$ to $t = 3$;
(*b*) differentiate to find $\mathbf{v}$;
(*c*) calculate the velocity when $t = 0, 1, 3$, and write the answer
(i) in one of the vector forms,
(ii) giving the magnitude and direction;
(*d*) mark the velocity on the curve, using lines roughly proportional to the velocity's magnitude and ended with a single arrow.

1. $\mathbf{r} = t\mathbf{i}$. **2.** $\mathbf{r} = t(\mathbf{i}-\mathbf{j})$. **3.** $\mathbf{r} = \sin \frac{1}{2}\pi t\mathbf{i}$.

4. $\mathbf{r} = \mathbf{i}+t^3(\mathbf{i}+2\mathbf{j})$. **5.** $\mathbf{r} = t\mathbf{i}+t^2\mathbf{j}$.

In the remaining questions of this exercise, we shall use the convention that **e**, **n**, **u** are unit vectors in the directions east, north and vertically upward from a point H on a flat earth.

6. (*a*) Given that $\mathbf{v} = \mathbf{e}+\mathbf{n}$ and $\mathbf{w} = 2\mathbf{e}-\mathbf{n}$, express the sum of these velocities in the vector form and as speed and direction.

(*b*) Given that $\mathbf{v}$ is a velocity of 20 km/h in the direction due north, and $\mathbf{w}$ is a velocity of 15 km/h in the direction due east, express the sum $\mathbf{v}+2\mathbf{w}$ in vector form and as speed and direction.

(*c*) Given that $\mathbf{v}$ is a velocity of 30 km/h in the direction north 30° west and $\mathbf{w}$ is a velocity of 40 km/h in the direction north 60° east, express the sum $\mathbf{v}$ and $\mathbf{w}$ in vector form and as speed and direction.

7. The position of an aircraft relative to the point H is given by

$$\mathbf{r} = 5\mathbf{u}+1000\sqrt{2}\,t(\mathbf{n}+\mathbf{e});$$

t being measured in hours and the magnitudes of the vectors in km. Describe its altitude, speed and course and calculate its distance from H five minutes after passing over H.

8. A dog and its master are exercising in a field. The position of the master is given by $\mathbf{r} = 2t(2\mathbf{n}+\mathbf{e})$; the position of the dog is given by

$$\mathbf{r} = (t \cos \tfrac{1}{2}\pi t+t)\mathbf{n}+(t^2+\sin \tfrac{1}{2}\pi t)\mathbf{e}.$$

How far apart are they and what are their velocities (in vector form) when $t = 0$ and $t = 4$?

9. A bullet has a velocity $\mathbf{v} = 2000\mathbf{e}-32t\mathbf{u}$. Is the speed increasing or decreasing? What is the new velocity if the bullet is deflected through 60° clockwise in the horizontal plane? (The vertical component remains constant.)

10. Write down expressions for the position and velocity of the go-kart of Section 1 (*a*) along the straight and (*b*) along the semicircular arc of radius 168 m. Assume in (*a*) that when $t = 0$, both $\mathbf{r}$ and $\mathbf{v}$ are $\mathbf{0}$, and $\mathbf{a} = 2\mathbf{e}$; in (*b*) assume that when $t = 0$, $\mathbf{r} = 168\mathbf{e}$ and $\mathbf{v} = 26\mathbf{n}$.

3. AVERAGE ACCELERATION

Just as we have taken average velocity to be the vector change in position divided by the time interval, so we now define the average acceleration over an interval of time as the vector change in velocity divided by the change in time.

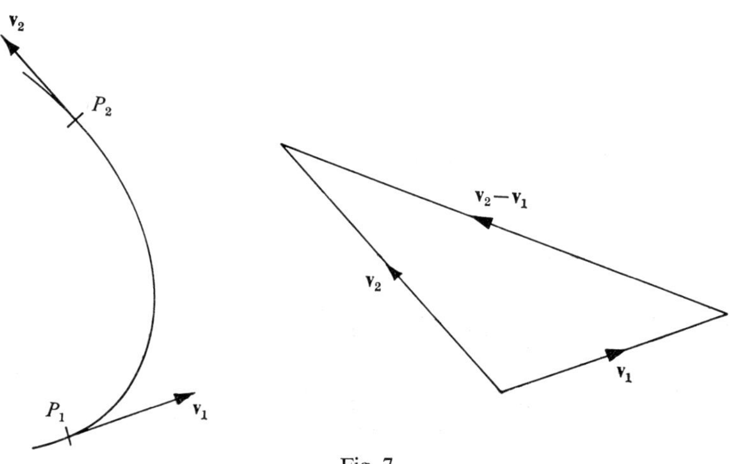

Fig. 7

If the velocities at P_1 and P_2 (see Figure 7) are $\mathbf{v}_1$ and $\mathbf{v}_2$, then the vector change in velocity is $\mathbf{v}_2-\mathbf{v}_1$; and hence the average acceleration in the corresponding interval t_1 to t_2 is

$$\frac{\mathbf{v}_2-\mathbf{v}_1}{t_2-t_1}.$$

Using S.I. units, the magnitude of the vector change of velocity is in metres per second units, the time interval in seconds, giving a unit for the magnitude of the acceleration in metres per second per second. This is written in standard notation as m/s^2 or m s^{-2}.

Example 1. A boy slides down a curved chute. When all directions are taken from the downward vertical, his velocities in positions *A*, *B* and *C* are 2 m/s at 20°, 4 m/s at 60°, and 8 m/s at 90°. If it takes him one second to slide from *A* to *B* and the same from *B* to *C*, find his average acceleration for each of the parts *AB*, *BC* and *AC* of the slide.

Figure 8 shows vectors $\mathbf{p}$, $\mathbf{q}$ and $\mathbf{r}$ representing the three velocities. By measurement $\mathbf{x}$ $(= \mathbf{q}-\mathbf{p})$ is 3 m/s in direction 88° and, as this is the change in velocity in 1 s, the average acceleration from *A* to *B* is 3 m/s^2 in direction 88°.

Similarly, by measuring **y**, the average acceleration from B to C is 5 m/s² in direction 115°. Again, by measuring **z** (7·6 m/s), which is the change in velocity in 2 s, the average acceleration from A to C is 3·8 m/s² in direction 105°.

Example 2. A stone thrown at 24 m/s at an angle of 30° above the horizontal experiences an average acceleration of 9 m/s² for 2 s in a direction 10° (backwards) from the downward vertical. What is its final velocity?

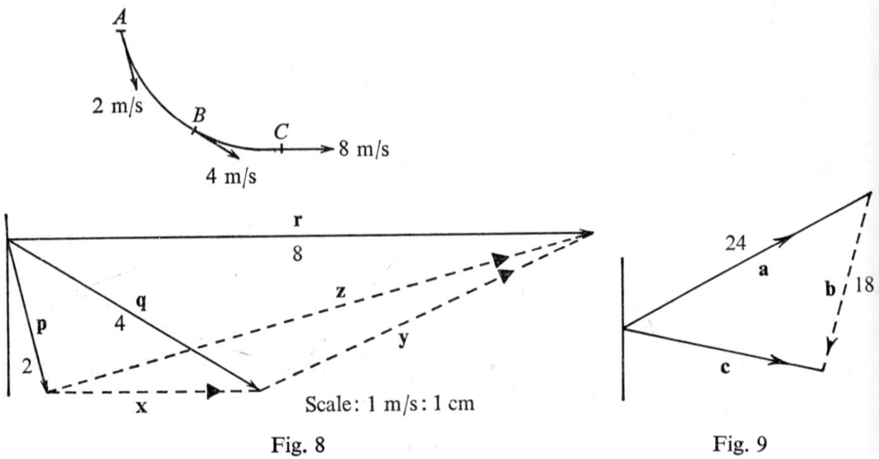

Fig. 8

Fig. 9

The vector **a** in Figure 9 represents the original velocity and **b** the change in velocity in 2 s, that is 2×9 m/s. The final velocity is therefore represented by **c** (= **a**+**b**) and is 19 m/s at 18° below the horizontal.

If instead of being given the average acceleration we had been told that the actual acceleration was constantly 9 m/s² in the same direction, the final velocity would have been the same.

Exercise C

(Some questions may be solved by drawing.)

1. In each of the following, calculate the vector change in velocity and hence the average acceleration over the given interval of time. Express the answers both in vector and in magnitude and direction form.

(*a*) $\mathbf{v} = t\mathbf{i}$ between $t = 0$ and $t = 2$;
(*b*) $\mathbf{v} = \mathbf{j}$ between $t = 0$ and $t = 3$;
(*c*) $\mathbf{v} = \mathbf{i}+2t\mathbf{j}$ between $t = 1$ and $t = 4$;
(*d*) $\mathbf{v} = \mathbf{i}+t^2(\mathbf{i}+2\mathbf{j})$ between $t = 2$ and $t = 3$.

2. A stone thrown horizontally with a speed of 20 m/s over a cliff edge experiences a constant acceleration of 10 m/s² vertically downwards. What is its velocity after $\frac{1}{2}$ s, 1 s, 2 s, 10 s?

3. A jet of water issues at 20 m/s at an upward angle of 70° to the horizontal. If each particle of water has a downward acceleration of 9·8 m/s², how long does it take such a particle to reach its highest point?

4. An electron moving at 8×10^6 m/s enters an electric field which gives it an acceleration of 2×10^{15} m/s² at right angles to its original direction for a period of 3×10^{-9} s. What is its final velocity?

5. What is the average acceleration of a cricket ball, moving horizontally, if its direction of motion is changed in 1/20 s through an angle of 120° and its speed increased from 15 to 18 m/s? In approximately what direction do you think the batsman played the ball?

6. A model aircraft is flying at 9 m/s in a horizontal circle of radius 15 m. What is the average acceleration in the interval in which its velocity changes direction from 000° to 030°? In what direction would you expect the acceleration to be at the instant when it is flying in the direction 000°?

4. ACCELERATION $a = dv/dt$

In Figure 10 suppose a particle having velocity $\mathbf{v}$ in position P at time t moves along some path to P' at time $t+\delta t$. If the vector change in velocity in this interval δt is denoted by $\delta\mathbf{v}$, so that the velocity at P' is $\mathbf{v}+\delta\mathbf{v}$, then we know the average velocity over this interval is $\delta\mathbf{v}/\delta t$.

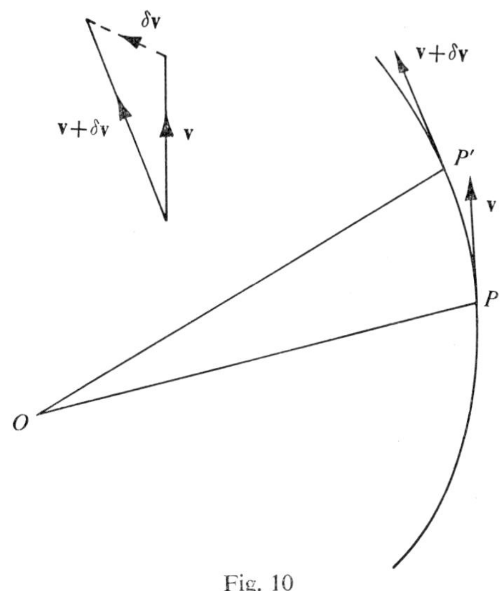

Fig. 10

We define the acceleration at the instant t to be the limiting value, if it exists, of this ratio as δt tends to zero. If we denote the acceleration by $\mathbf{a}$ and the limiting value of $\dfrac{\delta\mathbf{v}}{\delta t}$ by $\dfrac{d\mathbf{v}}{dt}$, then $\mathbf{a} = \dfrac{d\mathbf{v}}{dt}$.

The reader for whom the notion of acceleration is linked most closely with the increasing road speed of a car moving along either a straight or curved road, may wonder why we have not defined acceleration as the rate of change of speed regardless of direction. If this had been done, the average acceleration would have been

$$\frac{|\mathbf{v}+\delta\mathbf{v}|-|\mathbf{v}|}{\delta t},$$

where the numerator is the scalar difference between the magnitudes of the two velocities. Not only is this a scalar but in magnitude the numerator is in general not the same as the magnitude of $\delta\mathbf{v}$, and therefore this definition would be quite different from the one given. In particular, for a constant speed the second definition would lead to a zero acceleration, which the first does not unless the path is straight. The importance of the choice of definition will become apparent in Chapter 24 when Newton's law of motion is considered.

Example 3. Applying the rule to the motion specified by:

$$\mathbf{r} = 4t^2\mathbf{i}+t^3\mathbf{j}$$

gives

$$\mathbf{v} = 8t\mathbf{i}+3t^2\mathbf{j}$$

and

$$\mathbf{a} = 8\mathbf{i}+6t\mathbf{j}.$$

Writing the vectors in column form:

Time	Position	Velocity	Acceleration
$t = 0$	$\begin{pmatrix}4t^2\\t^3\end{pmatrix} = \begin{pmatrix}0\\0\end{pmatrix}$	$\begin{pmatrix}8t\\3t^2\end{pmatrix} = \begin{pmatrix}0\\0\end{pmatrix}$	$\begin{pmatrix}8\\6t\end{pmatrix} = \begin{pmatrix}8\\0\end{pmatrix}$
1	$\begin{pmatrix}4\\1\end{pmatrix}$	$\begin{pmatrix}8\\3\end{pmatrix}$	$\begin{pmatrix}8\\6\end{pmatrix}$
2	$\begin{pmatrix}16\\8\end{pmatrix}$	$\begin{pmatrix}16\\12\end{pmatrix}$	$\begin{pmatrix}8\\12\end{pmatrix}$

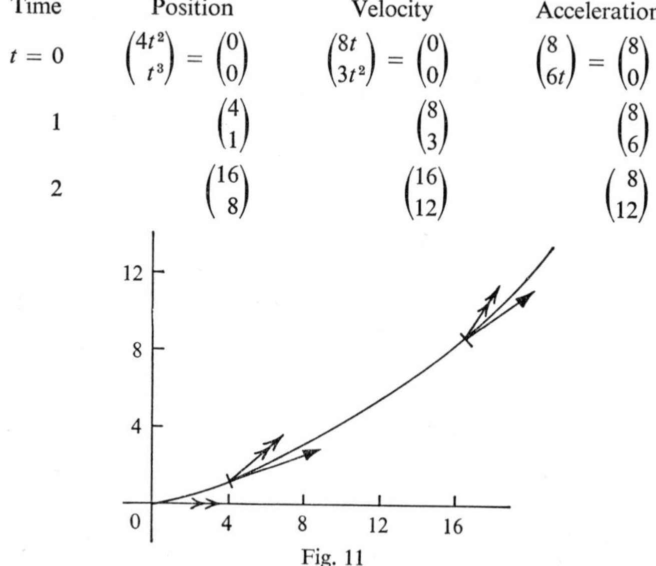

Fig. 11

Figure 11 is a sketch of the curve showing the velocities and accelerations.

As more complicated expressions are considered, it becomes convenient to refer to the components of the velocity (that is, $\dot{x}$ and $\dot{y}$) separately. For example, in the above curve, the position coordinates are $x = 4t^2$ and $y = t^3$, so the velocity components are $\dot{x} = 8t$ and $\dot{y} = 3t^2$, and similarly the acceleration components are $\ddot{x} = 8$ and $\ddot{y} = 6t$.

Example 4. A particle moves in a plane so that its Cartesian coordinates at time t are $x = \sin 2t$, $y = \cos t$. Discuss the motion.

The velocity and acceleration components are:

$$\dot{x} = 2\cos 2t, \qquad \dot{y} = -\sin t$$

and

$$\ddot{x} = -4\sin 2t, \qquad \ddot{y} = -\cos t.$$

The following table gives the components of position, velocity and acceleration vectors at a succession of times.

Time	Position	Velocity	Acceleration
$t = 0$	$A \begin{pmatrix} 0 \\ 1 \end{pmatrix}$	$\begin{pmatrix} 2 \\ 0 \end{pmatrix}$	$\begin{pmatrix} 0 \\ -1 \end{pmatrix}$
$t = \frac{1}{6}\pi$	$B \begin{pmatrix} \frac{1}{2}\sqrt{3} \\ \frac{1}{2}\sqrt{3} \end{pmatrix}$	$\begin{pmatrix} 1 \\ -\frac{1}{2} \end{pmatrix}$	$\begin{pmatrix} -2\sqrt{3} \\ -\frac{1}{2}\sqrt{3} \end{pmatrix}$
$t = \frac{1}{4}\pi$	$C \begin{pmatrix} 1 \\ 1/\sqrt{2} \end{pmatrix}$	$\begin{pmatrix} 0 \\ -1/\sqrt{2} \end{pmatrix}$	$\begin{pmatrix} -4 \\ -1/\sqrt{2} \end{pmatrix}$
$t = \frac{1}{3}\pi$	$D \begin{pmatrix} \frac{1}{2}\sqrt{3} \\ \frac{1}{2} \end{pmatrix}$	$\begin{pmatrix} -1 \\ -\frac{1}{2}\sqrt{3} \end{pmatrix}$	$\begin{pmatrix} -2\sqrt{3} \\ -\frac{1}{2} \end{pmatrix}$
$t = \frac{1}{2}\pi$	$E \begin{pmatrix} 0 \\ 0 \end{pmatrix}$	$\begin{pmatrix} -2 \\ -1 \end{pmatrix}$	$\begin{pmatrix} 0 \\ 0 \end{pmatrix}$

When these positions, together with other positions for times between $\frac{1}{2}\pi$ and 2π, are plotted, the path of the particle is as shown in Figure 12. The velocities and accelerations at these points, found from the tabulated components, are represented by arrows (a single head for velocity and a double head for acceleration) whose lengths are roughly proportional to their magnitudes.

From Q (at top left) the speed increases to A, where the acceleration is at right angles to the velocity; then decreases to a minimum somewhere between B and C, where again the acceleration and velocity are perpendicular and where the inward acceleration is large so that the turn is sharp; then increases to a maximum at E, where there is no acceleration; and similarly over the other sections of the path. A complete cycle takes 2π units of time.

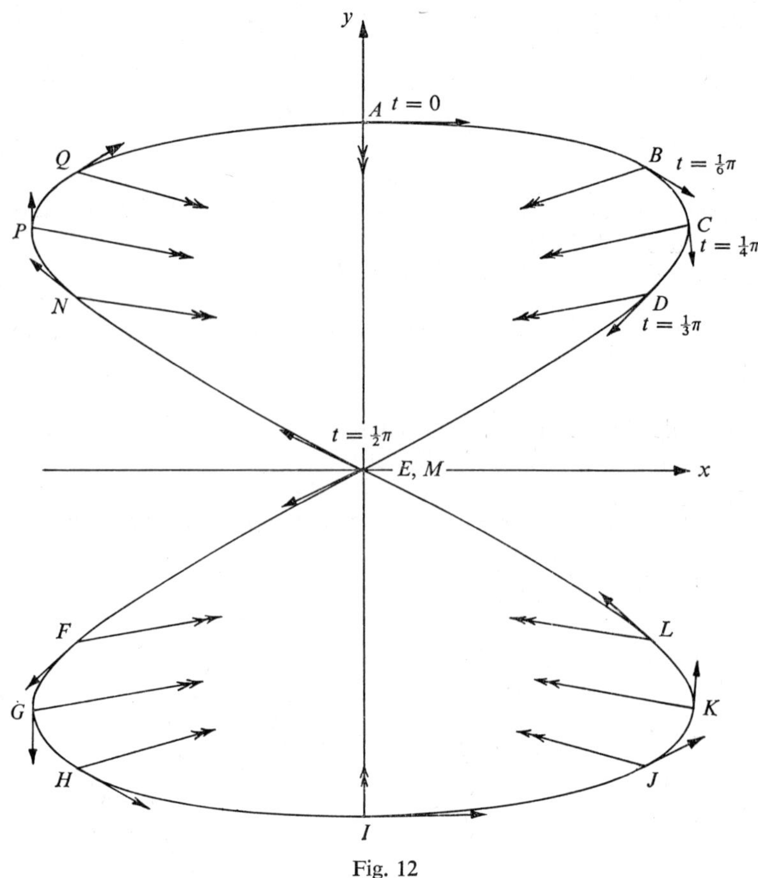

Fig. 12

Exercise D

1. A particle moves so that its position at time t is given by $x = 8t$, $y = 8t - t^2$. Find the velocity and acceleration coordinates when $t = 1$, 4 and 7, and hence, by drawing or calculation, the magnitude and direction of the velocity and acceleration at each of these times. Show these velocities and accelerations on a sketch of the path of the particle.

2. Repeat Question 1, but with $x = t^2$, $y = t^3$, for $t = -2, -1, 0, 1$ and 2.

3. Relative to perpendicular axes, the position vector of a particle at time t is given by

$$\mathbf{r} = \begin{pmatrix} t^3 \\ 10t^2 - 20t \end{pmatrix}.$$

Find $\mathbf{r}$, $\dot{\mathbf{r}}$ and $\ddot{\mathbf{r}}$, when $t = 0$, 1, 2 and 3, and hence, by drawing or calculation, obtain the magnitude and direction of the velocity and acceleration at each of these times. Show these vectors on a sketch of the path of the particle.

In general, at what type of point on the path of a moving particle do you expect the velocity and acceleration vectors to be in the same direction?

4. Sketch the path of the particle whose Cartesian coordinates are given parametrically in terms of the time t by $x = t^2$, $y = \sin t$. Calculate and show on the sketch the values of the velocity and acceleration at $t = 0, \frac{1}{2}\pi, \pi, \frac{3}{2}\pi$ and 2π. What is the gradient of the graph at $t = 2\pi$? Show that the acceleration and the velocity have the same direction when $\tan t = -1/t$ and give the approximate solutions of this equation when t is large.

5. What is the Cartesian equation of the path in Example 4?

6. Find, in terms of the time t, the magnitude and direction of the velocity and of the acceleration of the particle whose path is given by $x = \cos t$, $y = 1+\sin t$, and state any obvious relation between the velocity and acceleration. What sort of path do you think it is?

7. Explain why the motion of a particle whose position at time t is given by $x = \cos \omega t$, $y = \sin \omega t$, where ω is a constant, is one of constant speed in a circle. Find the magnitude and direction of the velocity and of the acceleration and draw any obvious conclusions about this type of motion.

8. If t denotes time, what type of motion of a particle P is represented by $x = \cos t^2$, $y = \sin t^2$?

Show that the velocity is perpendicular to OP, where O is the origin, and that the acceleration is equivalent to the sum of two accelerations, one of magnitude 2 perpendicular to OP and the other of magnitude $4t^2$ along PO.

9. An upright wheel, of radius 1 metre, rolls without slipping along the ground at 1 rad/s. The Cartesian coordinates of a point on the rim are (x, y) where $x = t-\sin t$, $y = 1-\cos t$. Sketch the locus of the point during two revolutions of the wheel and show on the sketch the velocities and accelerations at five or more points for each revolution.

10. Verify the values for x and y in terms of t in Question 9.

11. Show that the particle, whose motion is expressed in terms of the time parameter by $x = \sin t$, $y = t \cos t$, has its acceleration parallel to $y = x$ whenever it crosses the line $y = -x$. Sketch the path for $t = 0$ to $t = 4\pi$.

5. MOTION IN A CIRCLE

In the chapter so far, we have developed a technique for expressing velocity and acceleration by means of vectors, given in terms of their Cartesian components, and by differentiation of vectors. Now we shall consider a particular motion—motion in a circle—and we shall try to use the vector techniques to obtain simple expressions for velocity or acceleration so that, for example, we could immediately calculate the acceleration of an aircraft with a constant speed of 1200 km/h turning on an arc of radius of 1 km.

Although the speed of the aircraft is constant, its direction, and so its velocity, is changing. Furthermore, another very common example of circular motion is the rotation of a long-playing record. In this case, not only is the velocity of any point on the record visible for the reason given above, but also the speeds of points nearer the centre are different from the speed of the rim. There is, however, one thing constant and that is that the whole record is rotating at a constant $33\frac{1}{3}$ revolutions per minute. Its *angular velocity* is not changing.

5.1 Angular velocity of a position vector. When the position of a particle P in a plane is given in polar coordinates (r, θ) relative to a fixed point O and some fixed direction OA, its movement usually will involve changes in the angle θ. The rate at which the direction of the line OP

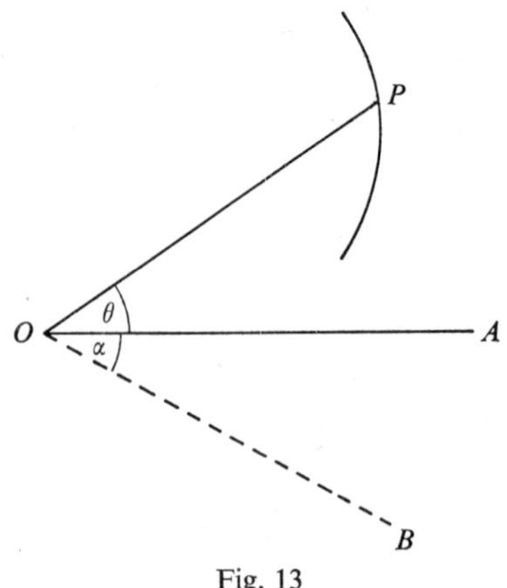

Fig. 13

changes with time, that is $\dot{\theta}$, is called the angular velocity of the line OP. It will frequently be denoted by the Greek letter ω (omega), so that $\omega = \dot{\theta}$. If, as is usual, θ is measured in radians and time in seconds, then ω is in rad/s. Other units which are sometimes employed are degrees per second, revolutions per minute (rev/min), and so on.

If some other fixed direction OB had been chosen instead of OA, where $\angle BOA = \alpha$, the angular velocity of OP would not have been affected since

$$\frac{d}{dt}(\theta+\alpha) = \frac{d\theta}{dt}.$$

Sometimes the angular velocity of OP is loosely referred to as the 'angular velocity of the point P about O', but more correctly it is a property of the line OP rather than the point P. To emphasize this distinction we shall consider the angular velocity of a lamina moving freely in a plane.

5.2 Angular velocity of a lamina. A lamina is a flat sheet of material, of negligible thickness, which can be considered to lie in a plane. At any instant of its motion, unless the motion is one of pure translation, it will have a rotational movement and all lines in the lamina will be changing direction at the same rate. This rate of change of direction is taken to be its angular velocity. Hence if PQ is some line in the lamina and AB is some fixed line of the plane, then the angular velocity of the lamina is defined to be $\dot{\theta}$ where θ is the angle between AB and PQ. It should be noticed that this angular velocity does not depend on the choice of AB or PQ—it is a property of the lamina's motion only.

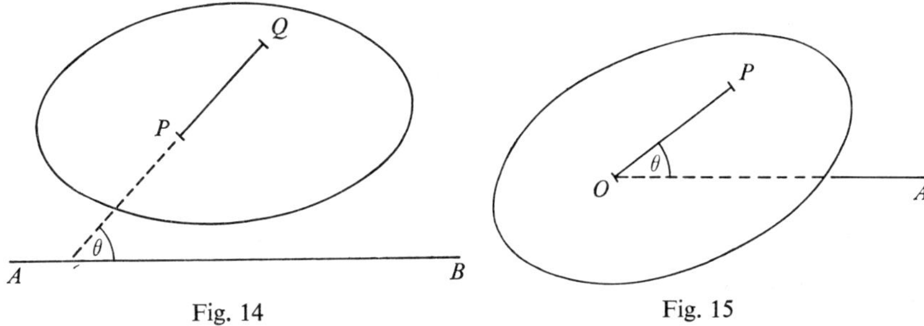

Fig. 14

Fig. 15

If the lamina is rotating about a fixed point O of the plane, then its angular velocity is the same as the angular velocity of OP, where P is any point of the lamina.

Note. The angular acceleration of a line or a lamina is $\ddot{\theta}$ if the angular velocity is $\dot{\theta}$.

5.3 Velocity in circular motion. With the centre of the circle at the origin, the magnitudes of the position vectors of all points on a circular path will be the same. Let the common magnitude be r. Then, from Figure 16, $x = r\cos\theta$, $y = r\sin\theta$.

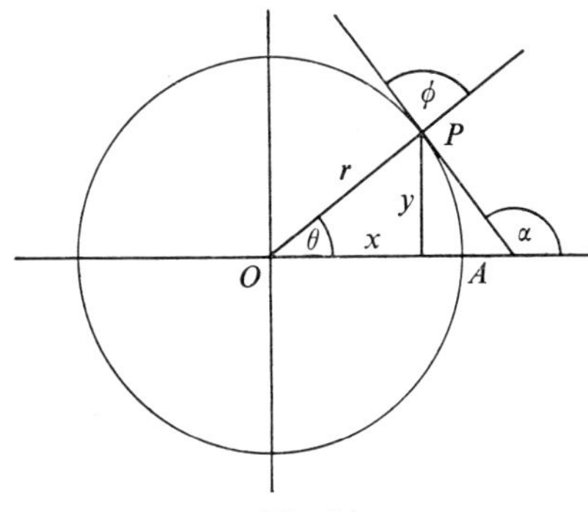

Fig. 16

Remember that if $z = \sin\theta$, then $\dfrac{dz}{d\theta} = \cos\theta$, where θ is measured in radians.

Then $$\frac{dz}{dt} = \frac{dz}{d\theta}.\frac{d\theta}{dt} = \cos\theta.\frac{d\theta}{dt}$$
$$= \dot{\theta}\cos\theta.$$

The position and velocity vectors become

$$\mathbf{r} = r\cos\theta\,\mathbf{i}+r\sin\theta\,\mathbf{j},$$
$$\mathbf{v} = \dot{\mathbf{r}} = r\dot{\theta}(-\sin\theta)\mathbf{i}+r\dot{\theta}\cos\theta\,\mathbf{j}.$$

The magnitude of the velocity is

$$v = \sqrt{\{[r\dot{\theta}(-\sin\theta)]^2+[r\dot{\theta}\cos\theta]^2\}}$$
$$= r\dot{\theta}\sqrt{\{(-\sin\theta)^2+(\cos\theta)^2\}}$$
$$= r\dot{\theta}.$$

The direction of the velocity makes an angle α with the x-axis where

$$\tan\alpha = \frac{\cos\theta}{-\sin\theta} = \frac{1}{-\tan\theta},$$

that is, $$\tan\alpha.\tan\theta = -1.$$

We found in Chapter 14, that this shows that $\alpha-\theta = \frac{1}{2}\pi$, i.e. that the velocity is perpendicular to the radius vector.

As the velocity (and later the acceleration) can be best described relative to the radius vector, we can also find the angle between the velocity and radius using the scalar product. If ϕ is the required angle, then

$$\mathbf{r}.\dot{\mathbf{r}} = \cos\phi\times r\times r\dot{\theta}$$
$$= [r\cos\theta\,\mathbf{i}+r\sin\theta\,\mathbf{j}].[r\sin\theta\dot{\theta}\,\mathbf{i}+r\cos\theta\dot{\theta}\,\mathbf{j}].$$
$$= r^2\dot{\theta}(-\cos\theta\sin\theta+\cos\theta\sin\theta).$$

Hence $$\cos\phi = 0,$$

and $$\phi = \tfrac{1}{2}\pi.$$

In short, the velocity of a point moving in a circle is of magnitude $v = r\dot{\theta}$ and its direction is perpendicular to the radius, that is, along the tangent.

A simpler way of appreciating the result is as follows. Let the arc length AP (see Figure 16) be denoted by s, then $s = r\theta$. Since this is true for all times under consideration, $\dot{s} = r\dot{\theta}$, r being a constant. This agrees with $v = r\dot{\theta}$ provided we are prepared to identify $\dot{s}$ with v.

Example 5. Convert the angular velocity of the turntable of a record player from $33\frac{1}{3}$ rev/min to rad/s, and find the speed of a point on the rim of a 30 cm record. (Radius = 15 cm.)

Since $$1 \text{ rev} = 2\pi \text{ radians},$$

$$33\tfrac{1}{3} \text{ rev/min} = \frac{100}{3} \times \frac{2\pi}{60} \text{ rad/s} \simeq 3{\cdot}5 \text{ rad/s}.$$

Using the formula $v = r\dot{\theta}$, the speed of a point 15 cm from the centre of the turntable

$$\simeq 0{\cdot}15 \times 3{\cdot}5 = 0{\cdot}525 \text{ m/s}.$$

Exercise E

1. An outboard motor is started by pulling a cord wound round a grooved wheel of radius 10 cm. If the cord is pulled at 1 m/s, what is the angular velocity of the wheel in rad/s and rev/min?

2. A helicopter's rotor blade is 4 m long and is rotating at 50 rev/min. Express this rate in rad/s, and find the speed of the tip of the blade.

3. A tennis ball of radius 3·7 cm is moving at 25 m/s carrying top spin of 10 rev/s. What are the speeds of the top and bottom points of the ball?

4. A wheel of radius $\frac{1}{2}$ metre is rolling along the ground and its centre has a speed of 10 m/s. What is the angular velocity of the wheel (in radians per second)? What are the linear velocities of (*a*) the top point, and (*b*) the foremost point (level with the centre) of the wheel?

5. What is the speed in m/s relative to the water of the tip of a ship's propeller which is 2·1 m from the centre of the shaft, when the propellor rotates at 1 rev/s and the ship's speed is 9·9 m/s? At what angle to the plane of the propeller would the blade near the tip have to be set if under the given conditions it was exerting no propulsive pressure on the water?

6. Assuming the planets move in circular orbits, one of Kepler's laws states that T^2/D^3 is constant, where T is the time for a complete revolution of a planet about the sun and D is its distance from the sun. If the angular velocity of the line from the sun to a planet is ω and the speed of the planet is v (assumed constant), find similar laws relating ω with D, v with D, and ω with v.

7. In Figure 14 explain why any PQ and AB suffice to determine the angular velocity.

8. Discuss the angular velocity of the line joining an observer to an athlete who is running at a steady speed round a circular track, where the observer is standing very close to the track but just inside. Illustrate with a graph.

9. A crane lifts one end of a girder directly upwards at a steady speed while the other end trails on the ground. Find a formula for the angular velocity of the girder in terms of its angle of slope and illustrate the relationship between these two quantities graphically.

10. A small cloud is moving with constant horizontal velocity v at a height h above an observer, and is at H as it passes over him. Express, in terms of h and θ, the horizontal distance x of the cloud from H when the angle of elevation is $\frac{1}{2}\pi - \theta$. Hence express v in terms of h, θ and $\dot{\theta}$. Sketch a graph of the angular velocity of the line from the observer to the cloud against θ, for values of θ from 0 to $\frac{1}{2}\pi$.

5.4 Acceleration in circular motion. Continuing the argument of Section 5.3, and differentiating a second time:

$$x = r\cos\theta, \qquad y = r\sin\theta,$$
$$\dot{x} = r\dot{\theta}(-\sin\theta), \qquad \dot{y} = r\dot{\theta}(\cos\theta),$$
$$\ddot{x} = r\{\dot{\theta}^2(-\cos\theta)+\ddot{\theta}(-\sin\theta)\}, \quad \ddot{y} = r\{\dot{\theta}^2(-\sin\theta)+\ddot{\theta}(\cos\theta)\}.$$

First, consider the case where the angular velocity is constant, that is when $\ddot{\theta} = 0$ and

$$\begin{aligned}\ddot{\mathbf{r}} &= \ddot{x}\mathbf{i}+\ddot{y}\mathbf{j}\\ &= r\dot{\theta}^2(-\cos\theta)\mathbf{i}+r\dot{\theta}^2(-\sin\theta)\mathbf{j}.\end{aligned}$$

Compare this with

$$\mathbf{r} = r\cos\theta\mathbf{i}+r\sin\theta\mathbf{j}.$$

and you will see that the acceleration has magnitude $r\dot{\theta}^2$ and direction parallel to the radius vector but opposite in direction, i.e. towards the centre of the circle.

Secondly, if the angular velocity is not constant, then

$$\ddot{\mathbf{r}} = [-r\dot{\theta}^2\cos\theta-r\ddot{\theta}\sin\theta]\mathbf{i}+[-r\dot{\theta}^2\sin\theta+r\ddot{\theta}\cos\theta]\mathbf{j}.$$

We can rearrange this expression in a most useful way as

$$\ddot{\mathbf{r}} = [-r\dot{\theta}^2\cos\theta\mathbf{i}-r\dot{\theta}^2\sin\theta\mathbf{j}]+[-r\ddot{\theta}\sin\theta\mathbf{i}+r\ddot{\theta}\cos\theta\mathbf{j}].$$

Now the first part is the same as the acceleration above when $\dot{\theta}$ is constant, and it represents an acceleration of $r\dot{\theta}^2$ along the radius vector towards the centre. The second part is another vector, whose magnitude is $r\ddot{\theta}$ and whose direction is parallel to the velocity, i.e. along the tangent.

The whole acceleration is equal to:

> One component of $r\dot{\theta}^2$ towards the centre and another component of $r\ddot{\theta}$ along the tangent.

Example 6. A space station in orbit rotates steadily so that a man at 12 m from the axis of rotation experiences an acceleration of 10 m/s²—about equivalent to that in the earth's gravitational field. What is the rate of rotation and how does the acceleration vary with the rate of rotation?

Using the formula $r\dot{\theta}^2$ for the acceleration towards the centre (there is no tangential acceleration since the speed is constant)

$$12\dot{\theta}^2 = 10,$$

and therefore $$\dot{\theta} = \surd(0{\cdot}83) \approx 0{\cdot}9.$$

So the space station rotates at 0·9 rad/s, or about 7 s for one rotation.

Since the acceleration is $r\dot{\theta}^2$ it varies as the square of the angular velocity; in fact, if the angular velocity were doubled, the acceleration would be about 10 m/s^2 at 3 m from the axis.

***5.5 An alternative proof: derivative of a unit vector.** When using Cartesian coordinates to describe the motion of a point it has been useful to express position in terms of unit vectors in fixed directions. Now when we use polar coordinates we shall find it convenient to express position in terms of a unit vector which can change its direction. As a preliminary to this we now investigate the derivative of such a vector.

The derivative of a unit vector, which is a function of time, is zero only if it is in a constant direction—when it is a constant vector. We shall find an expression for the derivative when the direction varies in some way with the time t.

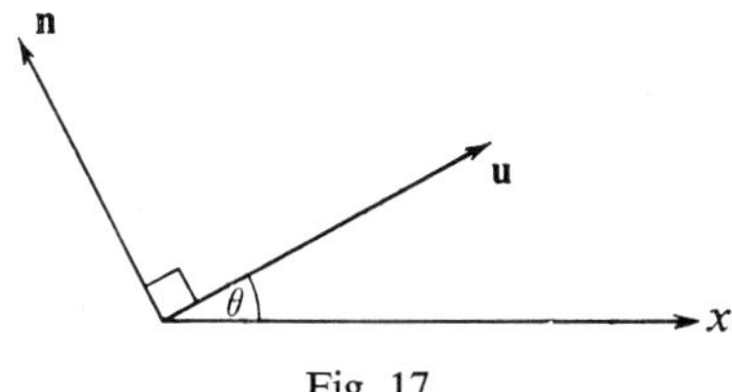

Fig. 17

Denote the unit vector whose derivative is to be found by **u**, and suppose it makes an angle θ with the x-axis (see Figure 17). Let the unit vector which makes an angle $\frac{1}{2}\pi+\theta$ with the x-axis be denoted by **n** (with the usual sign convention for angles). Then, if **i** and **j** represent unit vectors in the directions of the x- and y-axes,

$$\mathbf{u} = \cos\theta\,\mathbf{i}+\sin\theta\,\mathbf{j} \quad \text{and} \quad \mathbf{n} = -\sin\theta\,\mathbf{i}+\cos\theta\,\mathbf{j}.$$

Now

$$\begin{aligned}\dot{\mathbf{u}} &= \frac{d}{dt}(\cos\theta)\,\mathbf{i}+\frac{d}{dt}(\sin\theta)\,\mathbf{j}\\ &= -(\sin\theta)\,\dot{\theta}\,\mathbf{i}+(\cos\theta)\,\dot{\theta}\,\mathbf{j} \quad \left[\text{since}\,\frac{d(\cos\theta)}{dt} = \frac{d(\cos\theta)}{d\theta}\,\frac{d\theta}{dt} = -(\sin\theta)\,\dot{\theta}\right]\\ &= \dot{\theta}(-\sin\theta\,\mathbf{i}+\cos\theta\,\mathbf{j}).\end{aligned}$$

Hence

$$\dot{\mathbf{u}} = \dot{\theta}\mathbf{n}.$$

It is important to note that $\dot{\theta}$ has to be in *radians* per second, since

$$d/d\theta\,(\cos\theta) = -\sin\theta$$

only if θ is in radians.

***5.6 An alternative proof: velocity and acceleration in circular motion.** We shall show that for a particle moving in a circular path, its acceleration has components $r\dot{\theta}^2$ towards the centre and $r\ddot{\theta}$ tangentially.

Suppose the centre of the circular path of radius r is O, and at time t the particle has position vector $\mathbf{OP}(\mathbf{r})$ making an angle θ with a fixed radius OA. Then $\mathbf{r} = r\mathbf{u}$, where $\mathbf{u}$ is a unit vector in the direction OP. From this, using the result of Section 5.5 and the fact that r is constant,

$$\dot{\mathbf{r}} = r\dot{\theta}\mathbf{n},$$

where $\mathbf{n}$ is a unit vector perpendicular to OP (in the direction shown in Figure 18). Differentiating again, and treating the right side as the product of $r\dot{\theta}$ and $\mathbf{n}$,

$$\ddot{\mathbf{r}} = r\dot{\theta}\dot{\mathbf{n}} + r\ddot{\theta}\mathbf{n}.$$

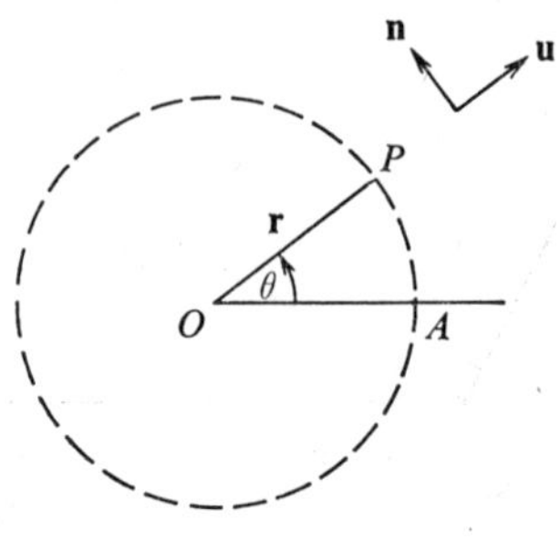

Fig. 18

But, since $\mathbf{n}$ is a unit vector, $\dot{\mathbf{n}} = -\dot{\theta}\mathbf{u}$. (Here we use again the result $\dot{\mathbf{u}} = \dot{\theta}\mathbf{n}$ and remember that the unit vector perpendicular to $\mathbf{n}$ in a positive direction is $-\mathbf{u}$.) Hence

$$\ddot{\mathbf{r}} = -r\dot{\theta}^2\mathbf{u} + r\ddot{\theta}\mathbf{n}.$$

So the acceleration has components in the *inward* radial and tangential directions of magnitudes $r\dot{\theta}^2$ and $r\ddot{\theta}$.

Exercise F

(Some questions may be solved by drawing.)

1. Show that the radial acceleration of $r\dot{\theta}^2$ can be expressed as v^2/r where v is the tangential speed.

2. If $\dot{\theta} = 3t^2$ radians per second and $r = 6$ m, what are the radial and tangential accelerations in m/s² when $t = 2$ s and $t = 3$ s? What are the total accelerations in these cases?

3. What is the acceleration of the go-kart of Section 1 when moving at a constant speed of 26 m/s along a circular arc of radius 168 m?

4. What is the acceleration of an aeroplane turning at constant speed of 1200 km/h in a circular arc of radius 5 km?

5. A car is travelling at a constant speed of 120 km/h round a bend consisting of part of a circular arc. The radial acceleration is 30 m/s^2. What is the radius of the bend?

6. A car enters a corner, which is an arc of a circle of radius 49 m, at 14 m/s (50·4 km/h) but slowing down at 5 m/s^2. Find the magnitude and direction of its acceleration.

7. (*a*) A bead threaded on a straight wire is distance x from a fixed point of the wire at time t, where $x = a \sin 2t$. Discuss the way in which the acceleration and the velocity vary for the motion.

(*b*) Discuss, in general terms, the way in which the acceleration and the velocity vary for a child on a swing.

8. A small bucket of water is being whirled round in a vertical circle at arm's length, with a speed of 2 m/s at the top and 3 m/s at the bottom of its path. What is the ratio of the magnitudes of the radial components of acceleration (the other components being tangential) in these two positions?

9. When trying to move a car parked on muddy ground one rear wheel is made to rotate at 3 rev/s whilst the car is stationary. What is the acceleration (in m/s^2) of a point on the tread of the tyre 30 cm from the centre of the axle? What would it be for a smaller wheel of radius 22·5 cm rotating at 4 rev/s? What would be the road speeds corresponding approximately to these two rates of rotation for the two sizes of wheel if there were no slipping?

($\pi^2 \approx 10$.)

10. Calculate the acceleration in m/s^2 towards the polar axis due to the earth's rotation, of a person (*a*) on the equator, and (*b*) in latitude 60°. (Radius of the earth is 6380 km.)

11. What is the acceleration of an aircraft which on coming out of a 'loop' is flying along a vertical circular path of radius 800 m, if its speed is 160 m/s and the speed is increasing at 10 m/s^2?

12. A pendulum of length L rotates about a vertical axis at a constant angular velocity ω with the pendulum rod inclined at the constant angle α to the vertical. Find a formula for the acceleration of the bob of the pendulum.

13. A man 1·8 m tall in a space station which is rotating at 1 rad/s has the top of his head 12 m from the centre of rotation. How far from the centre are his feet? If when he is standing with his head and feet along a radius from the centre of rotation he holds a small but massive body in front of him at head height and lets it go, will it hit his feet?

6. CONSTANT ACCELERATION

In Section 4, the special instance of motion along a given path was considered. In this section the particular condition of motion is that the acceleration should be constant. Again we need to find some formulae that can be used without reference to coordinate axes.

This time we shall start with $\ddot{\mathbf{r}} = \mathbf{a}$, the given constant acceleration. This could have been obtained by differentiation from $\mathbf{v} = \dot{\mathbf{r}} = t\mathbf{a}+\mathbf{b}$ (where $\mathbf{b}$ is another constant vector, to be found). When $t = 0$, $\mathbf{b}$ equals the particular value of $\dot{\mathbf{r}}$ at that instant; this initial velocity is usually denoted by $\mathbf{u}$. So

$$\mathbf{v} = \dot{\mathbf{r}} = t\mathbf{a}+\mathbf{u}.$$

Again, this could have been obtained from:

$$\mathbf{r} = \tfrac{1}{2}t^2\mathbf{a}+t\mathbf{u}+\mathbf{c}.$$

It is customary to assume a choice of origin such that $\mathbf{r} = \mathbf{0}$ when $t = 0$. This implies that

$$\mathbf{c} = \mathbf{0} \quad \text{and} \quad \mathbf{r} = \tfrac{1}{2}t^2\mathbf{a}+t\mathbf{u}.$$

Here we have two formulae connecting $\mathbf{v}$, $\mathbf{u}$, $\mathbf{a}$, t and $\mathbf{r}$, $\mathbf{u}$, $\mathbf{a}$, t. Two others are sometimes needed, connecting $\mathbf{r}$, $\mathbf{u}$, $\mathbf{v}$, t and $\mathbf{r}$, $\mathbf{a}$, u^2, v^2:

$$\mathbf{r} = \frac{\mathbf{u}+\mathbf{v}}{2}t \quad \text{from} \quad \mathbf{r} = \frac{t}{2}(2\mathbf{u}+t\mathbf{a}) = \frac{t}{2}(\mathbf{u}+\mathbf{v});$$

hence

$$\mathbf{v}+\mathbf{u} = \frac{2}{t}\mathbf{r}$$

and

$$\mathbf{v}-\mathbf{u} = t\mathbf{a}$$

$$\Rightarrow \quad v^2-u^2 = (\mathbf{v}+\mathbf{u}).(\mathbf{v}-\mathbf{u}) = 2\mathbf{a}.\mathbf{r}.$$

6.1 List of formulae for constant acceleration. For convenience the formulae we have found (with an extra one whose proof is left as an exercise) are listed below.

(i) $\mathbf{v} = \mathbf{u}+\mathbf{a}t$;
(ii) $\mathbf{r} = \tfrac{1}{2}(\mathbf{u}+\mathbf{v})t$;
(iii) $\mathbf{r} = \mathbf{u}t+\tfrac{1}{2}\mathbf{a}t^2$;
(iv) $\mathbf{r} = \mathbf{v}t-\tfrac{1}{2}\mathbf{a}t^2$;
(v) $v^2 = u^2+2\mathbf{a}.\mathbf{r}$.

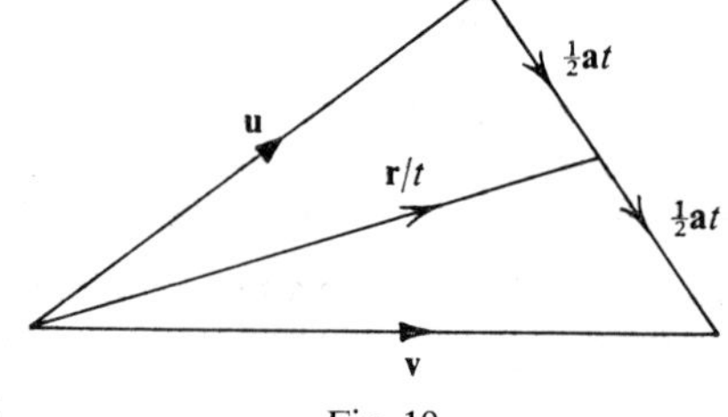

Fig. 19

All these formulae, except the last one, are incorporated in Figure 19.

These formulae apply, of course, in the special case where the motion is one-dimensional and the particle moves in a straight line, but it is simpler then to rewrite them as

$$v = u+at, \quad v^2 = u^2+2as$$

and so on, where u, v, a, s, are now understood to be simply directed quantities. (Traditionally displacement in one-dimensional problems is denoted by s and not r.)

Example 7. Find the velocity after 4 s of a particle whose initial velocity is $\begin{pmatrix}8\\-3\end{pmatrix}$ m/s, if it has constant acceleration of $\begin{pmatrix}2\\1\end{pmatrix}$ m/s². Find also the displacement in this time interval and check the formula $v^2 = u^2+2\mathbf{a}.\mathbf{r}$. Show the initial and final velocities in a sketch and give a rough indication of the path of the particle.

If the velocity after 4 s is $\mathbf{v}$ m/s, then

$$\mathbf{v} = \begin{pmatrix}8\\-3\end{pmatrix}+\begin{pmatrix}2\\1\end{pmatrix}4 = \begin{pmatrix}16\\1\end{pmatrix},$$

and using $\mathbf{r} = \mathbf{u}t+\frac{1}{2}\mathbf{a}t^2$, the displacement is given in metres by

$$\mathbf{r} = \begin{pmatrix}8\\-3\end{pmatrix}4+\frac{1}{2}\begin{pmatrix}2\\1\end{pmatrix}16 = \begin{pmatrix}32\\-12\end{pmatrix}+\begin{pmatrix}16\\8\end{pmatrix} = \begin{pmatrix}48\\-4\end{pmatrix}.$$

Hence the final velocity is $\begin{pmatrix}16\\1\end{pmatrix}$ m/s and the displacement $\begin{pmatrix}48\\-4\end{pmatrix}$ m. Now

$$v^2 = 16^2+1^2 = 257; \quad u^2 = 8^2+(-3)^2 = 73;$$

and $$2\mathbf{a}.\mathbf{r} = 2\begin{pmatrix}2\\1\end{pmatrix}.\begin{pmatrix}48\\-4\end{pmatrix} = 2(96-4) = 184;$$

and the relation $v^2 = u^2+2\mathbf{a}.\mathbf{r}$ is verified in this case.

Note. The displacement could equally well have been found from

$$\mathbf{r} = \tfrac{1}{2}(\mathbf{u}+\mathbf{v})\,t = \frac{1}{2}\left[\begin{pmatrix}8\\-3\end{pmatrix}+\begin{pmatrix}16\\1\end{pmatrix}\right]4 = \begin{pmatrix}48\\-4\end{pmatrix}.$$

Figure 20 shows the required sketch.

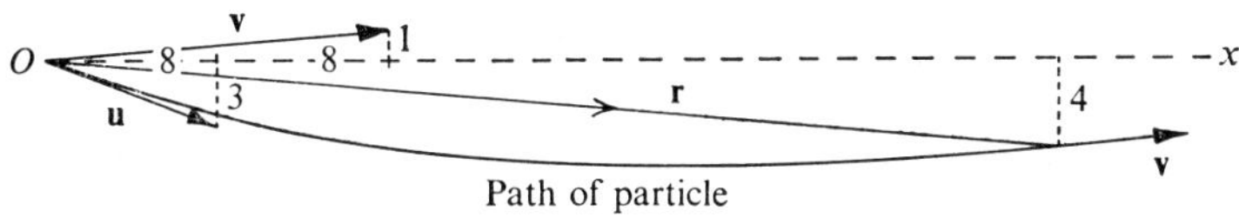

Fig. 20

Example 8. Find with what constant acceleration a skier travelling in a straight line increases her speed from 4 m/s to 10 m/s in a distance of 21 m.

Here we are relating u, v, a and s, so using $v^2 = u^2+2as$ we have (in metre-second units)

$$10^2 = 4^2+2a.21,$$

so that $$a = (100-16)/42 = 84/42 = 2.$$

The acceleration is therefore 2 m/s².

An alternative approach to the problem is by means of a velocity-time graph (see Figure 21). As the acceleration is constant the velocity increases steadily with time so that the graph is a straight line. The area under the graph represents the distance travelled, so that if t s is the time taken for this increase, then

$$\tfrac{1}{2}(10+4)t = 21,$$

or

$$t = 3.$$

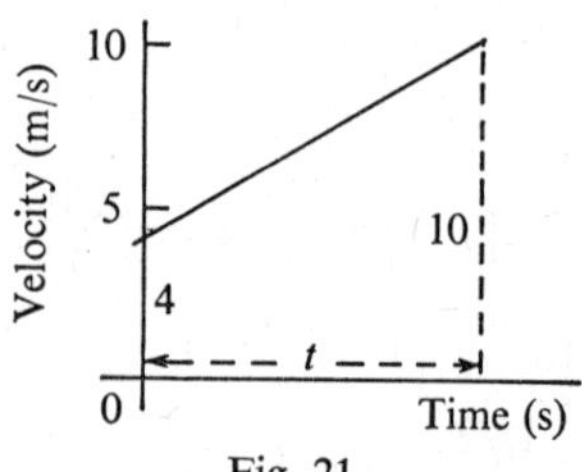

Fig. 21

Hence the velocity increases by 6 m/s in 3 s, which corresponds to a constant acceleration of 2 m/s^2.

Example 9. A train accelerates from rest at 810 kilometres per hour per hour. How far does a man move relative to the track if he walks steadily down the corridor towards the rear of the train at 6 km/h for 2 minutes from the time the train starts?

Let the forward direction be positive and the units be minutes and kilometres. Then, relative to the track, $u = -6/60$, $a = 810/(60)^2$, $t = 2$ and we are finding s.

$$s = ut + \tfrac{1}{2}at^2 = -\frac{6}{60}.2 + \tfrac{1}{2}.\frac{810}{(60)^2}.4$$

$$= -\tfrac{1}{5} + \tfrac{9}{20} = \tfrac{1}{4}.$$

So the man moves $\frac{1}{4}$ of a kilometre in the first 2 minutes.

Exercise G

(In this exercise acceleration is constant.)

1. The initial velocity of a particle is $\begin{pmatrix}4\\3\end{pmatrix}$ cm/s and the velocity after 6 s is $\begin{pmatrix}7\\-3\end{pmatrix}$ cm/s. Draw a vector diagram to represent these velocities and mark them **OA** and **OB**. What is **OM** if M is the mid-point of AB and what does it represent? Show in your figure the displacement vector for the 6 s interval. What are the velocity and acceleration after 3 s?

2. Find the velocity after 3 s of a particle whose initial velocity is $\begin{pmatrix}2\\4\end{pmatrix}$ m/s, if it has a constant acceleration of $\begin{pmatrix}6\\6\end{pmatrix}$ m/s^2. Find also the displacement in this time interval and check that $v^2 = u^2 + 2\mathbf{a}.\mathbf{r}$.

3. A car starting from rest has an acceleration of 8 kilometres per hour per second for the first 5 s and 5 kilometres per hour per second for the next 10 s. Use formulae to find its final speed and how many metres it has travelled in the 15 s. Show also how the results can be found from a velocity-time graph.

4. A body is travelling in direction 060° at 10 m/s. Express this as a vector with two components, one to the east and the other to the north. Find the components in these directions of the velocity after 5 s if it has a constant acceleration of 3 m/s² in a direction 210°. Express this velocity also in speed and direction.

5. An electron entering an electric field experiences a constant acceleration of 2×10^{15} m/s² in a direction 60° from its direction of entry. If its entry speed is 5×10^{6} m/s, find by drawing, and check by calculation, its speed after 2×10^{-9} s and the change in its direction of motion in this time. What is its displacement over a time interval of 4×10^{-9} s?

6. A particle has the constant acceleration

$$\begin{pmatrix}2\\-1\\3\end{pmatrix}\text{ cm/s}^2$$

relative to a set of mutually perpendicular axes in three dimensions. If its initial velocity is

$$\begin{pmatrix}-2\\4\\6\end{pmatrix}\text{ cm/s},$$

what are its velocities after 2, 4 and 8 s? What are the average velocities and what are the displacements in these intervals of 2, 4 and 8 s?

7. If

$$\mathbf{u} = \begin{pmatrix}1\\2\\3\end{pmatrix}\text{ mm/s and } \mathbf{a} = \begin{pmatrix}6\\2\\-3\end{pmatrix}\text{ mm/s}^2,$$

find $\mathbf{v}$ and $\mathbf{r}$ when $t = 2$ s, and check that $v^2 = u^2+2\mathbf{a}.\mathbf{r}$.

8. For a parachutist losing height steadily at 15 m/s, the wind changes from 12 m/s in direction 000° at 1500 m to 6 m/s in direction 090° at 900 m. Between these heights the wind changes so that the parachutist experiences a constant acceleration. Taking the northerly direction for the x-axis, the easterly direction for the y-axis, and vertically downwards for the z-axis, state his velocities at 1500 m and 900 m and his constant acceleration as column vectors. Find his displacements during each 150 m drop between these levels. Sketch the shape of the locus of his shadow on the ground. Find also his total displacement and check that $v^2 = u^2+2\mathbf{a}.\mathbf{r}$.

9. (*a*) For a particle moving in a straight line, $u = 6$ and $a = 2$. Sketch the velocity-time graph of this motion for the interval $t = 0$ to $t = 5$. What features of this graph represent the acceleration and the distance travelled? Find v and s when $t = 5$.

(*b*) If $u = 6$ and $a = -2$, sketch the velocity-time graph for the interval $t = 0$ to $t = 5$. Calculate the area under the graph for the intervals $t = 0$ to $t = 3$ and $t = 3$ to $t = 5$. What is the significance of the sum and difference of these areas in terms of displacements and distances travelled? Explain how the formula $s = \frac{1}{2}(u+v)t$ can be obtained from a velocity-time graph.

10. Draw the velocity-time graph for the movement of the man in Example 9 who starts with a velocity of -6 km/h and has an acceleration of 810 kilometres per hour per hour for 2 minutes. From your graph find when the velocity is zero.

What is represented by the areas under the two parts of the graph separated at the time for zero velocity? Hence find how far the man is from his starting point, relative to the track, after 2 minutes.

11. A bead on a straight wire has a speed of 12 cm/s in one direction (take this as the positive direction) and an acceleration of 3 cm/s² in the opposite direction. What is its velocity after 6 s and how far is it then from its initial position? Answer the same questions for 10 s instead of 6 s, and find for how long and for what distance it moves in the positive direction before reversing its movement. Find its velocity when its displacement from its initial position is (*a*) 20 cm, (*b*) -60 cm (use $v^2 = u^2+2as$).

7. MOTION UNDER GRAVITY—PROJECTILES

For a body moving freely in a small region of space near the earth's surface as, for example, a cricket ball, a car falling over a cliff, a rifle bullet or a bomb, the acceleration, if air resistance is neglected, is very nearly constant. This constant is the same for all bodies. The acceleration varies slighly in magnitude at different places on the earth's surface—from 9·78 metres per second per second at the equator to 9·83 metres per second per second at the north pole—and decreases with height. Its direction defines what we mean by vertically downward at each place, although because of the earth's rotation and for other reasons it is not exactly directed towards the centre of the earth.

Over any particular locality of the earth's surface we shall represent the acceleration by the constant vector **g**, taking its magnitude to be 9·8 metres per second per second; its direction is vertically downward. With these assumptions the effects of air resistance must be neglected. This is quite an important factor to omit, particularly at high speeds, so that the theory of the motion of projectiles (a general name to describe such freely moving bodies) developed on these assumptions can only be expected to be a first approximation to reality.

7.1 The path of a projectile by drawing. If the initial velocity is **u** and the velocity after t units of time is **v**, where the constant acceleration is **g** vertically downwards, then the relationship between these vectors is that shown in Figure 22(*a*). When this triangle is enlarged by the factor t we get triangle PQS of Figure 22(*b*). Now the displacement **r** in this time t is given by

$$\mathbf{r} = \tfrac{1}{2}(\mathbf{u}+\mathbf{v})t = \tfrac{1}{2}(\mathbf{u}t+\mathbf{v}t)$$

and is found by joining P to the mid-point R of QS. This method lends itself to a mass-production technique as in the following example.

We shall sketch the path of a stone thrown at 36 m/s at an angle of 40° above the horizontal, where the gravitational constant is 10 m/s², by plotting its position at second intervals. AB is drawn to represent the initial velocity; then down the vertical line BK are marked off equal segments each representing g, so that the velocity when $t = 3$, for example, is

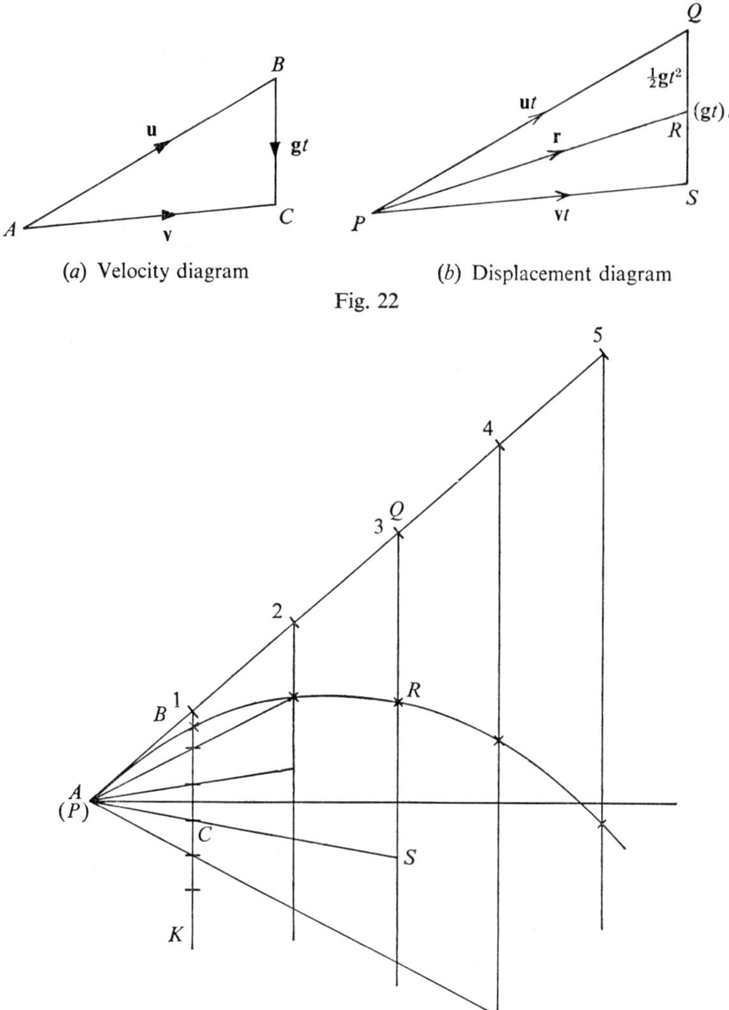

(*a*) Velocity diagram (*b*) Displacement diagram

Fig. 22

Scale: 1 cm represents 20 m/s

Fig. 23

represented by AC where BC is three of these segments. To find the displacement at this time (and therefore the position of the projectile) ABC is enlarged three times to give PQS (compare triangles ABC and PQS in Figure 22) and the displacement is then given by AR where R is the mid-point of QS. Similarly other points on the path can be plotted.

Exercise H

(Take $\mathbf{g}$ to be 10 m/s² vertically downwards, and neglect air resistance.)

1. Sketch the path of a ball thrown at 15 m/s at an angle of 40° above the horizontal, by plotting its positions after 1, 2, 3, 4 and 5 s. Use a scale of 10 m/s to 1 cm.

2. Sketch the path of a ball thrown at 30 m/s at an angle of 40° above the horizontal, by plotting its positions after 1, 2, 3, 4 and 5 s. Use a scale of 10 m/s to 1 cm.

3. Sketch the path of a car driven horizontally at 108 km/h (30 m/s) straight over a cliff 30 m high. Use the fact that the displacement vertically in t s is $\frac{1}{2}gt^2$ m to check the position of the point of impact by calculation.

4. Sketch the shape of a concentrated jet of water which leaves the nozzle at 35 m/s at 30° above the horizontal. If it leaves the nozzle at ground level, and the ground is horizontal, use a displacement diagram to find the time each water particle is in the air, and hence the horizontal range of the jet (see $\triangle PQS$ of Figure 22). Calculate the range of the water jet if the nozzle is pointed at (*a*) 60°, and (*b*) 45° above the horizontal. Comment on your results.

5. A boy standing on a hillside which slopes at 20° to the horizontal, throws a stone straight up the slope at an angle of 55° above the horizontal at 15 m/s. Draw a displacement diagram and use the sine formula to calculate the time the stone is in the air; hence find its range up the hill.

6. A marble is rolled across an inclined plane whose slope is such that the marble accelerates at 5 m/s² in the direction of the steepest slope of the plane. If its initial velocity is 10 m/s at 30° from the upward direction of steepest slope, calculate its speed and direction after 3 s. When does it reach its highest point up the plane and what is its speed then?

7. If a particle is projected at V, $\theta°$ above the horizontal, show that its range in a horizontal direction is $V^2 \sin 2\theta°/g$. For what angle is the range a maximum?

***8.** A particle is projected at V, from a point on a plane inclined at α to the horizontal, and its initial direction lies in a vertical plane which cuts the inclined plane along a line of greatest slope and is at θ above the plane. Show that the range up the plane is

$$\frac{V^2}{g\cos^2\alpha}[\sin(\alpha+\theta)-\sin\alpha].$$

Deduce that the maximum range up the plane occurs when the direction of projection bisects the angle between the vertical and the line of the slope.

7.2 Motion in terms of components. From the vector equations $\mathbf{v} = \mathbf{u}+t\mathbf{a}$ and $\mathbf{r} = t\mathbf{u}+\frac{1}{2}t^2\mathbf{a}$ we can deduce the scalar equations connecting the components

$$v_1 = u_1+ta_1, \quad r_1 = tu_1+\tfrac{1}{2}t^2a_1,$$

and

$$v_2 = u_2+ta_2, \quad r_2 = tu_2+\tfrac{1}{2}t^2a_2,$$

Now these equations are the special cases of the vector equations applied to vectors of the form

$$\begin{pmatrix} u_1 \\ 0 \end{pmatrix}, \quad \begin{pmatrix} a_1 \\ 0 \end{pmatrix}, \quad \begin{pmatrix} v_1 \\ 0 \end{pmatrix}, \quad \begin{pmatrix} r_1 \\ 0 \end{pmatrix}$$

and

$$\begin{pmatrix} 0 \\ u_2 \end{pmatrix}, \quad \begin{pmatrix} 0 \\ a_2 \end{pmatrix}, \quad \begin{pmatrix} 0 \\ v_2 \end{pmatrix}, \quad \begin{pmatrix} 0 \\ r_2 \end{pmatrix}$$

respectively. We conclude therefore that, for a particle whose acceleration is constant and equal to $\begin{pmatrix} a_1 \\ a_2 \end{pmatrix}$, and whose velocity at $t = 0$ is $\begin{pmatrix} u_1 \\ u_2 \end{pmatrix}$, the velocity and displacement at any time t will have components which are the velocities and displacements at time t of imaginary particles moving along the axes with the component accelerations and the component initial velocities.

Example 10. An aircraft flying horizontally at 140 m/s releases a bomb. Describe the path of the bomb (*a*) in space, and (*b*) relative to the aircraft.

Take axes Ox, Oy horizontally and vertically downwards with the origin O at the position where the bomb is released. At the instant of release the bomb has the same velocity as the aircraft, that is

$$\begin{pmatrix} 140 \\ 0 \end{pmatrix}$$

(the units being metres and seconds, in which case $g = 9{\cdot}8$).

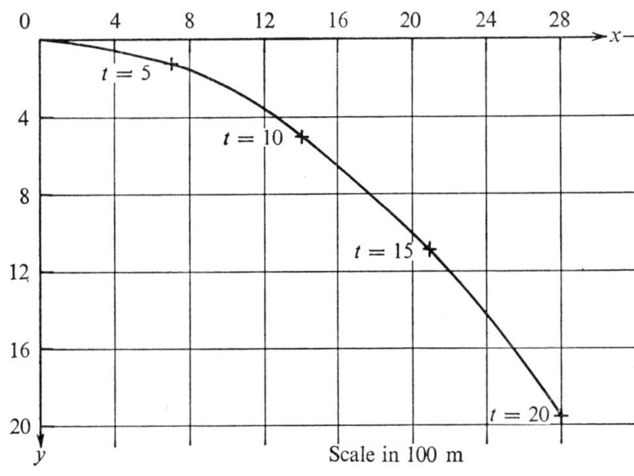

Fig. 24

The bomb's component of velocity horizontally remains constant since the acceleration component in this direction is zero. So $x = 140t$. Vertically, using $s = ut + \frac{1}{2}at^2$, $y = 4{\cdot}9t^2$.

Figure 24 shows the graph of these Cartesian parametric equations

($x = 140t$, $y = 4{\cdot}9t^2$) with points plotted for $t = 0, 5, 10, 15, 20$, where the scale on both axes is in hundreds of metres.

The Cartesian equation of the graph is found, by eliminating t between the two equations, to be

$$y = 4{\cdot}9\left(\frac{x}{140}\right)^2, \quad \text{that is} \quad y = 2{\cdot}5\times 10^{-4}x^2,$$

which is a parabola. This is the path of the bomb in space.

The path of the aircraft is along the x-axis with speed 140 m/s, so that the bomb is always vertically below it. Hence relative to the aircraft the bomb falls vertically with acceleration 9·8 m/s^2, and its depth is given at any time by the formula $4{\cdot}9t^2$.

Example 11. A golf ball is hit with velocity 36 m/s in a direction making 30° with the horizontal ground. If its path takes it over the edge of a cliff, how far will it have gone horizontally and vertically when it strikes the sea after 5 s? What will be its greatest height?

We choose the origin to be at the original position of the ball and x- and y-axes to be horizontally and vertically upwards through it. The units will be feet and seconds.

The initial velocity

$$\mathbf{u} = \begin{pmatrix} 36 \cos 30° \\ 36 \sin 30° \end{pmatrix} = \begin{pmatrix} 18\sqrt{3} \\ 18 \end{pmatrix},$$

and the acceleration is $\begin{pmatrix} 0 \\ -9{\cdot}8 \end{pmatrix}$.

In the x-direction the movement is equivalent to one with an initial velocity of $18\sqrt{3}$ and no acceleration. Hence at time t, $x = 18\sqrt{3}\,t$. In the y-direction the movement is equivalent to one with an initial velocity of 18 and an acceleration of $-9{\cdot}8$. Hence $y = 18t - 4{\cdot}9t^2$.

When it strikes the sea $t = 5$, and then

$$x = 90\sqrt{3} = 156 \text{ (approximately)} \quad \text{and} \quad y = 90 - 122{\cdot}5 = -32{\cdot}5;$$

that is, the sea is 32·5 m below the golf course.

To find the height of the top of the flight path we can use *either* $v = u - gt$ for the vertical motion, where $u = 18$, $v = 0$ and t is the time to reach this point and then with this value of t evaluate the height from $y = ut - \frac{1}{2}gt^2$, *or* we can use $v^2 = u^2 - 2gy$ with the same values for v and u and where y measures the greatest height, thus:

$$0 = 18^2 - 19{\cdot}6y,$$

so the greatest height is $\dfrac{18^2}{19{\cdot}6} = 16{\cdot}5$ m.

Exercise I

(For the acceleration due to gravity use 9·8 m/s².)

1. A boy in a coach which is travelling at 20 m/s throws a ball vertically upwards relative to himself at 14 m/s. How long is it in the air before he catches it and how far has the coach moved in this time? Sketch the shape of the path of the ball relative to the ground. What is the velocity of the ball relative to the ground as it is about to be caught? What is the maximum height of the ball?

2. A stone is thrown horizontally at a speed of 21 m/s from the top of a vertical cliff 90 m high. How long will it take to fall into the sea and how far from the foot of the cliff will it fall? At what speed and in what direction would it have to be thrown back from this position in order to reach the top of the cliff with a horizontal velocity of 21 m/s?

3. How far away (horizontally) from his target should a bomb-aimer release a bomb when he is flying horizontally at 1000 km/h at 2000 m?

4. A ball is thrown vertically upwards at 14 m/s.

(*a*) What is its velocity at half its maximum height on the way up and on the way down?

(*b*) What is its velocity at 'half time' on the way up?

(*c*) What would these velocities have been if the ball had been thrown so that the components of its velocity vertically and horizontally were 14 m/s and 7 m/s?

5. A fielder catches a cricket ball 42 m from the place where it was hit and 5 s after it left the bat. What was the initial velocity of the ball and how high did it rise?

6. How far does a bullet drop, if it is fired horizontally at 600 m/s, by the time it reaches a target at a horizontal range of 100 m?

7. A jet of water leaves the nozzle at 28 m/s at 30° above the horizontal. If it is then 30 m above the horizontal ground, what is the horizontal range of the jet?

***8.** A stone is thrown at 21 m/s to hit a target 10 m higher up and at a horizontal distance of 30 m. Write down equations for the horizontal and vertical motions in terms of the time of flight t s and the angle of projection α. Eliminate t between these equations and hence form a quadratic in $\tan\alpha$ (use $1/\cos^2\alpha = 1+\tan^2\alpha$). Solve this to find the two possible angles of projection.

***9.** A ball is thrown so that it hits the ground with a speed of 9 m/s at an angle of 30° to the horizontal. If at each bounce the magnitude of the component of the velocity in the vertical direction is reduced by a third, while the horizontal component is unaltered, find how far it goes horizontally between the first and second bounce. What fraction of this distance does it go between the second and third bounce? Find also how far it moves horizontally before it stops bouncing.

***10.** A bomb explodes in mid-air and pieces are scattered in all directions with speeds up to V m/s. Within what smallest region of space do they all lie t s later?

*8. INSTANTANEOUS CENTRE OF ROTATION

The position of a lamina in a plane can be described completely in terms of the position in the plane of any two of its points. Its motion is therefore determined by the motion of these two points.

If $\overline{PQ}$ and $\overline{P'Q'}$ are the positions of a line segment in the lamina at times t and $t+\delta t$, then $\overline{PQ}$ can be moved onto $\overline{P'Q'}$ by a single rotation about the point I' where the mediators of $\overline{PP'}$ and $\overline{QQ'}$ intersect—unless the mediators are parallel, in which case the single movement is one of translation.

If as $\delta t \to 0$, I' tends to a position I, then at time t the body can be said to be rotating about this point I which is called the 'instantaneous centre' (of rotation) at that time.

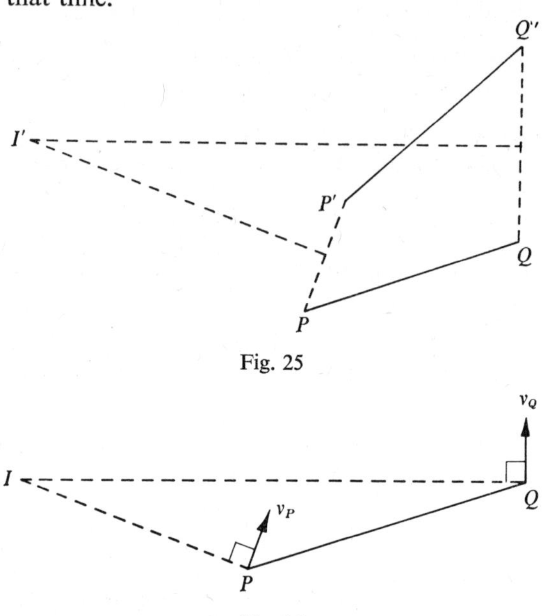

Fig. 25

Fig. 26

If P and Q have velocities $\mathbf{v}_P$ and $\mathbf{v}_Q$ at time t, then I is the intersection of the perpendiculars to $\mathbf{v}_P$ and $\mathbf{v}_Q$ at P and Q, because the limiting directions of the chords PP' and QQ' are the directions of $\mathbf{v}_P$ and $\mathbf{v}_Q$. Now suppose that at this time the lamina has an angular velocity of ω; it is then rotating about I with this angular velocity, and therefore

$$v_P = IP.\omega \quad \text{and} \quad v_Q = IQ.\omega,$$

where v_P and v_Q are the speeds of P and Q.

If R is any other point of the lamina its velocity is perpendicular to IR and of magnitude $IR.\omega$.

Example 12. A rod AB 3 m long passes through a ring at D, where D is a fixed point, and the end A moves at 5 m/s in a circle, centre C and radius 1 m with $CD = 2$ m. Find the velocity of B when $\angle ACD = 30°$.

Since A moves at right-angles to AC, the instantaneous centre (I) of rotation for AB lies somewhere on the line $\overleftrightarrow{CA}$. The point of the rod within the ring at D, since it cannot move sideways, moves along the length of the rod, that is, the velocity of D is along DA so that I lies on the perpendicular to AD at D. The point I is now determined by these two conditions (see Figure 27).

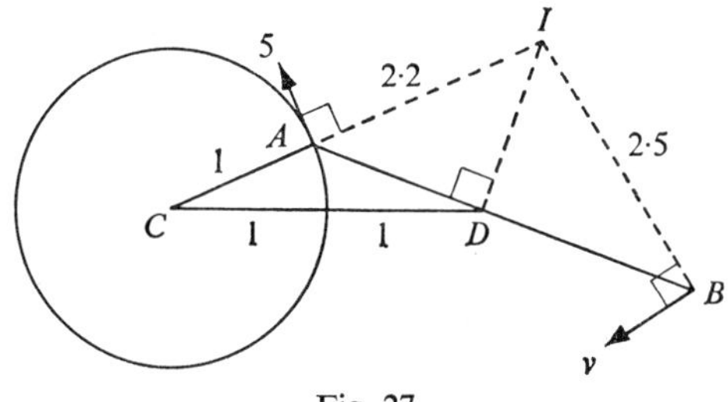

Fig. 27

Let the angular velocity of AB be ω; then using $v = r\omega$,

$$5 = IA\omega$$

and if v is the velocity of B,

$$v = IB\omega.$$

Hence $\quad \dfrac{v}{5} = \dfrac{IB}{IA} \quad$ so that $\quad v = 5\times\dfrac{2\cdot5}{2\cdot2} \simeq 5\cdot7$ m/s,

and the direction of $\mathbf{v}$ is 81° counterclockwise from the direction of A's velocity.

**Exercise J*

1. A ladder 8·5 m long reaches 7·5 m up a wall. If the foot is moved along the ground at 1·5 m/s directly from the wall, find the velocity of (i) the top, (ii) the mid-point of the ladder. Find also the position of the point of the ladder whose velocity is along the ladder.

2. A cylinder of radius r can rotate about its axis which is horizontal. A rod in a vertical plane rests across the cylinder. If an end of the rod is moved with speed v in a direction making an angle θ with the rod, show that the cylinder rotates with angular velocity $v \cos \theta/r$, if there is no slipping.

3. Discuss the way in which the front wheels of a car should turn when cornering, if none of the wheels is to side slip.

4. A rod OA is pivoted at O and when hanging vertically A just touches a table top. A rod AB (half the length of OA) is freely hinged to OA and initially lies flat on the table. Sketch the locus of the instantaneous centre of AB as OA moves so that OAB always lies in a fixed vertical plane and B remains on the table.

5. By finding the instantaneous centre of the circle C whose arc XY (of fixed length) moves so that X and Y remain in contact with the fixed lines p and q which intersect at A on the circle (see Figure 28), show that the point of C, which at the instant considered is at A, moves tangentially to C. What do you deduce about C in relation to A as X and Y move?

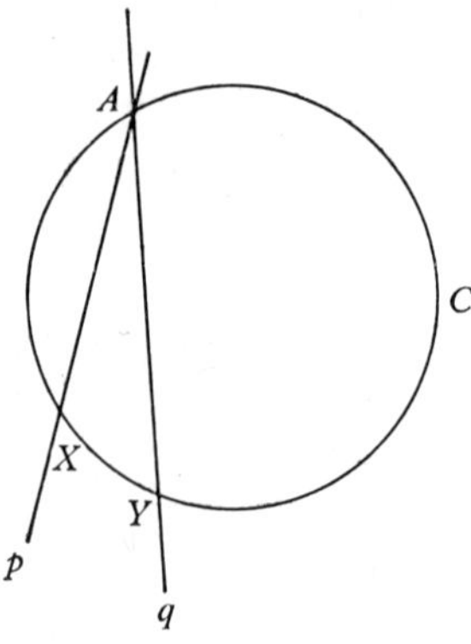

Fig. 28

Summary.

Units

	Metric
Length	1 metre (m)
Time	1 s
Velocity	1 metre per second (m/s)
Acceleration	1 metre per second per second (m/s^2)
Acceleration of gravity (**g**) (approx.)	9·8 m/s^2

	In space	In a straight line
Motion with uniform acceleration	$\mathbf{v} = \mathbf{u}+\mathbf{a}t$	$v = u+at$
	$\mathbf{r} = \mathbf{u}t+\frac{1}{2}\mathbf{a}t^2$	$s = ut+\frac{1}{2}at^2$
	$\mathbf{r} = (\mathbf{u}+\mathbf{v})t/2$	$s = (u+v)t/2$
	$v^2 = u^2+2\mathbf{a}.\mathbf{r}$	$v^2 = u^2+2as$

Motion in a circle of radius **r**

$\mathbf{v} = r\dot{\theta}$ along the tangent

$\mathbf{a} = r\dot{\theta}^2$ towards the centre $+ r\ddot{\theta}$ along the tangent

$= v^2/r$ towards the centre $+ dv/dt$ along the tangent

When letters are used without units attached, they stand for the quantities themselves.

REVISION EXERCISES

16. LOCAL APPROXIMATION

1. Find a quadratic approximation for $1/(4+\alpha)^2$ when α is small, and obtain, in its simplest form, a formula for the error involved in using this approximation.

2. The diagram (Figure 1) shows a toggle mechanism for opening windows. Show that the height (x cm) of the slider S above the point A is given by the positive root of the equation

$$x^2-6x\cos\theta-7=0,$$

where the angle BAS is θ radians. Find a linear approximate relation between x and θ when $x=5$, and hence find the distance the knot K must be moved in this position to raise S by 0·1 cm.

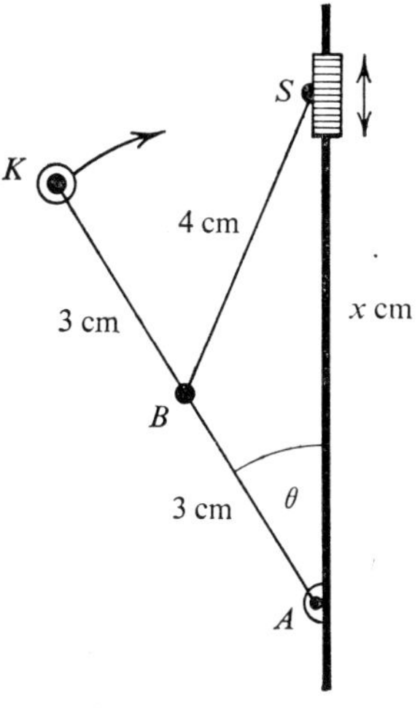

Fig. 1

3. Newton's formula is to be used to find a root of $3x^4-4x^3-13=0$. If $x=2$ is taken as the first approximation, what is the next approximation given by the formula?

4. By considering the graph of $\sin x$, show that the smallest positive root of $\sin x=\alpha x$ (where α is small) is nearly equal to π. Show that $\pi(1-\alpha)$ is a better approximation, and find an approximation to the order of α^2.

5. Obtain an approximation for $\tan x$ as a polynomial in x of the fifth degree, when x is small.

6. $y=f(x)$ is the solution of the differential equation $dy/dx=x-y^2$ for which $y=1$ when $x=3$.

(*a*) Prove that for this function

$$\frac{d^2y}{dx^2}=1-2xy+2y^3,$$

and obtain a similar expression for d^3y/dx^3 in terms of x and y.

(*b*) Find an approximate expression for the value of y when $x=3+h$, in the form $y=A+Bh+Ch^2+Dh^3$.

17. THE TECHNIQUE OF DIFFERENTIATION

1. Differentiate:

(*a*) $(2x+1)^5$; (*b*) $\cos^2 x$; (*c*) $\cos(2x-\pi)$;

(*d*) $\sqrt{(3+x)}$; (*e*) $x+(5/x)$; (*f*) $x^2\sin x$.

2. A curve is given as the locus

$$\{(x, y)\colon\ x = t^3,\quad y = t^4+t^2,\quad t \in R\}.$$

(*a*) Find the gradient of the curve where $t = -1$.
(*b*) Find points on the curve where the tangent is parallel to $y = 3x+7$.
(*c*) Show that y is never negative, and that $x/y \to 0$ as $x \to 0$.
(*d*) Sketch the curve.

3. (*a*) The period T of a compound pendulum is given by $T = 2\pi\sqrt{(I/mgh)}$, where h is the distance of the centre of mass from the point of suspension and g is a constant. I, the moment of inertia, may be expressed in the form $m(h^2+k^2)$, where k is a constant. Express T^2 in terms of h and find the value of h for which T^2 is a *minimum*.

(*b*) The formula $W = 144R/(R+12)^2$ gives the power developed in a certain electric circuit. By putting $R+12 = x$ and considering the function $f\colon x \to W$, find the value of R for which W is a *maximum*.

4. (*a*) If $y = \dfrac{\cos x}{1-\sin x}$, prove that $\cos x\dfrac{dy}{dx} = y$.

(*b*) If $y = \dfrac{\sin 2x}{x}$, prove that $x\dfrac{d^2y}{dx^2}+\dfrac{2dy}{dx}+4xy = 0$.

[Write $xy = \sin 2x$ and differentiate twice.]

5. Find the average scale factor for the function $f\colon x \to \log_{10} x$ over the interval $[a, aK]$, and deduce that $f'(a) = c/a$, where c is a number independent of a. Estimate the value of c by taking $K = 1{\cdot}05$ and using your tables.

Use this result to obtain the derived function of the inverse function of f, namely $g\colon x \to 10^x$.

6. Find the area of the largest rectangle with sides parallel to the coordinate axes whose vertices lie on the curves

$$y = \frac{1}{x^2+1} \quad\text{and}\quad y = \frac{-1}{x^2+1}.$$

18. UNITS AND DIMENSIONS

1. In each of the following physical situations, rewrite the equation connecting the variables in a dimensionally consistent form by inserting symbols for the units, and suggest reasonable values for these units:

(*a*) The height above the beach of a ball thrown from the top of a cliff, after time t, is given by $100+10t-5t^2$.

(*b*) A train pulls out from a station so that its speed after time t is given by $4500v = t^2(90-t)$.

(*c*) The turntable of a record-player, at a time t after the brakes are applied, has turned through an angle of $10\pi(t/9-t^2/18)$.

(*d*) The speed of a ball rolling down a slope is given by $v = 2\sqrt{s}$, where s is the distance it has rolled.

2. If new units are chosen, λ metres and τ seconds, what will the units of velocity and of acceleration be in the new system? Using this result, translate into metre-second units:

(*a*) an acceleration of 300 km/h^2;

(*b*) an acceleration of 981 cm/s^2;

(*c*) a speed of 0·1 km/min;

(*d*) a speed of 300000 km/s; and

(*e*) find the speed of the Moon in m/s, if it describes a circle of radius 385000 kilometres in 27·3 days.

3. In this and subsequent questions, we shall use the group generated by **M**, **L**, and **T**, where **M** is the dimension of mass.

Write down the dimension of each of the following quantities, which are physically related to more familiar quantities by the defining equations given below; we use x, r, a, b to denote lengths; t to denote time; f, g to denote accelerations; m to denote mass; u, v, c to denote velocity; and θ to denote angle:

(*a*) angular velocity, ω, given by $\omega = d\theta/dt$;

(*b*) force, P, given by $P = mf$;

(*c*) kinetic energy, E, given by $E = \frac{1}{2}mv^2$;

(*d*) potential energy, V, given by $V = mg(a-b)$;

(*e*) elastic constant of a spring, k, given by $P = kx$;

(*f*) work, W, given by $dW/ds = P$;

(*g*) momentum, mv, given by $(d/dt)(mv) = P$;

(*h*) universal constant of gravitation, G, given by $mg = Gmm'/r^2$;

(*i*) moment of inertia, I, given by $I = \Sigma m_i r_i^2$;

(*j*) viscosity, η, given by $P/A = \eta . dv/dx$, where A is an area;

(*k*) rotational energy, E', given by $E' = \frac{1}{2}I\omega^2$;

(*l*) frequency, n, given by $na = c$, where a is the wavelength and c the velocity of wave propagation (in this case, the velocity of light).

4. Suggest corrections to any of the following statements which need them. The notation of Question 3 is used throughout.

(*a*) The terminal velocity of a raindrop is given by $6\pi\eta\rho v = \frac{4}{3}\pi r^3\rho' g$, where ρ, ρ' are the densities of the air and of the water.

(*b*) The escape velocity for a body from a planet of radius R and density ρ is $R\sqrt{(\frac{8}{3}G\rho r)}$.

(*c*) The lift force on an aeroplane wing is $k\rho v^2 A$, where k is a number, ρ the density of the air, and A the wing area.

(*d*) The period of torsional oscillations is $\sqrt{(Ib^2/nr^4)}$.

5. A pendulum of length a and mass m swings θ radians either side of the vertical, making a complete oscillation in time t; the acceleration due to gravity is g. If it is assumed that $t = m^p a^q g^r \theta^s$, find possible values for p, q, r, s, and deduce that $t = f(\theta).\sqrt{(a/g)}$.

Can you combine m, g, a, t together to form a dimensionless quantity—that is to say, one with dimension $\mathbf{M}^0\mathbf{L}^0\mathbf{T}^0$—and can this be used to deduce the result given above?

6. What dimensionless variables can be formed from the following physical variables: V (velocity), D (length), ρ (density), η (viscosity, of dimension $\mathbf{ML}^{-1}\mathbf{T}^{-1}$), and F (force)?

Show that F must be given by an equation of the form

$$F = \rho V^2 D^2 f\left(\frac{\rho VD}{\eta}\right).$$

(This equation applies to bodies moving through fluids; $\rho VD/\eta$ is called the *Reynolds number*.)

19. KINEMATICS

1. The position of an electron at time t referred to a fixed set of axes is given by the position vector

$$\mathbf{r} = (t^2-7)\mathbf{i}+t^3\mathbf{j}.$$

At what time is the electron moving parallel to the vector $\mathbf{i}+\mathbf{j}$?

2. A car C is rounding a corner, which is a circular arc with centre O and radius 30 m, at a steady 25 m/s. Find the angular velocity of OC and the acceleration of the car.

3. The position vector $\begin{pmatrix} x \\ y \end{pmatrix}$ of a particle at time t is given by the equations

$$\begin{cases} x = 2t^3+3t, \\ y = 20t-t^3. \end{cases}$$

Find:

(*a*) the magnitude and direction of the velocity vector $\mathbf{v}$ after 1 second;

(*b*) the acceleration vector $\mathbf{a}$ at this moment;

(*c*) the scalar product $\mathbf{v}.\mathbf{a}$.

Show that $d/dt(v^2) = 2\mathbf{v}.\mathbf{a}$, and discover whether the speed is increasing or decreasing.

4. The position vector $\mathbf{r}$ of a particle can be expressed in terms of the constant orthogonal unit vectors $\mathbf{i}$, $\mathbf{j}$ by means of the relation

$$\mathbf{r} = \mathbf{i}\cos nt+\mathbf{j}\sin nt.$$

Find the speed of the particle at time t.

Show that its acceleration at time t is the vector $-n^2\mathbf{r}$.

What is the path of the particle? (OC)

5. A ball can be thrown with a fixed speed of 17·5 m/s at a variable angle α to the horizontal. It is required to hit a target 20 m away horizontally and 2 m above the level at which it is thrown. Show that

$$10\tan\alpha - 3{\cdot}2\sec^2\alpha = 1,$$

and solve this equation.

6. The diagram (Figure 2) shows the path of a ball struck from 0 with a velocity $\begin{pmatrix} 14 \\ 19{\cdot}6 \end{pmatrix}$ m/s as recorded on film exposed at intervals of 0·2 s. The scale of the diagram is 1 cm to 3 m on both axes.

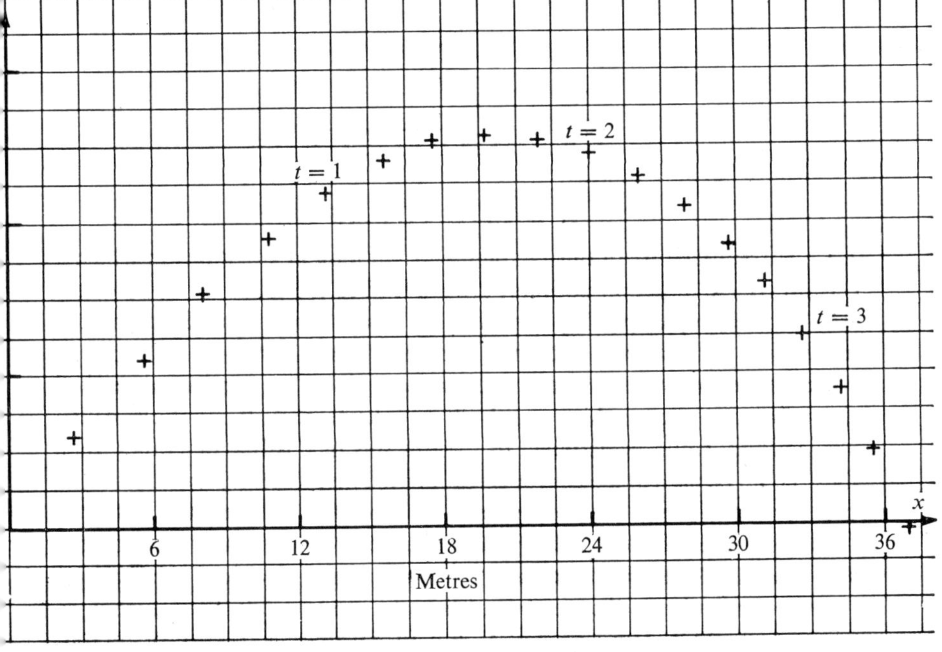

Fig. 2

(*a*) Use the formula

$$f'(a) \approx \frac{f(a+h)-f(a-h)}{2h}$$

to estimate the velocity at $t = 1$ and $t = 2$.

(*b*) Hence estimate the average acceleration from $t = 1$ to $t = 2$.

(*c*) Find approximately the acceleration at $t = 2$.

(*d*) Find the theoretical answers to (*a*), (*b*) and (*c*) if the motion were given by

$$\mathbf{r} = t\begin{pmatrix}14\\19{\cdot}6\end{pmatrix}+\tfrac{1}{2}t^2\begin{pmatrix}0\\-9{\cdot}8\end{pmatrix},$$

and comment on the discrepancies.

7. A point moves so that its position vector at time t referred to rectangular axes is

$$\mathbf{r} = (t-\sin t)\mathbf{i}+(1-\cos t)\mathbf{j}.$$

(*a*) When is its velocity parallel to $\mathbf{j}$? To $\mathbf{i}$? To $\mathbf{i}+\mathbf{j}$? To $\mathbf{i}-\mathbf{j}$?

(*b*) Find the magnitude and direction of the acceleration at each of these times.

(*c*) Sketch the path of the point in the interval $0 \leqslant t \leqslant 2\pi$, and mark on your sketch arrows representing the velocities and accelerations at the times you have considered.

20

PROBABILITY

1. BASIC IDEAS

1.1 Introduction. In this chapter we shall look at situations in which a certain course of action does not always lead to the same result. I make a *trial*—for example, placing a shilling in a slot machine and pulling the lever; and the trial can lead to a number of *possibilities*—I get a bar of chocolate, or my money is returned, or the machine jams, or the alarm bell rings (because the machine was built to take francs). If numbers, called *probabilities*, could be assigned to various sets of possible outcomes, then these could be used as a basis for certain decisions; whether, for example, to use the machine or to buy chocolate at the kiosk further down the platform.

In a complex modern society an assessment of numerical probabilities associated with particular events influences many decisions: the size of insurance premiums, the number of lines to run to a telephone exchange, where to build a new warehouse, etc. In calculating these probabilities various theoretical laws are applied, and it is our purpose in this chapter to derive some of these laws.

We shall do this for the most part by examining a number of conventional situations: coin-tossing, dice-throwing, drawing a card from a pack, etc. Not that these activities are important in themselves (though it may be recalled that gaming provided the incentive for the first studies of probability theory), but that their analysis is relatively simple. Wider application of the theory rests on the assumption that the results of this analysis remain valid for more sophisticated situations.

1.2 Trials and possibilities. We begin, then, with some incident such as:

I toss a coin,

or I roll a die,

or I roll a pair of dice (one green, one red).

The incident itself is of no significance unless a result is recorded; and what I decide to record depends on my particular interest at the time. If I am rolling a die, then I shall probably record the number of pips on the top face; but I might be interested only in whether or not I have thrown a six, and record simply 'yes' if a six is thrown and 'no' otherwise. I might even record whether the die shatters or not when it lands; or whether or not it rolls under the bed. Thus before recording the result I shall have had to decide the type of outcome with which I am concerned.

We shall use the word *trial* for the combination of an incident and making a record of the result; and this result will be one of a pre-selected list of possibilities. Examples of trials are:

(i) I toss a coin and record whether it comes up 'head' or 'tail';
(ii) I roll a pair of dice and record the numbers of pips on the top faces of the green and red die respectively;
(iii) I roll a pair of dice and record the larger of the numbers of the pips on the two top faces (or either one if the two numbers are equal);
(iv) I draw a card from a pack and record its suit;
(v) I draw a card from a pack and record whether or not it is a face card.

Suppose, for example, that six cards in succession are drawn from a pack, and that these are

$$\diamondsuit A,\quad \clubsuit 4,\quad \heartsuit K,\quad \heartsuit 10,\quad \spadesuit J,\quad \diamondsuit 3.$$

Then if I were conducting trial (iv), my record of results would be

$$\diamondsuit,\quad \clubsuit,\quad \heartsuit,\quad \heartsuit,\quad \spadesuit,\quad \diamondsuit;$$

whilst if I were conducting trial (v), it would be

no, no, yes, no, yes, no.

It will be obvious that these results must all be drawn from the set of all the possibilities of the type selected. In trial (iv) we record suits, and the set of all possibilities is

$$\{\clubsuit, \diamondsuit, \heartsuit, \spadesuit\};$$

whereas in trial (v) the set is merely

{yes, no}.

This set of all possibilities is called the *possibility space* for the trial.

1.3 Representing possibility spaces. The idea of a possibility space is central in the theory of probability. For each of the trials described above, there is only a finite number of possibilities, so that the possibility space is a finite set; this constitutes the universal set for discussion of the trial.

When talking about sets we have often found it useful to draw diagrams in which the elements are represented by points. If the set is a possibility space, then each point will correspond to a particular possibility for the trial. For example, in trial (i) the possibility space {head, tail} has two elements; it might therefore be represented by Figure 1.

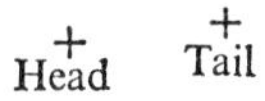

+ Head   + Tail

Fig. 1

For larger possibility spaces it may be helpful to display the points in an orderly fashion. Trial (ii), for example, yields a possibility space of

36 elements; each is an ordered pair of numbers (g, r), where g is the score on the green die and r that on the red die. It seems natural to use this ordered pair as the Cartesian coordinates of the corresponding point, and to represent the possibility space as in Figure 2.

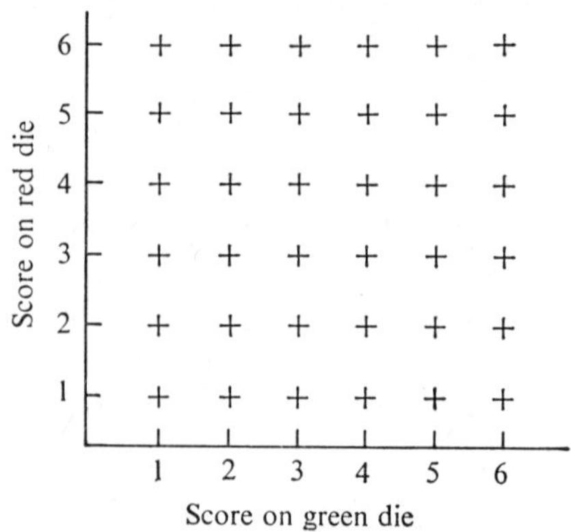

Fig. 2

In this example there is an obvious order in which to arrange the elements, that of increasing scores on either die. A similar array can still be useful, however, when there is no such order. Figure 3 shows a convenient way of representing the possibility space for a trial in which a card is drawn

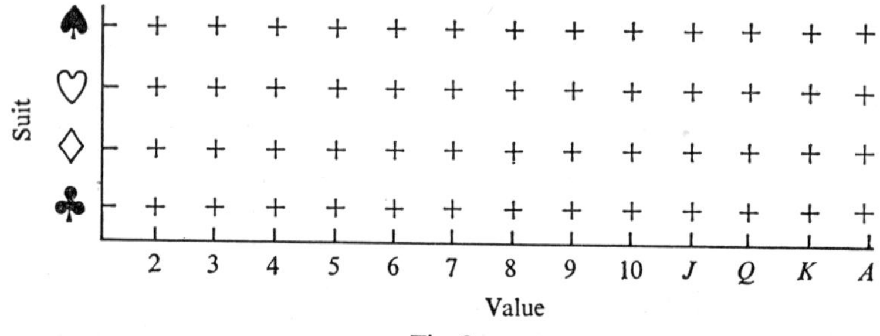

Fig. 3

from a pack and its name (i.e. its value and suit) recorded. The order in which the suits are listed is a matter of convenience (that of bidding precedence in bridge has in fact been selected), as is the decision to show 'ace high' rather than 'ace low'. If for any reason there appeared to be some advantage in describing the possibility space numerically, then some kind of number code could, of course, be invented for the purpose, such as:

$$\clubsuit \leftrightarrow 1, \quad \diamondsuit \leftrightarrow 2, \quad \heartsuit \leftrightarrow 3, \quad \spadesuit \leftrightarrow 4$$
$$J \leftrightarrow 11, \quad Q \leftrightarrow 12, \quad K \leftrightarrow 13, \quad A \leftrightarrow 14.$$

The possibility space could then be written

$$\{(v, s): v, s \text{ integers}, 2 \leqslant v \leqslant 14, 1 \leqslant s \leqslant 4\}.$$

The use of such a code does not essentially change the trial itself; we are merely recording the results in a different notation.

1.4 Equally likely possibilities. Let us now consider in more detail the trials (ii) and (iii) described in Section 1.2:

(ii) I roll a pair of dice and record the numbers of pips on the top faces of the green and red die respectively;

(iii) I roll a pair of dice and record the larger of the numbers of the pips on the two top faces (or either one if the two numbers are equal).

These two trials could be carried out simultaneously; the same roll will serve for both, and they will differ only in what is recorded. For (ii) the possibility space has 36 elements:

$$\{(g, r): g, r \text{ integers}, 1 \leqslant g \leqslant 6, 1 \leqslant r \leqslant 6\}.$$

The possibility space for (iii), however, has just six elements:

$$\{1, 2, 3, 4, 5, 6\}.$$

These two trials were actually carried out twenty times in succession, using the same roll for each, and the following results were recorded:

Trial (ii)

(1, 6) (3, 1) (6, 4) (1, 5) (4, 6) (4, 2) (1, 4) (1, 6) (4, 5) (1, 4)
(3, 1) (6, 5) (1, 1) (4, 5) (2, 6) (3, 4) (4, 2) (1, 1) (1, 5) (5, 1)

Trial (iii)

6 3 6 5 6 4 4 6 5 4
3 6 1 5 6 4 4 1 5 5

An important difference between the trials soon becomes obvious. Although the results of trial (ii) include certain repetitions, and some scores have occurred more frequently than others, yet by and large they give us no cause to doubt what we expected before we started: that no possibility is specially favoured, so that it is more likely to occur than any other. If successive results are traced on Figure 2, it will appear that the corresponding points are scattered randomly over the diagram. With trial (iii), however, the situation is very different. There would seem from the results to be a strong bias towards the higher numbers of the possibility space; for example, the outcome 6 occurs six times, 5 and 4 five times each, whilst 1 occurs only twice and 2 not at all.

We need not go far to see why. The only roll which will give the possibility 1 in trial (iii) is (1, 1); but the possibility 6 will arise from any of the eleven rolls

(1, 6) (2, 6) (3, 6) (4, 6) (5, 6) (6, 6)
(6, 1) (6, 2) (6, 3) (6, 4) (6, 5).

If therefore we expect that all the possibilities for trial (ii) are 'equally likely', then we might say that in trial (iii) 6 is 'eleven times as likely' as 1.

Whether or not all the possibilities for a trial can be regarded as equally likely depends, therefore, on the choice of what is recorded as well as on the apparatus with which the trial is conducted. Where there is no reason *a priori* (i.e. on the evidence available before any trials are carried out) to favour any possibility in preference to any other, then we say that all the elements of the possibility space are 'equally likely on grounds of symmetry'. Our first definition of probability (see Section 2.4) will be restricted to trials for which all the possibilities are equally likely.

Exercise A

For each trial outlined in this exercise, give a description of the possibility space; make a suitable diagrammatic representation; and state whether or not the possibilities are equally likely on grounds of symmetry.

1. Tossing a coin and recording the number of heads visible.

2. Tossing a pair of coins and recording the number of heads visible.

3. Tossing three coins and recording the number of heads visible.

4. Rolling a die and recording the score on the top face.

5. Rolling a pair of dice and recording the sum of the scores on the two top faces.

6. Rolling a die having one red, two green and the three blue faces, and recording the colour of the top face.

7. Drawing a card from a pack lacking the ♢ *A* and recording its name.

8. Drawing a card from a pack lacking the ♢ *A* and recording its suit.

9. Drawing a card from a pack lacking all the aces and recording its value.

10. Drawing a succession of cards (without replacing them) from a pack until the ♡ *K* appears and recording the number that have been drawn.

11. Drawing a succession of cards (without replacing them) from a pack until a king appears and recording the number that have been drawn.

12. Tossing a coin repeatedly until a head first appears and recording the number of times that it has been tossed.

2. PROBABILITY OF AN EVENT

2.1 Events. In the theory of probability we are concerned to assign numbers, called probabilities, to events. An *event* is something which may or may not occur as the result of a particular action. For example, the action might be the monthly draw of Premium Bonds, and the event 'I win a prize'. This event will occur if the number of one of my bonds appears in the list of winning numbers for the month in question. ERNIE (the device for randomly selecting winning numbers) can produce a very large number of different possible winning lists for a particular draw; the set of all such lists constitutes the possibility space, and if the draw is fair all lists should be equally likely. Some of these lists will include one or more of my bond numbers, and if one of these is selected then the event 'I win a prize' occurs.

We see, then, that with the occurrence of an event is associated a subset of elements of the possibility space. This correspondence forms the basis of our definition of the probability of an event.

Consider another example:

Trial. I roll a pair of dice and record the numbers of pips on the top faces of the green and red die respectively.

Event. The sum of the scores is at least 10.

Possibility space. $\{(g, r): g, r \text{ integers}, 1 \leqslant g \leqslant 6, 1 \leqslant r \leqslant 6\}$.

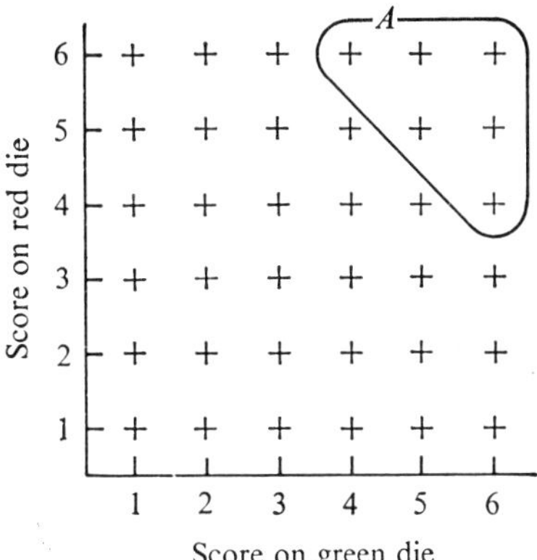

Fig. 4

In this example the event occurs if I roll a double six, a six and a five, and so on; that is, if the scores belong to the subset

$$\{(4, 6), (5, 6), (6, 6), (5, 5), (6, 5), (6, 4)\}$$

of the possibility space. This subset, which we will denote by A, is shown diagrammatically in Figure 4.

Denoting the possibility space itself by $\mathscr{E}$, we find that

$$n(\mathscr{E}) = 36, \quad n(A) = 6.$$

Thus the event occurs for 6 out of the 36 possibilities for the trial.

2.2 An alternative analysis. The situation in the last example could, however, be looked at in other ways. For example, instead of recording the separate scores on the green and red dice we might decide to record the sum of the scores directly. We should still be investigating the same event, but the trial would be different:

Trial. I roll a pair of dice and record the sum of the scores on the two top faces.

Event. The sum of the scores is at least 10.

Possibility space. $\{2, 3, 4, 5, 6, 7, 8, 9, 10, 11, 12\}$.

The event is now associated with just three elements of the possibility space, forming the subset $\{10, 11, 12\}$; let this be denoted by A'. Writing the possibility space as $\mathscr{E}'$, we see that $n(\mathscr{E}') = 11$, $n(A') = 3$, so that the event occurs for 3 out of the 11 possibilities for the trial.

2.3 Frequencies. Which of these two analyses is to be preferred? It seems more natural to adopt the one in which the space consists of equally likely possibilities; and the reason can be seen if we consider the results of a large number of repetitions of the trials.

Suppose that I were to roll a pair of dice 900 times and record the separate scores, as in the first trial. The results would give a population† of 900 outcomes, such as

$$((1, 6), (3, 1), (6, 4), \ldots, (2, 5)).$$

Now the possibility space consists of 36 equally likely possibilities, so we would expect each of these to appear about $\frac{900}{36}$, or 25, times in the population. Since the event 'the sum of the scores is at least 10' is associated with six of these possibilities, we would expect this to occur about 6×25, or 150 times. Thus we are prepared to make decisions in the belief that:

$$\text{The number of occurrences of the event} \approx \tfrac{6}{36} \times 900.$$

In Chapter 12 we defined the frequency of an observation in a population. It is now convenient to extend this in the obvious way and to define the frequency of a set of observations. We take this to be the sum of the frequencies of the observations which are members of the set. That is, if $A = \{a_i\}$, then we write

$$\operatorname{fr} A = \sum_i \operatorname{fr} a_i.$$

In particular the frequency $\operatorname{fr}\mathscr{E}$ of the possibility space $\mathscr{E}$ is equal to the total number of observations, that is the number of repetitions of the trial.

† In Chapter 12 the only populations discussed were of numbers, but there was no special significance in this restriction.

The result of the calculation performed previously can now be expressed in more general form. It is that, if $\text{fr}\,\mathscr{E}$ is large, we expect to find that

$$\text{fr}\,A \approx \frac{n(A)}{n(\mathscr{E})} \times \text{fr}\,\mathscr{E};$$

that is

$$\frac{\text{fr}\,A}{\text{fr}\,\mathscr{E}} \approx \frac{n(A)}{n(\mathscr{E})}.$$

The fraction $\text{fr}\,A/\text{fr}\,\mathscr{E}$ is called the *relative frequency* of the subset A of possibilities for the trial. Its precise value cannot, of course, be found theoretically; indeed, it will have a fresh value each time a new series of trials is carried out. On the other hand, this is the quantity which we wish to be able to predict in any practical application. The importance of the approximation rests in the possibility of determining the fraction on the right by purely theoretical means: if a trial yields a space of equally likely possibilities, then $n(A)/n(\mathscr{E})$ is the proportion of these possibilities associated with the specified event.

It will now be clear why the analysis of the dice-rolling situation in Section 2.2 is unsatisfactory. Here the possibilities are not all equally likely: we would expect to get a total of 7 far more frequently than a total of 2, for example. We can certainly calculate the fraction $n(A')/n(\mathscr{E}')$ to be $\frac{3}{11}$, but this fraction has no significance. There is no reason at all to expect $\text{fr}\,A'/\text{fr}\,\mathscr{E}'$ to be approximately $\frac{3}{11}$; indeed, we know that it is the same as $\text{fr}\,A/\text{fr}\,\mathscr{E}$ [why?], so that its value is approximately $\frac{1}{6}$.

2.4 Probability. We are now in a position to give the *a priori*, or 'classical', definition of probability:

> If, for a certain trial, there is a finite set $\mathscr{E}$ of possibilities, *all equally likely on grounds of symmetry*, and if a subset A of these possibilities is associated with an event **A**, then the *probability* of the event **A** is $n(A)/n(\mathscr{E})$.

The probability of the event **A** is usually written $p(\mathbf{A})$.

The result of Section 2.3 can now be stated:

> If a trial is repeated a large number of times, the relative frequency of the set of possibilities associated with a particular event will be approximately equal to the probability of that event.

It might be thought that the reference to 'equally likely possibilities' in the definition of probability involves a circular argument, but this is not so. Just as it is possible to say that two objects are 'equally massive' without having defined mass, or that two sets are equivalent without having met the idea of cardinal number, so it is possible to know what is meant by 'equally likely' without having a measure of likelihood.

It is important to notice that a distinction has been made between an event and the corresponding subset of the possibility space. In our notation the same letter is used for both, but when the event is referred to we use a different typeface. Thus we have $n(A)$, the number of possible outcomes in the subset; but $p(\mathbf{A})$, the probability of the event. Such distinctions are common in mathematics; consider, for comparison:

The set of numbers between 0 and 1	The inequalities $0 < x < 1$
The number 0	The equation $x = 0$
The null set ø	The number 0
The number 0	The set {0}
The point (2, 1)	The vector $\begin{pmatrix}2\\1\end{pmatrix}$
The circle bounding a disc	The disc itself

Finally, it must be realized that, although the nouns 'possibility' and 'probability' are derived from the adjectives 'possible' and 'probable', their technical usages here are quite different. A 'possibility' is something which might happen and which you will record; a probability is a number between 0 and 1. In ordinary English a possibility suggests something that might happen but is unlikely, whereas a probability suggests something that might happen and is more likely. No such meanings are relevant here.

Exercise B

In each question of this exercise a certain event is described relevant to some situation. State what you would record in order to obtain a space of equally likely possibilities; calculate the probability of the event; represent your findings in a diagram; and say how many times approximately you would expect the event to occur in 1000 repetitions of the trial.

1. Drawing a card from a pack and getting a face card.

2. Rolling a pair of dice and getting at least one six.

3. Tossing three coins and getting exactly two heads.

4. Drawing two coins from a pocket containing two francs and three new pence, and getting two new pence.

***5.** Drawing two cards simultaneously from a pack and getting two clubs.

***6.** Winning a prize with at least one of five tickets in a raffle for which 100 tickets are sold and two prizes awarded.

3. COMPOUND EVENTS

3.1 The basic compounding operations. From any event **A** can be derived its *negation*, the event '**A** does not occur'. Thus the negation of 'I draw a face card' is 'I do not draw a face card', i.e. 'I draw a number card'. The negation of **A** is called not-**A**, and written $\sim$ **A**. If **A** is associated with the subset A of the possibility space, then $\sim$ **A** is associated with the complement A'.

From two events **A**, **B** we can derive two important compound events:

(i) (**A** and **B**), the event that **A** and **B** both occur. For example, if **A** is 'I draw an ace' and **B** is 'I draw a heart', then (**A** and **B**) is 'I draw the ace of hearts'. (**A** and **B**), often written **A** $\wedge$ **B**, is the event associated with the intersection $A \cap B$ of the subsets A, B of the possibility space.

(ii) (**A** or **B**), the event that at least one of **A**, **B** occurs. (**A** or **B**), often written **A** $\vee$ **B**, is the event associated with the union $A \cup B$ of the subsets A, B.

These new events also, of course, have probabilities, given by the definition as

$$p(\sim \mathbf{A}) = \frac{n(A')}{n(\mathscr{E})}, \quad p(\mathbf{A} \wedge \mathbf{B}) = \frac{n(A \cap B)}{n(\mathscr{E})}, \quad p(\mathbf{A} \vee \mathbf{B}) = \frac{n(A \cup B)}{n(\mathscr{E})}.$$

Other compounds can also be formed, such as $\sim$ **A** $\vee$ **B**, $\sim$ (**A** $\wedge$ **B**), $\sim$ ($\sim$ **A**), **A** $\wedge$ (**B** $\vee$ **C**); their probabilities can be calculated similarly. Notice that $\sim$ **A** $\vee$ **B** means (not-**A** or **B**) rather than not-(**A** or **B**); the symbol $\sim$ is attached to the event that immediately follows it.

The symbol $\vee$ originated as the first letter of the Latin *vel*, meaning 'or'. The similarities of $\wedge$ and $\cap$, $\vee$ and $\cup$, make the meanings easy to remember.

3.2 Contingency tables. When calculating the probabilities of various compound events derived from **A**, **B**, it is often helpful to begin by tabulating the numbers of elements in the relevant subsets A, A', $A \cap B$, etc., of the possibility space. An illustration will make the method clear.

Figure 5 represents the possibility space for a trial in which a pair of

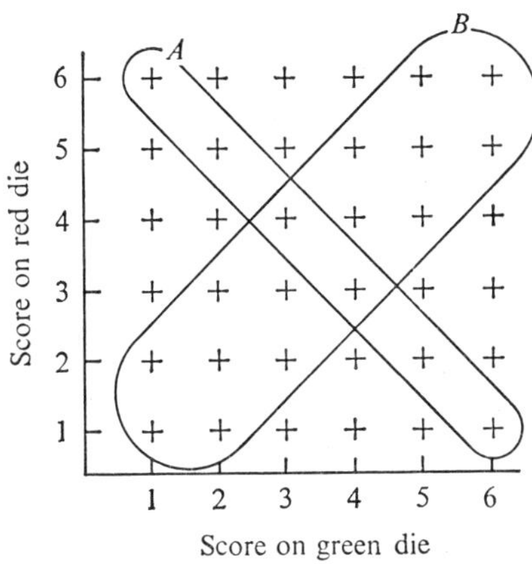

Fig. 5

dice are rolled and the separate scores recorded. We define two events as follows:

A: The sum of the two scores is 7.

B: The two scores differ from each other by not more than 1.

It is simple to calculate

$$n(\mathscr{E}) = 36; \quad n(A) = 6, \; n(B) = 16; \quad n(A') = 30, \; n(B') = 20;$$

$$n(A \cap B) = 2, \quad n(A' \cap B) = 14, \quad n(A \cap B') = 4, \quad n(A' \cap B') = 16.$$

This information is more easily taken in if set out in a table as follows:

	B	B'	
A	2	4	6
A'	14	16	30
	16	20	36

Thus the number entered in row A and column B is the number of elements in the intersection $A \cap B$; the marginal totals give the numbers of elements in the subsets A, B and their complements; and the grand total in the bottom right corner is the number of elements in the whole possibility space. A table of this kind is called a *contingency table* for set sizes.

To find the probabilities of the associated events the entries in this table must all be divided by $n(\mathscr{E})$. This gives a contingency table for probabilities:

	B	**~B**	
A	$\frac{1}{18}$	$\frac{1}{9}$	$\frac{1}{6}$
~A	$\frac{7}{18}$	$\frac{4}{9}$	$\frac{5}{6}$
	$\frac{4}{9}$	$\frac{5}{9}$	1

We read from this $p(\mathbf{A}) = \frac{1}{6}$, $p(\sim \mathbf{A} \wedge \mathbf{B}) = \frac{7}{18}$, and so on.

Exercise C

The questions in this exercise will be developed further in Exercise E. The solutions should therefore be kept for further reference.

In each question of this exercise a trial is proposed and two events **A**, **B** are described. The following probabilities are to be evaluated:

$p(\mathbf{A})$, $p(\mathbf{B})$, $p(\sim \mathbf{A})$, $p(\sim \mathbf{B})$;

$p(\mathbf{A} \wedge \mathbf{B})$, $p(\mathbf{A} \wedge \sim \mathbf{B})$, $p(\sim \mathbf{A} \wedge \mathbf{B})$, $p(\sim \mathbf{A} \wedge \sim \mathbf{B})$, $p(\mathbf{A} \wedge \mathbf{A})$, $p(\mathbf{A} \wedge \sim \mathbf{A})$;

$p(\mathbf{A} \vee \mathbf{B})$, $p(\mathbf{A} \vee \sim \mathbf{B})$, $p(\sim \mathbf{A} \vee \mathbf{B})$, $p(\sim \mathbf{A} \vee \sim \mathbf{B})$, $p(\mathbf{B} \vee \mathbf{B})$, $p(\mathbf{B} \vee \sim \mathbf{B})$.

1. The following cards are available: ♠ *A*, ♡ *K*, ♡ *Q*, ♣ *Q*, ♣ 8, ♡ 5, ♡ 3. One card is drawn and its name recorded.

A: The card is a heart.
B: The card is a queen.

2. George rolls a die and Harry draws a card from a pack. The score on the die and the suit of the card are recorded.

A: George rolls a 'two'.
B: Harry draws a club.

3. A card is drawn from a pack and its suit recorded.

A: The card is of a major suit (i.e. spade or heart).
B: The card is of a red suit.

4. A domino is drawn from a set, and its number-pair is recorded.

A: The domino is a 'double'.
B: The domino has at least one 2 or one 3.

(There are 28 dominoes in a set, each having a number between 0 and 6 on either end. The ends are indistinguishable, and no repetitions of number-pairs occur.)

5. A bag contains three 5p coins and two 1p coins. One coin is taken in each hand, and the colour of each is recorded.

A: The left hand holds a 'silver' coin.
B: The right hand holds a 'copper' coin.

6. A pair of dice is rolled and the separate scores recorded.

A: The score on the green die is less than 4.
B: The scores on the dice differ by not more than 2.

3.3 Probability laws. In working Exercise C the reader will have noticed that many of the probabilities calculated are linked with each other. For example, in each case the sum of $p(\mathbf{A})$ and $p(\sim \mathbf{A})$, and of $p(\mathbf{B})$ and $p(\sim \mathbf{B})$, is 1; also the sum of $p(\mathbf{A} \wedge \mathbf{B})$ and $p(\sim \mathbf{A} \wedge \mathbf{B})$ is $p(\mathbf{B})$; and so on. These are examples of general laws which hold for any events **S**, **T**:

Law 1. $p(\mathbf{S})+p(\sim \mathbf{S}) = 1.$

Law 2. $p(\mathbf{S} \wedge \mathbf{T})+p(\sim \mathbf{S} \wedge \mathbf{T}) = p(\mathbf{T}).$

Using these laws, all the compound probabilities involving the connective 'and' can be calculated from $p(\mathbf{A})$, $p(\mathbf{B})$ and $p(\mathbf{A} \wedge \mathbf{B})$. Suppose, for example, that $p(\mathbf{A}) = 0{\cdot}3$, $p(\mathbf{B}) = 0{\cdot}6$ and $p(\mathbf{A} \wedge \mathbf{B}) = 0{\cdot}1$. First Law 1, taking in turn $\mathbf{S} = \mathbf{A}$ and then $\mathbf{S} = \mathbf{B}$, gives

$$p(\sim \mathbf{A}) = 1-p(\mathbf{A}) = 1-0{\cdot}3 = 0{\cdot}7,$$

and $$p(\sim \mathbf{B}) = 1-p(\mathbf{B}) = 1-0{\cdot}6 = 0{\cdot}4.$$

Then Law 2, taking $\mathbf{S} = \mathbf{A}$ and $\mathbf{T} = \mathbf{B}$, gives

$$p(\sim \mathbf{A} \wedge \mathbf{B}) = p(\mathbf{B})-p(\mathbf{A} \wedge \mathbf{B}) = 0{\cdot}6-0{\cdot}1 = 0{\cdot}5;$$

and Law 2, taking $\mathbf{S} = \mathbf{B}$ and $\mathbf{T} = \mathbf{A}$, gives

$$p(\mathbf{A} \wedge \sim \mathbf{B}) = p(\mathbf{A}) - p(\mathbf{A} \wedge \mathbf{B}) = 0{\cdot}3 - 0{\cdot}1 = 0{\cdot}2.$$

(Here we use the commutative law, that $\mathbf{A} \wedge \mathbf{B}$ is the same event as $\mathbf{B} \wedge \mathbf{A}$, and $\mathbf{A} \wedge \sim \mathbf{B}$ the same as $\sim \mathbf{B} \wedge \mathbf{A}$.) Finally Law 2, taking $\mathbf{S} = \mathbf{A}$ and $\mathbf{T} = \sim \mathbf{B}$, gives

$$p(\sim \mathbf{A} \wedge \sim \mathbf{B}) = p(\sim \mathbf{B}) - p(\mathbf{A} \wedge \sim \mathbf{B}) = 0{\cdot}4 - 0{\cdot}2 = 0{\cdot}2.$$

These calculations are very easily followed with the help of a contingency table of probabilities in which the initial entries are:

	B	~ B	
A	0·1		0·3
~ A			
	0·6		1

To bring in the probabilities involving 'or', we have recourse to another result from the algebra of sets:

$$n(S \cup T) = n(S) + n(T) - n(S \cap T).$$

Again dividing by $n(\mathscr{E})$, and interpreting as probabilities, this gives:

Law 3. $p(\mathbf{S} \vee \mathbf{T}) = p(\mathbf{S}) + p(\mathbf{T}) - p(\mathbf{S} \wedge \mathbf{T})$.

***3.4 The algebra of events.** Besides the laws about probabilities, there are also certain laws about events themselves: laws which state that two different symbols involving events in fact stand for the same event. For example, we have already referred to the commutative law, that $\mathbf{S} \wedge \mathbf{T}$ is the same event as $\mathbf{T} \wedge \mathbf{S}$; and similarly $\mathbf{S} \vee \mathbf{T}$ is the same as $\mathbf{T} \vee \mathbf{S}$. Again, in working Exercise C, the laws

$$\mathbf{S} \wedge \mathbf{S} = \mathbf{S} \quad \text{and} \quad \mathbf{S} \vee \mathbf{S} = \mathbf{S}$$

emerged.

Important in this theory is the pair of laws known as *de Morgan's laws*:

$$\sim (\mathbf{S} \vee \mathbf{T}) = \sim \mathbf{S} \wedge \sim \mathbf{T} \quad \text{and} \quad \sim (\mathbf{S} \wedge \mathbf{T}) = \sim \mathbf{S} \vee \sim \mathbf{T}.$$

For example, if a man is not 'either-English-or-bespectacled', then he is not English *and* he is not bespectacled; and if he is not 'both-English-and-bespectacled', then either he is not English *or* he is not bespectacled (or both). These laws are easily verified with the aid of Venn diagrams for the associated subsets of the possibility space.

The first of de Morgan's laws gives another method of finding $p(\mathbf{S} \vee \mathbf{T})$. For it states that $\sim \mathbf{S} \wedge \sim \mathbf{T}$ is the negation of $\mathbf{S} \vee \mathbf{T}$, so that by Law 1

$$p(\mathbf{S} \vee \mathbf{T}) + p(\sim \mathbf{S} \wedge \sim \mathbf{T}) = 1.$$

Let us apply this to the numerical example discussed in the preceding section, in which we found that $p(\sim \mathbf{A} \wedge \sim \mathbf{B}) = 0{\cdot}2$. It follows that

$$p(\mathbf{A} \vee \mathbf{B}) = 1 - p(\sim \mathbf{A} \wedge \sim \mathbf{B}) = 1 - 0{\cdot}2 = 0{\cdot}8.$$

We can easily verify that this is the same value as is given by Law 3.

It is also sometimes useful to define events **E** and **O** corresponding to the special subsets $\mathscr{E}$ and ø of the possibility space: an event which always occurs, and an event which never occurs. Clearly, from the definitions,

$$p(\mathbf{E}) = 1, \quad p(\mathbf{O}) = 0.$$

Also, for any event **S**,

$$\mathbf{S} \wedge \mathbf{E} = \mathbf{S}, \quad \mathbf{S} \vee \mathbf{E} = \mathbf{E}; \quad \mathbf{S} \wedge \mathbf{O} = \mathbf{O}, \quad \mathbf{S} \vee \mathbf{O} = \mathbf{S};$$

and

$$\mathbf{S} \wedge \sim \mathbf{S} = \mathbf{O}, \quad \mathbf{S} \vee \sim \mathbf{S} = \mathbf{E}.$$

As an application of these definitions, consider the effect of substituting $\mathbf{T} = \mathbf{E}$ in the statement of Law 2. This gives

$$p(\mathbf{S} \wedge \mathbf{E}) + p(\sim \mathbf{S} \wedge \mathbf{E}) = p(\mathbf{E}),$$

or

$$p(\mathbf{S}) + p(\sim \mathbf{S}) = 1.$$

Thus Law 1 appears as a special case of Law 2.

The algebra of events which has now been built up is an example of *Boolean algebra*. It is isomorphic to the algebra of sets, with **S** written for S, $\wedge$ for $\cap$, $\vee$ for $\cup$, **E** for $\mathscr{E}$ and **O** for ø.

Exercise D

In Questions 1–4, complete the contingency table of probabilities from the information given; state the particular form of Laws 1,2 or 3 which is used in making each fresh entry; and draw a diagram of a possibility space with subsets A, B to which the data might apply.

1. $p(\mathbf{A}) = \frac{1}{3}, \quad p(\mathbf{B}) = \frac{1}{4}, \quad p(\mathbf{A} \wedge \mathbf{B}) = \frac{1}{6}.$

2. $p(\mathbf{A} \wedge \mathbf{B}) = 0{\cdot}2, \quad p(\mathbf{A} \wedge \sim \mathbf{B}) = 0{\cdot}3, \quad p(\sim \mathbf{A} \wedge \mathbf{B}) = 0{\cdot}4.$

3. $p(\mathbf{A}) = \frac{1}{3}, \quad p(\mathbf{B}) = \frac{2}{5}, \quad p(\sim \mathbf{A} \wedge \sim \mathbf{B}) = \frac{2}{5}.$

4. $p(\mathbf{A}) = 0{\cdot}6, \quad p(\mathbf{B}) = 0{\cdot}5, \quad p(\mathbf{A} \vee \mathbf{B}) = 0{\cdot}9.$

5. If $p(\mathbf{A}) = a$, $p(\mathbf{B}) = b$ and $p(\mathbf{A} \wedge \mathbf{B}) = c$, use Laws 1 and 2 to express $p(\sim \mathbf{A} \wedge \sim \mathbf{B})$ in terms of a, b, and c; then use Law 1 and de Morgan's law to find $p(\mathbf{A} \vee \mathbf{B})$, and verify that the answer agrees with Law 3.

6. With the notation of Question 5, prove that

$$0 \leqslant c \leqslant a \leqslant 1, \quad 0 \leqslant c \leqslant b \leqslant 1 \quad \text{and} \quad a+b \leqslant 1+c.$$

Describe the special situations for which:

(*a*) $a = c$, (*b*) $a+b = 1+c$, (*c*) $a = 1$.

4. CONDITIONAL PROBABILITY

4.1 Definition. In Section 2 we discussed the trial of rolling a pair of dice and recording the separate scores on the two top faces; and we saw that the probability of the event **A**, 'the sum of the scores is at least 10', was $\frac{6}{36}$, or $\frac{1}{6}$. Thus in a large number of repetitions of the trial we would expect to get such a total on about one-sixth of the throws; a gambler would think it fair to offer odds of 5 to 1 against a favourable result.

Imagine that when the trial is carried out the green die is examined first, and that it registers a score of 6. The situation immediately becomes far more hopeful, for of the six possible scores on the red die (still to be examined) three—scores of 4, 5 or 6—will bring success. Since all scores on the red die are equally likely, we would at this juncture assign a probability of $\frac{3}{6}$, or $\frac{1}{2}$, to the event 'the sum of the scores is at least 10'.

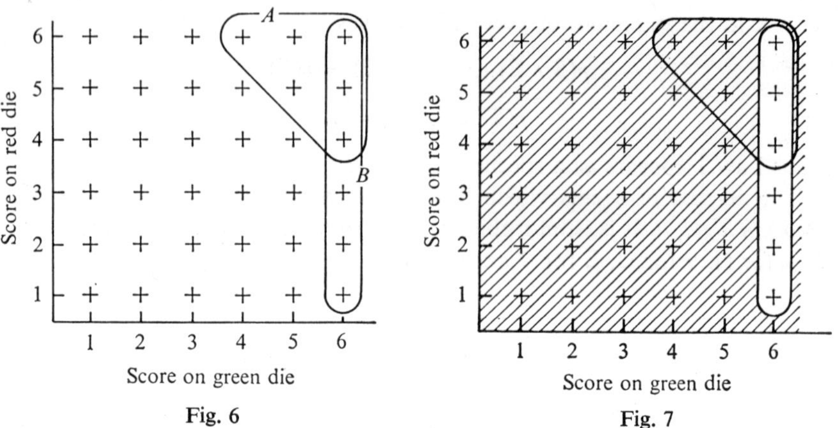

Fig. 6 Fig. 7

Let us denote by **B** the event 'the score on the green die is 6' (see Figure 6). Then the probability $\frac{1}{2}$ just calculated is called the *conditional probability of* **A** *given* **B**, and written $p(\mathbf{A}|\mathbf{B})$. It is found by concentrating on the subset B of the possibility space, i.e. on those scores for which the event **B** occurs. Imagine a piece of paper with a slot in it placed over Figure 6 so as to obscure all possibility points except those in B (see Figure 7). This then shows the new possibility space, with three outcomes (6, 4), (6, 5) and (6, 6) for which the event **A** occurs; a moment's reflection will convince the reader that these are the elements of the subset $A \cap B$. We are therefore led to the formal definition

$$p(\mathbf{A} \mid \mathbf{B}) = \frac{n(A \cap B)}{n(B)}.$$

It must be emphasized that this idea is not really a new one, since all probabilities are evaluated only after some initial conditions have been laid down (often implicitly). We cannot find the probability of drawing a spade from a pack of cards unless we know whether or not the joker is included in the pack; the set of equally likely possibilities must be given before probabilities can be defined. The difference here is merely that we are imposing a further condition, and thus restricting the set of possibilities within which we are interested whether or not the event occurs.

What is new is the notation $p(\mathbf{A} \mid \mathbf{B})$. By comparison, what we have so far denoted by $p(\mathbf{A})$ might be written as $p(\mathbf{A} \mid \mathbf{E})$, where $\mathbf{E}$ is the event defined by the whole possibility space (see Section 3.4).

The use of the word 'given' in referring to conditional probability should not mislead the reader into thinking that any idea of time is necessarily involved. The quantity $p(\mathbf{A} \mid \mathbf{B})$ is defined completely by the numbers of elements in the two subsets B and $A \cap B$ of the possibility space.

Exercise E

1–6. For each of the trials and pairs of events described in Questions 1–6 of Exercise C, evaluate the following conditional probabilities:

$$p(\mathbf{A}|\mathbf{B}),\quad p(\sim \mathbf{A}|\mathbf{B}),\quad p(\mathbf{A}|\sim \mathbf{B}),\quad p(\sim \mathbf{A}|\sim \mathbf{B}),$$
$$p(\mathbf{B}|\mathbf{A}),\quad p(\mathbf{B}|\sim \mathbf{A}),\quad p(\sim \mathbf{B}|\mathbf{A}),\quad p(\sim \mathbf{B}|\sim \mathbf{A}).$$

Among these probabilities are various pairs whose sum is unity in every case. Show that a general result is exemplified by these relations, and state this result in terms of events **S** and **T**.

4.2 A law for conditional probability. The definition of conditional probability can be re-cast simply in terms of probabilities alone. For two general events **S**, **T** we may write

$$p(\mathbf{S} \mid \mathbf{T}) = \frac{n(S \cap T)}{n(T)}$$
$$= \frac{n(S \cap T)}{n(\mathscr{E})} \Big/ \frac{n(T)}{n(\mathscr{E})}.$$

This leads at once to:

$$\textit{Law } 4.\quad p(\mathbf{S} \mid \mathbf{T}) = p(\mathbf{S} \wedge \mathbf{T})/p(\mathbf{T}).$$

It is often helpful to think of this in the alternative form

$$p(\mathbf{S} \wedge \mathbf{T}) = p(\mathbf{T}).p(\mathbf{S} \mid \mathbf{T}).$$

That is, to calculate the fraction of the possibilities for a trial that are in both S and T, we first find what fraction of the possibilities are in T, and multiply this by the fraction of the possibilities which, being in T, are also in S.

For instance, let us consider the probability that on any particular day it is cloudy and I shall be carrying an umbrella. Suppose that $\frac{2}{5}$ of all days are cloudy and that on $\frac{3}{7}$ of cloudy days I carry an umbrella; then on $\frac{2}{5}\times\frac{3}{7}$, that is $\frac{6}{35}$, of all days it is cloudy and I am carrying an umbrella.

4.3 Tree diagrams. In the elementary course we frequently used tree diagrams to illustrate situations in which conditional probabilities were involved. To demonstrate this, let us take the example just quoted a stage further; and let us add one more piece of information, that on days when it is not cloudy I carry an umbrella with a probability of only $\frac{1}{7}$. Then the whole situation can be summed up by the tree diagram of Figure 8.

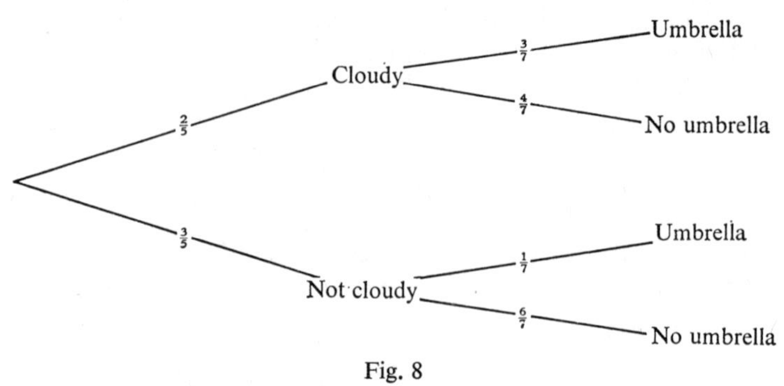

Fig. 8

Denoting by $\mathbf{C}$ the event 'it is cloudy', and by $\mathbf{U}$ the event 'I carry an umbrella', the probabilities along the two branches on the left are (reading downwards) $p(\mathbf{C})$ and $p(\sim \mathbf{C})$; and the probabilities along the four branches on the right are $p(\mathbf{U} \mid \mathbf{C})$, $p(\sim \mathbf{U} \mid \mathbf{C})$, $p(\mathbf{U} \mid \sim \mathbf{C})$ and $p(\sim \mathbf{U} \mid \sim \mathbf{C})$. We have seen that Law 4 justifies the practice of finding the probability of a combined event such as 'it is cloudy and I carry an umbrella' by multiplying the probabilities along the appropriate branches.

Now we know that in a tree diagram the probabilities on any set of branches emerging from the same point must add up to 1. For example

$$p(\mathbf{U} \mid \mathbf{C})+p(\sim \mathbf{U} \mid \mathbf{C}) = \tfrac{3}{7}+\tfrac{4}{7}= 1,$$

and similarly for $p(\mathbf{U} \mid \sim \mathbf{C})$ and $p(\sim \mathbf{U} \mid \sim \mathbf{C})$. These are examples of a general result, which the reader will already have observed in his solutions for Exercise E and which we shall now prove:

Theorem. $p(\mathbf{S} \mid \mathbf{T})+p(\sim \mathbf{S} \mid \mathbf{T}) = 1.$

Proof.
$$\begin{aligned} p(\mathbf{S} \mid \mathbf{T})+p(\sim \mathbf{S} \mid \mathbf{T}) &= \frac{p(\mathbf{S}\wedge\mathbf{T})}{p(\mathbf{T})}+\frac{p(\sim \mathbf{S}\wedge\mathbf{T})}{p(\mathbf{T})} \quad \text{(by Law 4)} \\ &= \frac{p(\mathbf{S}\wedge\mathbf{T})+p(\sim \mathbf{S}\wedge\mathbf{T})}{p(\mathbf{T})} \\ &= \frac{p(\mathbf{T})}{p(\mathbf{T})} \quad \text{(by Law 2)} \\ &= 1. \end{aligned}$$

4.4 Calculation of other probabilities. A tree diagram such as Figure 8 has significance only if it is read from left to right. It is not possible to read directly from this diagram, for example, the probability that it is cloudy given that I am carrying an umbrella. This can, however, be calculated from the information at our disposal.

By Law 4,
$$p(\mathbf{C} \mid \mathbf{U}) = p(\mathbf{C} \wedge \mathbf{U})/p(\mathbf{U}).$$

We know already that $p(\mathbf{C} \wedge \mathbf{U}) = \frac{6}{35}$. It therefore remains to evaluate $p(\mathbf{U})$, the overall probability that I am carrying an umbrella.

This is a problem with which we are familiar; and we solve it by adding the probabilities leading to the word 'umbrella' in the tree diagram by various routes. Thus

$$\begin{aligned} p(\text{umbrella}) &= p(\text{cloudy and umbrella}) \\ &\quad + p(\text{not-cloudy and umbrella}) \\ &= \tfrac{2}{5} \times \tfrac{3}{7} + \tfrac{3}{5} \times \tfrac{1}{7} \\ &= \tfrac{9}{35}, \end{aligned}$$

so that
$$p(\mathbf{C} \mid \mathbf{U}) = \tfrac{6}{35}/\tfrac{9}{35} = \tfrac{2}{3}.$$

So far we have regarded this method of calculating $p(\mathbf{U})$ as 'intuitively obvious'; but we can now display it as a consequence of the laws of probability. Again we state a general result and prove it:

Theorem. $p(\mathbf{T}) = p(\mathbf{S}).p(\mathbf{T} \mid \mathbf{S}) + p(\sim \mathbf{S}).p(\mathbf{T} \mid \sim \mathbf{S})$.

Proof.
$$\begin{aligned} p(\mathbf{T}) &= p(\mathbf{S} \wedge \mathbf{T}) + p(\sim \mathbf{S} \wedge \mathbf{T}) && \text{(by Law 2)} \\ &= p(\mathbf{T} \wedge \mathbf{S}) + p(\mathbf{T} \wedge \sim \mathbf{S}) && \text{(by the commutative law)} \\ &= p(\mathbf{S}).p(\mathbf{T} \mid \mathbf{S}) + p(\sim \mathbf{S}).p(\mathbf{T} \mid \sim \mathbf{S}) && \text{(by Law 4).} \end{aligned}$$

An alternative way of calculating $p(\mathbf{C} \mid \mathbf{U})$ would be to use a diagram of 35 points to represent a possibility space for the situation, as in Figure 9. We first circle off $\frac{2}{5} \times 35$ points to represent the set of cloudy possibilities, and then within this set and its complement we select the appropriate numbers of points to lie within the set U. From this diagram we read off

$$p(\mathbf{C} \mid \mathbf{U}) = \frac{n(C \cap U)}{n(U)} = \frac{6}{9} = \frac{2}{3}.$$

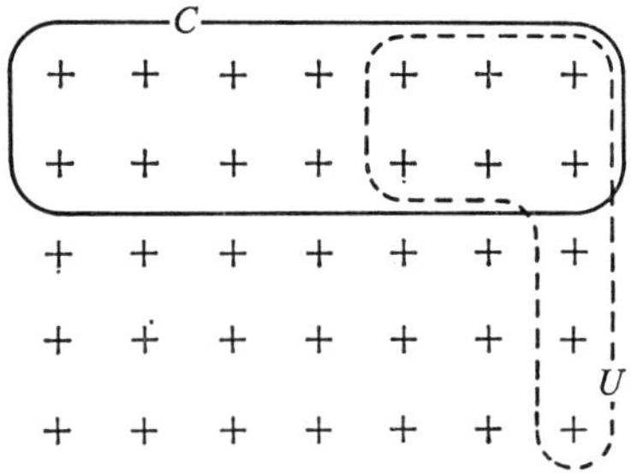

Fig. 9

Exercise F

1. A boy who has not done his homework thoroughly knows that there is a 60% chance that it will be tested, and that if there is a test he has a 70% chance of failing. Express the information given in probability notation, and deduce the probability that his negligence comes to the attention of his schoolmaster.

2. A member of a television audience has a probability of 0·002 of being invited up to the stage, and if she is invited she has a probability of one-quarter of winning a new car. What is the probability that she wins the car?

3. I go to London by car with probability 0·8, and by train with probability 0·2. If I go by car, the probability that I shall be on time for my appointment is 0·6; if I go by train, it is 0·3. Write this information in probability notation. Find the probability that I arrive early for an appointment in London, stating any properties of probabilities that you use.

In Questions 4–8:

(*a*) draw a tree diagram with $\mathbf{A}$ preceding $\mathbf{B}$, marking all the branch probabilities;

(*b*) calculate $p(\mathbf{A} \wedge \mathbf{B})$, $p(\mathbf{A} \wedge \sim \mathbf{B})$, $p(\sim \mathbf{A} \wedge \mathbf{B})$, $p(\sim \mathbf{A} \wedge \sim \mathbf{B})$;

(*c*) draw a diagram to represent a possibility space to fit the data;

(*d*) calculate $p(\mathbf{B})$ and $p(\sim \mathbf{B})$;

(*e*) calculate $p(\mathbf{A}|\mathbf{B})$, $p(\sim \mathbf{A}|\mathbf{B})$, $p(\mathbf{A}|\sim \mathbf{B})$, $p(\sim \mathbf{A}|\sim \mathbf{B})$;

(*f*) draw a tree diagram with $\mathbf{B}$ preceding $\mathbf{A}$, marking all the branch probabilities.

4. $p(\mathbf{A}) = \frac{3}{5}$, $p(\mathbf{B}|\mathbf{A}) = 0$, $p(\sim \mathbf{B}|\sim \mathbf{A}) = 0$.

5. $p(\sim \mathbf{A}) = \frac{1}{5}$, $p(\sim \mathbf{B}|\sim \mathbf{A}) = 0$, $p(\sim \mathbf{B}|\mathbf{A}) = \frac{2}{5}$.

6. $p(\mathbf{A}) = \frac{1}{6}$, $p(\sim \mathbf{B}|\mathbf{A}) = 1$, $p(\sim \mathbf{B}|\sim \mathbf{A}) = \frac{3}{5}$.

7. $p(\mathbf{A}) = \frac{3}{10}$, $p(\sim \mathbf{B}|\mathbf{A}) = \frac{2}{3}$, $p(\mathbf{B}|\sim \mathbf{A}) = \frac{3}{7}$.

8. $p(\mathbf{A}) = \frac{1}{4}$, $p(\mathbf{B}|\mathbf{A}) = \frac{1}{3}$, $p(\sim \mathbf{B}|\sim \mathbf{A}) = \frac{2}{3}$.

9. In a certain group of 1000 people 20% are men and 80% are women. Of the men 4% are colour blind, and of the women 1% are colour blind. What are the probabilities of selecting from the group (*a*) a colour blind man, (*b*) a colour blind person. If an individual is selected at random from the colour blind members of the group, what is the probability that the person chosen will be male?

10. Prove that $p(\mathbf{R} \wedge \mathbf{S} \wedge \mathbf{T}) = p(\mathbf{T}).p(\mathbf{S}|\mathbf{T}).p(\mathbf{R}|\mathbf{S} \wedge \mathbf{T})$.

At a party I have a $\frac{3}{4}$ chance of having a cracker to pull, but a $\frac{2}{3}$ chance that there is not a paper hat in the cracker even if I get a cracker at all. If there is a hat in the cracker I have only a 50% chance of reaching it first. What is the probability that I shall get a hat?

11. Prove that $p(\mathbf{S}|\mathbf{T})/p(\mathbf{T}|\mathbf{S}) = p(\mathbf{S})/p(\mathbf{T})$.

12. Prove that $p(\mathbf{R} \wedge \mathbf{S}|\mathbf{T}) = p(\mathbf{R}|\mathbf{S} \wedge \mathbf{T}).p(\mathbf{S}|\mathbf{T})$.

13. Prove that $p(\mathbf{S} \wedge \mathbf{T}|\mathbf{T}) = p(\mathbf{S}|\mathbf{T})$.

***14.** If $p(\mathbf{A}), p(\sim \mathbf{A}), p(\mathbf{B}|\mathbf{A})$ and $p(\mathbf{B}|\sim \mathbf{A})$ are given, prove that $p(\mathbf{A}|\mathbf{B})$ can be calculated from the formula

$$p(\mathbf{A}|\mathbf{B}) = \frac{p(\mathbf{A}).p(\mathbf{B}|\mathbf{A})}{p(\mathbf{A}).p(\mathbf{B}|\mathbf{A})+p(\sim \mathbf{A})\,p(\mathbf{B}|\sim \mathbf{A})}.$$

(This result, which expresses in general form the results of Questions 4–8, is known as *Bayes's Theorem*. If **A** precedes **B** in time or causally, then the given probabilities are sometimes referred to as *a priori* probabilities, and $p(\mathbf{A}|\mathbf{B})$ is called an *a posteriori* probability.)

5. DIFFICULTIES IN THE DEFINITION OF PROBABILITY

5.1 Frequency definition of probability. The reader will have noticed that in the last section we began to use the word 'probability' in situations for which the *a priori* definition given in Section 2.4 could hardly be said to apply. We suggested, for example, that the probability that 'on any particular day it is cloudy' might be taken as $\frac{2}{5}$; but this statement is unlikely to be made by considering possibilities which are 'equally likely on grounds of symmetry'. Clearly the extension of the theory of probability to cover this wider range of situations raises several new questions, such as:

Can numerical probabilities still be assigned to events?

If so, how can they be evaluated?

Do probabilities thus calculated obey the same laws as those derived from the *a priori* definition?

The usefulness of the theory in many applications rests on the assumption that the answer to the first question is 'yes'; that is, that we may assign a probability to an event even if it is impossible practically to consider the complete set of possibilities in such a way that they could be described as equally likely. For example, we say that there is a probability that the chocolates produced by a factory are correctly filled; but the only way of finding this exactly might be to examine every chocolate by bisecting it—thereby destroying it as a saleable product.

In practice we estimate this probability by a process known as 'sampling'. That is, we examine as many chocolates as we can conveniently and economically, and assume that the proportion of badly filled chocolates amongst those examined is nearly enough equal to the proportion in the total output of the factory. We must, of course, take care to keep the selection random; for example, we should not take too many of one particular flavour, or of those made at a certain time of day.

What we are doing here is to look at the approximation

$$\frac{\text{fr}\,A}{\text{fr}\,\mathscr{E}} \simeq \frac{n(A)}{n(\mathscr{E})},$$

given in Section 2.3, from the opposite point of view. Previously we defined $p(\mathbf{A})$ as $n(A)/n(\mathscr{E})$, which was known exactly from theoretical considerations; and this approximation then led us to expect that, if a large number of trials was carried out, then

$$\text{fr}\,A \approx p(\mathbf{A}).\text{fr}\,\mathscr{E}.$$

In this section we have assigned to $p(\mathbf{A})$ the value $\text{fr}\,A/\text{fr}\,\mathscr{E}$ for some *particular* large number of trials; and again we do this in the expectation that, for any other large number of trials, we shall find that

$$\text{fr}\,A \approx p(\mathbf{A}).\text{fr}\,\mathscr{E}.$$

It remains to discuss how, from this new point of view, probabilities of compound events and conditional probabilities can be found. Since $p(\sim \mathbf{A})$, $p(\mathbf{A} \wedge \mathbf{B})$, $p(\mathbf{A} \vee \mathbf{B})$ and $p(\mathbf{A} \mid \mathbf{B})$ can no longer be related to the sizes of sets of equally likely possibilities, the definitions previously given are no longer relevant. However, Laws 1–4 which have been derived from them are expressed entirely in terms of probabilities, and we make the assumption that these laws remain true with the extended meaning of probability. The laws are no longer deducible from results of set theory; rather they must be regarded as axioms of a more general theory of probability. But they can be applied exactly as they were before; and from these axioms we can then deduce other results, such as the theorems given in Sections 4.3 and 4.4.

This branch of mathematics has given rise to much discussion of fundamental logical and philosophical issues. But the practical justification for the assumptions made rests on their successful application in many areas of science, industry and commerce.

5.2 Infinite possibility spaces. Another difficulty arises if the possibility space consists of an infinite set of possibilities; for then the *a priori* definition is inapplicable since there is no finite number $n(\mathscr{E})$. Moreover, the frequency definition is fraught with difficulty, since the method of selecting the sample is of critical importance.

Consider the problem of selecting an angle between 0° and 45°, when all acute angles are possible. We might specify a sample which gives equal chances to all magnitudes of angle between 0° and 90°, or to all magnitudes of sine between 0 and 1, or to all magnitudes of cosine between 1 and 0, or to all magnitudes of the tangent of the half-angle (a frequently used parameter) between 0 and 1. We could then reasonably assign, on these bases, any of the probabilities $\frac{1}{2}$, 0·707, 1–0·707, or 0·414 to the same event; and the number of other approaches is legion.

A branch of pure mathematics called 'measure theory' has been developed to deal with this kind of problem, but it falls beyond the scope of this course. When we wish to deal with infinite possibility spaces we shall always allocate the probabilities unambiguously.

6. INDEPENDENT EVENTS

6.1 Definition. In the example of Section 4 the probability of my carrying an umbrella on cloudy days was different from that on bright days; we say that whether or not I carry an umbrella 'depends on' whether or not it is a cloudy day. On the other hand, an event such as 'I have kippers for my breakfast' (denoted by **K**) might not be influenced at all by the state of the weather. In this case the probability that I have kippers on cloudy days will be the same as the probability that I have kippers on bright days; that is,

$$p(\mathbf{K} \mid \mathbf{C}) = p(\mathbf{K} \mid \sim \mathbf{C}).$$

This thinking leads to the definition:

> An event **A** is said to be *statistically independent* of an event **B** if the conditional probabilities $p(\mathbf{A} \mid \mathbf{B})$ and $p(\mathbf{A} \mid \sim \mathbf{B})$ are equal.

6.2 Independence and statistical independence. The reason for adding the word 'statistically' to the description of independence is as follows. Whilst it is true that events which are independent in ordinary usage are also statistically independent, the converse is false: that is, statistically independent events may or may not be independent in the ordinary sense of the word.

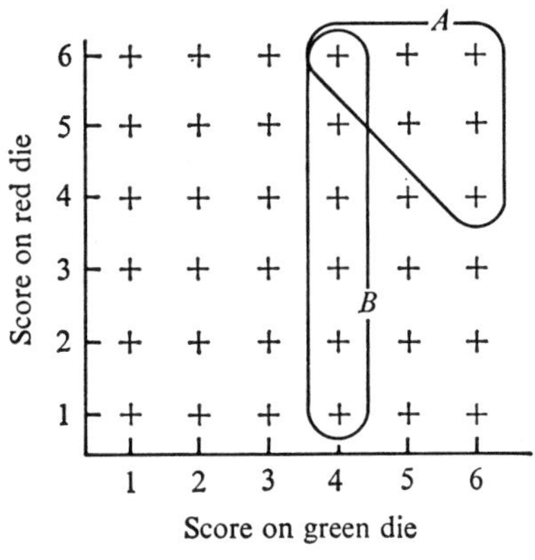

Fig. 10

As an illustration of this, consider the trial discussed in Section 4.1 in which two dice are rolled and the separate scores recorded, with the event **A** 'the sum of the scores is at least 10'. We saw that if the green die is examined first, the result of this examination might affect our estimate of the probability of **A**. For example, if the green die shows a score of 6, we would now wish to assign a probability of $\frac{1}{2}$ to getting the desired total; but if it showed 1, 2 or 3 there would be no point in looking at the red die, since we could not then possibly get a total of 10. We would say that whether or not we get the desired total depends on the score shown on the green die. If therefore we defined the event **B** as 'the score on the green die is 4' (see Figure 10), it would be natural to say that **A** is not independent of **B**.

In the statistical sense, however, **A** is independent of **B**. For

$$n(A \cap B) = 1, \quad n(B) = 6, \quad n(A \cap B') = 5, \quad n(B') = 30,$$

so that $$p(\mathbf{A}|\mathbf{B}) = \tfrac{1}{6} \text{ and } p(\mathbf{A}| \sim \mathbf{B}) = \tfrac{5}{30} = \tfrac{1}{6}.$$

6.3 Another form of the condition. If **A** is independent of **B**, so that the probability of **A** given **B** is equal to the probability of **A** given not-**B**, then it is natural to expect that these two probabilities will both be equal to $p(\mathbf{A})$. For instance, in the example just quoted,

$$p(\mathbf{A}) = \frac{n(A)}{n(\mathscr{E})} = \frac{6}{36} = \frac{1}{6},$$

which is the same as each of the two conditional probabilities. The general result is easily proved from the laws of probability:

Theorem. *If* **S** *is statistically independent of* **T**, *then the conditional probabilities* $p(\mathbf{S}|\mathbf{T})$ *and* $p(\mathbf{S}| \sim \mathbf{T})$ *are both equal to* $p(\mathbf{S})$.

Proof. By Law 4,
$$p(\mathbf{S} \wedge \mathbf{T}) = p(\mathbf{S}|\mathbf{T}).p(\mathbf{T});$$
and, replacing **T** by $\sim$ **T**,
$$p(\mathbf{S} \wedge \sim \mathbf{T}) = p(\mathbf{S}| \sim \mathbf{T}).p(\sim \mathbf{T}).$$
The argument will be clarified if we denote the common value of $p(\mathbf{S}|\mathbf{T})$ and $p(\mathbf{S}| \sim \mathbf{T})$ by the single letter λ. The equations then become
$$p(\mathbf{S} \wedge \mathbf{T}) = \lambda p(\mathbf{T}),$$
and $$p(\mathbf{S} \wedge \sim \mathbf{T}) = \lambda p(\sim \mathbf{T}).$$
Adding, $$p(\mathbf{S} \wedge \mathbf{T}) + p(\mathbf{S} \wedge \sim \mathbf{T}) = \lambda\{p(\mathbf{T}) + p(\sim \mathbf{T})\}.$$

Now we know, by Law 1, that
$$p(\mathbf{T}) + p(\sim \mathbf{T}) = 1;$$
and also, by Law 2 (interchanging **T** and **S**, and using the commutative law), that
$$p(\mathbf{S} \wedge \mathbf{T}) + p(\mathbf{S} \wedge \sim \mathbf{T}) = p(\mathbf{S}).$$
We have therefore proved that
$$p(\mathbf{S}) = \lambda,$$
which is the result required.

It is important to notice that this theorem has a converse, whose formal statement is:

Theorem. *If* $p(\mathbf{S}|\mathbf{T}) = p(\mathbf{S})$, *then* $\mathbf{S}$ *is statistically independent of* $\mathbf{T}$.

This can be proved by a direct reversal of the argument above. Writing λ now for the common value of $p(\mathbf{S})$ and $p(\mathbf{S}|\mathbf{T})$, we have

$$p(\mathbf{S}) - p(\mathbf{S} \wedge \mathbf{T}) = \lambda - \lambda p(\mathbf{T}),$$

so that

$$p(\mathbf{S} \wedge \sim \mathbf{T}) = \lambda p(\sim \mathbf{T});$$

that is

$$p(\mathbf{S}| \sim \mathbf{T}) = \lambda,$$

so that $p(\mathbf{S}|\mathbf{T}) = p(\mathbf{S}| \sim \mathbf{T})$, the condition for independence.

This result gives a different criterion for independence; and it is sometimes simpler to verify in a particular application that $p(\mathbf{S}|\mathbf{T})$ and $p(\mathbf{S})$ are equal, without calculating the other conditional probability $p(\mathbf{S}| \sim \mathbf{T})$.

6.4 Compounding independent events. The theorem of the preceding section leads at once to a result which the reader will recall from the elementary course, but which at that stage could only be justified intuitively—the 'product rule' for the probability of the coincidence of two independent events. For we know that in general, by Law 4,

$$p(\mathbf{S} \wedge \mathbf{T}) = p(\mathbf{S}|\mathbf{T}).p(\mathbf{T});$$

and we have now shown that, if $\mathbf{S}$ is independent of $\mathbf{T}$,

$$p(\mathbf{S}|\mathbf{T}) = p(\mathbf{S}).$$

In this case, therefore,

$$p(\mathbf{S} \wedge \mathbf{T}) = p(\mathbf{S}).p(\mathbf{T}),$$

which is the product rule referred to above.

Moreover, the argument can be reversed. For *if*

$$p(\mathbf{S} \wedge \mathbf{T}) = p(\mathbf{S}).p(\mathbf{T}),$$

then

$$p(\mathbf{S}) = p(\mathbf{S} \wedge \mathbf{T})/p(\mathbf{T})$$
$$= p(\mathbf{S}|\mathbf{T}),$$

so that $\mathbf{S}$ is statistically independent of $\mathbf{T}$.

These results are summarized in the following theorem:

Theorem. $\mathbf{S}$ *is statistically independent of* $\mathbf{T}$

$$\Leftrightarrow p(\mathbf{S} \wedge \mathbf{T}) = p(\mathbf{S}).p(\mathbf{T}).$$

6.5 Symmetry of the independence relation. A striking feature of this last theorem is its symmetry as between the events $\mathbf{S}$ and $\mathbf{T}$; and this suggests that the relation 'is statistically independent of' is a symmetric one.

Theorem. *If* $\mathbf{S}$ *is statistically independent of* $\mathbf{T}$, *then* $\mathbf{T}$ *is statistically independent of* $\mathbf{S}$.

Proof. **S** is statistically independent of **T**

$$\Rightarrow p(\mathbf{S} \wedge \mathbf{T}) = p(\mathbf{S}).p(\mathbf{T})$$
$$\Rightarrow p(\mathbf{T} \wedge \mathbf{S}) = p(\mathbf{T}).p(\mathbf{S})$$

$\Rightarrow$ **T** is statistically independent of **S**.

This is, perhaps, hardly surprising; for it ties in with our use of the word 'independent' in ordinary English. Nevertheless, since statistical independence has been defined mathematically, a mathematical proof of the symmetry of the relation is necessary. Now that it has been established, we are entitled to describe a pair of events as being 'independent of each other', without having to specify which is independent of which.

Exercise G

In Questions 1–6 a trial is proposed and two events **A**, **B** are described. By evaluating the appropriate conditional probabilities, determine whether **A** is independent of **B**, and also whether **B** is independent of **A**. Verify in each case the results of the theorem of Section 6.5. Evaluate also $p(\mathbf{A})$, $p(\mathbf{B})$ and $p(\mathbf{A} \wedge \mathbf{B})$, and hence verify the results stated in Sections 6.3 and 6.4. (Notice that each of these gives a 'necessary and sufficient condition': if **S** and **T** are independent, then a certain conclusion follows; and if not, it doesn't.)

1. A die is rolled and the score on the top face recorded.
A: The score is 6.
B: The score is 3.

2. Two dice are rolled and the separate scores recorded.
A: The score on the green die is 6.
B: The score on the red die is 3.

3. Two dice are rolled and the separate scores recorded.
A: The score on the green die is 1.
B: The sum of the scores on the two dice is 7.

4. Two dice are rolled and the separate scores recorded.
A: The score on the green die is 1.
B: The sum of the scores on the two dice is 8.

5. A card is drawn from a complete pack, and its name recorded.
A: The card is a spade.
B: The card is a face card.

6. A card is drawn from a pack including the Joker, and its name recorded.
A: The card is a spade.
B: The card is a face card.

7. Twenty-four people went on a picnic; eight got sunburned in the morning, six got stung by mosquitoes in the afternoon. What was the largest number of people who could have got home unscathed? Show that if twelve people got home unscathed, then getting sunburned and getting stung were statistically independent events; but that if eleven were unscathed, the events were not independent.

8. 343 patients are habitual sufferers from chilblains. One autumn 96 of them are given a new treatment. Seven of these do not develop chilblains during the winter, whilst of the untreated patients 229 do develop chilblains. Do these figures give any support to the theory that the treatment is effective?

9. A roulette wheel is numbered 0 to 36. Find the probabilities:

(*a*) that the first appearance of 13 is on the second spin;
(*b*) that 13 does not come up in the first two spins;
(*c*) that 13 comes up at least once in the first two spins.
State at each stage which law of probability you are applying.

10. The local bus company employs as conductors 350 men and 150 women, under the same conditions of service. I can get home from school either on an 18 or a 23 bus; the 18 buses run on average once every 15 minutes, and the 23 buses once every 10 minutes, but to no set schedule. In a school term of 70 days, how often would I expect to travel on a number 23 bus with a male conductor?

11. I drop 1000 identical buttons on the floor, and 300 of them land curved side up, 700 flat side up. If I now pick up a pair of buttons at random, what are the probabilities that they will be

(*a*) both curved side up;
(*b*) both flat side up;
(*c*) one of each?
Explain the steps of your argument in terms of the theory of probability.

12. If **S** is statistically independent of **T**, prove that

(*a*) **S** is statistically independent of ~ **T**,
(*b*) ~ **S** is statistically independent of **T**.
(Do not use (*a*) to prove (*b*), or vice versa.)

13. Complete the contingency table of probabilities, given that **A** and **B** are independent events:

	B	~ **B**	
A			*a*
~ **A**			
	b		

14. In what ways could you recognize from a contingency table of set sizes that the related events were statistically independent?

15. Prove that the relation 'is statistically independent of' is neither reflexive nor transitive.

16. A regular tetrahedral die has its faces marked (*a*), (*b*), (*c*) and (*abc*). When any face whose mark includes the letter *a* is in contact with the plane on which the die is thrown, we say that the event **A** has occurred; and similarly for *b* and *c*. Which of the following statements are true?

(i) **A** and **B** are independent events;
(ii) **A** and **C** are independent events;
(iii) **A** and (**B** and **C**) are independent events;
(iv) $p(\mathbf{B} \wedge \mathbf{C}) = p(\mathbf{B}).p(\mathbf{C})$;
(v) $p(\mathbf{A} \wedge \mathbf{B} \wedge \mathbf{C}) = p(\mathbf{A}).p(\mathbf{B}).p(\mathbf{C})$.

17. Answer as in Question 16 for a trial in which a penny and a 2p coin are tossed simultaneously and the results recorded, the events being as follows:
A, the penny comes down 'heads';
B, the 2p coin comes down 'heads';
C, the coins match (i.e. both 'heads' or both 'tails').

18. Answer as in Question 16 for a trial in which a penny, a 5p coin and a 10p coin are tossed simultaneously and the results recorded, the events being as follows:
A, the penny comes down 'heads';
B, the 5p coin comes down 'heads';
C, the 10p coin comes down 'heads'.

(Questions 16–18 suggest that special care about the meaning of 'independence' is required when three or more events are involved. Situations of this kind are examined in more detail in Miscellaneous Exercise, Question 10.)

19. I am going on holiday on 6 August and have left my arrangements rather late. It is possible that my railway ticket, my passport and my traveller's cheques will fail to arrive on time. These events are completely independent, and on a large survey of delay times their probabilities are assessed as $\frac{1}{3}$, $\frac{1}{4}$ and $\frac{3}{5}$. What is the probability that on 6 August
(*a*) I shall be without all three things;
(*b*) I shall be without my traveller's cheques but otherwise complete?
What do you think 'completely independent' means in the statement of this problem?

7. THE EVENT (S or T)

We need not devote much special discussion to the event (**S** or **T**), since its probability can be expressed in terms of that of the event (**S** and **T**) using Law 3:

$$p(\mathbf{S} \vee \mathbf{T}) = p(\mathbf{S})+p(\mathbf{T})-p(\mathbf{S} \wedge \mathbf{T}).$$

There are, however, two special situations which deserve notice because they give particularly simple expressions for $p(\mathbf{S} \vee \mathbf{T})$.

7.1 Exclusive events. We remarked in Section 6.2 that if in rolling a pair of dice we were interested in obtaining a total of at least 10, and if on examining the green die we found the score to be 3, then there would be no point in examining the red die. The events **A**, that the sum of the scores is at least 10, and **B**, that the score on the green die is 3, cannot occur in the same trial (see Figure 11).

In this case the subsets A, B of possible outcomes are disjoint; that is,

$$A \cap B = \varnothing.$$

It follows that
$$p(\mathbf{A} \wedge \mathbf{B}) = 0.$$

We say that the events **A**, **B** are *exclusive*, since the occurrence of either of them excludes the possibility of the occurrence of the other.

Law 3 now leads immediately to the result:

Theorem. *If* **S** *and* **T** *are exclusive events, then*

$$p(\mathbf{S} \vee \mathbf{T}) = p(\mathbf{S})+p(\mathbf{T}).$$

This is again familiar from the elementary course.

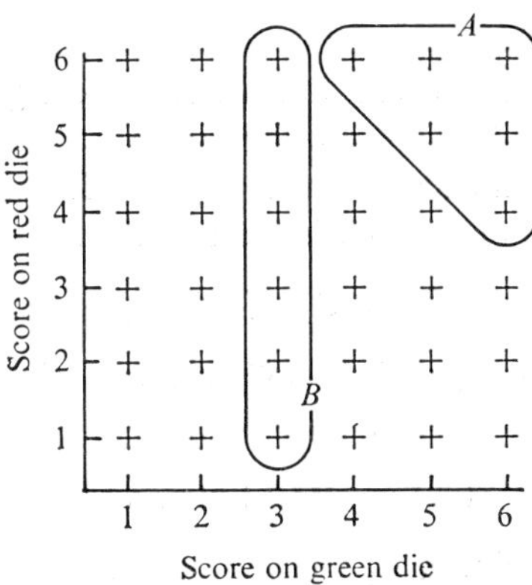

Fig. 11

It is important not to confuse exclusive events with independent events, as people are apt to do if they think loosely of 'events that have nothing to do with each other'.

7.2 Exhaustive events. If two events **S, T** are such that at least one of them is bound to occur, then

$$S \cup T = \mathscr{E}.$$

We then say that the events are *exhaustive*, since between them they exhaust all the possible outcomes. In this case

$$p(\mathbf{S} \vee \mathbf{T}) = 1,$$

so that Law 3 takes the form

$$p(\mathbf{S})+p(\mathbf{T}) = 1+p(\mathbf{S} \wedge \mathbf{T}).$$

7.3 Exclusive and exhaustive events. If **S** and **T** are both exclusive and exhaustive, then clearly

$$p(\mathbf{S})+p(\mathbf{T}) = 1.$$

This is not, however, a new result; for in this case **T** occurs if and only if **S** does not occur, so that **T** is the same as $\sim$ **S**. We have therefore arrived at a re-statement of Law 1, that

$$p(\mathbf{S})+p(\sim \mathbf{S}) = 1.$$

7.4 Worked examples. We end the chapter with two examples illustrating the application of the special results associated with independent, exclusive and exhaustive pairs of events.

Example 1. A bag contains 6 red and 4 green discs. Two are randomly removed in turn, and not replaced. Find the probability that there is at least one green disc amongst them.

Let us denote by $\mathbf{R}_1$, $\mathbf{G}_2$, etc., the events 'the first disc removed is red', 'the second is green'. The event 'at least one disc is green' will be denoted by $\mathbf{X}$. Two methods of solution will be suggested.

First solution. $\mathbf{X}$ will occur if either the first disc is green (whatever the colour of the second) or the first is red and the second green. Thus

$$\mathbf{X} = \mathbf{G}_1 \vee (\mathbf{R}_1 \wedge \mathbf{G}_2).$$

Moreover, the events $\mathbf{G}_1$ and $\mathbf{R}_1 \wedge \mathbf{G}_2$ are exclusive, since the first disc cannot be both red and green. Therefore, by the theorem of Section 7.1,

$$p(\mathbf{X}) = p(\mathbf{G}_1)+p(\mathbf{R}_1 \wedge \mathbf{G}_2).$$

Now $p(\mathbf{G}_1) = \frac{4}{10}$. To find $p(\mathbf{R}_1 \wedge \mathbf{G}_2)$ we use Law 4 for conditional probabilities (see Section 4.2), which gives

$$p(\mathbf{R}_1 \wedge \mathbf{G}_2) = p(\mathbf{R}_1).p(\mathbf{G}_2|\mathbf{R}_1).$$

In this product, $p(\mathbf{R}_1) = \frac{6}{10}$; and since, when a red disc has been removed, there remain 5 red and 4 green discs in the bag, $p(\mathbf{G}_2|\mathbf{R}_1) = \frac{4}{9}$. Putting these results together, we find

$$p(\mathbf{X}) = \tfrac{4}{10}+\tfrac{6}{10}\times\tfrac{4}{9} = \tfrac{2}{3}.$$

Second solution. Another way of saying 'at least one' is 'not none'. It follows that $\mathbf{X}$ and $\mathbf{R}_1 \wedge \mathbf{R}_2$ form a pair of exhaustive and exclusive events. Therefore, as in Section 7·3,

$$p(\mathbf{X})+p(\mathbf{R}_1 \wedge \mathbf{R}_2) = 1.$$

Now we find $p(\mathbf{R}_1 \wedge \mathbf{R}_2)$ by Law 4 for conditional probabilities,

$$p(\mathbf{R}_1 \wedge \mathbf{R}_2) = p(\mathbf{R}_1).p(\mathbf{R}_2|\mathbf{R}_1),$$

where $p(\mathbf{R}_1) = \frac{6}{10}$ and $p(\mathbf{R}_2|\mathbf{R}_1) = \frac{5}{9}$ by an argument similar to that used in the first solution. We deduce that

$$p(\mathbf{X}) = 1-\tfrac{6}{10}\times\tfrac{5}{9} = \tfrac{2}{3}.$$

The reader may find it instructive to follow these two solutions with the aid of a tree diagram.

Example 2. A game is played between two players throwing a die alternately. Ann wins if she throws a one or a two before Bob throws a one or a two or a three. Bob wins if he throws a one or a two or a three before Ann throws a one or a two. Ann throws first, and the game stops as soon as either player has won. If neither has won after two throws each, the game is drawn. What are the probabilities of either player winning and of a draw?

A small difficulty arises in this example over the independence of the results of successive throws. For if this is determined by considering conditional probabilities, what meaning can be given to 'the probability that Ann wins on the second throw given that Bob wins on the first throw'? For if Bob wins on the first throw, Ann will not have a second throw.

We therefore adopt the device of changing the conditions of the game slightly in such a way that the answer is not altered. We shall allow each player two throws (alternately) whether or not a winning throw occurs in the sequence, and then adjudicate the game afterwards, even though this might mean that some later throws were a waste of time. Thus the sequences:

(i) 3, 5, 1, 2; (ii) 3, 5, 3, 2; (iii) 3, 5, 3, 4

give respectively (i) Ann wins on her second throw; (ii) Bob wins on his second throw; (iii) the game is drawn.

We now define a 'good' throw as one which will win if it has not been preceded by a winning throw; and we denote by $\mathbf{A}_2$, $\mathbf{B}_1$, etc., events such as 'Ann's second throw is good', 'Bob's first throw is good'. Thus the sequences above would correspond to:

$$\text{(i)}\ \sim \mathbf{A}_1 \wedge \sim \mathbf{B}_1 \wedge \mathbf{A}_2 \wedge \mathbf{B}_2; \quad \text{(ii)}\ \sim \mathbf{A}_1 \wedge \sim \mathbf{B}_1 \wedge \sim \mathbf{A}_2 \wedge \mathbf{B}_2;$$

$$\text{(iii)}\ \sim \mathbf{A}_1 \wedge \sim \mathbf{B}_1 \wedge \sim \mathbf{A}_2 \wedge \sim \mathbf{B}_2.$$

Any of these events is certainly independent of the others, or of any combination of the others. This is easily seen by considering the sets of possibilities. (The possibility space might be represented by the points of a $6\times 6\times 6\times 6$ 'cube' in four dimensions!) Clearly $p(\mathbf{A}_1) = p(\mathbf{A}_2) = \frac{1}{3}$ and $p(\mathbf{B}_1) = p(\mathbf{B}_2) = \frac{1}{2}$.

We can now calculate the required probabilities. Ann can win in either of two ways: on her first throw, or on her second throw. They correspond to events $\mathbf{A}_1$ and $\sim \mathbf{A}_1 \wedge \sim \mathbf{B}_1 \wedge \mathbf{A}_2$ respectively, and these are exclusive events. Therefore

$$\begin{aligned} p(\text{Ann wins}) &= p(\mathbf{A}_1)+p(\sim \mathbf{A}_1 \wedge \sim \mathbf{B}_1 \wedge \mathbf{A}_2) \\ &= p(\mathbf{A}_1)+p(\sim \mathbf{A}_1 \wedge \sim \mathbf{B}_1).p(\mathbf{A}_2) \\ &= p(\mathbf{A}_1)+p(\sim \mathbf{A}_1).p(\sim \mathbf{B}_1).p(\mathbf{A}_2) \\ &= \tfrac{1}{3}+\tfrac{2}{3}\times\tfrac{1}{2}\times\tfrac{1}{3} \\ &= \tfrac{4}{9}. \end{aligned}$$

Here we use the fact that events $\sim \mathbf{A}_1 \wedge \sim \mathbf{B}_1$ and $\mathbf{A}_2$ are independent, and then that $\sim \mathbf{A}_1$ and $\sim \mathbf{B}_1$ are independent, applying each time the 'product rule' proved in Section 6.4. Similarly,

$$\begin{aligned} p(\text{Bob wins}) &= p(\sim \mathbf{A}_1 \wedge \mathbf{B}_1) + p(\sim \mathbf{A}_1 \wedge \sim \mathbf{B}_1 \wedge \sim \mathbf{A}_2 \wedge \mathbf{B}_2) \\ &= p(\sim \mathbf{A}_1).p(\mathbf{B}_1) + p(\sim \mathbf{A}_1).p(\sim \mathbf{B}_1).p(\sim \mathbf{A}_2).p(\mathbf{B}_2) \\ &= \tfrac{2}{3} \times \tfrac{1}{2} + \tfrac{2}{3} \times \tfrac{1}{2} \times \tfrac{2}{3} \times \tfrac{1}{2} \\ &= \tfrac{4}{9}; \end{aligned}$$

and

$$\begin{aligned} p(\text{game is drawn}) &= p(\sim \mathbf{A}_1 \wedge \sim \mathbf{B}_1 \wedge \sim \mathbf{A}_2 \wedge \sim \mathbf{B}_2) \\ &= p(\sim \mathbf{A}_1).p(\sim \mathbf{B}_1).p(\sim \mathbf{A}_2).p(\sim \mathbf{B}_2) \\ &= \tfrac{2}{3} \times \tfrac{1}{2} \times \tfrac{2}{3} \times \tfrac{1}{2} \\ &= \tfrac{1}{9}. \end{aligned}$$

Exercise H

1. If $\mathbf{S}$ and $\mathbf{T}$ are exhaustive, prove that $p(\mathbf{S}) + p(\mathbf{T}) \geq 1$.

2. How would you recognize from a contingency table of probabilities whether a pair of events is (i) exclusive, (ii) exhaustive, (iii) independent? State, with a reason, whether it is possible for a pair of events to be both

(*a*) exhaustive and independent;
(*b*) exclusive and independent;
(*c*) exhaustive and exclusive.

3. State in set language what is meant by saying that three events $\mathbf{A}, \mathbf{B}, \mathbf{C}$ are mutually exclusive, and deduce from the theorem of Section 7.1 that in this case

$$p(\mathbf{A} \vee \mathbf{B} \vee \mathbf{C}) = p(\mathbf{A}) + p(\mathbf{B}) + p(\mathbf{C}).$$

4. Generalize to n events $\mathbf{A}_i$ the definitions of exclusive events and exhaustive events. Write down the generalization of the result given in Section 7.3, and use the method of mathematical induction to prove it.

5. Generalize the theorems of Sections 4.3 and 4.4, replacing $\mathbf{S}$ and $\sim \mathbf{S}$ by a set of n exclusive and exhaustive events $\mathbf{A}_i$.

6. Is it true that

$$p(\mathbf{S}) + p(\mathbf{T}) = p(\mathbf{S} \vee \mathbf{T}) \Rightarrow \mathbf{S} \text{ and } \mathbf{T} \text{ are exclusive?}$$

If so, prove it; if not, give a counter-example. (You may find that you need to use explicitly the fact that the possibility space is finite. Why?)

7. Prove that, if $\mathbf{S}$ and $\mathbf{T}$ are independent, Law 3 can be put into the form

$$1 - p(\mathbf{S} \vee \mathbf{T}) = \{1 - p(\mathbf{S})\}\{1 - p(\mathbf{T})\}.$$

Interpret this equation in terms of the events $\sim \mathbf{S}$ and $\sim \mathbf{T}$.

8. Another form of Law 3, if **S** and **T** are independent, is

$$p(\mathbf{S} \vee \mathbf{T}) = p(\mathbf{S}) + p(\mathbf{T})\,\{1 - p(\mathbf{S})\}.$$

Give an interpretation of the law in this form.

9. A die is loaded so that the chance of throwing a four is $\frac{1}{3}K$ and the chance of throwing a three is $\frac{1}{3}(1-K)$. The chances of throwing each of the other faces are all $\frac{1}{6}$. If the die is thrown twice, what values of K maximize the chances of throwing a total of (*a*) 6, (*b*) 7, (*c*) 8, (*d*) 9, (*e*) 10?

10. A manufacturer supplies tumblers in boxes of 50. A buyer examines a sample of five, and if none of the five is cracked he accepts the box; if any of them is cracked he rejects it. If there are 10 cracked tumblers in a certain box, what is the probability that he will reject it?

11. A quarter of the population of Muddleton supports the Anarchist party. The party agent takes a poll of 3 people in the town. What is the probability that he finds at least one of them to be Anarchist (thereby overestimating Anarchist support in the town)?

12. Five dice are thrown. What is the probability of getting two or more sixes?

13. A die has the faces marked Ace, King, Queen, Jack, Ten. Nine. With five such dice, what are the probabilities of throwing:
(*a*) exactly four aces;
(*b*) exactly four faces the same;
(*c*) at least four faces the same?

14. Archer, Baker and Cutler have equal claims for a prize. They arrange that each will throw a coin, and that the boy whose coin falls unlike the other two will win. If all three coins fall alike they will throw again. If there is still no decision they will wait until the next day, and repeat the process. At the start of the procedure what are the probabilities that:
(*a*) Archer will win at the first attempt;
(*b*) there will be no winner at the first attempt;
(*c*) Baker will win at the second attempt;
(*d*) someone will win at the second attempt;
(*e*) Archer wins on the first day;
(*f*) no decision will be reached on the first day;
(*g*) a decision will be reached by the end of the second day;
(*h*) no decision will ever be reached?

Miscellaneous Exercise

1. If the probabilities of three events **P**, **Q**, **R** are p, q, r respectively, and the events are completely independent of each other (that is, the occurrence of any combination of two of them does not affect the occurrence of the third), find the probabilities that:
(*a*) **P**, **Q** occur and **R** does not;
(*b*) **Q** occurs and **P**, **R** do not;
(*c*) at least one of them occurs;
(*d*) exactly two of them occur.

2. A bag contains six discs, each of which is known to be either red or green. A random sample of four discs is drawn from the bag, and it is found to contain three red and one green. What mixture of discs in the bag gives the highest probability of this sample being drawn? (This is called the 'maximum-likelihood estimate' of the contents of the bag on the evidence of the sample.)

3. On average Lady Bracknell comes to tea once a fortnight and Ernest comes once a week. The cook produces cucumber sandwiches for tea on one day in twelve; but Lady Bracknell notices that on days when she comes to tea the probability of cucumber sandwiches is $\frac{7}{8}$.

(*a*) What is the probability that one or other of them comes to tea if their diaries are independent?

(*b*) Establish inequalities for the probability that one or the other comes to tea if nothing is known about the relationship between their diaries.

(*c*) What is the probability that there will be cucumber sandwiches on a day when Lady Bracknell does not come to tea?

4. The probability that any particular day in July is fine at Puddling Regis is $\frac{3}{4}$, and the weather on one day is no guide to the weather on the next day. What number of fine days has the highest probability if you are taking a holiday in

(*a*) the first two days of July;
(*b*) the next two days of July;
(*c*) the first four days of July;
(*d*) the first three days of July?

If you were the manager of an insurance company, and a client insured himself for £20 for each wet day of his holiday, what would be a fair premium to charge for each of these four holiday periods?

5. In a certain machine the following actions are possible. The top can blow or not; the spiggots can go up or go down or remain still; and the cam-lever can wiggle or thump. The top blows with probability $\frac{1}{5}$. The spiggots go up with probability $\frac{1}{2}$ if the top blows; they cannot go down if the top blows; otherwise they go up or go down or remain still with equal probabilities. The cam lever wiggles if the spiggots go up, otherwise it wiggles with probability $\frac{1}{6}$. The machine is robust and works provided the cam-lever is thumping.

(*a*) What is the probability that the machine works?
(*b*) What is the probability that the top blows and the cam-lever wiggles?
(*c*) If the machine breaks down, what is the probability that the top is blowing?

6. I write four letters and address four envelopes. If I now place the letters in the envelopes at random, find the probability that they will all be in the wrong envelope.

7. Which is more likely to occur:

(*a*) a throw of six at least once in 4 throws of a single die, or
(*b*) a throw of double-six at least once in 24 throws of two dice?

(The Chevalier de Méré noticed a difference in the two frequencies and wrote to Pascal for an explanation, His argument was that a six should occur on average once in 6 throws, and a double-six once in 36 throws; and since 24 is to 36 as 4 is to 6, the odds for the two occurrences should be the same. Pascal's resulting correspondence with Fermat (1654) opened the subject of probability. Poisson described it as 'un problème relatif aux jeux de hasard, proposé à un austère janséniste par un homme du monde'.)

8. 'A point is chosen in a line. Divide the line into n equal parts. The probability that the point is not in the first part is $1-(1/n)$. Similarly for the other parts. Hence the probability that the point is not on the line at all is

$$\left(1-\frac{1}{n}\right)^n.\text{'}$$

Expose the fallacy and provide a correct argument.

9. What is the probability of throwing a score that differs by more than 2 from the mean score (7) in a throw of two dice? What is the probability that in four games, each consisting of a throw of two dice, such a score will occur at least once? How many games of two throws each are needed to make the occurrence of at least one such score '95 % certain'?

10. Three events **R**, **S**, **T** are 'pairwise independent'—that is, any two of them are independent of each other. Show that it is not necessarily true that

$$p(\mathbf{R} \wedge \mathbf{S} \wedge \mathbf{T}) = p(\mathbf{R}).p(\mathbf{S}).p(\mathbf{T}).$$

If **R**, **S**, **T** are pairwise independent, and if in addition

$$p(\mathbf{R} \wedge \mathbf{S} \wedge \mathbf{T}) = p(\mathbf{R}).p(\mathbf{S}).p(\mathbf{T}),$$

prove that **R** is independent of each of the events $\mathbf{S} \wedge \mathbf{T}$, $\sim \mathbf{S} \wedge \mathbf{T}$, $\mathbf{S} \wedge \sim \mathbf{T}$ and $\sim \mathbf{S} \wedge \sim \mathbf{T}$; and similarly for **S** and **T** by interchange of letters.

(In this latter case the events are said to be *completely independent*. Compare Exercise G, Questions 16–19.)

11. (*a*) In a certain queue people join at the exact end of a minute if at all, and at most one person joins at a time. At the beginning the queue is empty, and at the end of each minute the probability that someone joins it is $\frac{1}{3}$. Find the probabilities of queues of various lengths at the end of each of the first four minutes.

(*b*) Repeat the question if, in addition, the person at the head of the queue during any minute (if there is one) may leave at the end of that minute, and does so with probability $\frac{1}{4}$.

(*c*) If $q(n, t)$ denotes the probability that there are n people in the queue at the end of the tth minute, prove that, in case (*a*),

$$q(n, t+1) = \tfrac{1}{3}q(n-1, t)+\tfrac{2}{3}q(n, t).$$

What initial conditions would be needed, in addition to this equation, to define the function completely? Find a similar equation for case (*b*).

12. If $\phi(n, r)$ denotes the probability of obtaining a total score of n with r dice, prove that

$$\phi(n, r+1) = \frac{1}{6}\sum_{i=1}^{6}\phi(n-i, r).$$

How could $\phi(n, 0)$ be defined so that this formula can be used to obtain $\phi(n, r)$ inductively for $r > 0$? Calculate the probabilities for $r = 1, 2, 3, 4, 5$ and display the results in a sequence of histograms.

13. A certain system can be in either of two states, called L and R. At the end of each unit interval of time it may or may not switch instantaneously from one state to the other; the probabilities of transition from L to R and from R to L are a, b respectively. At the nth instant the probabilities of finding the system in states L, R are u_n, v_n.

(*a*) Prove that $u_1 = (1-a)u_0 + bv_0$, and find a similar expression for v_1.

(*b*) If $\mathbf{w}_n$ denotes the probability vector $\begin{pmatrix} u_n \\ v_n \end{pmatrix}$, find a matrix $\mathbf{A}$ such that $\mathbf{w}_{n+1} = \mathbf{A}\mathbf{w}_n$, and deduce that $\mathbf{w}_n = \mathbf{A}^n\mathbf{w}_0$.

(*c*) If $a = \frac{1}{2}$, $b = \frac{1}{4}$ and $\mathbf{w}_0 = \begin{pmatrix} 1 \\ 0 \end{pmatrix}$, calculate $\mathbf{A}^n$ and $\mathbf{w}_n$ for $n = 1, 2, 3, 4$.

(*d*) Find an 'equilibrium' probability vector for which $\mathbf{w}_{n+1} = \mathbf{w}_n$, and deduce that if $\mathbf{w}_0$ has this value then the probability vector remains constant throughout the operation of the system.

(*e*) If, from any initial state, the vector $\mathbf{w}_n$ has a limiting value as $n \to \infty$, explain why this value must be the equilibrium vector found in (*d*).

(A process of the kind described in this question, with constant probabilities a, b is called a *Markov process*, and the chain of successive states is a *Markov chain*.)

14. A recruit takes one pace forward, one pace backward or stands still when the sergeant-major gives a command, with the following probabilities:

$$p(\text{one pace forward}) = p(\text{one pace backward}) = x,$$
$$p(\text{stands still}) = 1-2x,$$

where $0 \leqslant x \leqslant \frac{1}{2}$. Find the probabilities that, after two successive commands, he is 0, 1 and 2 paces away from his initial position. Sketch the graphs of these three probabilities, and give the most likely distances of the recruit from his initial position for different values of x.

15. Prove that

$$\begin{pmatrix} p(\mathbf{B}) \\ p(\sim \mathbf{B}) \end{pmatrix} = \begin{pmatrix} p(\mathbf{B}|\mathbf{A}) & p(\mathbf{B}|\sim \mathbf{A}) \\ p(\sim \mathbf{B}|\mathbf{A}) & p(\sim \mathbf{B}|\sim \mathbf{A}) \end{pmatrix} \begin{pmatrix} p(\mathbf{A}) \\ p(\sim \mathbf{A}) \end{pmatrix}.$$

If the square matrix above is written $\begin{pmatrix} e & f \\ g & h \end{pmatrix}$, prove that its determinant has the value $e-f$ and that this lies between -1 and 1. What relationships exist between the events $\mathbf{A}$ and $\mathbf{B}$ if the value is (*a*) -1, (*b*) 0, (*c*) 1?

16. A security firm on a regular run carries valuables in one car and a dummy box in another car. One car is sent by a town route and the other by a country route. The robbers have only the resources to ambush one of the routes. If they ambush the town route, the car will escape with probability 0·8; if they ambush the country route the car will escape with probability 0·6. The probability, x, that valuables are on the town route is selected by the firm; the probability, y, that the town route is ambushed is selected by the robbers. Firm and robbers act at random within the framework of these probabilities in order to prevent a leakage of information. Prove that the probability, z, that the valuables get through can be put into the form

$$z = \frac{13-(3x-2)(3y-2)}{15}.$$

(*a*) Make a table of values of z for values of x and y between 0 and 1 at intervals of $\frac{1}{6}$, and hence draw some typical contour lines for the three-dimensional graph of z against (x, y). How would you describe the point $(\frac{2}{3}, \frac{2}{3})$ on this surface?

(*b*) The firm can choose x, and realize that the robbers wish to minimize z. Show that if $x < \frac{2}{3}$ then z increases with y, and that its least value is $\frac{1}{5}(2x+3)$; but that if $x > \frac{2}{3}$ then z decreases as y increases and its least value is $\frac{1}{5}(5-x)$. Let this least value of z for given x be denoted by $m(x)$. What value of x should the firm select and fix in order to maximize $m(x)$? What is then the probability that the valuables get through?

(*c*) What value of y should the robbers select and fix in order to minimize $M(y)$, where $M(y)$ is the greatest value of z attainable by varying x for given y? What is then the probability that the valuables get through?

(*d*) Identify your results in terms of the surface considered in (*a*).

(This is an example of the 'theory of games', of which the first extensive account was published in 1944 by von Neumann and Morgenstern in *Theory of Games and Economic Behaviour*.)

21

LINEAR EQUATIONS

1. A REVIEW OF AVAILABLE METHODS OF SOLUTION

'The girl two places in front of me in the queue at the snack counter asked for a cup of coffee and three biscuits and was charged 17 p. The man who was next paid 14p for two cups of coffee and a biscuit. How much shall I have to pay for a cup of coffee and one biscuit?'

To solve this, we first construct a mathematical model by letting x pence be the cost of a biscuit and y pence that of a cup of coffee. We have two relations connecting x and y, namely

$$3x+\ y = 17$$

and

$$x+2y = 14,$$

and we need to find numbers x and y, if possible, for which these are simultaneously true. This, in its simplest form, is the basic problem of linear equations.

1.1 Elimination. This is our first available method. Multiplying the second equation by 3, we obtain

$$3x+\ y = 17$$

and

$$3x+6y = 42,$$

from which, by subtracting, we find $5y = 25$, and $y = 5$. Substitution now gives, in the first equation, $3x+5 = 17$, so that $x = 4$.

I shall have to pay $x+y$ pence, or ninepence in all.

1.2 Matrices. The second way is to write the equations in matrix form as

$$\begin{pmatrix} 3 & 1 \\ 1 & 2 \end{pmatrix} \begin{pmatrix} x \\ y \end{pmatrix} = \begin{pmatrix} 17 \\ 14 \end{pmatrix},$$

and then to premultiply each side by

$$\begin{pmatrix} 2 & -1 \\ -1 & 3 \end{pmatrix}.$$

This gives

$$\begin{pmatrix} 5 & 0 \\ 0 & 5 \end{pmatrix} \begin{pmatrix} x \\ y \end{pmatrix} = \begin{pmatrix} 20 \\ 25 \end{pmatrix}, \quad \text{whence} \quad \begin{pmatrix} x \\ y \end{pmatrix} = \begin{pmatrix} 4 \\ 5 \end{pmatrix}.$$

Both these methods extend to more than two equations; we shall see that they are basically the same.

1.3 Graphical method. Yet a third method is to draw the graphs of the sets $\{(x, y): 3x+y = 17\}$ and $\{(x, y): x+2y = 14\}$, which are straight lines, and to read off the solution which is given by the coordinates of their point of intersection, i.e. (4, 5). This method is impracticable for more than two equations, but it provides a valuable illustration of the various things that can happen when more than two unknown numbers are involved. The following exercise is designed to show some of the complications which may arise in this situation. Meanwhile the reader may care to ask himself which, if any, of these methods would have enabled him to produce the correct change for his cup of coffee.

Exercise A

1. Solve (i) by elimination, (ii) by matrix methods the following pairs of equations:

(*a*) $3x+2y = 13,\quad 5x-\ y = 39;$ (*b*) $5x+0y = 7,\quad 8x-3y = 11;$

(*c*) $2x-\ 3y = 5,\quad 34x-51y = 60;$ (*d*) $ax+by = p,\quad cx+dy = q.$

Check that your answers do in fact satisfy the equations.

2. Find the coordinates of the vertices of the triangle formed by the lines $x-y = 4$, $x+3y = 8$, $7x+y+4 = 0$.

3. Find P and Q in terms of W and α if

$$P\cos\alpha+Q\sin\alpha = 5W,$$
$$P\sin\alpha-Q\cos\alpha = 3W.$$

4. Find the point of intersection of the lines

$$\frac{x}{2}+\frac{y}{3} = 1 \quad\text{and}\quad \frac{x}{7}+\frac{y}{5} = 1.$$

5. Find x, y and z if

(*a*) $2x+3y-z = 12,\quad 2y+z = 7,\quad z = 1;$ (*b*) $2x+3y-z = 12,\quad 2y+z = 7,\quad 2y-z = 5.$

6. Find x, y and z if

$$x+4y-5z = 8,$$
$$2x+3y+z = -1,$$
$$3x-y+2z = 3.$$

(First eliminate x from the second and third equations.)

7. What happens if you attempt the same method for the equations:

$$x+4y-5z = 8,$$
$$2x+3y+\ z = -1,$$
$$3x+7y-4z = 5?$$

8. Find a solution of the equations:

$$\begin{aligned} x+4y-5z &= 8, \\ 2x+3y+z &= -1, \\ 3x+7y-4z &= 7. \end{aligned}$$

Is there more than one triple (x, y, z) which satisfies these equations?

2. THREE EQUATIONS IN x, y, AND z

2.1 Elimination. If we have three equations in three unknowns, we try to use one of the equations to remove one of the unknowns from the other two equations. This leaves us with two equations in two unknowns which we know how to solve. It does not matter which unknown we eliminate: we take the easiest.

Example 1. Consider:

$$\begin{aligned} (1)\quad x+2y+3z &= 13, \\ (2)\quad -x-y+2z &= 2, \\ (3)\quad -x+3y+4z &= 26. \end{aligned}$$

Here x is the easiest unknown to remove. Take the first equation and add it to each of the others, so obtaining:

$$\begin{aligned} (1)\quad x+2y+3z &= 13, \\ (2')\quad y+5z &= 15, \\ (3')\quad 5y+7z &= 39. \end{aligned}$$

Now take (2′) and (3′) and eliminate y between them, by subtracting $5\times(2')$ from (3′). This gives us the set of equations:

$$\begin{aligned} (1)\quad x+2y+3z &= 13, \\ (2')\quad y+5z &= 15, \\ (3'')\quad -18z &= -36, \end{aligned}$$

or

$$\begin{aligned} (1)\quad x+2y+3z &= 13, \\ (2')\quad y+5z &= 15, \\ (3''')\quad z &= 2. \end{aligned}$$

The rest is now rapid: from (2′) $y = 5$, and from (1) $x = -3$.

Example 2. But now try to do the same with the equations:

$$\begin{aligned} (1)\quad x+2y+3z &= 13, \\ (2)\quad -x-3y+2z &= 2, \\ (3)\quad -x-4y+7z &= 11. \end{aligned}$$

If you carry out the process correctly, you will arrive at:

$$(2')\quad -\ y+\ 5z = 15,$$

$$(3')\quad -2y+10z = 24,$$

and any attempt to proceed further produces (3″) $0z = 6$, for which no value of z can be found to make it true.

When something like this happens, the mathematician asks, is this the fault of the method, or is there something about the equations which leads inevitably to this impasse?

Before we answer this question, here are some examples for practice.

Exercise B

1. 'Solve' the above three equations in Example 2 by eliminating y first. Does the method lead to a solution?

2. Consider the equations:

$$x+2y+3z = 13,$$
$$-x-3y+2z = 2,$$
$$-x-4y+7z = 17.$$

(*a*) Show that they are satisfied by the triple $(-9, 5, 4)$.
(*b*) Put $y = 5t$, $z = 3+t$, and find x from the first equation. Show that this set of values of x, y, and z satisfies the other two equations whatever the value of t.
(*c*) If you attempt to solve these three equations as in Example 2, what do you get for (3″)?

3. What is c if:

$$x+y = 2,$$
$$y+z = 3,$$
$$x-z = c$$

have a solution?

4. If there are values of x, y, z for which:

$$x+y+\ z = 5,$$
$$3x-y+2z = 11,$$

what is the value of $4x+3z$

and of $5x-3y+3z$?

Do the equations:

$$x+\ y+\ z = 5,$$
$$3x-\ y+2z = 11,$$
$$5x-3y+3z = 13$$

have a solution?

5. Find x, y and z if:

(*a*) $x+y = 5$,

$y+z = 7$,

$z+x = 12$;

(*b*) $2x-y+z = 6$,

$5x+y-z = 22$,

$3x-2y+z = 11$;

(*c*) $x+y-z = 2$,

$y+z-x = 5$,

$z+x-y = 8$.

2.2 Matrix representation. It requires only a moment's consideration to realize two important facts: first, that the nature of the solution of a set of linear equations depends in some way on the coefficients of x, y, and z, and the constants on the right-hand side of the equations—these twelve numbers determine whether the equations have a unique solution, an infinity of solutions, or no solution; and second, that the solution depends only on these numbers—it makes no difference whether we call the 'unknowns' x, y, z or p, q, r or K, G, V or any other symbols we like to invent. If therefore we want to instruct a computer to solve such a set of equations, we need to supply it with (i) a programme for carrying out the solution, and (ii) the data in the form of this set of twelve numbers to put in its stores. We therefore separate the coefficients from the names of the variables by writing the set of equations in matrix form.

Example 1 can now be written as

$$\begin{pmatrix} 1 & 2 & 3 \\ -1 & -1 & 2 \\ -1 & 3 & 4 \end{pmatrix}\begin{pmatrix} x \\ y \\ z \end{pmatrix} = \begin{pmatrix} 13 \\ 2 \\ 26 \end{pmatrix}.$$

Referring back to the process of solution, we see that when we add the first equation to the second we simply add the first rows of these two matrices—the 3×3 matrix on the left and the 3×1 matrix or column vector on the right—to their second rows. In the same way, every step in the solution by elimination can be represented as a manipulation of these matrices: the various steps are set out in this way below.

We have

$$\begin{pmatrix} 1 & 2 & 3 \\ -1 & -1 & 2 \\ -1 & 3 & 4 \end{pmatrix}\begin{pmatrix} x \\ y \\ z \end{pmatrix} = \begin{pmatrix} 13 \\ 2 \\ 26 \end{pmatrix},$$

hence

$$\begin{pmatrix} 1 & 2 & 3 \\ 0 & 1 & 5 \\ -1 & 3 & 4 \end{pmatrix}\begin{pmatrix} x \\ y \\ z \end{pmatrix} = \begin{pmatrix} 13 \\ 15 \\ 26 \end{pmatrix}, \quad \text{adding row 1 and row 2;}$$

then
$$\begin{pmatrix}1 & 2 & 3\\0 & 1 & 5\\0 & 5 & 7\end{pmatrix}\begin{pmatrix}x\\y\\z\end{pmatrix}=\begin{pmatrix}13\\15\\39\end{pmatrix}, \text{ adding row 1 and row 3;}$$
next
$$\begin{pmatrix}1 & 2 & 3\\0 & 1 & 5\\0 & 0 & -18\end{pmatrix}\begin{pmatrix}x\\y\\z\end{pmatrix}=\begin{pmatrix}13\\15\\-36\end{pmatrix}, \text{ taking 5 times row 2 from row 3;}$$
and finally
$$\begin{pmatrix}1 & 2 & 3\\0 & 1 & 5\\0 & 0 & 1\end{pmatrix}\begin{pmatrix}x\\y\\z\end{pmatrix}=\begin{pmatrix}13\\15\\2\end{pmatrix}, \text{ dividing row 3 by } -18.$$

We have reduced the original matrix to a form in which there are only zeros to the left of the main diagonal, when it is said to be in *echelon form*.

Once this form is reached, it is a simple matter to complete the solution by substitution, working from the last equation upwards; thus, in turn, we have
$$z = 2$$
$$y+5z = 15 \Rightarrow y = 15-5\times 2 = 5,$$
$$x+2y+3z = 13 \Rightarrow x = 13-2\times 5-3\times 2 = -3.$$

2.3 Solution by premultiplication. Each of these 'row operations' on the two sides of the matrix equations can clearly be justified by referring back to the original method of solution; but can it also be justified in matrix terms? We can show very easily that it can, by showing that each step is effected by premultiplying both sides of the matrix equations by a suitable matrix and using the associative law for matrix multiplication. Thus the first step, in which we added the first row to the second, could have been effected by premultiplying both matrices by
$$\mathbf{E}=\begin{pmatrix}1 & 0 & 0\\1 & 1 & 0\\0 & 0 & 1\end{pmatrix},$$
as is easily verified. If we assume for the moment that there is a matrix corresponding in this way to each step, its form is easily found. For if $\mathbf{I}$ is the identity matrix
$$\mathbf{I}=\begin{pmatrix}1 & 0 & 0\\0 & 1 & 0\\0 & 0 & 1\end{pmatrix},$$
then $\mathbf{EA} = (\mathbf{EI})\mathbf{A}$, so that if $\mathbf{E}$ adds row 1 to row 2, then
$$\mathbf{E}=\mathbf{EI}=\begin{pmatrix}1 & 0 & 0\\1 & 1 & 0\\0 & 0 & 1\end{pmatrix},$$

by adding row 1 of **I** to row 2 of **I**. Similarly, the step of taking 5 times row 2 from 3 is effected by premultiplying by the matrix obtained from **I** by the same process, i.e.

$$\begin{pmatrix} 1 & 0 & 0 \\ 0 & 1 & 0 \\ 0 & -5 & 1 \end{pmatrix}.$$

Let us now examine this process in general terms.

2.4 Elementary matrices. It will be convenient to adopt a standard procedure—a permutation of the letters may be necessary to ensure this.

1. Use the first equation to eliminate x from the second and third.
2. Use the new second equation to eliminate y from the third.
3. Solve the third equation for z and substitute back to find y and x.

In order to do this we repeatedly use two processes: (*a*) multiply an equation through by a number k, (*b*) add one equation to another. These correspond, in matrix terms, to (*a*) multiplying a row by k, and (*b*) adding one row to another. The following two theorems show that these steps are effected by matrix premultiplication.

Theorem A. *If a matrix is premultiplied by*

$$\mathbf{E} = \begin{pmatrix} k & 0 & 0 \\ 0 & 1 & 0 \\ 0 & 0 & 1 \end{pmatrix}$$

it is unchanged except that its first row is multiplied by k. Similar results hold for the other rows.

The proof is immediate.

Theorem B. *If a matrix is premultiplied by*

$$\mathbf{E}' = \begin{pmatrix} 1 & 0 & 0 \\ 1 & 1 & 0 \\ 0 & 0 & 1 \end{pmatrix}$$

it is unchanged except that row 2 *is replaced by row* 2+*row* 1.

Again the proof is immediately completed by carrying out the multiplication. Similar results hold for the other rows.

The **E**-matrices are called *elementary matrices*, and they are obtained by performing operations (*a*) and (*b*) on the identity matrix

$$\begin{pmatrix} 1 & 0 & 0 \\ 0 & 1 & 0 \\ 0 & 0 & 1 \end{pmatrix}$$

in each case.

Since multiplication of matrices is associative, we can combine any number of these elementary row-operations together and the effect of multiplying together the corresponding elementary matrices will be to produce a matrix obtained from the identity matrix by the same sequence of operations. This is

Theorem C. *The effect on a matrix of a sequence of elementary row-operations (addition of rows and multiplication of rows by scalars) is to pre-multiply it by a matrix obtained from the identity matrix by the same sequence of operations.*

Example 3. Consider the equations:

$$\begin{aligned} x+\ y+\ z &= 15, \\ x+2y+3z &= 28, \\ x+4y+5z &= 46. \end{aligned}$$

Write these as
$$\begin{pmatrix} 1 & 1 & 1 \\ 1 & 2 & 3 \\ 1 & 4 & 5 \end{pmatrix}\begin{pmatrix} x \\ y \\ z \end{pmatrix} = \begin{pmatrix} 15 \\ 28 \\ 46 \end{pmatrix}.$$

(*a*) Subtract row 1 from row 2

$$\begin{pmatrix} 1 & 1 & 1 \\ 0 & 1 & 2 \\ 1 & 4 & 5 \end{pmatrix}\begin{pmatrix} x \\ y \\ z \end{pmatrix} = \begin{pmatrix} 15 \\ 13 \\ 46 \end{pmatrix}.$$

(*b*) Subtract row 1 from row 3

$$\begin{pmatrix} 1 & 1 & 1 \\ 0 & 1 & 2 \\ 0 & 3 & 4 \end{pmatrix}\begin{pmatrix} x \\ y \\ z \end{pmatrix} = \begin{pmatrix} 15 \\ 13 \\ 31 \end{pmatrix}.$$

(*c*) Subtract $3 \times$ row 2 from row 3

$$\begin{pmatrix} 1 & 1 & 1 \\ 0 & 1 & 2 \\ 0 & 0 & -2 \end{pmatrix}\begin{pmatrix} x \\ y \\ z \end{pmatrix} = \begin{pmatrix} 15 \\ 13 \\ -8 \end{pmatrix}.$$

(*d*) Multiply row 3 by $-\frac{1}{2}$

$$\begin{pmatrix} 1 & 1 & 1 \\ 0 & 1 & 2 \\ 0 & 0 & 1 \end{pmatrix}\begin{pmatrix} x \\ y \\ z \end{pmatrix} = \begin{pmatrix} 15 \\ 13 \\ 4 \end{pmatrix}.$$

At this point we may easily solve the equations, since we have $z = 4$, $y+2z = 13$, $x+y+z = 15$, giving $z = 4$, $y = 5$, $x = 6$.

Now step (*a*) could have been effected by premultiplication by

$$\mathbf{E}_a = \begin{pmatrix} 1 & 0 & 0 \\ -1 & 1 & 0 \\ 0 & 0 & 1 \end{pmatrix};$$

step (b) by premultiplication by

$$\mathbf{E}_b = \begin{pmatrix} 1 & 0 & 0 \\ 0 & 1 & 0 \\ -1 & 0 & 1 \end{pmatrix};$$

for step (c) the elementary matrix is

$$\mathbf{E}_c = \begin{pmatrix} 1 & 0 & 0 \\ 0 & 1 & 0 \\ 0 & -3 & 1 \end{pmatrix}$$

and finally

$$\mathbf{E}_d = \begin{pmatrix} 1 & 0 & 0 \\ 0 & 1 & 0 \\ 0 & 0 & -\frac{1}{2} \end{pmatrix}.$$

Hence

$$\mathbf{E}_d\mathbf{E}_c\mathbf{E}_b\mathbf{E}_a \begin{pmatrix} 1 & 1 & 1 \\ 1 & 2 & 3 \\ 1 & 4 & 5 \end{pmatrix} = \begin{pmatrix} 1 & 1 & 1 \\ 0 & 1 & 2 \\ 0 & 0 & 1 \end{pmatrix},$$

and the whole process could just as well have been carried out by premultiplying by this single product, which can in its turn be evaluated by carrying out the same operations on the identity.

$$\mathbf{E}_d\mathbf{E}_c\mathbf{E}_b\mathbf{E}_a = \mathbf{E}_d\mathbf{E}_c\mathbf{E}_b\mathbf{E}_a\mathbf{I} = \mathbf{E}_d\mathbf{E}_c \begin{pmatrix} 1 & 0 & 0 \\ -1 & 1 & 0 \\ -1 & 0 & 1 \end{pmatrix} = \mathbf{E}_d \begin{pmatrix} 1 & 0 & 0 \\ -1 & 1 & 0 \\ 2 & -3 & 1 \end{pmatrix}$$

$$= \begin{pmatrix} 1 & 0 & 0 \\ -1 & 1 & 0 \\ -1 & +\frac{3}{2} & -\frac{1}{2} \end{pmatrix}.$$

There is, however, no easy way of writing down this matrix without carrying out the separate steps. Notice that at this stage we have

$$\begin{pmatrix} 1 & 0 & 0 \\ -1 & 1 & 0 \\ -1 & \frac{3}{2} & -\frac{1}{2} \end{pmatrix} \begin{pmatrix} 1 & 1 & 1 \\ 1 & 2 & 3 \\ 1 & 4 & 5 \end{pmatrix} = \begin{pmatrix} 1 & 1 & 1 \\ 0 & 1 & 2 \\ 0 & 0 & 1 \end{pmatrix},$$

which is of the form $\mathbf{LA} = \mathbf{U}$, where $\mathbf{L}$ is 'lower triangular' and $\mathbf{U}$ is 'upper triangular'.

Exercise C

1. Solve the equations:

$$\begin{aligned} x - y + z &= -1, \\ 3x - 2y + z &= 1, \\ 4x + y - 3z &= 10. \end{aligned}$$

2. If

$$\mathbf{A} = \begin{pmatrix} 1 & -1 & 1 \\ 3 & -2 & 1 \\ 4 & 1 & -3 \end{pmatrix},$$

write down in turn the elementary matrices used in reducing this to echelon (upper triangular) form, **U**. By performing these same elementary row-operations on

$$\mathbf{I} = \begin{pmatrix} 1 & 0 & 0 \\ 0 & 1 & 0 \\ 0 & 0 & 1 \end{pmatrix},$$

find a matrix **L** such that **LA** = **U**.

3. Use the matrix **L** of Question 2 to solve the equations:

$$\begin{aligned} x - y + z &= 3, \\ 3x - 2y + z &= 10, \\ 4x + y - 3z &= 20, \end{aligned}$$

and to write down the general solution of the equations:

$$\begin{aligned} x - y + z &= a, \\ 3x - 2y + z &= b, \\ 4x + y - 3z &= c. \end{aligned}$$

4. Find elementary matrices $\mathbf{E}_1$, $\mathbf{E}_2$, $\mathbf{E}_3$, ... so that

$$\dots \mathbf{E}_3 \mathbf{E}_2 \mathbf{E}_1 \begin{pmatrix} 3 & 2 \\ 4 & 3 \end{pmatrix} = \begin{pmatrix} 1 & 0 \\ 0 & 1 \end{pmatrix}.$$

What is the product matrix ... $\mathbf{E}_3 \mathbf{E}_2 \mathbf{E}_1$?

5. Write down the inverses of the matrices $\mathbf{E}_1$, $\mathbf{E}_2$, ... in Question 4, and verify that

$$\mathbf{E}_1^{-1} \mathbf{E}_2^{-1} \mathbf{E}_3^{-1} \dots = \begin{pmatrix} 3 & 2 \\ 4 & 3 \end{pmatrix}.$$

6. Draw the parallelogram $ABCD$, where A is (0, 0), B (3, 4), C (5, 7), and D (2, 3). Sketch the positions of this parallelogram when the transformations corresponding to $\mathbf{E}_1$, $\mathbf{E}_2$, ... are applied successively to the position vectors of its vertices, and show that they transform $ABCD$ ultimately to the unit square.

Describe this succession of transformations in geometrical terms.

7. Evaluate the matrix product

$$\begin{pmatrix} a & 0 \\ 0 & 1 \end{pmatrix} \begin{pmatrix} 1 & 0 \\ c & 1 \end{pmatrix} \begin{pmatrix} 1 & 0 \\ 0 & \Delta/a \end{pmatrix} \begin{pmatrix} 1 & b/a \\ 0 & 1 \end{pmatrix} \begin{pmatrix} 1 & 0 \\ 0 & 1 \end{pmatrix},$$

where $\Delta = ad - bc$. Describe geometrically a series of one-way stretches and shears which will transform the unit square into the parallelogram determined by the position vectors

$$\begin{pmatrix} a \\ c \end{pmatrix}, \quad \begin{pmatrix} b \\ d \end{pmatrix}.$$

What happens if $ad - bc = 0$?

8. Show that premultiplying by

$$\begin{pmatrix} 0 & 1 & 0 \\ 1 & 0 & 0 \\ 0 & 0 & 1 \end{pmatrix}$$

interchanges the first two rows of a matrix. What is the effect of premultiplying by

$$\begin{pmatrix} 0 & 1 & 0 \\ 0 & 0 & 1 \\ 1 & 0 & 0 \end{pmatrix}?$$

Is it possible to permute the *columns* of a matrix by premultiplying by a matrix of this kind? How can it be done?

9. If **B** is the matrix

$$\begin{pmatrix} 1 & 1 & 1 \\ 1 & 3 & 7 \\ 1 & 4 & 10 \end{pmatrix}$$

and the echelon process is carried out, giving $\mathbf{LB} = \mathbf{U}$ as in Question 2, what is the matrix **U**?

When do the equations

$$\begin{pmatrix} 1 & 1 & 1 \\ 1 & 3 & 7 \\ 1 & 4 & 10 \end{pmatrix} \begin{pmatrix} x \\ y \\ z \end{pmatrix} = \begin{pmatrix} 4 \\ 7 \\ c \end{pmatrix}$$

have a solution?

3. THE INVERSE OF A MATRIX

When we have only a single set of equations to solve, there is no point in proceeding beyond the echelon form; the solution can be completed simply by direct substitution. But if we have a number of equations to solve with the same coefficient matrix, or if for any other reason we wish to find the inverse of the coefficient matrix, it is useful to carry the process on to a further stage in which the matrix is reduced to a form in which all the elements are zero except those on the main diagonal. When this is the case it is said to be in diagonal form. From here it is a short step to reduce the matrix to the identity matrix; when this is done, both the inverse matrix and the solution of the equations will immediately appear. We illustrate the process by continuing Example 3.

We had arrived at a stage where we had

$$\mathbf{LA} = \mathbf{U},$$

where **A** is the original matrix, **U** is upper triangular with 1's on its diagonal, and **L** is lower triangular, a product of elementary matrices. Provided that

U *has no zeros on its diagonal*, we can continue the process as follows: (From Example 3),

$$\begin{pmatrix} 1 & 0 & 0 \\ -1 & 1 & 0 \\ -1 & \frac{3}{2} & -\frac{1}{2} \end{pmatrix} \begin{pmatrix} 1 & 1 & 1 \\ 1 & 2 & 3 \\ 1 & 4 & 5 \end{pmatrix} = \begin{pmatrix} 1 & 1 & 1 \\ 0 & 1 & 2 \\ 0 & 0 & 1 \end{pmatrix}.$$

We perform the elementary row operation 'row $2-2\times$row 3' by pre-multiplying each side by the elementary matrix

$$\begin{pmatrix} 1 & 0 & 0 \\ 0 & 1 & -2 \\ 0 & 0 & 1 \end{pmatrix}.$$

This will effect the operation on the first and third matrices above, giving

$$\begin{pmatrix} 1 & 0 & 0 \\ 1 & -2 & 1 \\ -1 & \frac{3}{2} & -\frac{1}{2} \end{pmatrix} \begin{pmatrix} 1 & 1 & 1 \\ 1 & 2 & 3 \\ 1 & 4 & 5 \end{pmatrix} = \begin{pmatrix} 1 & 1 & 1 \\ 0 & 1 & 0 \\ 0 & 0 & 1 \end{pmatrix}.$$

Finally 'row $1-$row $2-$row 3' (which can also be justified as a pre-multiplication) gives

$$\begin{pmatrix} 1 & \frac{1}{2} & -\frac{1}{2} \\ 1 & -2 & 1 \\ -1 & \frac{3}{2} & -\frac{1}{2} \end{pmatrix} \begin{pmatrix} 1 & 1 & 1 \\ 1 & 2 & 3 \\ 1 & 4 & 5 \end{pmatrix} = \begin{pmatrix} 1 & 0 & 0 \\ 0 & 1 & 0 \\ 0 & 0 & 1 \end{pmatrix},$$

and since the matrix on the right is now the identity, the first matrix is *the inverse of the matrix* **A**. Thus the inverse of a matrix **A** is obtained from the identity matrix **I** by the same sequence of elementary row operations as is used to reduce **A** to **I**. In the language of elementary matrices, if

$$\ldots \mathbf{E}_2\mathbf{E}_1\mathbf{A} = \mathbf{I},$$

then $$(\ldots \mathbf{E}_2\mathbf{E}_1\mathbf{I})\mathbf{A} = (\ldots \mathbf{E}_2\mathbf{E}_1)\mathbf{I}\mathbf{A} = (\ldots \mathbf{E}_2\mathbf{E}_1)\mathbf{A} = \mathbf{I},$$

so that $$\ldots \mathbf{E}_2\mathbf{E}_1\mathbf{I} = \mathbf{A}^{-1}.$$

This means that we can solve a set of equations *and* construct the inverse matrix (provided this exists) by a single set of elementary row operations. An example should make the whole process clear.

Example 4. Consider a particular problem, originating in Lewis Carroll's *Tangled Tale*:

A lunch consisting of one glass of lemonade, a sandwich and a biscuit, costs 8p; a glass of lemonade, three sandwiches and seven biscuits costs 14p, and a glass of lemonade, four sandwiches and twelve biscuits costs 18p. Find the cost of the separate items.

If lemonade costs xp a glass, a sandwich yp and a biscuit zp, we have:

$$\begin{aligned}(1)\quad x+\ y+\ \ z &= 8,\\ (2)\quad x+3y+\ 7z &= 14,\\ (3)\quad x+4y+12z &= 18.\end{aligned}$$

The equations can be written in matrix form

$$\begin{pmatrix}1 & 1 & 1\\ 1 & 3 & 7\\ 1 & 4 & 12\end{pmatrix}\begin{pmatrix}x\\ y\\ z\end{pmatrix} = \begin{pmatrix}8\\ 14\\ 18\end{pmatrix}$$

If we write the coefficient matrix and the identity side by side and perform row-operations, we obtain first the 'echelon' (triangular) matrix and then the inverse. If in an additional column we set down the vector which gives the constants on the right of the three equations and perform the row-operations on this also, we obtain the solution of our original problem too. The whole process can be written down in this way:

Operation	*Coefficient matrix*	*Identity*	*Constant vector*
	$\begin{pmatrix}1 & 1 & 1\\ 1 & 3 & 7\\ 1 & 4 & 12\end{pmatrix}$	$\begin{pmatrix}1 & 0 & 0\\ 0 & 1 & 0\\ 0 & 0 & 1\end{pmatrix}$	$\begin{pmatrix}8\\ 14\\ 18\end{pmatrix}$
row 2 − row 1 row 3 − row 1	$\begin{pmatrix}1 & 1 & 1\\ 0 & 2 & 6\\ 0 & 3 & 11\end{pmatrix}$	$\begin{pmatrix}1 & 0 & 0\\ -1 & 1 & 0\\ -1 & 0 & 1\end{pmatrix}$	$\begin{pmatrix}8\\ 6\\ 10\end{pmatrix}$
$\frac{1}{2}\times$ row 2	$\begin{pmatrix}1 & 1 & 1\\ 0 & 1 & 3\\ 0 & 3 & 11\end{pmatrix}$	$\begin{pmatrix}1 & 0 & 0\\ -\frac{1}{2} & \frac{1}{2} & 0\\ -1 & 0 & 1\end{pmatrix}$	$\begin{pmatrix}8\\ 3\\ 10\end{pmatrix}$
row 3 − 3 × row 2	$\begin{pmatrix}1 & 1 & 1\\ 0 & 1 & 3\\ 0 & 0 & 2\end{pmatrix}$	$\begin{pmatrix}1 & 0 & 0\\ -\frac{1}{2} & \frac{1}{2} & 0\\ \frac{1}{2} & -1\frac{1}{2} & 1\end{pmatrix}$	$\begin{pmatrix}8\\ 3\\ 1\end{pmatrix}$
$\frac{1}{2}\times$ row 3	$\begin{pmatrix}1 & 1 & 1\\ 0 & 1 & 3\\ 0 & 0 & 1\end{pmatrix}$	$\begin{pmatrix}1 & 0 & 0\\ -\frac{1}{2} & \frac{1}{2} & 0\\ \frac{1}{4} & -\frac{3}{4} & \frac{1}{2}\end{pmatrix}$	$\begin{pmatrix}8\\ 3\\ \frac{1}{2}\end{pmatrix}$
row 1 − row 3 row 2 − 3 × row 3	$\begin{pmatrix}1 & 1 & 0\\ 0 & 1 & 0\\ 0 & 0 & 1\end{pmatrix}$	$\begin{pmatrix}\frac{3}{4} & \frac{3}{4} & -\frac{1}{2}\\ -1\frac{1}{4} & 2\frac{3}{4} & -1\frac{1}{2}\\ \frac{1}{4} & -\frac{3}{4} & \frac{1}{2}\end{pmatrix}$	$\begin{pmatrix}7\frac{1}{2}\\ 1\frac{1}{2}\\ \frac{1}{2}\end{pmatrix}$
row 1 − row 2	$\begin{pmatrix}1 & 0 & 0\\ 0 & 1 & 0\\ 0 & 0 & 1\end{pmatrix}$	$\begin{pmatrix}2 & -2 & 1\\ -1\frac{1}{4} & 2\frac{3}{4} & -1\frac{1}{2}\\ \frac{1}{4} & -\frac{3}{4} & \frac{1}{2}\end{pmatrix}$	$\begin{pmatrix}6\\ 1\frac{1}{2}\\ \frac{1}{2}\end{pmatrix}$
	Identity	*Inverse*	*Solution*

The meaning, for example, of the fourth line in this working is that

$$\begin{pmatrix} 1 & 0 & 0 \\ -\frac{1}{2} & \frac{1}{2} & 0 \\ \frac{1}{2} & -1\frac{1}{2} & 1 \end{pmatrix} \begin{pmatrix} 1 & 1 & 1 \\ 1 & 3 & 7 \\ 1 & 4 & 12 \end{pmatrix} = \begin{pmatrix} 1 & 1 & 1 \\ 0 & 1 & 3 \\ 0 & 0 & 2 \end{pmatrix}$$

and
$$\begin{pmatrix} 1 & 0 & 0 \\ -\frac{1}{2} & \frac{1}{2} & \frac{1}{2} \\ \frac{1}{2} & -1\frac{1}{2} & 1 \end{pmatrix} \begin{pmatrix} 8 \\ 14 \\ 18 \end{pmatrix} = \begin{pmatrix} 8 \\ 3 \\ 1 \end{pmatrix};$$

and of the final line that

$$\begin{pmatrix} 2 & -2 & 1 \\ -1\frac{1}{4} & 2\frac{3}{4} & -1\frac{1}{2} \\ \frac{1}{4} & -\frac{3}{4} & \frac{1}{2} \end{pmatrix} \begin{pmatrix} 1 & 1 & 1 \\ 1 & 3 & 7 \\ 1 & 4 & 12 \end{pmatrix} = \begin{pmatrix} 1 & 0 & 0 \\ 0 & 1 & 0 \\ 0 & 0 & 1 \end{pmatrix}$$

and
$$\begin{pmatrix} 2 & -2 & 1 \\ -1\frac{1}{4} & 2\frac{3}{4} & -1\frac{1}{2} \\ \frac{1}{4} & -\frac{3}{4} & \frac{1}{2} \end{pmatrix} \begin{pmatrix} 8 \\ 14 \\ 18 \end{pmatrix} = \begin{pmatrix} 6 \\ 1\frac{1}{2} \\ \frac{1}{2} \end{pmatrix},$$

so that if
$$\begin{pmatrix} 1 & 1 & 1 \\ 1 & 3 & 7 \\ 1 & 4 & 12 \end{pmatrix} \begin{pmatrix} x \\ y \\ z \end{pmatrix} = \begin{pmatrix} 8 \\ 14 \\ 18 \end{pmatrix},$$

then
$$\begin{pmatrix} x \\ y \\ z \end{pmatrix} = \begin{pmatrix} 1 & 0 & 0 \\ 0 & 1 & 0 \\ 0 & 0 & 1 \end{pmatrix} \begin{pmatrix} x \\ y \\ z \end{pmatrix}$$

$$= \begin{pmatrix} 2 & -2 & 1 \\ -1\frac{1}{4} & 2\frac{3}{4} & -1\frac{1}{2} \\ \frac{1}{4} & -\frac{3}{4} & \frac{1}{2} \end{pmatrix} \begin{pmatrix} 1 & 1 & 1 \\ 1 & 3 & 7 \\ 1 & 4 & 12 \end{pmatrix} \begin{pmatrix} x \\ y \\ z \end{pmatrix}$$

$$= \begin{pmatrix} 2 & -2 & 1 \\ -1\frac{1}{4} & 2\frac{3}{4} & -1\frac{1}{2} \\ \frac{1}{4} & -\frac{3}{4} & \frac{1}{2} \end{pmatrix} \begin{pmatrix} 8 \\ 14 \\ 18 \end{pmatrix}$$

$$= \begin{pmatrix} 6 \\ 1\frac{1}{2} \\ \frac{1}{2} \end{pmatrix}$$

from which $x = 6$, $y = 1\frac{1}{2}$, $z = \frac{1}{2}$.

The reader should check that (as will be proved in a later chapter) the matrices commute with their inverses.

Exercise D

1. Use the method above to find the inverse of the matrix

$$\begin{pmatrix} 1 & 3 & -2 \\ 4 & -5 & 1 \\ -4 & 7 & -2 \end{pmatrix}.$$

Use this inverse to write down the solutions of the sets of equations

$$\begin{pmatrix} 1 & 3 & -2 \\ 4 & -5 & 1 \\ -4 & 7 & -2 \end{pmatrix}\begin{pmatrix} x \\ y \\ z \end{pmatrix} = \begin{pmatrix} 10p \\ 10p+1 \\ 10p-1 \end{pmatrix}$$

for values of p from 0 to 5.

2. Follow the method through for the matrix

$$\begin{pmatrix} 1 & 5 & 8 \\ 1 & 7 & 12 \\ 1 & 6 & 10 \end{pmatrix}$$

and note carefully where it breaks down. Does every 3×3 matrix have an inverse?

3. Use the same method to find the inverses of:

(*a*) $\begin{pmatrix} 1 & 3 \\ 2 & 5 \end{pmatrix}$; (*b*) $\begin{pmatrix} 4 & 3 \\ 5 & 4 \end{pmatrix}$; (*c*) $\begin{pmatrix} 3 & 4 \\ -1 & 7 \end{pmatrix}$; (*d*) $\begin{pmatrix} a & b \\ c & d \end{pmatrix}$.

4. What are the inverses of the following *elementary* matrices?

(*a*) $\begin{pmatrix} k & 0 \\ 0 & 1 \end{pmatrix}$; (*b*) $\begin{pmatrix} 1 & 0 \\ -3 & 1 \end{pmatrix}$; (*c*) $\begin{pmatrix} 1 & 0 & 0 \\ 0 & k & 0 \\ 0 & 0 & 1 \end{pmatrix}$;

(*d*) $\begin{pmatrix} 0 & 1 & 0 \\ 1 & 0 & 0 \\ 0 & 0 & 1 \end{pmatrix}$; (*e*) $\begin{pmatrix} 1 & 0 & 0 \\ 3 & 1 & 0 \\ 0 & 0 & 1 \end{pmatrix}$; (*f*) $\begin{pmatrix} 1 & 0 & 0 \\ 0 & 1 & 0 \\ a & 0 & 1 \end{pmatrix}$.

Can you interpret your results geometrically?

4. RELAXATION

This is the official name of an entirely different method of solving linear equations, but it may also provide some light relief from the main work! The name arose because the method, which is essentially a kind of intelligent trial-and-error method, was the invention of an engineer (Southwell) who used it to find the stresses in complicated frameworks by relaxing the constraints of the framework in turn. It is best understood from an example.

4.1 Solution by relaxation.

Example 5. To solve the equations:

$$8x - y + 3z = 11,$$
$$3x + 5y - z = 8,$$
$$x + y + 6z = 10.$$

Write the equations:

$$R_1 = 8x - y + 3z - 11 = 0,$$
$$R_2 = 3x + 5y - z - 8 = 0,$$
$$R_3 = x + y + 6z - 10 = 0.$$

We have to find values of x, y, z which make R_1, R_2, R_3, the so-called *residuals*, zero. To do this we shall guess values of x, y, z and then modify our guesses one at a time in order to make R_1, R_2, and R_3 as small as possible.

We first tabulate the effects on R_1, R_2, R_3 of changes in x, y, z.

			ΔR_1	ΔR_2	ΔR_3
$\Delta x = 1$	$\Delta y = 0$	$\Delta z = 0$	8	3	1
$\Delta x = 0$	$\Delta y = 1$	$\Delta z = 0$	-1	5	1
$\Delta x = 0$	$\Delta y = 0$	$\Delta z = 1$	3	-1	6

(This is the transpose of the coefficient matrix.)

This table is called the *relaxation table* and guides all our future actions.

Next we put $x = 0$, $y = 0$, $z = 0$ and then modify x, y, z in succession so as to reduce the residuals. To change R_1 it is best to change x; to change R_2, y; while a change in z most affects R_3. Each time we try to reduce the largest residual. The work is set out as follows.

	x	y	z	R_1	R_2	R_3
Set	0	0	0	-11	-8	-10
Changes	$+1$			-3	-5	-9
			$+1$	0	-6	-3
		$+1$		-1	-1	-2

At this point $x = 1$, $y = 1$, $z = 1$ and we check that in fact $R_1 = -1$, $R_2 = -1$, $R_3 = -2$. No further reduction in R_1, R_2, R_3 can be made without fractional changes in x, y, z. We therefore consider changes in x, y and z in the first place of decimals.

	x	y	z	R_1	R_2	R_3
	1	1	1	-1	-1	-2
Changes			$+0{\cdot}3$	$-0{\cdot}1$	$-1{\cdot}3$	$-0{\cdot}2$
		$+0{\cdot}3$		$-0{\cdot}4$	$+0{\cdot}2$	$+0{\cdot}1$

Again check, and proceed to the next decimal place.

	1	1·3	1·3	−0·4	+0·2	+0·1
Changes	+0·05			0	0·35	0·15
		−0·07		0·07	0	0·08
			−0·01	0·04	0·01	0·02

At this stage we have $x = 1{\cdot}05$, $y = 1{\cdot}23$, $z = 1{\cdot}29$. The process can be continued as long as required. In fact the answers to six figures are $x = 1{\cdot}04598$, $y = 1{\cdot}22988$, $z = 1{\cdot}28736$.

These equations behaved well because each row of the relaxation table had a dominating coefficient—i.e. one numerically greater than the others, and these were in different columns. This meant that we could concentrate on reducing one residual at a time—the largest one—merely by altering one of the variables x, y and z. If this is not the case, we may have to choose combinations of changes which will have the effect of reducing one residual more than the others.

Thus for the equations:

$$\begin{aligned} 2x+\ y+2z &= \ 5, \\ 3x+4y+5z &= 11, \\ x-\ y+8z &= \ 3, \end{aligned}$$

no simple change will affect R_1 more than R_2 and R_3; but if we take $\Delta x = 2$, $\Delta y = -1$ simultaneously we get $\Delta R_1 = 3$, $\Delta R_2 = 2$, $\Delta R_3 = 3$; and if we take $\Delta x = 5$, $\Delta y = -3$, $\Delta z = -1$ simultaneously we get $\Delta R_1 = 5$, $\Delta R_2 = -2$, $\Delta R_3 = 0$ which is even better.

Alternatively, we may be able to produce a better relaxation table by combining the equations in some way; thus in the example above, replacing the first equation by the second minus four times the first gives

$$5x+0y+3z = 9,$$

which is preferable because it enables us to change R_1 by a change in x alone, without affecting the rest of the table unduly.

This process is called *conditioning* the equations for solution. Sometimes, however, nothing very much can be done to make the process converge rapidly, and the equations are then said to be *ill-conditioned*. The meaning of this can be seen most simply from geometrical ideas.

4.2 Geometrical interpretation. Consider the equations

$$\begin{aligned} 8x+\ 6y-31 &= 0, \\ 5x+12y-38 &= 0. \end{aligned}$$

These are the equations of two straight lines, and the problem is to find their point of intersection. Given any numbers x, y, the residuals

$$R_1 = 8x+6y-31, \quad \text{and} \quad R_2 = 5x+12y-38$$

are related to the perpendicular distances of the point (x, y) from these two lines. In fact, if these perpendiculars are p_1 and p_2, then $R_1 = 10p_1$ and $R_2 = 13p_2$. The process of relaxation then consists of starting anywhere, usually at the origin, and making changes in x and y so that at each stage the perpendicular distances to the lines are reduced. The first few stages for these two equations are illustrated in Figure 1.

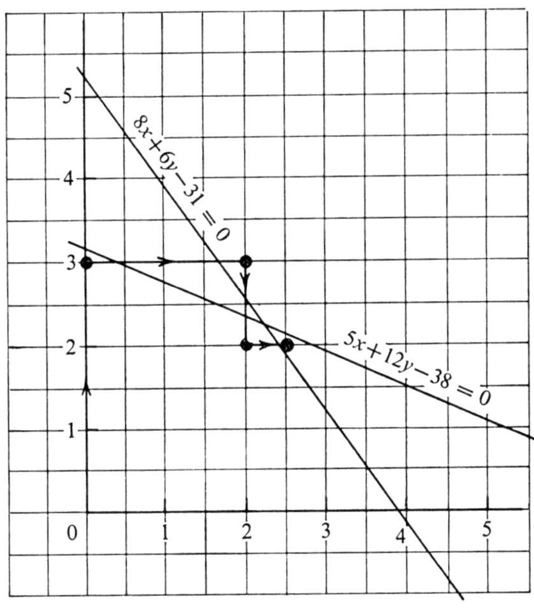

Fig. 1

If the lines meet at a very narrow angle, as in Figure 2, then it is possible, as, for example, at the point P shown, to have both residuals quite small while in fact being a long way from the solution. These lines have ill-conditioned equations like

$$11x+8y-32 = 0,$$

$$7x+5y-23 = 0,$$

their gradients, $-11/8$ and $-7/5$, being very nearly equal. For the two equations

$$ax+by-p = 0,$$

$$cx+dy-q = 0,$$

this situation will occur when $-a/b$ is nearly equal to $-c/d$; i.e. when the determinant $ad-bc$ is small compared with a, b, c, and d.

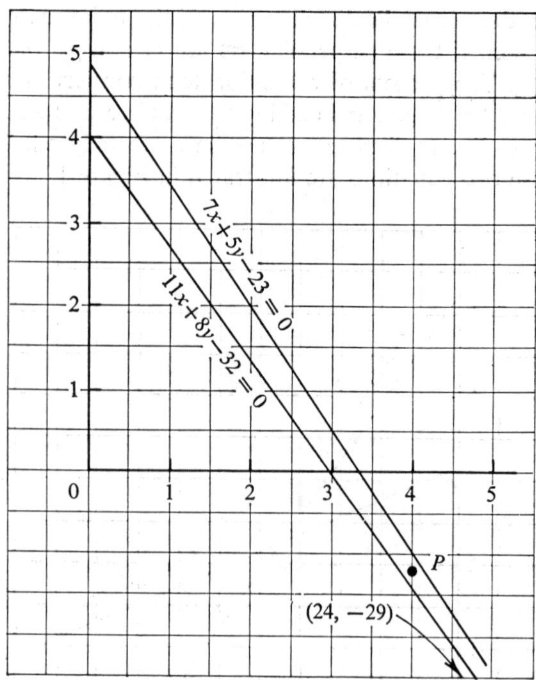

Fig. 2

Exercise E

1. Solve by relaxation the equations $4x+2y = 21$, $x+3y = 3$.

2. Find by relaxation the exact solution of the equations

$$5x-3y = 11, \qquad 8x-5y = 7.$$

($\Delta x = 2$, $\Delta y = 3$ will change both residuals equally.)

3. Draw the graphs representing the equations in Questions 1–2, and show the steps of your solutions, as in Figure 1.

4. Solve by relaxation the equations $4x+y+7 = 0$, $x+3y+1 = 0$. Begin with $x = 0$, $y = 0$, and show that when $x = 2$, $y = -0{\cdot}3$, both residuals have been reduced to $-0{\cdot}1$ of their previous values. Can you use this fact to write down the solution?

5. Solve by relaxation the equations:

$$\begin{aligned} 5x-\ y-\ \ z &= 11,\\ 2x+7y-\ 3z &= \ 4,\\ x-3y+10z &= 12 \end{aligned}$$

giving your answers to two decimal places.

6. Condition the equations:

$$49x - 50y + 51z = 52,$$

$$50x - 56y + 52z = 55,$$

$$103x - 110y + 100z = 111$$

for solution by relaxation by subtracting the first from the second and twice the second from the third. Hence solve them to two decimal places.

[You may find it easier to write $x - z = u$, $x + z = v$ and solve for u, v and y.]

7. Condition and solve the equations:

$$x + \tfrac{1}{2}y + \tfrac{1}{3}z = 1,$$

$$\tfrac{1}{2}x + \tfrac{1}{3}y + \tfrac{1}{4}z = 0{\cdot}75,$$

$$\tfrac{1}{3}x + \tfrac{1}{4}y + \tfrac{1}{5}z = 0{\cdot}55.$$

Solve by relaxation and check by another method.

8. Solve exactly, by elimination, the system of equations:

$$x + 0{\cdot}5y + 0{\cdot}33z = 1,$$

$$0{\cdot}5x + 0{\cdot}33y + 0{\cdot}25z = 0{\cdot}75,$$

$$0{\cdot}33x + 0{\cdot}25y + 0{\cdot}2z = 0{\cdot}55.$$

How much does the solution differ from that of the equations in the last question? Explain this result.

Miscellaneous Exercise

1. Find the inverses of the following matrices by row-operations and check by calculating the determinant of the original matrix:

(*a*) $\begin{pmatrix} 1 & -1 \\ 4 & 6 \end{pmatrix}$; (*b*) $\begin{pmatrix} 1 & 3 \\ 5 & 7 \end{pmatrix}$; (*c*) $\begin{pmatrix} 2 & -3 \\ 5 & -7 \end{pmatrix}$;

(*d*) $\begin{pmatrix} 3 & -8 \\ 2 & 3 \end{pmatrix}$; (*e*) $\begin{pmatrix} -4 & 9 \\ 2 & -5 \end{pmatrix}$; (*f*) $\begin{pmatrix} 0 & 4 \\ -7 & 3 \end{pmatrix}$.

2. Write down, by the use of Theorem C, the inverses of the elementary matrices:

(*a*) $\begin{pmatrix} 1 & 0 \\ -1 & 1 \end{pmatrix}$; (*b*) $\begin{pmatrix} 1 & 1 \\ 0 & 1 \end{pmatrix}$; (*c*) $\begin{pmatrix} k & 0 \\ 0 & 1 \end{pmatrix}$;

(*d*) $\begin{pmatrix} 1 & 0 \\ p & 1 \end{pmatrix}$; (*e*) $\begin{pmatrix} 1 & q \\ 0 & 1 \end{pmatrix}$; (*f*) $\begin{pmatrix} k & 0 \\ 0 & l \end{pmatrix}$.

3. Find, by row-operations, or otherwise, a matrix X for which

$$X\begin{pmatrix} 3 & 2 \\ 1 & -1 \end{pmatrix} = \begin{pmatrix} 4 & 1 \\ 2 & 3 \end{pmatrix}.$$

4. Find a value of λ for which

$$\left.\begin{aligned} x+5y &= 8 \\ 2x+\lambda y &= 11 \end{aligned}\right\}$$

have no solution.

What can you then say about the lines represented by these equations?

5. Show by the echelon process that the third row of the matrix

$$\begin{pmatrix} 1 & 3 & 4 \\ 1 & 4 & 7 \\ 2 & 1 & -7 \end{pmatrix}$$

is a linear combination of the first two rows, and find this combination.

For what value of c do the equations:

$$\begin{aligned} p+3q+4r &= 8, \\ p+4q+7r &= 9, \\ 2p+\ q-7r &= c \end{aligned}$$

have solutions?

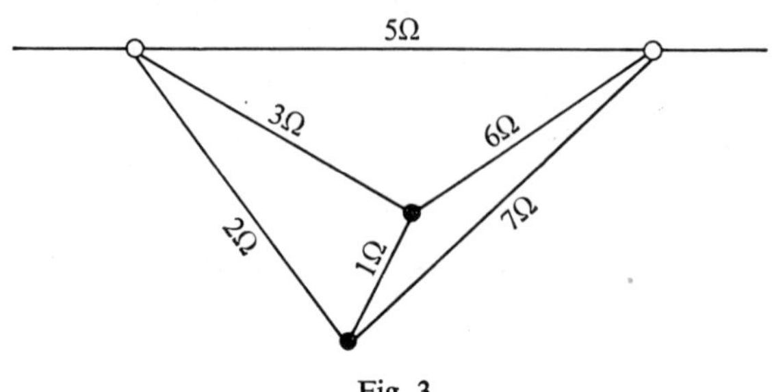

Fig. 3

6. A voltage of 20·5 volts is applied across the terminals of this network (Figure 3). Find the currents in the various wires.

7. Find the vertices of the tetrahedron formed by the planes:

$$\begin{aligned} x+5y+z &= 4, \\ 3x-\ y-z &= 3, \\ x-11y+z &= 0, \\ 3x+\ 7y-z &= 1. \end{aligned}$$

8. There are 24 children in the local convalescent home, and I propose to give them each a jig-saw puzzle for Christmas. There are three types to choose from: the simple Totshapes at 35p, the Jig-geogs at 50p, and the difficult Puzzlepics at 40p. The matron tells me that on the average it takes a child 50 minutes to complete a Totshape, an hour to do a Jig-geog, and an hour and a half for a Puzzlepic. She urges me, for the peace of the staff, to ensure that my gifts occupy altogether at least 24 child-hours. I shall give as many Jig-geogs as I can, for they are so educational; I would like some change out of a £10 note. What should I buy?

22

AREA

We have an intuitive idea of associating with a region of a surface a number, which we call the *area* of the region, which measures the amount of surface covered by the region. In this chapter we shall examine this concept in greater detail, and develop ways of calculating areas bounded by curves other than straight lines and circles.

For simplicity we shall confine attention to regions of a plane, and it will be useful to specify rather more precisely what we mean by the word 'region'. For the purpose of the discussion which follows, a *region* is a set of points consisting of all the points within a 'simple closed curve'—that is, a continuous curve that does not cross itself. It will be convenient to specify that the closed curve itself, which is the boundary of the region, is counted as part of the region. Thus, the set of points

$$\{(x, y): 0 \leqslant x \leqslant 1 \quad \text{and} \quad 0 \leqslant y \leqslant 1\}$$

would be called a region, but not the set

$$\{(x, y): 0 \leqslant x \leqslant 1 \quad \text{and} \quad 0 < y < 1\}.$$

We make this restriction solely to simplify the statement of certain results.

The preceding paragraph introduces a number of terms whose precise definition is far from easy, such as the 'boundary' of a region and the 'inside' of a curve. The resolution of these difficulties forms the starting point of some important theories in topology. It is not proposed to pursue such investigations here, since our applications will be solely to regions for which the meaning to be assigned to such terms is intuitively 'obvious'.

When we associate an area with each region, we define a function having the set of all possible regions of the plane as its domain and the set of positive real numbers as range. We shall denote this function by the letter A. If we then denote a region by R, we write

$$A: R \rightarrow A(R).$$

For example, if R_1 is to mean the set of points P whose distance from a fixed point O does not exceed r, then $A(R_1) = \pi r^2$; and if

$$R_2 = \{(x, y): 0 \leqslant x \leqslant 1 \quad \text{and} \quad 0 \leqslant y \leqslant 1\},$$

then $A(R_2) = 1$.

1. PROPERTIES OF THE AREA FUNCTION

We shall begin by listing a number of properties that, on the basis of our intuitive ideas about area, we should expect such a measure to possess. These properties will be the basis of our subsequent work on evaluating areas, but the list which follows is not a formal minimum list of axioms. It leads to a function unique except for the choice of unit area.

(*a*) *All regions have positive area.*

This is another way of saying that the range of the area function is the set of positive numbers; or, if R is any region, $A(R) > 0$.

(*b*) *Area is additive.*

By this we mean that, if two regions R_1 and R_2 do not 'overlap' each other, but combine to form a single region, R, then the area of R is the sum of the areas of R_1 and R_2. It is clear that, to form a single region bounded by a simple closed curve, R_1 and R_2 must possess some common boundary points; by saying that the regions do not overlap we mean that the *only* common points are boundary points (Figure 1).

Thus, the property can be stated as follows: If the only points common to R_1 and R_2 are boundary points of both regions, then

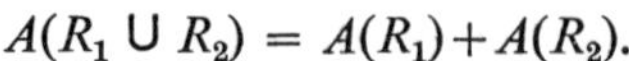

$$A(R_1 \cup R_2) = A(R_1)+A(R_2).$$

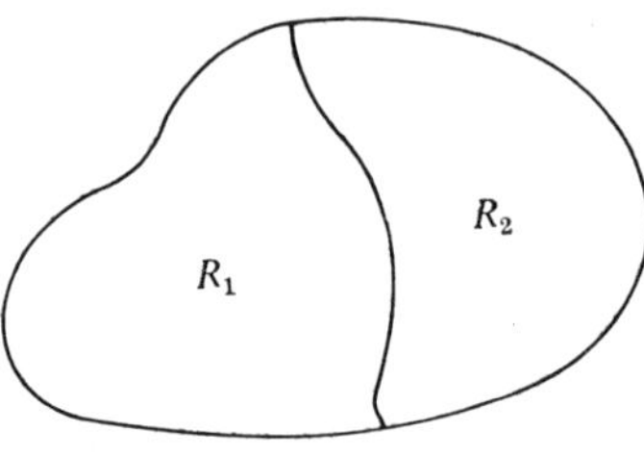

Fig. 1

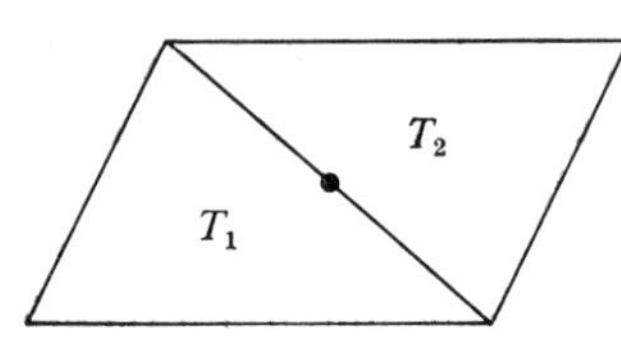

Fig. 2

(*c*) *Congruent regions have the same area.*

Thus, if any isometry transformation is applied to the points of a plane, the image of any region under this transformation has the same area as the original region. We say that 'area is invariant under isometry transformations'.

We use properties (*b*) and (*c*), for example, when we assert that the diagonal of a parallelogram divides it into two triangular regions, each of which has an area one-half of that bounded by the parallelogram. For if these two triangular regions are denoted by T_1 and T_2 (Figure 2), then a half-turn about the mid-point of the diagonal transforms T_1 into T_2, so that $A(T_1) = A(T_2)$.

Moreover, T_1 and T_2 have in common only the points of the diagonal, which is a boundary of both regions, and together they form the parallelogram region R. Therefore, from the additive property,

$$A(R) = A(T_1)+A(T_2).$$

These two results together show that $A(T_1) = A(T_2) = \frac{1}{2}A(R)$.

(*d*) *Area is invariant under shearing transformations.*

By a shearing transformation we mean one in which each point of the plane moves parallel to a given line through a distance which depends only on its distance from that line. For example, if the line is taken as the y-axis (Figure 3), the transformation can be described by the mapping $(x, y) \rightarrow (x, y+a)$, where a is a function of x. The most familiar example

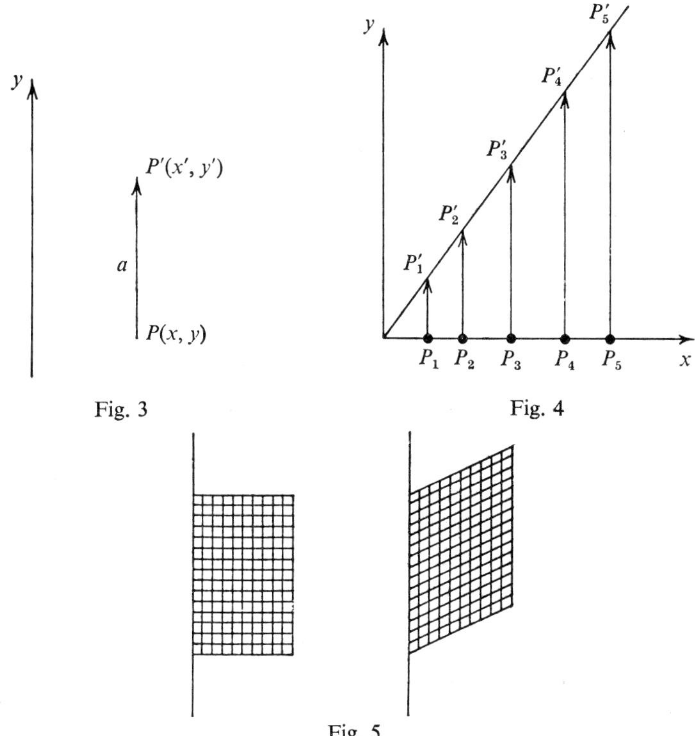

Fig. 3

Fig. 4

Fig. 5

of this uniform shearing which we met in earlier books and for which a is proportional to x (Figure 4). This transformation was used, for example, to map a rectangle onto a parallelogram (Figure 5), and we deduced that the regions bounded by the rectangle and the parallelogram have the same area.

Figure 6 shows an example of a more general shearing transformation. In this a region with a curved boundary is transformed into a region having part of its boundary along the x-axis, by choosing for a the displacement needed to map a point of the 'lower part' of the curved boundary onto a point of the x-axis.

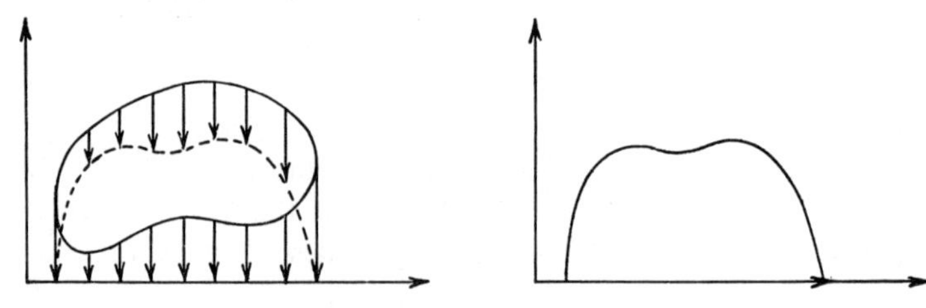

Fig. 6

(*e*) *If one region lies inside another, it has the smaller area.*

By 'lies inside', we do not preclude the possibility that the two regions may have boundaries that coincide in part; but since a region is defined by its boundary, they cannot coincide completely. This property can be stated:

If a region R_1 is a proper subset of a region R_2, then $A(R_1) < A(R_2)$.

In fact, we shall later tacitly modify the definition of 'region' to include 'regions' of zero area, and in certain contexts make conventions about the signs of areas. However, properties (*a*)–(*e*) allow us to proceed to the practical measurement of the plane.

2. THE CALCULATION OF AREA

2.1 A unit of area. Before a numerical value can be assigned to the area of a particular region, it is necessary to choose a region that will be said to have *unit* area. For this purpose, we always select a *square* whose side has unit length; since all such squares are congruent to one another, it is immaterial which particular one is chosen. It should, however, be realized that there is nothing to force us to make this choice; we could equally well decide to have an equilateral triangle of unit side ('triangular centimetres'), or a disc of unit radius ('circular centimetres'), and express all other areas relative to these units.

2.2 Simple closed polygons. Once this unit area has been established, it is possible, by using the properties (*a*) to (*e*) listed in Section 1, to evaluate the area of any region bounded by a simple closed polygon. The calculation can be broken down by stages as follows:

(i) The region can be displayed as a combination of a number of non-overlapping triangular regions having only boundary points in common, so that by the additive property its area will be the sum of the areas of the separate triangular regions (Figure 7).

(ii) Under property (*c*) it was shown that the area of any triangular region is one-half of that of a region bounded by a parallelogram.

(iii) A parallelogram can be transformed by shearing into a rectangle, and the regions contained within these two figures will have the same area (property (*d*)).

The problem therefore reduces to that of finding the area of any region bounded by a rectangle. Suppose, first, that the sides of the rectangle are rational multiples of the unit length; then the properties (*b*) and (*c*) can be used to show that its area is measured by the product of the lengths of the sides. For example, if the sides have lengths $\frac{4}{3}$ and $\frac{2}{5}$, then we can arrange 15 such rectangular regions so that they have only boundary points in common and combine to form a rectangular region with sides 4 units and

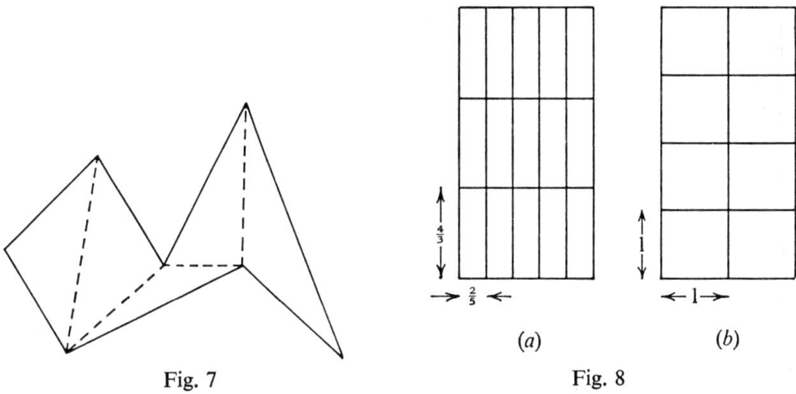

Fig. 7

Fig. 8

2 units (Figure 8(*a*)); but we can also arrange 8 'unit regions' to cover the same rectangular region (Figure 8(*b*)). It follows that 15 times the area of one of the original rectangles is equal to 8 times the unit area, so that each region has $\frac{8}{15}$ of the unit area.

For rectangles having one or both sides incommensurable with the unit length we must use property (*e*). Consider, for example, a rectangle whose sides have lengths $\sqrt{2}$ and $\sqrt{3}$ units. Since

$$1{\cdot}4 < \sqrt{2} < 1{\cdot}5 \quad \text{and} \quad 1{\cdot}7 < \sqrt{3} < 1{\cdot}8,$$

the rectangle can be made to lie outside one with sides 1·4 and 1·7 units, whose area is 2·38 units, and inside one with sides 1·5 and 1·8 units, whose area is 2·70 units.

Similarly, by taking closer bounds 1·41 and 1·42 to the value of $\sqrt{2}$, and 1·73 and 1·74 to the value of $\sqrt{3}$, we can enclose the given rectangular region within regions of area $1{\cdot}41 \times 1{\cdot}73 = 2{\cdot}4393$, and $1{\cdot}42 \times 1{\cdot}74 = 2{\cdot}4708$; and so on. We therefore set up a sequence of nesting intervals within which the required area S lies:

$$2{\cdot}38 < S < 2{\cdot}70$$

$$2{\cdot}4393 < S < 2{\cdot}4708, \text{ etc.}$$

It can be shown that the only number common to all such intervals is the number $\sqrt{6}$. In this way it can be shown that the areas of rectangles with sides measured by irrational numbers are found also as the product of the lengths of their sides.

From the complete chain of calculation, it now appears that the area of any region bounded by a simple closed polygon can be found.

2.3 Regions with curved boundaries. When we come to consider regions with curved boundaries the situation is less simple. Suppose, for example, that we wish to find the area within a circle of unit radius. We can no longer dissect the region into non-overlapping triangular regions, since any dissection is bound to give some regions part of whose boundary is curved. Moreover, we cannot combine a number of congruent circular discs in a non-overlapping manner to make up some figure whose area we already know. Nor is it possible to transform a circle by shearing into a region bounded by a closed polygon. Thus, none of the simple methods based on properties (*b*), (*c*) and (*d*) can be used to solve this problem. The only property which offers any hope of progress is property (*e*), since we can find regions bounded by polygons which enclose the circle completely, and others which are completely contained by the circle. It is therefore possible to find bounds within which the area of the circular region must lie.

One method of doing this is illustrated in Figure 9. A very rough estimate can be made by putting squares inside and round the circle, of sides $\sqrt{2}$ and 2 respectively, thus showing that the area lies between 2 and 4 units (Figures 9(*a*) and (*b*)). For a closer pair of bounds, we may inscribe and circumscribe octagons to the circle; since these are formed by bisecting the arcs between the vertices in Figure 9(*a*), and between points of contact in Figure 9(*b*), it is clear that, by adding pieces to the inscribed square or taking pieces off the circumscribed one, the areas of these octagons will lie within the interval bounded by the areas of the squares (Figures 9(*c*) and (*d*)).

It can be shown that these areas are respectively $2\sqrt{2}$ and $8(\sqrt{2}-1)$, so that the area of the circle lies between 2·828 and 3·314. A further bisection gives inscribed and circumscribed 16-gons (Figures 9(*e*) and (*f*)), of areas 3·061 and 3·183; and so on. We therefore have a sequence of nesting intervals within which the area S of the disc must lie:

$$2 < S < 4,$$

$$2{\cdot}828 < S < 3{\cdot}314,$$

$$3{\cdot}061 < S < 3{\cdot}183, \quad \text{and so on.}$$

It can be shown that these intervals have a single common number; this is the number which we denote by π, and evaluation of further terms of the sequence enables us to find the value of this number to within any specified degree of accuracy.

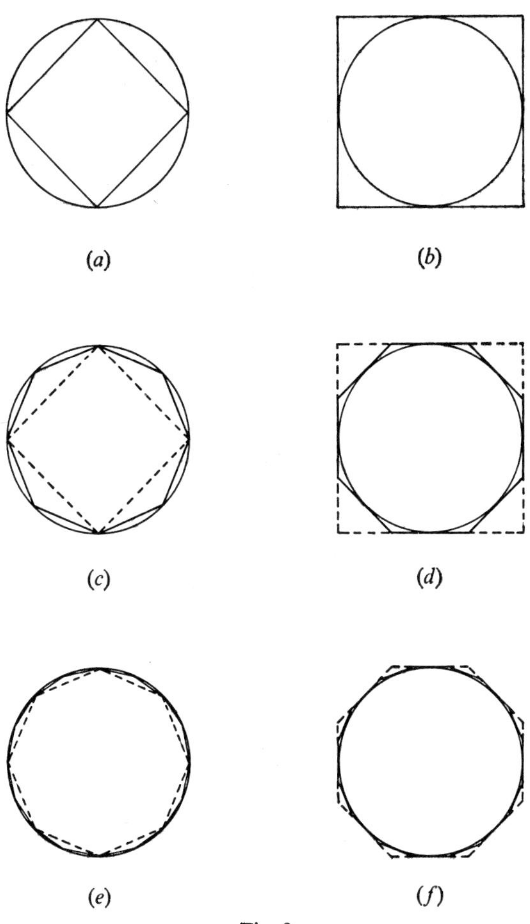

Fig. 9

Exercise A

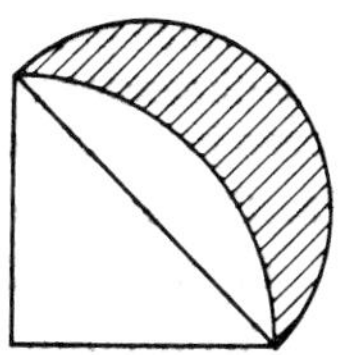

Fig. 10

1. Figure 10 shows a region whose boundary consists of a semi-circle and a quadrant of a circle, described on a hypotenuse and a side respectively of an isosceles right-angled triangle. Show, by using the additive property of area, that the area of the region is equal to that of the triangle. (A region like this is called a 'lune'. This result was discovered by Hippocrates in the latter part of the fifth century B.C.)

2. Sketch on the same diagram the graphs of $y = x^2$ and $y = (x-1)^2$. Find the area of the region whose boundary consists of parts of these two graphs and of the y-axis.

(*Hint*. Use a shearing transformation to convert this into a region with straight sides.)

3. Show that property (*e*) of Section 1 follows from properties (*a*) and (*b*).

4. Sets of points such a those illustrated in Figure 11 are not 'regions' within the definition given in the text. Use the properties of Section 1 to suggest how the concept of area might be extended to cover sets of points such as these.

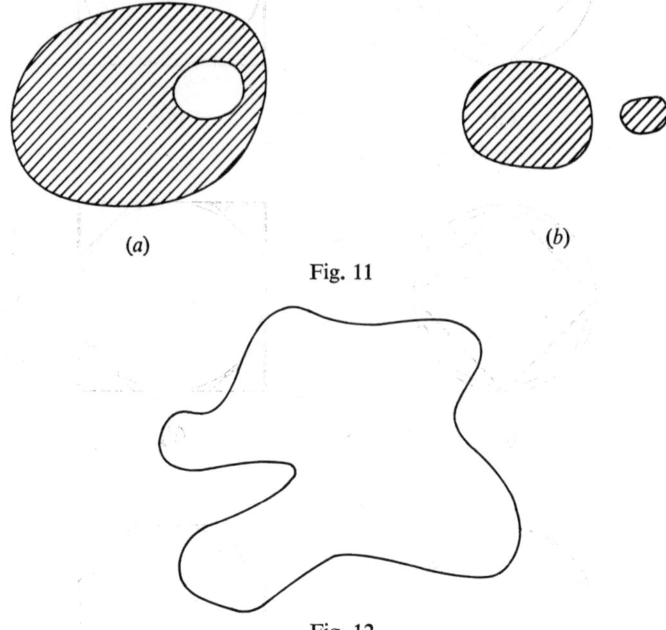

(*a*) (*b*)

Fig. 11

Fig. 12

5. Figure 12 shows a region whose area is required. Trace it on graph paper, and by finding suitable polygonal regions obtain upper and lower bounds within which the area must lie. How could the closeness of your estimate be improved?

***6.** How can the properties (*a*) to (*e*) of Section 1 and the argument of Section 2 be adapted to three-dimensional Euclidean space? Would it be possible to define a 'hyper-volume' in four-dimensional Euclidean space?

***7.** Which parts of Sections 1 and 2 are necessary for consideration of length in a one-dimensional Euclidean space? Can you think of a curved one-dimensional space in which length can be defined in this way?

***8.** Can area be defined in this way on:

(*a*) a sphere? (*b*) an ellipsoid? (*c*) a cylinder? (*d*) a cone?

***9.** Write down the areas of the 2^n-gons inscribed and circumscribed to the circle in the sequence defined in Section 2.3. What assumptions must be made to prove from this that the area of the disc is π?

3. AREAS UNDER GRAPHS

3.1 It was shown in Section 1 (*d*) (see Figure 6) that a region with a curved boundary can be transformed into one for which part of the boundary is a straight line. Considerable simplification of this kind can be effected even for regions with boundaries of a more complicated shape, such as that shown in Figure 13 (*a*), by a succession of shears. The regions R_1 and R_2 can first be transformed (leaving the rest of the region unaltered) into the regions R_1' and R_2' of the same area. A further transformation, indicated by the arrows in Figure 13 (*c*), will finally convert the region into one with part of its boundary a straight line of the form shown in Figure 13 (*d*).

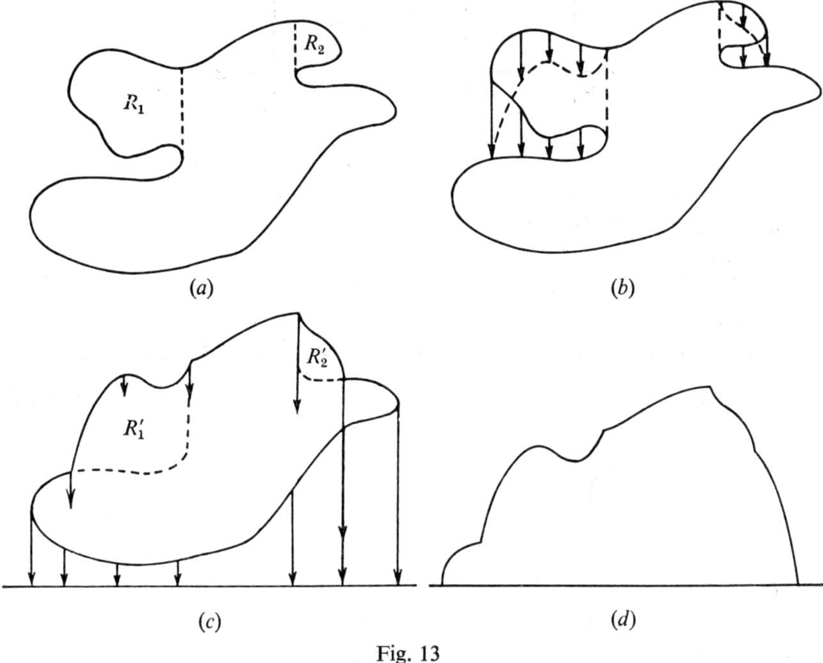

Fig. 13

3.2 Areas under graphs. It will, therefore, suffice in devising general methods for calculating areas, to consider regions of this special shape. It is convenient to set up a coordinate system with the straight part of the boundary forming part of the *x*-axis, the whole of the region lying within the strip of the plane: $\{(x, y): a \leqslant x \leqslant b, y \geqslant 0\}$ (see Figure 14).

The shape of the region then determines, for each given *x*-coordinate, the width in the direction of the *y*-axis. Thus a function f is established, such that the region under discussion is bounded on the upper side by the graph of the equation $y = f(x)$, on the lower side by the *x*-axis, and to left and right, where necessary, by parts of the lines $x = a$ and $x = b$. The region can be designated symbolically by

$$\{(x, y): a \leqslant x \leqslant b, 0 \leqslant y \leqslant f(x)\}.$$

The area of this region is called the *area under the graph* of $y = f(x)$.

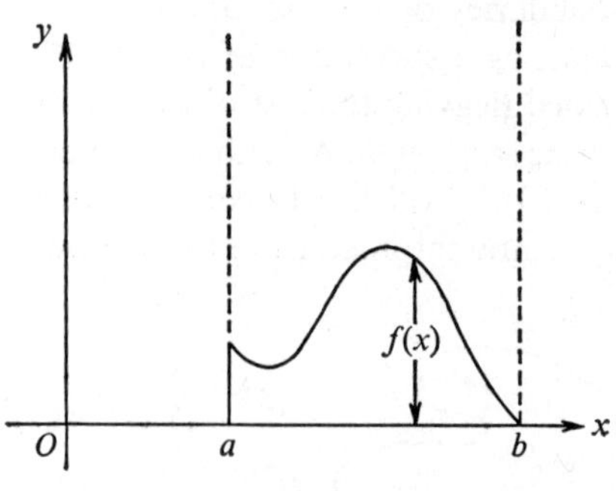

Fig. 14

3.3 The area under the graph of the square function. As an example, we shall apply a method similar to that of Section 2.3 to calculate the area under the graph of $y = x^2$ over the interval $[0, b]$, that is, the set $\{x: 0 \leqslant x \leqslant b\}$. In the course of it, we shall need the formula (established in Chapter 11):

The sum of the squares of the first n integers is $\frac{1}{6}n(n+1)(2n+1)$.

Example 1. Find the area under the graph of $y = x^2$ over the interval $[0, b]$.

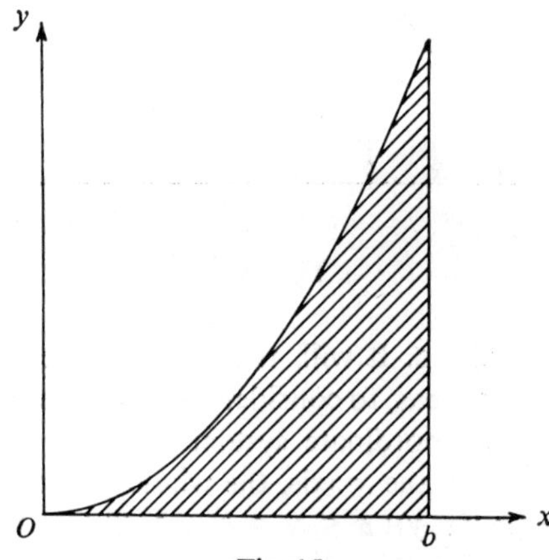

Fig. 15

The region whose area is to be found is illustrated in Figure 15. Our method will be to find two regions bounded by closed polygons, of which one completely surrounds the given region and the other is completely within it. We shall use for this purpose regions composed of a number of rectangular regions, all of width b/N; these are illustrated, for the case $N = 6$, in Figures 16(*a*) and (*b*). Those vertices of the rectangular regions indicated in Figure 16 by small crosses lie on the graph of $y = x^2$, and therefore have coordinates

$$\left(\frac{b}{N}, \frac{b^2}{N^2}\right), \quad \left(\frac{2b}{N}, \frac{4b^2}{N^2}\right), \quad \left(\frac{3b}{N}, \frac{9b^2}{N^2}\right), \text{ etc.}$$

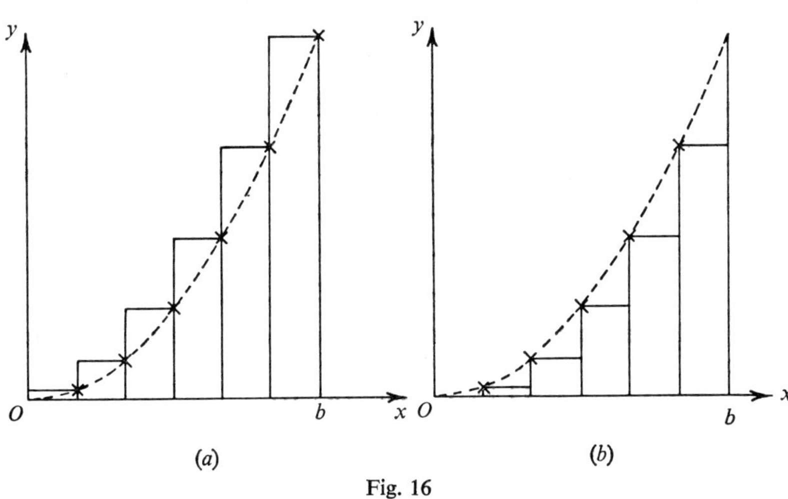

Fig. 16

In Figure 16(*a*), the region is composed of N rectangles, and the total area is:

$$\frac{b}{N}\cdot\frac{b^2}{N^2}+\frac{b}{N}\cdot\frac{4b^2}{N^2}+\frac{b}{N}\cdot\frac{9b^2}{N^2}+\ldots+\frac{b}{N}\cdot\frac{(N-1)^2b^2}{N^2}+\frac{b}{N}\cdot b^2,$$

which can be written as

$$\frac{b^3}{N^3}\cdot(1+4+9+\ldots+(N-1)^2+N^2).$$

Using the result given above, we can write this as

$$\frac{b^3}{N^3}\cdot\frac{1}{6}N(N+1)(2N+1)$$

or

$$\frac{b^3}{6}\left(1+\frac{1}{N}\right)\left(2+\frac{1}{N}\right).$$

This gives an upper bound for the value of the area; whatever the value of N, the area is certainly less than this.

A similar calculation applied to Figure 16(*b*) gives a lower bound. There are now only $(N-1)$ rectangles, and inspection of the figure shows that they are in fact congruent to the first $(N-1)$ rectangles of Figure 16(a). Their area is therefore

$$\frac{b^3}{N^3}.(1+4+9+\ldots+(N-1)^2).$$

Using the result again, with $(N-1)$ written for n, this formula can be simplified to:

$$\frac{b^3}{N^3}.\tfrac{1}{6}(N-1)\{(N-1)+1\}\{2(N-1)+1\}$$

$$=\frac{b^3}{N^3}.\tfrac{1}{6}(N-1)\,N(2N-1)$$

$$=\frac{b^3}{6}.\left(1-\frac{1}{N}\right)\left(2-\frac{1}{N}\right).$$

Whatever the value of N, the area is certainly greater than this.

By giving different values to N, we obtain a sequence of nesting intervals within which the area S must lie. Thus, $N = 10$, $N = 100$, $N = 1000$ give respectively:

$$0{\cdot}285b^3 < S < 0{\cdot}385b^3$$

$$0{\cdot}32835b^3 < S < 0{\cdot}33835b^3$$

$$0{\cdot}3328335b^3 < S < 0{\cdot}3338335b^3.$$

It is easily seen that the only number common to all these intervals is $\frac{1}{3}b^3$. For

$$\left(1+\frac{1}{N}\right) \text{ and } \left(2+\frac{1}{N}\right)$$

are always greater than 1 and 2 respectively, but can be made as close to them as we please, so that their product can be made to exceed 2 by as little as we please. Similarly, the product

$$\left(1-\frac{1}{N}\right)\left(2-\frac{1}{N}\right)$$

can be made to fall short of 2 by as little as we please. The upper and lower bounds for the area therefore both converge on the value $\frac{1}{6}b^3.2$, or $\frac{1}{3}b^3$. It follows that the area under the graph of $y = x^2$ is $\frac{1}{3}b^3$.

3.4 Definite integral—definition and notation. The method used to find the area in Example 1 (which is due, in essence, to Archimedes) can be applied to the areas under a number of other graphs. The difficulty is usually to find a formula, like the one above, by which the sum of the areas of the rectangular regions can be simplified.

From this method we derive an important piece of mathematical notation. In Figure 17 is illustrated one of the rectangular regions whose area forms part of the sum. The height of such a region is equal to the value of the function f for some number in the interval $[a, b]$, which we denote by $f(x)$; the width is a small portion of the x-axis, denoted by δx. The area of the rectangle is then denoted by $f(x).\delta x$, and the sum of all the areas, which makes up the area of one of the bounding regions, is written

$$\underset{x=a}{\overset{x=b}{\mathsf{S}}} f(x).\delta x.$$

In the notation for the area under the curve itself, rather than the bounding rectangular areas, the δx is replaced by dx (since a process of convergence is involved), and the letter S is 'straightened out' into the symbol $\int$, which is known as an 'integral sign'. The final form of the notation is then:

> The area under the graph of $y = f(x)$ over the interval $[a, b]$ is denoted by the symbol
> $$\int_a^b f(x)\, dx.$$

We call this the *definite integral* of the function f over the interval $[a, b]$. The symbol is sometimes abbreviated $\int_a^b f$, for general (or unspecified) functions; it is not, however, correct to write $\int_0^b x^2$.

Thus, the result of Example 1 can be written

$$\int_0^b x^2\, dx = \tfrac{1}{3}b^3.$$

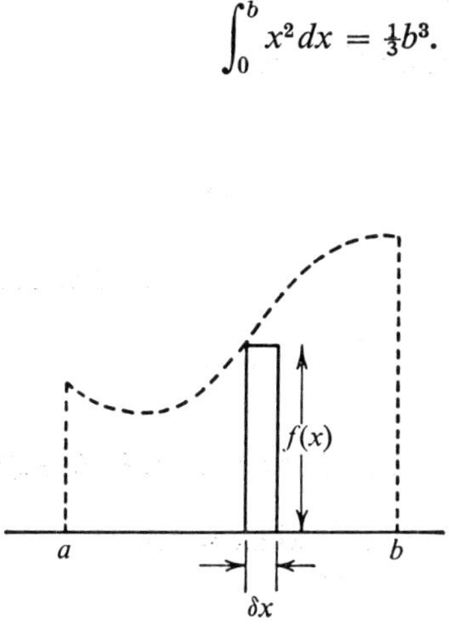

Fig. 17

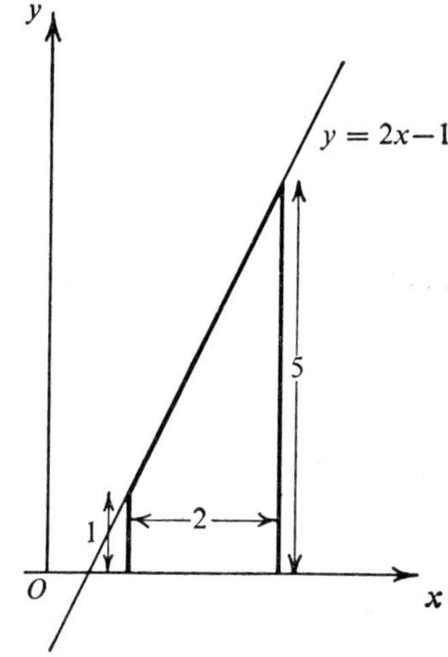

Fig. 18

Example 2. Find the value of

$$\int_1^3 (2x-1)\, dx.$$

Since the function $x \to 2x-1$ is linear, its graph is a straight line. The area required is that of a region bounded by a trapezium, as shown in Figure 18. From the usual formula, the area of this trapezium is $\frac{1}{2}.2.(1+5)$, or 6 units. Therefore

$$\int_1^3 (2x-1)\, dx = 6.$$

Exercise B

1. Draw graphs to illustrate the following definite integrals, and find their values.

(*a*) $\int_1^2 (x+2)\,dx$; (*b*) $\int_1^2 x^2\,dx$;

(*c*) $\int_1^2 |3x-4|\,dx$; (*d*) $\int_1^2 x(x+2)\,dx$.

2. What is the value of $\int_a^b x^2\,dx$?

3. Use the properties of area in Section 1 to establish the following results:

(*a*) $\int_a^b f + \int_b^c f = \int_a^c f$; (*b*) $\int_a^b f + \int_a^b g = \int_a^b (f+g)$.

4. Draw a figure to illustrate $\int_0^c \sqrt{x}\,dx$. Use the result of Example 1, together with the additive property of area, to evaluate this integral.

5. Draw a diagram showing the graph of $y = px+q$, where $pa+q$ and $pb+q$ are both positive; and hence prove that

$$\int_a^b (px+q)\,dx = (\tfrac{1}{2}pb^2+qb)-(\tfrac{1}{2}pa^2+qa).$$

Use another graph to find the value of

$$\int_a^b |px+q|\,dx, \quad \text{if} \quad (pb+q) > 0 > (pa+q).$$

6. Use the method of Example 1 to show that, whatever the value of N,

$$\tfrac{1}{4}b^4\left(1-\frac{1}{N}\right)^2 < \int_0^b x^3\,dx < \tfrac{1}{4}b^4\left(1+\frac{1}{N}\right)^2,$$

and find the value of the integral.

(It was proved in Chapter 11 that the sum of the first n cubes is $\tfrac{1}{4}n^2(n+1)^2$.)

7. Deduce from the result of Question 6 that $\int_0^c x^{\frac{1}{3}}\,dx = \tfrac{3}{4}c^{\frac{4}{3}}$.

8. Use the result (established in Chapter 14) that

$$2\cos\frac{rb}{n}\sin\frac{\frac{1}{2}b}{n} = \sin(r+\tfrac{1}{2})\frac{b}{n} - \sin(r-\tfrac{1}{2})\frac{b}{n}$$

to sum the series $$1+\cos\frac{b}{n}+\cos\frac{2b}{n}+\ldots+\cos\frac{(n-1)b}{n}$$

and $$\cos\frac{b}{n}+\cos\frac{2b}{n}+\ldots+\cos b.$$

Hence prove that $$\int_0^b \cos x\,dx = \sin b.$$

(To simplify the argument, assume that $b < \pi/2$.)

9. Use a method similar to the one suggested in Question 8 to find

$$\int_0^b \sin 2x\,dx.$$

10. A transformation of the form $(x, y) \to (x, ky)$ is called a 'stretch' (if $k > 1$) or a 'squash' (if $k < 1$) of ratio k parallel to the y-axis. What is the effect of such a transformation on the area of a region?

Show that a stretch of ratio b parallel to the y-axis, followed by a squash of ratio $1/b$ parallel to the x-axis, transforms a portion of the graph of $y = 1/x$ into another portion of the same graph.

Deduce that

$$\int_b^{ab} \frac{1}{x}\,dx = \int_1^a \frac{1}{x}\,dx,$$

and hence that

$$\int_1^a \frac{1}{x}\,dx + \int_1^b \frac{1}{x}\,dx = \int_1^{ab} \frac{1}{x}\,dx.$$

What function have you previously encountered for which

$$F(a)+F(b) = F(ab)?$$

4. APPROXIMATE METHODS

In this section we shall approach the problem of finding areas from a slightly different standpoint. Given a region whose area is required, we shall ask whether it is possible to find another region whose area is susceptible to exact calculation and which approximates closely to the area of the given region.

We shall suppose that the region has been transformed into a form similar to that of Figure 14, so that we require to find an approximate value for $\int_a^b f(x)\,dx$.

4.1 Approximation by trapezia. The simplest kind of region for this purpose is one with a polygon as its boundary, with vertices at points of

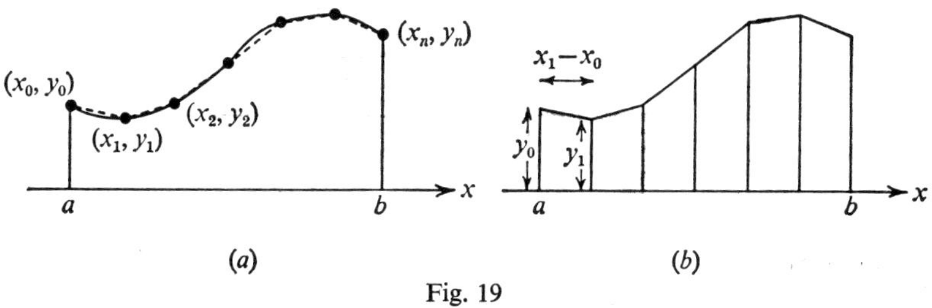

Fig. 19

the graph of $y = f(x)$, as shown in Figure 19(a). The area of this polygonal region is simple to calculate, since it can be seen as the combination of a number of trapezium regions (Figure 19(b)) with sides parallel to the

y-axis. If there are n trapezia in all, it is convenient to denote the vertices by (x_0, y_0), (x_1, y_1), (x_2, y_2), ..., (x_n, y_n), where x_0 and x_n are written for a, b for consistency of notation. The area of the first trapezium region is then $\frac{1}{2}(x_1-x_0)(y_0+y_1)$, and similarly for the others. The total area can be written as

$$\sum_{i=1}^{i=n} \tfrac{1}{2}(x_i-x_{i-1})(y_{i-1}+y_i).$$

This formula is greatly simplified if the vertices are chosen along the curve so that the x-coordinates are evenly spaced. If the spaces are denoted by h, so that $h = (b-a)/n$, the formula for the area becomes

$$\tfrac{1}{2}h(y_0+y_1)+\tfrac{1}{2}h(y_1+y_2)+\ldots+\tfrac{1}{2}h(y_{n-1}+y_n),$$

that is,

$$\boldsymbol{A \approx \tfrac{1}{2}h(y_0+2y_1+2y_2+\ldots+2y_{n-1}+y_n).}$$

This is known as the *Trapezium Rule.*

In applying this formula, it will be found convenient to list the values of y in two columns, and to evaluate the expression in brackets as

$$(y_0+y_n)+2(y_1+y_2+\ldots+y_{n-1}).$$

We then have

$$\int_a^b f(x)\,dx \approx \tfrac{1}{2}h(\text{'ends'}+2\text{ 'middles'}).$$

Example 3. Find an approximate value for

$$\int_0^{\frac{1}{2}\pi} \cos x\,dx.$$

Figure 20(a) shows the area to be evaluated, and Figure 20(b) a polygonal region having vertices at (0, 1), $(\frac{1}{12}\pi, 0{\cdot}966)$, $(\frac{1}{6}\pi, 0{\cdot}866)$, $(\frac{1}{4}\pi, 0{\cdot}707)$, $(\frac{1}{3}\pi, 0{\cdot}500)$, $(\frac{5}{12}\pi, 0{\cdot}259)$, $(\frac{1}{2}\pi, 0)$, which are all on the graph of $y = \cos x$.

The calculation is set out as follows:

	y	
x	Ends	Middles
0	1·000	
$\frac{1}{12}\pi$		0·966
$\frac{1}{6}\pi$		0·866
$\frac{1}{4}\pi$		0·707
$\frac{1}{3}\pi$		0·500
$\frac{5}{12}\pi$		0·259
$\frac{1}{2}\pi$	0·000	
	1·000 × 1	3·298 × 2
	1·000	6·596

The approximate area of the polygonal region is therefore

$$\tfrac{1}{2}\times\tfrac{1}{12}\pi\times(1{\cdot}000+6{\cdot}596) = 0{\cdot}994.$$

It follows that
$$\int_0^{\frac{1}{2}\pi}\cos x\,dx \approx 0{\cdot}994.$$

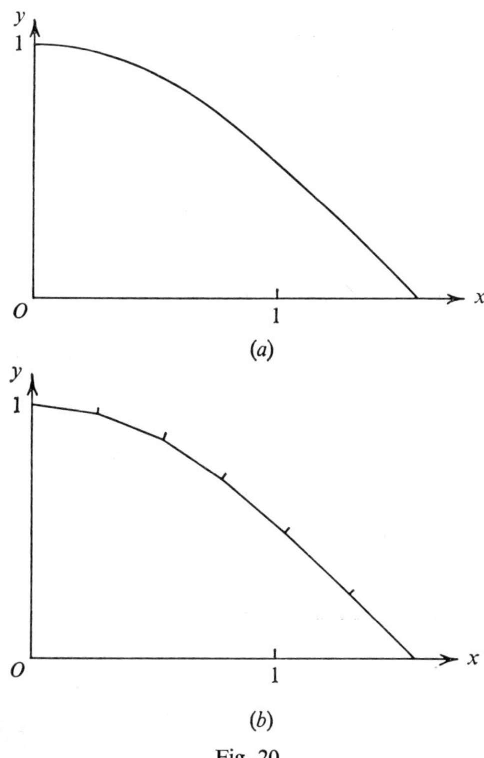

Fig. 20

The result of Exercise B, Question 8 shows that the exact value of this integral is in fact $\sin\frac{1}{2}\pi$, or 1, so that the approximate method gives an answer which is accurate to within 0·6%. It is clear from the shape of the curve that in this example the approximate value is likely to be rather too small.

4.2 Approximation by quadratic trapezia. The drawback of the Trapezium Rule is that it takes no account of the curvature of the graph. To do this, it would be necessary to consider at least three points together, rather than taking pairs of points and joining them with straight lines.

We are therefore led to the problem: given three points (x_0, y_0), (x_1, y_1), (x_2, y_2), to find the area under a curve through these points over the interval $x_0 \leqslant x \leqslant x_2$.

There are many curves through these points, but amongst the simplest is the graph whose equation has the form $y = px^2+qx+r$. Given three points, there is just one set of numbers p, q, r such that the graph passes through the points. We shall call a figure such as Figure 21, where the curve is the unique graph of this kind through the three points, a *quadratic trapezium.*

Our objective in the work which follows is to improve on the approximation described in Section 4.1 by finding a region composed of quadratic trapezia whose area is very close to that of the region whose area is required.

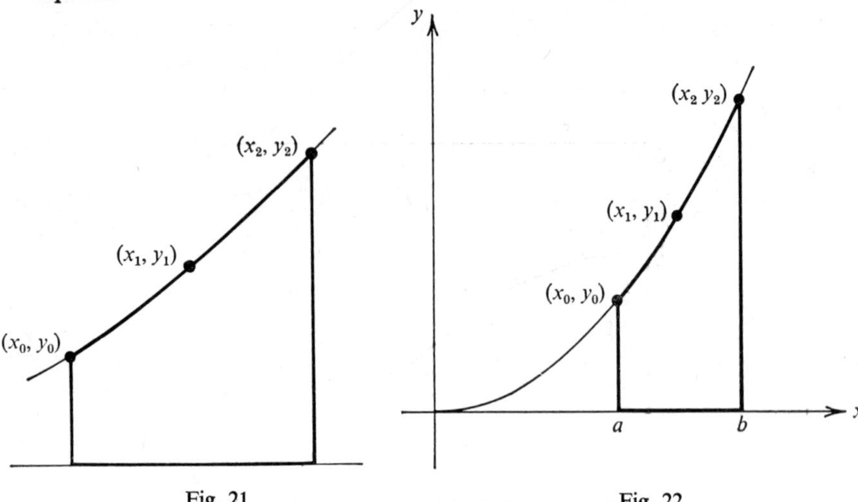

Fig. 21

Fig. 22

4.3 A special quadratic trapezium. Consider first the quadratic trapezium whose boundary consists of parts of the graph of $y = x^2$, the x-axis, and the lines $x = a$ and $x = b$ (Figure 22).

Since

$$\int_0^b x^2\,dx = \tfrac{1}{3}b^3 \quad\text{and}\quad \int_0^a x^2\,dx = \tfrac{1}{3}a^3,$$

it follows from the additive property that

$$\begin{aligned}\int_a^b x^2\,dx &= \tfrac{1}{3}b^3-\tfrac{1}{3}a^3\\ &= \tfrac{1}{3}(b-a)(b^2+ab+a^2)\\ &= \tfrac{1}{6}(b-a)\,\{a^2+(a^2+2ab+b^2)+b^2\}\\ &= \tfrac{1}{6}(b-a)\,\{a^2+(a+b)^2+b^2\}.\end{aligned}$$

We shall now express this result in the notation of Section 4.2. Denote the three points on the graph at the ends and the middle of the interval by

(x_0, y_0), (x_1, y_1) and (x_2, y_2), and write $(x_2-x_1) = (x_1-x_0) = h$. Then, since $x_0 = a$ and $x_2 = b$, we have

$$y_0 = a^2, \quad y_2 = b^2,$$

$$b-a = 2h$$

and
$$x_1 = \frac{a+b}{2},$$

so that
$$(a+b)^2 = 4x_1^2 = 4y_1.$$

The formula for the area above can therefore be re-written in the form

$$\tfrac{1}{6}.2h(y_0+4y_1+y_2) = \tfrac{1}{3}h(y_0+4y_1+y_2).$$

We shall show in the following section that this formula holds for the area of *any* quadratic trapezium. From this we shall derive, in Section 4.5, a practical method of calculating areas (known as Simpson's Rule), which, with only slight increase in the labour of computation, achieves substantially more accurate estimates than the Trapezium Rule.

4.4 Formula for any quadratic trapezium. There are two possible types of quadratic trapezium—'up', when p is positive, and 'down', when p is negative. (We exclude the special case in which the points are collinear,

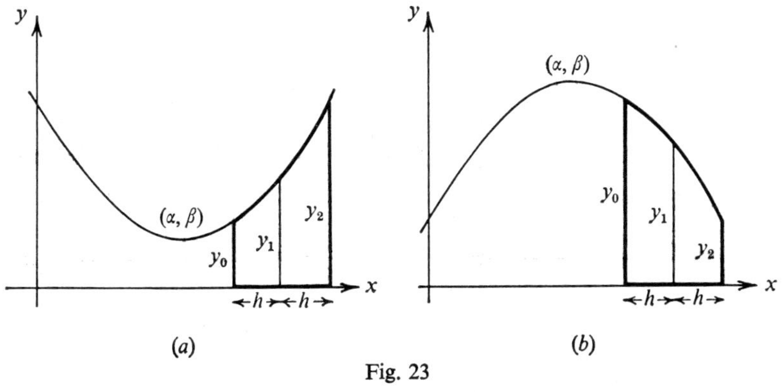

Fig. 23

when $p = 0$; it is easy to show that the formula for the area still holds in this case.) The coordinates of the maximum or minimum on the graph are denoted by (α, β); this is known as the *vertex* of the graph of the parabola. Figure 23 illustrates the two types, with the graph produced beyond the ends of the interval; if α lay between x_0 and x_2, some modification of this work would be needed.

Either of these graphs can be transformed into that of $y = x^2$ by the successive application of three transformations:

(i) A translation of amount α to the left (Figure 24); this maps the vertex onto a point on the y-axis.

(ii) *Either* a translation of amount β downwards (Figure 25(a)), *or* a reflection in the line $y = \frac{1}{2}\beta$ (Figure 25(b)); this maps the vertex onto the origin.

(iii) A stretch or squash parallel to the y-axis (Figure 26).

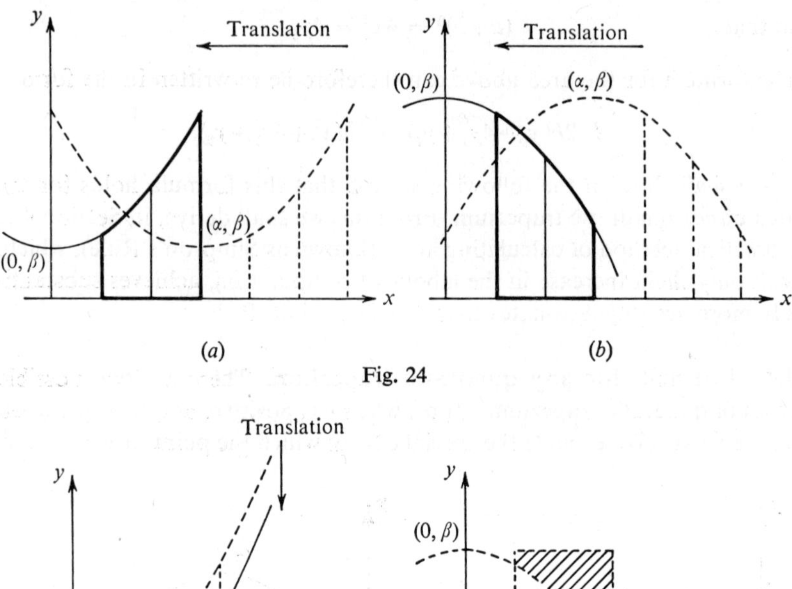

Fig. 24

Fig. 25

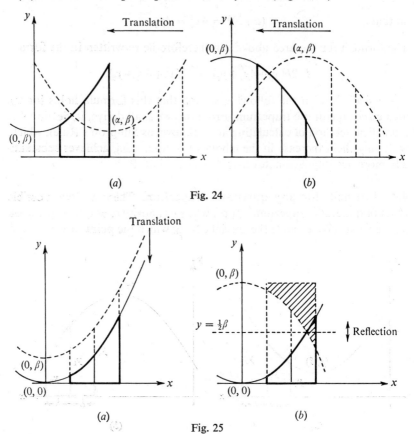

We shall show that each of these transformations has the same effect on the area of the region bounded by the quadratic trapezium as on the value of the formula $\frac{1}{3}h(y_0+4y_1+y_2)$.

(i) This is obvious for the transformation (i), since neither the area nor the values of y_0, y_1, y_2, h are affected by it.

(ii) The effect of the translation in Figure 25(a) is to reduce the region by a rectangle of height β and width $2h$, and so to reduce the area by $2h\beta$.

It also reduces all the values of y by β, and so reduces the expression for the area by $\frac{1}{3}(\beta+4\beta+\beta)h$, that is, by $2h\beta$.

In the case of Figure 25(b), the transformed region is congruent to another (shown shaded in the figure), which makes up with the original rectangle a rectangle of area $2h\beta$. Also, each value of y is replaced by $(\beta-y)$, so that the expression becomes

$$\tfrac{1}{3}h\{(\beta-y_0)+4(\beta-y_1)+(\beta-y_2)\},$$

which is equal to $2h\beta-\frac{1}{3}h(y_0+4y_1+y_2)$. The effect on the area and on the value of the formula is once again the same.

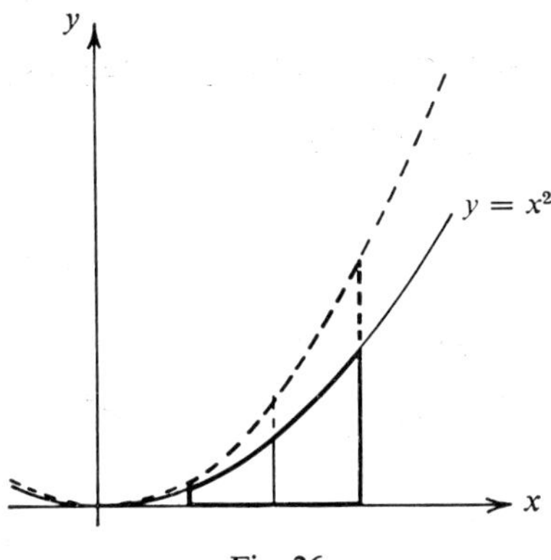

Fig. 26

(iii) A stretch or squash of ratio k multiplies the area by k; and since each value of y is multiplied by k, the value of the formula is also changed in the same way.

It follows, by combining these transformations, that the area of any region bounded by a quadratic trapezium is given by the formula

$$\tfrac{1}{3}h(y_0+4y_1+y_2), \quad \text{where} \quad x_2-x_1 = x_1-x_0 = h.$$

4.5 Simpson's Rule. This result furnishes a better method of approximating to the area of a given region than the result of Section 4.1. As in that section, we take a number of points along the graph of $y = f(x)$. It is now necessary to divide the interval $a \leqslant x \leqslant b$ into an *even* number of intervals, each of length h, so that the number of points taken must be odd. We denote these points by $(x_0, y_0), (x_1, y_1), (x_2, y_2), \ldots, (x_{2n}, y_{2n})$, where x_0 and x_{2n} are written in place of a and b for the sake of uniformity, and $h = (b-a)/2n$.

We then approximate to the area of the region by the sum of the areas of

n regions bounded by quadratic trapezia over the intervals $[x_0, x_2]$, $[x_2, x_4]$, ..., $[x_{2n-2}, x_{2n}]$, as in Figure 27. This gives the value

$$\tfrac{1}{3}h(y_0+4y_1+y_2)+\tfrac{1}{3}h(y_2+4y_3+y_4)+\ldots+\tfrac{1}{3}h(y_{2n-2}+4y_{2n-1}+y_{2n}),$$

which is equal to

$$\tfrac{1}{3}h(y_0+4y_1+2y_2+4y_3+2y_4+\ldots+4y_{2n-1}+y_{2n}).$$

It is convenient for the purpose of calculation to re-arrange the expression in brackets and write

$$A \approx \tfrac{1}{3}h[(y_0+y_{2n})+4(y_1+y_3+\ldots+y_{2n-1})+2(y_2+y_4+\ldots+y_{2n-2})],$$

or, in words,

$$\textbf{Area} \approx \tfrac{1}{3}h(\text{'ends'}+4\times\text{'odds'}+2\times\text{'evens'}).$$

This is known as Simpson's Rule.

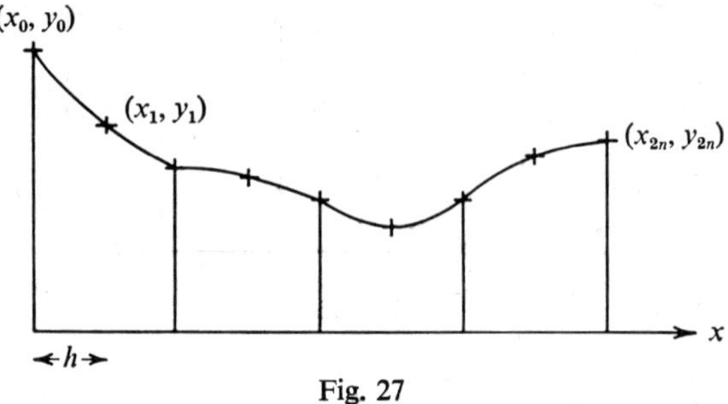

Fig. 27

Example 4. Find a value for the integral of Example 3 by Simpson's Rule.

We now arrange the calculation in three columns:

x	y: Ends	Odds	Evens
0	1·000		
$\frac{1}{12}\pi$		0·966	
$\frac{1}{6}\pi$			0·866
$\frac{1}{4}\pi$		0·707	
$\frac{1}{3}\pi$			0·500
$\frac{5}{12}\pi$		0·259	
$\frac{1}{2}\pi$	0·000		
	1·000	1·932 × 4	1·366 × 2
	1·000	7·728	2·732

Simpson's Rule therefore gives

$$\int_0^{\frac{1}{2}\pi} \cos x \, dx \approx \tfrac{1}{3} \times \tfrac{1}{12}\pi \times (1{\cdot}000 + 7{\cdot}728 + 2{\cdot}732)$$
$$= 1{\cdot}000,$$

which is accurate to three places of decimals.

It is a common mistake to take an odd number of intervals, and to end with '$\ldots + 2y_{2n-1} + y_{2n}$'. This is *always* wrong, as can be seen by considering a linear function, and shows a clear misunderstanding of the nature of the approximation.

It has probably occurred to the reader that it is much harder to find areas under graphs than to find gradients. Simpson's Rule, however, ensures that we can find a value in principle, as accurately as we please, for *any* function we may encounter.

Exercise C

1. Show that the error involved in using the Trapezium Rule to evaluate the area in Example 1 is $b^3/6n^2$, where n is the number of trapezia used.

2. The mean value of a function f over $[a, b]$ is defined as the constant which has the same definite integral over the interval as the function f. Show that the mean value of f is given approximately by the formula

$$\frac{(y_0 + 2y_1 + 2y_2 + \ldots + 2y_{n-1} + y_n)}{2n},$$

where $y_0, y_1, \ldots, y_n$ are the values at equally spaced intervals. What does this give for the mean value of the constant function $f: x \to 1$?

3. Show that Simpson's Rule (with just two intervals, so that $n = 1$) applied to the evaluation of $\int_0^b x^3 \, dx$ gives the answer exactly (see Exercise B, Question 6). Illustrate this result by drawing with the same axes the graphs of $y = x^3$ and of the approximating quadratic function.

4. By applying Simpson's Rule with just two intervals to the integral in Example 4, prove that an approximate value for π is given by

$$\frac{12}{(2\sqrt{2}+1)}.$$

5. Use Simpson's Rule to estimate the value of

$$\int_0^1 \frac{4}{1+x^2} \, dx.$$

(This is in fact another integral whose exact value is π.)

6. Use Simpson's Rule to find approximate values for

$$\int_1^2 \frac{1}{x} \, dx, \quad \int_1^3 \frac{1}{x} \, dx, \quad \text{and} \quad \int_1^6 \frac{1}{x} \, dx.$$

(Use the result of Exercise B, Question 10 as a check on accuracy.)

7. Find the percentage error in using Simpson's Rule with two intervals to obtain an approximate value for $\int_0^c \sqrt{x}\,dx$ (see Exercise B, Question 4). Give a reason why the error in this application is so large.

8. Prove that the graph of $y = \sqrt{(1-x^2)}$ is a semi-circle, and show how to deduce from this that

$$\int_0^{\frac{1}{2}} \sqrt{(1-x^2)}\,dx = \frac{\pi}{12}+\frac{\sqrt{3}}{8}.$$

Hence use Simpson's Rule to find an approximate value for π.

Explain why Simpson's Rule should not be expected to give a good approximation to the area of a quadrant.

9. The function

$$f\colon x \to \frac{1}{\sqrt{2\pi}}\, e^{-\frac{1}{2}x^2},$$

and the area under the graph of f, are very important in the theory of sampling. Estimate $\int_0^1 f(x)\,dx$, given the table of values:

x	0·0	0·1	0·2	0·3	0·4	0·5
$f(x)$	0·399	0·397	0·391	0·381	0·368	0·352

x	0·6	0·7	0·8	0·9	1·0
$f(x)$	0·333	0·312	0·290	0·266	0·242

Can you form an estimate of $\int_{-1}^1 f(x)\,dx$?

10. Use Simpson's Rule to evaluate the area of the region shown in Figure 12 (see Exercise A, Question 5).

11. A marksman firing at a target scatters his shots, and the distribution is described by a 'probability function' p; this associates with each distance r inches from the centre of the target a number $p(r)$ such that the probability of getting within a narrow ring of radius r and thickness δr is $p(r).\delta r$. The table of values for this function is:

r	0	1	2	3	4	5	6	7	8
$p(r)$	0	0·181	0·268	0·244	0·162	0·082	0·033	0·010	0·003

It can be shown that the probability of getting the shot into a ring between two circles of radii a and b centimetres is $\int_a^b p$. Estimate the probability of hitting the target between two circles of radii 3 and 7 cm, and also that of hitting within the 3-cm circle. (For the second part, assume that the function p is linear over [0, 1].)

12. The time taken for an object dropped from a height in an atmosphere producing a resistance proportional to the αth power of the velocity, to reach a fraction k of its terminal velocity is given by the formula

$$t = \frac{u}{g}\int_0^k \frac{1}{1-z^\alpha}\,dz.$$

Obtain from this a numerical formula (in terms of u and g) for the time to reach 0·8 of the terminal velocity: (*a*) if $\alpha = 1$, (*b*) if $\alpha = \frac{3}{2}$, (*c*) if $\alpha = 2$.

13. The periodic time for an oscillating pendulum of length l swinging through an angle α on either side of the vertical is given by the formula:

$$T = 4\sqrt{\left(\frac{l}{g}\right)}\int_0^{\frac{1}{2}\pi}(1-k^2\sin^2\phi)^{-\frac{1}{2}}\,d\phi,$$

where $k = \sin\frac{1}{2}\alpha$. For small angles of swing, the approximate formula

$$T = 2\pi\sqrt{(l/g)}$$

is often used. Estimate the percentage error in using this approximation (*a*) if $\alpha = 6°$, (*b*) if $\alpha = 60°$.

5. EVALUATING INTEGRALS

5.1 Integral functions. In Section 4.3 (Figure 22) we saw that, since we had proved

$$\int_0^b x^2\,dx = \tfrac{1}{3}b^3,$$

the more general result $\int_a^b x^2\,dx = \tfrac{1}{3}b^3-\tfrac{1}{3}a^3$

could be obtained by the additive property.

A similar generalization can be made for the integration of any function f. Suppose that the definite integral of f is known over an interval from L to b, where L is some fixed left-hand boundary. Then for each value of b this integral has a specific value, so that an 'integral function' F is established, which maps the number b onto the integral $\int_L^b f$. We can then write $F(b) = \int_L^b f$; this is illustrated in Figure 28.

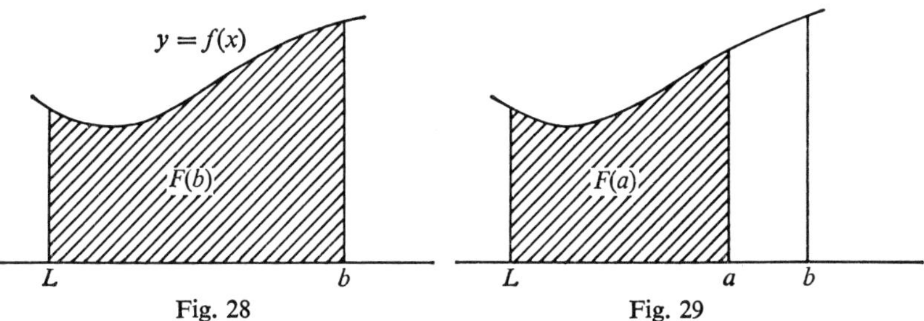

Fig. 28 Fig. 29

For example, if L is taken to be zero, and f is defined by $f: x \to x^2$, then we have seen that $F(b) = \frac{1}{3}b^3$, so that F is defined by $F: x \to \frac{1}{3}x^3$.

In the general case, since

$$F(b) = \int_L^b f \quad\text{and}\quad F(a) = \int_L^a f,$$

it follows at once from the additive property (compare Figures 28 and 29) that

$$\int_a^b f = F(b)-F(a).$$

The expression on the right of this last equation is of sufficiently common occurrence to warrant the introduction of a special notation. We write

$$F(b)-F(a) = \Big[F(x)\Big]_a^b.$$

Thus, the expression $\frac{1}{3}b^3-\frac{1}{3}a^3$ would be written $\Big[\frac{1}{3}x^3\Big]_a^b$, so that

$$\int_a^b x^2\,dx = \Big[\tfrac{1}{3}x^3\Big]_a^b.$$

In the general case, we have similarly

$$\int_a^b f = \Big[F\Big]_a^b,$$

where F is an integral function defined from f.

5.2 The fundamental theorem of analysis. The problem of evaluating definite integrals therefore comes down to the determination of this function F. This has already been done for a number of functions f by special methods, and it will be helpful at this stage to make a list of the results obtained. In these examples the left-hand boundary L has always been zero, but this is not essential.

$f(x)$	$F(x)$	Reference
x^2	$\frac{1}{3}x^3$	Section 3.3, Example 1
$x^{\frac{1}{2}}$	$\frac{2}{3}x^{\frac{3}{2}}$	Exercise B, Question 4
$px+q$	$\frac{1}{2}px^2+qx$	Exercise B, Question 5
x^3	$\frac{1}{4}x^4$	Exercise B, Question 6
$x^{\frac{1}{3}}$	$\frac{3}{4}x^{\frac{4}{3}}$	Exercise B, Question 7
$\cos x$	$\sin x$	Exercise B, Question 8

Careful study of this table will reveal an important relation between the functions f and F: *in each case, f is the derived function of F.*

This result, which is true in general, is fundamental in the theory of integration. It implies that the definite integral of a function f over an interval can be found if we can discover a function F which has f as its derived function. This depends on the following theorem.

The fundamental theorem of analysis. *If f is a continuous function, and a function F is defined by the equation $F(x) = \int_L^x f$ (where L is some fixed left-hand boundary), then $F' = f$.*

We recall that $F'(p)$, the derivative of a function F at a value p of the domain, is defined as the limit of the expression

$$\frac{F(q)-F(p)}{q-p}, \quad \text{as } q \text{ tends to } p.$$

In the present context, we have seen (Section 5.1) that

$$F(q)-F(p) = \int_p^q f,$$

and this measures the area under the graph of $y = f(x)$ from p to q, the shaded region shown in Figure 30.†

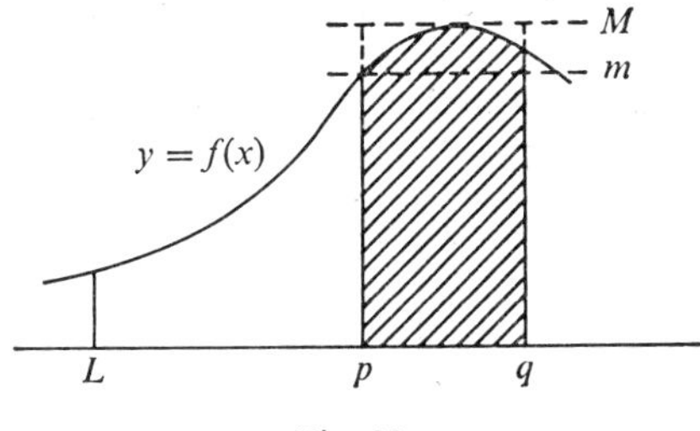

Fig. 30

Suppose now that over this interval the upper and lower bounds of the values of the function f are M and m. Then the region is contained completely within a rectangle of area $M(q-p)$, and lies outside one of area $m(q-p)$, so that

$$m(q-p) \leqslant F(q)-F(p) \leqslant M(q-p).$$

It follows that

$$m \leqslant \frac{F(q)-(Fp)}{q-p} \leqslant M.$$

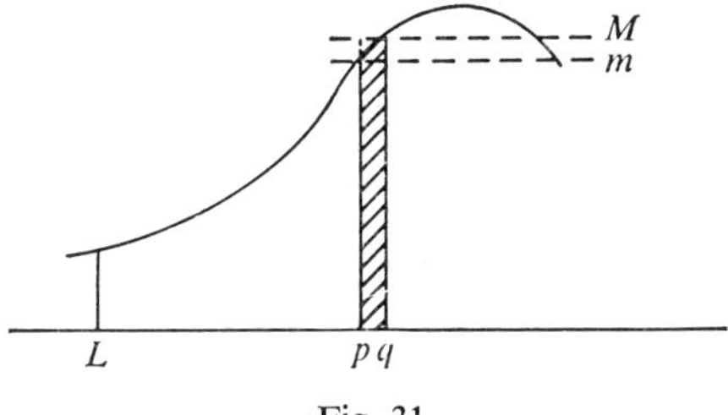

Fig. 31

We now consider the effect of varying q. Figure 31 shows the situation when q is much closer to p than in Figure 30. It is clear that, since f is continuous, M and m must both tend to the value $f(p)$ as q tends to p. It follows that

$$\frac{F(q)-F(p)}{q-p}$$

must also tend to $f(p)$, so that

$$F'(p) = f(p).$$

Since this holds for each separate value of p, we can assert that the functions F' and f are in fact the same.

† The proof which follows is based on the assumption that $q > p$. It is left as an exercise to consider what modifications are needed if $q < p$.

5.3 Application of the theorem. The results of the preceding sections furnish an important method of evaluating integrals, applicable to a large number of functions.

If the value of $\int_a^b f$ is required, we first look for a function F which has f for its derived function.† The value of the integral is then given by $\Big[F\Big]_a^b$.

Example 5. Find the area under the graph of $y = 1/(1+x^2)$ over the interval [1, 2] (see Figure 32).

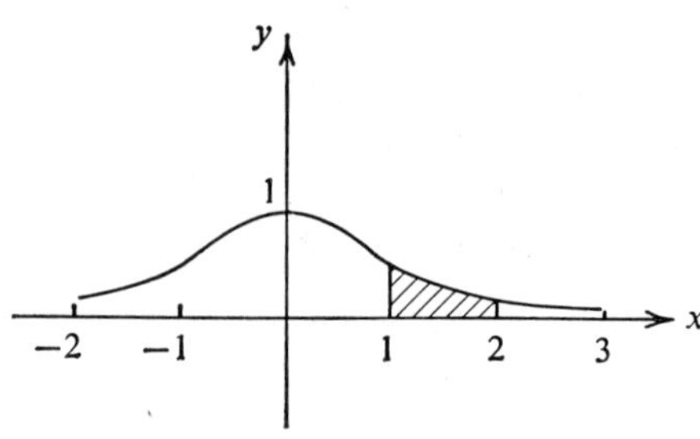

Fig. 32

We require to calculate $\displaystyle\int_1^2 \frac{1}{1+x^2}\,dx.$

It was shown in Chapter 17 that

$$\frac{d}{dx}(\tan^{-1} x) = \frac{1}{1+x^2},$$

so that the function F defined by the formula $F(x) = \tan^{-1} x$ will serve the purpose. The value of the integral is therefore

$$\Big[\tan^{-1} x\Big]_1^2$$

$$= \tan^{-1} 2 - \tan^{-1} 1$$

$$= 1{\cdot}107 - 0{\cdot}785$$

$$= 0{\cdot}322.$$

The area is therefore 0·322 units.

5.4 Indefinite integrals. It should be remarked that in Example 5 the function $\tan^{-1}$ is not the only one with the required property. For example, the function F_1 defined by

$$F_1(x) = 5 + \tan^{-1} x$$

† We have not, strictly, proved that $\int_a^b F' = F(b) - F(a)$, and this cannot be done until Rolle's Theorem has been established.

also has this property; and clearly any number k could be written in place of 5.

Any function F whose derived function is f is called a *primitive* or an *indefinite integral* of f. The notation used to describe this relationship is

$$\int f(x)\,dx = F(x),$$

which may be abbreviated to $\int f = F.$

Thus, we may write

$$\int \frac{1}{1+x^2}\,dx = k+\tan^{-1} x,$$

whatever numerical value is assigned to k.

This ambiguity in specifying the primitive of a function is linked with the fact that, in the theorem of 5.2, the integral function was assigned an arbitrary left-hand boundary L. By giving different values to L, we obtain different integral functions F, all of which have the property that $F' = f$.

In evaluating a definite integral, it is immaterial which of the primitives is used. In Example 5, had we taken for F the function defined by

$$F(x) = k+\tan^{-1} x,$$

our rule would have given for the area the value

$$\begin{aligned}\Big[k+\tan^{-1} x\Big]_1^2 & \\ &= (k+\tan^{-1} 2)-(k+\tan^{-1} 1)\\ &= \tan^{-1} 2-\tan^{-1} 1,\end{aligned}$$

as in the previous calculation.

Thus, the value of $\int_a^b f$ is given by $\Big[F\Big]_a^b$, where F is *any* primitive of f. In practice, we normally choose the primitive with the simplest formula.

Exercise D

1. Write out in full:

(*a*) $\Big[\tfrac{4}{3}\pi x^3\Big]_r^R$; (*b*) $\Big[\frac{1}{x}\Big]_a^b - \Big[\frac{1}{x}\Big]_c^b$; (*c*) $\Big[x^2-3x\Big]_1^2$; (*d*) $\Big[\mathbf{r}\Big]_{\mathbf{r}_2}^{\mathbf{r}_1}$,

where $\mathbf{r}$, $\mathbf{r}_1$, $\mathbf{r}_2$ are vectors in three dimensions.

2. Use the notation of Section 5.1 to write

(*a*) $\pi R_2^2-\pi R_1^2$; (*b*) $1-\dfrac{1}{n+1}$;

(*c*) The rise in the temperature $\theta(t)$ of a body from time t_1 to time t_2;

(*d*) The displacement from the point $(x_1, 0)$ to $(x_2, 0)$.

3. Use the results obtained in Chapters 7 and 17 to evaluate the following definite integrals; in each case check the reasonableness of your answer by drawing a graph and examining the corresponding area.

(*a*) $\int_1^2 x^3\,dx$; (*b*) $\int_{-1}^{+1} x^4\,dx$; (*c*) $\int_0^2 (4-x^2)\,dx$;

(*d*) $\int_0^{\frac{1}{3}\pi} \sin x\,dx$; (*e*) $\int_0^{\frac{1}{8}\pi} 2\cos 2x\,dx$; (*f*) $\int_1^2 \frac{1}{x^2}\,dx$;

(*g*) $\int_1^2 \frac{1}{x^3}\,dx$; (*h*) $\int_1^2 x^{\frac{1}{3}}\,dx$; (*i*) $\int_0^{\frac{1}{2}\pi} 4\sin x\cos^3 x\,dx$.

(*Hint*. What is $d(\cos^n x)/dx$?)

4. Evaluate:

(*a*) $\int_{-2}^{2} (x^3+3x)\,dx$; (*b*) $\int_1^2 (x-1)(x-2)\,dx$;

(*c*) $\int_0^{\frac{1}{4}\pi} (\cos x - \sin x)\,dx$; (*d*) $\int_0^{\pi} \sin \tfrac{1}{2}x\,dx$;

(*e*) $\int_{-\frac{1}{2}\pi}^{\frac{1}{2}\pi} 4\sin x\cos^2 x\,dx$; (*f*) $\int_0^{\frac{1}{2}\pi} \cos^3 x\,dx$.

5. What is the area under the graph of $y = x^m$ over the interval $0 \leqslant x \leqslant a$, where m is a positive rational number? Why is it necessary to include the condition that m is (*a*) positive, (*b*) rational?

6. Write down the derived function of $x \to x\cos x$ and of $x \to x \sin x$.
Find the values of

$$\int_0^{\frac{1}{4}\pi} (x\cos x + \sin x)\,dx \quad \text{and of} \quad \int_0^{\frac{1}{4}\pi} \sin x\,dx,$$

and deduce the value of
$$\int_0^{\frac{1}{4}\pi} x\cos x\,dx.$$

Find by a similar method the value of

$$\int_0^{\frac{1}{4}\pi} x\sin x\,dx.$$

7. We know that the derivative of $\sin^2 x$ is $2\sin x\cos x$, and that of $\cos^2 x$ is $-2\sin x\cos x$. Moreover, the derivative of $\cos 2x$ is

$$-2\sin 2x = -4\sin x\cos x.$$

Does it follow from this that the indefinite integral of the function defined by $f(x) = 2\sin x\cos x$ can be given as any one of: $\sin^2 x$, $-\cos^2 x$, or $-\frac{1}{2}\cos 2x$? If so, does this imply that the three expressions are equal to one another?

8. Write expressions for:

(*a*) $\int \cos x\,dx$; (*b*) $\int x^m\,dx$ (where $m \neq -1$);

(*c*) $\int \frac{1}{(x+1)^2}\,dx$; (*d*) $\int \cos ax\,dx$ (where $a \neq 0$);

(*e*) $\int (ax^2+2bx+c)\,dx$; (*f*) $\int (1/x^m)\,dx$.

9. By considering the area represented by $\int_0^a \sqrt{(1-x^2)}\, dx$, find the indefinite integral $\int \sqrt{(1-x^2)}\, dx$. Check your answer by differentiation.

10. The definite integrals of functions over a given interval $a \leqslant x \leqslant b$ satisfy the *linear relations*

$$\int_a^b f + \int_a^b g = \int_a^b (f+g) \quad \text{and} \quad \int_a^b kf = k\int_a^b f.$$

Does the indefinite integral $\int f$ have the same property? If not, can you make a more precise statement along these lines which is true?

What other examples of these linear relations have you met before?

6. SOME GENERALIZATIONS

So far, the definite integral $\int_a^b f$ has been defined only when $a < b$ and when f is positive and bounded over the interval $[a, b]$. It is convenient to extend the definition to cover other cases, and we now consider a generalization to integrals for which $a \geqslant b$, for functions with negative values over the interval, and for certain regions which are unbounded.

6.1 The integral $\int_a^b f$ when $a \geqslant b$. The extension to the case $a \geqslant b$ is effected by making use of the result of Exercise B, Question 3(a), and supposing this holds when a, b and c are not related so that $a < b < c$.

First, substitution of $b = a$ in the equation

$$\int_a^b f + \int_b^c f = \int_a^c f \quad \text{gives} \quad \int_a^a f + \int_a^c f = \int_a^c f,$$

which suggests that we define

$$\int_a^a f = 0.$$

Then, substitution of $c = a$ in the same equation gives

$$\int_a^b f + \int_b^a f = \int_a^a f,$$

which suggests that

$$\int_a^b f = -\int_b^a f.$$

Now, if $a > b$, the definite integral on the right has a well-understood meaning. We use this equation to *define* $\int_a^b f$ when $a > b$.

6.2 The integral $\int_a^b f$ when f takes negative values. A similar method can be used to define the integral of a function which has negative values over the interval of integration. We now make use of the result of Exercise B, Question 3(*b*).

Substitution of the zero function for g in the equation

$$\int_a^b f + \int_a^b g = \int_a^b (f+g) \quad \text{gives} \quad \int_a^b f + \int_a^b 0 = \int_a^b f,$$

which suggests that we define $\int_a^b 0 = 0.$

We next substitute the function $(-f)$ for g in the same equation and obtain

$$\int_a^b f + \int_a^b (-f) = \int_a^b 0,$$

which suggests that
$$\int_a^b f = -\int_a^b (-f).$$

Now, if the function f has negative values over the interval, $(-f)$ has positive values, so that the integral on the right side of this equation is meaningful. We therefore use this equation to *define* $\int_a^b f$ when the values of f over the interval are negative.

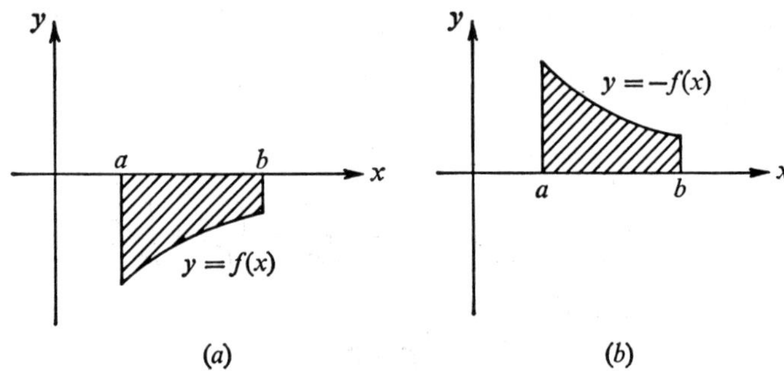

Fig. 33

The geometrical significance of this result is illustrated in Figure 33. The graph of $y = -f(x)$ is the reflection in the x-axis of the graph of $y = f(x)$, and the areas of the regions shown in Figure 33(*a*) and Figure 33(*b*) are clearly equal. It follows that

$$\int_a^b f = -\int_a^b (-f),$$

so that the integral measures *minus* the area bounded by parts of the graph $y = f(x)$, the x-axis, and the lines $x = a$ and $x = b$.

If the function f has a primitive F, so that $F' = f$, then we know that $(-F)' = (-f)$, so that $-f$ has a primitive $-F$. Therefore

$$\begin{aligned}\int_a^b f &= -\int_a^b (-f) = -\Big[(-F)\Big]_a^b \\ &= -\{-F(b)+F(a)\} = F(b)-F(a) \\ &= \Big[F\Big]_a^b.\end{aligned}$$

This shows that the evaluation of the integral by means of the primitive is still valid as it was seen to be when the function took positive values.

Example 6. Evaluate the definite integral $\int_0^3 (x^2-2x)\,dx$, and interpret the result by means of a diagram.

A primitive for the function to be integrated is given by

$$F(x) = \tfrac{1}{3}x^3 - x^2,$$

so that formal evaluation gives

$$\begin{aligned}\int_0^3 (x^2-2x)\,dx = \Big[\tfrac{1}{3}x^3-x^2\Big]_0^3 &= (9-9)-(0-0) \\ &= 0.\end{aligned}$$

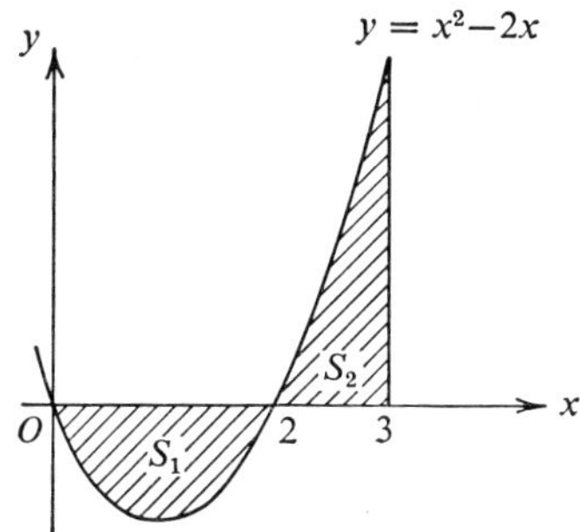

Fig. 34

The graph of the equation $y = x^2-2x$ is shown in Figure 34. It crosses the x-axis at $x = 2$, and so makes two regions over the relevant interval, whose areas are denoted by S_1 and S_2.

For the first region, we have shown that the definite integral over the interval gives the value of $-S_1$:

$$\begin{aligned}-S_1 &= \int_0^2 (x^2-2x)\,dx = \Big[\tfrac{1}{3}x^3-x^2\Big]_0^2 \\ &= (2\tfrac{2}{3}-4)-(0-0) = -1\tfrac{1}{3},\end{aligned}$$

so that $$S_1 = 1\tfrac{1}{3}.$$

For the second region, since the values of f over the interval are positive,

$$S_2 = \int_2^3 (x^2-2x)\,dx = \left[\tfrac{1}{3}x^3-x^2\right]_2^3$$
$$= (9-9)-(2\tfrac{2}{3}-4) = 1\tfrac{1}{3}.$$

Thus the areas S_1 and S_2 are equal. The definite integral from 0 to 3 measures the sum $(-S_1)+S_2$, and this is zero.

6.3 Unbounded regions. A further generalization which is sometimes possible is to regions whose extent is unbounded, either because the interval over which the integral is taken is allowed to be infinite, or because the set of values of the function over the interval is unbounded. These situations are most easily described by means of examples.

Example 7. Find the area under the graph of $y = 1/x^2$ over the interval $[1, N]$, and consider the result of the allowing N to tend to infinity.

The area required is

$$\int_1^N x^{-2}\,dx = \left[-x^{-1}\right]_1^N$$
$$= \left(-\frac{1}{N}\right)-(-1) = 1-\frac{1}{N}.$$

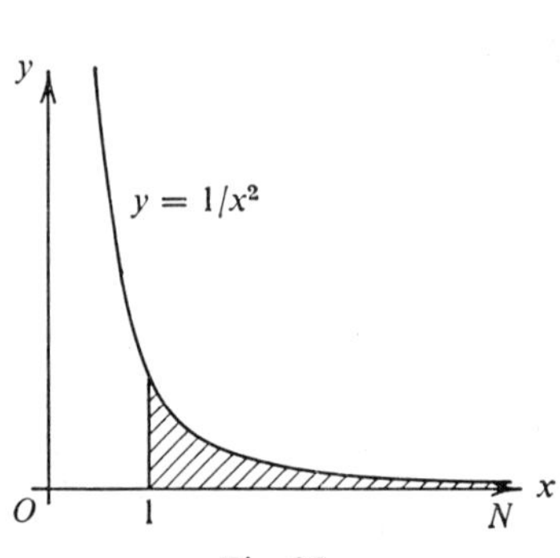

Fig. 35

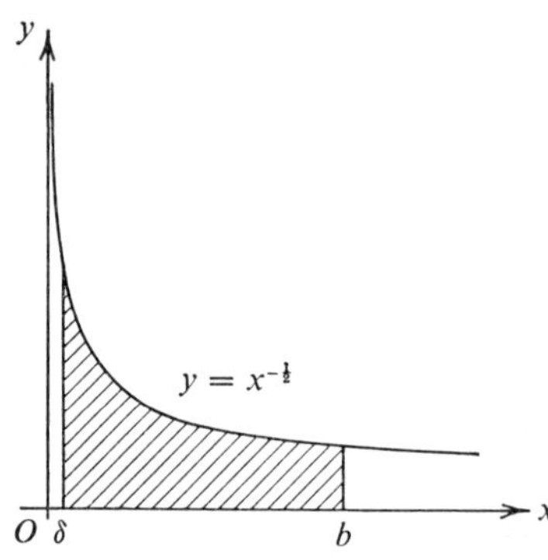

Fig. 36

We observe that, however large the value of N, this area is always less than 1; but that it can be made as close to 1 as we please by the choice of a large enough value of N. Thus, as N tends to infinity, the area tends to 1. The region is depicted in Figure 35.

We write this result in the form

$$\int_1^\infty x^{-2}\,dx = 1.$$

Example 8. Find the area under the graph of $y = x^{-\frac{1}{2}}$ over the interval $[\delta, b]$, and consider the result of allowing δ to tend to zero.

The graph is shown in Figure 36, and the area under the graph is

$$\int_\delta^b x^{-\frac{1}{2}}\,dx = \Big[2x^{\frac{1}{2}}\Big]_\delta^b$$
$$= 2\sqrt{b}-2\sqrt{\delta}.$$

This area is always less than $2\sqrt{b}$; but by making δ sufficiently small we may find an interval over which the value of the integral is as close to $2\sqrt{b}$ as we please, so that it tends to $2\sqrt{b}$ as δ tends to zero.

We write this in the form

$$\int_0^b x^{-\frac{1}{2}}\,dx = 2\sqrt{b}.$$

The notation $\int_a^\infty f$ is used only when the value of $\int_a^b f$ has a limit as b tends to infinity; and the definite integral is then defined to be the value of this limit.

Definition. $\int_a^\infty f = \lim_{b\to\infty} \int_a^b f$, provided this limit exists.

Similarly, if f tends to infinity at a, but $\int_{a+\delta}^b f$ tends to a limit as δ tends to zero through positive values, then we write the value of this limit as $\int_a^b f$.

Exercise E

1. Evaluate the following definite integrals, and interpret their meaning with the aid of graphs;

(*a*) $\int_0^1 (x^3-x)\,dx$; (*b*) $\int_0^\pi \cos x\,dx$; (*c*) $\int_{-2}^2 (x^2-3)\,dx$;

(*d*) $\int_0^{-\frac{1}{2}\pi} \sin x\,dx$; (*e*) $\int_{-2}^{-3} x\,dx$; (*f*) $\int_{-2}^{-3} \frac{1}{x^2}\,dx$.

2. Prove that

$$\int_a^b f = \int_b^a (-f).$$

3. What is the connection between

$$\int_{-1}^{-2} \frac{1}{x}\,dx \quad\text{and}\quad \int_1^2 \frac{1}{x}\,dx?$$

4. For what values of m can a meaning be given to

(*a*) $\int_1^\infty x^{-m}\,dx$; (*b*) $\int_0^1 x^{-m}\,dx$?

5. Find a meaning for

$$\int_{-\infty}^{+\infty} \frac{1}{1+x^2}\,dx,$$

and illustrate your answer with the aid of a graph.

6. Repeat Question 5 for the integral

$$\int_{-1}^{+1} \frac{1}{\sqrt{(1-x^2)}}\,dx.$$

7. By considering the effect of letting a tend to infinity in the last equation of Exercise B, Question 10, prove that no meaning can be attached to the integral

$$\int_1^\infty \frac{1}{x}\,dx.$$

Miscellaneous Exercise

1. If f and g are two functions such that

$$x \in [a, b] \Rightarrow f(x) \leqslant g(x),$$

show that

$$\int_a^b f \leqslant \int_a^b g.$$

Deduce that, if α is between 0 and $\frac{1}{2}\pi$,

$$\sin\alpha < \int_0^\alpha \frac{\sin x}{x}\,dx < \alpha.$$

(You may assume that, if $0 < x < \frac{1}{2}\pi$, then $0 < \sin x < x$.)

2. Use the fact that $(1+x^2)(1-x^2) \leqslant 1$ to prove that $\tan^{-1} 0{\cdot}1$ lies between $0{\cdot}0996$ and $0{\cdot}1$.

Use a similar method to obtain bounds within which the value of

$$\int_0^{0\cdot1} \frac{1}{1+x}\,dx$$

must lie.

3. If f is a function for which $\int_a^\infty f$ has a meaning, and if g is an integrable function such that $x > a \Rightarrow 0 < g(x) < f(x)$, show that $\int_a^\infty g$ has a meaning.

Deduce that $\int_1^\infty (1+x^2)^{-\frac{2}{3}}\,dx$ has a meaning, and find bounds within which its value must lie.

4. Two boys were discussing the formula used in Simpson's Rule. One said he thought it was $\frac{1}{3}h(y_0+3y_1+y_2)$, the other $\frac{1}{4}h(y_0+4y_1+y_2)$. Why are both these formulae obviously wrong?

5. If α lies between 0 and $\frac{1}{2}\pi$, explain why

$$0 < x < \alpha \Rightarrow \frac{\sin\alpha}{\alpha}x < \sin x < x.$$

Use this result to prove that $\int_0^\alpha \sqrt{(\csc x)}\,dx$ has a meaning, and give bounds within which this integral lies.

By choosing a suitable small value for α (a convenient choice would be $\frac{1}{18}\pi$), and using Simpson's Rule to find an approximate value for the integral over the interval $\alpha \leqslant x \leqslant \frac{1}{2}\pi$, estimate the value of $\int_0^{\frac{1}{2}\pi} \sqrt{(\csc x)}\,dx$.

6. If f is an odd function, prove that $\int_{-a}^{a} f = 0$. By applying this to the function defined by $f(x) = k(x^3 - a^2x)$, and applying a suitable transformation, prove that, if $x_2 - x_1 = x_1 - x_0$,

$$\int_{x_0}^{x_2} k(x-x_0)(x-x_1)(x-x_2)\,dx = 0.$$

Hence show that if Simpson's Rule is applied to evaluate the integral of any cubic function, the result obtained is exact.

7. Suggest ways of extending the definition of $\int_a^b f$ to include some functions which are not continuous over the relevant interval.

23

TECHNIQUES OF INTEGRATION

1. NOTATION

It is convenient to begin by collecting together here some of the results obtained in previous chapters, and by recalling some of the notation that we use.

We frequently describe a function by a single letter, such as f, say. Some functions can be specified by an algebraic formula; for example, the square function can be written as

$$f: x \to x^2.$$

Every member of the domain of the function has just one image, denoted by $f(x)$. We often refer to this image by a single letter, such as y, especially in applications; the function is then described by an equation, such as

$$y = x^2.$$

There is not always an inverse function, unless we restrict the domain of the original function; for instance, if $y = x^2$, we have to specify which of the two possible values of x is to correspond to a particular positive value of y.

If the ratio

$$\frac{f(x)-f(a)}{x-a}$$

has a limit as x tends to a, we call this limit the derivative of f at a. It is written $f'(a)$. For the set of points of the domain at which the derivative exists, a new function is defined, mapping each number a onto its derivative $f'(a)$; this is the derived function

$$f': x \to f'(x).$$

If $f(x)$ is replaced by the single letter y, then $f'(x)$ can be written as dy/dx. Thus, we may write that the derived function of

$$f: x \to x^2$$

is

$$f': x \to 2x;$$

or that

$$y = x^2 \Rightarrow \frac{dy}{dx} = 2x.$$

Two results which allow us to differentiate (that is, to find the derived functions of) combinations of previously differentiated functions are:

(*a*) the *Chain Rule*: $\quad (fg)' = (f'g) \cdot g'$,

or
$$\frac{dy}{dx} = \frac{dy}{du} \times \frac{du}{dx}.$$

This is best illustrated by Figure 1, in which we use the alternative phrase 'local scale factor' (L.S.F.) for the derivative, to remind ourselves how the result was reached.

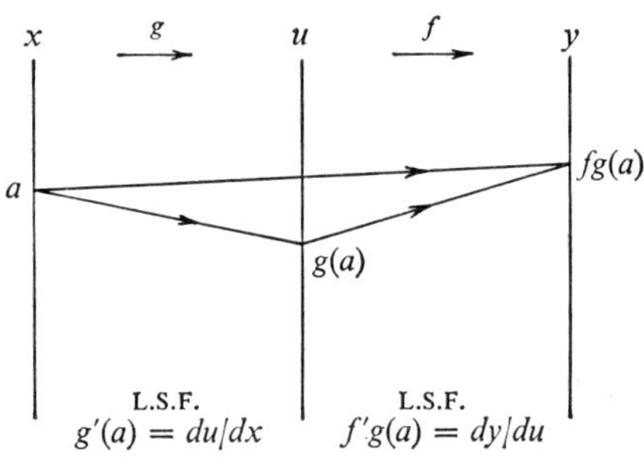

Fig. 1

(*b*) the *Product Rule*:
$$(f.g)' = f.g' + f'.g,$$

or
$$\frac{d}{dx}(uv) = u\frac{dv}{dx} + v\frac{du}{dx}.$$

The area under the graph of $y = f(x)$ over $[a, b]$ (that is, the set of points $\{x: a \leqslant x \leqslant b\}$) is denoted by $\int_a^b f(x)\,dx$. If F is any function such that $F' = f$, then
$$\int_a^b f(x)\,dx = \Big[F(x)\Big]_a^b = F(b) - F(a).$$

All such functions F differ from each other only by a constant. We use the notation
$$F = \int f,$$

or
$$F(x) = \int f(x)\,dx$$

to describe this relationship between the functions F and f.

We say that an indefinite integral of
$$f: x \to x^2$$

is
$$\int f: x \to \tfrac{1}{3}x^3 + c,$$

or that
$$\int x^2\,dx = \tfrac{1}{3}x^3 + c.$$

Exercise A

1. Find the derived functions of:

(*a*) $f\colon x \to x^5$; (*b*) $f\colon x \to (2x-1)^3$;

(*c*) $f\colon x \to \dfrac{1}{\sqrt{(3x+2)}}$; (*d*) $f\colon x \to (x^2+1)^3$;

(*e*) $f\colon x \to (3x^5-4)^4$; (*f*) $f\colon x \to x^2+\sin 2x$;

(*g*) $f\colon x \to \sin^3 x$; (*h*) $f\colon x \to \tan(\tfrac{1}{2}x+\tfrac{1}{4}\pi)$.

2. Find indefinite integrals of:

(*a*) $f\colon x \to x^5$; (*b*) $f\colon x \to 2(2x-1)^2$;

(*c*) $f\colon x \to \dfrac{1}{\sqrt{(3x+2)^3}}$; (*d*) $f\colon x \to 2x(x^2+1)^3$;

(*e*) $f\colon x \to x^4(3x^5-4)^3$; (*f*) $f\colon x \to x+\cos 2x$;

(*g*) $f\colon x \to \sin^2 x \cos x$; (*h*) $f\colon x \to \sec^2(\tfrac{1}{2}x+\tfrac{1}{4}\pi)$.

3. Find dy/dx when:

(*a*) $y = x^{\frac{2}{3}}$; (*b*) $y = x^{-\frac{1}{2}}$;

(*c*) $y = \sqrt{(ax+b)}$; (*d*) $y = \sqrt{(ax^2+bx+c)}$;

(*e*) $y = \cos^2 3x$; (*f*) $y = \dfrac{1}{1+x^2}$;

(*g*) $y = \sqrt{(4-x^2)}$; (*h*) $y = (x^3-3x+1)^5$.

4. Evaluate:

(*a*) $\int x^{\frac{1}{2}}\,dx$; (*b*) $\int x^{-\frac{2}{3}}\,dx$;

(*c*) $\int (x-1)^{\frac{1}{4}}\,dx$; (*d*) $\int x\sqrt{(x^2+1)}\,dx$;

(*e*) $\int \sin 3x \cos^2 3x\,dx$; (*f*) $\displaystyle\int \frac{x}{(1+x^2)^2}\,dx$;

(*g*) $\int (2x+3)(x^2+3x)^3\,dx$; (*h*) $\int 2x\cos(x^2)\,dx$.

5. We know that $y = (2x+1)^3 \Rightarrow \dfrac{dy}{dx} = 6(2x+1)^2$.

Does it follow that $\int (2x+1)^2\,dx = \tfrac{1}{6}(2x+1)^3+c$? Why?

We also know that $y = (x^2+1)^3 \Rightarrow \dfrac{dy}{dx} = 6x(x^2+1)^2$.

Does it follow that: $\displaystyle\int (x^2+1)^2\,dx = \frac{1}{6x}(x^2+1)^3+c$? Why?

6. Evaluate:

(*a*) $\int_0^4 x^{-\frac{1}{2}}\,dx$; (*b*) $\int_0^{0\cdot 3} x(1-x^2)^2\,dx$;

(*c*) $\int_0^3 x\sqrt{(x^2+16)}\,dx$; (*d*) $\int_0^{\frac{1}{2}\pi} \sin x\cos^3 x\,dx$;

(*e*) $\int_0^{\frac{1}{4}} (4x+1)^3\,dx$; (*f*) $\int_{-\pi}^{\pi} \sin^2 2x\cos 2x\,dx$;

(*g*) $\int_{1\cdot 25}^{2\cdot 60} x(x^2-1)^{-\frac{1}{2}}\,dx$; (*h*) $\int_0^{0\cdot 6} \dfrac{x}{\sqrt{(1-x^2)^3}}\,dx$.

2. SOME USEFUL DEVICES

2.1 Use of algebraic identities. Examples 1 and 2 illustrate how an algebraic formula may sometimes be manipulated so that the integral of the corresponding function can be seen immediately.

Example 1. Integrate $\dfrac{x+1}{x^3}$.

Since $$\frac{x+1}{x^3} = \frac{1}{x^2}+\frac{1}{x^3},$$

$$\int \frac{x+1}{x^3}\,dx = \int\left(\frac{1}{x^2}+\frac{1}{x^3}\right)dx$$
$$= -\frac{1}{x}-\frac{1}{2x^2}+c.$$

Example 2. Evaluate $\int_0^4 x\sqrt{(2x+1)}\,dx$.

Since $$x = \tfrac{1}{2}(2x+1)-\tfrac{1}{2},$$

$$\int_0^4 x\sqrt{(2x+1)}\,dx = \int_0^4 \{\tfrac{1}{2}(2x+1)^{\frac{3}{2}}-\tfrac{1}{2}(2x+1)^{\frac{1}{2}}\}\,dx$$
$$= \left[\tfrac{1}{10}(2x+1)^{\frac{5}{2}}-\tfrac{1}{6}(2x+1)^{\frac{3}{2}}\right]_0^4$$
$$= (\tfrac{1}{10}.3^5-\tfrac{1}{6}.3^3)-(\tfrac{1}{10}.1^5-\tfrac{1}{6}1^3)$$
$$= 24\tfrac{1}{5}-4\tfrac{1}{3} = 19\tfrac{13}{15}.$$

2.2 Use of trigonometrical identities. Sums are easy to integrate, but products are not. The next two examples illustrate the use of trigonometrical identities established in Chapter 14, which convert products of trigonometrical functions into sums.

Example 3. Evaluate $\int \sin^2 x\, dx$.

Since
$$\sin^2 x = \tfrac{1}{2}(1-\cos 2x),$$
$$\int \sin^2 x\, dx = \int \tfrac{1}{2}(1-\cos 2x)\, dx$$
$$= \tfrac{1}{2}x - \tfrac{1}{4}\sin 2x + c,$$
or
$$\boldsymbol{\int \sin^2 x\, dx = \tfrac{1}{2}(x-\sin x \cos x + c).}$$
$\int \cos^2 x\, dx$ may be found in the same way, or by use of the identity
$$\sin^2 x + \cos^2 x = 1.$$

Example 4. Evaluate $\int_0^{\frac{1}{2}\pi} \cos x \cos 3x\, dx$.

We know that
$$2\cos A \cos B = \cos(A+B) + \cos(A-B).$$
Writing A, B as $3x$, x respectively, we have
$$2\cos 3x \cos x = \cos 4x + \cos 2x.$$
Therefore
$$\int_0^{\frac{1}{2}\pi} \cos 3x \cos x\, dx = \int_0^{\frac{1}{2}\pi} \tfrac{1}{2}(\cos 4x + \cos 2x)\, dx$$
$$= \left[\tfrac{1}{8}\sin 4x + \tfrac{1}{4}\sin 2x\right]_0^{\frac{1}{2}\pi}$$
$$= 0.$$

Example 5. Integrate $\tan^2 x$.

This is by no means easy, until we recall that
$$\frac{d}{dx}(\tan x) = \sec^2 x,$$
and that
$$\sec^2 x - \tan^2 x = 1.$$
Thus,
$$\boldsymbol{\int \tan^2 x\, dx} = \int (\sec^2 x - 1)\, dx$$
$$= \boldsymbol{\tan x - x + c}.$$

2.3 Symmetry. Functions that are odd, even, or periodic can often be integrated simply. In applications, intervals of integration such as $[-a, +a]$, $[0, \pi]$, and $[0, 2\pi]$ occur frequently. In such cases, it is often helpful to look for symmetries of the function to be integrated.

Example 6. Evaluate $\int_0^{\frac{1}{2}\pi} \sin^2 x\, dx$.

Since the graph of $\sin^2 x$ is the image of the graph of $\cos^2 x$ in the line $x = \frac{1}{4}\pi$, the integrals of these functions over the interval $[0, \frac{1}{2}\pi]$ are equal. But
$$\int_0^{\frac{1}{2}\pi} (\sin^2 x + \cos^2 x)\, dx = \int_0^{\frac{1}{2}\pi} 1.dx = \tfrac{1}{2}\pi;$$

Therefore $$\int_0^{\frac{1}{2}\pi} \sin^2 x\,dx = \int_0^{\frac{1}{2}\pi} \cos^2 x\,dx = \tfrac{1}{4}\pi.$$

Example 7. Evaluate $\displaystyle\int_{-1}^{+1} (x^3+3x^2-2x-1)\,dx.$

An odd function (one for which $f(-x) = -f(x)$) has $\displaystyle\int_{-a}^{+a} f = 0$, provided the integral exists; and an even function (for which $f(-x) = f(x)$) has
$$\int_{-a}^{+a} f = 2.\int_0^{+a} f \quad \text{(see Figure 2).}$$

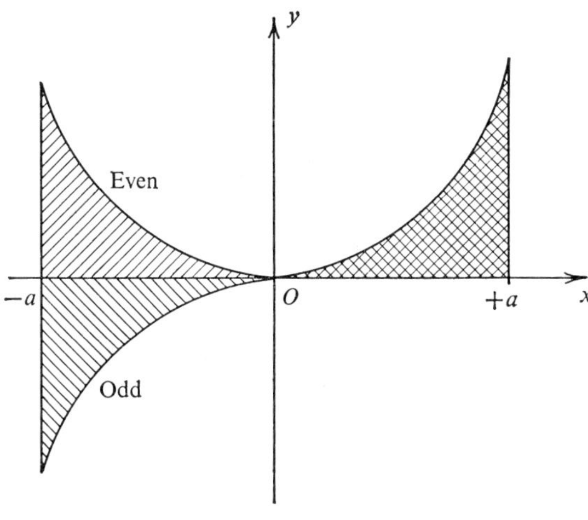

Fig. 2

But $f\colon x \to x^3-2x$ is odd, and $g\colon x \to 3x^2-1$ is even, so that
$$\int_{-1}^{+1} (x^3-2x)\,dx = 0$$
and
$$\begin{aligned}\int_{-1}^{+1} (3x^2-1)\,dx &= 2.\int_0^{+1} (3x^2-1)\,dx \\ &= 2\Big[x^3-x\Big]_0^1 \\ &= 0.\end{aligned}$$

**Example* 8. Evaluate $\displaystyle\int_0^{\pi} x \sin x\,dx.$

Although $x \sin x$ is not symmetrical in the interval $[0, \pi]$, the graph of $(\pi-x)\sin x$ is the image of the graph of $x \sin x$ in the line $x = \frac{1}{2}\pi$ (see Figure 3).

Hence $$\int_0^{\pi} x \sin x\,dx = \int_0^{\pi} (\pi-x)\sin x\,dx.$$

The sum of these integrals is

$$\int_0^{\pi} \pi \sin x \, dx = 2\pi;$$

therefore

$$\int_0^{\pi} x \sin x \, dx = \tfrac{1}{2}.2\pi = \pi.$$

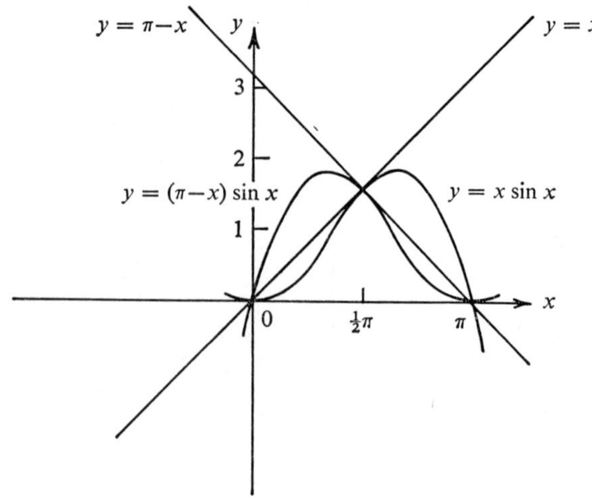

Fig. 3

Exercise B

1. Evaluate:

(*a*) $\int \frac{x^3-3x+1}{x^3} dx$; (*b*) $\int x(x+1)^4 \, dx$;

(*c*) $\int \frac{x}{(x+2)^3} dx$;

(*d*) $\int (x+1)(x+2)(x+3) \, dx$ (express in terms of $(x+2)$);

(*e*) $\int_1^2 \frac{x}{(2x-1)^4} dx$; (*f*) $\int_0^1 x\sqrt{(1-x)} \, dx$.

2. Evaluate:

(*a*) $\int \cos 3x \sin x \, dx$; (*b*) $\int \sin \tfrac{5}{2}x \sin \tfrac{3}{2}x \, dx$;

(*c*) $\int_0^{\frac{1}{4}\pi} \cos x \sin x \, dx$; (*d*) $\int_0^{\frac{1}{4}\pi} \cos^2 2x \, dx$;

(*e*) $\int_{\frac{1}{4}\pi}^{\frac{1}{2}\pi} \cot^2 x \, dx$ (compare the graphs of $\tan x$ and $\cot x$);

(*f*) $\int_0^{\frac{1}{2}\pi} \cos^2 x \sin^2 x \, dx$;

(*g*) $\int_0^{\frac{1}{2}\pi} \cos^3 x \, dx$ (note that $\cos 3x = 4\cos^3 x - 3\cos x$).

3. Evaluate:

(*a*) $\int_{-2}^{+2} (x^3-3x+1)\,dx$; (*b*) $\int_{-h}^{+h} (ax^3+bx^2+cx+d)\,dx$;

(*c*) $\int_{-\frac{1}{2}\pi}^{\frac{1}{2}\pi} x\cos^2 x\,dx$; (*d*) $\int_{\frac{1}{4}\pi}^{2\frac{3}{4}\pi} \cos^3 x\,dx$ (use symmetry);

(*e*) $\int_{-1}^{+1} \frac{x}{1+x^2}\,dx$; *(*f*) $\int_0^{\pi} x\sin^2 x\,dx$;

*(*g*) $\int_0^{\pi} x(1-\sin x)^2\,dx$.

3. INTEGRATION BY SUBSTITUTION

3.1 Deductions from the Chain Rule. If we have a composite function, so that, for example, y is a function of x, which is itself a function of u, the Chain Rule states that

$$\frac{dy}{du} = \frac{dy}{dx}\times\frac{dx}{du}$$

Thus, if $y = x^3$ and $x = (1+u^2)$, and therefore $y = (1+u^2)^3$,

$$\frac{dy}{du} = \frac{dy}{dx}\times\frac{dx}{du} = 3x^2.2u$$

$$= 6u(1+u^2)^2.$$

If we know that $dy/dx = f(x)$, we can often replace x by $g(u)$, and find a simpler problem of the form $dy/du = h(u)$. Examples 9 and 10 illustrate this process.

Example 9. Evaluate $\int x\sqrt{(x+1)}\,dx.$

By definition,

$$y = \int x\sqrt{(x+1)}\,dx \Leftrightarrow \frac{dy}{dx} = x\sqrt{(x+1)}.$$

We can integrate powers of x, but not of $(x+1)$; so some substitution needs to be made by means of which powers of u replace powers of $(x+1)$. The substitution $u = x+1$ would do perfectly well, but to avoid fractional powers of u we prefer

$$u^2 = x+1;$$

we therefore change the variable to u, and write $x = u^2-1$.

Now, applying the rule, we find

$$\frac{dy}{du} = \frac{dy}{dx}\times\frac{dx}{du}$$

$$= x\sqrt{(x+1)}\times 2u$$

$$= (u^2-1)\,u\times 2u$$

$$= 2u^4-2u^2.$$

This is a very much simpler problem. We deduce

$$y = \tfrac{2}{5}u^5 - \tfrac{2}{3}u^3 + c,$$

and so, changing back to the original variable,

$$y = \tfrac{2}{5}(x+1)^{\frac{5}{2}} - \tfrac{2}{3}(x+1)^{\frac{3}{2}} + c.$$

Example 10. Evaluate $\int \sqrt{(1-x^2)}\, dx.$

Again, the problem is to find y such that

$$\frac{dy}{dx} = \sqrt{(1-x^2)}.$$

The substitution to make this time is not immediately obvious; but, since $1-\sin^2 u = \cos^2 u$, we try $x = \sin u$ (where u is, for the moment, between 0 and $\tfrac{1}{2}\pi$).

Then, applying the rule,

$$\begin{aligned}\frac{dy}{du} &= \frac{dy}{dx}\times\frac{dx}{du}\\ &= \sqrt{(1-x^2)}\times\cos u\\ &= \sqrt{(1-\sin^2 u)}\times\cos u\\ &= \cos u\times\cos u, \quad \text{since} \quad 0 \leqslant u \leqslant \tfrac{1}{2}\pi,\\ &= \cos^2 u.\end{aligned}$$

But this is a problem whose solution we already know (cf. Example 3); we deduce

$$\frac{dy}{du} = \tfrac{1}{2}(1+\cos 2u)$$

and hence

$$\begin{aligned}y &= \tfrac{1}{2}u + \tfrac{1}{4}\sin 2u + c\\ &= \tfrac{1}{2}(u + \sin u \cos u) + c.\end{aligned}$$

It only remains to express y in terms of the original variable, x. Since $\sin u = x$, it follows that $\cos u = \sqrt{(1-x^2)}$ and that $u = \sin^{-1} x$. Therefore we deduce that

$$y = \tfrac{1}{2}(\sin^{-1} x + x.\sqrt{(1-x^2)}) + c.$$

Exercise C

1. Evaluate the following, using the suggested substitutions:

(*a*) $\int x(x+1)^3\, dx;\ x = u-1;$ (*b*) $\int x\sqrt{(1-x)}\, dx;\ x = 1-u^2;$

(*c*) $\displaystyle\int \frac{1}{\sqrt{(1-x^2)}}\, dx;\ x = \sin u;$ (*d*) $\displaystyle\int \frac{1}{1+x^2}\, dx;\ x = \tan u;$

(e) $\displaystyle\int \frac{x}{(x+1)^3}\,dx$; $x = u-1$; (f) $\displaystyle\int \sqrt{\left(\frac{x}{1-x}\right)}\,dx$; $x = \sin^2 u$.

(Assume in (b) that u is positive, and in (c), (d) and (f) that u lies between 0 and $\frac{1}{2}\pi$.)

2. Evaluate:

(a) $\displaystyle\int \frac{1}{\sqrt{(1-x)}}\,dx$; (b) $\displaystyle\int \frac{x}{\sqrt{(4-x)}}\,dx$;

(c) $\displaystyle\int \frac{1}{\sqrt{(4-x^2)}}\,dx$; (d) $\displaystyle\int \frac{3}{9+x^2}\,dx$;

(e) $\displaystyle\int \frac{1}{x\sqrt{(x^2-1)}}\,dx$ (put $x = \sec u$);

(f) $\displaystyle\int \frac{1}{x^2\sqrt{(1+x^2)}}\,dx$.

3. Show that by the method of Section 3.1 we are converting

$$\int f(x)\,dx \quad \text{into} \quad \int fg(u).g'(u)\,du,$$

and

$$\int w\,dx \quad \text{into} \quad \int w\frac{dx}{du}\,du.$$

3.2 A formal method of substitution. In the examples above, the argument has run as follows:

$$y = \int f(x)\,dx \Leftrightarrow \frac{dy}{dx} = f(x),$$

by definition; so, substituting $g(u)$ for x, and noticing that

$$\frac{dy}{du} = \frac{dy}{dx}\times\frac{dx}{du},$$

we have

$$\begin{aligned}\frac{dy}{dx} = f(x) \Leftrightarrow \frac{dy}{du} &= f(x)\times\frac{dx}{du}\\ &= f(g(u))\times\frac{dx}{du}\\ \Leftrightarrow y &= \int fg(u)\times\frac{dx}{du}\,du.\end{aligned}$$

It is therefore possible to convert one integral into the other formally by substituting $g(u)$ for x wherever it occurs, and replacing dx by $(dx/du)\,du$. Examples 9 and 10 are repeated to demonstrate this formal method of substitution.

Example 9. Evaluate $\int x\sqrt{(x+1)}\,dx.$

Substitute (u^2-1) for x (u being positive). Then $dx/du = 2u$, so we replace dx by $2u\,du$ in the integral. This gives

$$\begin{aligned}\int x\sqrt{(x+1)}\,dx &= \int (u^2-1)\,u\times 2u\,du\\ &= \int (2u^4-2u^2)\,du\\ &= \tfrac{2}{5}u^5-\tfrac{2}{3}u^3+c\\ &= \tfrac{2}{5}(x+1)^{\frac{5}{2}}-\tfrac{2}{3}(x+1)^{\frac{3}{2}}+c.\end{aligned}$$

Example 10. Evaluate $\int\sqrt{(1-x^2)}\,dx.$

Substitute $\sin u$ for x (where $0 \leqslant u \leqslant \frac{1}{2}\pi$), and replace dx by $\cos u\,du$. Then

$$\begin{aligned}\int\sqrt{(1-x^2)}\,dx &= \int\cos u\cos u\,du\\ &= \int\tfrac{1}{2}(1+\cos 2u)\,du\\ &= \tfrac{1}{2}(u+\tfrac{1}{2}\sin 2u)+c\\ &= \tfrac{1}{2}(u+\sin u\cos u)+c\\ &= \tfrac{1}{2}\sin^{-1}x+\tfrac{1}{2}x\sqrt{(1-x^2)}+c.\end{aligned}$$

Example 11. Evaluate $\int(1+x^2)^{-\frac{3}{2}}\,dx.$

In this case, the $(1+x^2)$ once again suggests the use of $\tan u$. Let us therefore try substituting $\tan u$ for x (where $0 \leqslant u < \frac{1}{2}\pi$), and replacing dx by $\sec^2 u\,du$. Then

$$\begin{aligned}\int(1+x^2)^{-\frac{3}{2}}\,dx &= \int(\sec^2 u)^{-\frac{3}{2}}\sec^2 u\,du\\ &= \int(\sec u)^{-3}\sec^2 u\,du\\ &= \int(\sec u)^{-1}\,du\\ &= \int\cos u\,du\\ &= \sin u+c.\end{aligned}$$

It only remains to express this as a function of x. This may be done by noting that

$$\sin u = \tan u/\sec u = x/\sqrt{(1+x^2)},$$

$$\int(1+x^2)^{-\frac{3}{2}}\,dx = \frac{x}{\sqrt{(1+x^2)}}+c.$$

3.3 Substituting in definite integrals. When the method of substitution is applied to definite integrals (that is, to integrals of the form $\int_a^b f(x)\,dx$) it is unnecessary to perform the last step of converting back to the original variable. Instead, when the integral for x is turned into an integral for u, the interval of integration $\{x: a \leqslant x \leqslant b\}$ is also changed into the corresponding interval of integration for u. We merely find values of u which give rise to the ends of the interval of integration (so that x is a continuous function of u over this interval), and these determine the interval of integration for the transformed integral.

Example 12. Evaluate

$$\int_0^3 x\sqrt{(x+1)}\,dx. \quad \text{(cf. Example 9).}$$

When we substitute u^2-1 for x (u being positive), we notice that

$$x = 0 \Leftrightarrow u = 1 \quad \text{and} \quad x = 3 \Leftrightarrow u = 2.$$

Therefore
$$\int_0^3 x\sqrt{(x+1)}\,dx = \int_1^2 (u^2-1)\,u.2u\,du$$
$$= \left[\tfrac{2}{5}u^5 - \tfrac{2}{3}u^3\right]_1^2,$$

which simplifies to $7\tfrac{11}{15}$.

This is more direct than converting the integral back into the form

$$\left[\tfrac{2}{5}(x+1)^{\frac{5}{2}} - \tfrac{2}{3}(x+1)^{\frac{3}{2}}\right]_0^3$$

(cf. Example 9) before carrying out the necessary calculation.

If, then, $x_1 = g(u_1)$ and $x_2 = g(u_2)$, where g is continuous over the interval $[u_1, u_2]$, we can now give the rule:

$$\int_{x_1}^{x_2} f(x)\,dx = \int_{u_1}^{u_2} fg(u)\frac{dx}{du}\,du.$$

Example 13. Evaluate
$$\int_0^{\frac{1}{2}} \frac{1}{\sqrt{(1-x^2)}}\,dx.$$

The obvious substitution is $x = \sin u$; we replace dx by $\cos u\,du$, and take the values $u_1 = 0$, $u_2 = \frac{1}{6}\pi$.

Then the value of the integral is

$$\int_0^{\frac{1}{6}\pi} \frac{\cos u\,du}{\cos u} = \int_0^{\frac{1}{6}\pi} 1\,du$$
$$= \tfrac{1}{6}\pi = 0{\cdot}5234, \quad \text{approximately.}$$

Exercise D

1. Evaluate (cf. Exercise C, Question 1):

(*a*) $\int x(x+1)^3\,dx$; $x = u-1$; (*b*) $\int x\sqrt{(1-x)}\,dx$; $x = 1-u$;

(*c*) $\int \frac{1}{1+x^2}\,dx$; $x = \tan u$; (*d*) $\int \sqrt{\left(\frac{x}{1-x}\right)}\,dx$; $x = \sin^2 u$.

2. Evaluate:

(*a*) $\int \frac{x}{(2x-1)^3}\,dx$; $x = \frac{1}{2}(u+1)$; (*b*) $\int (x+1)\sqrt{(x+2)}\,dx$; $x = u-2$;

(*c*) $\int \sqrt{(1-4x^2)}\,dx$; $x = \frac{1}{2}\sin u$; (*d*) $\int \frac{1}{(4+x^2)^2}\,dx$; $x = 2\tan u$.

3. Evaluate:

(*a*) $\int_1^5 x\sqrt{(3x+1)}\,dx$; (*b*) $\int_0^1 \frac{1-x}{(1+x)^4}\,dx$;

(*c*) $\int_0^3 \frac{3}{9+x^2}\,dx$; (*d*) $\int_0^{\frac{1}{4}} \frac{1}{\sqrt{(1-4x^2)}}\,dx$.

4. Evaluate:

(*a*) $\int_0^{\frac{1}{2}} \sqrt{\left(\frac{1+x}{1-x}\right)}\,dx;\quad x = \cos 2u;$

(*b*) $\int_0^1 \frac{1}{(1+x)\sqrt{x}}\,dx;\ x = \tan^2 u;$

(*c*) $\int_1^3 \frac{1}{\sqrt{\{(3-x)(x-1)\}}}\,dx;\quad x = 3\cos^2 u+\sin^2 u;$

(*d*) $\int_{\frac{1}{2}}^1 \frac{1}{\sqrt{(x-x^2)}}\,dx;\ x = \frac{1}{2}(1+\sin u).$

***5.** In Question 4(*d*), how does the identity $x-x^2 = \frac{1}{4}-(x-\frac{1}{2})^2$ help? For what values of a, b, c can you now evaluate

(*a*) $\int \frac{1}{\sqrt{(c+2bx-ax^2)}}\,dx$; (*b*) $\int \frac{1}{ax^2+2bx+c}\,dx$?

3.4 Integration by replacement of functions of *x*. The rule for substitution given in Section 3.2 is, perhaps, even more useful when applied the other way round, for it often offers a means of reducing a complicated problem to a simpler one. It involves, in effect, a direct use of the chain rule in reverse, and is best illustrated by examples.

Example 14. Integrate $6x(x^2+1)^2$.

The key to this problem is to recognize that for the function

$$g: x \to x^2+1,$$

the derived function is $g': x \to 2x,$

and that $g'(x)$ appears explicitly in the integrand.

Now, the Chain Rule tells us that the derivative of fg is

$$f'g(x).g'(x),$$

and the integrand appears to be of this form. If, then, we write

$$u = g(x) = x^2+1,$$

and therefore $\frac{du}{dx} = g'(x) = 2x,$

$$6x(x^2+1)^2 = 3(x^2+1)^2.2x$$
$$= 3u^2.\frac{du}{dx},$$

so that the problem has been reduced to the integration of $3u^2$. Now, we can recognize at once that the right-hand side of the equation above is simply $d(u^3)/dx$; therefore, if

$$\frac{dy}{dx} = 6x(x^2+1)^2, \quad \text{and we put} \quad (x^2+1) = u,$$

$$\frac{dy}{dx} = 3u^2 . \frac{du}{dx}$$

$$= \frac{d}{dx}(u^3),$$

so that

$$y = u^3+c = (x^2+1)^3+c.$$

If we think of the Chain Rule in the form

$$\frac{dy}{dx} = \frac{dy}{du} \times \frac{du}{dx},$$

this means effectively that we have reduced the problem to the form

$$\frac{dy}{du} = 3u^2;$$

and, in general, if we replace $g(x)$ by u, we conclude from the fact that

$$\text{the derivative of } \quad fg(x) \quad \text{is} \quad f'g(x).g'(x)$$

the fact that

$$\text{the integral with respect to } x \text{ of } \quad f'(u).\frac{du}{dx} \quad \text{is} \quad f(u).$$

Formally,

$$\int f'g(x).g'(x).dx = \int f'(u).\frac{du}{dx}.dx = \int f'(u).du = f(u).$$

If therefore we can recognize an appropriate u, we may replace the expression $(du/dx) \times dx$ by du, and carry out the integration with respect to u. We can therefore write:

$$I = \int 6x(x^2+1)^2 \, dx;$$

replacing (x^2+1) by u,

$$I = \int 3u^2 . \frac{du}{dx} \, dx$$

$$= \int 3u^2 \, du$$

$$= u^3 + c$$

$$= (x^2+1)^3+c.$$

Example 15. Evaluate $\displaystyle\int_0^{\frac{1}{2}\pi} \cos^4 x \sin x \, dx.$

If we write $u = \cos x$, so that $(du/dx) = -\sin x$, we may replace $-\sin x \, dx = \dfrac{du}{dx} \times dx$ by du.

Also, $u_1 = \cos 0 = 1$, $u_2 = \cos \frac{1}{2}\pi = 0$. Therefore

$$\int_0^{\frac{1}{2}\pi} \cos^4 x \sin x \, dx = \int_1^0 -u^4 \, du$$

$$= \left[-\tfrac{1}{5}u^5\right]_1^0$$

$$= \tfrac{1}{5}.$$

This is, even more obviously than Example 14, a direct reversal of the Chain Rule; what we are effectively doing is noticing that differentiating $\cos^5 x$ gives a result very similar to the integrand. This was the process used in Exercise A, where a number of results of this type were anticipated.

Exercise E

1. Evaluate:

(*a*) $\int x\sqrt{(1-x^2)}\, dx;\ u = 1-x^2;$ (*b*) $\int \frac{x^2}{\sqrt{(x^3+1)}}\, dx;\ u = x^3+1;$

(*c*) $\int_0^{\frac{1}{4}\pi} \frac{\sin x}{\cos^2 x}\, dx;\ u = \cos x;$ (*d*) $\int_0^{\frac{1}{4}\pi} \tan x \sec^2 x \, dx;\ u = \tan x;$

(*e*) $\int_0^4 \frac{x}{(x^2+4)^2}\, dx;\ u = x^2+4.$

2. Evaluate:

(*a*) $\int \sin^2 x \cos x \, dx;$

(*b*) $\int \cos^3 x \, dx$ [use $\cos^2 x + \sin^2 x = 1$];

(*c*) $\int x(1-x^2)^3 \, dx;$ (*d*) $\int x^3\sqrt{(1-x^2)}\, dx;$

(*e*) $\int (a \cos x + b \sin x) \times (b \cos x - a \sin x)\, dx.$

3. Evaluate:

(*a*) $\int_0^{0\cdot 6} \frac{x^3}{\sqrt{(1-x^2)}}\, dx;$ (*b*) $\int_{\frac{1}{6}\pi}^{\frac{1}{2}\pi} \frac{\cos^3 x}{\sqrt{(\sin x)}}\, dx;$

(*c*) $\int_0^{\frac{1}{4}\pi} \sec^4 x \, dx$ [use $\sec^2 x - \tan^2 x = 1$];

(*d*) $\int_0^{\frac{1}{3}\pi} \tan^4 x \, dx;$ (*e*) $\int_0^1 (x-1)(x^2-2x)^2 \, dx.$

4. Substitute $u^2 = 1-x^2$ in the integral $\int_0^{\frac{1}{2}} \sqrt{(1-x^2)}\, dx$, and explain how it could be useful in solving another problem. Draw a graph, and evaluate the required area with its help.

4. INTEGRATION BY PARTS

The Chain Rule and the Product Rule between them provide means of differentiating any function made up of others whose derived functions are already known. We studied the analogue of the Chain Rule in the previous section, and it is reasonable to hope that the analogue of the Product Rule will achieve a further extension of power.

It does not, however, provide a general method. There are many simple functions of considerable importance which cannot be integrated by these or any other analytical techniques; we have to proceed by approximate methods, such as Simpson's Rule, including considerable refinements; expansion in series; and so forth. Examples of such functions are

$$\int e^{-x^2}\,dx \quad\text{and}\quad \int \frac{\sin x}{x}\,dx.$$

Exercise F

1. Differentiate $f: x \to x \sin x$. What light does this throw on $\int x \cos x\, dx$?

2. Find the integrals of $x \sin 2x$ and of $x \cos \tfrac{1}{2}x$.

3. Differentiate:

(*a*) $x \sin^{-1} x$; (*b*) $x^2 \cos x$.

What results about integrals can you deduce?

4.1 Deductions from the Product Rule. The rule for differentiating a product tells us that

$$(f.g)' = f'.g + f.g'$$

or, writing $f(x)$ and $g(x)$ as u and v,

$$\frac{d}{dx}(uv) = u\frac{dv}{dx} + v\frac{du}{dx}.$$

If we integrate these expressions over the interval $[a, b]$, we have

$$\Big[f.g\Big]_a^b = \int_a^b f'.g + \int_a^b f.g'.$$

From this we deduce the rule for *integration by parts*

$$\int_a^b f.g' = \Big[f.g\Big]_a^b - \int_a^b f'.g$$

or

$$\int_a^b u\frac{dv}{dx}\,dx = \Big[uv\Big]_a^b - \int_a^b v\frac{du}{dx}\,dx.$$

Example 16. Evaluate $$\int_0^{\frac{1}{2}\pi} x\cos x\,dx.$$

In the formula above, put $u = x$, and choose for v a function such that $dv/dx = \cos x$. The obvious choice is $v = \sin x$. Then $du/dx = 1$. Applying the formula,

$$\int_0^{\frac{1}{2}\pi} x\cos x\,dx = \Big[x\sin x\Big]_0^{\frac{1}{2}\pi} - \int_0^{\frac{1}{2}\pi} 1.\sin x\,dx$$

$$= \tfrac{1}{2}\pi + \Big[\cos x\Big]_0^{\frac{1}{2}\pi}$$

$$= \tfrac{1}{2}\pi - 1 = 0{\cdot}571,$$

approximately.

Here, we had to choose whether to take u as x or $\cos x$. The corresponding choices for v are $\sin x$ and $\frac{1}{2}x^2$. Now, if we had made the latter choice, we should have had to integrate $\frac{1}{2}x^2 \cos x$, which is harder than the original problem. We therefore made the choice which made v no more complicated, while simplifying u.

Example 17. Evaluate $$\int \sin^{-1} x\,dx.$$

This does not, at first sight, look like a product at all. The integral can, however, be integrated by taking u as $\sin^{-1} x$, and choosing v so that $dv/dx = 1$.

In the formula, therefore, put $u = \sin^{-1} x$, $v = x$, and note that

$$\frac{du}{dx} = \frac{1}{\sqrt{(1-x^2)}}.$$

Then
$$\int \sin^{-1} x\,dx = x\sin^{-1} x - \int \frac{x}{\sqrt{(1-x^2)}}\,dx$$

$$= x\sin^{-1} x + \sqrt{(1-x^2)} + c.$$

Exercise G

1. Evaluate:

(*a*) $\int x\sin x\,dx$; (*b*) $\int_0^{\frac{1}{2}\pi} x\cos 2x\,dx$;

(*c*) $\int_0^{\pi} x\sin\frac{1}{2}x\,dx$; (*d*) $\int x\tan^{-1} x\,dx$.

2. Evaluate:

(*a*) $\int x^2 \sin x\,dx$ (use the process of Section 4.1 twice);

(*b*) $\int x^3 \cos x\,dx$; (*c*) $\int x\sin^2 x\,dx$;

(*d*) $\int x\sin 3x\cos x\,dx$.

(For (*c*) and (*d*), use a formula which will convert the trigonometrical expressions into sums.)

3. Use the method of Section 4.1 to evaluate:

(*a*) $\int x\sqrt{(x+1)}\,dx$; (*b*) $\int_0^{\frac{1}{2}} \sqrt{(1-x^2)}\,dx$.

(You will need the identity $x^2 = 1-(1-x^2)$ in (*b*).)

4. Find a method for evaluating

$$\int_0^{\frac{1}{2}\pi} x^n \sin x\,dx.$$

5. Show that $\int_0^{\frac{1}{2}\pi} \sin^3 x \cos^4 x\,dx = \frac{2}{7}\int_0^{\frac{1}{2}\pi} \sin x \cos^4 x\,dx.$

(Start by taking $u = \sin^2 x$ and $\frac{dv}{dx} = \sin x \cos^4 x$.)

Find its value.

Show also that

$$\int_0^{\frac{1}{2}\pi} \sin^n x \cos^4 x\,dx = \frac{n-1}{n+4}\int_0^{\frac{1}{2}\pi} \sin^{n-2} x \cos^4 x\,dx \quad (n \text{ integer} > 1),$$

and use this result to evaluate

$$\int_0^{\frac{1}{2}\pi} \sin^7 x \cos^4 x\,dx.$$

Can you find the value of $\int_0^{\frac{1}{2}\pi} \sin^6 x \cos^2 x\,dx$?

What general formula do these results suggest for

$$\int_0^{\frac{1}{2}\pi} \sin^m x \cos^n x\,dx?$$

6. Show how to express

$$\int \frac{\cos x}{x^2}\,dx \quad \text{in terms of} \quad \int \frac{\sin x}{x}\,dx.$$

(Neither of these functions can be integrated analytically.)

7. If $$\int_1^y \frac{dt}{t} = F(y),$$

show that $$\int_0^1 \tan^{-1} x\,dx = \tfrac{1}{4}\pi - \tfrac{1}{2}F(2).$$

5. SOME STANDARD INTEGRALS AND THEIR EXTENSION

The following integrals, in which arbitrary constants are omitted and a is assumed positive, are printed in your tables, together with others which depend upon two principal functions which we have not yet considered. They can be adapted quite trivially to give a number of fresh results, but with a little practice the results of such adaptation should be obvious.

$$\int x^n\,dx = \frac{1}{n+1}\,x^{n+1} \quad (\text{if } n \neq -1);$$

$$\int \sin x\,dx = -\cos x; \qquad \int \cos x\,dx = +\sin x;$$

$$\int \sin^2 x\,dx = \tfrac{1}{2}(x-\tfrac{1}{2}\sin 2x); \quad \int \cos^2 x\,dx = \tfrac{1}{2}(x+\tfrac{1}{2}\sin 2x);$$

$$\int \frac{dx}{x^2+a^2} = \frac{1}{a}\tan^{-1}\left(\frac{x}{a}\right); \qquad \int \frac{dx}{\sqrt{(a^2-x^2)}} = \sin^{-1}\left(\frac{x}{a}\right);$$

$$\int \sec^2 x\,dx = \tan x.$$

Example 18. Evaluate $\int 4\sec^2(2x+3)\,dx.$

This can of course be solved by writing $u = 2x+3$, but it is easier to see by inspection that the answer is some multiple of $\tan(2x+3)$. Now,

$$\frac{d}{dx}(\tan(2x+3)) = 2\sec^2(2x+3);$$

so, by adjusting the constant,

$$\int 4\sec^2(2x+3)\,dx = 2\tan(2x+3)+c.$$

Similar working would lead to the conclusion that

$$\int a\sec^2(bx+k)\,dx = \frac{a}{b}\tan(bx+k)+c.$$

**Example* 19. Evaluate $\displaystyle\int_0^1 \frac{1}{2x^2+8x+16}\,dx.$

The quadratic form in the denominator can be rearranged by completing the square in the more useful form $2\{(x+2)^2+4\}$, so that the integral is

$$\int_0^1 \frac{1}{2\{(x+2)^2+4\}}\,dx = \left[\tfrac{1}{4}\tan^{-1}\left(\frac{x+2}{2}\right)\right]_0^1$$

$$= \tfrac{1}{4}(0{\cdot}983-0{\cdot}785)$$

$$= 0{\cdot}05, \quad \text{approximately.}$$

It is almost as easy to see immediately that

$$\int \frac{dx}{a\{(x+b)^2+k^2\}} = \frac{1}{ak}\tan^{-1}\left(\frac{x+b}{k}\right)+c;$$

the next section introduces a useful way of checking such results.

Exercise H

1. Write down the answers to:

(*a*) $\int (2x-1)^{-\frac{1}{3}}\,dx;$ (*b*) $\int \sin(\tfrac{1}{2}x+\tfrac{1}{4}\pi)\,dx;$

(*c*) $\displaystyle\int \frac{3}{x^2+9}\,dx;$ (*d*) $\displaystyle\int \frac{1}{\sqrt{(25-x^2)}}\,dx;$

(*e*) $\int \sec^2 3x\,dx.$

2. Evaluate:

(*a*) $\int_0^{\frac{1}{6}} (1-3x)^{-3}\,dx$; (*b*) $\int_0^{\frac{1}{2}\pi} \sec^2 \tfrac{1}{2}x\,dx$;

(*c*) $\int_3^4 \cos \tfrac{1}{6}\pi(x-3)\,dx$; (*d*) $\int_1^2 \frac{1}{\sqrt{(4-(x-2)^2)}}\,dx$;

(*e*) $\int_{-1}^{+1} \frac{1}{(x+1)^2+4}\,dx$.

3. Evaluate:

(*a*) $\int (ax+b)^n\,dx$; (*b*) $\int a \sin(bx+c)\,dx$;

(*c*) $\int \sec^2 (px+q)\,dx$; (*d*) $\int (qx+r)^{-m}\,dx$;

(*e*) $\int \frac{1}{a^2(x+b)^2+c^2}\,dx$; (*f*) $\int \frac{1}{\sqrt{(p^2-(qx+r)^2)}}\,dx$.

***4.** Evaluate:

(*a*) $\int \frac{1}{\sqrt{(2x-x^2)}}\,dx$; (*b*) $\int \frac{1}{x^2+2x+2}\,dx$;

(*c*) $\int \frac{1}{3x^2-12x+15}\,dx$; (*d*) $\int \frac{1}{\sqrt{(36-16x-x^2)}}\,dx$;

(*e*) $\int \frac{1}{\sqrt{(1+6x-2x^2)}}\,dx$.

6. DIMENSIONAL CONSISTENCY

6.1 Consistency of derivatives and integrals. In Chapter 18, there was an introduction to the group of dimensions generated by **L** and **T**, the dimensions of length and time. The identity of this group is $\mathbf{L}^0\mathbf{T}^0$, which we may abbreviate to **1**, the dimension of a number. The principle of dimensional consistency was introduced, and it was remarked that the derivative dy/dx has the same dimension as the expression y/x. A similar result for integrals may be used, for $\int y\,dx$ has the same dimension as yx, as the following example illustrates.

Example 20. What can you say about $\int x^n\,dx$ if x has dimension **L**?

$$\int x^n\,dx \text{ has dimension } \mathbf{L}^n \times \mathbf{L} = \mathbf{L}^{n+1}.$$

Thus, since x is the only dimensional quantity involved,

$$\int x^n\,dx = f(n)\,x^{n+1},$$

where $f(n)$ is a numerical function of n, which in fact we know from our previous analysis to be $1/(n+1)$.

It follows that we have a partial check on our evaluation of integrals which arise from physical problems. If, say, v denotes a velocity and so is of dimension $\mathbf{LT}^{-1}$, and t denotes time, then $\int v\,dt$ has dimension **L**, and any answer which does not conform to this must be wrong.

6.2 Working with dimensionless quantities. It was also remarked that functions from R to R, such as sin, $\tan^{-1}$, log, deal essentially with dimensionless quantities; thus, an equation such as $p = \sin^{-1} q$ carries with it the implication that p, q both have dimension **1**. This implication will be of great importance in the next section.

Equations are often formulated, however, which appear to transgress the law of dimensional consistency; and in such cases the introduction of suitable dimensional constants to achieve dimensional consistency may carry advantages. Thus, for example, the equation $y^2 = 4x$ is not a satisfactory form for the equation of a parabola since, if x and y are to be interpreted as lengths and 4 as a number, it is dimensionally inconsistent. But if we introduce the constant a, a length characteristic of the given parabola, and write $(y/a)^2 = 4(x/a)$, we have a form which is dimensionally consistent; it suggests the parametric coordinates $(at^2, 2at)$ where t is a number, and reduces at once to the homogeneous form $y^2 = 4ax$. Dimensional consistency once established may be maintained. For example, the reciprocal of the gradient at $(at^2, 2at)$, being the ratio of two lengths, is a number and in fact is equal to t, which is indeed a number as already noted.

6.3 Application to integrals arising from physical problems. In Examples 21 and 22 we consider integrals which arise from a simple type of oscillation. The work is done by change of variable, and checked by dimensional consistency.

Example 21. If $v = ap \cos pt$, where v is a velocity and t a time, find the displacement $x = \int v\, dt$, and check that your answer is dimensionally consistent.

Now, v has dimension $\mathbf{LT^{-1}}$, and t dimension $\mathbf{T}$. We first use the given relation to deduce the dimensions of a and p.

Since the function cos maps numbers onto numbers, pt and $\cos pt$ are both dimensionless quantities; thus p has dimension $\mathbf{T^{-1}}$, and a has dimension $\mathbf{L}$.

If we denote pt by y (so that y is dimensionless) then

$$\begin{aligned} x = \int ap \cos pt\, dt &= \int a \cos (pt)\, d(pt) \\ &= \int a \cos y\, dy \\ &= a \sin y \\ &= a \sin pt. \end{aligned}$$

(i) x, being a displacement, has dimension $\mathbf{L}$;

(ii) $ap \cos pt\, dt$ has dimension $\mathbf{LT^{-1}.L^0T^0.T = L}$;

(iii) $a \sin pt$ has dimension $\mathbf{L.L^0T^0 = L}$. The answer is therefore dimensionally consistent.

Example 22. If u is a velocity and x a length, integrate the expression

$$\frac{1}{\sqrt{(u^2-p^2x^2)}}$$

with respect to x, and check the dimensional consistency of your results. (Assume $u > 0$, $p > 0$.)

As in Example 21, we try to isolate non-dimensional combinations and to concentrate the dimensional character of the expression into a single dimensional factor. Now u has dimension $\mathbf{LT}^{-1}$ and x dimension $\mathbf{L}$, so that p has dimension $\mathbf{T}^{-1}$ for consistency; $\sqrt{(u^2-p^2x^2)}$ has dimension $\mathbf{LT}^{-1}$, while (px/u) is a number. Thus

$$\int \frac{1}{\sqrt{(u^2-p^2x^2)}}\,dx = \int \frac{1}{u\sqrt{(1-(px/u)^2)}}\cdot\frac{u}{p}\,d\left(\frac{px}{u}\right)$$

$$= \int \frac{1}{p}\cdot\frac{1}{\sqrt{(1-y^2)}}\,dy$$

where $y = px/u$, and is non-dimensional.

Thus
$$\int \frac{1}{\sqrt{(u^2-p^2x^2)}}\,dx = (1/p)\sin^{-1} y$$
$$= (1/p)\sin^{-1}(px/u).$$

So:

(i) the integral has dimension $\mathbf{L}^{-1}\mathbf{T}.\mathbf{L} = \mathbf{T}$;
(ii) the answer has dimension $\mathbf{1}/\mathbf{T}^{-1} = \mathbf{T}$, which is consistent.

6.4 An extension of the principle of dimensional consistency. In physical problems, this principle is implicit in every equation we use. It may, however, be extended slightly to deal with integrals containing expressions whose dimensions are not stated. Thus, in Example 23, it might well be that x and u represent a length and a velocity respectively as above. But if we consider only an abstract dimensional group, generated by **A**, **B**, say, and take these 'dimensions' to obey laws identical with those for the usual group generated by **L** and **T**, the result may still be usefully checked, although the method fails if either **A** or **B** is allowed to be a neutral element.

Example 23. Evaluate
$$\int \frac{1}{p^2x^2+u^2}\,dx,$$

and confirm your answer by a dimensional check. (Assume $u > 0$, $p > 0$.)

Here, px and u must be of the same dimensions for the integrand to make sense. We therefore create the dimensionless variable $y = px/u$. Then

$$\int \frac{1}{p^2x^2+u^2}\,dx = \int \frac{1}{u^2(1+(px/u)^2)}\cdot\frac{u}{p}\,d\left(\frac{px}{u}\right)$$
$$= \frac{1}{up}\int\frac{1}{1+y^2}\,dy$$
$$= (1/up)\tan^{-1} y$$
$$= (1/up)\tan^{-1}(px/u).$$

If p has dimension **A** and x dimension **B**, the integrand suggests that u has dimension **AB**.

(i) The integral has dimension

$$\mathbf{A}^{-2}\mathbf{B}^{-2}.\mathbf{B} = \mathbf{A}^{-2}\mathbf{B}^{-1}.$$

(ii) The answer has dimension

$$\frac{1}{\mathbf{AB}.\mathbf{A}} = \mathbf{A}^{-2}\mathbf{B}^{-1},$$

which is therefore dimensionally consistent.

This technique guards against the accidental omission of, say, u or p, and even suggests the correction that might be needed if the calculated answer is found to be in error by being dimensionally inconsistent. Also, whenever a new integral is considered, it is interesting to generalize it; for example

$$G(x) = \int\frac{1}{x^2-1}\,dx \quad \Rightarrow \int\frac{1}{a^2x^2-b^2}\,dx = \frac{1}{ab}G\left(\frac{ax}{b}\right),$$

and

$$H(x) = \int\frac{1}{\sqrt{(1+x^4)}}\,dx \Rightarrow \int\frac{1}{\sqrt{(a^4+x^4)}}\,dx = \frac{1}{a}H\left(\frac{x}{a}\right).$$

**Exercise I*

1. Assuming that x, y are lengths, consider the dimensions of the other quantities which occur in the usual equations for a line, and confirm your answer by interpreting them geometrically if possible:

(*a*) $y = mx+c$; (*b*) $x\cos\theta+y\sin\theta = p$;

(*c*) $\frac{x}{a}+\frac{y}{b} = 1$; (*d*) $lx+my+n = 0$;

(*e*) $x = p+qt,\ y = r+(1-q)\,t$.

2. If a curve is represented parametrically by $(ct, c/t)$, what can you say about the dimensions of c and of t? If the tangent at the point whose parameter is t is $y = mx+k$, can you say anything about the way c and t occur in m and k? Repeat for $(a\cos t, b\sin t)$ and for (at^2, at^3).

3. Express the following equations as relations between numbers in each case, and suggest a suitable parametric representation if you can. ($\cos^2 t+\sin^2 t = 1$ and $y/x = t$ often give useful leads.)

(*a*) $x^2+y^2 = a^2$; (*b*) $x^{\frac{2}{3}}+y^{\frac{2}{3}} = a^{\frac{2}{3}}$;

(*c*) $x^2-y^2 = a^2$; (*d*) $x^3+y^3 = 3axy$;

(*e*) $ay = x^2$; (*f*) $y = \dfrac{a^3}{a^2+x^2}$;

(*g*) $y^2(2a-x) = x^3$; (*h*) $x^2+y^2 = 2a(x+y)$.

4. Write down the answers to the following (compare Exercise H, Question 3):

(*a*) $\int (ax+b)^n \, dx$; (*b*) $\int a \sin(bx+c) \, dx$;

(*c*) $\int \sec^2 (px+q) \, dx$; (*d*) $\int (qx+r)^{-m} \, dx$;

(*e*) $\displaystyle\int \frac{1}{4x^2+25} \, dx$; (*f*) $\displaystyle\int \frac{1}{\sqrt{(9-4x^2)}} \, dx$.

5. If x is a length, and if, for all values of x,

$$(x-p)(x-q)(x-r) = x^3+ax^2+bx+c,$$

so that p, q, r are the roots of the equation $x^3+ax^2+bx+c = 0$, is it possible that $p^3+q^3+r^3 = 3ab-3c-a^2$? If not, suggest a more likely relationship.

Show that $p^2+q^2+r^2$ must be $m.b+n.a^2$, for some numbers m and n, and, by considering $(x-1)^3$ and $(x-1)x(x+1)$, find the numbers m, n. Similarly, find expressions for

$$pq+qr+rp, \quad \text{for} \quad \frac{1}{p}+\frac{1}{q}+\frac{1}{r}, \quad \text{and for} \quad pq^2+p^2q+qr^2+q^2r+rp^2+r^2p,$$

in terms of a, b and c.

6. Invent and solve some problems like Examples 21 and 22, and check that your answers are dimensionally consistent.

7. New functions are defined such that:

(*a*) $G(x) = \displaystyle\int \frac{1}{\sqrt{(x^2-1)}} \, dx$; (*b*) $H(x) = \displaystyle\int \frac{1}{\sqrt{(x^2+1)}} \, dx$;

(*c*) $K(x) = \displaystyle\int \frac{1}{1-x^2} \, dx$; (*d*) $L(x) = \int \tan^{-1} x \, dx$.

Examine the effect of generalizing as suggested after Example 23.

*7. PRINCIPAL VALUES

7.1 Inverse functions. We saw in earlier chapters how to construct inverse functions, by restricting the domain of the original function to a particular interval. We need now to consider how they can be used in integration, and Examples 24 and 25 show some of the dangers involved in using them uncritically.

Example 24. Sketch the graph of $y = \sin^{-1}(x/a)$, if (i) $a > 0$; (ii) $a < 0$.

The natural choice for the function $\sin^{-1}$ is to restrict its range to $[-\frac{1}{2}\pi, +\frac{1}{2}\pi]$. (This choice is discussed in more detail in Example 25.) Now the domain of the function is $[-a, +a]$ if a is positive, but $[+a, -a]$ if a is negative. In either case the image of $+a$ is $+1$, for example, so that the graphs appear as in Figures 4 and 5 respectively.

This indicates that the gradient is $+1/\sqrt{(a^2-x^2)}$ if a is positive, but $-1/\sqrt{(a^2-x^2)}$ if a is negative.

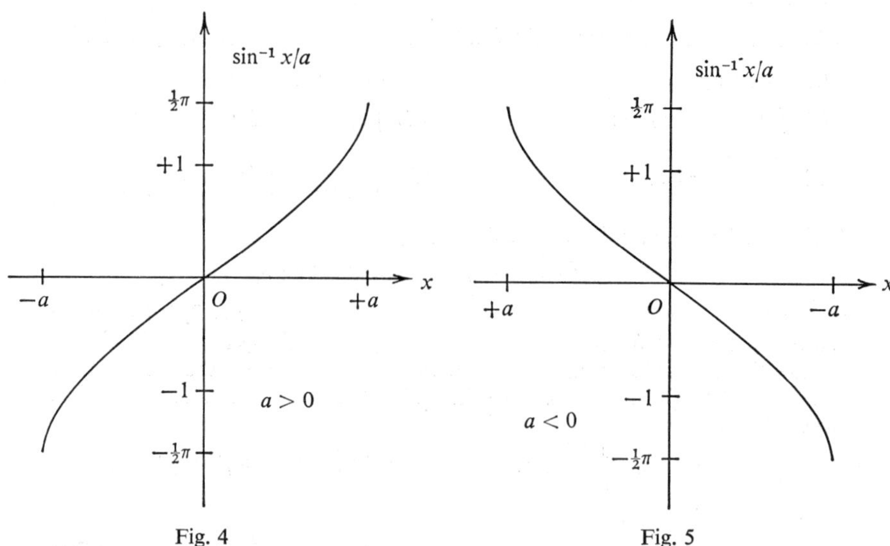

Fig. 4

Fig. 5

This means that the formula

$$\int \frac{1}{\sqrt{(a^2-x^2)}}\,dx = \sin^{-1}\left(\frac{x}{a}\right)$$

will only be true if $a > 0$. What will the corresponding formula be if $a < 0$?

A similar difficulty has already been indicated in Example 10, p. 648. There, if the variable u had been allowed to take values from $\frac{1}{2}\pi$ to π, say, it would not have been true that $\sqrt{(1-\sin^2 u)} = \cos u$, for $\cos u$ would then have been negative; the equation would have been

$$\frac{dy}{du} = -\cos^2 u$$

instead of

$$\frac{dy}{du} = +\cos^2 u,$$

although the answer in terms of x would not have been affected. (Look back and find out why.)

Example 25. Discuss the meaning of $\cos^{-1} x$, and use it to evaluate

$$\int_{-a}^{+a} \frac{1}{\sqrt{(1-x^2)}}\,dx \quad \text{for} \quad |a| < 1.$$

Since $\cos x$ is periodic (see Figure 6), every element of the range $[-1, +1]$ is the image of infinitely many different points of the domain. Thus, the inverse image of the number $\frac{1}{2}$ under the function cosine is

$$\{\ldots, -2\pi-\tfrac{1}{3}\pi, -2\pi+\tfrac{1}{3}\pi, -\tfrac{1}{3}\pi, +\tfrac{1}{3}\pi, 2\pi-\tfrac{1}{3}\pi, 2\pi+\tfrac{1}{3}\pi, \ldots\}$$

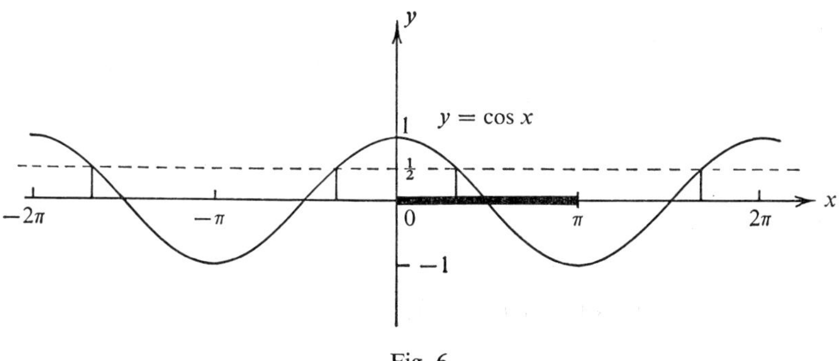

Fig. 6

If, however, we restrict the domain to $[0, \pi]$, each value in the co-domain is covered just once, and we have established a one-to-one mapping which determines an inverse function $\cos^{-1}$. We can then write $\cos^{-1}\frac{1}{2} = \frac{1}{3}\pi$, the principal value of the inverse image of the function with an unrestricted domain.

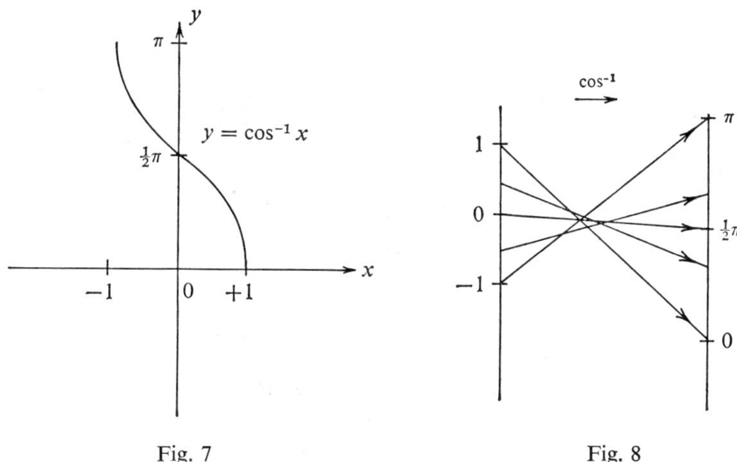

Fig. 7 Fig. 8

The choice of restriction is arbitrary. Figure 7 shows that $[0, \pi]$ is the natural interval to choose; and similar conventions are made whereby both sin and tan have their domains restricted to $[-\frac{1}{2}\pi, +\frac{1}{2}\pi]$ for the definition of their inverse functions. Figures 7 and 8 display the function $\cos^{-1}$ in the form of a graph and of a mapping.

Now the scale factor of the function cos at a is $-\sin a$; if $\cos a = b$, $\sin^2 a = 1-\cos^2 a = 1-b^2$. The derivative $-\sin a$ is therefore equal to $-\sqrt{(1-b^2)}$ if $\sin a$ is positive, and to $+\sqrt{(1-b^2)}$ if $\sin a$ is negative. But, over $[0, \pi]$, $\sin a$ is always positive or zero; and Figure 4 confirms that the gradient of the graph of $\cos x$ over $[0, \pi]$ is always negative or zero. The derivative of cos may thus always be expressed as $-\sqrt{(1-b^2)}$, over this restricted domain, and therefore the derivative of $\cos^{-1}$ will be its reciprocal, $-1/\sqrt{(1-b^2)}$, except when $b = \pm 1$, in which case the derivative does not exist. We deduce that

$$\frac{d}{dx}(\cos^{-1} x) = \frac{-1}{\sqrt{(1-x^2)}} \quad \text{for} \quad -1 < x < +1.$$

This means that (for example)

$$\begin{aligned}\int_{-\frac{1}{2}}^{\frac{1}{2}} \frac{1}{\sqrt{(1-x^2)}}\,dx &= \Big[-\cos^{-1} x\Big]_{-\frac{1}{2}}^{+\frac{1}{2}} \\ &= -\cos^{-1}(\tfrac{1}{2})+\cos^{-1}(-\tfrac{1}{2}) \\ &= -\tfrac{1}{3}\pi+\tfrac{2}{3}\pi = \tfrac{1}{3}\pi.\end{aligned}$$

Similarly, the original integral has the value $\pi-2\cos^{-1} a$.

7.2 Problems of substitution. Unfortunately, it is not quite safe to apply this process without careful thought; see Exercise J, Question 1. It is better to apply the general result for integration by substitution quoted below; for the same problem arises in substituting $x = g(u)$ whenever g is not one-to-one.

We therefore state, without proof, sufficient conditions to give the appropriate result; this covers substitutions both for x and for $g(x)$ (see Sections 3.3 and 3.4 respectively).

If (*a*) $fg(u)$ is continuous over $[u_1, u_2]$, and
(*b*) $g'(u)$ is continuous over (u_1, u_2),
then, if $x_1 = g(u_1)$ and $x_2 = g(u_2)$,

$$\int_{x_1}^{x_2} f(x)\,dx = \int_{u_1}^{u_2} fg(u).g'(u)\,du.$$

Example 25 may then be handled as follows:
In the integral

$$\int_{-a}^{+a} \frac{1}{\sqrt{(1-x^2)}}\,dx,$$

we substitute $x = \cos u$, where

$$u_1 = \cos^{-1}(-a) = \pi-\cos^{-1}(a), \quad \text{and} \quad u_2 = \cos^{-1}(a).$$

The conditions of the theorem are both met; for
(*a*) $1/\sqrt{(1-\cos^2 u)}$ is continuous over $[u_1, u_2]$ (provided that $a^2 < 1$), and
(*b*) $-\sin u$ is continuous over (u_1, u_2). Therefore

$$\begin{aligned}\int_{-a}^{+a} \frac{1}{\sqrt{(1-x^2)}}\,dx &= \int_{u_1}^{u_2} \frac{-\sin u}{\sqrt{(1-\cos^2 u)}}\,du \\ &= \int_{u_1}^{u_2} -1.du, \quad \text{since} \quad u \in (0, \pi), \\ &= -u_2+u_1 \\ &= \pi - 2\cos^{-1} a.\end{aligned}$$

**Exercise J*

1. Confirm that the following results are correct, by the method of Section 7.2:

(*a*) $\displaystyle\int_{-\frac{1}{2}}^{+\frac{1}{2}} \frac{1}{\sqrt{(1-x^2)}}\,dx = \tfrac{1}{3}\pi$ (substituting $x = \sin u$);

(*b*) $\displaystyle\int_{-1}^{+1} \frac{1}{1+x^2}\,dx = \tfrac{1}{2}\pi$ (substituting $x = \tan u$);

(*c*) $\displaystyle\int_{0}^{+1} \sqrt[4]{x}\,dx = \tfrac{4}{5}$; (*d*) $\displaystyle\int_{-\sqrt{2}}^{-1} \frac{1}{x\sqrt{(x^2-1)}}\,dx = \tfrac{1}{4}\pi$ (see p. 363).

2. Confirm that
$$\frac{d}{dx}(\cot^{-1} x) = \frac{-1}{1+x^2},$$
and point out the errors in the following:

(*a*) $\displaystyle\int_{-1}^{+1} \frac{1}{1+x^2}\,dx = \Big[-\cot^{-1} x\Big]_{-1}^{+1} = -\tfrac{1}{4}\pi + (-\tfrac{1}{4}\pi) = -\tfrac{1}{2}\pi$;

(*b*)
$$\begin{aligned}\int_0^{\pi} \frac{1}{a^2\sin^2 u + b^2\cos^2 u}\,du &= \int_0^{\pi} \frac{\sec^2 u}{a^2\tan^2 u + b^2}\,du \\ &= \int_0^0 \frac{1}{a^2x^2+b^2}\,dx \quad (\text{writing } \tan u = x) \\ &= \left[\frac{1}{ab}\tan^{-1}\left(\frac{ax}{b}\right)\right]_0^0 \\ &= 0;\end{aligned}$$

(*c*) $\displaystyle\int_{-1}^{+1} \frac{dx}{x^2} = \int_{-1}^{+1} u^2.\left(-\frac{1}{u^2}\right)du = \int_{-1}^{+1} -du = -2$ (writing $u = 1/x$).

3. Evaluate:

(*a*) $\displaystyle\int_{-2}^{-1} \frac{1}{\sqrt{(9-x^2)}}\,dx$; (*b*) $\displaystyle\int_{-\infty}^{-2} \frac{1}{4+x^2}\,dx$;

(*c*) $\displaystyle\int_{-1}^{+1} \sqrt{(x^4)}\,dx$; (*d*) $\displaystyle\int_{-2}^{-1} \frac{\sqrt{(4-x^2)}}{x^2}\,dx$;

(*e*) $\displaystyle\int_{-\frac{1}{4}\pi}^{\frac{3}{4}\pi} \cos^3 x \sin^4 x\,dx$.

Miscellaneous Exercise

(These questions are generally not in groups—any of the methods of this or previous chapters may be appropriate. A few of them can not be integrated by any of these methods; they are included to emphasize the difference between integration and differentiation.)

In Questions 1–18, evaluate the definite integrals, and find expressions for the rest:

1. $\int x(x^2+1)^4\,dx.$

2. $\int x^2\sqrt{(1-x)}\,dx.$

3. $\int x\sqrt{(2x+3)}\,dx.$

4. $\int (x^2/(x^2+1))\,dx.$

5. $\int (x-1)(x+1)^4\,dx.$

6. $\displaystyle\int \frac{x\,dx}{(x+1)^3}.$

7. $\int ((x^2+1)/x^2)\,dx.$

8. $\int x^3\sqrt{(x^2+1)}\,dx.$

9. $\int (2x+1)^{-\frac{1}{4}}\,dx.$

10. $\displaystyle\int \frac{x^2dx}{\sqrt{(x+1)}}.$

11. $\int (1-x^2)^{-\frac{1}{2}}\,dx.$

12. $\displaystyle\int \frac{\sqrt{(1+x)}}{\sqrt{(1-x)}}\,dx.$

13. $\displaystyle\int \frac{dx}{(x^2+1)^2}.$

14. $\displaystyle\int \frac{x}{4-x^2}\,dx.$

15. $\int x.(x^2+4)^{-\frac{1}{2}}\,dx.$

16. $\displaystyle\int \frac{x^2}{x^2+4}\,dx.$

17. $\displaystyle\int_0^a (a^2-x^2)^{\frac{3}{2}}\,dx.$

18. $\displaystyle\int_1^4 \sqrt{\left(\frac{4-x}{x-1}\right)}\,dx.$

Perform the following trigonometrical integrations, Questions 19–30: (it is worth remembering that 'sec' and 'tan' are very closely linked together in integrals):

19. $\displaystyle\int_0^{\frac{1}{2}\pi} \frac{\cos x}{1+\sin^2 x}\,dx.$

20. $\displaystyle\int_0^{\frac{1}{4}\pi} \sec^2 x\sqrt{(1+\tan x)}\,dx.$

21. $\int (1-\tan^4 x)\,dx.$

22. $\int \sec^2 x\tan x\,dx$ (express your answer in two ways).

23. $\int \sin^2 x\sec^6 x\,dx.$

24. $\int \sin x\sec^6 x\,dx.$

25. $\int \sec^6 x\,dx.$

26. $\int x\tan^2 x\,dx.$

27. $\int \tan^{-1} x\,dx.$

28. $\int x\tan^{-1} x\,dx.$

29. $\displaystyle\int_{-1}^{+1} \frac{dx}{\sqrt{(4-x^2)}}.$

30. $\displaystyle\int_0^3 \frac{dx}{\sqrt{(36-x^2)}}.$

In evaluating the integrals in Questions 31–42, the trigonometrical formulae, such as $2\cos A\cos B = \cos(A+B)+\cos(A-B)$, $2\sin^2 x = 1-\cos 2x$, etc., are likely to prove useful.

31. $\int \cos x \cos 3x\, dx.$

32. $\int x^2 \sin 2x\, dx.$

33. $\int x \sin x \cos x\, dx.$

34. $\int \sin^2 x\, dx.$

35. $\int \sin^2 x \cos^4 x\, dx.$

36. $\int \sin^3 x \cos^6 x\, dx.$

37. $\int \cos^2 x \cos 2x\, dx.$

38. $\int \sin^4 x \cos^5 x\, dx.$

39. $\int_0^{\pi} \cos x \cos 5x\, dx.$

40. $\int_0^{\pi} \cos mx \cos nx\, dx.$

(In Question 40, does it matter whether m and n are equal?)

41. $\int_0^{\frac{1}{2}\pi} \sin^6 x\, dx.$

42. $\int_0^{\frac{1}{2}\pi} \cos^6 x\, dx.$

In Questions **43–46**, the substitution $t = \tan x$ will be useful, as always for integrals of even powers of $\sin x$ and $\cos x$.

43. $\int_0^{\frac{1}{4}\pi} \frac{dx}{1+3\sin^2 x}.$

44. $\int_0^{\frac{1}{3}\pi} \frac{\cos^2 x\, dx}{(1+\cos^2 x)^2}.$

45. $\int_{\frac{1}{8}\pi}^{\frac{3}{8}\pi} \sec^2 x \operatorname{cosec}^2 x\, dx.$

46. $\int \frac{\sin^2 x\, dx}{2\cos^2 x + \sin^2 x}.$

In Questions **47–52**, without performing the integration, state whether the integral is positive, negative, or zero.

47. $\int_{-\frac{1}{2}\pi}^{\frac{1}{2}\pi} \cos^3 x\, dx.$

48. $\int_{-\pi}^{\pi} \sin \tfrac{1}{3}x\, dx.$

49. $\int_{-\pi}^{\pi} x \cos x\, dx.$

50. $\int_0^{\pi} \cos^3 x\, dx.$

51. $\int_{-1}^{1} (x^3 - 3x^2 + 2x)\, dx.$

52. $\int_{-1}^{1} \frac{x-1}{x^4+1}\, dx.$

**Harder Miscellaneous Exercise*

1. Evaluate:

(*a*) $\int_0^{2\pi} x \cos^2 x\, dx;$

(*b*) $\int_0^{4\pi} \cos^3 x\, dx;$

(*c*) $\int_0^{2\pi} x \sin^2 \tfrac{1}{2}x\, dx;$

(*d*) $\int_0^{2\pi} \sin \tfrac{3}{2}x \sin \tfrac{5}{2}x\, dx.$

2. Find the ratio of

$$\int_0^1 x^m (1-x)^n\, dx \quad \text{to} \quad \int_0^1 x^{m+1} (1-x)^{n-1}\, dx,$$

and hence evaluate
$$\int_0^1 x^4 (1-x)^3\, dx.$$

(This is a typical Beta-function, useful in sampling theory.)

3. Differentiate $\cos^{n-1} x . \sin^{m+1} x$, and hence show that

$$\int_0^{\frac{1}{2}\pi} \cos^n x . \sin^m x \, dx = \frac{(n-1)}{(m+n)} \int_0^{\frac{1}{2}\pi} \cos^{n-2} x . \sin^m x \, dx.$$

Evaluate (by repeating the process)

$$\int_0^{\frac{1}{2}\pi} \sin^2 x \cos^4 x \, dx.$$

4. Can you find a similar formula which will reduce m instead of n? What happens when either m or n is zero? What happens when either m or n is unity? Evaluate the original integral:

(*a*) for $m = 3, n = 4$; (*b*) for $m = n = 5$;

(*c*) for $m = 4, n = 6$; (*d*) for $m = 6, n = 4$.

5. Show that $\displaystyle\int_0^{\frac{1}{2}\pi} \cos^n x . \cos nx \, dx = \frac{1}{2} \int_0^{\frac{1}{2}\pi} \cos^{n-1} x . \cos (n-1) x \, dx$ and evaluate

$$\int_0^{\frac{1}{2}\pi} \cos^6 x \cos 6x \, dx.$$

6. Evaluate

$$\int_0^{\pi} \sin nx \sin mx \, dx,$$

where (*a*) m, n are different integers; (*b*) m, n are the same integer. Do similar results hold for cosines? For a sine and a cosine?

7. For what range of values of n can a meaning be attached to the area under the graph of $y = x^n$ over:

(*a*) the interval $(0, 1)$; (*b*) the interval $(1, +\infty)$;

(*c*) the interval $(0, +\infty)$?

8. Integrate (by parts):

$$\int_0^a \frac{x^2 \, dx}{(1+x^2)^2}.$$

Does

$$\int_{-\infty}^{+\infty} \frac{x^2 \, dx}{(1+x^2)^2}$$

have a meaning?

9. Evaluate

$$\int_0^{\frac{1}{2}\pi} \frac{\cos x \, dx}{\sqrt{\sin x}}.$$

What is the difficulty about it?

10. Can a meaning be attached to:

(*a*) $\displaystyle\int_{-1}^{+1} \frac{dx}{\sqrt{x}}$; (*b*) $\displaystyle\int_0^1 \sqrt{\left(\frac{x}{1-x}\right)} \, dx$;

(*c*) $\displaystyle\int_{-1}^{+1} \frac{dx}{\sqrt{(1-x^2)}}$; (*d*) $\displaystyle\int_{-\infty}^{\infty} \frac{dx}{1+x}$?

11. Show that

$$\int_0^{\pi} x f(\sin x) \, dx = \pi \int_0^{\frac{1}{2}\pi} f(\sin x) \, dx,$$

and evaluate:

(*a*) $\displaystyle\int_0^{\pi} x \sin^2 x \, dx$; (*b*) $\displaystyle\int_0^{\pi} \frac{x \sin x}{1+\cos^2 x} \, dx$.

12. Find numbers a, b, c such that

$$\int_{-2h}^{+2h} f(x)\,dx = af(-2h)+bf(-h)+cf(0)+bf(h)+af(2h)$$

for the general quintic function.

Compare the accuracy of this rule with the accuracy of Simpson's Rule, using four strips, in integrating $\sin x$ over the interval $\{x: 0 \leqslant x \leqslant \pi\}$.

13. Show that, although g is not one-one over $[-1, 2]$, the substitution

$$u = g(x) = x^2+1$$

correctly evaluates
$$\int_{-1}^{+2} x^3(x^2+1)^4\,dx.$$

Show also that the same integral integrated over $[1, 2]$ has the same value.

14. Show that
$$\int_{\frac{1}{2}}^{2} \left(1-\frac{1}{t^2}\right) f\left(t+\frac{1}{t}\right) dt = 0.$$

Can you explain why the substitution $x = t+(1/t)$ makes this obvious?

24

INTRODUCTION TO MECHANICS

In Chapter 19, mathematical expressions were developed to describe motion. This chapter deals with the causes or circumstances of motion and their expression in mathematical terms.

As a preliminary to this, it will be useful to discuss the general idea of 'applied' mathematics.

1. APPLIED MATHEMATICS

1.1 The description of events. Suppose that you had taken up parachute jumping and that you wished to discover your terminal velocity, that is the constant, maximum velocity you might achieve while falling before the parachute opens. How could you possibly find this velocity if no instruments were available that would give you a direct reading?

One method would be to obtain the relation between the height and the time during that period of free falling. This could be done using an altimeter and a watch. The results could be plotted, a line drawn through the region of the points and the velocity estimated from the tangent at the appropriate times. Alternatively, an algebraic expression of the relation could be sought by plotting height against time; from this the velocity could be deduced by differentiation.

A completely different approach would be to attempt an analysis of the physical circumstances of the fall in the hope of discovering another lead to the velocity. The idea can be simply illustrated.

Obviously the parachutist experiences a downward pull and, further, it is generally observed that the harder anything is pulled, the sharper is its movement, that is, the greater its acceleration. So, if you measure the pull, you will find the acceleration and, by integration, you can then deduce the velocity.

This would be an excellent idea if it were not so difficult to think of a good way to measure the downward pull on yourself while free falling. Even if this could be done, the exact connection between acceleration and pull still has to be found. Perhaps we could simulate the fall under experimental conditions so that each factor can be varied at will. What factors should be considered? The basic, downward pull (but this cannot be varied in a laboratory) and the air resistance. What other things might affect these two factors? The position, shape, size, clothing, mass, temperature, or velocity of the parachutist, and perhaps the height, or humidity of the air? (What other things might be suggested?)

1.2 Models in mathematics. Before trying to deal with these experiments, it will be necessary to spend a great deal more time on understanding the things that have been described. To help us do that, it will be necessary to simplify. For example, let us consider a stone falling and let us think of it falling without air to resist it. Even that leaves the consideration of the pull of the earth about which we know little as yet, so let us go further; let us consider a small object under the action of a pull. How would it behave? We should imagine that it would be given an acceleration proportional to the pull.

The development of this discussion is the main purpose of this chapter. Though we shall not completely return to the falling parachutist, some of the complications will be re-introduced as soon as the simple ideas have been expressed mathematically.

The process has been to make a model of a situation and to imagine how things would happen in the model assuming that they would happen in the same way as in the real world. Such assumptions about the model are called 'postulates'.

Applied mathematics is the mathematics associated with these models; it involves the construction of concepts such as 'force', 'momentum', 'energy' in this field of mechanics; 'current', 'voltage', 'potential' in the field of electricity; 'mean', 'deviation', 'significance' in the field of statistics. It also involves the application of 'ordinary' pure mathematics to these situations. (We must take care that the right pure mathematics is applied at any time. It is no good trying to solve equations of motion with Boolean algebra.)

The model is considered to be a good one if events predicted in the model turn out to agree with observed facts. If you predict that your terminal velocity will be 45 m/s and it is so, as far as your accuracy goes, then you may have a good model. When a model has been well tested (as Newton's has over the last three hundred years) then the postulates are called laws.

2. NEWTON'S MODEL

2.1 Mass and force. In making a model for an object under the effect of a pull, Newton suggested the following postulates.

(i) *The particle.* Whenever we can ignore the extension of a body in space and can just consider it as matter concentrated at a point, we shall refer to a 'particle'. A planet in its motion round the sun, a go-kart accelerating along a track, a falling parachutist may be considered as particles, provided we are not concerned with their movements about their own centres. This idea cannot be used without modification when discussing a spinning wheel or a planet revolving about its axis. We shall postulate the existence of particles that occupy a point in space at an instant of time, so that we can use the equations developed in Chapter 19.

(ii) *Mass.* Associated with each particle there will always be a constant which will be called its 'mass'. Whatever the position or time, the same mass will be associated with a given particle. We can think of the mass as representing in some way the quantity of matter belonging to the body—we cannot say what mass really is any more than we can say what time is—and we shall have to consider how it can be measured.

(iii) *Natural behaviour.* At one time it was considered that, if physical objects were left to themselves, they would naturally come to rest: after all everything we experience on earth slows up and stops eventually. It would follow that, to keep a body steadily moving, some external agent would be needed to push it along its path. Newton's idea, inherited from Galileo, was to suppose that the natural state for a body was for it to continue moving in the same direction with a constant speed (or, if at rest, to remain so). He looked for agencies that altered *that* state. The agent that causes changes from the natural state of constant velocity (or rest) is described as a 'force'.

So, if a particle moves from rest, or if, when moving, it changes its speed either with or without change of direction, then a force is acting: or if it is at constant speed but it changes its direction, then again, a force is acting.

This qualitative definition of a force is given as Newton's First Law:

> 'Every body remains stationary or in uniform motion in a straight line unless it is made to change that state by external forces.'

Have we done enough analysis? Is the model quite clearly defined before we move on to Newton's Second Law which gives the quantitative definition of force, that is, the relation between force and acceleration? The answer is that for most every-day, terrestrial purposes, we *have*, but the following will show that the ideas are not yet clear enough for all purposes. A straightforward model will show that the ideas of a particle at rest or moving with constant velocity need more study.

Suppose a ball is rolling outwards at a steady speed along a radial groove of a rotating stage; then to a person standing on the stage or walking straight across it at a steady speed, the ball would be seen to have a constant velocity and he would infer that no force was acting on it. To an observer standing off the stage the ball would appear to move in a spiral path and he would infer that there was some force acting on it. In general, a particle having a constant speed and direction for one 'frame of reference' (that is, some origin and set of axes) is in the same condition for any other which is not accelerating or rotating relative to it, but not so for other frames of reference. So, either one must know which frames are permissible or accept the fact that force cannot have an absolute existence. Implicit in Newtonian mechanics is the assumption that forces are absolute entities.

For a study of the solar system, the basic frame of reference used is one whose origin is at the centre of the sun and whose axes are fixed relative to the fixed stars. Force defined relative to this system would differ from that defined for a frame of reference fixed relative to the earth, but as the earth's path curves slowly and its rotation on its axis is slow the difference is slight.† So for terrestrial problems we shall define force relative to a frame of reference fixed to the earth or to one whose motion relative to this is non-rotating and of constant velocity.

2.2 Equation of motion. We state the following as our first law:

> The force acting on a particle is proportional to its mass and to its acceleration, and has the direction of the acceleration.
>
> (This is Newton's Second Law and is sometimes written: Acceleration is proportional to the impressed force, and acts along the same straight line.)

If the force, mass and acceleration are denoted by F, m and a, then the statement is equivalent to $F = \lambda ma$, where λ is some constant, and F has the same direction as a. By a suitable choice of units, λ can be put equal to 1, so that

$$F = ma.$$

This relation we shall refer to as the 'equation of motion'.

The question of what units will be employed is postponed for a while. It is worth observing that if equal forces are applied to different particles, those with smaller masses have the larger accelerations, as we might have hoped.

To discuss the implications of the equation of motion it is simpler if we shed some of the difficulties due to our earthly existence and transport ourselves to a laboratory in the depths of space (making sure, of course, that it represents a permitted frame of reference). Let us take a particle and ascribe to it a unit of mass. We notice, let us say, that it stays freely wherever it is put, so we know no force is acting on it.

Now suppose that by some mechanism we make it move in a straight line with an acceleration which is measured to be 1 m/s^2; then by the equation of motion we can say that the mechanism has exerted a force of 1 unit on it. If instead it had accelerated at 10 m/s^2 then 10 units of force must have been exerted on it; and in each case the direction of the force must have been the direction of the acceleration.

† The difference between the two systems shows up when one observes the behaviour of Foucault's pendulum or a freely mounted gyroscope, maintaining its direction in space.

Next it is put in a solenoid (a spring-like winding of wire) through which an electric current is passed and it is observed to accelerate at 5 m/s^2 along the axis of the solenoid. We immediately deduce that the electromagnetic field of the solenoid has exerted a force of 5 units in the direction of the axis.

Thirdly, suppose it is set in motion at the end of a piece of string 1 metre long, with the other end fixed so that it describes a circle at a measured angular rate of 3 radians per second. Since it will have an acceleration of $r\omega^2$, in this case 9 m/s^2, towards the centre we can say that the string is always exerting a force of 9 units on it towards the centre.

2.3 Vector equation of motion: $F = ma$. So far we have encountered single forces defined in terms of measurable acceleration and mass, and we are thinking of forces as having an absolute existence. By experiment, observation and hypothesis, we can predict what force will be exerted by a particular agent, for example, a spring under a certain compression or the attraction by the earth on a body at a certain distance away. Now suppose a particle is acted on by a number of such agents simultaneously; how would we expect it to accelerate? By experiment and observation we find that the acceleration is the vector sum of what would be the accelerations due to each force separately, and this we therefore take as a further postulate in our model.

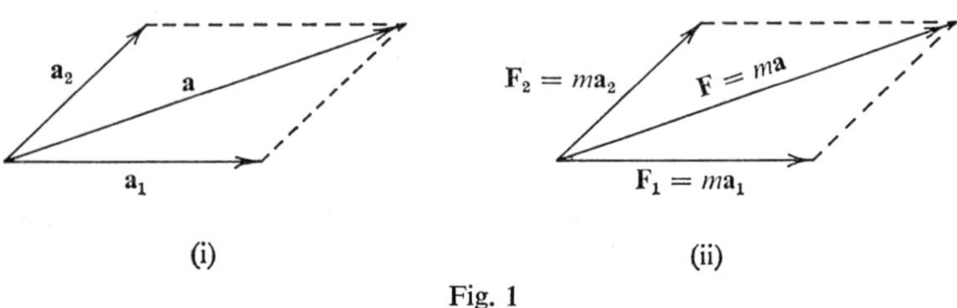

Fig. 1

Suppose forces F_1 and F_2 give a particle of mass m accelerations $\mathbf{a}_1$ and $\mathbf{a}_2$, respectively, and let F be the single force which gives the mass the acceleration $\mathbf{a}$, which it has when the forces act together. Then F_1, F_2, F have the magnitudes and directions of $m\mathbf{a}_1$, $m\mathbf{a}_2$, $m\mathbf{a}$ respectively. But $\mathbf{a}$ is the vector sum of $\mathbf{a}_1$ and $\mathbf{a}_2$, and therefore F is the sum of F_1 and F_2 added as vectors.

Since forces have magnitude and direction and are added by the rule for the addition of vectors, we can say that a force is a vector quantity. The equation of motion can now be written as the vector equation

$$\mathbf{F} = m\mathbf{a},$$

where $\mathbf{F}$ is the vector sum of the forces—called the resultant force—and $\mathbf{a}$

is the actual acceleration of the mass. This result is easily extended to cases where more than two forces act.

Example 1. If a mass of 2 units is acted on by forces of 5, 10 and 8 units in directions north, east and S 60° W, find the resultant force and hence the acceleration (Figure 2).

The simplest way to find the vector sum of the forces (that is, the resultant) is by drawing, as shown in Figure 2(ii), where the resultant is **AD**, which by measurement is 3·23 units in a direction N 72° E.

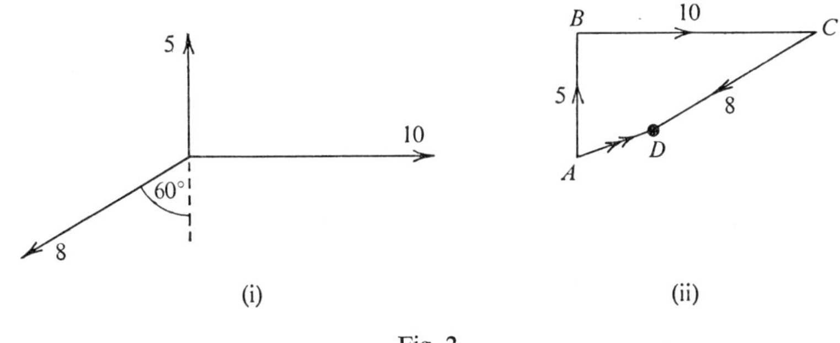

Fig. 2

Since the mass is 2 units, the acceleration is 1·62 units in the direction N 72° E.

So far the equation of motion has been applied to single particles. Under certain simple conditions the same equation can be applied to systems of particles. This extension will be considered after the interaction principle has been described.

Exercise A

In this exercise, a unit force will be one which gives to a unit mass an acceleration of 1 m/s².

For all the questions, the action takes place in a space away from any gravitational field.

In the vector questions, solution by drawing will be acceptable.

1. What is the acceleration of a particle of mass 100 units when pushed with a force (*a*) of 10 units; (*b*) of 100 units?

2. What force must be exerted on a particle of mass 2000 units in order to give it an acceleration (*a*) of 1 unit? (*b*) of 10 units? (*c*) of 1/2000 units?

3. Figure 3 (overleaf) is a graph of the velocity of a particle of mass 200 units moving in a straight line over a period of 20 seconds. From the sketch, estimate the force that is being exerted upon the particle when

(*a*) $t = 1$ s; (*b*) $t = 10$ s; (*c*) $t = 18$ s.

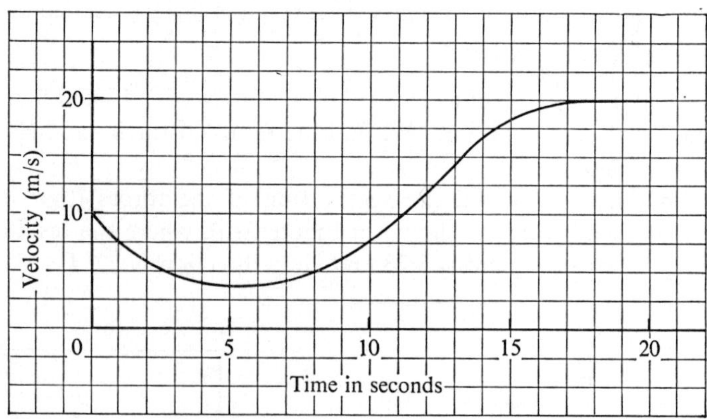

Fig. 3

4. A particle of mass 25 units is moving with a constant velocity of magnitude 10000 m/s and is then pushed with a force of 100 units.

(*a*) Does the initial velocity make any difference to the change of velocity?

(*b*) Can any information about the change of velocity be deduced if the initial velocity is not given?

(*c*) What is the magnitude of the change in velocity, if the force is exerted for 1 s? What can be stated about its direction?

5. A particle of mass 1 unit is moving with constant velocity of 500 m/s when it is pulled by a force.

(*a*) If the force is of magnitude 100 units making an angle of 45° with the original path, what will the new velocity be after (i) 1 s, (ii) 3 s?

(*b*) If the final velocity after 1 s is 500 m/s at right-angles to the original path, what was the magnitude and direction of the constant force exerted?

6. A particle of mass 5 units moves in a circle of radius 12 units at a speed of 5 m/s. What force must be exerted on the particle?

7. A force is causing a particle of mass 2 units to move in a circle of radius 0·2 m with an angular velocity of 3 rev/s. What is the magnitude of the force? In what ratio is the force increased if (*a*) the mass is doubled, or if (*b*) the angular velocity is doubled?

8. A particle of mass 10000 units is being pulled by two forces of 2000 and 1000 units respectively. The angle between the forces is 60°. What is the particle's acceleration?

9. Three coplanar forces act on a particle. They are inclined at 120° with each other and have magnitudes of 2, 2 and 3 units. If the magnitude of the resultant acceleration is $\frac{1}{2}$ m/s, what is the mass of the particle?

10. A particle of mass 10 units, in position *A*, is acted on by forces of 4, 6, 1 units in directions which make angles of 0°, 120°, 210° with a fixed direction *AB*. What is its acceleration?

11. A moving particle of mass 6 units is acted on by a force of 5 units in a direction of 40° from the direction of its velocity.

(*a*) What additional force at 90° to its velocity will keep the particle moving in a straight line?

(*b*) In what direction should an additional force of 3 units be applied to keep the particle moving in a straight line?

(*c*) What additional force will give the particle an instantaneous acceleration of 2 m/s^2 in a direction of 70° from the direction of its velocity?

12. A particle of mass 5 units is moving on a circular course of radius 2 m. If at some instant its speed is 1 m/s, and its speed is decreasing at $\frac{1}{4}$ m/s^2, what is the total force exerted on the particle?

13. A particle of mass 1 unit is moving in a circle of radius 1 m. Its angular velocity is 1 rad/s. What force is being exerted on it?

If the angular velocity is increased by 1 rad/s in 1 second, what force is being exerted along the tangent? What is now the total force acting upon the particle?

14. A particle of mass 5 units is moving along a path whose vector equation is given by

(*a*) $\mathbf{r} = t(\mathbf{i}+\mathbf{j})$; (*b*) $\mathbf{r} = t\mathbf{i}+t^2\mathbf{j}$;

(*c*) $\mathbf{r} = \mathbf{i}+t^3(\mathbf{i}+\mathbf{j})$; (*d*) $\mathbf{r} = t\mathbf{i}+(\sin t)\mathbf{j}$.

What forces must be acting on the particle in each case at the moments when $t = 0, 1, \frac{1}{2}\pi$?

15. A particle of mass 3 units is moving on a wire whose vector equation is

$$\mathbf{r} = t\mathbf{i}+16t^2\mathbf{j};$$

what force must be acting on the particle?

If the wire itself is moving with a velocity given by

$$\dot{\mathbf{r}} = t^2\mathbf{i},$$

what is the total force that must be acting on the particle?

2.4 The interaction principle. In the model we are constructing, we have laid down the basic elements, particles with mass and position at any given time, and we have stated their 'natural' behaviour and how this may be altered by forces. The relation between force and acceleration has been stated and the way in which forces can be combined. There remains one other consideration with regard to forces which can be illustrated in the following way.

If you stand still, you push downwards onto the ground and, to keep you there, the ground has to push upwards with the same force. The downward pull of the earth on the falling parachutist is equalled by the upward pull of the falling parachutist on the earth. If you whirl a dancing partner round, a force must be exerted upon her to make her move in a circle; an equal but opposite force pulls you towards her. All these are instances of the fact that all forces are 'two-ended'; no body can exert a force in one direction on another body without the second body exerting an equal force on it in the opposite direction. This principle or postulate is equally true whether the bodies are at rest, moving uniformly, or being accelerated. If you stand with your hand on a trolley and give the trolley a push so that it moves away from you, while you pushed, it was accelerating away, yet it was at the same time exerting an equal and opposite force upon your hand.

The following analysis will help to make this clear.

A particle A of mass m units is set in motion with acceleration a units by means of a rod which is pushed against it. Imagine this particle to be split, by a plane section at right-angles to the rod, into two parts which we assume can be considered to be particles B and C of masses m_1 and m_2 units, where $m = m_1+m_2$ (see Figure 4).

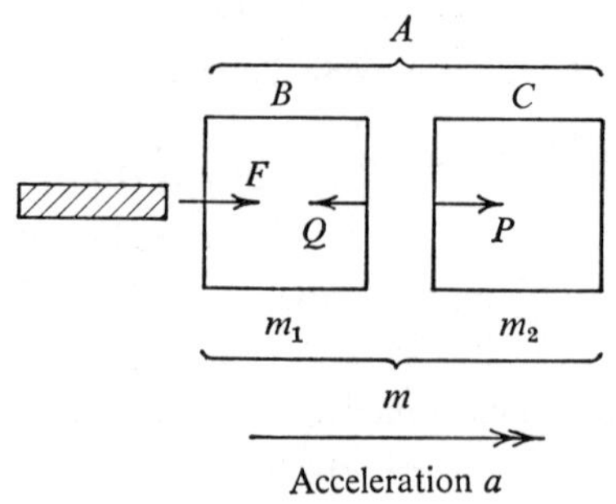

Fig. 4

If the rod exerts a force F units on A, then

$$F = (m_1+m_2)\,a. \tag{1}$$

For the particle C, if the force which B exerts on it is P units,

$$P = m_2 a.$$

Now, if the only force on B were F units, then F would be equal to $m_1 a$, in contradiction to (i). It follows that C must exert some force, say Q units, backwards on B.

Then $$F-Q = m_1 a,$$

and hence
$$\begin{aligned} Q &= F-m_1 a \\ &= (m_1+m_2)\,a-m_1 a \\ &= m_2 a \\ &= P. \end{aligned}$$

That is, the force which C exerts on B is equal in magnitude and opposite in direction to the force which B exerts on C.

To arrive at this result we have had to make certain assumptions, so that nothing has been proved even though the assumptions may seem reasonable; and in any case we have here dealt with a particular situation where forces of contact exist between particles and other cases will arise which are not so simple to analyse. The general statement that when one system of particles exerts a force on another, then the second system exerts an equal and opposite force on the first, will be taken as a postulate.

> *The interaction principle.* Forces arise only when bodies are acting on one another; when a body A exerts a force on a body B, then body B exerts an equal and opposite force on body A (acting in the same straight line).

This is Newton's Third Law.

2.5 Bodies. By a body we shall mean a solid piece of matter which we conceive as composed of a large number of particles bound together in fixed relative positions by internal forces which obey the interaction principle.

If we now consider a collection of particles forming a body and study the forces, both internal and external, acting on them when the system moves *without rotation*, so that all the particles have the same velocity at any instant and therefore the same acceleration, we shall find that the system can be treated dynamically as if it were a single particle whose mass equals the total of the masses of the constituent particles and having the acceleration common to these particles. The argument is simple.

The sum of all the internal forces between the particles of the system is zero because, by the interaction principle, to each force there is an equal and opposite force which annuls it in the total. Now if the common acceleration of the particles is $\mathbf{a}$, and the particles have masses m_1, m_2, ..., m_n, then

$$\text{the sum of the internal and external forces on mass } m_1 = m_1\mathbf{a};$$
$$\text{the sum of the internal and external forces on mass } m_2 = m_2\mathbf{a};$$

and so on. Adding vectorially all the forces for all the particles and equating to zero the sum of all the internal forces, we have,

$$\text{the vector sum of the external forces} = (m_1+m_2+\ldots+m_n)\,\mathbf{a}.$$

The acceleration of the body is therefore the same as if the external force system acted on a particle of mass M where $M = m_1+m_2+\ldots+m_n$.

Exercise B

In this exercise, a unit force will be one that gives to a unit mass an acceleration of 1 m/s.

In all the questions, the action will take place away from any gravitational field.

1. A particle is split into two parts of mass 10 and 20 units. A force of 30 units is pushing the smaller part against the larger in the manner of Figure 4.

What is the acceleration of the whole particle and what are the forces of reaction between the two parts?

2. A body in the shape of a rod of uniform cross-section and length 3 m is being pulled from one end in the line of its length. It has an acceleration of 1 m/s^2 and a total mass of 3 units. What force is being exerted across the sections at one and two metres from the leading end?

3. A, B, C and D are four cubical blocks in contact in a straight line. The mass of each block is 8 units. An experimenting spaceman pushes on block A with a force along $\overrightarrow{AD}$. If A exerts a force of 12 units on B, find:

(*a*) the acceleration of the four blocks;
(*b*) the force exerted by the spaceman;
(*c*) the force which block B exerts on block A;
(*d*) the force which block D exerts on block C.

4. A force of attraction of 10 units exists between two bodies of masses 50 and 80 units. If they are free to move, what will their acceleration of approach be?

5. Two bodies, A and B with masses 5 and 10 units respectively, are joined by a wire of negligible mass. A force on B moves both bodies in the direction AB with an acceleration of 30 m/s^2. What is the magnitude of the force and what force does the wire exert on each block? What is the force across any section of the wire?

6. Repeat Question 5 assuming that the wire has a mass of 5 units, a length of 1 m and a uniform cross-section. Give the force across any section in terms of its distance d from B.

7. A particle of mass 60 units is attached to a pivot and made to move in a circular path of radius 2 units with an angular velocity of 2 rev/s. What force is being exerted upon the pivot? What would the acceleration of the particle relative to the pivot be, if the connection broke?

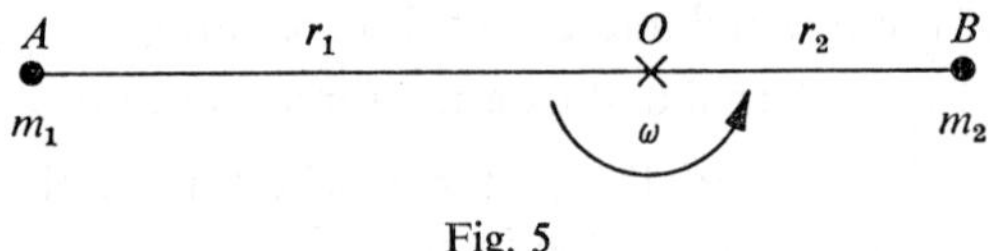

Fig. 5

8. Suppose in our laboratory out in space we have a system of two particles A and B of masses m_1 and m_2, joined by a fine string whose mass is small enough to be neglected, which is set in steady rotary motion, so that a point O of the string is at rest. Let the measured distances from O to the two particles be r_1 and r_2 metres, and let the angular velocity of the string be ω rad/s. Write down the acceleration of the particle A towards O and also the force that the string must be exerting on A. Write down the acceleration and force acting on B. From these expressions and the interaction principle, find an expression for the ratio of the masses of A and B in terms of the distances r_1 and r_2.

3. THE APPLICATION OF NEWTON'S MODEL

3.1 Newton's law of gravitation. The foundation and the main confirming test of his laws in Newton's time was to be found in observations of the planets and moon.

In the early part of the seventeenth century, Kepler announced three kinematical laws of planetary motion which he unfolded after many years of arduous calculation based on the observational data given by the astronomer Tycho Brahe shortly before. The laws can be stated thus:

1. The planets move in ellipses with the sun at one focus.
2. The line joining the sun to a planet sweeps out equal areas in equal times.
3. $T^2 = kr^3$, where T is the time of revolution, r is the mean distance of the planet from the sun, and k is a constant for all planets.

From his laws of motion Newton showed that Kepler's empirical laws required that the sun should exert an attractive force on the planets which varies as their mass and inversely as the square of their distance from the sun at any point in their orbit. Furthermore, he showed that the acceleration of the moon towards the earth as she pursues her almost circular orbit, compared with the acceleration of a body falling freely near the earth's surface, was in the inverse ratio of the square of the distances of the moon and the terrestrial body from the earth's centre. So the law of attraction which accounted for the motion of the planets around the sun could also be applied to the gravitational force which the earth exerts on any object at its surface and on the moon.

It appeared to be a law of nature that an attracting body exerts a force of km/d^2, where m is the mass of the attracted body and d its distance away, while k is a constant depending on the attracting body.

Since, by the interaction principle, the gravitational attraction between two bodies is a mutual force, the role of attracting and attracted bodies are interchangeable. So Newton was led to propound his universal law of gravitation. Effectively this states that between any two particles of masses m and m', at a distance d apart, there is a mutual attractive force of $G.(mm'/d^2)$, where G is a universal constant (for a particular system of units). It can be deduced from this, as Newton showed, that the gravitational force between spherical bodies of masses m and m' (of any radius) is given by the same formula where d is the distance between their centres.

We have the fact that the earth exerts a force of km/d^2 on a body of mass m, a distance d from its centre, where the force acts towards the centre of the earth, and k is a constant. By the weight of a body we mean this gravitational force towards the earth's centre. The term weight is not used except for bodies close to the earth's surface (and not of course for the earth itself!). Weight is not an absolute property of a body (as mass is) because it decreases as the body moves further away from the earth and indeed varies over the earth's surface; since the earth is not an exact sphere, some places are nearer to the centre than others.

This gives us a simple, practical way of measuring mass. For two bodies in the same locality (so that d is near enough the same for both) their weights will be proportional to their masses; so that, for instance, if one has three times the weight of the other, it will have three times the mass. Hence, after choosing our unit of mass, we can determine the mass of any other body by comparing its weight (as shown on a weighing machine) with the weight of the unit mass.

It follows immediately from the law of gravitation that all bodies near the earth's surface have the same acceleration, if free to fall, for the gravitational force (weight) on a body of mass m is km/d^2, where d is now the radius of the earth, and its acceleration is therefore k/d^2 which is independent of the mass. The constancy of the acceleration can be checked experimentally in a vacuum; and, indeed, gave Newton further evidence for his law.

3.2 Inertial and gravitational mass. If different particles are subjected to equal forces (for example, that provided by a spring under a certain compression) their accelerations depend on their masses—the more massive the particle, the smaller its acceleration. This was our original understanding of mass as a property of matter determined by the fundamental equation of motion, $F = ma$. We can describe this property as the *inertial* mass of the particle, that is, its resistance to change in the state of motion.

If different particles are placed one after another in some definite position relative to the earth, they are found to experience different gravitational forces, the magnitudes being proportional to their masses. This property of matter—the ability to experience a force in a gravitational field—we can describe as the *gravitational* mass of the particle.

It is rather remarkable that the gravitational mass of a body is the same as its inertial mass; as one can realize if one thinks of the particle being placed in an electromagnetic field instead of a gravitational field, when the force it experiences does not depend on its mass but on the electric charge it carries.

3.3 Unit of mass. In the metric system, the unit of mass is the *kilogram* (kg) which is equal to the mass of a cubic decimetre of distilled water at the temperature of its maximum density (4° C). The kilogram is defined as the mass of a platinum–iridium standard, a solid cylinder of height equal to its diameter, which is preserved at the International Bureau of Weights and Measures at Paris.

3.4 Unit of force. A unit force is a force which gives a unit mass a unit of acceleration. (This makes $\lambda = 1$ in Section 2.2.) In the metric system we take a unit length to be a *metre* and a unit time to be a *second*; a unit force is called a *newton*. Hence, 1 newton gives a mass of 1 kg an acceleration of 1 metre per second per second, and therefore

$$1 \text{ newton} = 1 \text{ kg} \frac{1 \text{ metre}}{(1 \text{ second})^2} = 1 \text{ kg m/s}^2.$$

(The standard abbreviation for a newton is 'N'.)

3.5 Weight. At the earth's surface a free body accelerates at approximately 9·8 m/s². If its mass is m kg, the gravitational force on it is

$$(m \text{ kg}) \times (9{\cdot}8 \text{ m/s}^2),$$

that is, its weight is $9{\cdot}8m$ N.

In general, if g is the acceleration due to gravity, the weight of a body of mass m is mg, and as g varies so does the weight.

Weighing suggests the idea of a body resting on a scale pan. If the body were free to fall it would have an acceleration g and the earth's attractive force would be mg, where m is its mass. On the scale pan the earth still exerts this force on it, but it remains at rest because an exactly equal and opposite force N is exerted upwards on it by the scale pan.

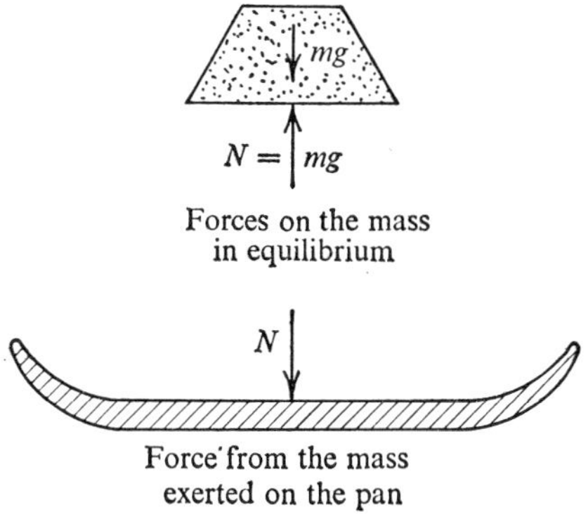

Fig. 6

Now by the interaction principle the body exerts an equal and opposite force to this—that is, a force N downwards—on the scale pan, and it is this force (which is equal to mg) which the weighing machine measures. If the same force were exerted by some different means, such as pressing down on the pan with one's hand, the reading would be the same.

Exercise C†

(The radius of the earth is approximately $6{\cdot}4 \times 10^6$ metres.)

1. Stating the units, find the forces required to propel:
(*a*) a mass of 3 kg with an acceleration of 50 m/s²;
(*b*) a mass of 5000 kg with an acceleration of 10 m/s²;
(*c*) a mass of 300 gm with an acceleration of 20 m/s²;
(*d*) a mass of 3000 kg with an acceleration of 50 cm/s².

2. Stating the units, give the acceleration of the following:
(*a*) a mass of 3 kg under a force of 30 N;
(*b*) a mass of 10 kg under a force of 6 N;
(*c*) a mass of 3000 kg under a force of 60 N.

The following 4 questions repeat the ideas of Exercise A and should be considered just as an exercise in the use of units.

3. A particle of mass 5 kg increases its speed from 3 m/s to 17 m/s in 3 s. What force was acting on it?

4. A force of 70 N acts upon a mass of 5 kg to retard its initial speed of 70 m/s. If the force acts for 1/200 s, what distance does the mass cover in that time?

5. The force acting on a body of mass of 50 kg is given by the relation $P = 20t$ where P is measured in newtons. If, when $t = 0$, the speed is 3 m/s, what is the speed when $t = 5$ s?

6. The position of a mass of 3 gm is given by the vector equation $\mathbf{r} = t^2(\mathbf{i}+\mathbf{j})$, where r is measured in cm and t in s. What force is acting on the mass? Answer in newtons.

The remaining questions of this exercise are about weight.

7. What is the weight at the earth's surface of a body of mass 10 kg? With what force does the earth attract it when its height above the surface of the earth is

(*a*) 3200 km; (*b*) 6400 km; (*c*) 100000 km?

8. If a man moves from sea level to the top of a mountain 8 km high, by approximately what ratio has his weight decreased? (Compare p. 452.)

9. The height of a body is 1600 kilometres above the surface of the earth. If its mass is 2000 kg, what is its weight? What is the mass of another body that has this weight when at the surface of the earth?

10. If a man of mass 60 kg were to stand on the surface of the moon, what would his weight be, relative to the moon, given that the mass of the moon is approximately $\frac{1}{80}$ the mass of the earth and that its radius is $\frac{3}{11}$ the radius of the earth?

11. Sketch graphs showing the general way in which the gravitational forces to the earth and the moon vary with position during a rocket flight directly to the moon. Sketch also the way in which the acceleration varies with position, and from this deduce the graph of the speed against position, assuming the rocket quickly attains its maximum speed away from the earth and then the propulsive force ceases.

† We use 'a mass of 3 kg' as a convenient, though loose, abbreviation for 'a body of mass 3 kg'.

4. FORCE AND MASS-ACCELERATION VECTOR SYSTEMS

For the remainder of this chapter, the model we have developed will be used so that mathematics can be applied to situations concerning forces acting on various objects. In each case, the parachutist, balloon or goldfish will be considered as a particle and the pressures, buoyancies or tensions will be the forces acting upon them. Situations where the model does not apply will not be mentioned.

The method of solution will be to equate the sum of the force vectors to the sum of the mass × acceleration vectors (which will in future be written mass-acceleration). In most of the examples, several forces are combined and equated to a single mass-acceleration vector.

It is often useful to draw diagrams showing each of the forces acting on the body, its mass and acceleration(s). Sometimes it is clearer to show the two systems on separate diagrams.

4.1 Types of forces. Pressure forces, such as those considered in the previous example, are referred to as 'normal contact forces', where normal is used in the mathematical sense of perpendicular—the forces are perpendicular to the surfaces in contact. Normal contact force will often be abbreviated to 'normal force'.

Most forces we shall meet are contact forces, that is, forces due to matter in contact; the exceptions being gravitational and electromagnetic forces. It is a useful, if not consistent, practice to give special names to such contact forces.

If an agent such as a ram rod or a spring is designed to exert a continuous force on a body, that force is often called a thrust. If a string or rod or a stretched spring is pulling on the body, the force is usually called a tension. If two bodies in contact are in relative motion, then in addition to the normal force there is a so-called frictional force between them; and a frictional force sufficient to prevent motion can also exist. Other names used for contact forces, when the agent is a fluid or gas, are: lift, drag, air resistance, buoyancy and so on.

Apart from the exceptions mentioned, all the forces in a mechanical problem are contact forces. When drawing a diagram to show the forces acting on a body one must insert, in addition to the non-contact forces (usually gravity), a force *from each* of the material contacts.

4.2 Parallel forces on a single body. When the forces are known to be parallel, the equating of vector systems reduces to the statement of the equation of motion, that is to equations between the scalar magnitudes of the forces and mass-acceleration vectors.

Example 2 (Figure 7). A balloon of total mass 5500 kg (including the occupants and gear) is rising steadily at 1 m/s when 500 kg of sand are jettisoned. How fast is the balloon rising 10 s later? If gas is then released from the balloon which reduces its buoyancy by $700g$ N, at what rate will it be descending after a further minute? (Neglect the mass of the released gas and the air resistance to the balloon. g here and in metric examples is a numerical constant equal to 9·8.)

When it has a constant upward speed the buoyancy (B N) is equal to the weight $5500g$ N, since there is no acceleration. That is

$$B = 5500g.$$

After dropping 500 kg of sand the balloon's mass is reduced to 5000 kg. The forces acting are now the weight $5000g$ N down and the buoyancy $5500g$ N up. If it accelerates upwards at a m/s², the equation of motion is

$$5500g - 5000g = 5000a,$$

and therefore

$$a = g/10 = 9{\cdot}8.$$

The acceleration is therefore 0·98 m/s² upwards. Originally it had an upward speed of 1 m/s, so with this acceleration its speed after 10 s is $1+9{\cdot}8 = 10{\cdot}8$ m/s upwards.

Now when the buoyancy has been reduced by $700g$ N the forces acting are the buoyancy $4800g$ N and the weight $5000g$ N (since the mass of 5000 kg is assumed to be unchanged by the loss of gas). If its upward acceleration is now a', the equation of motion is

$$4800g - 5000g = 5000a',$$

and therefore

$$a' = -g/25.$$

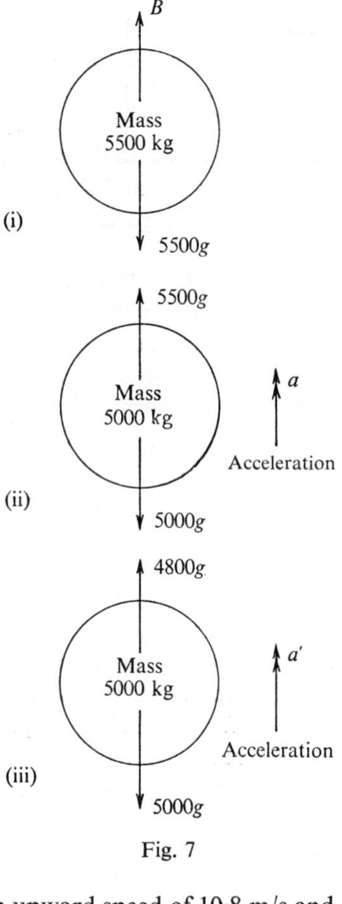

Fig. 7

The situation now is that the balloon has an upward speed of 10·8 m/s and an upward acceleration of $-g/25$ m/s². Its speed in m/s after 60 s is therefore v m/s, where

$$v = 10{\cdot}8 - \frac{g}{25}.60 = 10{\cdot}8 - \frac{9{\cdot}8}{25}.60 \simeq -12{\cdot}7,$$

that is, a downward speed of about 12·7 m/s.

Example 3 (Figure 8). A man of mass 75 kg is in a lift which is accelerating downwards at $1{\cdot}8\ \mathrm{m/s^2}$. What force does he exert on the lift?

If the man exerts a downward force of P N on the floor of the lift, then the lift exerts an upward force of P N on the man. The forces on the man are therefore P N upwards and the weight $75g$ N downwards. Since his mass is 75 kg and the acceleration is $1{\cdot}8\ \mathrm{m/s^2}$ downwards, the equation of motion is

$$75g - P = 75 \times 1{\cdot}8 \quad (\text{where } g = 9{\cdot}8).$$

Therefore, $$P = 75.9{\cdot}8 - 75.1{\cdot}8 = 75{\cdot}8 = 600.$$

Hence the man exerts a downward force on the lift of 600 N.

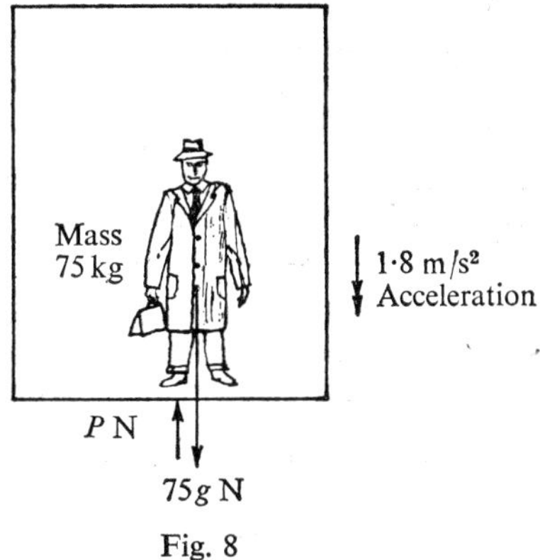

Fig. 8

Had the lift been stationary or moving up or down at a steady speed, the pressure force would have been equal to the weight of the man, which is $75g$ N, or 735 N. If the lift accelerates downwards, the force between his feet and the lift is decreased; and if the lift were dropping freely at $9{\cdot}8\ \mathrm{m/s^2}$ the force would of course be zero. When the man no longer feels a force of reaction on his feet he is in a state of apparent weightlessness.

Exercise D

1. A rock of mass 2 kg is to be given an acceleration of $3\ \mathrm{m/s^2}$. What force must be exerted upon it if the direction of the acceleration is to be (*a*) vertically upward, (*b*) vertically downward?

2. A body of mass 10 kg is falling with a downward acceleration of $a\ \mathrm{m/s^2}$. What is the value of a, if the resisting force is 13 N?

3. A boy of mass 50 kg is in a lift which is being brought to rest on its way down at a retardation of $3\ \mathrm{m/s^2}$. How does the contact force on the boy from the lift change as the lift comes to rest?

4. A metal canister of mass 3 kg is released underwater. If the buoyancy is 60 N, what is its initial acceleration? If, later on when it is moving, the water offers a resistance of 15 N, what is its acceleration then?

5. A crane is lifting a mass of 1 tonne. How quickly can the mass be accelerated upwards if the coupling must not bear a strain of more than $1{\cdot}1 \times 10^4$ N?

6. A goldfish in a bowl placed on a weighing machine accelerates upwards from rest. In what way, if any, does the machine reading change? What can you say about the reading when the fish swims upwards at a steady speed?

7. A buoy of mass 2000 kg is supporting a length of cable of weight 10000 N, when it breaks free. What is its initial acceleration?

8. A parachutist, of total mass 90 kg, at the end of a free fall has a constant speed of 40 m/s. What is the air resistance? When the parachute opens there is an additional resistance of 2000 N for the next $1\frac{1}{2}$ s. What is his speed at the end of this time? If instead of opening, the parachute had broken free, would his speed have increased or decreased?

9. A mass of 0·2 kg is swung round in a vertical circular path of radius 1 m at the end of a piece of string. What is the tension in the string when the mass is at its lowest point if its speed there is 2 m/s?

10. A boy catches a cricket ball of mass 160 g which is moving vertically downwards at 15 m/s. In the process his hands move downwards with the ball for 75 cm, and while doing so exert a constant force on the ball. Calculate this force.

11. A body of mass 100 kg is re-entering the earth's atmosphere vertically at a speed of 300 m/s and at a height of 10^5 metres. If the average air resistance over the next 2 s is 400 N, what is its velocity at the end of this time?

12. Analyse the forces and accelerations on an astronaut in a condition of 'weightlessness' when orbiting the earth.

13. What is the gravitational force on a mass m at d km above the earth's surface (radius of the earth is approximately 6400 km)? Calculate the height of a hovering (Early Bird) satellite.

4.3 Springs and elastic strings. Springs and elastic strings provide another source of examples of the application of Newton's Second Law.

It can be shown by experiments that, when a spring or an elastic string is stretched, the extension is proportional to the tension. (This supposes that the material has not been so far extended that it has been broken or deformed and unable to return to its original shape.) The extension is also proportional to the original length if specimens of different length are subjected to the same tension, but this fact will not be used here. A spring under compression has similar properties: the compression being proportional to the thrust. These facts are known as *Hooke's Law*.

In any problem involving springs or elastic strings, the elastic properties will be given by stating the extension (or compression) for a particular tension (or thrust).

Example 4. The top end of a spring is fixed and the lower end is extended by 3 cm and attached to a mass of 10 kg. Given that the spring is extended by 2 cm under a tension of 80 N, what will be the acceleration of the mass immediately it is released? (Figure 9.)

The force T exerted by the spring $= 80 \times \frac{3}{2} = 120$ N.

The forces acting on the mass are

$$120 \text{ N upward} \quad \text{and} \quad 98 \text{ N downward.}$$

If the acceleration is a m/s² upwards, the equation of motion is

$$120-98 = 10a.$$

Hence $a = 2{\cdot}2$; the acceleration is therefore 2·2 m/s² upwards.

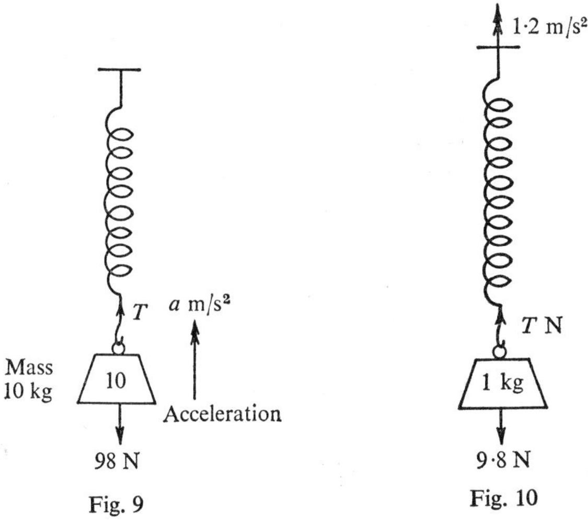

Fig. 9

Fig. 10

Example 5. Suppose that a spring is such that it is initially stretched by 20 cm when supporting a mass of 1 kg. What will the extension be, if the upper end is moving upward with an acceleration of 1·2 m/s²? (Figure 10.)

When at rest the forces on the mass are T_0 N and 9·8 N. So

$$T_0 - 9{\cdot}8 = 1 \times 0 \Rightarrow T_0 = 9{\cdot}8.$$

When accelerating let the new tension be T N. So

$$T - 9{\cdot}8 = 1 \times 1{\cdot}2 \Rightarrow T = 11.$$

The new extension will be

$$\frac{11}{9{\cdot}8} \times 20 = 22{\cdot}5 \text{ cm.}$$

In the last example, when the top of the spring was first accelerated, the spring would not *gradually* open another 2·5 cm and remain at that extension. Instead, the mass would oscillate about the new extension. At first, when the upper end accelerates, the lower end is left behind, but it gradually acquires more acceleration under the increasing tension as the spring stretches. Even when the acceleration of the lower end *does* reach $1{\cdot}2\ \text{m/s}^2$, the spring will continue to stretch, for it will be moving more slowly than the top end. As the spring stretches further, and the acceleration of the mass consequently increases, the mass will eventually acquire a greater velocity than the top end and the spring will start to contract. . . . and so on. Forces within the spring will damp the oscillations and will then cease to operate. The second part of the working of the example assumes that this has happened.

Exercise E

1. A spring is extended by 2 cm when under a tension of 40 N. By how much will it be extended under tensions of 60 N, 80 N, 10 N?

2. A spring of unstretched length 20 cm becomes 22 cm when held vertically and supporting a mass of 5 kg at its lower end. What will its length be when supporting 3 kg?

3. An elastic string is 0·6 m in length when unstretched and extends by 1 cm when under a tension of 8 N.

(*a*) What will its length be when held vertically and made to support a mass of 2 kg at the lower end?

(*b*) What would the acceleration of the mass be immediately after release, if the string had been extended by 5 cm beyond its unstretched length and released?

4. A spring that requires a thrust of 100 N to compress it by 8 cm, is compressed by 12 cm and locked in that position. It is placed vertically on a table and a mass of 4 kg is fixed to the top end. What would the initial acceleration of the mass be when the spring is released?

5. If the locked spring of Question 4 is placed between two blocks with masses of 1·5 kg and 2·5 kg, what will the initial accelerations of the blocks be if

(*a*) no other forces are acting on the blocks;

(*b*) the blocks are held one above the other in the gravitational field (the 1·5 kg block above the spring) and are released when the spring is released?

6. A mass of 20 kg will extend the spring supporting it by 3 cm. What will the extension be if the top of the spring is given a *downward* acceleration of $2\ \text{m/s}^2$?

7. A mass of 3 kg resting on a light vertical spring, compresses it 21 mm. What further compression is necessary if there are to be no oscillations when the lower end of the spring is given a steady upward acceleration of $2{\cdot}8\ \text{m/s}^2$?

8. A mass is oscillating at the end of a light spring, whose other end is fixed. Neglecting gravitational forces, sketch a graph of the acceleration against the extension during one-half oscillation.

9. A catapult consists of a light elastic string of length 6 cm fixed to the ends of prongs 5 cm apart. The elastic stretches 1 cm under a force of 16 N. If a mass of 10 g is held at the mid-point of the elastic string which is then pulled back until the angle between the two parts of it is 40°, find by drawing and measurement the extensions of the string at a number of positions during the propulsive movement. Hence calculate the accelerations at these positions and sketch a graph of the acceleration against the distance moved by the mass.

4.4 Systems of bodies. We shall now consider some problems in which the motion of more than one body is involved, and in which we have to take into account the interactions between the bodies. We shall include only those bodies which are particles or can be treated as such (that is, if they are sizable bodies they must not rotate) or are of negligible mass; this will be implied when it is not explicitly stated. When more than one main body is involved it is advisable to draw separate figures, one for each, showing the forces acting *on* each one. In addition, except in the simplest cases, it is advisable to draw another figure for each body to show its mass $\times$ acceleration and then the equation of motion merely expresses the equality of the total force and the mass-acceleration vectors.

Example 6. A man of mass 75 kg is in a lift of mass 1000 kg, which is accelerating upwards at 1·2 m/s². Find:

(*a*) the force exerted by the floor on the man, and

(*b*) the total tension in the cables raising the lift.

Figure 11 (ii) shows the forces on the man, where P N is the force from the floor on the man. By the equation of motion $P-75g = 75\times 1{\cdot}2$, so that $P = 825$.

Hence the upward force from the floor on the man is 825 N.

Figure 11 (iii) shows the forces on the lift: the weight $1000g$ N, the force P N downwards from the man, and the tension T N in the cables. By the equation of motion

$$T-P-1000g = 1000\times 1{\cdot}2,$$

from which, since $P = 825$, $T = 11\,825$. Hence the tension in the cables, where they are fixed to the lift, is 11 825 N.

In this example, the cable tension could equally well have been found by considering the lift and the man as a single body. The equal and opposite contact forces (P) are then internal forces which annul one another. The forces on the composite body are the tension T N upwards and the total weight $1075g$ N downwards; and the total mass is 1075 kg. Hence the equation of motion is $T-1075 = 1075\times 1{\cdot}2$, which gives the same value for T as before.

Example 7. A rod OA of length a and of negligible mass is pivoted to a fixed point at O and has a mass m attached at A. Another rod AB, of length a and of negligible mass, is rigidly fixed to the mass m so that O, A, B are collinear; it carries a mass m' at B. The system is let fall from an inclined position so that when OAB is vertical the rods have an angular velocity ω. Find the tensions in the rods.

Neglecting air resistance we should expect the rods to have their maximum angular velocity when in the vertical position, so that at this time there is no angular acceleration.

Consider first the mass m', for which two diagrams Figure 12(ii), (iii) have been drawn: one for the forces and the other for the mass-acceleration, that is, the product of the mass and the acceleration. The only contact force is from the rod AB; let this be T'. Then the force system is T'

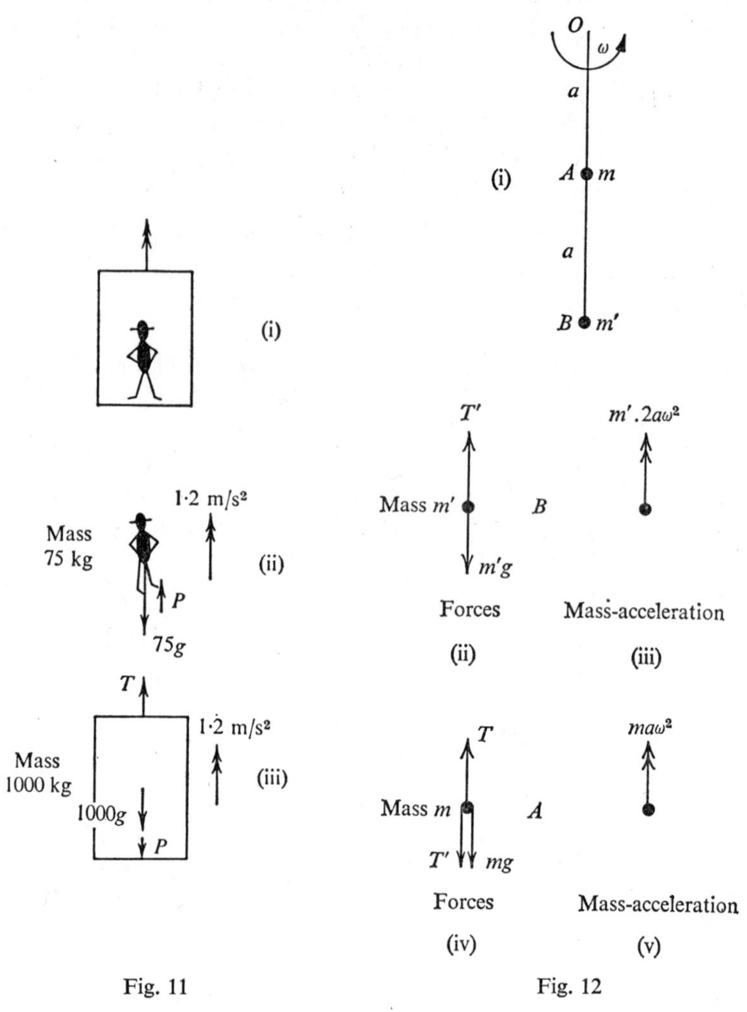

Fig. 11

Fig. 12

upwards and the weight $m'g$ downwards. For the other diagram, since m' is moving in a circle of radius $2a$ with angular velocity ω, its acceleration is $2a\omega^2$, so that its mass-acceleration is $m'.2a\omega^2$ upwards.

Applying the equation of motion to the mass m' is to equate these two vector systems. Thus:
$$T'-m'g = m'.2a\omega^2,$$
and therefore
$$T' = m'g+2m'a\omega^2.$$

Now consider the mass m, again drawing two diagrams Figure 12(iv), (v). Contact forces arise from the two rods. AB exerts a tension T' downwards (the tension at the two ends of the rod are equal because the mass of the rod is negligible. Compare Section 2.1); and we let the tension in OA be T. There is also a gravitational force mg. The mass acceleration diagram consists of the single vector $ma\omega^2$ upwards.

Now equating the two vector systems we have

$$T-T'-mg = ma\omega^2,$$

so that

$$T = T'+mg+ma\omega^2,$$

and, inserting the value for T',

$$T = m'g+mg+(m+2m')a\omega^2.$$

Exercise F

1. In each of the following parts list the main forces acting on each body of the system of bodies, show them in separate diagrams for each body, labelling each force with a letter. Describe the forces (tension, resistance, and so on) and state any obvious inequalities or equalities that necessarily hold between them.

(*a*) Man and parachute when the parachute is first open.

(*b*) A bullet and rifle during the passage of the bullet down the barrel when the rifle points horizontally. Consider only the horizontal forces.

(*c*) Two railway trucks when one is shunted into the other.

(*d*) A space-ship and man when the man is hauling himself back to the space-ship.

(*e*) Lorry towing a car (include the towing chain). Consider the cases (i) when the speed of the vehicles is constant; (ii) when the vehicles are accelerating together.

2. Outside any gravitational field, a force of 300 N is pushing a mass of 56 kg against another of 144 kg. What is the thrust between the two masses?

3. A lorry of mass 1500 kg is towing a car of mass 1000 kg connected to it by a steel bar. In slowing down, the force along the tow bar is 600 N. What is the magnitude of the retarding force on the system, if it is (*a*) entirely due to the car and (*b*) entirely due to the lorry?

4. A, B and C are points on a straight line. At A and B are bodies of mass 10 and 90 kg respectively; at C there is a source of attraction. The bodies at A and B are touching.

(*a*) If the source at C attracts the bodies with forces proportional to their masses, the constant of proportionality being 18 newtons per kg, what is their acceleration?

(*b*) If the source at C attracts A and B each with a force of 900 N, what will their resultant acceleration be?

5. A load of mass 40 kg is retarded at 5·2 m/s^2 by a newly opened parachute of mass 2 kg. If the air resistance to the load is 40 N what vertical force does the parachute exert on it, and what is the air resistance to the parachute?

6. A piece of string 1·5 m long, fixed at one end to a peg, carries a mass of 2 kg at the other end. If the mass swings through the vertically downwards position with a speed of 3 m/s, what force does the string exert on the peg?

7. A mass of 1 kg is fixed to the end of a light rod of length 2 metres and a mass of 2 kg is attached to the mid-point. The system is revolved freely in a vertical plane about the other end as centre. What force does the bar exert on the pivot there, when the rod is upright above the pivot point, if it then has an angular velocity of 3 rad/s?

8. A lift of mass 1000 kg, carrying a load of 250 kg, is descending at 2·8 m/s, and slowing down. If the tension in the supporting cables is 1500g N, find the contact force between the load and the lift floor. How much farther will the lift descend before coming to rest?

9. A humming bird is perched in an airtight cage placed on a weighing machine. If later the bird is seen hovering, what changes, if any, will there have been in the weight reading?

10. Two men, of masses m_1 and m_2 (m_1 above m_2), holding on firmly at different points of a light rope, are given an acceleration a vertically up a cliff face. Show in a diagram the forces on each man and on the vertical part of the rope. If now the man of mass m_2 lets the rope slip roughly through his hands, so that his acceleration drops to zero, what are the forces on the vertical part of the rope? Is there any prospect now that he will reach the top of the cliff?

11. A man of mass 90 kg is in the cabin suspended below a balloon, and the total mass of the balloon and cabin (excluding the man) is 800 kg. A steady downward drift at 8 m/s is stopped by throwing out 50 kg of ballast. What is the change in the upward force on the man's feet when the ballast is jettisoned? What will be the speed of the balloon 30 s later?

12. A rifleman holds a rifle of mass 4 kg, pointing horizontally, and fires a bullet of mass 25 g which then accelerates at $1{\cdot}5\times10^5$ m/s^2 for 3×10^{-3} s while it travels along the barrel. What are the speeds of the bullet and the rifle as the bullet is ejected if the rifleman does nothing during this time to prevent the recoil of the rifle, and the mass of the gas generated is neglected?

4.5 Pulley systems. As a further illustration of the motion of systems of bodies we shall consider the behaviour of masses connected by light strings of fixed length passing over smooth pulleys or pegs. It will be assumed that the tension in a string whose mass can be neglected is constant throughout its length, provided the constraints over which it passes can be considered to be perfectly smooth.

Example 8. A light string carrying masses of 1 kg and 2 kg at its ends passes over a smooth block of mass $\frac{1}{2}$ kg. The block is accelerated upwards at 2·2 m/s^2. Find the accelerations of the two masses, the tension in the string, and the external force required to give the block its acceleration (Figure 13).

Let the 1 kg mass accelerate upwards at a m/s^2 relative to the block, so that the 2 kg mass has the same relative acceleration downwards. Then the actual acceleration of the 1 kg mass is $(a+2{\cdot}2)$ m/s^2 upwards, and of the

2 kg mass is $(a-2{\cdot}2)$ m/s² downwards. Let the tension in the string be T N throughout its length. The forces acting on the 1 kg mass are T N up and $1g$ N down, and on the 2 kg mass are T N up and $2g$ N down. The equations of motion for these masses are therefore

$$T-g = a+2{\cdot}2,$$

and

$$2g-T = 2(a-2{\cdot}2);$$

from which

$$a = 4 \quad \text{and} \quad T = 16.$$

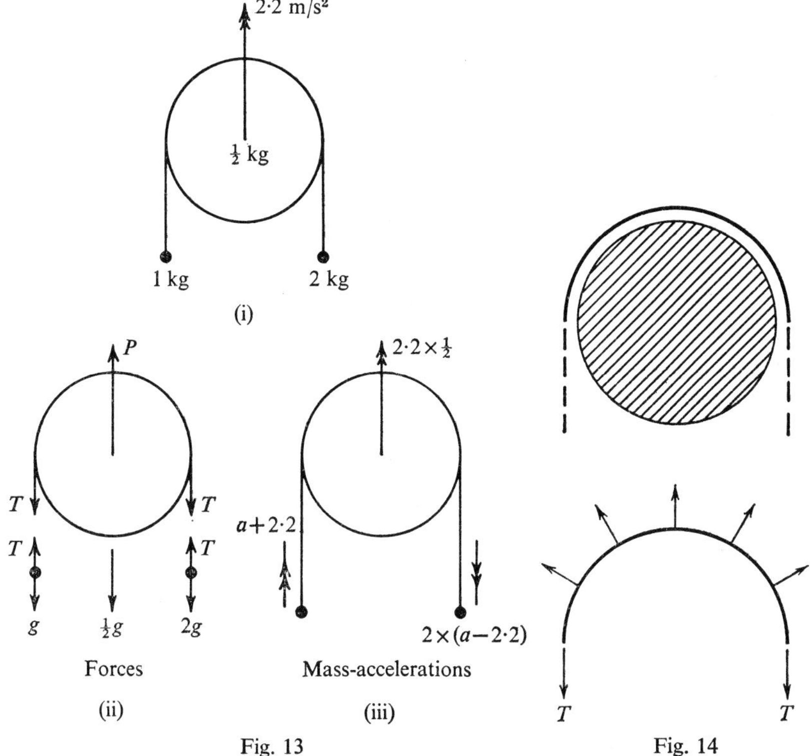

Fig. 13

Fig. 14

Hence the 1 kg mass accelerates upwards at 6·2 m/s², the 2 kg mass accelerates downwards at 1·8 m/s², and the tension in the string is 16 N.

The forces on the block are, say, P N upwards and $2T$ N downwards (the justification for this is given later). Hence

$$P-2T-\tfrac{1}{2}g = \tfrac{1}{2}\times 2{\cdot}2, \quad \text{so that} \quad P = 38.$$

The external force on the block is therefore 38 N upwards.

We have assumed above that the string exerts a force of $2T$ N downwards on the block, and it is interesting to analyse the force systems between the block and the string in more detail (Figure 14).

Consider first the part of the string which is in contact with the block. In addition to the two downward tensions at its ends, there are outward radial contact forces from the block acting on it. Now on each particle of the string the total force is zero, since the whole mass of the string is taken to be negligible, and therefore the vector sum of all the external forces on this part of the string is zero (the internal forces cancelling out). It follows that the sum of the contact forces is $2T$ upwards, and, by the interaction principle, the sum of the contact forces from the string onto the block is $2T$ downwards.

It is worth noticing that, by taking a smooth block, we have avoided difficulties which would arise if instead the string had passed over a pulley which would be rotated by the movement of the string. The rotary acceleration of a pulley turning with the string would be caused by a difference in tension between the two vertical parts of the string. Mechanics problems involving rotary accelerations are outside our present range, so we must limit ourselves to non-rotating smooth blocks or pulleys of negligible mass.

Exercise G

1. A light string runs horizontally to a smooth ring through which it passes and carries a mass of 10 kg at its lower end. With what force must the other end be pulled to give the mass an acceleration of 2 m/s² (*a*) upwards, and (*b*) downwards?

2. Masses of 3 kg and 5 kg are at the ends of a light string which passes over a smooth fixed peg. Calculate the accelerations of the system and the tension in the string.

3. Two masses, each of 2 kg, are at the ends of a light string which passes over a smooth peg. What is the tension in the string when one mass moves up and the other down at a steady speed of 1 m/s? If half of one mass is now removed, what is the change in the tension?

4. If in Question 2 the peg had been fixed to a lift which was falling (*a*) at a constant speed of 3 m/s, and (*b*) at a constant acceleration of 1·4 m/s², what would the accelerations and tensions have been?

5. A piece of light string, with one end fixed to the ground, passes through a smooth ring and supports a mass of 2 kg at the other end, so that the two parts of the string are vertical. What is the tension in the string when the ring is given an acceleration of 3 m/s² upwards?

6. A light string, passing over a smooth block of mass 200 g, carries masses of 800 g and 1200 g at its ends. Find the tension in the string and the accelerations of the masses when the block is pulled upwards with a force of 26·5 N.

7. Two caterpillars find themselves hanging stationary at the ends of a fine string which passes over a smooth branch. Explain what motion you think will ensue when one of them climbs upwards.

4.6 Systems of non-parallel forces. The methods used so far in Section 4 will still be used here. The new factor is that, with non-parallel forces, the vector sum must be found either by drawing, as in Section 2.3, or by sketching the diagrams and using trigonometry to work out the sides or angles, or by using resolved parts of the forces. This last method will be discussed in the next subsection.

Example 9. A body of mass m on a piece of light string suspended from the ceiling of a railway carriage, is inclined at a fixed angle α from the vertical when the train has a steady acceleration a. Express α in terms of m and a, and find the tension T in the string.

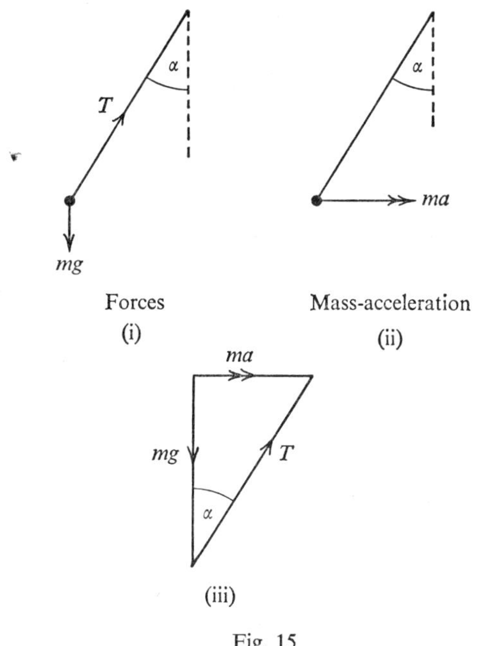

Fig. 15

In Figure 15, (i) shows the forces acting on the body, and (ii) its mass-acceleration vector. By the equation of motion, the vector sum of the two forces equals the mass-acceleration; and this is shown in (iii).

From (iii) it is clear that

$$\alpha = \tan^{-1}(a/g),$$

and

$$T = m(a^2+g^2)^{\frac{1}{2}}.$$

Note that the same result would arise if we considered the situation relative to the railway carriage with a gravitational acceleration compounded of g downwards and a backwards.

[*Note.* When a problem involves only literal quantities, as in this one, we shall usually suppose that the letters stand for quantities and not just numbers. These quantities may then be expressed as numbers of units in any consistent system. When the problem is given in numerical terms we shall usually not do this.]

Exercise H

(In this Exercise draw separate figures for forces and mass-accelerations.)

1. A body of mass m is sliding down a smooth plane inclined at an angle θ to the horizontal. Find the acceleration of the body and the normal contact force from the plane.

2. A pendulum, consisting of a mass on the end of a light rod, hangs from the roof of a car. If it is inclined at a constant backward angle of 10° from the vertical, what is the car's acceleration? What would be the behaviour of the pendulum if the car accelerated at this rate from rest?

3. A mass m is swung as a pendulum at the end of a light string of length l through 60° either side of the vertical. Find an expression for the acceleration of the mass when at either extreme point.

4. A mass of 1·5 kg is constrained to slide on a smooth vertical wire. If a force of 29·4 N is applied to the mass at an angle of 30° from the upward vertical, calculate the acceleration of the mass and the normal contact force from the wire.

5. A toboggan of mass 50 kg is pulled by a force of 40 N at an angle of 40° above the horizontal. Assuming the snow surface to be perfectly smooth and horizontal, calculate the acceleration of the toboggan and the force upwards on it.

6. A load of mass 90 kg is hung from a fixed point by a light rope which stays at rest inclined at 20° from the vertical when a certain horizontal force is applied to the load. Find this force and the tension in the rope.

7. A hemispherical bowl is fixed with its rim in a horizontal plane. A small ball-bearing rolls steadily around the smooth inside surface of the bowl in a horizontal plane half-way between the plane of the rim and the bottom of the bowl. What is the speed of the ball-bearing?

8. A skier is moving down a slope inclined at 25° to the horizontal. The only forces acting on her are her weight, the normal contact force, and the resistances parallel to the plane. If her mass is 50 kg, what will the total of the resistances be when she moves with (*a*) constant speed; (*b*) a retardation of 1·2 m/s^2?

9. Two boys are hauling a boat up a stream with ropes. On one side, the rope is at 30° to the line of the stream, on the other it is at 40°. Both are horizontal. If the tension in the first rope is 250 N and if the boat is moving straight up the stream, what is the tension in the second rope and what is the resultant pull on the boat?

10. A 'stage' fairy is supported by two wires and moves horizontally across the stage. Her mass is 45 kg and, when accelerating at 3 m/s^2 across the stage the wires are inclined at 60° and 150° to the direction of motion. What are the tensions in the wires?

11. A car of mass 500 kg is travelling at 28 m/s on the banked surface of a circular track of radius 240 m. At what angle to the horizontal is the surface banked if the car has no tendency to sideslip?

12. An aircraft of mass 3000 kg is flying at a constant speed in a horizontal circle of radius 3000 m, banked over at 30° from the horizontal. If there is no tendency to sideslip, at what speed is it flying and what is the lift force? (Take the lift force to lie in the plane of symmetry of the aircraft at right-angles to the direction of motion.)

13. A figure skater of mass 50 kg is moving in a circle of radius 12 m at 6 m/s, slowing down at $0{\cdot}8$ m/s^2. What total force does she exert on the ice?

14. A body of mass *m* attached to a fixed point by a light string of length *l* is moving in a horizontal circle with constant angular velocity ω, so that the string is always inclined at an angle α from the vertical.
Prove that

$$\omega^2 = \frac{g}{l\cos\alpha}.$$

Write down an expression for the tension in the string in terms of m, g and α. Also make a sketch graph to show how ω varies with α.

4.7 Resolved parts.

Example 10. A bead of mass m is threaded on a smooth straight wire and a force P is applied to it in a direction making a constant angle α with the wire. Find the acceleration of the bead.

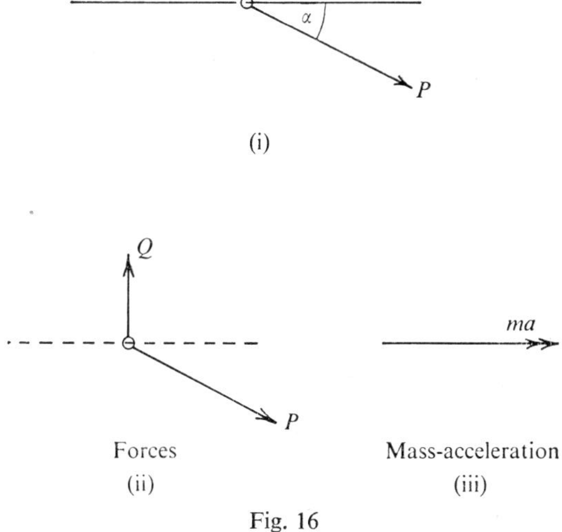

Fig. 16

Let the acceleration be **a**. We draw two vector diagrams, one showing all the forces acting on the bead and the other showing the mass-acceleration $m\mathbf{a}$ as in Figure 16.

Since the wire is smooth the only force apart from P is a normal force Q, say.

In (iii) the vector $m\mathbf{a}$ is along the wire because the bead can only move this way.

The equation of motion is equivalent to the statement that the vector sum of the forces equals the mass-acceleration vector. Now in the force system we can replace P at an angle α by a force $P \cos \alpha$ horizontally and a force $P \sin \alpha$ vertically downwards without altering the vector sum of the force system (see Figure 17(i)). This gives us the situation shown in Figure 17(ii) and (iii) where the vector sum of the three forces in (ii) equals the mass-acceleration vector $m\mathbf{a}$ in (iii).

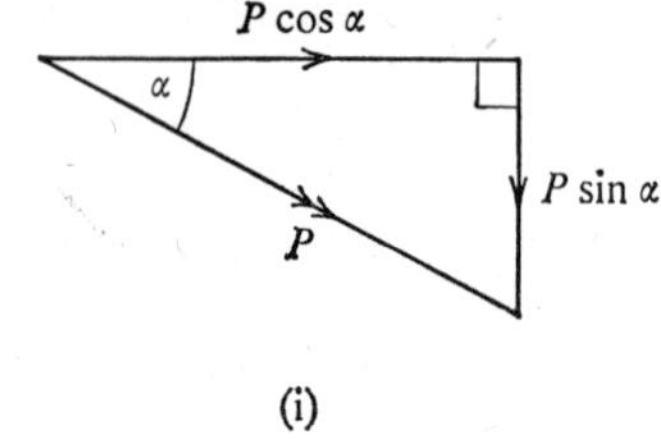

(i)

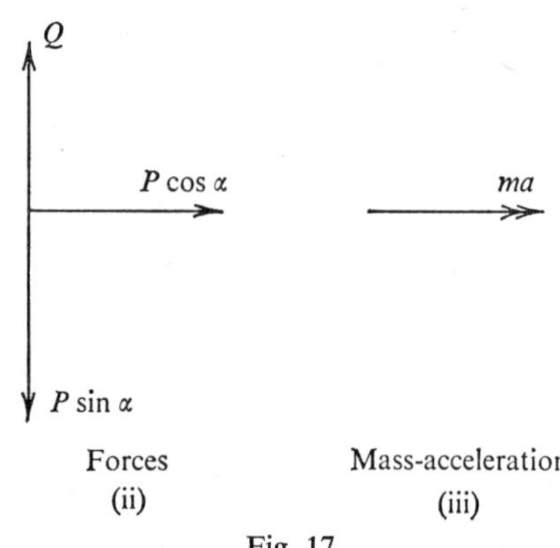

Forces (ii) Mass-acceleration (iii)

Fig. 17

This can only be so if

$$P \sin \alpha = Q \quad \text{and} \quad P \cos \alpha = ma.$$

Hence the required acceleration is

$$\frac{P \cos \alpha}{m}.$$

Now looking back at this example we might say—a little loosely perhaps—that the acceleration is caused by 'the part of P which is effective in the horizontal direction'.

It is this idea which will now be analysed formally.

The principles we are about to establish hold in three dimensions but we shall only apply them in this chapter to situations in which the vectors involved are parallel to a plane.

The reader will recall that the scalar product of a vector $\mathbf{v}$ with a unit vector $\hat{\mathbf{u}}$, written $\mathbf{v}.\hat{\mathbf{u}}$, is the scalar quantity $v \cos \theta$, where v is the magnitude of $\mathbf{v}$ and θ the angle between the vectors; and that scalar multiplication is distributive over addition.

Definition. By the *resolved part* of a vector $\mathbf{v}$ in the direction of a unit vector $\hat{\mathbf{u}}$, we shall mean the scalar product $\mathbf{v}.\hat{\mathbf{u}}$.

We first examine the case of two vectors $\mathbf{a}_1$ and $\mathbf{a}_2$ and what we shall show is that if $\mathbf{s}$ is their resultant, then the sum of the resolved parts of $\mathbf{a}_1$ and $\mathbf{a}_2$ in the direction of an arbitrary unit vector $\hat{\mathbf{u}}$ is equal to the resolved part of $\mathbf{s}$ in that direction (Figure 18). That is

$$\mathbf{s}.\hat{\mathbf{u}} = \mathbf{a}_1.\hat{\mathbf{u}}+\mathbf{a}_2.\hat{\mathbf{u}}. \qquad \text{(i)}$$

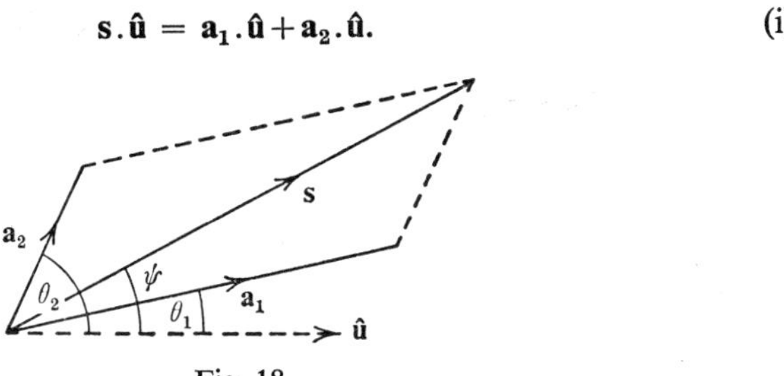

Fig. 18

This is an immediate deduction from the distributive law which states that

$$(\mathbf{a}_1+\mathbf{a}_2).\hat{\mathbf{u}} = \mathbf{a}_1.\hat{\mathbf{u}}+\mathbf{a}_2.\hat{\mathbf{u}}.$$

Equation (i) is equivalent to

$$s \cos \psi = a_1 \cos \theta_1+a_2 \cos \theta_2,$$

where $\mathbf{s}$, $\mathbf{a}_1$, $\mathbf{a}_2$ make angles ψ, θ_1, θ_2 with $\hat{\mathbf{u}}$ and s, a_1, a_2 are the magnitudes of $\mathbf{s}$, $\mathbf{a}_1$, $\mathbf{a}_2$. It is in this latter form that the result is usually employed.

The generalization of these results to the case where $\mathbf{s}$ is the resultant of a set of vectors $\mathbf{a}_1, \mathbf{a}_2, \ldots, \mathbf{a}_n$ is straightforward and the proof is simple enough to be omitted. The general statement of the result in the form in which it will usually be employed is

$$s \cos \psi = a_1 \cos \theta_1+a_2 \cos \theta_2+\ldots+a_n \cos \theta_n$$

with the obvious notation.

We may now go further and say that if there is a second set of m vectors $\mathbf{b}_1, \mathbf{b}_2, \ldots, \mathbf{b}_m$ having the same sum as the first set of n vectors, then

$$b_1 \cos \phi_1+b_2 \cos \phi_2+\ldots+b_m \cos \phi_m$$
$$= a_1 \cos \theta_1+a_2 \cos \theta_2+\ldots+a_n \cos \theta_n,$$

where $b_1, b_2, \ldots, b_m$ are the magnitudes of $\mathbf{b}_1, \mathbf{b}_2, \ldots, \mathbf{b}_m$ and $\phi_1, \phi_2, \ldots, \phi_m$ are the angles these vectors make with $\hat{\mathbf{u}}$. This follows directly from the previous result since $\mathbf{s}$ is the same for both sets of vectors, or it can be proved thus:

$$\mathbf{b}_1+\mathbf{b}_2+\ldots+\mathbf{b}_m = \mathbf{a}_1+\mathbf{a}_2+\ldots+\mathbf{a}_n;$$

so, taking the scalar multiple of each side with $\hat{\mathbf{u}}$ and expanding by the distributive law, we get

$$\mathbf{b}_1.\hat{\mathbf{u}}+\mathbf{b}_2.\hat{\mathbf{u}}+\ldots+\mathbf{b}_m.\hat{\mathbf{u}} = \mathbf{a}_1.\hat{\mathbf{u}}+\mathbf{a}_2.\hat{\mathbf{u}}+\ldots+\mathbf{a}_n.\hat{\mathbf{u}},$$

which is equivalent to the required result.

This setting up of the equality between the sums of the resolved parts we shall describe as 'resolving in the direction $\hat{\mathbf{u}}$'; and a phrase such as 'resolving horizontally' will be used to mean 'resolving in the direction $\hat{\mathbf{u}}$ where $\hat{\mathbf{u}}$ is a unit vector in the horizontal direction', and written sometimes more briefly as '$\mathscr{R}$ horizontally'.

We are now in a position to tackle Example 1, Section 1.4, in an alternative way. The problem will be repeated in a slightly different form.

Example 11. If a mass of 2 kg is acted on by forces of 5 N, 10 N, 8 N in directions north, east, and S 60° W, calculate the resultant force and hence the acceleration.

In Figure 19 two diagrams are drawn, one for the forces and the other, in this case, for the resultant force which we shall assume is of magnitude R N in a direction θ from north.

Equating resolved parts we have:

resolving in a northerly direction

$$R\cos\theta = 5-8\cos 60°,$$

and resolving in an easterly direction

$$R\sin\theta = 10-8\sin 60°.$$

Hence
$$R\cos\theta = 1 \qquad \text{(i)}$$
and
$$R\sin\theta = 3{\cdot}07. \qquad \text{(ii)}$$

Dividing (ii) by (i),

$$\tan\theta = 3{\cdot}07 \quad \left(\text{since } \frac{\sin\theta}{\cos\theta} = \tan\theta\right).$$

Now as $\cos\theta$ and $\sin\theta$ are both positive, since R is positive, θ is acute. Therefore,

$$\theta = 72°.$$

Squaring (i) and (ii) and adding

$$R^2\cos^2\theta+R^2\sin^2\theta = 1+(3{\cdot}07)^2,$$

and, as $\cos^2\theta+\sin^2\theta = 1$,
$$R^2 = 1+(3{\cdot}07)^2 = 10{\cdot}43,$$
so
$$R = 3{\cdot}23.$$

Now the mass is 2 kg and therefore the acceleration is $1{\cdot}62$ m/s² in the direction N 72° E.

Note. If equations (i), (ii) had been $R\cos\theta = 1$, $R\sin\theta = -3{\cdot}07$, then, since R is positive, θ would have been in the fourth quadrant; and from $\tan\theta = -3{\cdot}07$ we should have derived $\theta = 288°$.

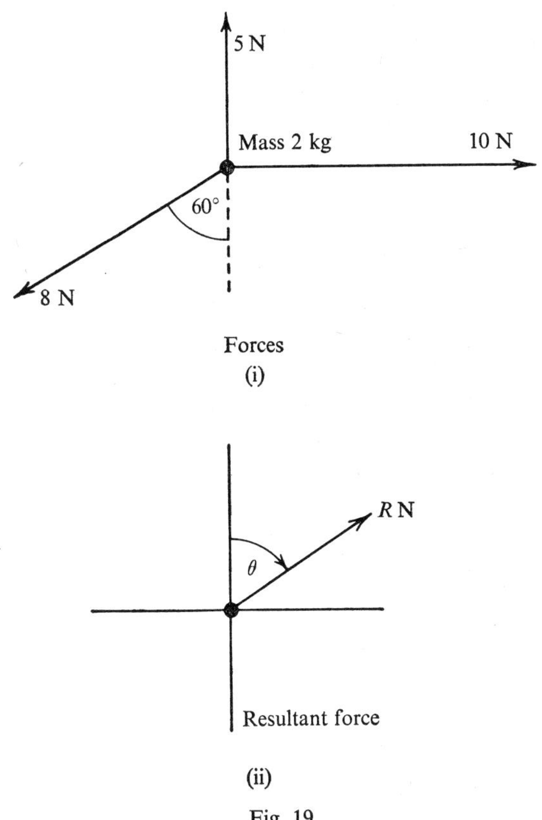

Fig. 19

Exercise I

The ideas of this section should be used to answer some of the questions of the last exercise, Exercise H. It would be useful to compare the efficiency of the method of resolving with that of the addition of vectors for each different sort of question so that you can decide which you prefer to use.

The following offer some preliminary practice.

1. Using the method of Example 9, find the resultant of the following sets of coplanar forces acting at a point O, where the directions are measured from some fixed direction OA:

(*a*) 9 N at 0°, 6 N at 60°, 3 N at 270°;
(*b*) 5 N at 0°, 4 N at 125°, 3 N at 320°;
(*c*) 2 N at 0°, 10 N at 170°, 12 N at 250°.

2. A box is being pulled along a horizontal board by a rope. The tension in the rope is 60 N. Resisting forces parallel to the board are 30 N. What will be the sum of the resolved parts of all the forces acting on the box parallel to the board given that the angle between the board and the rope is: (*a*) 60°, (*b*) 30°, (*c*) 0°?

If the mass of the box is 16 kg, what will the acceleration be in each case?

3. Answer the questions in Question 2, given that the board is inclined at 10° to the horizontal and that the rope tends to pull the box *up* the slope.

4. Two wires are clipped to a ring in the top of a block of stone of weight $1000g$ N. The wires are each inclined to the vertical at an angle of 15°. What is the tension in each wire? What would the new tension be, if the wires gave the stone an upward acceleration of 1 cm/s^2?

If one wire had been passed through the ring to support the stone in place of the two that were clipped on, what difference would it make to the answers?

5. Three forces in a vertical plane are acting on a mass of 10 kg. One force of 5 N is acting vertically downward. One of 10 N is inclined at 60° to the upward vertical. One of 8 N is inclined at 20° on the opposite side of the upward vertical.

Find the sum of the resolved parts of these forces in:

(*a*) the vertical and the horizontal directions;

(*b*) directions parallel and perpendicular to the force of 8 N.

Check that the resultant forces obtained from these two pairs are equal. What is the final acceleration of the mass?

6. A mass of 20 kg is swinging at the end of a string 4 m long as though it were a pendulum. When the string is inclined at 20° to the vertical, the mass is moving at 1 m/s.

(*a*) What are the resolved parts of the weight of the mass, along and perpendicular to the line of the string?

(*b*) What is the acceleration of the mass along the line of the string?

(*c*) What is the tension of the string?

(*d*) What are the resolved parts of the forces acting on the mass in the vertical and horizontal directions?

5. FRICTION

When there is relative motion between two bodies, or a body moves over a rough surface, in addition to the normal force between them there is a frictional force in their common tangent plane in the opposite direction to that of the relative motion. The magnitude of this frictional force depends on what materials are in contact and upon the pressure forces between the surfaces in contact (the normal contact forces) but is little affected by the amount of area in contact.

> We shall accept as an approximate experimental result that, for given materials in contact, this frictional force is proportional to the normal force; the constant of proportionality being denoted by μ, and called the *coefficient of friction*. When there is no motion between the surfaces, the frictional force cannot exceed a maximum value, called *limiting friction*. This value is usually taken to be equal to that of sliding friction, although experimentally it may be somewhat greater.

Consider what happens when a boy skids on his bicycle when applying his back brake so as to lock the wheel. If the coefficient of friction μ is 0·6, and the normal contact force, R, from the ground is 250 N, then the frictional force F is μR, that is, $F = 150$ N (see Figure 20). From this, knowing the mass of the boy and bicycle, the retardation can be found, assuming that the other forces acting on the bicycle which have a horizontal resolved part are negligible in comparison with the friction. These forces are the air resistance and the small forward frictional force on the front wheel which is required to slow down its rotation.

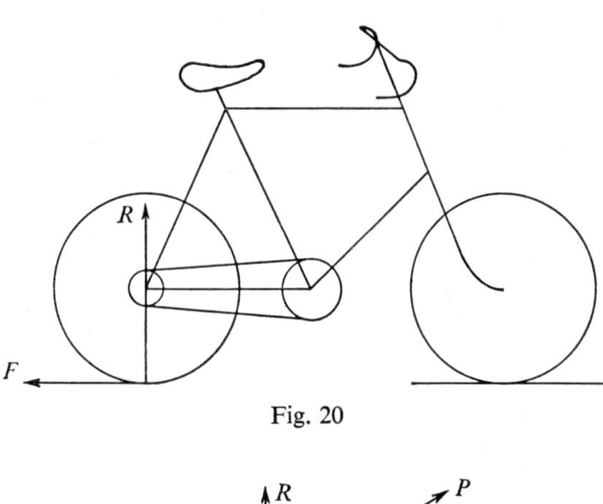

Fig. 20

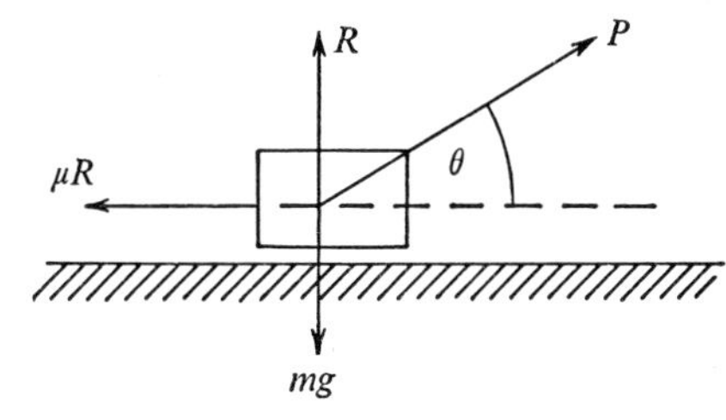

Fig. 21

Example 12. What is the direction of the smallest force needed to move a body of mass m over a rough horizontal surface, if the coefficient of friction is μ?

Let the force be P in a direction θ above the horizontal (Figure 21). Clearly P will be least when the mass is moving without acceleration; so the vector sum of the force P, the normal force R, the frictional force μR, and the weight mg, is zero.

$\mathscr{R}$ horizontally:

$$P \cos \theta - \mu R = 0, \quad \text{so that} \quad P \cos \theta = \mu R.$$

$\mathscr{R}$ vertically:

$$P \sin \theta + R - mg = 0, \quad \text{so that} \quad P \sin \theta = mg - R.$$

Hence, by squaring and adding,

$$P^2 = \mu^2R^2+(mg-R)^2.$$

By calculus, P^2 is least when

$$dP^2/dR = 2\mu^2R-2(mg-R) = 0,$$

that is, when $2\mu P\cos\theta-2P\sin\theta = 0$ or $\mu = \tan\theta$.

The least possible force therefore acts at $\tan^{-1}\mu$ above the horizontal.

If we think of the force P replaced by its horizontal and vertical components, so that as θ increases the horizontal one decreases and the vertical one increases, then as the vertical component increases the normal pressure R is reduced, thereby reducing the frictional force which is proportional to it; but as this happens, so the forward propulsive force is reduced. The direction $\tan^{-1}\mu$ is the best compromise.

5.1 Angle of friction. A geometrical argument provides a simpler alternative approach to the problem of the previous section.

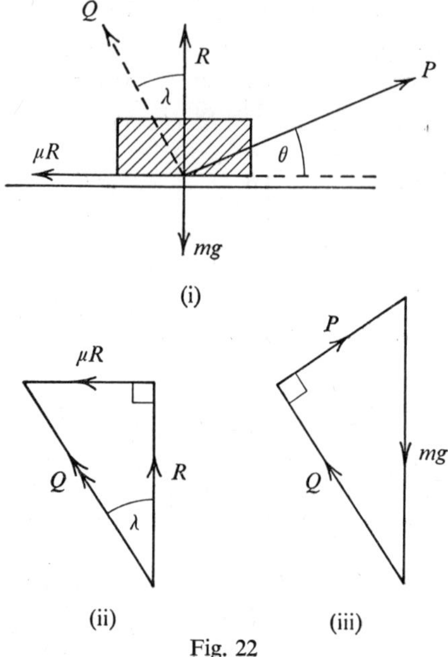

Fig. 22

Since the friction is proportional to the normal force R, the resultant $\mathbf{Q}$ of these two forces will be in a fixed direction. If we denote this direction by the angle λ from the normal, then $\tan\lambda = \mu$ (see Figure 22(ii)). For different forces $\mathbf{P}$ at different angles θ, $\mathbf{Q}$ will vary in magnitude, but for zero acceleration, the sum of mg, $\mathbf{Q}$ and $\mathbf{P}$ is zero, as shown in Figure 22 (iii).

Clearly the least value of P occurs when $\mathbf{P}$ is at right-angles to $\mathbf{Q}$; that is, when $\mathbf{P}$ acts at the angle λ above the horizontal.

The angle λ, which equals $\tan^{-1}\mu$, is called the 'angle of friction'. So when a body is sliding over a rough surface, the total contact force (that is, the sum of the normal and frictional forces) makes an angle with the normal equal to the angle of friction.

Exercise J

1. A block of mass 10 kg is pulled along a horizontal surface by a horizontal force of 100 N. The coefficient of friction between the block and the surface is 0·4.

(*a*) What is the magnitude of the limiting friction between the block and the surface?

(*b*) Work out the acceleration of the block.

(*c*) If a second block, also of mass 10 kg, is placed on top of the first one, will the acceleration be halved? What will the new acceleration be?

(*d*) If a third block of mass 10 kg is added to the other two, what will the magnitude of the resisting friction be?

2. A car of mass 800 kg is accelerating at 1·5 m/s^2. What is the nature of the external forces causing the acceleration and what is their total magnitude (neglecting external resistances)? Would this force give the car the same acceleration on the moon? If 1·5 m/s^2 is the maximum acceleration on the earth without back-wheel skidding, could the car have this acceleration on a similar lunar surface?

3. A crate of mass 500 kg is resting on a slope whose angle with the horizontal is $\sin^{-1}\frac{3}{5}$. The coefficient of friction between the crate and the slope is 0·2. Work out the following:

(*a*) the normal reaction of the slope on the crate;

(*b*) the limiting friction along the slope;

(*c*) the force required to move the crate with an acceleration of 9·8 m/s^2

(i) directly down the slope,

(ii) directly up the slope,

assuming that the force is parallel to the slope.

4. A puppy on a lead is resisting progress by sitting down. Its mass is 3 kg. The angle between the lead and the horizontal ground is 75°. The tension in the lead is to be increased until the puppy begins to slide along the ground. If the tension at some moment is T N, express the following in terms of T, if $\mu = 0{\cdot}8$:

(*a*) the normal reaction between the ground and the puppy (take into account the effect of the vertical component of the tension in the lead);

(*b*) the limiting friction;

(*c*) the horizontal component of the tension in the lead.

From (*b*) and (*c*), find the value of the tension when the puppy is just about to slide along.

5. A box of mass 10 kg is pulled across the floor by the tension in a string attached to it which makes an angle of 40° with the horizontal. What is its acceleration if the tension in the string is $8g$ N, and the coefficient of friction is 0·6?

6. A horizontal force of 800 N is pulling a block of mass 200 kg over a horizontal surface. If the angle of friction is 14°, what is the acceleration of the block?

7. A cupboard of weight $150g$ N is standing on a rough, horizontal floor. If the coefficient of friction is 0·7, what is the angle of friction? What horizontal force would keep the cupboard sliding over the surface at a constant speed?

What is the angle between the vertical and the resultant of the normal and frictional forces? What is the angle between the vertical and the resultant of the normal and the pushing force? If the horizontal force had failed to move the cupboard, what could be said about this angle?

8. Cars and cycles are caused to change direction by frictional forces between the tyres and the road.

A car is moving at 28 m/s round a curve which is part of a circular arc of radius 160 m. The road is horizontal. Find the minimum value of the coefficient of friction.

*6. OTHER UNITS OF FORCE

Although the newton (N) and its multiples and submultiples—principally the meganewton (MN, 10^6 N), kilonewton (kN, 10^3 N) and millinewton (mN, 10^{-3} N)—are the only units of force recognized officially in the Système Internationale d'Unités which is the standard system adopted in this course, there are other obsolete and obsolescent units which will take time to disappear, and with which the student may need to be familiar. Agreement has been reached, however, in Britain that no units other than S.I. will be required for examination purposes from 1972 onwards.

The unit of force depends on two things: first, on the units of mass, length and time; secondly, on the form taken for Newton's Second Law. Up to now, we have considered that unit force gives unit acceleration to unit mass, and have taken $\lambda = 1$ in the equation of Section 2.2. We first consider systems for which this remains true.

The obsolete c.g.s. system is now rarely met with. In it the unit of length was the *centimetre*, and of mass the *gram*. (The unit of time is the *second* in all systems.) The unit of force was called the *dyne*. Thus 1 dyne gives an acceleration of 10^{-2} m/s^2 to a mass of 10^{-3} kg. Hence 1 dyne $= 10^{-5}$ N. This is a minute unit of force.

There are major economic problems to be overcome before the British (imperial) system finally disappears, so that it may be with us for some time. In it, the unit of length is one *foot* (ft) defined to be 0·3048 m exactly, and the unit of mass is one *pound* avoirdupois (lb), defined to be

0·453 592 37 kg exactly. The corresponding unit of force is the *poundal* (pdl), which gives a mass of 1 lb an acceleration of 1 ft/s². Thus

$$1 \text{ poundal} = 0{\cdot}138 \text{ N, approximately.}$$

$$1 \text{ poundal} = 1 \text{ lb} \frac{1 \text{ foot}}{(1 \text{ second})^2} \approx (0{\cdot}454 \text{ kg}) \frac{(0{\cdot}305 \text{ m})}{(1 \text{ second})^2} \approx 0{\cdot}138 \text{ N}.$$

The poundal is still rather small for practical purposes, and even a man of mass 10 stone weighs 4480 pdl; a car may weigh about 40 000 pdl, and the tensions and thrusts involved in the construction of houses, bridges or skyscrapers appear to be astronomical when measured in these units. Consequently it is often convenient to choose a different unit of mass, for example 1 *ton* (2240 lb), the unit of force then being 1 *tonnal.*

Engineers have, however, in the past adopted a rather more tiresome expedient. Since, prior to the advent of the space-ship, most of their operations were conducted near the earth's surface, and involved mainly the static effects of gravity, they chose as a unit of force the gravitational pull of the earth on a unit mass placed at its surface. This, of course, is not properly defined; to make it precise, we must say that it is placed at sea level at Sèvres in France, where the acceleration due to gravity is

$$g_0 = 9{\cdot}80665 \text{ m/s}^2 \approx 32{\cdot}174 \text{ ft/s}^2.$$

This is 'standard gravity'; a force which gives this acceleration to a kilogram is called a *kilogram-force* (kgf); a force which gives this acceleration to a pound is called a *pound-force* (lbf), to a ton, a *ton-force* (tonf), and so on.

$$1 \text{ kgf} = 9{\cdot}80665 \text{ N}.$$

$$1 \text{ lbf} \approx 32{\cdot}174 \text{ pdl} \approx 445 \text{ N}.$$

In such systems the constant in Newton's Second Law is no longer unity, but the reciprocal of the numerical value of g_0 in the system. It is, however, better to argue as follows:

5 lbf acting on 5 lb gives an acceleration of about 32 ft/s²;

5 lbf acting on 1 lb gives an acceleration of about 32×5 ft/s²;

5 lbf acting on 9 lb gives an acceleration of about $\dfrac{32 \times 5}{9}$ ft/s²;

5 tonf acting on 9 ton gives an acceleration of about $\dfrac{32 \times 5}{9}$ ft/s²;

5 kgf acting on 9 kg gives an acceleration of about $\dfrac{9{\cdot}8 \times 5}{9}$ m/s².

Example 13. A full bucket of total mass 24 lb is being raised by a winch. The tension in the rope is five times the force on the handle of the winch. If a man presses on the winch-handle with a force of 5 lbf, what is the acceleration of the bucket?

The earth's pull on the bucket (its weight) is 24 lbf. The net upward accelerating force is therefore 1 lbf = g poundals. Hence, if the acceleration is a ft/s²,

$$32 = 24a,$$

giving

$$a = 4/3.$$

The acceleration of the bucket is therefore $\frac{4}{3}$ ft/s².

Example 14. A mass of 300 gm is being pushed along a horizontal plane against a resistance to motion of 70 gmf by a force of 500 gmf. What is its acceleration?

When we use the equation of motion in the form $F = ma$, we must ensure that we are using a consistent system of units; our unit force must give unit mass unit acceleration. Now 1 gmf gives a mass of 1 gm an acceleration of 9·8 m/s² (approximately). There are therefore two courses open to us. (*a*) We may choose a unit acceleration of 9·8 m/s²—i.e. we may measure accelerations in units of g_0. This is sometimes a convenient thing to do anyway; accelerations of space-capsules and jet aircraft are often given in such units. (*b*) The other alternative, which we shall adopt in this course, is to continue to use 1 m/s² as our unit of acceleration, and to convert the measure of the force so that the unit is consistent with this: 1 gmf = 1 gm × (9·8 m/s²) = 9·8 gm.m/s².

Using (*b*) then, we let the acceleration be a m/s², and write

$$(500-70)\,9{\cdot}8 = 300a,$$

giving

$$a = \frac{430 \times 9{\cdot}8}{300} = 14 \text{ (to 2 significant figures).}$$

The acceleration is therefore 14 m/s².

Example 15. A body of mass 26 tons lies on a plane inclined at $\sin^{-1}(\frac{5}{13})$ to the horizontal. If the coefficient of friction between the plane and the body is 0·05, what force parallel to the plane is required to stop it sliding down the plane? If this force were removed, what would be its acceleration down the plane? (Figure 23.)

There is obviously no sense here in expressing the mass of the body in lb and its weight in pdl. We can set up a consistent system by taking a new unit of force: let the force which gives a mass of 1 ton an acceleration of 1 ft/s² be 1 *tonnal*. Then the weight of 1 ton is 32 tonnals. Name the normal and frictional forces N and F, as in the diagram.

(Note that we have named the *forces*, not the number of units in each, on this occasion.)

(*a*) When the body is at rest on the plane, let P be the force acting;

$\mathscr{R}$ perpendicular to the plane $\quad N - \frac{12}{13}Mg = 0; \qquad (1)$

$\mathscr{R}$ down the plane $\quad \frac{5}{13}Mg - F - P = 0. \qquad (2)$

The condition on F is

$$-0{\cdot}05N \leqslant F \leqslant 0{\cdot}05N. \qquad (3)$$

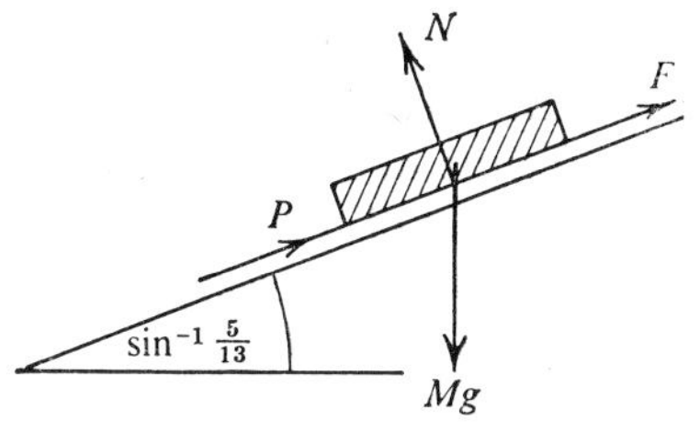

Fig. 23

Now $M = 26$ tons; hence (1) gives

$$N = \tfrac{12}{13} \times 26 \times 32 \text{ ton ft/s}^2$$
$$= 768 \text{ tonnals.}$$

(3) now gives $\quad -38{\cdot}4$ tonnals $\leqslant F \leqslant 38{\cdot}4$ tonnals.

Finally, from (2), $\quad P = 320 \text{ tonnals} - F,$

so that P lies between 280 and 360 tonnals (to 2 significant figures).

The *least* force needed will be about 280 tonnals.

(*b*) When the body is sliding down the plane with acceleration a, the first equation is the same as before, but the other two are replaced by

$$\tfrac{5}{13}Mg - F = Ma \qquad (2')$$

and

$$F = 0{\cdot}05N, \qquad (3')$$

since the friction is now limiting.

From these we find

$$a = \frac{5g}{13} - 0{\cdot}05 \times \frac{12g}{13}$$
$$= \frac{4{\cdot}4}{13} \times 32 \text{ ft/s}^2$$
$$= 11 \text{ ft/s}^2\text{, to 2 significant figures.}$$

7. DIMENSIONS

7.1 The dimension of force. In Chapter 18 we discussed the various physical quantities that could be derived from the fundamental quantities of length and time. Mass and force are not among these quantities, and in order to include them and other related quantities some additional physical entity must be admitted to the basic list. There are difficulties in the way of admitting force to this distinction: most forces are transient, variable things, and there is no obvious natural unit of force which is reproducible at will. The electrostatic attraction between a proton and an electron separated by a fixed interval of empty space might conceivably be used, but the electrical ideas introduced are obviously alien to the basic idea of mechanical force. The gravitational attraction of two such particles is far too minute and difficult to measure to be any use. These and other considerations lead to the preference of mass as the candidate for admission to the basic list. A standard mass of useful size—the kilogram—is easily preserved, and the mass of a hydrogen, oxygen or carbon atom or molecule is a natural unit which is always available.

We therefore assign a dimension **M** to mass, and seek to express force in terms of it. This we can do through the medium of Newton's second law; which tells us that a force is measured by the product of the mass and the acceleration it causes in that mass. Now the dimension of acceleration is $\mathbf{LT^{-2}}$, and from this it follows at once that

force has dimension $\mathbf{MLT^{-2}}$.

From this the dimensions of other mechanical quantities can be immediately derived. Work (force × distance) will have dimension $\mathbf{ML^2T^{-2}}$, the same as that of energy (mass × velocity × velocity); impulse (force × time) has dimension $\mathbf{MLT^{-1}}$, the same as that of momentum, which is mass × velocity.

7.2 Dimensional consistency. When all the physical quantities appearing in any problem are represented by letters, the dimensional consistency of formulae and equations can be immediately checked. Consider, for example, the formula in Exercise H, Question 14: $\omega^2 = g/(l \cos \alpha)$. The left-hand side is the square of an angular velocity ω; an angle is dimensionless, being the ratio of two lengths, arc:radius. ω, therefore, has dimension $\mathbf{T^{-1}}$, and ω^2 has dimension $\mathbf{T^{-2}}$. Now consider the right-hand side. $\cos \alpha$ is a dimensionless number, so that the dimension of $g/(l \cos \alpha)$ is that of acceleration ÷ length; i.e. $\mathbf{LT^{-2}} \div \mathbf{L} = \mathbf{T^{-2}}$, the dimension of the left-hand side. The formula is therefore dimensionally consistent.

There are two courses open to us to preserve the dimensional consistency of the equations in numerical work. (Compare the note in Section 4.6.) If you are observant you will have noticed that we have used both, and you may also have realized the differences between them. Look again at the worked Examples 14 and 15. In Example 14 we denoted the acceleration by a m/s^2, so that a is a dimensionless number. All subsequent equations are dimensionless, and the conclusion is that $a = 14$. Note carefully that a is *not* 14 m/s^2; this is the acceleration, and a is a number. In Example 15, however, we adopted the other plan: P, N and F are forces, not numbers-of-units, and the equations are dimensional. Thus equation (2′)

$$\tfrac{5}{13}Mg-F = Ma$$

has every term of dimension $\mathbf{MLT^{-2}}$, and when we come to insert numerical measures in this equation we should strictly insert the units as well. In this case $M = 26$ tons, and we should write

$$\tfrac{5}{13}\,(26\text{ tons})\,(32\text{ ft/s}^2)-F = (26\text{ tons})\,a;$$

when we have inserted the value of F we should then have

$$a = \frac{(320-38{\cdot}4)\,(\text{tons ft/s}^2)}{(26\text{ tons})} = 11\text{ ft/s}^2,$$

where the units are manipulated by the arithmetic along with the numbers. This second system, in which the symbols stand for quantities, is called the Stroud system, and is preferred by many engineers and applied mathematicians. It has everything to commend it, but it will not appeal to the lazy or slipshod.

The two systems are of course equivalent. If, using the Stroud system, we write the equation of motion in the form $F = Ma$, where every term is dimensioned, we may divide by the units of measure and obtain

$$\left(\frac{F}{\text{kg.m/s}^2}\right) = \left(\frac{M}{\text{kg}}\right)\left(\frac{a}{\text{m/s}^2}\right),$$

where every term is a dimensionless number.

Finally, we must confess to some inconsistency in the use of the letter g. Strictly, g is an acceleration, that of local gravity. It is therefore true to say that, approximately,

$$g = 9{\cdot}8\text{ m/s}^2 = 32\text{ ft/s}^2.$$

We are not then at liberty to say (as we have done in Example 2) that the weight of 1 kg is g newtons, or (as we have done in Example 13) that the weight of 1 lb is g poundals. These statements contradict one another and also contradict the statement above. What we should say is that the weight of 1 kg is $\left(\frac{g}{\text{m/s}^2}\right)$ newtons, and the weight of 1 lb is $\left(\frac{g}{\text{ft/s}^2}\right)$ poundals. But this is clumsy, and provided there is no confusion we have used g in numerical examples to stand for the *numerical* constants 9·8 and 32 respectively.

The pound-force (lbf) and kilogram-force (kgf) are defined, not in terms of the local gravity, g, which would make them variable units, but in terms of *standard gravity* g_0, which by international agreement is defined to be the dimensioned quantity

$$g_0 = 9{\cdot}80665 \text{ m/s}^2 = 32{\cdot}174 \text{ ft/s}^2.$$

Then

$$1 \text{ kgf} = \left(\frac{g_0}{\text{m/s}^2}\right) \text{ newtons} \quad \text{and} \quad 1 \text{ lbf} = \left(\frac{g_0}{\text{ft/s}^2}\right) \text{ poundals.}$$

Exercise K

1. Find the acceleration produced in each of the following cases:
(*a*) a body of mass 4 kg is acted on by a force of 2 kgf;
(*b*) a body of mass 7 lb is acted on by a force of 7 lbf;
(*c*) a body of mass 7 lb is acted on by a force of 91 lbf;
(*d*) a body of mass 2 tons is acted on by a force of 100 lbf;
(*e*) a body of mass 8 kg is acted on by a force of 300 gmf.

2. Find, in the stated units, the force required to give:
(*a*) a mass of 4 kg an acceleration of 30 m/s² (kgf);
(*b*) a mass of 7 kg an acceleration of $3g$ (kgf);
(*c*) a mass of 2 tons an acceleration of $\frac{1}{4}$ ft/s² (tonf);
(*d*) a mass of 40 lb an acceleration of 5 ft/s² (lbf);
(*e*) a mass of 100 tons an acceleration of $g/10$ (tonnals).

3. A locomotive is pulling two trucks, the first of mass 20 tons and the second of mass 12 tons. If the whole train moves with constant acceleration and reaches the speed of 20 ft/s in 25 s from rest, what will be the tensions in the couplings over that period? (Give your answers in tonf.)

4. A spring requires the application of 1 tonf to compress it by 1 inch. It is fixed vertically, compressed by 3 in., and loaded with a mass of $\frac{1}{8}$ ton resting on it. When the spring is released, what will be the initial upward acceleration of the load?

5. The force which gives a mass of 1 gm an acceleration of 1 cm/s² is called a *dyne*.
(*a*) Find the number of dynes in a newton.
(*b*) Express 1 kgf in dynes.
(*c*) If two masses, one of 3 gm and the other of 7 gm, are joined by a string of negligible mass which is hung over a smooth peg, find the tension of the string in dynes.

***6.** A dynamometer car, of mass 30 tons, is attached to the rear of a train of 10 coaches, each of mass 40 tons, drawn by a locomotive of mass 90 tons with twelve driving-wheels (Co–Co). The resistances may be taken to be 15 lbf/ton for every vehicle in the train, including the locomotive. On level track, 10 s after starting, the tension in the coupling of the dynamometer car is found to be 1290 lbf. Find:
(*a*) the acceleration of the train;
(*b*) the drawbar pull of the locomotive on the train;
(*c*) the frictional force between each driving-wheel and the rails (assuming that all twelve wheels are equally loaded);
(*d*) the necessary coefficient of friction to make this possible.
Give a simple formula expressing the acceleration in terms of the tension in the coupling of the dynamometer car.

Miscellaneous Exercise

1. Show in a diagram the nature of the external forces which act on a bicycle which is being accelerated.

2. (*a*) Show in a sketch the lift, weight, propulsion and resistance forces on an aircraft in level flight at a steady speed. How are they related?

(*b*) An aircraft of mass m diving along a straight path at angle α to the vertical has an acceleration f along the path. What is the resistance?

3. A car of mass 500 kg is freewheeling down a slope of 30° to the horizontal. What is its acceleration if the total resistance to motion is 700 N?

4. Two boys are dragging a 150 kg victim by the legs. They pull with forces of 620 N and 800 N in horizontal directions 50° apart. If the victim's total resistance is entirely frictional and of amount 750 N, what is his acceleration?

5. A mass of 2 kg hung from a fixed point on a light string is pulled aside and held with the string at 40° to the vertical. What is the least force necessary? What force is needed if the mass is pulled downwards in a direction making 50° with the vertical?

6. A tug is towing three barges each of mass 40000 kg. If the tension in the tow-line to the first barge is 20000 N and the water resistance to each barge is 5500 N, what is the tension in the last tow-line?

7. A lorry of mass 3000 kg is towing a trailer of mass 1000 kg up a hill inclined to the horizontal at $\sin^{-1}\frac{1}{5}$. Frictional forces at the driving wheels of the lorry give a thrust parallel to the road of $2000g$ N. What is the tension in the towing bar?

8. Particles of mass m and M lie one on each of two smooth surfaces inclined at α to the horizontal which meet in a horizontal ridge line. They are joined by a light string which runs smoothly at right-angles over the ridge. Find the tension in the string.

9. A mass of 6 kg is resting on a table. The frictional force between the mass and the table is 10 N. A horizontal string leads from this mass, over a smooth peg and down to a 2 kg mass which is hanging freely. What is the tension in the string? (The string has negligible mass.)

10. A book of mass 500 g is held vertically between finger and thumb. What total force is exerted by the finger on the book if the coefficient of friction is $\frac{1}{3}$ and the book is allowed to slip downwards at 3 m/s^2?

11. A box of mass 200 kg, starting at rest slides 12·5 m down a slope of $\sin^{-1}(\frac{3}{5})$ to the horizontal. If the coefficient of friction is 0·5, what is the velocity at the bottom of the slope?

12. A particle slides down a rough plane surface at a constant speed. Show that the angle of slope equals the angle of friction.

13. A small ring of mass m runs smoothly on a vertical wire. It is connected by a light string to a mass M after passing through a fixed smooth ring. What is the slope of the inclined part of the string when the system is in equilibrium? If it is now pulled down and released, explain in general terms what motion ensues and show that the acceleration of the masses is zero as they pass through the equilibrium position.

14. A bead of mass m is threaded on a rough vertical ring of radius r and coefficient of friction μ. If it is released when the radius to it is inclined at θ to the vertical, what is its acceleration? If instead it were released higher up and passed through this position with a velocity v, what would be its tangential acceleration?

15. Two rings, each of mass m, threaded on a smooth horizontal wire are held at a distance $2b$ apart. They are joined by a light string of length $2a$ on which is threaded another smooth ring of mass m. What forces are required to hold the two rings in position on the wire? If one is released show that its acceleration is less than $gb/2\sqrt{(a^2-b^2)}$. Sketch the path of the lowest ring in the ensuing motion.

16. A particle of mass m is at rest on a plane surface sloping at α to the horizontal when a horizontal force F is applied to it at right-angles to the line of greatest slope. Assuming it moves, what is its acceleration if the coefficient of friction is μ?

17. A pendulum consisting of a mass m on a light string of length l is hung in a railway compartment which has an acceleration a. At what angle to the vertical will it be at relative rest? What will be its initial angular acceleration if a horizontal force P is now applied in the direction of the acceleration a and what will be the increase in the tension in the string?

18. At what angle to the vertical would a pendulum, consisting of a mass m on a light rod, lie in a rocket having an acceleration a in a direction θ from the direction of the line joining the earth's centre to the rocket when it is a distance r from the centre? Give the answer in terms of a, θ, r, g, d where d is the radius of the earth.

19. A bob-sleigh is moving with speed v in a horizontal circle of radius r. If there is no frictional resistance, find by resolving along the surface of the run at right-angles to the direction of motion, the angle of slope of the surface. Sketch the shape of the graphs of the angle of slope against r for constant v, and against v for constant r.

20. Two light strings AB and CB, each of length l are tied together at B and arranged with $\angle ABC = 2\theta$. Particles of mass m are secured at the ends A and C, and then B is given constant acceleration a in the direction bisecting the reflex angle ABC. If the strings have initial angular acceleration α, show in a diagram the acceleration components of A. Find α and the tension in AB in terms of the other quantities. If A has acquired a velocity v relative to B when $\angle ABC = 2\phi$, find the tension in the string there and the angular acceleration.

21. A particle of mass m is sliding down the smooth, sloping surface of a wedge of mass M which stands on a smooth table, the angle of slope being α to the horizontal. Find the acceleration of the two masses. (Introduce the acceleration of m relative to M.)

22. A bead of mass m is threaded on a smooth vertical ring of radius a and centre O, and joined by a light elastic string to the top point A of the ring. The natural length of the string is a and its tension is mg when the extension is a. The bead is held in a position P such that $\angle AOP = 2\theta$ and released. What is its initial acceleration? If it had been released from a point nearer A so that it passed through P with velocity v, find what normal force the ring would have exerted in this position.

REVISION EXERCISES

20. PROBABILITY

1. The probability of each stocking of a certain brand laddering in less than a month's use is 3/5. I buy two pairs of these stockings. What is the probability of my not having an unladdered pair in two months' time, if I wear them on alternate days, laddered or not? What can you say about this probability if I discard a stocking as soon as it is laddered?

2. Driving through a certain town I have to pass three sets of (unlinked) traffic lights. The probabilities of passing these at green are 3/4, 1/3, 1/2 respectively. What is the probability of my getting through with not more than one hold up?

3. In the circuit shown (Figure 1), one of the three switches is closed at random. What is the probability that:

(*a*) *A* only will light up?

(*b*) *B* will light up?

Answer the same questions if two switches are closed at random.

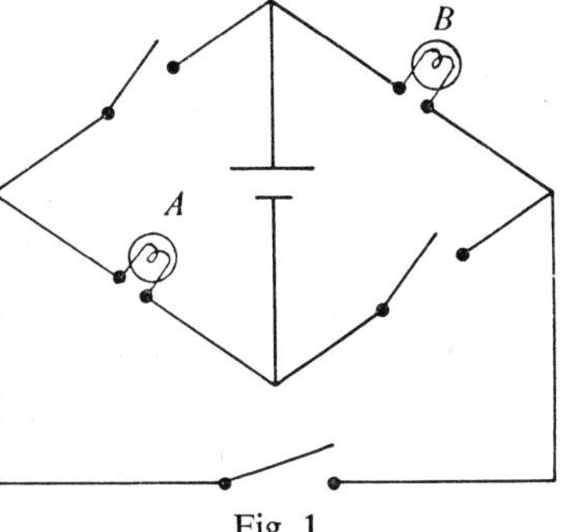

Fig. 1

4. An anti-aircraft missile destroys its target $\frac{1}{2}$ of the time, damages it $\frac{1}{3}$ of the time, and misses $\frac{1}{6}$ of the time. Suppose that two 'damaging' shots will destroy the target.

(*a*) Find the probability that an aircraft will escape total destruction if 4 missiles are fired at it. [Use a tree diagram.]

(*a*) What is the probability that the aircraft will be damaged but not destroyed?

(*c*) If two missiles are fired at each aircraft of a squadron of 36, how many would you expect to survive?

5. A test which might prove useful in the detection of cancer is applied to all the patients in a large hospital in which 4% of the patients have the disease. Of the patients with cancer, 94% react positively to the test but only 3% of the other patients do so. If $P[\mathbf{T}]$ is the probability of reacting positively to the test, and $P[\mathbf{C}] = 0{\cdot}04$ is the probability of having cancer, represent on a Venn diagram or otherwise, the four probabilities

$$P[\mathbf{T} \wedge \mathbf{C}], \quad P[\mathbf{T} \wedge \sim \mathbf{C}], \quad P[\sim \mathbf{T} \wedge \mathbf{C}], \quad P[\sim \mathbf{T} \wedge \sim \mathbf{C}].$$

Find the probability that a patient, selected at random, reacts positively to the test.

6. A drunken man emerges from the 'Lobster Pot' into a narrow passage which leads down to the quayside, 18 steps away. He takes ten steps at a time and then sits down (if he is not already over the edge). He begins with ten steps towards the quay. There is then a $\frac{2}{3}$ chance that he will start off towards the 'Lobster Pot' and a $\frac{1}{3}$ chance that he walks into the water. If he returns to the 'Lobster Pot' there is a fifty-fifty chance that a pal will take him home. Otherwise he will be slung out. Find the probability that after a maximum of six 'walks' he is:

(*a*) in safe custody;
(*b*) on the steps of the 'Lobster Pot';
(*c*) in the drink.

Estimate the probability of (*c*) if this goes on all night.

21. LINEAR EQUATIONS

1. Premultiply
$$\begin{pmatrix} 2 & 1 & 1 \\ 1 & -2 & -2 \\ 1 & 3 & 2 \end{pmatrix} \text{ by } \begin{pmatrix} 2 & 1 & 0 \\ -4 & 3 & 5 \\ 5 & -5 & -5 \end{pmatrix},$$
and hence solve the equations:
$$\begin{aligned} 2x+y+z &= 1, \\ x-2y-2z &= -1, \\ x+3y+2z &= 1. \end{aligned}$$

2. Solve by the echelon process:
$$\begin{aligned} x+2y+3z &= 1, \\ 2x+3y+4z &= 5, \\ 3x+5y+2z &= 4, \end{aligned}$$
(*a*) if the coefficients are in the field of rational numbers;
(*b*) if the coefficients are in the field of integers modulo 7.

3. Invert the matrix
$$\begin{pmatrix} 1 & 2 & 3 \\ 4 & 6 & 7 \\ 5 & 8 & 9 \end{pmatrix}.$$

4. Show that the three planes with equations $p_1 = 0$, $p_2 = 0$, and $p_3 = 0$, where
$$\begin{aligned} p_1 &= x+y+z-\tfrac{1}{5}, \\ p_2 &= 10x-5y+15z-7, \\ p_3 &= 5x+8y+4z, \end{aligned}$$
have a whole line in common, and find the coordinates of two points on it.
Find λ, μ and ν if $\lambda p_1+\mu p_2+\nu p_3$ is identically zero.

5. Find for what values of K the equations:
$$\begin{aligned} x+y+Kz &= 4K, \\ x+Ky+z &= -2, \\ 2x+y+z &= -2, \end{aligned}$$
have (*a*) no solution, (*b*) one solution, (*c*) an infinity of solutions. Illustrate geometrically.

6. The quartermaster for an expedition to climb Mt Matrix by the echelon route, seeking relaxation in Cramer's gully, is working out high-altitude rations. He has three food-packs available: tins of Tummican of mass 360 g, packets of Datamix of mass 240 g, and blocks of Krout mint cake of mass 210 g. Analysis of the food values of these three yields the following table.

	Units per pack		
Food	Protein	Carbo-hydrate	Vitamins
Tummican	10	7	2
Datamix	6	11	5
Krout	0	12	9

Each man needs at least 140 units of protein, 280 units of carbohydrate, and 160 units of vitamins. Owing to the intricacies of the notorious Elimination traverse, it is desirable that the mass of food carried is kept below 7·2 kg. Advise the quartermaster.

22. AREA

1. Evaluate: $I = \int_2^3 |4x-11|\,dx$ and $J = \int_2^3 (4x-11)^2\,dx$.

Is I^2 more than, less than, or equal to J?

2. The velocity of a train leaving a station is given in the table:

Time (min)	0	2	4	6	8	10	12	14	16
Speed (m/min)	0	150	330	500	730	890	1070	1230	1370

Use Simpson's Rule to find the distance travelled in the 16 min.

3. By considering a suitable approximation to

$$\int_0^1 x^3\,dx,$$

find

$$\lim_{n\to\infty} \frac{1^3+2^3+\ldots+n^3}{n^4}.$$

Check by using the formula

$$4\sum_{i=1}^{n} i^3 = n^2(n+1)^2.$$

4. Find the mean value of

$$\frac{1}{x^2+4} \quad \text{between} \quad x=4 \quad \text{and} \quad x=6,$$

and compare it with the average of the extreme values. Illustrate your result with a rough sketch.

5. Find the area enclosed between the three curves whose equations are

$$a^2y = 4x^3, \quad 4ay = x^2, \quad x^2y = 4a^3 \quad (x > 0).$$

[Take care: the first two curves meet in *two* places.]

6. The probability that a policeman, chosen at random from the Cauchyville police force, wears boots whose size is between $10-t$ and $10+t$ is approximately

$$\frac{2}{\pi}\int_{-t}^{t}\frac{1}{1+4u^2}\,du.$$

Find the probability that a particular policeman wears boots:

(*a*) between size 8 and size 12; (*b*) of size larger than 12.

23. TECHNIQUES OF INTEGRATION

1. Prove that $$\int_0^8 \frac{x\,dx}{\sqrt{(x^2+9)}} = \sqrt{73}-3.$$

Apply Simpson's Rule, with ordinates at $x = 0, 4, 8$, to this integral to estimate the value of $\sqrt{73}$.

2. Evaluate:

(*a*) $\displaystyle\int \frac{x\,dx}{(1+x^2)^2}$; (*b*) $\displaystyle\int_0^1 x^2(1+x)^2\,dx$;

(*c*) $\displaystyle\int_0^{\frac{1}{2}\pi} x \sin 2x\,dx$; (*d*) $\displaystyle\int_0^{\pi} \cos x \cos 5x\,dx$.

3. Use the method of integration by parts:

(*a*) to show that

$$\int_0^{\frac{1}{2}\pi} \sin^2 x \cos^5 x\,dx = \tfrac{1}{6}\int_0^{\frac{1}{2}\pi} \cos^7 x\,dx;$$

(*b*) to evaluate $$\int_0^{\frac{1}{2}\pi} x^2 \cos x\,dx.$$

4. Show that $16 < (4+\sin x)^2 < (4+x)^2$ for $0 < x < \frac{1}{2}\pi$.

Deduce that $$\frac{\pi}{32} > \int_0^{\frac{1}{2}\pi}\frac{dx}{(4+\sin x)^2} > \frac{\pi}{32+4\pi}.$$

5. Find polynomials $p(x)$ and $q(x)$ such that

$$\int\{(3x-1)\cos x + (1-2x)\sin x\}\,dx = p(x)\cos x + q(x)\sin x.$$

6. Evaluate
$$\int_0^{\pi} \sin mx \sin nx \, dx$$
(*a*) if $m \neq n$; (*b*) if $m = n$.

Evaluate $\displaystyle\int_0^{\frac{1}{2}\pi} x \sin nx \, dx$ and hence $\displaystyle\int_{\frac{1}{2}\pi}^{\pi} (\pi - x) \sin nx \, dx$,

(*a*) if n is odd; (*b*) if n is even.

It is required to approximate to a function f over the interval $\{x: 0 \leqslant x \leqslant \pi\}$, so that for each x
$$f(x) \simeq a_1 \sin x + a_2 \sin 2x + \ldots + a_n \sin nx.$$
What is the effect of multiplying each side by $\sin nx$ and integrating over the interval? (Assume that the process is legitimate.)

f is defined so that
$$\left.\begin{aligned} f(x) &= x && \text{for} \quad 0 \leqslant x \leqslant \tfrac{1}{2}\pi, \\ f(x) &= \pi - x && \text{for} \quad \tfrac{1}{2}\pi \leqslant x \leqslant \pi. \end{aligned}\right\}$$
For this function, evaluate the a_n, and draw the graphs of $f(x)$ and of the sum of the first three terms of the series which are not zero.

This is called a *Fourier Series*.

24. INTRODUCTION TO MECHANICS

1. (*a*) An electron of mass 9×10^{-27} g in a magnetic field has a momentary acceleration of 6×10^{22} cm/s². What is the force acting on it?

(*b*) A two-tonne truck on smooth rails is pulled with a force of 600 N at an angle of 60° to the rails. Find its acceleration and the reaction between the wheel flanges and the rails caused by this force.

2. A man whose mass is 100 kg is travelling in a lift. If the thrust on the floor is 1200 N at a certain instant, what is the lift's acceleration?

3. A body of mass 2 kg, initially moving with velocity 10 m/s on a bearing of 120°, is acted on by a constant force of 14 N on a bearing of 180°. Find its velocity after 2 seconds.

4. A mass of 2 kg is swung round in a vertical circle so that its speed at the lowest point is 10 m/s. If the string attaching it to a fixed point is 1 metre long, find the tension in it.

5. A packing-case of mass 100 kg stands on a ramp making an angle of 30° with the horizontal, the coefficient of friction being $1/2\sqrt{3}$. What is the least force applied parallel to the ramp that will

(*a*) prevent the case from sliding down;
(*b*) cause it to move steadily up?

6. Four 20 tonne trucks are being pushed, by a diesel shunter, up an incline of 1 in 100 with an acceleration of 30 mm/s².

All have similar buffers with springs which obey Hooke's Law. The uppermost truck's buffers are compressed 16 mm each. Find the amount of compression in the upper and lower buffers of the lowest truck, and the force needed to compress one of the springs 1 cm.

Miscellaneous Problems

1. Write $10\cos\theta+2\sin\theta$ in the form $R\cos(\theta-\alpha)$, where R is a positive number and α an acute angle. Show that, in this case, $10\sin\theta+2\cos\theta$ is equal to $R\sin(\theta+\alpha)$.

I have a piece of paper 9×8 cm out of which I want to cut a rectangle 10×2 cm (see Figure 2). Show that in order to do this the quantities

$$10\cos\theta+2\sin\theta \quad \text{and} \quad 10\sin\theta+2\cos\theta$$

must satisfy certain inequalities. (θ is the angle at which the rectangle is inclined to the edges of the paper, as shown in the diagram.) Using the alternative forms found above, solve these inequalities for acute angles θ, and hence find the possible range of values of θ.

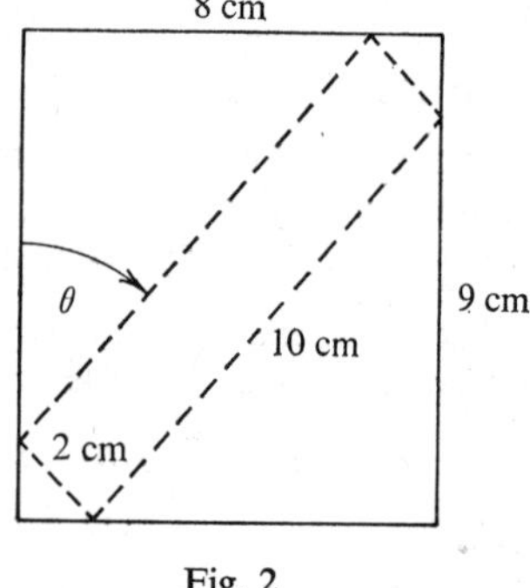

Fig. 2

2. An ice-skater describes an elliptic path, her position vector $\mathbf{r}$, with respect to O at time t (in metre-second units) being

$$\mathbf{r} = \begin{pmatrix} 18\cos\frac{1}{3}t \\ 13{\cdot}5\sin\frac{1}{3}t \end{pmatrix}.$$

(i) How long does she take to go right round the ellipse?

(ii) Show accurately, on a scale diagram on graph paper, her position and the directions of her velocity and acceleration at time $t = 2\pi$.

(iii) Prove that her speed can be expressed as $1{\cdot}5\sqrt{(16-7\cos^2\frac{1}{3}t)}$. Hence find the points at which her speed is greatest.

(iv) Prove that the acceleration is a scalar multiple of $\mathbf{r}$, and hence find where her acceleration is greatest. Find the magnitude of the greatest acceleration.

(v) What coefficient of friction would be necessary to enable her to describe the path in this way?

3. The mathematics marks of candidates for two similar examinations are shown in the following frequency tables:

Marks (Exam. A):	30–39	40–49	50–59	60–69	70–79
No. of candidates:	5	15	30	15	5

Marks (Exam. B):	30–39	40–49	50–59	60–69	70–79	80–89	90–99
No. of candidates:	3	5	5	11	22	10	4

(*a*) Find the mean and standard deviation of each population.

(*b*) Discuss how the marks of the second set of candidates could be scaled to give a population with the same mean and standard deviation as the first.

4. Figure 3 shows a brick with sides 3 cm, 4 cm, 5 cm in isometric projection (i.e. with lengths correctly portrayed in the direction of each edge). Copy the figure accurately, and show on it the section of the brick by the perpendicular bisector plane of the diagonal XY, setting down any calculation you do in the course of your work.

5. A transformation of a plane is described by the equation

$$\begin{pmatrix} x' \\ y' \end{pmatrix} = \begin{pmatrix} 2 & 6 \\ 1 & 1 \end{pmatrix} \begin{pmatrix} x \\ y \end{pmatrix}.$$

Are there any vectors $\begin{pmatrix} x \\ y \end{pmatrix}$, other than $\begin{pmatrix} 0 \\ 0 \end{pmatrix}$, which are transformed into themselves? Prove that the vector $\begin{pmatrix} 3 \\ 1 \end{pmatrix}$ is transformed into a multiple of itself, and find another vector in a different direction which has a similar property. State the appropriate multiple in each case.

Use your results to give a simple construction for the point P' into which any point P of the plane is transformed.

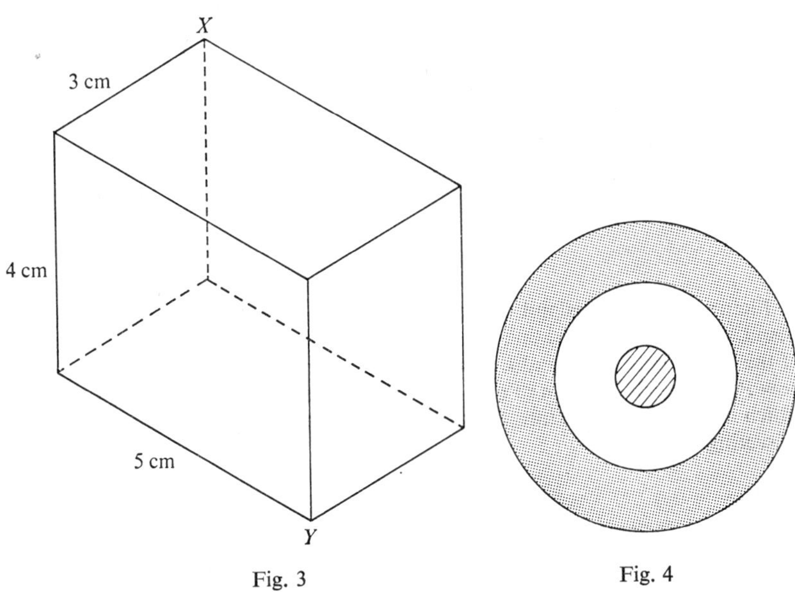

Fig. 3

Fig. 4

6. The diameters of the rings on a target at a fair (Figure 4) are in the ratio 1:3:5, and the scores from the outside inwards are 1, 2, 3. There is a one-sixth chance that you will miss the target completely, and an equal chance of getting your shot anywhere on the target area. If the stallholder charges the customers 6*d.* for 4 shots, and offers a prize for a score of 10 or more, what value can he afford to make the prizes if he is to pocket 99% of the takings?

7. Prove that $$(a^2+b^2)(x^2+y^2) = (ax+by)^2+(ay-bx)^2.$$

Write down a pair of natural numbers whose squares add up to 10, and another pair whose squares add up to 25. Use the result given above to deduce two pairs of numbers whose squares add up to 250. Then find as many pairs as you can whose squares add up to 250^2.

8. You are given that
$$y = \tan^{-1}x \Rightarrow \frac{dy}{dx} = \frac{1}{1+x^2}.$$
Use this fact to find a linear approximation for $\tan^{-1}(1+\alpha)$, where α is small.

Find d^2y/dx^2, and hence prove that
$$d^3y/dx^3 = \frac{6x^2-2}{(1+x^2)^3}.$$
Deduce a cubic approximation for $\tan^{-1}\beta$, where β is small.

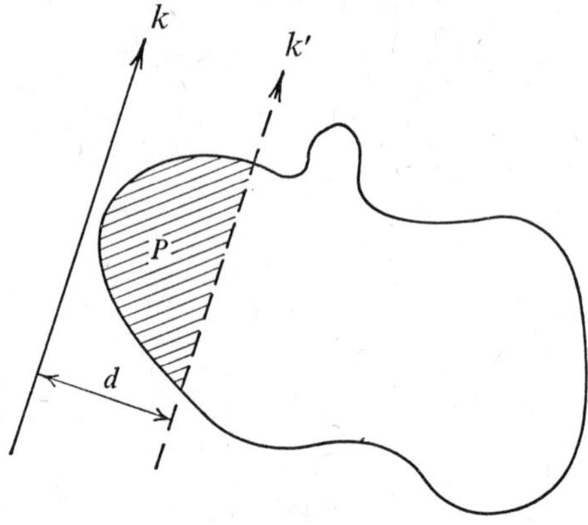

Fig. 5

9. Figure 5 shows an island of area A. k is a fixed line which does not cross the island, and k' is a parallel line at a distance d away from k. If the area of the part of the island between k and k' is denoted by P, draw a rough graph illustrating how P varies as a function of d. Deduce that there is a line in any given direction which divides the island into two parts of equal area. We shall call such a line a 'bisecting line'.

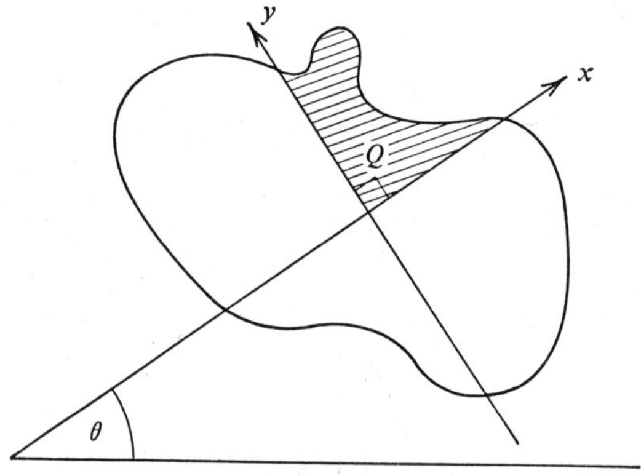

Fig. 6

Figure 6 shows the same island with a pair of bisecting lines forming a pair of axes, such that the x-axis makes an angle θ with a fixed direction. Let Q denote the area in the positive quadrant, so that Q is a function of θ. Explain carefully why the values of Q corresponding to $\theta = 0°$ and $\theta = 90°$ add up to $\frac{1}{2}A$. Deduce that it is always possible to find two lines at right angles to each other which divide the island into four equal areas.

Explain briefly where the idea of continuity enters into your arguments.

10. i, a, b, c, are members of a set on which an operation denoted by $*$ is defined. This operation is associative, and i is a neutral element.

Using the information in the following table, show that $a * b = b * a$. Then complete the table, justifying each entry, and show that the set is closed under this operation.

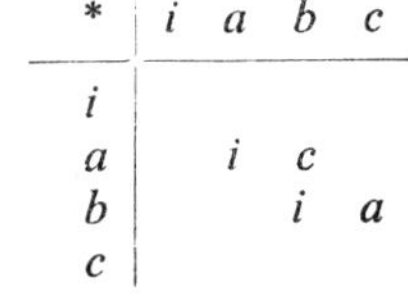

$*$	i	a	b	c
i				
a		i	c	
b			i	a
c				

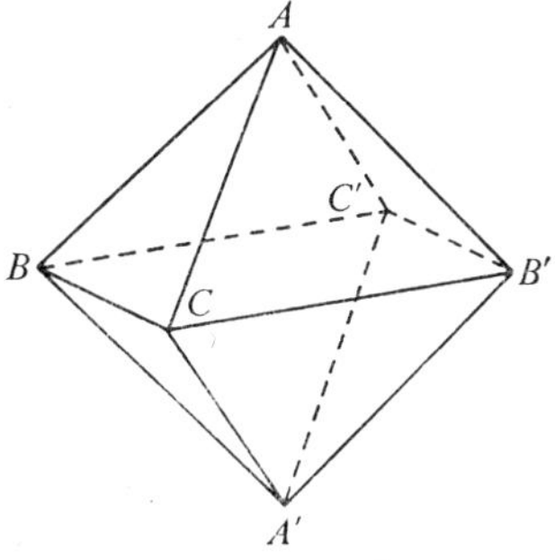

Fig. 7

11. $ABCA'B'C'$ is a regular octahedron (Figure 7). How many different isometry transformations are there which map the octahedron onto itself? Explain why half of these must be direct isometries and half of them indirect; and show (by listing the possibilities or otherwise) that all the direct isometries (except the identity) can be obtained by rotation about suitable axes. How many of the indirect isometries can be obtained by reflection in a plane? Give an example of one which cannot be obtained in this way, and show how it *can* be effected by combining a reflection with a rotation.

The 4-dimensional equivalent of the octahedron is called a 'cross polytope'. It may be thought of as having eight vertices with coordinates $(\pm 1, 0, 0, 0)$, $(0, \pm 1, 0, 0)$, $(0, 0, \pm 1, 0)$, $(0, 0, 0, \pm 1)$. How many isometry transformations are there which map this figure onto itself? Generalize your answer to n dimensions.

(*Hint.* Try matrices.)

12. Prove that the two vectors

$$\begin{pmatrix} \frac{1}{3} \\ \frac{2}{3} \\ \frac{2}{3} \end{pmatrix} \quad \text{and} \quad \begin{pmatrix} \frac{2}{3} \\ -\frac{2}{3} \\ \frac{1}{3} \end{pmatrix}$$

are (i) each of unit length, and (ii) at right-angles to each other.

A unit cube is originally placed with a vertex at the origin and three edges along the axes, represented by vectors

$$\begin{pmatrix}1\\0\\0\end{pmatrix},\quad \begin{pmatrix}0\\1\\0\end{pmatrix}\quad \text{and}\quad \begin{pmatrix}0\\0\\1\end{pmatrix}.$$

The cube is then moved into a new position with the same vertex at the origin and with its edges along

$$\begin{pmatrix}\frac{1}{3}\\\frac{2}{3}\\\frac{2}{3}\end{pmatrix},\quad \begin{pmatrix}\frac{2}{3}\\-\frac{2}{3}\\\frac{1}{3}\end{pmatrix}\quad \text{and}\quad \begin{pmatrix}a\\b\\c\end{pmatrix}$$

respectively; so that $\begin{pmatrix}a\\b\\c\end{pmatrix}$

is at right-angles to each of the other vectors and is of unit length. Find the vector

$$\begin{pmatrix}a\\b\\c\end{pmatrix}.$$

(An algebraic method will give two answers, with opposite signs. Use a diagram or a rough model to decide which is the right one.)

This transformation of the cube can in fact be carried out by a rotation about some axis through O. If (x, y, z) is a point on this axis, explain why

$$\begin{pmatrix}x\\y\\z\end{pmatrix}$$

is transformed into itself. Write down the matrix of the transformation and use the fact just stated to make up a set of equations. Deduce that points on the axis satisfy the equations

$$\tfrac{1}{2}x = y = z.$$

What value would you expect the determinant of the transformation matrix to have, and why? Verify this by direct calculation.

13. A schoolmaster plans his work as follows. If there is a test on a certain day, then there is a probability of 0·7 that there will be a test on the next day as well. If on the other hand there is no test on the first day, then the probability of a test on the next day is 0·9. Let x_n denote the probability of a test on the nth day of term, and y_n the probability that there is not a test. Express x_{n+1}, y_{n+1}, the corresponding probabilities for the $(n+1)$th day, in terms of x_n and y_n; and then write your answer in the form of a matrix equation connecting

$$\begin{pmatrix}x_{n+1}\\y_{n+1}\end{pmatrix}\quad \text{with}\quad \begin{pmatrix}x_n\\y_n\end{pmatrix}.$$

If there will certainly not be a test on the first day of term, what are the probabilities of a test on the second, third and fourth days?

Show that if there were a probability of $\frac{3}{4}$ that there is a test on the first day of term, then the probability of a test on every day of the term would be the same.

In this last event, a boy plans his strategy as follows. He knows that if he spends K hours on his prep. each night, where $0 \leqslant K \leqslant 1$, his probability of passing the test next morning (if there is one) is K. If he fails the test, he will be kept in for N hours. He regards any time spent either on prep. or on being kept in as time wasted. Prove that he could expect on average to waste W hours per day, where W is given by the formula

$$W = K(1-\tfrac{3}{4}N)+\tfrac{3}{4}N.$$

Find how long he should spend on prep. each night, so as to waste as little time as possible in the long run (i) if $N = 1$, (ii) if $N = 2$. What is the shortest duration of the keep-in which will ensure that the boy will do a full hour's prep. every night?

14. $OABC$, $OPQR$ are any two lines meeting at O, and $A, B, C; P, Q, R$ are any points on them. BR, QC meet at X; CP, RA meet at Y; AQ, PB meet at Z.

Take $\mathbf{i}$, $\mathbf{j}$ as unit vectors along OA, OP and let $OA = a\mathbf{i}$, $OB = b\mathbf{i}$, etc.

(*a*) Prove that $(qb-cr)\mathbf{x} = bc(q-r)\mathbf{i}+qr(b-c)\mathbf{j}$.

(*b*) Use algebraic symmetry to write down $\mathbf{y}$ and $\mathbf{z}$ in terms of $\mathbf{i}$ and $\mathbf{j}$.

(*c*) Find a linear relation connecting $\mathbf{x}$, $\mathbf{y}$, and $\mathbf{z}$, and hence show that X, Y, Z are collinear. [*Hint*. Divide the equation in (*a*) by $bcqr$.]

INDEX

acceleration, 515–17, 675; angular, 521; average, 513–15, 516; in circular motion, 519, 524–5, 526; constant, 527–30, 540; under gravity, 532, 684, 685, 715; unit of, 540
addition formula for tangents, 386–8
algebra, Boolean, 559; of events, 558–9; vector, in terms of components, 351–2
algebraic irrationals, 433
amplitude, of a wave, 392
analysis, fundamental theorem of, 628–31; harmonic, 392; of variance, 335
angle, auxiliary, 399; of friction, 709–10; multiple, 388–91; between two lines, 371; between two vectors, 363–4, 386–7; between velocity and radius, in circular motion, 522
angular acceleration, 521
angular velocity, 520–1
approximations, for finding area, 617–25; higher degree, 465–8; linear, to a function, 447–53, 462–4, 469; local, 445–70; local quadratic, 466, 468, 470; by maps, 445–7.
Archimedean spiral, 411
area, 603–39; unit of, 606
area function, properties of, 604–6
Argand diagram, 438–9
arithmetic progressions, 311, 315
auxiliary angle, 399
average acceleration, 513–15, 516
average error, 343–4; in approximation, 464
average velocity, 505–6
axes, 348; intercepts on, 378–9; isometric, 349–50; right-handed (three-dimensional), 349
axial planes, 378; intercepts on, 378–9

base vectors, 367; and coordinates, 347–8
Bayes's Theorem, 565
bodies, in mechanics, 681; systems of, 693–5
Boolean algebra, 559

cardioid, 411
Cartesian coordinates, 407; connection between polar coordinates and, 409–10
centroid, 356
chain rule, for differentiating composite functions, 472–4; 640–1; deductions from, 647–9
Charlier's checks, 339, 340
circle, area within, 608–9
circular motion, 519–27; acceleration in, 519, 524–5, 526; velocity in, 519, 521–3, 525–6
cissoid, 411
classes, statistical, 323–5
coefficient of friction, 707
combined functions, 391–4
comparison, use of statistics in, 316–17, 320
completing the square, 423–4, 428
complex number plane, 439
complex numbers, 438
components of vectors, 351; scalar product in terms of, 362–3; vector algebra in terms of, 351–2
composite functions, 471–2; chain rule for differentiation of, 472–4, integration of 640–1, 647–9
compound events, 554–9, 569
compression, of a spring, 494, 691
computer, use of, for calculation of standard deviation 332; for solution of linear equations, 586
conditional probability, 560–5
conditioning equations for solution, 598
constant acceleration, 527–30, 540
contingency tables, 555–6, 558
continuous domain, 322–3
coordinates, base vectors and, 347–8; Cartesian, 407; connection between Cartesian and polar, 409–10; polar, 407–9, 525; of position, velocity, and acceleration, 516–17; three-dimensional, 348–50
cosecant, 404
cosine rule, for solution of triangles, 412–13, 414
cotangent, 404
cube root, 459–60
cubic approximations, local, 468, 470
cycloid, 482–3

definite integrals, 614–15; substituting in, 651
de Morgan's Laws, 558–9
derivative (derived function), 471, 473; dimensional consistency of, 659; of polynomials, 503; of products, 477, 486; of quotients, 479, 483; of sin x, 402–3; of square-root function, 448; of trigonometrical functions, 487; of vectors with respect to scalars, 510, 525
description of events, 627–3

descriptive statistics, 317
deviation, 328; mean absolute, 329, 342, 345; mean square, 329, 342, 345; root mean square or standard, 329–40
diagonal form, matrices in, 592
differentiation, technique of, 471–92; *see also* derivative
dimension, 498; of force, 713–14; of products, 499–500; of quotients, 500; of sums 497–9
dimensional consistency, 498, 500, 660–2, 714–16; of derivatives and integrals, 659–62
dimensionless quantities, working with, 660
discrete domain, 322–3
discriminant, 435
displacement, 507
domains, discrete and continuous, 322–3
dot product (scalar product), 360–3
'dropping the dashes', 418
dummy variable, 305, 307

echelon form, matrices in, 587, 592
elementary matrices, 588–90
elimination, solution of linear equations by, 582, 584–5
energy, dimension of, 714
equation of motion (Newton's Second Law), 675–7
equations, 598; linear, planes defined by, 376–7; linear, solution of, 582–602; linear trigonometrical, 399–400; local approximation in solution of, 455–60; parametric, 353, 380–2; of planes, 356, 376–7; polar, 410; quadratic, 426–9; simple trigonometrical, 396–400; use of tan $\frac{1}{2}x$ formulae in, 403–4
error, average, 343–4; average, in approximation, 464; fractional, 475
events, compounds, 554–9; exclusive and exhaustive, 572–6; independent, 567–70, 573; probability of, 551–4
experiments, design of, 335
extension, of a spring, 690–2

factor formulae, for sums and differences of sizes and cosines, 401–2
factors, solution of quadratic equations by, 426
field, of complex numbers, 438; of real numbers, 433
finite series, examples of, 309, 315
forces, acting on a particle, 675; as agent altering natural behaviour, 674; arising when a body acts on another, 679–81; dimension of, 713–14; non-parallel, 699–700; parallel, 688–9; types of, 688; work done by, 360, 365
forecasting, use of statistics in, 317
fractional change, fractional error, 475
frames of reference, in mechanics, 674–5
frequency, statistical, 306, 318–19, 552; relative, 553
frequency definition of probability, 565–6
frequency density, 325
frequency diagrams, 319
frequency functions, 318–20
frequency table, 318
friction (frictional force), 688, 706–9; angle of, 708; coefficient of, 706
function $a \sin x + b \cos x$, 384–6
fundamental theorem of analysis, 628–31

generator, probability, 346
geometric progressions, 314, 315
gradients, of perpendicular vectors in a plane, 367
graphs, areas under, 611–14; of quadratic functions, 417–22; of quadratic polynomials, 435; solution of linear equations by, 583; solution of quadratic equations by, 426–8; solution of quadratic inequalities by, 429–30
gravitation, Newton's Law of, 452, 683–4
gravitational mass, 684
gravity, acceleration under, 532, 684, 685, 715; motion under, 532–6, 540; standard, 685, 711
grouping of data, 323–4; effect of, on standard deviation, 338

harmonic analysis, 392
histograms, 324–5
hyperbola, 411

identities, use of, in integration, 643
impulse, dimension of, 714
increment notation, 452
indefinite integrals, 630–1
independence and statistical independence, 567–70
inequalities, in physical measurements, 492; quadratic, 429–31
inertial mass, 684
infinite possibility spaces, 566
infinite series, 309–10
instantaneous centre of rotation, 538–9
integral functions, evaluation of, 627–33
integrals, definite, 614–15, 651; dimensional consistency of, 659–62; generalizations about, 633–7; indefinite, 630–1; some standard, 658

integration, by parts, 655; by substitution, 647; techniques of, 640–71
intersection, of lines, 354–5, 357; of planes, 357
interaction principle, in mechanics, 679–81
inverse functions, differentiation of, 481–2, 486; in integration, 663–6
irrational numbers, 432–3
isometric axes, 349–50
isometry, area invariant under, 604
iterative methods, 437, 459, 461, 469 596–8

Kepler's Laws of planetary motion, 682
kilogram, as unit of mass. 684–5
kinematics, 504–40
kurtosis, 346

lamina, angular velocity of, 520–1, 538
Legendre's Equation, 490
lemniscate, 411
length, unit of, 493, 540
limaçon, 411
linear approximation, to a function, 447–53, 462–4, 469
linear equations, methods of solving, 582–602; planes defined by, 356, 376–7
lines, angle between, 371; intersection of, 354–5, 357; through the origin, 353; not through the origin, 353–4; parallel, 370; parallel to a plane, 382–3; perpendicular, 370–1; in three dimensions, 380–2; vectors and, 368
local approximation, 445–70
local quadratic approximations, 466, 468, 470
local scale factor, 447, 473–4, 641
locating the graph of a quadratic function, 421–2
loci, polar, 410–11
lune, 609

maps, approximation by, 445–7
Markov chain, 580
mass, 674, 675; gravitational and inertial, 684; units of, 684–5
matrices, in diagonal form, 592; in echelon form, 587, 592; elementary, 588–90; inverse of, 592–6; solution of linear equations by, 582, 586–92
mean, 321, 322, 332, 342; deviations from, 328–46; in discrete and continuous domains, 323; of extreme values, 321, 322; mean absolute deviation from, 329, 342, 345; mean square deviation from, 329, 342, 345; standard (root mean square) deviation from, 329–40
mean value, 342–3, 625
measure theory, 566
measurements, physical, 492–3
mechanics, introduction to, 672–718
median, 321, 322; in discrete and continuous domains, 323
metre, as unit of length, 493, 685
minimum property of variance, 345
mode, 321, 322
models, in mathematics, 498, 673
momentum, dimension of, 714
motion, in a circle, 519–27, 540; with constant acceleration, 527–30, 540; equation of (Newton's Second Law), 516, 675–7; under gravity, 532–6, 540;
multiple angles, 388–91

newton, as unit of force, 685
Newton–Raphson method, for solving equations by approximation, 459, 469; modified, 461
Newton's Laws, First, 674–5; Second, 516, 675–7; Third, 681
Newton's model for mass and force, 673–87
normal contact force (normal force), 688
Normal population, 336, 346
normal vector, 370
notation, for definite integral, 615; for differentiating a product, 476; for expressions of dimensions, 501; increment, 452; for integral of unbounded region, 637; for integration, 640–1; for mean of population, 337, 343; for probabilities, 553, 555; Sigma, 305–6, 315
numbers, complex, 438; irrational, 432–3; rational, 431–2; real, 433–4, 495

origin, 348; lines through, 353; lines not through, 363–4
orthocentres, 374–5
oscillations, periodic, 391–2

parabola, 418, 536, 621
parallel forces, 688–9
parallel lines, 370
parameters, 353; components in two dimensions in terms of, 353; differentiation of functions defined by, 482–3, 486; in one dimension, 353–6; in two dimensions, 356–8
parametric equations, 363, 380–2
parent populations, 317
particle, in mechanics, 673; force acting on, 675
parts, integration by, 655–6
periodic oscillations, 391–2

perpendicular distance, from a line, 369–70; from a plane, 376, 377–8
perpendicular lines (two dimensions), 370–1
perpendicular vectors (three dimensions), 372–3
perpendicularity, 367–76
phase difference, between waves, 392
planes, axial, 378–9; defined by linear equations, 356, 376–7; intersection of, 357–8; lines parallel to, 382–3; through the origin, 356–7; not through the origin, 357–8; perpendicular distance from, 376, 377–8; perpendicular vectors in, 367; sheaf and prism of, 383–5
planetary motion, Kepler's Laws of, 683
Poisson population, 346
polar coordinates, 407–11, 525; connection between Cartesian coordinates and, 409–10
polar loci, 410–11
polygons, simple closed, area of, 606–8
polynomial, quadratic, 417, 434–7
populations, 316–17, 332; J-shaped, 325; Normal, 336; Poisson, 346; skewed, 325, 346; symmetrical, 325
position, measures of, 320–1, 344
position vectors, 407, 509; angular velocity of, 520
possibilities, 554; equally likely, 549; trials and, 546–7
possibility spaces, 547; infinite, 566; representation of, 547–9
pound avoirdupois, as unit of mass, 710
pound-force, 710
poundal, as unit of force, 710
powers of x, differentiation of, 485–6
primitive (indefinite integrals), 630–1
prism of planes, 383–5
probability, 546–81; 'classical' definition of, 553, 554; conditional, 560–5; difficulties in definition of, 565–70; laws of, 557–8, 561, 566; *a priori* and *a posteriori*, 565
product, of roots of quadratic polynomials, 436–7; rule for differentiation of, 475–9, 480, 486, 641, 655–6; scalar (dot), 360–3, 511
projectiles, paths of, by calculation, 535; by drawing, 532–3
projection, of segment onto line, 359–60
pulleys, systems of, 697–9
Pythagoras, Theorem of, 362–3, 412

quadratic approximations, local, 466, 468, 470
quadratic equations, 426–9
quadratic functions, 417; domain and range of, 418, 431–4; graphs of, 417–22, 435; roots of, 434–5, 436–7; sign of, 435–6
quadratic inequalities, 429–31
quadratic surds, 433
quadratic trapezia, area of, 619–23
quotients, differentiation of, 479–80, 483; dimension of, 500–2

range, as measure of spread, 328; of quadratic functions, 418, 431–3
rational index, 486
rational numbers, 431–2
real numbers, 433–4
reciprocal functions, sec x, csc x, cot x, 404–5
reciprocal spiral, 411
rectangles, area of, 607–8
regions, area of, 603–8; of circle and plane, 313; with curved boundaries, area of, 608–9; unbounded, 636–7
regression lines, 343–4, 464
relative frequency, 553
relaxation, solution of linear equations by, 596–601
replacement of functions of x, integration by, 652–5
resolved parts, in mechanics, 701–5
Rietz pattern slide-rule, 414–15
right-handed axes (three-dimensional), 349
roots, of general equation, 455–60; of quadratic equation, 426, 434–5, 436–7; of trigonometrical equations, 396–400
rose-curve, 511
rotation, instantaneous centre of, 538–9

samples, statistics of, 317
sampling, in estimating probability, 565
scalar multiple, 351
scalar product (dot product), 360–2, 511; in terms of components, 362–3
scalars, differentiation of vectors with respect to, 510–11; as multipliers, 497
scale factors, local, 447, 473–4, 641
secant, 404, 405
second, as unit of time, 493, 685
semi-interquartile range of spread, 328
series, finite, 309–15; infinite 309; trigonometrical, 407
sheaf of planes, 383–5
shearing, area invariant under, 605–6
Sheppard's Correction, 338
Sigma notation, 305–6, 315
sign, of quadratic polynomial, 435–6
Simpson's Rule, 623–5

sine, derivative of, 402–3
  factor formulae for, 401–2
sine rule, for solution of triangles, 413–14
skewness, 346
slide-rule, Rietz pattern, 414–15
speed, and velocity, 504, 519
spiral, Archimedean, 411; reciprocal, 411
spread, measures of, 327–32, 344
springs, extension and compression of, 690–2
square, completing the, 423–4, 428; perfect, 424; as unit of area, 606
square function, 417, 481; area under graph of, 612–14
square root function, derivative of, 448, 481
standard deviation (root mean square deviation from mean), 329–36; aids to calculation of, 336–40
statistical independence, 567–9
statistics, descriptive, 317
stereographic projection, 446–7
substitution, integration by, 647–51; problems of, 666–7
suffixes, in terms of a sequence, 306–7
sums, by accumulation, 495, 497; of arithmetic progressions, 311; of different units, 497–9; of geometric progressions, 314; integration of, 643–4; partial, of infinite series, 309–10; of roots of quadratic polynomial 436–7; of vectors, 351
surds, quadratic, 433
symmetry, in integration, 644–6; of graphs of quadratic functions, 418; of statistical independence, 569–70

tan $\frac{1}{2}x$ formulae, use of, in equations, 403–4
tangent, 405
tangents, addition formula for, 386–8
Taylor's approximation, 467–8, 470, 473
Tchebychev's inequalities, 336
tension, in a spring, 688, 690–2
tetrahedron, with or without orthocentre, 374–5
thrust, 688; compression in a spring proportional to, 690
time, as a dimension, 500; unit of, 493, 540
trapezia, areas of quadratic, 619–23
Trapezium Rule, 618
tree diagrams, 562
trials, and possibilities, 546–7
triangles, area of, 604, 607; orthocentres of, 374; solution of, 412–15
trifolium, 411
trigonometrical equations, linear, 399–400; simple, 396–98
trigonometrical functions, derivatives of, 487
trigonometry, 386–416
two standard deviation check, 336–7, 340

units, of area, 606; and dimensions, 492–503, 540; of force, 494, 685, 710–13; of mass, 684–5; of variance, 333

variance (square of standard deviation), 333; average, within and between classes, 335; minimum property of, 345
vector algebra, in terms of components, 351–2
vector equation of motion, 676–7
vectors, angle between two, 363–4, 386–7; average velocities as, 505, 509; base, and coordinates, 347–8; differentiation of, 504, 507–11, 525; and lines, 368; normal, 370; perpendicular, 367, 372–3; position, 407, 509, 520; scalar product of two, 360–3; sum of, 351
velocity, 507–11; angular, 520–2; average, 505–6; in circular motion, 521–3, 526; and speed, 504, 519; unit of, 540
velocity diagram, 533
vertex, of parabola, 418, 621

waves, superposition of, 392–3
weight, 683–4, 685–6
weightlessness, 690
work, dimensions of, 714; done by a force, 360, 365
working zero, 337

zeros, of function, 455 (see roots)